KT-178-826

00184236

An Introduction to Film Studies

Particularly useful to undergraduates in giving an all-round introduction to the history and theory of film. It has been thoroughly updated and revised to include new themes and examples.
Linda Sever, *University of Central Lancashire*

Unrivalled in its ability to inform students of the development of cinema and send them off on exciting journeys to discover why they love film … The ideal book for anyone sta___ng Film Studies … Illustrations are plentiful and all important concepts and termi-
___y are ac___ y explained. I encourage students to make it their top priority ___ing.
___ Thor___ g Gwent, Pontypool

___ other introductory film text that covers so much ground, nor that so readily ___nnects up film theory and discourse with work in mass and popular culture. The revised edition keeps up with changes in technology … the discussions of Hollywood are particularly illuminating … I highly recommend *An Introduction to Film Studies*.
Denise Albanese, *George Mason University, Fairfax, Virginia*

An Introduction to Film Studies has established itself as a leading textbook for students of cinema. This completely revised and updated third edition guides students through the key issues and concepts in film studies and introduces some of the world's foremost national cinemas. Written by experienced teachers in the field and lavishly illustrated with 122 film stills and production shots, it will be essential reading for any student of film.

Key fe___res of the third edition are:

- co___ all the important topics for introductory level
- up___ed coverage of a wide range of concepts, theories and issues in film studies
- co___ehensive and up to date, with new case studies on recent films such as G___tor, *Spider-Man*, *The Blair Witch Project*, *Fight Club*, *Shrek* and *The Matrix*
- study questions, website resources and a glossary of terms
- annotated key reading, further viewing and a comprehensive bibliography and index

Contributors: Chris Darke, Lalitha Gopalan, Chris Jones, Mark Joyce, Searle Kochberg, Jill Nelmes, Patrick Phillips, Allan Rowe, Amy Sargeant, Paul Watson and Paul Wells

Editor: **Jill Nelmes** is a senior lecturer in film studies and cultural studies at the University of East London.

STRODE'S COLLEGE LIBRARY

Comments on the first edition:

'To me, it is simply the best introductory volume in the field so far'.
Jesus B. Sanchez, *Castilla La Mongha University, Ciudad Real, Spain*

'Indispensable for the A Level, degree student or lay reader in film communications or media courses … will indisputably be the standard text for many years to come … If I had to unreservedly tell a student at any level to buy one book, this is it: as close to the perfect film studies textbook as you're likely to see'.
John Lough, *Senior Lecturer in Media Theory, University of Humberside*

What readers said about the second edition:

'Another of the volume's enormous strengths is its respect for its student readers. In tackling complicated debates, intellectual lineages and concepts, the chapters and particularly the "think points" ask students to engage dynamically with the material. In presenting different ideas evenly, the book nonetheless encourages students to take positions, to reject orthodoxy, to examine their own responses to cinema critically … It's a wonderful book'.
Amy Villarejo, *Cornell University*

'Probably the clearest, most comprehensive and accessible introduction to film studies available'.
Martin Price, *Stratford-upon-Avon Sixth Form College*

An Introduction to Film Studies

Third edition

Edited by Jill Nelmes

Routledge
Taylor & Francis Group

LONDON AND NEW YORK

First published 1996 by Routledge

Second edition first published in 1999 by Routledge
Reprinted 2000 and 2001

Third edition first published 2003 by Routledge
11 New Fetter Lane, London EC4P 4EE

Simultaneously published in the USA and Canada
by Routledge
29 West 35th Street, New York, NY 10001

Routledge is an imprint of the Taylor & Francis Group

Selection and editorial matter © 1996, 1999, 2003 Jill Nelmes
Individual chapters (1996, 1999, 2003) © individual contributors

Typeset in Helvetica 55 by Taylor & Francis Books Ltd
Printed and bound in Great Britain by Bell & Bain Ltd, Glasgow

All rights reserved. No part of this book may be reprinted or
reproduced or utilised in any form or by any electronic,
mechanical, or other means, now known or hereafter
invented, including photocopying and recording, or in any
information storage or retrieval system, without permission in
writing from the publishers.

British Library Cataloguing in Publication Data
A catalogue record for this book is available from the British Library

Library of Congress Cataloging in Publication Data
A catalog record for this book has been requested

ISBN 0–415–26268–2 (hbk)
       0–415–26269–0 (pbk)

Contents

Illustrations

Contributors

Chris Darke has written on film and the arts for a variety of publications. A collection of his essays, *Light Readings: Film Criticism and Screen Arts*, was published in 2000 by Wallflower Press. He has lectured at the universities of Warwick, Middlesex and Kent and at the Art Academy in Malmö, Sweden.

Lalitha Gopalan teaches film studies at Georgetown University in Washington, DC. She is the author of *Cinema of Interruptions: Action Genres in Contemporary Indian Cinema* (BFI, 2002).

Chris Jones has taught literature, theatre and film studies at Brooklands College for a number of years. He has participated in gay-related theatre and video work. He wrote about Derek Jarman for his film MA. He has recently taught film theory and creative writing at the University of Greenwich.

Mark Joyce is a lecturer in film, media and communication studies at West Kent College of Further Education, Tonbridge. He also lectures in cultural studies on the West Kent College/University of Greenwich BA degree programme in media and communication.

Searle Kochberg is a senior lecturer in film studies and video production at the University of Portsmouth. He also works as a film critic and as a consultant to various media/arts operations.

Jill Nelmes is a senior lecturer in film studies and cultural studies at the University of East London and has taught a range of courses from access to A level and higher education. She has been an examiner for WJEC media studies and is on the subject panel for WJEC film and media studies. She is also a scriptwriter and has a variety of projects in development.

Patrick Phillips is senior lecturer and subject leader, film studies, at Middlesex University. He has taught extensively in sixth form and further education colleges and is currently responsible for A level film studies nationally as chief examiner.

Allan Rowe has lectured in film, media and sociology since the mid-1960s. He has taught film A level since the original consortium in 1984. At present he teaches film studies at Chelmsford College.

Amy Sargeant is a lecturer on the MA course in the Department for the History of Film and Visual Media at Birkbeck College, University of London. She has recently co-edited, with Claire Monk, *British Historical Cinema* (Routledge, 2002), and is currently working on a new book, *A Critical and Interpretative History of British Cinema*, commissioned by the British Film Institute.

Paul Watson is the programme leader for media studies at the University of Teeside, Middlesborough. He is the co-author of *The Animation Handbook* (forthcoming) and publishes in the areas of film theory and animation.

Paul Wells is head of the media portfolio at the University of Teeside, Middlesborough. He has published widely in the field of animation, including *Understanding Animation* (Routledge, 1998) and *Animation: Genre and Authorship* (Wallflower Press, 2002). He also recently made a Channel 4 documentary with Illuminations Television called *Cartoons Kick Ass*.

Acknowledgements

I would like to thank the contributors who have given their time so willingly and put so much hard work into the third edition. My thanks also to Rebecca Barden and Moira Taylor for their unstinting enthusiasm and encouragement throughout the production process. Finally I would like to thank readers and academics for their constructive and helpful suggestions as to how to improve the new edition.

Jill Nelmes

Introduction to the third edition

Jill Nelmes

Watching films is once again a popular form of entertainment. From the spiral of decline in the 1950s, film and cinema attendance has had something of a spectacular revival in its fortunes. The 1990s saw a rapid rise in cinema attendance in Britain and the USA. In February 2002 British cinema had its highest attendance since 1969. Although the audience may now be more eclectic in its tastes it is the mainstream Hollywood films such as *Titanic* (1997) and the *Star Wars* series which still have the highest box-office grosses in Britain and the USA. Hollywood blockbuster successes make millions of dollars for the studios and are the staple diet of the cineplexes. Many of the special-effects blockbusters target the young male audience yet films such as *Gosford Park* (2001) have attracted an older audience while still doing very well in terms of box-office takings in the UK.

It is perhaps surprising that the cinema experience is still so popular given that we have access to rapidly changing and evolving technologies which now allow home cinema with plasma screen, surround sound and digital video discs. DVDs, as they are popularly known, often include the director's cut plus many extra features. Yet surrendering oneself to the pleasures of the big screen, the anticipation of an event, a spectacle, and the atmosphere and excitement generated as the cinema screen stretches from widescreen to superscope, is an experience that still cannot be matched by any other medium. Family audience viewing has been regained, partly because of the success of animation, especially computer animation in such films as *Monsters Inc.* (2001), *Toy Story* (1995) and *Shrek* (2001). A cine-literate audience, admittedly small and generally only catered for in art cinemas, is increasingly aware of film from other countries such as Iran and Africa; think of the popularity of Bollywood film not just within the Asian diaspora but in Britain as a whole.

The term 'film' is not fixed but dependent on where it is viewed – many people watch film on videos or DVDs in the home. It is still difficult to watch non-mainstream film in multi-screen cineplexes and sales of world cinema videos are on the increase.

Movies, it is generally assumed, are filmed on 35mm film, but more and more film is now recorded on digital camera then transferred to film. This way of working is likely to increase as the quality and sensitivity of digital cameras more accurately mimics film. Since the mid-1990s virtually all film has been edited digitally rather than manually, and it is likely that film will be transferred digitally to cinemas in the very near future. We will then be looking at a digital world transferred to the cinema screen. An experience which is unlikely to be replaced by a new medium such as the internet, even though the two media may eventually compete. It was feared that the advent of video would mark the death knell of cinema, but video has instead complemented and even stimulated film viewing.

Alongside the revival of cinema attendance there has been an increase in the study of film. There are now many courses at the post-16 and undergraduate levels which either concentrate on film or include an element of the study of film. Although film is often seen as part of media studies it has particular qualities that separate it from other media. Film is the marriage of sound and vision presented in a larger-than-life viewing field. Film has its own conditions of production, its qualities as medium, its own history, development and culture that is specific to individual countries and regions in the world.

Yet film cannot be seen in isolation; films are shown on TV, satellite and video and it is only a matter of time before they are shown on the internet. Films are frequently referred to by the other media in a self-conscious, self-referential way such as in the US animation series *The Simpsons*. Audience familiarity with film texts is assumed: for example, we understand the Austin Powers series as a parody of the Bond films. Developments in computer technology and multimedia also affect film; thus film affects, and is affected by, other media and indeed by society. How images are put together, used and understood is of concern to all the visual media.

What it is then about film that attracts us so much to this medium that was invented over a century ago? Why do we enjoy film so much? Why indeed should we study film? Film is now an integral part of our culture. It is not only fascinating to look at how films are constructed and how they affect us, but also to ask what they tell us about our society, our understanding of the world around us and how this differs from nation to nation?

This book does not subscribe to one particular method of studying or analysis of film but draws the reader's attention to the diversity, discursive nature and range of opinion within the subject. Each chapter discusses a particular aspect of film theory, giving a sense of how film theory has developed, outlining both influential and contemporary debates about the placing of film study at particular moments in our history. To understand where we are now in terms of film theory it is useful to see what has influenced film studies in the past; the chapters on Soviet montage cinema (Chapter 11) and French New Wave (Chapter 12), for instance, look at key moments in the development of both film and film theory. The theories referred to in the book have, in the main, developed in the USA and Europe, although much interesting work is being carried out in other parts of the world such as Australia and India, where the Department of Film Studies in Jadavpur, Calcutta, has recently launched an academic periodical, *Journal of Moving Image*.

Film theory is influenced by contemporary thinking within society and by contemporary ways of seeing the world; it is therefore in a constant state of flux. It is now moving away from the 'grand theory' that so influenced philosophy, literature and film in the 1970s; the overarching psychoanalytic theories of Freud and Lacan, the political theories of Marx and Althusser, and the semiotic theories of Saussure. But that is not to say that those theorists should be discarded in their entirety; rather they should be reassessed. A strand of film studies has, more recently, explored the appeal that film has to the senses, cinema as spectacle, as visual image, as affecting the body directly, and importantly as having its own visual language. Postmodernism has encouraged criticism of the *grand narrative* approach and yet a cultural studies approach continues to exert its influence.[1]

Boundaries as to what film is are less clearly defined; technology has affected our understanding of film as has our understanding of the conventions of film; the classical model of Hollywood cinema no longer exists. We can look forward with interest to these new developments in the next century of film.

HOW TO USE THIS BOOK

The book is by no means definitive and is not meant to be read from cover to cover in one sitting. It is designed as a resource which the reader will be able to study at particular times, either as part of a course or for general interest. It is hoped that the reader will be inspired and encouraged to look further, and extensive cross-referencing to other chapters suggests where to look for related topics and concepts

Useful features

Features of this book which have helped to make it an accessible and useful tool for the reader in the first and second editions have been revised and extended to include the following

- Coverage of a wide range of concepts, theories and ideas about film studies.
- In-depth discussion of the film industry in Hollywood and Britain, with reference to other cinemas and their conditions of production.
- Reference to a wide range of films from different periods and different countries.
- Generous use of film stills as referents but also to give a sense of the pleasure of 'looking' at film.
- Self-contained chapters which can be seen as introductions to the areas discussed.
- Key terms highlighted in the text, with short definitions given in the margins the first time they are used.
- A glossary of key terms at the end of the book.
- Highlighted text which picks out particular areas of note in a chapter; this may be a particular point which is being identified.
- Case studies giving suggestions for the way a text may be approached. The third edition has a number of new case studies.
- Cross-referencing not only helps to unify the book but makes it easier for the reader to link concepts, terms and connections between chapters, and sometimes within a chapter.
- Annotated key reading at the end of each chapter to encourage the reader to look further afield. Other references in the text may appear in the Bibliography at the end of the book.
- Updated further viewing sections for each chapter, suggesting films which would further the reader's knowledge and understanding of the area under discussion. Where possible, video availability is given, although contemporary films may still be on general release at the time of publishing.
- Updated internet sites for each chapter. These are a useful resource tool but much of the material is non-academic; we try to steer the reader towards particularly helpful sites.
- Useful addresses are given as a resource for both lecturers and students.

New features of the third edition

- All the chapters have been revised and updated; some have changed focus and been substantially modified. Most chapters include new case studies.
- The chapters on Critical Approaches to Hollywood Cinema, British Cinema and Indian Cinema have new authors; each of these chapters has been updated and now presents a slightly different approach to the subject.
- A new chapter on the French New Wave outlines an important period of film history which has had a direct influence on contemporary film and film theory.
- Questions for further study are included with the aim of encouraging the reader to go beyond the chapter, to develop independent thinking and to encourage engagement with the book.

PART ONE: INSTITUTIONS AND AUDIENCES

This section explores the relationship between cinema as a cultural product and as an industry, since its existence as a business is dependent on gaining an audience to watch the films it produces. In Chapter 1 Searle Kochberg explains that the film industry is a complex organisation, an institution with set rules and methods of working which have evolved from the early days of cinema, to the rigour of a studio system dominated by five companies, to the much more flexible conditions of production which exist today. The focus is mainly on US film, which has so dominated film style and production in the twentieth century, although the state of the film industry in the UK is referred to and the chapter includes a discussion of the effect of funding from the British Film Council. Contemporary distribution and exhibition in the US and the UK is outlined and case studies of the production of US and UK films are given, including a new case study of *Gladiator* (2000). A section on cinema attendance discusses the renaissance of the film industry since the 1990s and how recent films such as the *Blair Witch Project* (1999) and *Harry Potter* (2001) have used the internet to market their films with enormous success. Finally, the chapter examines censorship in the US and the UK, with a short history of the topic and relevant case studies. The phenomenon of the 'moral panic' is described using two case studies: in the USA, generated by the Catholic League at the openings of *Priest* (1995) and *Dogma* (1999), and in the UK by the press against *Crash* (1996).

PART TWO: APPROACHES TO STUDYING FILM TEXTS

This section addresses methods of interpreting and analysing film and is probably the most theoretically focused section of the book, examining how a film text is understood by the audience.

Chapter 2, 'Film Form and Narrative', co-authored by Allan Rowe and Paul Wells, is an introduction to how film is constructed, shaped and formed. The codes and conventions used in film-making have evolved over a period of time and are accepted as 'real', as normal to an audience. The development of these filmic conventions is explored using Buster Keaton's *The General* (1925) as an example of the early studio film. This section breaks down, deconstructs the film-making process and looks at mise-en-scène, which creates the look of the film, editing, sound and the role of narrative. Narrative theory is applied to a wide range of films and features discussion of alternatives to mainstream narrative cinema.

Chapter 3, 'Spectator, Audience and Response', written by Patrick Phillips, explores how the audience makes sense of film. The chapter examines the relationship between the film and the audience, how the look of the audience is controlled by the camera, and whether this is natural or ideological. The chapter also asks what role the spectator has in relation to the film and whether the audience is passive or active. Differing theoretical approaches are discussed as well as how, as a spectator, we may read a film in varying ways. A new case study of D.W. Griffith's *Birth of a Nation* (1915) looks at audience response in terms of race, from a black and a white point of view. The case study of *Pulp Fiction* (1994) suggests how we might approach an analysis of film, looking at the way in which the audience responds to a sequence, how their reaction is manipulated and how the audience may align with particular characters in a film.

Chapter 4, a new chapter, written by Paul Watson is divided into three sections: Authorship, Genre and Stars. Although each section is written separately there is a certain amount of overlap and intersection. All three areas are often discussed outside academic study and are now seen as approaches rather than specific theories. The section on authorship points out that it is difficult to attribute a sole author to a film when so many people have an input; film-making is a collaborative process. The history of authorship is discussed and the change in meaning of the term 'auteur' from its early Romantic application of auteur as artist to more recently that of director as commodity, as a marketing tool.

The second section discusses genre and Hollywood cinema. It argues the term is not usable in the way it was referred to in the studio system. This section asks why genre is a useful term and how it works, suggesting that it is 'a form of difference in repetition'. Discussions of *Moulin Rouge* (2001) and *The Matrix* (1997) look at the notion of film as spectacle and the action blockbuster film, discussing the difficulties in defining genre and, indeed, whether it is useful to do so when so many other styles, genres and moments in film are brought together. This section argues that genre can be challenging and surprising and can push film to new levels of expression.

The section on Stars and Hollywood Cinema outlines three approaches to the subject: first is a discussion of the star as an industrial commodity; second, a look at the star as a sign, analysing the meaning of the image; and, finally, the consumption of the star, how the audience identify with stars, aspiring to be like them or finding them desirable. The notion of the term 'star' however has changed; there are now hierarchies of star and crossovers from other media have affected stardom too. Studies of Michael Douglas and Jodie Foster look at how they differ as stars: Douglas as 'star-as-professional' and celebrity with a consistent screen persona, and Foster as 'complex star', a single parent and career woman, with her own production company.

PART THREE: GENRE FORMS – REALISM AND ILLUSION

Part three examines two different and often neglected categories or genre of film: documentary and animation. The documentary form aspires to record 'reality' as opposed to fiction yet it is very much a construction of events. In Chapter 5 Paul Wells asks: 'What is documentary'? The chapter focuses on notions of 'truth and authenticity'. A history of the non-fiction film is given, covering the work of post-Russian Revolution documentary film-maker Dziga Vertov, and that of Robert Flaherty, who used the documentary as an ethnographic tool for recording different cultures such as the Eskimos in *Nanook of the North* (1922). In the UK John Grierson politicised the documentary, being influenced by Soviet film-makers such as Vertov and Eisenstein.

The impact of lightweight cameras in the1960s allowed the film-maker more mobility. In the USA this enabled film-makers such as Doon Pennebaker to develop a 'fly on the wall' style of documentary. More recently the cheapness of video cameras has allowed marginalised film-makers a voice. The documentary form is continually evolving and one of its most recent transformations has been as the 'docu-soap', which possibly exploits rather than explores its subjects. Yet documentary is able to make powerful points about society and our past, as discussed in the case study on the American film-maker Ken Burns.

In Chapter 6, Paul Wells suggests that animation should be recognised as a significant art form with its own codes and conventions. Often seen merely as cartoons, animation in fact demonstrates a wide range of styles. In recent years computer animation has enabled animators to work in different ways and to invent fresh approaches to their work whilst at the same time attracting huge audiences, as in the case of *Monsters Inc.* (2001) and *Shrek* (2001) for instance. The effect has been that animation is now one of the most significant art forms of the twenty-first century. The chapter outlines the development of animation from the first days of the moving image in the 1880s to the legacy of Disney and more contemporary processes. Differing styles of animation are discussed from orthodox animation to the experimental style of Len Lye. New case studies of *Ghost in the Shell* (1995), an example of Japanese adult animation, and *Shrek* (2001) are given.

PART FOUR: REPRESENTATION OF GENDER AND SEXUALITY

This section examines how different groups with different identities are represented on film. In Chapter 7, a newly titled and revised chapter 'Gender and Film', Jill Nelmes discusses how gender and concepts of femininity and masculinity are represented in film and understood by the audience. The chapter gives a brief history of women in film-making then looks at feminist film theory and how it evolved, partly out of feminist film practice and the avant-garde. The seminal theories of Mulvey, drawing on the psychoanalytic theories of Freud and Lacan, are concerned with the gendered relationship between the film and the look of the spectator. Their impact on feminist and gender studies are discussed. More recent feminist theory argues that this is only one way of analysing film and that other influences such as cultural studies should be incorporated. The new section on masculinity discusses Neale's revising of Mulvey's approach and points out that masculinity is not opaque and natural but full of tensions and contradictions. Changing representations of the male body are discussed as well as how anxieties within society regarding masculinity, and indeed femininity, are acted out in film. A case study of *Fight Club* (1999) demonstrates masculinity in crisis in the nineties film.

Chapter 8, written by Chris Jones, argues for a separate theory to account for lesbians and gays both in the way they are represented on screen and how they interpret film as an audience. Film theory generally assumes the viewer is heterosexual and film has tended to see homosexuality as a problem, as sickness. This chapter examines work by key theorists such as Vito Russo, Richard Dyer and Andrea Weiss. Russo points out that in Hollywood film lesbians and gays have been either invisible or marginalised. Dyer explains how sexual ideology is transmitted by cultural artefacts such as film, but points out that representation of social groups is by no means fixed and can change. Weiss is a feminist lesbian film-maker and writer who suggests that identification in film is a much more complex process than just being about binary opposites of either male or female. The 1990s saw an explosion of lesbian and gay films, termed the 'New Queer Cinema'. Such films reappropriate the term 'queer' in a positive sense. Two new case studies are included: *The Hanging Garden* (1997) and *Happy Together* (1997).

PART FIVE: NATIONAL CINEMAS

In Western society we tend to think of Hollywood as being the dominant form of cinema. Yet other national cinemas, past and present, have made an impact for many reasons, ranging from their productivity and popularity to their formal, aesthetic, political and social value. Cinema in countries as diverse as Brazil and Hong Kong have produced an exciting range of film that present fascinating alternatives to the dominance of Hollywood and its conventions of film-making which so predominates in the Western world. This section of the book focuses on four very different types of national cinema: two more general studies (British cinema and Indian cinema) and two particular moments in history (Soviet cinema in the 1920s and French New Wave).

Chapter 9, Amy Sargeant's new chapter, examines what we mean by British cinema, pointing out that most of the films we see in the cinema are not British and that the distributors and exhibitors are also, in the main, not British. The film industry in Britain has been, and still is, dependent on foreign, mostly US, funding. Because of this dependence an ambivalent relationship has developed between the UK and the USA, where many British film-makers have made their mark on Hollywood film. In return, US actors and film-makers have contributed to the British film industry, with directors such as Joseph Losey in *The Servant* (1963) and Robert Altman in *Gosford Park* (2001) providing us with fascinating insights into the changing class system. The relationship between British and European film is also explored. The difference between depictions of town and country, rural and city life is discussed, and the 'heritage' film is considered. A section on the relationship between television and film points out how television has made an important contribution to the British film industry. Finally two case studies, 'West End Girls' and 'East End Boys', look at the city in terms of geography and gender.

Chapter 10, written by Lalitha Gopalan, looks at Indian cinema's increasing popularity, its crossover audience and the influence of Bollywood film on contemporary Western film-makers such as Baz Luhrmann and his *Moulin Rouge* (2001). Narrative and genre in Indian popular cinema is discussed and compared with Hollywood, exploring the most popular genres: song and dance; the love story; the gangster film; and the importance of the interval in Indian cinemas as a narrative breaking point in the film. Censorship was introduced to Indian cinema by the British in 1918, although the film industry generally works through a system of self-censorship and accepted visual and aural codes which act as symbols of the sexual act. Post-colonial films are analysed and the recent increase in India of academic and critical writing on cinema is discussed. Case studies of recent critical and box-office successes *Monsoon Wedding* (2002) and *Lagaan* (2001) are given.

Soviet montage cinema of the 1920s emerged out of the Russian Revolution of 1917 as a vehicle for propaganda, spreading the message of socialism. As a form of film-making, Mark Joyce argues in Chapter 11, Soviet montage cinema has had a lasting impact and theories developed out of this cinema are still influential today. Film was seen as crucial to the success of communism and the climate was right for experimentation in film to take place, and for montage cinema to flourish, based on the concept of the audience creating meaning from viewing two unrelated pieces of film side by side. This chapter discusses key Soviet montage film-makers such as Kuleshov, Eisenstein, Pudovkin and Vertov, giving case studies and analysis of their films. Vertov experimented with documentary form, believing that the camera could capture the 'truth', and documented events around him. By the 1930s montage cinema was no longer supported by the Soviet authorities (Eisenstein was one of the few who continued to make films) and, combined with the coming of sound, this sounded the death knell for this experimental and innovative form of cinema.

Chapter 12, 'The French New Wave', is a new addition, written by Chris Darke. The French New Wave was in existence for a relatively brief period from the late 1950s to the mid-1960s but has had a profound influence on film worldwide. Many of the New Wave directors such as François Truffaut, Jean–Luc Godard and Eric Rohmer had been involved with film criticism and the French film magazine *Cahiers du cinéma*. The *Cahiers* critics argued that cinema should be seen as an art form and Hollywood film-makers such as Hitchcock, Ford and Hawks were seen as especially important. The chapter also looks at the conditions of production of New Wave films as well as their technological and aesthetic characteristics. Case studies of key films are given which include *A bout de souffle* (1959), *Les Quatre cent coups* (1959) and discussion of film-makers such as Jean-Luc Godard and Agnès Varda.

NOTE

1   For further discussion of film theory and the various philosophies which have influenced it, see Gledhill and Williams (2000).

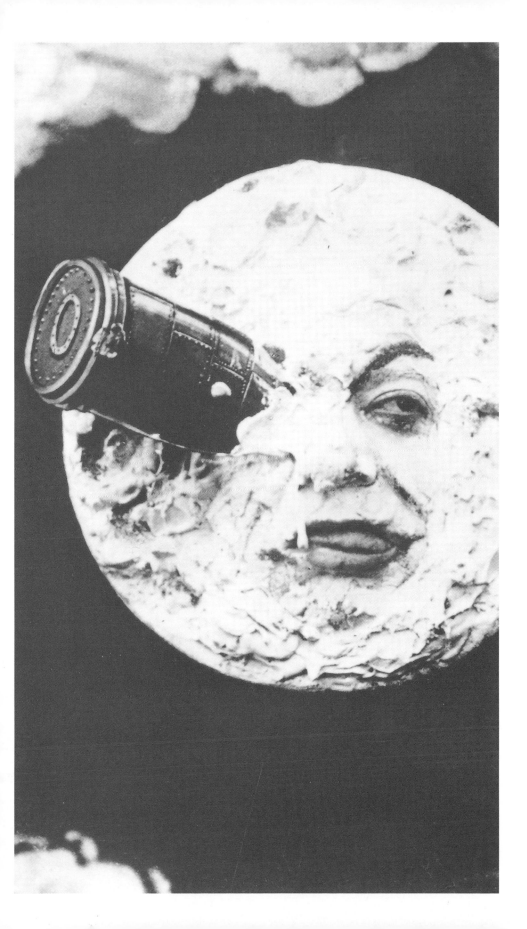

Part one

Institutions and audiences

Cinema as institution

Searle Kochberg

■ Cinema as institution

INTRODUCTION

Films do not exist in a vacuum: they are conceived, produced, distributed and consumed within specific economic and social contexts.

The chapter that follows is a journey through the mainstream institutional frameworks of US and UK film. The American film industry has dominated all others for the last 100 years and for this reason discussion here largely centres around it. I do not claim the itinerary to be definitive, but I have sought to cite some key issues in the socio-economic infrastructure of American and British film.

The origins and consolidation of the American industry are traced from 1900 to 1930, a period which saw a fledgling industry harness new industrial practices and quickly grow into an important popular medium, organised into highly defined exhibition, production and distribution components.

The Hollywood studio era (1930 to 1949) is the next stop on the tour. Monopolistic practice and the finely tuned industrial organisation of the Hollywood 'factories' are discussed at some length. This section looks specifically at Warner Brothers as an example of a vertically integrated film company during the studio era.

There follows an exploration of the contemporary institutional framework of US (global) and UK commercial film, starting with a review of the position of the 'majors' in the light of multimedia empires, new media technologies and (mainstream) independent production. The production/distribution histories of *Gladiator* (2000) and *The Crying Game* (1992) are taken as case studies.

The film-going habit is an important part of social history in the twentieth century. With this in mind, the changing nature of UK and US audiences since the Second World War is reviewed. The case studies focus on the contemporary context and are *The Blair Witch Project* (1999) and *Trainspotting* (1996).

The chapter ends with a review of the systems of censorship and classification that have operated in the USA and UK since the 1920s. Both contemporary and historical case studies are considered.

THE ORIGINS OF THE AMERICAN FILM INDUSTRY (1900–14)

exhibition
Division of the film industry concentrating on the public screening of film.

distribution
Division concentrating on the marketing of film, connecting the producer with the exhibitor by leasing films from the former and renting them to the latter.

production
Division concentrating on the making of film.

kinetograph
Edison's first movie camera.

The American film industry has been in existence as long as there has been American film. This section looks at how the film industry organised itself into three main divisions in the early years of the twentieth century, divisions that exist to this day – **exhibition**, **distribution** and **production**.

Exhibition until 1907

By 1894 the exhibition of moving pictures had been established in New York City with the introduction of the box-like **kinetoscope**. This allowed an individual customer to watch a fifty-foot strip of film through a slit at the top of the machine. In 1895, a projector called the Pantopticon was demonstrated, again in NYC, and for the first time more than one person could watch the same moving images simultaneously.

Once projectors were available, single-reel films started to be shown in vaudeville theatres as novelties. Exhibition outlets began to multiply and by the first years of this century small high-street stores and restaurants were being converted to small-scale cinemas or nickelodeons. As the name suggests, the cost of entry to these cinemas was 5 cents – an amount affordable to the (predominantly) working-class audience. By the end of 1905 there were an estimated 1,000 of these theatres in America; by 1908 there were 6,000.

Distribution until 1907

As the film industry expanded, exhibitors had a growing commercial need for an unbroken supply of films to show. To meet this need, the first film exchange was in operation by 1902 and acted as a go-between for the producers and exhibitors (Balio 1976: 14). The exchanges purchased (later leased) films from producers and distributed films to exhibitors by renting to them. By 1907 there were between 125 and 150 film exchanges covering the whole of the USA.

Production until 1907

Until 1900 the average length of films was around 50 feet. Three major companies dominated production in the USA: Edison, Biograph and Vitagraph. Although filming on location was very common at this stage, as early as 1893 the world's first 'kinetographic theatre' or film studio was in operation. This was built by the Edison Company and called the 'Black Maria'.

For an account of early UK film production see Chapter 9, pp 322–325.

After 1900, films started to get longer, and by 1903, films of 300 to 600 feet were fairly common. The Edison Company's *The Great Train Robbery* (1903) was over 1,000

• **Plate 1.1**
A nickelodeon (5¢ entry fee) in NYC in the first decade of the twentieth century. Converted high-street stores such as this one were typical of the first cinemas

feet long (ibid.: 7–9) and is an example of Early Cinema utilising increased running time and primitive continuity editing to tell what was for then a fairly ambitious story. By this time there were several major film producers in America, including (as well as the companies mentioned above) Selig, Kalem, Essanay and Lubin. These companies ensured their dominant position in the industry by holding patents in camera and projection equipment.

The industrial organisation of film production until 1907 has been referred to as the 'cameraman' system of production (Bordwell *et al*. 1985: 116–17). As the name suggests, films were largely the creation of one individual, the cameraman, who was responsible for planning, writing, filming and editing. Edwin Porter, working for the Edison Company, is a good example of such a craftsman.

Thus, by 1907, the American film industry was already organised into three main divisions: exhibition, distribution and production. The creation of these separate commercial divisions demonstrates pragmatic, commercial streamlining by a very young industry, a move designed to maximise profits in an expanding market.

The Motion Picture Patents Company and industry monopolies (1908–15)

In 1908, the Edison and Biograph companies attempted to control the fledgling film industry through the key patents they held in camera and projection technology. They set up the Motion Picture Patents Company (MPPC), a **patent pool**, which issued licenses for a fee to companies on a discretionary basis. Only licensed firms could legally utilise technology patented by or contracted to the MPPC without fear of litigation. The MPPC was soon collecting royalties from all sectors of the industry, including manufacturers of equipment, film producers and exhibitors. The MPPC's ultimate ambition was to monopolise the film industry in the USA. Its goal was a situation in which films would be shot on patented cameras, distributed through its General Film Company and screened on its patented projectors.

patent pool
An association of companies, operating collectively in the marketplace by pooling the patents held by each individual company.

Exhibition and audience during the MPPC era

An important contribution to the profits of the MPPC came from the licensing of projection equipment to exhibitors. In 1908 the most important exhibition outlet was the nickelodeon.

The year 1910 marked the peak of this type of theatre, with an estimated 26,000,000 people attending the 10,000 'nickels' in the continental US every week (Balio 1976: 63). The meteoric rise of the nickel theatres was remarkable and reflected the general expansion of popular entertainment during America's prosperous start to the twentieth century. Enormous expansion in film exhibition occurred throughout the USA and inner-city locations were particularly important due to their concentrated populations. The growth of the nickelodeon in large American cities has been well documented and may in part be attributable to mass working-class immigration to the USA at that time (Allen and Gomery 1995: 202–5).

The exhibition industry understood that its successful future lay in securing a wide audience-base. It appears to have accomplished this even in its nickelodeon years, by successfully positioning nickels in middle-class as well as working-class districts. Exhibitors realised, however, that even greater profit lay in larger theatres and more ambitious narratives. As early as 1909, large movie theatres were being constructed. Film producers were also being encouraged by exhibitors to provide films that would appeal to middle- as well as working-class audiences, including 'women's' stories and one-reel adaptations of literary classics. This process continued to gather momentum in the final years of the MPPC era, when large luxurious theatres began to supplant the nickels in movie exhibition, and audiences reached 49,000,000 per week (Balio 1976: 75). Feature-length films of an average length of 4–6 reels also became established.

Distribution in the MPPC era

Soon after its inception, the MPPC turned its attention to film distribution and licensed 70 per cent of the film exchanges operating in the USA. By 1910, the MPPC had set up its own distribution company – the General Film Company – which soon had nationwide cover through the purchase of forty-eight key exchanges in the USA (Elsaesser 1990: 192–3). By 1911, the MPPC had constructed the first effective example of **vertical integration** in the film industry through a combination of takeovers and patent rights.

Changing conditions were soon to challenge the MPPC's supreme position in the industry. First, independent distributors, exhibitors and producers quickly and success-fully organised themselves in response to the MPPC's attempted monopoly.[1] Then in 1912 a charge of anti-**trust** violation was filed against the MPPC by the Department of Justice. The outcome of the case (announced in 1915) was that the MPPC was ordered to break up. Ironically, by this time, other vertically integrated companies were being organised within the industry.

Production during the MPPC era

The years 1908 to 1915 were not only marked by the rise and fall of the industrial giant – the MPPC – but also by the rise of the multi-reel feature film and the relative demise of the single-reel film. Greater length and greater narrative complexity coincided with the application of scientific management principles to the industrial organisation of film production.

By 1908, the 'cameraman' system of production had already been discarded and replaced by the 'director system' (1907–9) (see Bordwell *et al.* 1985: 113–20). For the first time a director was responsible for overseeing a group of operative workers, including the cameraman. The director was central to the planning, filming and editing stages of film-making. Production was centralised in a studio/factory, permitting greater control of production, thus keeping costs down. Around 1909, this system was in turn discarded in favour of the 'director–unit' system (ibid.: 121–7). Directors were now in charge of autonomous production units within companies, each with a separate group of workers. Companies were subdivided into various departments, for ever-greater productivity and efficiency, informed no doubt by the then current 'scientific manage-ment' model of labour and workshop organisation popularised by F.W. Taylor.

By the end of the MPPC era, the 'central producer' system (ibid.: 128–41) had been introduced, which was to dominate as a model in production management until the start of the studio era around 1930. This was a fully structured hierarchical system, with a strict 'scientific' division of labour. Production line film-making was now the order of the day, all under the central control of a producer who used very detailed shooting scripts to plan budgets before giving the go-ahead to studio projects.

Summary

During the first twenty years of its life, the film industry increased in scale from a cottage-size enterprise to an established mass medium. Its rapid and enormous growth was largely driven by the explosion in exhibition, which in turn triggered a streamlining in distribution methods and the industrialisation of production. The predominant posi-tion of exhibition within the industry was also to be a hallmark of the studio era of American film.

THE STUDIO ERA OF AMERICAN FILM (1930–49)

This section looks at the studio era of film production. By 1930 the film industry in America was dominated by five companies – all vertically integrated – known as the 'majors' or the '*Big Five*': Warner Brothers, Loew's–MGM, Fox, Paramount and

vertical integration
Where a company is organised so that it over-sees a product from the planning/development stage, through produc-tion, through market distribution, through to the end-user – the retail consumer. In the case of the film industry, this translates to a company controlling the produc-tion, marketing and exhibition of its films.

trust
A group of companies operating together to control the market for a commodity. This is illegal practice in the USA.

oligopoly
Where a state of limited
competition exists
between a small group
of producers or sellers.

Radio–Keith–Orpheum (RKO). Three smaller companies, the '*Little Three*', were also part of the **oligopoly**: Columbia, Universal (both with production and distribution facilities) and United Artists (U.A., a distribution company for independent producers).

The origins of the studio-era oligopoly

Vertical integration made sense to the power brokers of the film industry: companies with the financial resources to organise themselves in this way stood to dominate the marketplace through their all-pervasive influence and their ability to block competition.

Despite the alarm bells of the MPPC anti-trust case verdict in 1915, film companies continued to seek out legal ways to construct vertically integrated companies through mergers and acquisitions. In December 1916 an industry merger occurred which became the cornerstone of the future Hollywood studio era. This involved the Famous Players and Jesse L. Lasky production companies and Paramount, a distribution company. By 1920 Famous Players–Lasky (as the new company was called) had established a pre-eminent position in the American film industry with the purchase of theatre chains throughout the USA and Canada (Gomery 1986: 26–8).

The trend set by Famous Players–Lasky was soon copied elsewhere in the industry. In 1922 the distribution–exhibition giant First National became vertically integrated with the construction of a large production facility in Burbank, California (Balio 1976: 114).[2] By 1924 Loew's Incorporated, the major exhibition firm, had acquired both Metro Pictures (producer–distributor) and Goldwyn Pictures (producer–exhibitor). Henceforth, Loew's production subsidiary would be known as Metro–Goldwyn–Mayer (MGM) (Gomery 1986: 54–5).

Exhibition during the studio era

Exhibition continued to be the most powerful and influential branch of the American film industry during the studio era. The reason for this was simple: it was where the money was made. Reflecting this, the majors channelled most of their investment into exhibition, which accounted for 90 per cent of the majors' total asset value during the years 1930 to 1949 (ibid.: 14).

In spite of the fact that the majors owned only 15 per cent of the movie theatres in the USA, they collected approximately 75 per cent of exhibition revenues in America during the studio era (ibid.: 12, 18). This was possible because the Big Five film companies owned 70 per cent of the **first-run** movie houses in the USA during this period. Their numbers were relatively small, but the first-run theatres accounted for most of the exhibition revenue because of their very large seating capacity (on average over 1,200 seats), prime locations (in key urban sites) and higher price of admission. The majors further strengthened their grip on exhibition by 'encouraging' the (30 per cent) independent first-run theatres to book their films, sight unseen, to the exclusion of competitors (see below). By bowing to the wishes of the majors, the independents safeguarded their access to the majors' popular films. All in all, it was the majors' control of cinemas during the years of vertical integration that ensured their profits.

first-run
Important movie theatres
would show films imme-
diately upon their
theatrical release (or
their 'first-run'). Smaller,
local theatres would
show films on subse-
quent runs, hence the
terms second-run, third-
run etc.

The successful theatre chains

By the 1920s, American innovations in national wholesaling and chain-store retailing had been absorbed into cinema exhibition methods. The introduction of scientific management methods and economies of scale led to the building up of chains of theatres, lower per-unit costs and faster, more efficient operations.

Exhibition and Balaban and Katz

By far the most financially successful and innovative of the exhibition companies in the lead up to the studio era was Balaban and Katz which had its corporate headquarters in Chicago (and was part of Paramount from 1925 onwards). Its success influenced the whole exhibition industry, especially at the top end of the market. Key innovations of Balaban and Katz included locating cinemas in outlying business and residential areas as well as downtown, building large, ornate, air-conditioned movie palaces (trips to which were 'events' in themselves for movie-goers) and accompanying screen presentations with quality vaudeville acts (Gomery 1992: 40–56).

The 1930s and 1940s saw a continuation of the scientific management practices inaugurated by innovators such as Balaban and Katz. Changes were made in exhibition during the studio era, some a direct result of the fall in attendance brought about by the Great Depression which followed the Wall Street Crash of 1929. Vaudeville acts were eliminated in all but the grandest of movie houses and replaced by talkie shorts, new movie theatres were less elaborate, double bills were introduced, air-conditioning was more universally adopted, and food and drink stands – in the form of popcorn (pre-Second World War onwards) and Coke/Pepsi (post-Second World War) – were introduced into foyers. These became major profit earners for exhibitors (ibid.: 70, 80–1).

The war years (1941–45) and the immediate postwar period were to mark the heyday of studio-era exhibition in the USA, with 1946 bringing in the greatest profits for the Big Five.

Distribution during the studio era

The distribution of films in the USA was effectively controlled by the Big Five during the studio era, even though the Little Three were also heavily engaged in the distribution business. The reason for this lay in the majors' complete domination of exhibition. To ensure access for their films to the nationwide cinema network controlled by the majors, the Little Three went along with the distribution system of the Big Five. Areas were zoned by the majors, and theatres designated first-run, second-run etc. The average period between runs, or clearance, was thirty days or more.

When booking films into their own theatres, each of the majors ensured that precedence was given to their own product, followed by films of the other majors. Any exhibition slots still available would be allocated to the Little Three.

Block-booking

In distributing films to independent theatres, the Big Five and Little Three utilised a system of *advance block-booking*[3] (films booked en masse and in advance). Under this system, independent exhibitors were often forced to book a full year's feature-film output of an individual film company, sight unseen, in order to secure likely box-office hits (Gomery 1992: 67–9).

It is worth noting that genre films and star vehicles of the studio era owed their popularity with distributors and exhibitors to the fact that they were useful marketing tools for distributors and at the same time helped provide box-office insurance for exhibitors.

For further discussion of stars and marketing, see Chapter 4, p 170 and of genre and pleasure see Chapter 4, pp. 158–160.

Production during the studio era

By the onset of the studio era, the major movie factories were each producing an average of fifty features per year to satisfy the voracious demands of the highly profitable exhibition end of the business. As in other areas of the film industry, production management was 'scientific': film studios were organised as assembly-line plants with strict divisions of labour and hierarchies of authority.

As early as 1931, Hollywood majors had begun to move away from the central-producer system which had dominated production since 1915. Columbia Pictures was the first company to announce the adoption of a producer–unit system in October 1931. Under the new organisational framework, the company appointed a head of production to oversee the running of the studio. Several producers were then appointed under the head, and each had the job of supervising the production of a group of films and of delivering the films on completion to the head of production (Bordwell *et al.* 1985: 321).

Those firms that adopted the new system (not all did)[4] were convinced that it was an advance in scientific management for several reasons. First, it was felt that the system saved money, since it allowed each producer to keep a closer control of individual budgets (overseeing far fewer films than a central producer). Second, the system was felt to foster 'better quality' films and encourage specialisms in individual units, by investing in the creativity of the delegated producers.

Certain production units were associated with particular genres: Jerry Wald's unit at Warner Brothers specialised in noir melodrama, e.g. *Mildred Pierce* (1945); Arthur Freed's unit at Metro–Goldwyn–Mayer specialised in the integrated musical, e.g. *Meet Me In St. Louis* (1944).

Contracts and unions

It was standard studio practice during the 1930s and 1940s to employ personnel on long-term or permanent contracts. Workers' unions had firmly established themselves in American film production by the early years of the Roosevelt administration (in the mid-1930s) under the auspices of the **National Recovery Administration (NRA)** and the Wagner Act (Gomery 1986: 10). Ironically, by defining and enforcing rigidly delineated areas of responsibility for specific jobs to protect their members' jobs, the unions were directly instrumental in reinforcing the hierarchical structure of film production practice.

NRA (The National Recovery Administration) programme
A 1930s government programme designed to rescue the US economy from the Great Depression (commonly known as the 'New Deal').

• Plate 1.2
An aerial view of Paramount's production facility in Hollywood in the 1930s. This studio was one of the most modern talking-picture production plants in the world. It covered an area of 26 acres, had 14 sound stages on the grounds, and had a working population of 2,000 persons

Stars

Long before the 1930s, a whole subsidiary industry had grown up promoting the Hollywood 'dream factory', its films and its stars. This continued throughout the studio era, fuelled by the publicity machines of the film companies themselves.

Long-term contracts (normally of seven years duration) secured the ongoing services of stars for the film companies. This was key to the financial security of corporations since the acting ability and personality of stars generated significant value for the films in which they appeared. Stars helped differentiate films that were otherwise very standard in content and format. Their popularity reinforced consumer brand loyalty for the films of individual film companies and provided the majors with the necessary 'carrot' with which to entice independent exhibitors into booking blocks of films sight unseen (or 'blind').

For further discussion of stars and Hollywood Cinema, see Chapter 3, pp. 169–181.

Summary

During the Hollywood studio era, a small group of manufacturers-cum-distributors-cum-retailers controlled the film market between them. Smaller US producers were forced to show their films in subsequent-run cinemas or to arrange distribution deals with the Big Five and Little Three. Likewise, foreign films could not get a foothold in the USA unless they too had arrangements with one of the eight US film companies comprising the oligopoly.

UK films and US distribution

Examples of UK production companies that had US distribution during the studio era were: London Films – distributing through U.A.; Imperator Films – distributing through R.K.O.; and Rank Organisation – distributing through Universal.

It wasn't until after 1948 that the majors were forced to divest themselves of their cinema chains, as a result of the Supreme Court's decision in the Paramount anti-trust case (see next section).

☐ CASE STUDY 1: WARNER BROTHERS

From its origins as a small production company in the mid-1920s, by the end of the decade Warner Brothers had risen to become one of the five major vertically integrated film companies. This was largely achieved through debt-financing – expansion financed through loans. Key to Warners' exponential growth were the following financial deals: its takeover of Vitagraph Corporation (with distribution and production facilities) in 1925; its exclusive licensing of Western Electric sound equipment for 'talking pictures' in 1926; and its purchase of the Stanley Company cinema chain with its associated film company, First National in 1928.

Vitaphone

Warner Brothers created a corporate subsidiary for its sound productions called Vitaphone Corporation in 1926. That year it premiered its Vitaphone 'shorts' and its first feature film with recorded musical accompaniment, *Don Juan*. 1927 saw the release of Warner's first feature-length part-talkie, *The Jazz Singer*.

The Great Depression seriously weakened Warners' financial base. The company could carry its enormous debt-load while big profits were being generated at the box-office. After 1930, however, box-office takings fell off so sharply that the company

• **Plate 1.3**
The Vitaphone sound system: a sound-on-disc system. An engineer monitors the wax disc during a recording in the late 1920s

began to lose money and had difficulty meeting its loan commitments. Warners was not to show a profit again until 1935.[5]

Warner Brothers' response to its financial crisis was to sell off assets (like cinemas), introduce production units (to help control film budgets) and to make feature films as cheaply as possible.[6] Its series of studio-bound, fast paced, topical films in the early 1930s were the direct result of this corporate policy.

By 1935, the fortunes of the company had improved sufficiently for it to return to profit again. As profits increased, so did film budgets. Studio genres changed too, with the entrenchment of the melodrama, biopic, Merrie England and film noir genres in the late 1930s and early 1940s. As with the other majors, profits reached record levels for Warners during and immediately after the Second World War.

Warner as auteur (authorial voice)

The Warners' house style – cast, subject, treatment, technical standards – is discernable in the work of all of its contract directors and over a wide variety of genres.

Warner Brothers style during the studio era

As discussed, film production during the studio era was all about standardised assembly-line manufacturing practice. This is why there is such impressive consistency in the physical make-up of the classic Hollywood film of the period. However, individual film companies needed to differentiate their product if they were to develop brand loyalty with their customers.

Senior management control over Warner house style is evident: staff workers were assigned projects by management, they did not choose them. Management retained ultimate authority on all matters concerning its productions, and the corporation had direct control over the final cut. This was extensively exercised, much to the chagrin of directors and stars.

Throughout the studio era, Warner films articulated a populist, liberal ethos. Several productions of the early 1930s were particularly hard-hitting social critiques. From 1933 onwards, however, Warner films discarded their anti-government position and whole-heartedly supported the new Roosevelt (Democratic) administration and its NRA programme. The ultimate endorsement of the New Deal and Roosevelt must be *Footlight Parade* (1933), with its 'Shanghai Lil' dance routine incorporating images of the NRA eagle and Roosevelt, and its leading protagonist (played by James Cagney) apparently inspired by Roosevelt himself (see Roth in Altman 1981: 41–56)!

From the mid-1930s onwards, the radical streak in Warner films may have been muted (due in part to a management eager for middle-class respectability), but the company's films still retained an 'edge' not apparent in the films of the other majors.

Warner Brothers (like most of the major film companies of the studio era) specialised in particular genres. Up until the mid-1930s, the company concentrated on low-budget contemporary urban genres such as the gangster cycle, the social-conscience film and the fast-talking comedy/drama. The one costly genre that Warners specialised in during this period was the musical. Later, from the mid-1930s onwards, new genres began to dominate: the Merrie England cycle, the biopic, the melodrama and the film noir.

For a list of key Warner Brothers genre films, see the Further viewing section at the end of this chapter.

• **Plate 1.4**
Still from *Footlight Parade* (Lloyd Bacon, 1933)
James Cagney's character at the helm in this NRA-inspired musical

• **Plate 1.5**
Production still from
Jezebel (1938)
Bette Davis and Henry
Fonda are directed by
William Wyler (seated on
the camera crane)

As one might expect, Warners' roster of players during the studio era reflected to a large extent the studio's reputation for straightforwardness and toughness. It is worth noting that Warners' stars tended to be very genre-specific; e.g. Bette Davis = melodrama; James Cagney = gangster film/musical; Humphrey Bogart = gangster film/film noir.

The factory-like regimentation of Warners' production methods meant that its studio style inevitably overwhelmed the individual creative talents of its contract directors. Pressure of work and division of labour meant that there was little active collaboration on projects between director and editor, or director and writer (Campbell 1971: 2). Directors were assigned projects and as soon as their task was done they moved on, leaving editors to complete the post-production work. It is thus particularly problematic to assign to Warners' contract directors such as Michael Curtiz, William Keighley, Mervyn Le Roy and Raoul Walsh[7] individual authorship of their films.

The cinematographic style of the company was very much in keeping with its tight-budget policy. Studio cameramen such as Tony Gaudio (*The Adventures of Robin Hood*, 1938), Sol Polito (*Now Voyager*, 1942) and Ernest Haller (*Mildred Pierce*, 1945) were exponents of a visual style based on low-key lighting, incorporating many night scenes. This aesthetic strategy suited Warners' genres and also helped to disguise cheap sets.

Art direction

Warners' art direction reflected a low-cost policy: location work was avoided, films were designed around a studio-bound look and sets were regularly reused. Anton Grot, a major art director at Warner Brothers during the studio era, typifies the studio's style. Grot not only designed sets, but also suggested camera angles and lighting for them. His sets conveyed a mood. They were not literal reproductions of life, but instead were impressionistic, using shadow, silhouette and angular perspective.[8] He is quoted as saying: 'I for one, do not like extremely realistic sets. I am for simplicity and beauty and you can achieve that only by creating an impression' (Deschner 1975: 22). The end result was art design that was both economic and atmospheric and in total sympathy with the studio's cinematography.

• **Plate 1.6**
Still from *Mildred Pierce*
(Michael Curtiz, 1945)
This shot typifies the
studio-bound cinemato-
graphic style and art
direction of Warners
during the studio era.
The scene,
photographed by Ernest
Haller, is shot with low-
key lighting; the art
direction by Anton Grot
conveys an impression
of a quay-side through
its use of space,
shadow, silhouette and
perspective

Costume design at Warners was very much in keeping with the contemporary stories of the films. The studio's principal designers, Orry-Kelly for instance, designed modern clothes for ordinary people, in keeping with Warners' up-to-date urban image.

Warners' films of the studio era, particularly in the early to mid-1930s, had a particular 'fast' editing style. Narratives were developed in a rapid succession of scenes, with extensive classic Hollywood montage sequences. The overall effect was one of dynamism and compression of time.

Finally, the background music of Warners' films was highly individual, and typified by the work of Max Steiner (*Now Voyager*) and *Mildred Pierce*) and Erich Wolfgang Korngold (*The Adventures of Robin Hood*, 1938 and *King's Row*, 1942). From the mid-1930s to the end of the studio era, both composers created scores very much in the Middle-European tradition of romantic composition, using Wagner-like leitmotifs (recurring melodic phrases used to suggest characters or ideas) throughout.

*For further discussion of
Mildred Pierce, see
Chapter 2, pp. 70, 77.*

Warners' style of the 1930s and 1940s can thus be identified as a composite, the product of its creative personnel working under the control and direction of corporate management. The various signifying elements that made up this style were reinforced film after film, year after year, producing what one now identifies as the studio-era Warner Brothers film.

As a useful summary exercise, consider the questions below in relation to the previous sections:

1 **What are the three main divisions of the film industry?**
2 **What do you understand by 'scientific management'? How did scientific management inform on the industrial practice of film production before and during the studio era?**
3 **How did vertical integration of the majors assist oligopolistic practice in the studio era?**
4 **In what sense did Warners foster a corporate identity in its films?**

THE CONTEMPORARY FILM INDUSTRY (1949 ONWARDS)

The early twenty-first-century film industry is a very different affair from the system in operation during the studio era. This section looks at the contemporary institutional framework of film, first by examining the specifics *within* the film industry itself, and then by looking at the wider media context within which film exists today.

The 'Paramount' case

In the late 1940s an anti-trust suit was brought against the Big Five and the Little Three by the Justice Department of the United States (in the pipelines since the late 1930s).

Paramount and R.K.O. were the first of the majors to agree to the terms of the government's **consent decrees** in 1949 (Balio 1976: 317), putting to rest the charge against them of monopolistic practice in exhibition. The terms agreed were the hiving off of their cinemas.

consent decree
A court order made with the consent of both parties – the defendant and the plaintiff – which puts to rest the lawsuit brought against the former by the latter.

1949 to the present: a brief review

The majors were finally forced to divest themselves of their theatres at the end of the 1940s as a result of the 'Paramount' anti-trust suit. This division of exhibition from production–distribution marked the end of the studio era.

The next few years saw a retrenchment of the majors. They no longer had a guaranteed market for their films and had to compete with independent producers for exhibition slots. Under the circumstances, they found their old studio infrastructure too expensive in the face of new market competition from the independents.

Meanwhile, for independents, things had never been better, with the majors only too willing to rent them studio space and distribute their (better) films, and exhibitors eager to show them. The 1950s was to see an enormous explosion in independent production in the USA. By 1957, 58 per cent of the films distributed by the erstwhile Big Five and Little Three were independent productions that they financed and/or distributed (ibid.: 353).

U.A. and distribution

In the 1950s, U.A. led the industry in the distribution of independent films. With no studios to restructure and no long-term contract players, U.A. was able to respond very quickly to the post-1949 reality. In 1957, for instance, only Columbia Pictures distributed more films than U.A.[9]

Another shock to the film industry around the early 1950s was the exponential growth of television, a product of TV's own popularity and a postwar focus on the home and consumer durables: between 1947 and 1950, the number of TV sets in the USA rose from 14,000 to 4 million (see section below on film audiences). The film industry's response was twofold: differentiation from and collaboration with TV.

In the 1950s, various film presentation strategies were introduced to emphasise the difference between the film-going experience and TV viewing in a bid to stave off the harmful competition from film's rival. Widescreen, colour, 3-D and stereophonic sound were all introduced in the period 1952 to 1954. However, at the end of the day it proved expedient for the industry to collaborate with 'the enemy'. Film companies began to sell (and later lease) their films to TV,[10] to make films for TV,[11] and to merge with TV companies.[12] By the late 1960s, the futures of the two media industries were inextricably linked. The situation by the mid-1980s was more complicated. The two industries had become integrated into multimedia conglomerates where they represented just two of the many associated interests of their parent corporations.

OLD STANDARD SCREEN

— C I N E M A S C O P E —

• **Plate 1.7** Early 1950s advertisement for the (then) new Twentieth Century Fox widescreen Cinemascope system. The ad is intended to give consumers an idea of how the Cinemascope image (married with stereophonic sound) vastly improves the experience of cinema-going

Cinema exhibition today

Throughout the studio era and before, the most powerful sector of the film industry was exhibition. In today's film economy, however, distribution is the dominant sector (see below).

Theatre ownership in the USA is still dominated by a small number of companies. For example, in 1987 twelve cinema circuits controlled 45 per cent of cinema exhibition in the USA (and 29 per cent of the market was accounted for by the four leading circuits alone) (see Jowett and Linton 1989: 43).

And history does repeat itself. In spite of the consent decrees of the late 1940s and early 1950s, the majors are once again amongst those companies with substantial interests in cinema chains. By the end of 1987 they had acquired interests in 14 per cent of US and Canadian theatre screens (ibid.: 46), and by 1989 four film companies (Universal, Columbia, Paramount and Warners) were subsidiaries of parent companies owning 3,185 screens in the USA and Canada.[13] The US government's view on this has been that the majors' ownership of theatre screens does not, in itself, constitute a threat to competition because of the diversified nature of the industry infastructure itself today – evidenced by independent production, pay-TV, DVD/video etc. However, even the majors would concede that their ownership of cinemas gives them a head start in the exploitation of their blockbusters (see below).

Theatrical presentation is no longer typified by large, select first-run movie theatres as in the studio era. Individual theatres are now usually small mini-theatres (average seating capacity, 200–300), and mainstream commercial films distributed by the majors generally open simultaneously at a large number of these 'screens'.[14] Several screens are commonly housed under one roof, in multiplex theatres, where economies of scale (several screens sharing overheads) allow for low per-unit costs. These cinemas are often purpose-built, located on major roads outside of town centres (where land is cheaper and more readily available) and associated with shopping-mall developments.

The multiplex theatre

The company to first realise the potential of the purpose-built, multi-screen theatre was American Multi-Cinema (AMC) in the 1960s. Its success with the multi-screen formula was so great that by the 1980s AMC was one of the five largest cinema chains in the USA. Based on the statements of AMC's senior management in 1983, its targeted audiences appeared to be the same as those of all exhibitors right back to the days of the nickelodeon theatres: 'we prefer to locate theatres in middle-class areas inhabited by college-educated families...These groups are the backbone of the existing motion picture audience and of our future audience' (Squire 1986: 329–30).

Another company notable for its development of the multi-screen concept is the Canadian company Cineplex. It opened its 18-screen Cineplex in Toronto's Eaton Centre in 1979, followed by a complex in the Beverly Centre, Los Angeles in 1982. After its purchase of the Odeon chain in Canada in the mid-1980s, it began its US acquisitions in earnest, so that by 1988 it was the largest theatre-chain in North America (Jowett and Linton 1989: 47). Cineplex–Odeon's UK acquisitions began in May 1988 with the purchase of the 10-screen Maybox Theatre in Slough. Within a year its Gallery Cinema chain in the UK consisted of eleven multiplexes.[15]

From the mid-1980s, Cineplex–Odeon has led the exhibition industry in its construction of several mini-picture palaces and the introduction of cafés and kiosks selling film-related materials. The company did find itself in a fragile financial position in 1989 when its debt-financing left it over-extended in a major recession (much like Warners in 1931). But by then the company's style and innovation had set the tone for contemporary mainstream exhibition practice.

More new screens: boom or bust?

Since the mid-1990s there has been a large investment in new screens in the USA (and elsewhere): in 1996 there were 26.5 thousand screens in the US sector, and by 2000 this figure had risen to 38 thousand (Parkes 2001: 10). As a consequence, cinema attendance has increased, but this construction boom has also led to overcapacity in the marketplace and bankruptcies in leading chains such as Regal Cinemas, the largest chain in the USA.

E-cinema and implications for exhibition

As of 2000, there were twelve commercial operators using e-cinema technologies worldwide, with projectors in the USA, UK, France and Mexico (Sanghera 2000: 18). And by 2020, media analysts generally agree that there will be a complete transition from 35mm to digital files in movie exhibition. The changeover offers many advantages to the industry, such as no more expensive prints to manufacture (currently 35mm prints for a feature cost US$1,000 – $2,000 apiece), relative ease and flexibility of delivery to theatres (by DVD, IP networks, cable or satellite) and the chance to expand into theatrical pay-per-view non-film content (e.g. football, pop concerts etc.). There are disadvantages as well, however, the leading one being the cost of the digital projector which currently runs at around $200,000 per machine (as opposed to $30,000 for film projectors). Also, there are challenges to overcome to ensure that the movies arrive at the theatre without being degraded, altered or stolen (La Franco 2001: 56–7).

Runs

It is worth noting that there are a variety of different types of cinema-run in operation today. A run can be **exclusive**, **multiple** or **saturation**. Combinations of runs are selected (largely at the discretion of distributors) on the basis of a film's likely performance. For instance, the exhibition of a word-of-mouth 'sleeper' – a small budget film that does unexpectedly well at the box-office – will usually begin with a semi-exclusive run, until it has built up enough of a reputation to warrant a wider run.

Harry Potter (2001)

Harry Potter and the Sorcerer's Stone (UK title, *Harry Potter and the Philosopher's Stone*) set a record in US exhibition history on Friday 16 November, 2001, by opening 'superwide' in a record number of theatres – 3,672 – and on around 8,000 screens (approximately 21 per cent of the nation's total). In the UK, the number was around 500 theatres and 1,140 screens (approximately 38 per cent of the nation's total). In both cases, openings were accompanied by huge marketing campaigns around the time of release (see below, pp. 32, on AOL Time Warner synergy and marketing).

The UK scenario[16]

In Britain, some of the international majors have shareholding relationships with exhibition companies; others do not. Thus, Paramount, Universal and Warner Brothers are represented in UK exhibition; Columbia, Disney and Twentieth Century Fox are not.

Despite there being around 350 exhibition companies in the UK, the four largest companies alone account for 55 per cent of UK screens and 65 per cent of the box-office returns according to industry estimates. These companies are Odeon, UGC (a French company part-owned by Vivendi, owner of Universal), UCI (largely owned by Paramount and Universal) and Warner Village (a joint venture between WB International Theatres and the (Australian) Village Roadshow International Theatres). Odeon is the biggest of the exhibitors with approximately 630 screens, followed by UGC and UCI each with approximately 350 screens and Warner Village with approximately 320 screens (as at end of 2000).

Independent cinemas account for only 20 per cent of box-office revenue in the UK. Under the label 'independent', are many different types of cinema organisation. Some independents are simply smaller chains showing mainstream fare. Others show a mixture of 'blockbuster', 'off-centre' (mainstream but not blockbuster) and 'art' films. Other cinemas specialise in the screening of minority interest/alternative films.

Schemes to offset the dominance of the blockbuster in UK cinemas include the Europa Scheme (administered by Media Plus[17] – the Third European Media Programme [2001–5]) which makes available to UK exhibitors public monies to assist in the showing of European films. However, there is a minimum target of 70 per cent non-national EU/Norway/Iceland/Liechtenstein films which must be shown for cinemas to qualify.

Finally, in the public sector, the regional film theatres (RFTs) provide a circuit of exhibition for minority interest/alternative cinema. They also provide excellent education on film through newsletters, lectures, conferences and workshops.

Power and control are two hotly disputed areas in the film industry in the UK today. Some parties argue that despite the renaissance in cinema-going in the UK,

---

exclusive run
Where a film is screened only in one movie theatre.

multiple run
Where a film is shown simultaneously at a number of cinemas. 'Platforming' a movie in a few cities, in up to 200 screens, can help build up word-of-mouth enthusiasm for 'off-centre' (mainstream but not blockbuster) movies.

saturation run
Where a film opens 'wide' and is shown simultaneously at an enormous number of cinemas, accompanied by heavy media promotion.
Increasingly, 'superwide' openings are becoming an entrenched strategy for 'event' films such as the big summer releases where a film can open in 3,000 plus US and Canadian screens simultaneously. 'Superwide' openings help ensure that big films reap big returns at the box-office, particularly on the opening weekend, before the reviews come out.

For further discussion of contemporary British films, see Chapter 9.

structural domination by the majors in distribution, and their influence on exhibitors (exhibitors will not endanger the main source of their revenue), mean that non-Hollywood product (including UK film) does not get a fair crack of the whip in UK cinemas.[18] Others dismiss the conspiracy theories and point out the obvious – that the Hollywood product has the advantage of high production costs, high marketing budgets and film stars, and that these are the films that the public want to see and exhibitors want to show.

Whatever lies behind exhibition practice in the UK today, the (new) British Film Council, mindful of the concerns of many in European production, is nudging big cinema chains to widen their exhibition base and show a greater variety of fare. How much the major exhibitors will do so will depend on whether they think there is a market there to exploit. *Amélie* (2001) has recently performed very well at the UK box-office. But should other Euro films do well and the larger exhibitors move into this market, it should be borne in mind that the art-house/specialist cinemas – who hitherto have dominated this sector – will see their low market share eroded even further than it is right now.

Whether considering large chains or small, most UK cinemas today are multiplexes. The turning point in UK exhibition is usually taken as November 1985 when the purpose-built multiplex, the Point, first opened its doors in Milton Keynes. However, it should be noted that the company, Screen 4, had been building four-screen cinemas in the north since the mid-1960s, cinemas which were effectively purpose-built. Nevertheless, the success of the Point and other early multiplexes, such as the Maybox in Slough, triggered new investment in British exhibition and a resurgence in the cinema-going habit in the UK. A year prior to the opening of the Point, cinema attendance was down to 52 million admissions per year. By 1996 that figure had risen to 123.5 million admissions, and an estimated 148 million by the end of 2001. The multiplex has played a crucial role in this renaissance of cinema-going by offering the punter a choice of viewing in a modern, comfortable environment.

See section on Film Audiences, pp. 35–37, for more information on cinema-going.

Distribution today

The role of the majors today embraces film production, distribution and (since the mid-1980s) exhibition. In the area of exhibition, the majors' participation is very significant but not completely dominant. In the fields of production finance and distribution, however, the majors rule supreme. Their names are all very familiar from the studio era: Paramount, Warner Brothers, Columbia, Universal, Disney and Twentieth Century Fox.

Since the consent decrees of the late 1940s, the power base in the industry has shifted from exhibition to production finance and distribution, i.e. from the power base of the pre-1949 majors to the power base of the post-1949 majors (Balio 1976: 458–67). This shift reflects the fact that film revenue is no longer purely a function of cinema receipts. With the increasing importance of other distribution 'windows' (e.g. DVD/video, subscription TV and terrestrial TV) and merchandising spin-offs, access to a major's worldwide distribution/marketing network has become the determining factor in a film's financial success. Through their domination of marketing and promotion, the majors ensure that it is their films that the public wants to see and that cinema owners want to secure for their cinemas. Witness the reaction of the public and the exhibitors to the beat of the distributors' tom-tom with blockbuster releases such as *Jurassic Park* (summer 1993) and *Harry Potter* (autumn 2001).

Today, a major financier–distributor stands between the producer (if not directly producing the film itself) and the exhibitor. It will largely dictate the business terms which shape a film's finance and exploitation. As noted by the ex-chairman of Cineplex–Odeon, Garth Drabinsky, in 1976:

If, but only if, a distributor...decides that the picture merits release and the kind of expenditures necessary to get it off the ground, the distributor will enter into a distribution agreement with the producer to govern their relationship.

(Cited in Jowett and Linton 1989: 56)

For the most part, the distributor dictates the terms of its deal with the exhibitor as well: the nature of the run, the length of the engagement, the advertising to be employed and the financial split of box-office receipts between the various parties. It has also been reported that it is common practice for distributors to exploit their upper hand with exhibitors and insist on blind-bidding and block-booking (ibid.: 43–4).

Distribution windows

Up until the mid-1970s, apart from the theatrical release, the only distribution windows were network and syndicated TV. The new age of film distribution began in 1975 with the introduction of Time Inc.'s Home Box-office cable pay-TV (HBO) and Sony's domestic Betamax videocassette recorder (VCR). The following year, Matsushita introduced the VHS format for domestic VCRs. This soon became the industry standard.

Today, a number of distribution windows play key roles in determining film profits. The most important is still the *theatrical window*. Failure to secure a theatrical release will severely restrict a film's profitability. Apart from the lost revenue, a film that hasn't secured a theatrical release cannot secure anything but poor deals for the other windows, because DVD/video, TV etc. rely on the publicity of a theatrical release to promote a film. Without one, the film is a far less valuable commodity. A typical distribution sequence for a major's film in the USA will be an initial theatrical release of around six months, followed by a DVD/video window (which remains open for an indefinite period). This is followed by pay-per-view telecasts anywhere from two to three weeks after a film goes on video release, and a premium cable movie channel window (for approximately one year), a network TV window and, finally, a syndicated TV window. Because of the enormous importance of rental and retail DVD/video software to film profits, the majors in recent years have increasingly marketed their own software labels, rather than sell on the DVD/video rights of their films.

For an interesting discussion on the importance of lesbian and gay film festivals in the area of distribution and exhibition see Chapter 8, pp. 283–284.

DVDs (digital versatile discs)

The first commercial DVD players appeared in Japan in 1996. Early manufacturers were Toshiba, Pioneer and Matsushita. DVDs were designed to compete with VHS and they are certainly doing that. Currently the DVD market is growing at ten times the VHS market, with Blockbuster Video estimating that 30 per cent of its US rental business is DVD.[19]

The recent phenomenal success of DVD lies in the high quality of the image and sound, the increased storage capacity compared to video (up to 8 hours of high quality video, up to 8 tracks of digital audio and interactive features) and DVD as a cross-platform format (DVD can be viewed on dedicated DVD players, PCs, Macs and game consoles) (see Angelini 2001). And yet, industry pundits do not expect DVD players to totally replace VCRs in the immediate future because recordable DVD is currently for computer data only and the costs are high. But this is bound to change with time. (For a discussion on DVDs and audiences, see Case study 2: *Gladiator*, pp. 26–28; see also below on film audiences, pp. 34–45.)

Marketing

One of the key roles of a financier–distributor is to successfully orchestrate the marketing of a film. The three main types of advertising used in film marketing are: **free publicity**, **paid advertising** and **tie-ins/merchandising** (see below, pp. 34–45, on film audiences).

free publicity
Free coverage of subjects which the media feel are newsworthy.

paid advertising
Promotion on TV, radio, billboards and printed media.

tie-ins
Mutually beneficial promotional liaisons between films and other consumer products and/or personalities.

merchandising
Where manufacturers pay a film company to use a film title or image on their products.

Universal's UK marketing of *Jurassic Park* (1993)

Free publicity in the UK media included reports on such diverse subjects as Spielberg profiles, reports on the making of the film (particularly with regard to its special effects), the film's premieres, genetic engineering, dinomania and the film's certification.

Paid advertising in the UK included promotion on TV, radio, billboards and in newspapers and magazines. The TV blitz the week before and the week of its opening is typical of saturation release patterns for 'big' movies.

Tie-ins in the UK included multimillion-dollar tie-ins with McDonalds and selected hotels.

Merchandising in the UK included JP holographic watches, JP vinyl model dinosaur kits, JP fantasy balls, JP pinball machines, JP socks, JP briefs, JP Christmas cards and JP building bricks.[20]

The UK scenario

The international majors dominate UK distribution: each has a UK subsidiary to handle its distribution. To offset the dominance of the majors in distribution, there are mechanisms available to assist independent distributors with the marketing and distribution of their films. Public assistance (in the form of a loan) is available through the Media Plus programme – headquartered in Brussels – which is designed to support the promotion of European films: European distributors of films and DVDs/videos receive loans to help with distribution and promotion costs within European markets. Welcome as this programme is, it hardly compensates for the domination of distribution by the multinational media companies.

Not surprisingly, given the dominance of the majors in UK distribution, patterns of distribution in the UK mirror those in the USA. There is normally a six-month theatrical window for a film, followed by a DVD/video window of the same length (the DVD/video agreement itself is normally for one year). There follow pay-per-view telecasts (normally twelve months after the initial theatrical release), and later telecasts on premium cable/satellite movie channels such as Sky Premier. This window normally extends for between twelve and fifteen months, after which films are available for terrestrial TV screening. It is important to note that *all* windows are contractually agreed with the parties concerned and are not subject to any regulatory framework. In the case of TV-financed UK feature-film production (currently a dominant model for UK commercial production), the terrestrial TV window may be brought forward contractually because TV financiers wish to show their product on TV as soon as possible. However, factors such as critical and public response will, inevitably, also affect distribution patterns even for these films.

Production today

Before examining those key players that dominate mainstream film production today – the majors, **independent** producers, agents/management groups and stars (see below) – it is useful to review the current industrial organisation of film production.

The industrial system in operation today is called the 'package-unit' system (Bordwell *et al*. 1985: 330–7). Under this system, the self-contained studio and long-term-contract studio employee of the studio era have been replaced by rented studio space and short-term-contract employment. Today, individual producers are responsible for bringing together all the components of a film's production – finance, personnel, the 'property', equipment, studio space – on a short-term, film-by-film basis.

independent
A highly problematic term, meaning different things in different situations. *Here*, the term simply implies a production realised outside one of the majors. *Here*, the term does not imply a production context outside the mainstream institutional framework altogether, *nor* does it imply a film produced in an alternative aesthetic format to 'Classic Hollywood'.

Why package units?

The shift to the package-unit system from the mid-1950s was a direct response to the combined effects of the 1949 consent decrees: the rise of independent production, cost-cutting and rationalisation at the majors' studios, and the majors leasing studio space to independent producers.

Majors vs independents

Despite the growth of independent production in the 1950s, by the early 1970s the majors had reclaimed their domination in production. Their hegemonic role in current film distribution and production is evidenced by the following statistic: between the years 1970 and 1987, films directly produced by the majors collected on average 84 per cent of the total US/Canadian box-office returns (Jowett and Linton 1989: 38).

In recent years, however, there has been some evidence to suggest that independent production is once again making inroads, at the expense of the majors' own produced features. In 1991 for instance, films produced independently accounted for one-third of the summer box-office grosses in the USA and Canada.[21] But, despite this recent success for independents, their continued dependence on the majors – particularly if they are 'picked up' for distribution only after production is completed – makes the return on investment for their backers more-than-somewhat precarious.

New media and independent production/distribution

Launched by Artisan Films at the 1999 Sundance Film Festival (a showcase for independent film), *The Blair Witch Project* (1999) was perhaps the first blockbuster to use extensive digital camera footage. Since then, industry interest in digital video-making has skyrocketed. This is partly a consequence of interest in innovation and partly an interest in low-budget production. Another digital production, *Chuck and Buck*, was launched at Sundance in 2000, also by Artisan Films (Haring 2000), and by 2001 more than 40 per cent of the projects submitted for the Sundance Festival were shot on digital formats.[22] Notable digital releases premiered at Sundance that year included the documentary feature *Startup.com*.

Today, not only is production informed by new media technologies, but so is distribution. Companies such as ifilm and atomfilms are revolutionising distribution of short films by releasing them via their web sites. A notable film to be distributed this way is *405* (2000), put out on ifilm.com. The industry is hoping that a future TV-like boom in online entertainment will generate big advertising revenues from such film-screening web sites.

Agents

The ending of long-term studio contracts for creative personnel in the early 1950s (a consequence of the rationalisation of studios by the majors after the consent decrees) meant that important stars, directors, writers and other talent could now negotiate very lucrative freelance deals with film companies.[23] Their increased negotiating power also strengthened the hand of their agents who negotiated their deals with the film companies. The most powerful agency at the time was MCA, controlled by Jules Stein and Lew Wasserman. So successful was the agency during the 1950s that it purchased Universal in 1959.

MCA's agency monopoly ended in 1962, when it closed down to concentrate on film production. Today there are three big talent agencies in Hollywood – Creative Artists Agency (CAA), William Morris, and International Creative Management (ICM). Apart from these three, there are many smaller 'boutique' agencies who handle a select number of important clients.

Agencies do occasionally get more directly involved in the production of film projects, as evidenced by the agency 'package', where big agents offer groups of creative personnel (with possibly a literary property as well) as a joint package to a production company for a single film or TV production. The most famous example of this in recent decades has been the agency packages put together by CAA for films such as *Ghostbusters II* (1989) (Kent 1991: 210–45).

Interestingly, recent evidence suggests that Hollywood talent may in part be forsaking agents in favour of representation by lawyers and management groups such as Artists Management Group (AMG), run by Michael Ovitz, ex-CAA.[24] This may be a consequence of the talent preferring a less intimate and more corporate relationship between themselves and their representatives in an era of superstar-producers.

Stars

For further discussion of the star in film see Chapter 4, pp. 169–181.

A star's association with a film project affects the ease with which it can be financed and marketed. A star's presence in a film is also held to be an important factor in a film's box-office performance. These three factors explain the huge salaries awarded stars today. However, some statistics suggest that stars are less a factor in a film's box-office success than was once the case.[25] Certainly, stars cannot ensure box-office success for films in which they appear (if they ever could); nonetheless, their position within the current Hollywood economic structure is central.

Arnold Schwarzenegger, star

Such was the popularity of this star in the early 1990s that for *Total Recall* (1990) he was able to command a $10 million fee, plus 15 per cent of the gross takings of the picture. However, even Arnie could not guarantee massive profits at the box-office all the time, and his 1993 summer release, *The Last Action Hero*, was a huge commercial flop in cinemas.

The UK scenario

British feature films today are generally made on low to medium budgets (up to UK£3.5 million, or approximately US$5 million at 2002 exchange rates) and are usually co-productions, where film finance comes from a range of sources. Dominant players are UK and foreign terrestrial TV companies, film companies and cable/ satellite companies. In addition, funding assistance in the form of a loan is available from the (British) Film Council.

TV money for UK film production

For further discussion of the funding and finance of British film, see Chapter 9, p. 332. For further reference to and analysis of contemporary British film see Chapter 9, pp. 349–351.

For twenty years Channel 4 has been the British channel most actively engaged in film production. Since its launch in 1982, it has participated in well over 300 films including *My Beautiful Laundrette* (1985), *The Crying Game* (1992; see pp. 29–31), *Four Weddings and a Funeral* (1994), *Trainspotting* (1996) and *Secrets and Lies* (1996). And, like the BBC – its terrestrial rival in film production – it favours co-productions. But recently Channel 4 has announced a huge cutback in film finance, partly as a consequence of the failure of its big budget films at the box-office: films such as *Charlotte Gray* (co-produced with Warners, 2001). It has also closed its film distribution company Film Four. Under the circumstances, one can only quote Steve Woolley (producer of *The Crying Game*) when he says that 'it is a really black day' for the British film industry (cited in Nathan 2002: 15).

For most low- to medium-budget productions, a typical sequence of events for developing and producing a feature film is as follows. Applications are first made by the creative team[26] for development money to produce a preliminary script and project budget: funding sources include the commissioning groups themselves, the Film Council and the Media Plus programme.

Having produced their preliminary script and budget, the creative team seeks sources to fund the production proper. 'Pack-of-cards' financing typifies these co-productions: each source of funding is dependent on the participation of the others. As each source of finance comes on board, the script is changed to fit in with the requirements of the specific investor. The backers are inevitably financiers-cum-distributors, and monies from the distribution deals made at this point for different 'territories' – i.e. USA, UK and the rest of the world – are used to fund the production. Once the budget is fixed, pre-production in earnest begins with the preparation of the final script and budget.

The Film Council

This agency, which was set up in May 2000, brings under its umbrella the British Film Institute, the British Film Commission and British Screen Finance. It replaces the Arts Council as the co-ordinator of National Lottery funds earmarked for British Film – and not a minute too soon for many people. Under the Arts Council stewardship – between 1996 and 2000 – the funds had supported mainly a string of poor quality flops such as *Janice Beard: 45 wpm* (1999) and had provided little in the way of long-term gains for the UK film industry, [27] although to be perfectly fair a few quality productions did materialise, for example *Hideous Kinky* (1999) and *Ratcatcher* (1999), even if they too lost money at the box-office.

The Film Council has a budget of UK £150 million to spend over three years, including £15 million for development money, £15 million for small-budget innovative films and £30 million to commission bigger films such as *Gosford Park* (2001), which received £2 million in Lottery funds. It has also set itself the challenge of overseeing structural changes in the UK film industry by giving makers more ready access to finance and by getting a broader range of films into UK cinemas. This will be achieved presumably by affecting changes in film distribution, where US companies currently represent 85 per cent of the market. Many in the UK industry hope that the Film Council will succeed in its aims.

....

Working Title Films

In spite of the efforts of the Film Council and TV commissioning groups, the British film industry is less protected than it has ever been from the demands of the global entertainment economy. The UK production company most successful in meeting those demands is currently Working Title Films, responsible for *My Beautiful Laundrette*, *Four Weddings and a Funeral*, *Notting Hill* and *Bridget Jones's Diary*. This company points one way forward for UK commercial feature production, with its focus on genre film-making (romantic comedy) and its move away from small-scale TV funding of the early hits, toward bigger budgets, international financing and global distribution. The recent production, *Bridget Jones's Diary*, for instance, was a $22 million production[28] distributed by Universal and Miramax (Disney).[29] But clearly such a recipe for UK production as a whole is too narrow, and doesn't guarantee success. Take, for instance, the recent co-production deal between Channel 4 and Warner Brothers: it failed both artistically and financially (see above, p.24). As a general aspiration, what is needed are popular films that are also distinctive and personal. British film-making needs to break away from its own somewhat entrenched position of pigeon-holing film as either 'genre' or 'cultural'.[30]

....

For case studies on contemporary British Film see Chapter 9, pp. 352–356.

☐ CASE STUDY 2: A US 'BLOCKBUSTER' PRODUCTION – *GLADIATOR* (RIDLEY SCOTT, 2000)

Script development and pre-production

*For a discussion of
Gladiator, amongst other
films in terms of
masculinity see Chapter
7, pp. 264–275.*

In 1996 David Franzoni (producer/writer) approached Dreamworks SKG with a story about gladiators in ancient Rome. The story was then developed by him in collaboration with the head of Dreamworks Pictures, Walter Parkes, and producer Douglas Wick. In the process they revived the 'ancient epic' genre, one that hadn't really seen the light of day since the mid-1960s in such films as *The Fall of the Roman Empire* (1964). This older film, in fact, was to share many of same protagonists as the future production, *Gladiator*.

The producers felt that their planned film needed a director who could manage the cinematic spectacle that would feature in it. Hence they approached Ridley Scott, who relished the prospect of recreating a detailed historical environment that would be realistic. The creation of detailed worlds that were believable on their own terms, irrespective of genre, had been a hallmark of earlier Scott productions such as *Alien* (1979), *Blade Runner* (1982) and *Someone to Watch Over Me* (1987). Once the great metteur-en-scéne agreed to direct, script development began in earnest.

Franzoni produced the first draft of the screenplay, with John Logan and William Nicholson working as collaborators later on. In the process, the games in the Roman arena came to occupy the central focus of the narrative. And for many months before production began, Scott worked on sketches of the key scenes and on storyboards with Sylvain Despretz. This production was to reflect Scott's long-held notion that direction is akin to orchestration, with incident, sound, movement, colour, sets and computer graphics all knitted together under his watchful eye (Bukatman 1997).

The film would be jointly produced, financed and distributed by Dreamworks and Universal, the former having had a long-standing distribution arrangement with the latter.[31]

It was decided that location shooting would bring down the cost of the production, rather than trying to construct everything in Hollywood. However, filming on the site of historical monuments was impossible because of the likely damage incurred during filming and because of the often poor condition of the sites to begin with. Therefore scouting commenced in Europe and North Africa for locations that could accommodate new sets. Such was the scale of the production that individual design departments were assigned to each of the major locations (UK, Morocco and Malta) by Arthur Max, the

• Plate 1.8
Still from *Gladiator*
(Ridley Scott, 2000)
Maximus (Russell
Crowe) and his fellow
gladiators – tensile,
hard-muscled and
armoured – salute the
roaring crowds in the
Colosseum as they and
their Dreamworks/
Universal picture enjoy
the sweet smell of
success

film's overall production designer. In each location 'sets, props and costumes were custom-made for the film', or sets were added to existing buildings (Landau 2000: 66).

The biggest set, that of 'ancient Rome', was built at Port Mifisalfi, Malta, over nineteen weeks in the winter of 1998/99, just prior to filming. The set included a full-scale section of the Roman Colosseum (the rest would be filled in using computer graphics), as well as sets for the emperor's palace, the Forum and the Roman marketplace. This huge complex of sets was built on to disused nineteenth-century barracks on the site to add an air of authenticity to the look of the production. This is a favoured technique of Scott's to add verisimilitude to the world he is creating, as per the sets of *Blade Runner* which were built on to old Warner Brother city sets to legitimise the film's noir mise-en-scène.

Production and post-production

From the beginning, the shoot was a very complex affair. The scale of the production – with a mammoth budget of over US$100 million, scenes involving thousands of extras and a four-month shoot in four countries – necessitated the use of four different crews.

Principal photography commenced at the beginning of February 1999, in Bourne Woods, Farnham, Surrey, after the construction of a Roman encampment, a stake barricade and a forest dwelling. The opening battle scene – set in Germania in the film – was a hugely involved affair incorporating replicas of Roman war machines and an army of 1,000 extras. Shooting was finally wrapped up in the UK on the 24 February, 1999[32] from where the production moved to Morocco.

Morocco was the setting in the movie for the gladiator school. In preparation for filming, the local production crew had been busy for nine weeks, since December 1998.[33] In all, the shoot took three weeks here, after which the production moved to Malta for the 'Rome' scenes.

Again, preparation of the sets had begun long before shooting: because of the scale of the set, construction had begun nineteen weeks earlier. And despite bad storms damaging the set,[34] filming commenced around mid-March and was completed by the end of May 1999.[35] This part of the shoot involved the large-scale Colosseum scenes incorporating 2,000 extras.

Finally, there followed a two-day shoot in Tuscany, which was the chosen location for the home of Maximus in the film. This work – involving Ridley Scott, the main crew (which travelled from location to location), doubles and stunt doubles – marked the end of the long location schedule.[36]

The film was then completed at Shepperton studios, but not before the extraordinary computer visual effects work of Mill Film (London) was incorporated into the film to create the composite shots of the Colosseum. Computer graphic imaging (CGI) was utilised to complete the circumference of the first tier of the stadium and to create the second and third tiers. CGI was also used to increase the number of spectators in the Colosseum from 2,000 to 35,000, and to extend other vistas on the Rome set.[37]

The film was edited by Ridley Scott and Pietro Scalia, and scored by Hans Zimmer (head of Dreamworks' film music division) and Lisa Gerrard. With the completion of post-production, Scott delivered the picture to Dreamworks on time and on budget (US$106 million[38]).

Distribution and exhibition

For the film's marketing poster, Dreamworks SKG (responsible for marketing the film in the USA/Canada) and United International Pictures (Universal's marketing arm and responsible for international distribution) promoted a low-angled, medium long shot of the film's star, Russell Crowe, in costume as Maximus. Here for all to see was the towering presence of a rectilinear, hard, tough male action star with classical adornments of armour and phallic sword. At his feet, literally, lay the Colosseum, across the base of the poster. The powerhouse epic, *Gladiator*, had been launched!

The movie's marketing campaign was standard for a blockbuster: saturation booking technique with simultaneous media promotion on a massive scale. The film opened superwide in the US/Canada market on the 5 May, 2000 in approximately 3,000 screens. With such a big opening, the film caught the imagination of the punters even before the reviews came out – which is of course the purpose of a big opening. But the makers needn't have worried for the reviews were very favourable. In its opening weekend the film grossed around US$35 million and went straight to number one at the box-office. This success was repeated the following weekend in the UK, where the film opened in around 400 screens and grossed approximately £3.5 million.[39]

Merchandising was kept to a minimum so as not to cheapen the film: available were the soundtrack, books on the film's production and the movie poster – which was soon becoming an iconic image. Tie-ins included Sega games and holidays to Rome.

By the end of the film's box-office run, *Gladiator* had grossed around US$452 million worldwide, with takings of $188 million in the US market alone.[40] But the story didn't end there. On 21 November, 2000, the DVD and video were released in the USA/Canada market. The DVD two-disc set included the following extras: audio commentary by Ridley Scott, eleven deleted scenes from the movie, a behind-the-scenes documentary, a history of gladiatorial games and a theatre trailer amongst others.

Evidently, large sales of the DVD were anticipated for the forthcoming holiday season because prior to the release date 2.6 million copies of DVD were shipped to retail outlets. *Gladiator* sales more than met expectations, for it went on to become the biggest-selling DVD in the USA. Sales everywhere were remarkable: in the UK too it became the biggest-selling DVD. Eventually, worldwide sales clocked in at around 4.5 million units – the biggest selling DVD up until that time.

And so, with the financial and critical momentum afforded the film, nothing could prevent it from being nominated for twelve Oscars or from winning five in March 2001: for best film, best actor (Russell Crowe), best costume design (Janty Yates), best sound and best visual effects.

The film was, of course, distributed to pay-per-view channels, and subsequently to premium cable/satellite movie channels. In the UK, the film debuted on Sky Premier movie channel in October 2001, and announcements were made in 2001 of a deal having been struck for its terrestrial TV debut in 2003. The keenly contested battle amongst UK broadcasters for the first-run terrestrial rights was further evidence – if indeed further evidence was necessary – of the global distribution phenomenon that *Gladiator* had become.

In summary, the UK distribution windows for *Gladiator* are to date as follows:

1st commercial theatrical release
12 May, 2000

DVD/video release date
20 November, 2000

Premium satellite movie channel premiere
Sky Premier
27 October, 2001

□ CASE STUDY 3: A MEDIUM-BUDGET UK PRODUCTION – *THE CRYING GAME* (NEIL JORDAN, 1992)

This film has been chosen as a case study because it is a high-profile example of the TV co-production feature which has dominated UK production in the recent past. The project was conceived, written and directed by Neil Jordan.

For an account of British cinema in the 1990s see Chapter 9, pp. 322.

Script development and pre-production

In 1982 Neil Jordan produced an outline and partial script for a project entitled *The Soldier's Wife*. The project was proposed to the then-new terrestrial TV channel, Channel 4, but was turned down.

Nearly ten years later, in 1991, the project was set in motion again: to be directed by Jordan and produced by Stephen Woolley of Palace Productions. Despite many potential backers (including Miramax, ultimately the film's US distributor) being put off by what were perceived as 'difficult' themes – race, transgressive sexuality and Northern Ireland politics – a 'pack-of-cards' finance package was arranged through the summer and autumn of 1991. The participants included British Screen, Eurotrustees (a pan-European distribution alliance which included Palace Pictures), Channel 4 and Nippon Development and Finance (a Japanese distribution company). Financing was very tight – a modest £2.7 million budget[41] – and hard won. Quoting Steven Woolley:

It was only after literally begging on my knees to Channel 4 and British Screen (which later became strong supporters of the film), and a handful of European distributors that we were able to finance the film at all, and then only because the entire cast and crew accepted substantial deferments.

(Woolley 1992)

After script changes were made (at the behest of the backers), shooting commenced at the beginning of November.

Production and post-production

Despite the fact that the financing of the picture was not fully completed until 10 November 1991, shooting of the picture commenced a week earlier, on location in

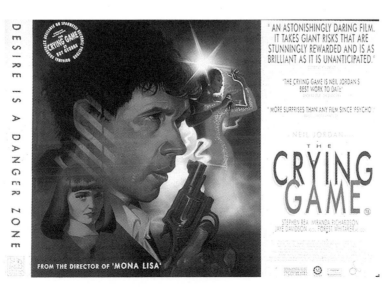

• Plate 1.9
UK poster for *The Crying Game* (Neil Jordan, 1992), utilising a noir visual vocabulary to promote the film

Ireland (Finney 1997: 25–8). As the film went into production, Palace Pictures – of which Palace Productions was a part – was in serious financial trouble. The majority of its companies would be formally put into administration in May 1992 (ibid.: 262). Despite Palace's problems, however, production proceeded.

After less than a week's shoot in Ireland, production shifted to London. Location work took place in central London (in, for instance, Eaton Square and Fournier Street, Spitalfields). The rest of the film was shot at Shepperton Studios. Shooting was completed just before Christmas 1991.

By the end of January 1992, a rough cut had been completed. Subsequently a new ending was shot at an extra cost of £45,000 (Giles 1997: 36–7). By April 1992 the film was completed, and had a new title, *The Crying Game*.

Initial UK distribution and exhibition

The film opened in the UK at the end of October 1992, having failed to secure a Cannes premiere, but having been seen at the Venice Film Festival that autumn.

Films with low budgets and no stars tend to have extended exclusive cinema runs upon release, to give the film the chance to build an audience through word of mouth. Not so here, unfortunately. Mayfair, the UK distributors, decided to book the film into cinemas across the country after only a few weeks' 'platform' exhibition in London (Finney 1997: 272–3).

Anecdotal evidence suggests that the unfortunate coincidence of the film's release with an IRA bombing campaign on the British mainland, on top of the poor marketing, severely hampered the film's chances. For despite generally favourable reviews, the film's initial box-office performance was weak (only around £680,000 gross by December 1992).[42]

US distribution and exhibition

In the spring of 1992, the partners in the film struck a US distribution deal with Miramax for $1.5 million. Miramax in the early 1990s was an independent distribution company (now owned by Disney) with a reputation for handling non-Hollywood product.

After screening the film at Telluride, Toronto and New York Film Festivals, the film was released in the USA at the end of November 1992. Miramax demonstrated its agility in non-blockbuster distribution with its careful marketing strategy. On its UK release, those marketing the film had requested that the press not reveal the film's 'secret' in their reviews. Miramax picked up on that idea as a promotional tool, and enlisted not only the media but the audience *as well* in a conspiracy of silence. The film was 'sold' to the public as an action thriller/film noir with a secret (the gay and IRA themes were played down). An inspired ad line – 'The movie everyone is talking about, but no one is giving away its secrets' – certainly helped to fire the imagination of the cinema-going public (Fleming and Klady 1993: 68). Meanwhile, Miramax also built a steady Oscar-nomination campaign for the film through late 1992/early 1993.

The promotional campaign was supported by a carefully orchestrated theatrical release pattern. The film debuted on only six screens in the USA (ibid.). By early February 1993, Miramax had taken the film 'wide' – it was now being shown at 239 screens (ibid.: 1) – and by the 17th of that month, when the Oscar nominations were announced, the film was booked into 500 screens (ibid.: 69). The film received six nominations (best film, best director, best screenplay, best actor, best supporting actor, best editing) and, on the weekend following the announcement of the nominations, grossed $5.2 million at the box-office: a '400 per cent increase over the previous week' (ibid.). By the week preceding Academy Award night – the 29 March – the number of screens had been increased to saturation level: 1,093 in total (ibid.: 1).

In the event, the film won only one academy award, that for best screenplay. Nevertheless, Miramax's effective handling of the film assured it continued box-office success. If US grosses for 1992 were a healthy $4.5 million,[43] grosses for 1993 were outstanding: at around $59.3 million.[44] In the end, the total US gross figure was estimated at around $68 million (Giles 1997: 50).

Miramax's handling of the film in the US proved to be a classic example of how to build an audience successfully for a relatively low budget, non-US feature (see below, pp. 34–40, on film audiences).

A footnote to UK distribution and exhibition: Although never outstanding, the UK box-office did pick up again as a consequence of the film's success in America. For the period December 1992–December 1993, the UK gross was around £1.4 million.[45]

In summary, the UK distribution windows for *The Crying Game* were as follows:

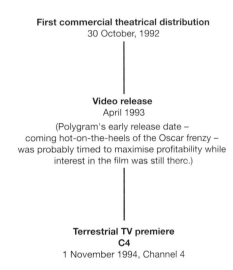

First commercial theatrical distribution
30 October, 1992

Video release
April 1993

(Polygram's early release date –
coming hot-on-the-heels of the Oscar frenzy –
was probably timed to maximise profitability while
interest in the film was still there.)

Terrestrial TV premiere
C4
1 November 1994, Channel 4

Multimedia empires

Today, it is not adequate to consider the film industry in isolation, for it is only one part of a network of media, entertainment and communications industries controlled by vertically and laterally integrated multimedia conglomerates,

Each company controlling a vast empire of media and entertainment properties that amounts to a global distribution system...[46]

Examples of such organisations are AOL Time Warner (owner of Warner Communications), Sony Corporation of Japan (owner of Columbia Pictures) and News Corporation (owner of Twentieth Century Fox).

AOL (America Online) merged with Time Warner in January 2001. The new global media giant is the largest in the world, and has interests in the internet, film and TV, publishing, cable and satellite systems and the music industry. The underlying philosophy behind the merger is to work across the corporation's holdings to create new business opportunities/associations, in other words a **synergy strategy**.

synergy strategy
Combined or related action by a group of individuals or corporations towards a common goal, the combined effect of which exceeds the sum of the individual efforts.

• **Plate 1.10**
Still from *Harry Potter and the Sorcerer's Stone* (Chris Columbus, 2001) Madame Hooch looks on as Neville Longbottom awkwardly takes to the skies. Box-office and merchandising, on the other hand, had no problem soaring due to the synergy strategy adopted by AOL Time Warner for the film's promotion

AOL Time Warner synergy and marketing

After the merger of AOL with Time Warner was completed in January 2001, the new corporation set up a 'marketing council' to optimise marketing opportunities across the whole corporation. *Harry Potter and the Sorcerer's Stone* (US title) was the first substantive evidence of this new synergy strategy in operation. Marketing was planned carefully across all media to take into account the fact that a series of films was planned for 'Harry Potter' (anywhere from three to seven films in the series[47]) and the corporation didn't want the series to suffer from overkill in the early stages.

As noted in the *Financial Times* on the film's opening weekend (16–18 November, 2001; see Grimes 2001: 17), the film was being promoted on the HBO and Warner Brothers networks in the USA, the music was being issued on Warner Music's Atlantic Records label, and a series of articles was appearing across the corporation's print media empire. Of particular note, however, was the promotional activity of AOL itself. The online service was offering merchandising (with 90 licensing partners and 700 products), ticket promotions and giveaways tied in with subscriptions to AOL services.

The combined, co-ordinated activities of the AOL Time Warner marketing council would seem to have paid off, for on the opening weekend the film took approximately $90 million in the US territory and approximately £16 million in the UK.[48] (For more examples of building audiences, see below, pp. 34–40, on film audiences.)

Sony Corporation of Japan purchased Columbia Pictures entertainment in 1989 for $5 billion. Underlying this purchase was a synergy strategy.[49] Sony bought Columbia to boost sales of its home electronics hardware and to achieve synergy between its software and hardware enterprises.[50] Since it acquired Columbia, Sony has used the studio to showcase its electronic high-definition technology such as high-definition TV and interactive multimedia video games.

The UK scenario

Rupert Murdoch's News Corporation is the media conglomerate with the highest visibility in the UK. As an example of its synergy strategy we need only look at its UK BSkyB digital satellite service comprising approximately 170 TV, CD quality radio and pay-per-view channels, interactive services, e-mail and so on. This service utilises press media and film and TV production companies owned by News Corporation across Europe, Asia and America to help promote it and provide programmes for it.

Summary

In a few years we will be looking at an integrated digital combination of TV, cable descrambler, personal computer, camcorder, and radio and phone set, which plugs into a telephone outlet.[51] Products such as these will revolutionise the communications business – of which film is a part.

The communications revolution is being orchestrated by only a handful of global players. Unless properly regulated, these few companies stand to enjoy an oligopolistic power not dreamed of in the far-off days of the MPPC and the studio era.

As a useful summary exercise, consider the questions below in relation to the previous section:

1 **What was the long-term effect of the 'Paramount' case on the film industry?**
2 **How many distribution windows can you think of for a typical blockbuster film such as *Gladiator* in today's viewing context?**
3 **To what extent do you think British films 'get a fair hearing' at the British box-office?**
4 **To what extent has the internet offered new opportunities for 'film'-making and promotion?**

FILM AUDIENCES

Fundamental to the study of cinema as institution is a study of cinema audience. This section reviews the changes in cinema audience patterns/profiles from the end of the Second World War to the present day, and considers their likely causes.

The section ends with a review of how film companies attempt to build audiences for their films.

For further discussion about the film spectator and the film audience, see Chapter 3.

The 1940s: cinema-going as recreation

Before the 1950s, cinema-going was a major recreational activity. According to one official report,[52] film-going was the number one recreational activity for most people in wartime America. The year 1946 marked the peak in cinema-going in the USA, unsurpassed to this day: in that year, the average weekly attendance in US cinemas was 95 million.[53]

From the late 1940s onwards

Studies of the composition of audiences in the 1940s identify certain key trends. Although men and women registered the same average monthly picture attendance,[54] a greater percentage of men were very high-frequency cinema-goers.[55]

Age was the major determinant in the frequency of attendance. All surveys of the 1940s point to the fact that young people attended the cinema much more frequently than older persons.[56]

Statistics from the 1940s also indicate that expenditure on motion pictures increased with annual income and that those with higher levels of education (i.e. high school and/or college) were more frequent cinema-goers than persons with only a grade-school education.[57]

By the 1950s, cinema attendance was in rapid decline. Average weekly attendance figures had dropped in 1950 to 60 million (from their 95 million peak four years earlier), and by 1956 that number had slipped to 46.5 million.[58] What happened to bring about this sudden decline? Two reasons are most often cited: the first is the change in living patterns of Americans after the Second World War, the second is TV.

'Being at home' explains the drop in cinema attendance after the peak of the mid- to late 1940s. There was a radical change in social trends in the USA after the war:

…home ownership, suburbanization of metropolitan areas, traffic difficulties, large families, family-centred leisure time activities, and the do-it-yourself movement.

(Bernstein 1957: 74)

These new trends placed the focus firmly on domestic lifestyle, to the detriment of 'outside-the-home' film entertainment. An exception to this was the rise of the outdoor drive-in theatre in the early 1950s – itself a consequence of postwar suburbanisation. Now parents could choose to have a night out at the movies in the comfort of their own car, with the kids in the back of the vehicle. By 1954 there were 3,800 drive-ins in America, whose box-office grosses accounted for 16 per cent of the total US box-office receipts.[59]

• **Plate 1.11**
Queue outside the Odeon Leicester Square, London, in the late 1940s. The years immediately following the Second World War were to be the last ones where film held the position of number-one mass medium of entertainment.

The early days of TV

The number of TV sets in America grew from 250,000 in 1947 to 8,000,000 by 1950 and to 42.2 million by 1956. TV's rise was directly proportional to the demise of movie theatres, particularly those situated in the residential neighbourhoods. It is thus logical to assume that the audiences who previously frequented local theatres were now at home watching TV instead (ibid.: 73).

The 1960s and 1970s saw an enormous growth in the leisure industry in the USA. Yet, despite this, film-going continued to decline: in 1960, the weekly attendance figure had been 40 million; by 1980, the average weekly attendance was down to 19.7 million (Austin 1989: 36, 40–1). A Gallup poll taken in 1977 underlined the dominance of home-based leisure pursuits as a 'favourite way to spend an evening'.[60] The survey also confirmed the long-standing trends of movie-going being more popular with younger persons,[61] those with higher incomes and those who were college-educated.

The 1970s and 1980s saw the expansion of home-based, 'TV-related' media entertainment in the form of VCRs, subscription cable and satellite services and video games, all of which weakened movie-going as a commercial leisure activity.

• **Plate 1.12**
Still showing Joanne Woodward in *No Down Payment* (Martin Ritt, 1957). The film industry in the 1950s would certainly have wished this fate on all domestic TV sets!

The UK scenario

The history of cinema attendance in the UK since the Second World War mirrors US statistics to a large degree. As in the USA, 1946 marked the peak in UK cinema-going. That year, the average weekly cinema attendance was 31.5 million (Docherty *et al.* 1987: 14–15), and as in the USA, high-frequency cinema-going in the 1940s was predominantly the habit of the young.[62] However, unlike US statistics, working-class people went to the cinema significantly more often than others.[63]

Attendance figures fell dramatically in the 1950s: by 1956 weekly attendance was down to 21.1 million and by 1960 to 9.6 million (ibid.). As in the USA, the precipitate drop correlated with the dramatic rise in the number of TV sets in circulation.[64] This phenomenon was symptomatic of a much larger social change of the 1950s: the growth of outlying residential areas[65] and the subsequent establishment of a home-based consumer culture. The decline in attendance amongst the frequent cinema-going age group (16–24 years) might also be a attributable to the sudden appearance of a distinct youth culture in the 1950s, which led to new forms of recreation for teenagers (ibid.: 26–7).

By the early 1970s, cinema-going was just one of many options in the expanding leisure industry. The long decline continued through the 1970s, so that by the mid-1980s weekly attendance had plummeted to just over 1 million (ibid.: 29). Other changes were apparent too: by the early 1980s the percentage of working-class people attending cinemas declined significantly for the first time ever.[66]

Recent and future trends

Attendance figures have improved in recent decades: take for instance the year 2000 when the weekly figure was 27 million for the US sector. This is partly a product of the growth in multiplexes and the resulting increase in screens since the 1990s (the number of which increased from 26.5 thousand to 38 thousand between 1996 and 2000) (Parkes 2001: 10).

Two factors that continue to be a focus of interest for film industry analysts are age and education level. Although the under 30s still account for the largest number of yearly admissions at movie theatres,[67] in recent years the percentage of the movie audience over the age of 30 has climbed significantly. For instance, between 1979 and 1987, the percentage of over-30s (in the USA) in the total movie audience increased from 24 per cent to 38 per cent.[68] And although the statistics are affected by fluctuations in age distribution within the population, this trend appears to have continued. Now the 30+ individual without kids, and indeed the older 'empty nester', are identified as important demographic categories in film industry statistics.

There has long been evidence supporting the claim that increased education translates to increased frequency of cinema-going. *If*, and it is a big if, the number of college-educated individuals continues to rise, as it has in recent years, we can suppose that movie attendance may also rise.

Currently, film-going is enjoying a renaissance with the public, with local multiplexes offering the 'supermarket' convenience of choice and car-parking facilities. But new films are also being delivered to their audience via pay TV and DVD/video. In the end, movie-going will continue as a social practice as long as the public and film industry show a willingness to support it.

DVDs and audiences as 'viewsers'

The number of DVD players in the USA has grown from around 350 thousand in 1997 to approximately 1.4 million in 1998, 5.5 million in 1999, 14 million in 2000 and to an estimated 30 million by the end of 2001.[69] This exponential growth mirrors the growth of TV sets in the late 1940s, with DVD now becoming the latest home-based entertainment phenomenon. It makes available to the consumer interactive features – multiple storylines, games, instant search controls, different camera angles for the same action[70] – that herald the new digital viewer, the 'viewser' or viewer-cum-user.

The UK scenario

In recent years, multiplexes have also been at the centre of a renaissance in movie-going in the UK: attendance has risen from a derisory 1 million per week in 1984 to 2.7 million per week by 1997 (Buncombe 1998: 9). Figures for 2001 are estimated at around 2.9 million per week.[71] Changes in audience profiles have also been noted. The 30+ individual without kids and the 'empty nester' are making impacts in the frequent cinema-goer categories as they are in the US. And amongst the most frequent cinema-goers, the 16- to 24-year-olds, demographic groups A, B and C1 are over-represented (in relation to their percentage in the general population), whereas C2 and D groups are under-represented. The shift toward better-off, better-educated young audiences is, in part at least, a consequence of the growth of purpose-built, out-of-town multiplexes which invariably need to be reached by car. This scenario is changing, however, as a consequence of new planning guidelines laid down by the government. Currently, new cinema developments are being directed away from out-of-town sites, and back into city centres, onto 'brown-field' sites, in a policy of urban revitalisation. We will have to wait and see whether this affects audience demographics.

Building an audience

Since the earliest days of the film industry, there have been attempts by makers, distributors and exhibitors to build audiences for their films. In today's film industry, building an audience is a sophisticated business: audience profiling, advertising (see above, pp. 36–37, on contemporary film industry), and psychological testing are all incorporated to help 'deliver' an audience for a film.

Audience profiling

Audience-profile data – age, sex, income level, education etc. – is influential in determining the kinds of films that receive finance and the shape such projects take.

Audience data is sought by film 'backers' seeking evidence of potential audiences for films. For instance, in recent years the percentage of the total movie audience over the age of 30 has increased significantly. The effect of this statistic has been to spur on Hollywood producers to make more films that appeal to a wider range of audiences than just the teen-market. The summer 1993 releases reflect this policy – films such as *The Firm*, *In the Line of Fire*, *Sleepless in Seattle*, *The Fugitive* and *Rising Sun*.

TV and other advertising

This topic has already been covered in the previous section on the contemporary film industry (see pp. 21–22). However, it is important to re-state that TV advertising is an essential tool in building audience interest for big-budget films. And because it is expensive, advertising budgets tend to be very high for such films: in recent years it has been noted that the total marketing costs of a US mainstream film can 'devour' up to 25 per cent of a film's total revenue.

Since the release of *Jaws* (in 1975), concentrated national TV promotion – allied with saturation booking strategies – has proven a most effective way to exploit big-budget films. To that we can add the recent successes of online, new media advertising (see, p. 32, on AOL Time Warner synergy and marketing), and to a lesser extent the efficacy of the print media.

Big-budget films need to show big returns at the box-office in the first week of release, before potentially bad reviews and word-of-mouth reduce these. *Jurassic Park* is a case in point: 'after taking $50 million in its first American weekend in June, [it] took half of that in weekend three...'[72] Thus, to maximise early box-office takings, TV advertising is at saturation level in the immediate weeks preceding and following a theatrical release.

this makes especially good sense since it is cheap to run and targets the 'lean-forward' young PC viewser/film-goer, rather than the stay-at-home 'lean-back' TV viewer.

More recently, the cross-media campaign for the blockbuster, *Harry Potter and the Sorcerer's Stone*, bears witness to the lessons learned by the industry from *The Blair Witch Project*. The campaign utilised to great effect the web, TV and the press to promote and publicise the movie.

Summary

Film as communication is not unidirectional, with the producer presenting the consumer with a fixed diet of consumables. Quite the contrary. Increasingly, new media allows market analysts to access accurate information from and about movie-goers – information which is then used to determine production decisions. Whether these decisions can help to sustain the recent renaissance of film-going remains to be seen.

As a useful summary exercise, consider the questions below in relation to the previous section:

1   What do you make of these statistics?

	US weekly attendance (millions)	UK weekly attendance (millions)
1946	95	32
1960	40	10
1980	20	1.5
2000	27	2.6

2   Who do you consider to be the typical frequent cinema-goer in the UK or USA today? Are audience demographics reflected in the choice of films shown at neighbourhood multiplexes?
3   How do film companies try to build an audience for low-budget films?

CENSORSHIP AND CLASSIFICATION

For further discussion of censorship and regulation in relation to the audience, see Chapter 3, pp. 124–126.

Embarking upon a review of censorship, even when limiting the discussion to films, is a daunting task given the size of the topic. For this reason the content of this section is limited to a discussion of contemporary censorship in the USA and the UK, followed by a look at specific examples from both countries.

Advocates versus critics of censorship

Those who argue in favour of censorship claim that it reflects and protects standards of morality generally held in society. Those who argue against it say that, rather than reflecting standards, it imposes them. There are strong arguments on both sides: advocates argue that depiction of graphic violence on film shapes social behaviour, especially in young people, and that therefore its circulation needs to be controlled. Critics, on the other hand, argue that film censorship is only one example of where ideals and morals are imposed on the public by powerful groups within society.

The contemporary US scenario

Since 1952, film has been protected under the first amendment to the constitution of the US, along with other communication media such as newspapers and magazines. Under American law, individual states have the power to censor adult material, but only if it is deemed '**obscene**' (Balio 1976: 438). However, where children are concerned state censors have extended legal powers to classify (or to rate) films as well.

The introduction of the 'ratings system' in 1968 is usually explained as an attempt by the film industry to offset the extended powers of state and municipal censors granted them that year by the supreme court which ruled that local authorities had the legal right to classify films for the protection of children.[76]

The ratings system is the film industry's 'voluntary' self-regulation system, and is administered by the Motion Picture Association of America (MPAA). The ratings in current use are G,[77] PG,[78] PG-13, R,[79] and NC-17.[80]

Some observers argue that there is little censorship in the USA, only classification. However, can one really argue that position with any confidence when film-makers are contractually obliged to deliver films to distributors that do not exceed an R rating, because exclusion of the pre-17 – frequent film-going – audience will mean that the films will do less well commercially? When this happens, as it does, censorship is in operation.

Other serious issues are raised by the current ratings system. First, what are the MPAA board's criteria for determining what children should and should not see? Second, do major film companies, as the backers of the MPAA, receive preferential treatment, as has been suggested?

Issues such as these need to be raised and discussed if we are to understand fully the motivation behind the promotion of certain moral positions in films seen in the USA and the suppression of others.

The contemporary UK scenario

In matters of censorship and classification, the UK shares many similar strategies to the USA: the only legally recognised censor bodies in the UK are local authorities; the nation's law cites 'obscenity' as a major reason for film censorship; and there exists a universally adopted system of film classification, administered by an industry-supported board – the British Board of Film Classification (BBFC) – which argues that the primary role of classification is the protection of children.

The BBFC operates a system of classification for film releases as well as for DVD/video releases and miscellaneous digital media material (such as action-oriented games or softcore erotica).[81] For the cinema, the ratings are as follows: U,[82] PG,[83] 12,[84] 15,[85] 18,[86] and R18.[87] For the DVD/video industry, an additional classification exists: Uc[88]. In the case of DVD/video releases, classification is more rigidly imposed because of the 'greater risk of underage viewing in a less controlled domestic environment…'.[89]

Unlike in the USA, however, films intended for adult consumption are subject to broad legal censorship as well as classification, and this job also falls to the BBFC, which applies a 'deprave and corrupt' test to the material it considers. Charges of obscenity or any of the following will likely result in cuts: sexual violence, glamorisation of violence, details of imitatable techniques that are dangerous and liable to cause significant injury (e.g. combat techniques), affirmation of illegal drug-taking as alluring, cruelty to animals or sexualised images of children.[90]

The BBFC is funded entirely by the film industry, and the appointment of the president and director have traditionally required the agreement of the local authorities, the industry trade associations and the Home Secretary of the day. Can the BBFC therefore claim independence as an organisation?

A case that brings out the sometimes anxious relationship between government and the BBFC is the recent 'R18' issue. In 1997, the BBFC decided to allow certain more

Key institution
The Motion Picture Association of America (MPAA) administers the classification (ratings) system in the USA.

obscene
A work, or part thereof, may be found 'obscene' if it has a tendency to deprave and corrupt (i.e. make morally bad) a significant proportion of the people likely to see it (as defined under the Obscene Publications Act [1959], and cited in the guidelines of the BBFC. See www.bbfc.co.uk.).

Key institution
The British Board of Film Classification (BBFC) is responsible for *both* classification and censorship of films shown in the UK.

explicit R18 videos which it deemed not harmful to be sold in licensed sex shops. For this the BBFC was criticised by the Home Office. Subsequently, the BBFC did a volte-face and demanded cuts in the relevant R18 videos. The company handling the films in the UK refused and made successful representation to the Video Appeals Committee. The irony is that despite initially supporting a liberalisation of censorship of R18 films, the BBFC now found itself challenging the decision by the Video Appeals Committee in the Courts at the behest of the Home Office. A landmark decision, in May 2000, found in favour of the Video Appeals Committee. As a consequence, the BBFC has now liber-alised its R18 guidelines: something it was trying to do in the first place, before the government intervened (Jones and Ford 2000; Tyler 1998: 3).

Recent public consultation in the form of questionnaires and citizens' juries evidences the widespread support for the BBFC's role where the protection of children is concerned. However, its function in the censorship of films intended for adult consumption continues to provoke a far less clear response. In the case of the R18 films, the public surveyed appear to have been in favour of liberalisation.

□ CASE STUDY 7: US – THE HAYS CODE

For a period of approximately twenty years, from the early 1930s to the early 1950s, American commercial film was subject to rigid regulation from within the industry itself. The Production Code, or Hays Code, laid down specific ideological and moral principles to which all films shown commercially in America had to subscribe.

Will Hays and the Production Code

The history of the Production Code dates back to 1922, and the appointment of Will Hays as president of the new industry-sponsored, Motion Picture Producers and Distributors of America. He was an ideal front man for the organisa-tion, having been a senior Republican politician – the ex-Postmaster-General. Hays' brief was twofold: to improve the public image of Hollywood (following a series of very public Hollywood scandals around that time[91] – the film industry feared a backlash from state censors), and to protect Hollywood's interests in Washington and abroad, through his strong ties with the Republican party.

Throughout the 1920s, Will Hays, as president of the MPPDA, saw to it that the influ-ence of his organisation increased steadily within the industry. In the first few years of his appointment, Hays focused his energies on heading off state censorship boards,[92] under the banner of free speech. In 1924, the MPPDA introduced advice to film-makers on 'the suitability for screening of current novels and stage plays' (Balio 1976: 308). In 1927 it produced a small document called *The Don'ts and Be Carefuls* for producers (Champlin 1980: 42). With the coming of 'talking pictures', a more formal code was announced (in 1930) – the Production Code.

The code proved difficult to enforce until 1934, because producers, faced with falling box-office receipts brought about by the onset of the Depression, would not adhere to its principles.[93] Film producers saw sex and violence as 'box-office' insurance. The Hays office was not yet powerful enough to force the issue.

1934, however, proved the decisive year. State censors, women's groups, education groups and religious groups were demanding action. The Roman Catholic Church formed its Legion of Decency whose 'oath of obedience not to attend condemned films was recited by millions across the country during Sunday mass' (ibid.: 44). In this climate of threatened mass-boycott of Hollywood films, the MPPDA could now rely on the complete support of the majors in implementing the Production Code.

Key films exceeding the provisions of the Code:
in their depiction of sex: *Red Dust* (1932), *She Done Him Wrong* (1932); and *Baby Face* (1933) in their depiction of violence: *Public Enemy* (1931) and *Scarface* (1932).

Universal implementation of the code was finally assured with the arrival of the Production Code Administration (PCA) that year, whereby the industry agreed that no film would be distributed or exhibited in the USA that did not carry a PCA seal.

Thus, from 1934 until just beyond the end of the studio era, the code defined the ideological limits of the classic Hollywood film.

The content of the Production Code[94]

When depicting crime, producers were not allowed to include scenes on how to commit a crime, which might inspire the audience to imitate the crime or which made criminals seem heroic or justified. *The Public Enemy* (1931), for instance, with its glorification of the gangster, would in all likelihood not have been granted a PCA seal after 1934.

The code, in keeping with its project of pacifying the religious groups in the country, took a hard line on religion. No film could 'throw ridicule on any religious faith'. Ministers of religion could not be depicted as villains or as comical and the depiction of religious ceremonies had to be handled with respect.

Under the terms of the code, representation of foreign countries and foreigners had to be respectful.[95] 'The history, institutions, prominent people and citizenry' of other nations had to be represented fairly.

Key film
compensating moral values:
Back Street (1941)

Any overt depiction of sex was banned *of course*. Other taboo subjects were sexual perversion, white slavery, miscegenation and sex hygiene! In the depiction of gender relations, films had to be sympathetic to marriage as an institution. 'Impure love' could not be represented as attractive, it could not be the subject of comedy, it could not be presented so as to 'arouse passion or morbid curiosity' in audiences, and it could not be portrayed as permissible. 'Compensating moral values' were required where the scenario depicted 'impure love': i.e. characters had to suffer in the scenario as a result of their behaviour.

Under the rules of the code, no adult nudity was permissible. Bedrooms had be treated with the utmost discretion because of their association with 'sexual life or with sexual sin'. Vulgarities, obscenities and profanities[96] of any kind were all banned. Producers could not depict dances which suggested 'sexual actions'.

With so many restrictions, it is a wonder that Hollywood was able to dispense any 'pleasure' from its dream factories during the studio era!

☐ CASE STUDY 8: CONTEMPORARY USA – RECENT MORAL PANICS

Catholic groups in the USA continue to this day in their crusade against films they feel are an affront to Catholicism. Two films which ran foul of Catholic groups in recent years are *Priest* (1995) and *Dogma* (1999). The first, a film depicting non-celibate priests – the central one of whom is gay – was accused by the American Life League and the Catholic League of being pornographic. Threats were then made to Disney, parent company of the US distributor Miramax, in the form of boycotts.[97]

A similar fate awaited *Dogma* (1999). Again, the Catholic League led other Catholic groups (thirty in all, ranging from Women for Faith and Family, to Sons of Italy) in a petition against Miramax, who handled this film also. The furore resulted in Miramax selling on the film rights to another distributor.

In both cases, the Catholic groups were fearful of the Church and its priests being depicted as 'objects of caricature and insult' (Campbell 1999). Their response however begs the question: 'whatever happened to freedom of speech?'

☐ CASE STUDY 9: UK CENSORSHIP – THE INTERWAR YEARS AND THE SECOND WORLD WAR

The British Board of Film Censors[98] was founded by the film industry in 1912 to neutralise the effect of local authority censorship (see above). From its inception, the BBFC operated a system of classification. It issued two categories: U[99] and A.[100] These categories were advisory until 1921, when the London County Council decided to adopt them. (An H category was introduced in 1933 for horror films [Robertson 1985: 58].)

Although not an official censor, the BBFC protected ruling values and interests. Indeed, its personnel had established links with government. For instance, Lord Tyrell – the president of the BBFC from 1935 to 1947 – had been Head of the Political Intelligence Department and Permanent Under-Secretary of State at the Foreign Office before taking up his post at the BBFC (Barr 1986: 44).

During the interwar years, most local authorities accepted a BBFC certificate as validation of a film's moral rectitude and therefore as fit for exhibition. Up until the end of the Second World War, the BBFC maintained a formal code of practice, like the MPPDA in the USA. The BBFC was nothing if not conscientious in its crusade and, predictable censor fodder aside (i.e. sex and crime), made sure that any filmic material that was in any way 'sensitive' did not get passed. To quote Julian Petley, in his essay 'Cinema and State' (ibid.: 44):

With its bans on the great Russian [Soviet film] classics, on...newsreels critical of Nazi Germany and Fascist Italy, on 'references to controversial politics', 'relations to capital and labour',[101] 'subjects calculated or possibly intended to foment social unrest or discontent',...it is perhaps hardly surprising that in 1937 Lord Tyrrell could say to the exhibitors association: 'We may take pride in observing that there is not a single film showing in London today which deals with any of the burning questions of the day'.

Examples of films banned or severely cut by the BBFC in the UK during the 1920s and 1930s

Film	Reason for Ban* / Cut**
Battleship Potemkin (1925)*	pro-revolutionary propaganda
Mother (1926)*	pro-revolutionary propaganda
La Chienne (1931)*	an unrepentant prostitute was the central character
The Public Enemy (1931)*	subversive depiction of crime and gangsterism
Spanish Earth (1937)**	reference to controversial foreign politics – the Spanish Civil War.

With the start of the Second World War, the state took a direct role in film censorship. The Ministry of Information was set up to control the flow of public information, for the sake of national security. In other words, it became the official censor. (The BBFC's role during wartime was vastly reduced as all films were first submitted to the MoI.) It was also responsible for presenting 'the national case to the public at home and abroad' and for 'the preparation and issue of national propaganda'.[102] Under the leadership of Jack Beddington (1940–46), the Films Division of the MoI conveyed the 'do-s and don't-s' to commercial film-makers, amongst others.

Around 1942, Jack Beddington initiated an Ideas Committee, included in which were eminent writers and directors of UK commercial film.[103] It operated as a forum for discussion, a kind of proactive censorship group, where the wartime ideological (propaganda) strategy was formulated. A film that definitely wasn't a product of the ideas committee, and seems to have 'slipped through the net' during the Second World War, was *The Life and Death of Col. Blimp* (1943). Winston Churchill, no less, attempted to stop the production, because he felt it was '…propaganda detrimental to the morale of the army'.[104] Despite his attempts, the film was made and shown: the Ministry of Information deemed it could not impose a ban on the film because it did not pose a threat to national security.[105]

☐ CASE STUDY 10: CONTEMPORARY UK – *CRASH* (DAVID CRONENBERG, 1996)

A review of the handling of the certification of *Crash* a few years ago reflects a Board that has abandoned a formal code of practice (eliminated after the Second World War), and is sensitive not to overstep the mark in its capacity as censor. Left to its own devices, it prefers the adult viewing public to debate provoking films in the public arena.

In 1996 *Crash* received the Special Jury prize at Cannes and was widely shown on the international circuit. In Britain, however, the tabloid press – particularly the *Daily Mail* and the *Evening Standard* – mounted a campaign against the film, picking up on rumours of the film's sensational storyline (concerning car crashes, disability and sexual excitement) even before the film had been publicly screened. Press attempts to encourage local authorities to ban the film were successful to a limited degree: it was banned by Westminster Council (London) for instance. Thus a lot of media pressure was brought to bear on the BBFC. However, after taking legal advice, consulting with a psychologist and arranging a screening for disabled people, the BBFC deemed the film neither obscene nor harmful. Therefore there was no reason to ban it, and the film was passed without cuts on 18 March, 1997.[106]

• **Plate 1.15**
David Cronenberg positions himself provocatively at the centre of the scenario of *Crash* (David Cronenberg, 1996), with its themes of sex, auto-collisions and death

Summary

There is no question that in the past dominant groups in society were able to impose a strict code of values on films consumed by US and UK film-goers. Today, however, media penetration and accessibility (eg through satellite), and the democratisation of culture, make a mockery of any attempt to fashion such a dogmatic policy. Nevertheless, the shaping of film texts to prescribed notions of what is 'suitable for children' or what is 'obscene' still goes on. It must be left to society to debate the correctness and appropriateness of such a policy.

As a useful summary exercise, consider the questions below in relation to the previous section:

1 Does film censorship reflect or impose standards?
2 Taking the studio era blockbuster *Gone with the Wind* (1939) as a case study, would you consider the film entirely in keeping with the spirit of the Production Code?
3 Does the BBFC underestimate the maturity of young audiences in the UK? (Do some research on the internet with regard to the cinema release of *Spiderman* (2002) in the UK.)

CONCLUSION

This chapter has centred on the institutional framework of mainstream film, and the historical relationship between text and context. Any change in production, exhibition or distribution practice, in communication technology (both hardware and software), in audience demographics or in censorship will have repercussions for the films we see and how we see them.

Films and their socio-economic contexts are part of a much broader history, that of the cultural history of the last 100 years. The purpose of this overview has been to go some way towards illuminating this point.

 **NOTES**

1 Immediately after the formation of the General Film Company, independents began operating their own distribution company – the Motion Picture Distributing & Sales Company (May 1910). This was superseded by the Film Supply Company of America, the Universal Film Manufacturing Company and Mutual Films in 1912. Later, the introduction of feature-length films further weakened the MPPC, when many of its own members began dissociating themselves from the GFC and distributed their features through alternative distribution organisations (Elsaesser 1990: 194–6, 201).

2 In 1928, First National was purchased by Warner Brothers Film Company.

3 An early form of block-booking existed during the days of the MPPC under the designation 'standing-orders' (Elsaesser 1990: 193).

4 This system was not universally adopted, nor did companies refrain from changing production systems periodically. Taking 1941 as an example, it is interesting to note that the three most financially successful companies, in terms of box-office receipts, were all operating different production systems:

   • United Artists had a system of director–units and producer–units
   • MGM operated a producer–unit system
   • Twentieth Century Fox used a central-producer system
                                       (Bordwell *et al*. 1985: 320–9).

5 See Warner Brothers' balance sheet for the studio era (Gomery 1986: 102).

6 In 1932, the average production cost per feature was US$200,000 at Warner Brothers, whereas at MGM it was $450,000 (see Campbell 1971: 2).

7 For a discussion on the relationship of this director to Warner studio style, see E. Buscombe's essay in Hardy (1974).

8 See his drawings for *Mildred Pierce* sets in Deschner (1975: 20).

9 More, 30 per cent of Columbia's releases were also produced by them (Balio 1976: 353).

10 The first major film company to sell its film library to TV was R.K.O., in December 1955 (Balio 1976: 322).

11 From the late 1940s onwards, film companies began producing programmes for TV, e.g. Warners' weekly series for ABC-TV, *Warner Bros. Presents* (1955). By the early 1960s, producing TV shows was standard film industry practice and a major source of its revenue. Shortly afterwards (from the mid-1960s onwards), TV networks began commissioning made-for-TV films from major studios and independent producers (Balio 1976: 322–4).

12 In 1956, United Paramount theatres (the ex-exhibition arm of Paramount) merged with ABC-TV (Balio 1976: 324).

13 See *Variety*, 6 December, 1989, p.3.

14 The pattern of exclusive first-run releases having been broken with *The Godfather* in 1972 (Jowett and Linton 1989: 59).

15 *Screen International*, no. 750, 31 March, 1990.

16 Many thanks to John Wilkinson, of the UK-based Cinema Exhibitors' Association, whose interviews with me assisted in the compilation of the following information.

17 An EU commission initiative and encompassing the 15 EU member states and the EEA countries (Norway, Iceland and Liechtenstein).

18 A useful precis of this argument was articulated in Wilf Stevenson's 1997 article in the *Daily Telegraph*.

19 Taken from 'DVD Rising', *Chicago Tribune*, 14/10/01.

20 Reported in 'The Sunday Review', *Independent On Sunday*, 11 July, 1993, p.15.

21 This constitutes US$600 million of the summer's $1.8 billion gross. The independent productions that were major box-office winners were *Terminator 2* (CAROLCO Productions), *Robin Hood* (Morgan Creek Productions), *City Slickers* (Castle Rock Productions), *Backdraft* (Imagine Productions) and *Point Break* (Largo Productions) (Biskind 1991: 6).

22 See Scott Smith's online article, 'Byte Me…'', dated 24/1/01, at www.atomfilms.com.

23 In 1950 James Stewart's agent, MCA (Music Corp. of America), arranged for him to be paid 50 per cent of the net profits of the Universal film, *Winchester '73*, in lieu of his normal salary of $250,000. This arrangement would not have been possible under the terms of his MGM contract during the studio era (Kent 1991: 86).

24 See online article, 'Hollywoodbuzz: The War Between the Agents', dated 2000, at www.tribute.ca/tribute/1000/hollywood buzz.html.

25 A 1989 audience survey reported that the presence of stars was not an important factor in movie attendance decisions, but only important as a means of publicising a film (Jowett and Linton 1989: 39).

26 In the form of writer/producer teams, writer/producer/director teams and unattached writers.

27 A particularly vociferous critic of the Arts Council's handling of the Lottery funds has been journalist Alexander Walker, of the *Evening Standard*: see, for instance, Walker (2000: 13).

28 Taken from the *Daily Telegraph*, 5/4/01, p.25.

29 Distribution in France was handled by StudioCanal.

30 See Chris Collins's comments in his 2001 *Guardian* essay 'British Film: The Next Generation'; also available online at http://film.guardian.co.uk/features/featurepages/

31 See www.hollywoodreporter.com/hollywoodreporter/wrap/wrap00/dreamworks.jsp, dated 24/10/01.

32 Source: www.upcomingmovies.com/gladiator.html.

33 Source: Ali Cherkaoui, 2nd Assistant Director.

34 Reported in an interview with Ridley Scott in the 'Magazine' section of *The Times*, Saturday 25 November, 2000, p.39.

35 Source: wwww.upcomingmovies.com/gladiator.html.

36 Source: Enrico Ballarin, Mestiere Cinema Productions.

37 See *Gladiator* UK press release produced by Media Enterprises, 2000, pp.15–16.

38 Source: the 'Magazine' section of *The Times*, 11 November, 2000, p.39.

39 Source: http://us.imdb.com/charts/.

40 Source: http://www.the-movie-times.com/thrsdir/top100 world.html.

41 Source: *Screen International*, no. 840, 17 January, 1992.

42 Source: *Screen International*, no. 888, 18–25 December, 1992.

43 Source: *Screen International*, no. 889, 8–14 January, 1993.

44 Source: *Screen International*, no. 940, 14–20 January, 1994.

45 Source: *Screen International*, no. 940, 14–20 January, 1994.

46 'Plenty of Fish in Pond Time–Warner Wants To Swim In', *The Wall Street Journal*, 7 March, 1989, p.B1, cited in Balio (1990: 315).

47 Warners owns the film rights to J.K. Rowling's first three books and has options on the next four. Reported in Reid and Peek (2001: 11).

48 Source: *Guardian*, 23 November, 2001, p.27.

49 See 'Will Sony Make It In Hollywood?', *Fortune*, 9 September, 1991.

50 Sony Corporation is convinced that its Betamax videotape format would have had greater success in the late 1970s if Sony had owned a studio and had thus secured for itself software for its hardware. (VHS succeeded as the standard format because it was promoted by European manufacturers – the first important domestic VCR market – and Hollywood studios adopted it as their standard format.) Source: 'Will Sony Make It In Hollywood?', *Fortune*, 9 September, 1991.

51 See 'Wiring The World', *Newsweek*, 5 April, 1993, pp.28–35. (The above scenario no doubt underlies the News Corporation/British Telecom partnership announced on 1 September, 1993.)

52 Report by the US Dept of Labour entitled *Family Spending and Saving in Wartime*, Bulletin No. 822. Cited in Handel (1950: 104).

53 Source: *Film Daily Year Book*, and cited in Handel (1950: 96). As a comparison, attendance figures for 1940 (pre-Second World War) were 80 million/week, and around 85 million/week for 1945 (end of the Second World War) (Austin 1989: 36).

54 Figures averaged: women: 3.75 times per month; men: 3.7 times per month. Source: Handel, *Studies of the Motion Picture Audience*, NYC, December 1941, cited in Handel (1950: 100).

55 Defined as attending ten times a month or more: figures for men were 11.8 per cent, as opposed to only 7.5 per cent for women. Source: A/A, cited in Handel (1950: 100).

56 In a state-wide survey conducted in Iowa in 1942, 31 per cent of men and 24.9 per cent of women aged 15 to 20 attended cinemas over five times/month, as opposed to only 11.4 per cent and 7.6 per cent respectively of those aged 21 to 35 years. Source: F. Whan and H. Summers, *The 1942 Iowa Radio Audience Survey*, Des Moines, 1942, cited in Handel (1950: 103).

57 NB: in actual numbers, persons with higher levels of education were a minority amongst cinema-goers in the 1940s (Handel 1950: 104–8).

58 Source: *Film Daily Year Book*, cited in Bernstein (1957: 2).

59 Source: Department of Commerce's Census of Business for 1954, cited in Bernstein (1957: 5).

60 Of those surveyed, 30 per cent cited watching TV as their favourite way to spend an evening. Only 6 per cent of those surveyed cited going to the movies. Source: *The Gallup Opinion Index*, Report 146, pp.14–15, September 1977, cited in Austin (1989: 40).

61 Defined in this survey as persons under the age of 30.

62 In a 1948 Gallup poll, 79 per cent of people surveyed between the ages of 18 and 20, and 76 per cent of those between the ages of 21 and 29, had been to the cinema within the last three weeks: This declined to 57 per cent for those aged 30–49 (cited in Docherty *et al.* 1987: 17).

63 In a survey in 1949, 19 per cent of the working-class people surveyed (i.e. those persons with low levels of income and

education) went to the cinema (at least) twice a week, as opposed to 13 per cent of middle-class people interviewed, and 8 per cent of upper-class people surveyed. Source: Hulton Research, cited in Docherty *et al*. (1987: 16).

64 'There was an increase in TV licences from 343k in 1950 to 10 million in 1960' (Docherty *et al*. 1987: 23).

65 Partly a product of 1950s prosperity and a move toward greater owner-occupation, and partly the result of the Town and Country Planning Act of 1947 which 'led to the clearing of slums, the growth of new towns…and, crucially, the resiting of large sections of the working class…around the edges of cities…' (Docherty *et al*. 1987: 25–6)

66 Dropping from half of the total audience to one-third between 1977 and 1983 (Docherty *et al*. 1987: 30–1).

67 For the year 1987, in the USA 12–15 year olds accounted for 11 per cent of yearly admissions; 16–20 years, 21 per cent ; 21–24 years, 15 per cent ; 25–29 years, 15 per cent. Source: MPPA, 1987, cited in Jowett and Linton (1989: 90).

68 Source: MPAA, cited in Jowett and Linton (1989: 90).

69 Source: 'DVD shipments seen reaching lofty heights', Reuters, 24 October, 2001.

70 Source: www.dvddemistified.com.

71 Source: the Cinema Advertisers Assoc. (CAA), cited in http://news.bbc.co.uk.

72 Quote from 'The Sunday Review', *Independent On Sunday*, 11 July, 1993.

73 'Every element of this heart-warming drama (*Grizzly Adams*), from the hair and eye colouring of the actors to the type of animals they frolic with, was pre-tested…your family's every 'Ooh' and 'Ahh' was anticipated in tests taken by other families demographically identical to yours'. Source: P. Morrisroe, 'Making Movies The Computer Way', *Parade*, vol. 16, 3 February, 1980, cited in Jowett and Linton (1989: 106).

74 Source: B. Farrow's article dated 8 October, 1999, 'Hollywood Runs Scared', on *The Times* web site.

75 Source: http://us.imdb.com/charts/worldtopmovies.

76 '…the choice was not between a rating system and no rating system, it was between an industry rating system and 50 state classification boards (more if you add municipalities such as Dallas)…' (Byron 1986: 76).

77 General audience.

78 Parental guidance suggested.

79 Persons under the age of 17 must be accompanied by a parent or adult guardian.

80 No one under 17 admitted.

81 As a result of the Video Recordings Act 1984, the BBFC exercises a statutory function on behalf of central govern-

ment whereby it is the designated authority appointed by the Home Secretary to classify videos.

82 Suitable for all.

83 Parental guidance advised.

84 Restricted to persons 12 years and over.

85 Restricted to persons 15 years and over.

86 Restricted to persons 18 years and over.

87 Restricted distribution only, through sex shops, specially licensed cinemas etc.

88 Particularly suitable for pre-school children.

89 See BBFC *Annual Report 2000*, p.24, at www.bbfc.co.uk.

90 See BBFC guidelines at www.bbfc.co.uk.

91 Examples of such scandals include the Fatty Arbuckle scandal (rape and murder trial), the murder of William Desmond Taylor and the death (through drug addiction) of Wallace Reid (Champlin 1980: 42).

92 'Reformer-inspired censorship legislation' was on the rise at that time in more than half the states in the USA (Balio 1976: 304).

93 Despite the introduction of mandatory script submission by producers to the Hays Office in 1931.

94 Reprinted in full in Leff and Simmons (1990: 283–92).

95 As early as 1922, the Mexican government negotiated with the MPPDA, over the representation of Mexicans in American films.

96 The dialogue, 'Frankly my dear, I don't give a damn', was only allowed in *Gone with the Wind* (1939) after a special appeal by the producer to the Hays Office.

97 Source: *The Advocate*, 2 May, 1995, p.11.

98 As it was called until 1985.

99 Universal.

100 Adult, denoting that the film was more suitable for adults. NB, in 1921, the classification was modified to stipulate that children under 16 had to be accompanied by a parent or guardian (Falcon 1994, part 2: 4).

101 For example, a ban was imposed on the scenario *Love on the Dole*, until the outbreak of the Second World War. In 1940, the project was given the go-ahead.

102 I. McLaine, *Ministry of Morale* (London, 1979), cited in Aldgate and Richards (1986: 18).

103 Including (at various times): M. Balcon, M. Powell, S. Gilliat, L. Howard, C. Frend and A. Asquith.

104 From the Prime Minister's personal minute M.357/2, 10 Sept/42, reprinted in Christie (1978: 107).

105 However, the film was cut at the request of the MoI before an export licence (for America) was granted (Christie 1978: 110).

106 See BBFC press release for the film, to be found on the web site www.bbfc.co.uk.

 **KEY TEXTS**

Algate, A. and Richards, J., *Britain Can Take It*, Basil Blackwell, London, 1986. A useful analysis of British films made during the Second World War, and their reception.

Austin, B., *Immediate Seating: A Look at Movie Audiences*, Wadsworth Publishing Company, Belmont, CA, 1989. A clear insightful examination of US film audiences in the recent past, before DVD.

Balio, T. (ed.), *The American Film Industry*, University of Wisconsin Press, Madison, 1976. An historical overview of the Hollywood film industry from its inception to the recent past.

—— *Hollywood in the Age of Television*, Unwin Hyman, Boston, 1990. A follow-up volume by Balio looking at structural developments in the Hollywood film industry in the recent past.

Barr, C. (ed.), *All our Yesterdays: Ninety Years of British Cinema*, British Film Institute, London, 1986. A series of useful essays on British film and its social context from the 1920s to the 1980s.

Bernstein, I., *Hollywood at the Crossroads: An Economic Study of the Motion Picture Industry*, Hollywood Film Council, Los Angeles, 1957. A book published in the 1950s looking at the Hollywood film industry at a moment of crisis: after the consent decrees, and audiences preferring to stay at home.

Bordwell, D. Staiger, J. and Thompson, K., *The Classical Hollywood Cinema*, Routledge and Kegan Paul, London, 1985. A classic textbook examining Hollywood film style and its mode of production from 1900 to 1960.

Docherty, D., Morrison, D. and Tracey, M., *The Last Picture Show?*, British Film Institute, London, 1987. A useful sociological review of UK audience demographics from the Second World War to the recent past.

Finney, A., *The Egos Have Landed*, Mandarin, London, 1997. An informative and interesting history of the rise and fall of Palace Pictures through the 1980s to the early 1990s.

Giles, J., *The Crying Game*, British Film Institute, London, 1997. One of the BFI Modern Classics Series, looking at the production history and themes of *The Crying Game*.

Gomery, D., *The Hollywood Studio System*, Macmillan, London, 1986. A very useful slim volume on the eight film companies that dominated the industry during the studio era of the 1930s and 1940s.

—— *Shared Pleasures*, British Film Institute, London, 1992. A useful history of how Americans watch their films: from the nickelodeon era, to the movie palaces, to cable TV and video.

Handel, L., *Hollywood Looks at its Audience*, University of Illinois Press, Urbana, 1950. An early examination of American film audiences written just after the Second World War, around the time of the consent decrees.

Jowett, G. and Linton, J., *Movies as Mass Communication*, Sage, Newbury Park, CA, 1989. A useful volume focusing on US film as business and film as a means of social interaction.

Kent, N., *Naked Hollywood*, BBC Books, London, 1991. Kent's book, based on his TV series for the BBC, examines the recent make-up of the Hollywood film industry.

Landau, D. (ed.), *Gladiator: The Making of the Ridley Scott Epic*, Boxtree, London, 2000. A fan book produced to accompany the release of the film, *Gladiator*; despite its superficiality, it is full of good images and interesting background to the film's production.

Leff, L. and Simmons, J., *The Dame in the Kimono*, Grove Weidenfeld, New York, 1990. A clear and entertaining book on the history of the US Production Code in operation from the studio era until the 1960s.

Merritt, G., *Celluloid Mavericks*, Thunder's Mouth Press, New York, 2000. An examination of non-Hollywood independent film from the birth of the movies to the present day, looking at mainstream to art to documentary film.

Robertson, J., *The British Board of Film Censors: Film Censorship in Britain, 1896–1950*, Croom Helm, Kent, 1985. Rather an empirical examination of the BBFC's policy from its earliest days until after the Second World War – but full of useful facts and figures.

Roddick, N., *A New Deal in Entertainment*, British Film Institute, London, 1983. A classic polemical study of the themes of Warner Brothers films during the studio era: particularly the 1930s/1st and 2nd terms of the Roosevelt Administration.

FURTHER VIEWING

Key Warner Brothers (genre) films

Gangster film

Little Caesar (1930)
The Public Enemy (1931)
Bullets or Ballots (1935)
Marked Woman (1937)
The Roaring 'Twenties (1939)

Social conscience film

I am a Fugitive from a Chain Gang (1932)
Wild Boys of the Road (1933)

Fast-talking comedy/drama

Five-Star Final (1931)
Lady Killer (1933)
Hard to Handle (1933)

Musical

42nd Street (1933)
Gold Diggers of 1933 (1933)
Dames (1934)

Biopic

The Story of Louis Pasteur (1936)
The Life of Emile Zola (1937)
Juarez (1939)

Merrie-England cycle

Captain Blood (1935)
The Adventures of Robin Hood (1938)
The Sea Hawk (1940)

Melodrama

Jezebel (1938)
The Letter (1940)
Now Voyager (1942)
Mildred Pierce (1945)

Film noir

The Maltese Falcon (1941)
The Big Sleep (1946)
Dark Passage (1947)

RESOURCE CENTRES

British Board of Film Classification
3 Soho Square
London W1V 5DE
Tel: 0207 287 0141

British Film Institute Library
21 Stephen Street
London W1P 1PL
Tel: 0207 255 1444

British Screen Advisory Council
19 Cavendish Square
London W1M 9AB
Tel: 0207 499 4177

The Cinema Exhibitors' Association
22 Golden Square
London W1R 3PA
Tel: 0207 734 9551

Dodona Research
12 The Crescent, King Street
Leicester LE2 2YE
Tel: 0116 285 4550

The Film Council
10 Little Portland Street
London W1W 7JG
Tel: 0207 861 7861

BBFC, at www.bbfc.co.uk
The official web site of the British Board of Film Classification
and full of useful things.

Part two

Approaches to studying film texts

Film form and narrative

Allan Rowe and Paul Wells

• **Plate 2.1**
Spider-Man (Sam Raimi, 2002)

immediately established by the introductory voiceover, which the audience assumes to be Peter Parker (aka Spider-Man, played here by Tobey Maguire), who tells his story in retrospect, posing the key question of 'Who Am I?' about his identity, and announcing that while this is not going to be 'a happy little tale', it nevertheless, 'like any story worth telling is all about a girl'. This line is juxtaposed with the appearance of Mary Jane 'MJ' Watson (Kirsten Dunst) who is, of course, the unknown object of Parker's desire, and the person who prompts most of his affective narrative events throughout the film – when he seeks to impress her; when he seeks to support and reassure her about her ambition to be an actress; when he saves her from falling with a lunch tray, from rape and assault and from his eventual antagonist, the Green Goblin.

Parker is first established as class 'nerd' chasing after the school bus, and being humiliated by his colleagues, but this is partially redressed in the following scene in which his scientific knowledge is acknowledged by his best friend Harry's father, Norman Osborn (Willem Dafoe), scientist and CEO of OsCorps, a company seeking to sell the US military a biological performance enhancer for its personnel. Parker's world is to change by the end of this scene: following a lecture about spiders which the class have attended at the University of Columbia science department, he is bitten by a genetically enhanced 'super-spider', suspensefully played out as Raimi cuts between Parker's besotted attempt to photograph MJ for the school magazine and the slowly descending thread of the spider towards his hand. The most 'comic book' aspect of this sequence, however, is a close-up of the bite itself, and the concentration on the wound which is to provoke Parker's transformation into the 'super-powered', Spider-Man.

Norman Osborn, meanwhile, threatened by the potential withdrawal of funding for his project – drawing upon many 'mad scientist' narratives of the 1930s and 1940s – decides to trial his performance enhancer on himself, resulting in his becoming a split-personality, one part Osborn, father-figure and progressive innovator, one part the Green Goblin, an evil avenger of all things denied him in his desire for success. This is essentially a 'parallel' narrative which directly echoes the story of Peter Parker and creates 'an antagonist' for Spider-Man. Osborn's role as a 'father-figure' is important, because of Parker's relationship to his own guardians, Uncle Ben and Aunt May.

Parker's Uncle Ben understandably mistakes Peter's physical, emotional and psychological changes as the transition from puberty to full-blown adolescence rather than the result of a spider bite; his parental advice – 'with great power comes great responsibility' (effectively the core 'theme' of the film) – is petulantly rejected by Peter, who hurts his uncle by telling him to 'stop pretending to be' his father. Raimi is careful to foreground the issue of personal transition and confusion in Peter by locating him in the privacy of his bedroom, narcissistically approving his own new-found muscularity; alluding to masturbatory privacy in Peter's practised ejaculation of his 'web', and the clumsy attempts to control his faculties. His new powers are also used to settle scores with the 'jocks' who persecute him at school, and to impress MJ, but even when he catches her when she slips and saves the food on her lunch tray in a tour-de-force of agility, reflex and dexterity, he still cannot speak to her, let alone articulate his feelings.

This urgency to impress leads him to try and buy a car. Parker becomes 'The Human Spider', renamed 'Spider-Man' by an exasperated MC, in a wrestling-for-cash contest, a thinly veiled parody of the WWF theatre-cum-thuggery, which draws Peter from the naivety of his high school world and into the urban mêlée, a short step from the dystopic chaos that sees the murder of his uncle by a car-jacker, ironically a thief whom Parker had not prevented from stealing the takings from the wrestling contest. In terms of narration, this is all very important. Parker has entered a world of brutality and injustice; he is overwhelmed with guilt at having rejected his uncle as his 'father'; and his 'powers' now have a purpose. To compound this transition, Parker graduates from school, and prepares to move to the city and to find work as a photographer; meanwhile he becomes Spider-Man. On the one hand, in the perception of some, he is the heroic crime-fighting avenger; on the other, he is viewed by others as a vigilante and a public menace. In the terms of 'classical narrative', this is the end of 'Act One', with everything established, to be advanced in 'Act Two', the middle section of the film, which sees Parker's consolidation as Spider-Man, and the emergence of the Green Goblin as his adversary.

This takes place when the Board of Directors of Osborn's company, OsCorps, seek to oust him as CEO as part of a buy-out agreement with their rivals for the US military contract, Quest. Osborn's alter-ego, the Green Goblin, emerges at the company's annual parade and bombs the proceedings, killing all the Board of Directors and having his first aerobatic encounters with Spider-Man, who arrives to remedy the chaos. This sequence develops the earlier dynamics of Parker's first flight across the city, testing his web, which was largely about enjoying the speed of movement through space; in the context in which Spider-Man now encounters the Green Goblin, the sequence seeks to reveal the nature of the conflict between a 'protagonist' armed with heightened senses and reflexes, a web, physical strength and intelligence, and an 'antagonist' armed with an armoured, high-powered, multi-weaponed exoskeleton and glider. Although Spider-Man is already established as 'empowered', and has demonstrated this process of empowerment, this has largely been achieved by Raimi through encouraging identification and *empathy* in the viewer; this sequence shifts the emphasis, and requires that the audience move to a point of *sympathy* with Spider-Man because initially he seems to be less well-equipped to defeat his adversary. He temporarily blinds the Green Goblin with his web and disables the wiring in the glider, thus winning the first battle between the two, but this, like the death of his uncle, becomes a significant 'turning point', as this new figure poses a greater threat, and 'Whatever it is, somebody has to stop it'. This is obviously the imperative for Spider-Man in this part of the story.

The descent into an immediate battle between the two is prevented, however, by the recognition on the part of Osborn/the Green Goblin, that Spider-Man could defeat him, and that a first option would be to proposition him into coalition. This enables Raimi to explore the moral themes in the story, rather than merely descend into an archetypal story of 'good versus evil'. The 'split-personalities' in both characters are a strong indication of the moral contradictions, ambiguities and ambivalence that inform the story – there is no clarity or certainty in this contemporary environment, and both figures represent the struggle with this fact, and the different ways of dealing with it. At this stage in the story, too, the adversaries only know themselves to be Spider-Man and the Green Goblin – only we as the audience are privileged with the information of knowing both their identities – and narratively, the threat/promise of revelation to 'someone' remains an important imperative in the remainder of the story. 'When' and 'to who' this happens becomes crucial in postponing the seemingly inevitable outcome of this kind of narrative, and in providing what Steve Neale has called 'regulated difference' (Neale 1990: 64). The Green Goblin kidnaps Spider-Man and seeks to persuade him that the world is so unjust that whatever good he were to do there, the public seek only gratification in seeing the heroic fall and fail, in maintaining the unexceptional, and in resenting those who try to make things better: 'eventually they will hate you'. Spider-Man, despite knowing something of the truth of this argument, rejects the Green Goblin. He continues his vigil against crime, saving MJ from assault, and in the film's one erotic interlude, drenched from the storm, MJ peels down the mask from Spider-Man's face as he hangs upside down before her, and kisses him in gratitude, teasing herself with the revelation of Spider-Man's true identity but preserving the arousing excitement of an infatuation with a heroic stranger. The audience, of course, sees this as another stage in what it hopes will be the consummation of Peter and MJ's relationship, which is narratively implied, generically inscribed and seemingly inevitable as a model of a 'happy ending'. Spider-Man's re-engagement with the Green Goblin in the midst of a blazing fire delays this further, however, and sees Spider-Man injured; the cut on his arm is the clearest demonstration of his humanity and mortality beneath the spandex suits. This incident prefigures the end of Act Two in the story, a 'Thanksgiving Meal' which takes place at Peter's house. Harry is bringing MJ to the meal – throughout the audience has known MJ is going out with Harry, even though the viewer has seen only scenes of intimacy between MJ and Peter/Spider-Man, and recognises that it is likely Peter, through some narrative circumstance, will replace Harry as MJ's object of affection. Most romantic stories, and certainly most romantic comedy, has a 'dupe' partner, who even if perfectly acceptable, is not the partner 'preferred' and 'privileged' by the narrative. Harry wishes to introduce MJ to his father, but during the meal Osborn cannot successfully repress his Green Goblin alterego. This results in him abusing MJ – 'broom her fast' – revealing a deep-seated misogyny, but more importantly, in Peter's initial absence from the meal, searching his room suspiciously. Once he discovers a drop of blood – dripping from Peter's arm as he hangs precariously, and unseen, on the ceiling above – and sees Peter's wound later when he 'arrives' at the meal, Osborn knows that this is the injury he inflicted on Spider-Man during their fight in the fire, and consequently, he knows who Spider-Man is. Peter suspects, too, that he has been discovered.

This is the prelude to Act Three. Peter realises that his identity must remain secret, and that the Green Goblin must be defeated. Osborn, however, knows that there is now an Achilles heel to Spider-Man. He can defeat him through 'his heart', by attacking the ones Peter loves. The Green Goblin hospitalises Aunt May. This is an important narrative choice because Aunt May could have easily been killed; rather it affords the opportunity to avoid a seemingly unnecessary callousness in having another of Peter's parents killed, and creates an opportunity for a bedside scene in which Peter and MJ visit May, and Peter describes his own feelings for MJ but pretends that these are his description of her to Spider-Man. This is observed obliquely by Harry, her boyfriend, who also visits, and provokes his realisation that Peter is finally getting closer to MJ, and that his own relationship with MJ is over. May too, reinforces this final transition in Peter's progress towards winning MJ by recalling Peter's childhood observation of MJ as 'an angel', and encouraging him to finally share his feelings with her. Harry meanwhile has told his father Osborn that Peter is now with MJ, fuelling the final 'showdown' as the Green Goblin seeks to harm MJ and destroy Spider-Man.

The key requirements of Act Three in classical narrative are 'crisis', 'climax' and 'resolution'. These are played in this instance in the following ways. The Green Goblin provokes 'crisis' by destroying a city bridge and endangering a tram-car full of people at the very same time as he threatens to drop MJ from a great height. He tells Spider-Man to choose between saving MJ or saving the people. Inevitably, Spider-Man saves both in an extraordinary action sequence which prefigures the 'climax', the final fight between the Green Goblin and Spider-Man in which both reveal their identities to each other, and when, on the edge of defeat, Osborn tries to persuade Peter that he has been a 'father' figure to him. The first resolution then comes as Peter redeems himself and assuages his guilt by saying 'I have a father – his name is Ben Parker'. Osborn is then killed by his own glider, and utters his final wish that Harry shouldn't be told that he was indeed the Green Goblin. The ultimate denouement to the film follows recent trends in both resolving many aspects of the story that have taken place, but leaving enough unresolved elements which might lead to a sequel. Harry, for example, swears revenge on Spider-Man because he believes him to be the cause of his father's death, at the very same moment as he acknowledges that Peter Parker is 'the only family I have'. Similarly, in a scene set at Ben's grave, MJ's declaration of love for Peter and the audience's expected 'happy ending' is denied by Peter's rejection of her, not of course because he doesn't love her, but because he has to accept 'my gift, my curse', of being Spider-Man. He kisses her, however, and in this, she suspects that Peter and Spider-Man may be in some way related, and an obvious story 'thread' is opened up. Ultimately, the 'resolution' is the acceptance of the role of Spider-Man as social redeemer and the selfless denial of 'Peter', the wholesome nerd – the acceptance of great power and great responsibility over personal satisfaction, however much desired. For the audience, this is a satisfactory replacement for romantic consummation as this seems to serve the greater need and the greater good, however amorphous this may be. The classical narrative has assured its 'happy ending' and attained a populist consensus which is a highly charged ideological acceptance of the 'status quo'. Spider-Man swoops into the sky – 'spectacle' once more over-riding the intimacies of the 'two-shot' and 'close-up', uplifting and optimistic, if in some ways not fulfilling the expectations of the audience at one level, careful to inspire at another.

THE READING OF FILM

Such a reading of *Spider-Man* rests on a number of social, cultural and aesthetic perceptions of the content by the viewer, but also on a reading of 'film' itself and its conventions. It appears relatively easy for us to read such a film because we have seen it all, or nearly all, before. The film has been made recently and, for people like ourselves, there is general agreement among members of the audience as to what it is about, what is happening, how we identify with characters and so on. The reading of early films, made a hundred years ago, is different, and perhaps appears on first sight to be easier, because they are less 'busy'. The language of the films of Lumière Brothers and Georges Méliès appears simpler – the visual equivalent of children's picture-books – and it may be tempting to regard the early film-makers and their audiences with condescension. It is crucial, though, that the contemporary viewer recognises that what has become known as the 'Primitive Mode of Representation' (Burch 1973), readily seen in films made within the first two decades of 'cinema', encourages us to read these as the first faltering steps to the irresistible final product of the modern Hollywood movie.

See Chapter 1, pp. 4–7, for discussion on early cinema, and Chapter 6, pp. 214–215 for Méliès; see also Chapter 3, pp. 97–105, for a discussion of early cinema in relation to spectatorship.

Although the first extant movies are documentary records of either public or private events, such as the Lumières' home movie of feeding a baby or the reconstruction of events as in Edison's early boxing pictures for the Kinetoscope – a 'peepshow' system that predated the Lumière's projection process – the normal format soon became fictional narrative. The earliest fiction films are the so-called 'tableau' films, including most of the work of Georges Méliès (see Frazer 1979). These films are characterised by a succession of scenes recorded in long shot, square on to the action. Each scene begins with a cut to black and is replaced by another scene in a different (later) time and place. Characters walk on and off either from the side of the frame, or alternatively through stage doors in the frame, like the 'crew' walking into the spaceship in Méliès' *Voyage to the Moon*. These films draw strongly on a theatrical tradition. They appear to be shot from the 'best seat in the stalls', and represent a series of scenes, albeit short ones, without the need to wait for the scene to be shifted.

Such films can still be enjoyed as 'spectacle' – the special effects, the hand-painted colour, the sets and costumes – basically, Gunning's 'cinema of attractions'. These are connected by a narrative linking each shot to the whole, and usually each shot to the next one, by a pattern of cause and effect. However, the narrative is hard to follow for the contemporary viewer. This is in part due to the absence of close-up or identification with character. However, in a number of instances Méliès relies upon our knowledge of the narrative. *Ali Baba* (Méliès, 1905, from the BFI Early Cinema video) depends on the audience's pre-knowledge of the story. The individual tableaux appear to be operating as illustrations of the narrative rather than driving it

The shift to a cinematic narrative and formal structure occurred fairly swiftly, so that by the mid-1910s most films are recognisable to a contemporary audience as fiction films. While there may be some dispute about who 'invented' the language of film – most accounts ascribing a major role to D.W. Griffith, who directed about 400 single reel (11 minute) films between 1908 and 1913, and subsequently developed the full-length feature with *The Birth of a Nation* in 1915 – it is generally accepted that changes that had occurred by the end of that decade make the films of the late silent period resemble modern films more than the 'primitive' cinema. Inevitably, this was as a consequence of the confluence of further economic investment, technological innovation and creative endeavour which evolved the potential of cinema as a distinctive 'language' of expression (film form) and as a particular storytelling engine (narrative) (see Allen and Gomery 1985).

☐ CASE STUDY 2: THE BEGINNING OF KEATON'S *THE GENERAL* (1925)

Institutional Mode of Representation
The IMR is a broad categorisation of systems of film form and narrative characterising mainstream cinema from around 1915 onwards. It was perceived as replacing the Primitive Mode of Representation (a set of conventions used in early film between 1895 and 1905) as a gradual process in the first twenty years of cinema.

For further discussion of the IMR and spectatorship, see Chapter 3, p. 102

Directed by Buster Keaton, this 1925 film is an example of the **Institutional Mode of Representation (IMR)** (see Burch 1973). Many of the conventions of mainstream cinema had already been established. Despite being a silent film it has a complex narrative structure: it tells a story set in a concrete historical setting, and lasts for nearly an hour and a half. It is also strongly based on identification with character. We get to know the world of the film through the experience of a single player. In this sense the mainstream film is drawing on the conventions of the nineteenth-century novel which is focused on the psychological experience of one or two 'rounded' characters.

The credits prioritise Keaton as both star and co-director. The film starts with a title establishing place (Marietta, Ga) and time (1861), a device that continued into the sound era. The title does suggest that the spectator is able to 'read' this, the time being just prior to the American Civil War, and the 'Ga' signifying Georgia and the South. This message, however, is subsequently reinforced by dialogue, uniforms and indeed, the whole narrative. A classical narrative film using the IMR aspires for *closure*: it is complete and understandable in its own right.

The title is followed by an establishing, long panning shot of a train, cutting to a medium shot to identify Johnny Gray (Keaton) as driver, and continuing to track forward to identify 'The General' – the name of the train. It then cuts ahead to the arrival of the train at the station.

There is then a reverse shot of the other side of the train. As Johnny descends he is admired by two children and checks with a colleague the time of the arrival of the train (implying the high status of the job and his proficiency).

This is followed by an inserted title – 'There were 2 loves in his life his engine and…'

– and a cut to a close-up of a portrait of a young woman which he has in his cab. This title suggests an external narrative commentary; the 'writer' is telling us what to think. This is a 'primitive' device that was destined to disappear from mainstream cinema, although it has reappeared recently in the work of Martin Scorsese, for example in *The Age of Innocence* where Edith Wharton's words are read by a narrator as a commentary on the action. Classical narrative, that which was in effect to become 'Classic Hollywood', aspired to tell its stories through what we see and hear immediately. The narrator is absent and the story 'tells itself'.

After the title, Keaton walks off towards frame right. The following fade to black implies a different place or time and cuts to Annabelle (Marion Mack), identifiable as the woman in the portrait. She is looking away to frame right, the opposite direction from Johnny, and receives a look from an unseen admirer(?). The viewer can read that this is not Johnny, who should have appeared from the left of the frame as he walked off from the right of the previous frame. This was one of the conventions of editing that had been adopted by early film-makers, and which by the 1920s seemed 'natural' to the audience.

Keaton is discovered walking from left to right followed by the two children (the same direction as from which he left the previous frame and the same direction as the train). Annabelle hides and deceives him by following the children (parallel to her deception of him with the admirer). She ends the joke and invites him in, with the children following. This creates a 'family', but not a real one and Johnny has to tell the children to leave. (This parallels her trick on him and suggests a similarity between them – they are a 'proper couple'.) He gives her a picture of himself standing in front of the train, a parallel of her portrait but significantly different: he is active and in control, the driver of The General.

There is a cut to an older man in a different room who, after looking off frame right, moves into the sitting room and a younger man enters from the door (right). The exchange that follows is 'in depth' and on a different plane to the 'lovers'. The first dialogue title appears, announcing the war and the wish to enlist. After the two men leave we get a subjective shot from Annabelle to Johnny, who is left alone and on the sofa (due to her absence they are no longer a couple). The shot places him on the edge and suggests imbalance and discomfort.

As Johnny leaves to try to enlist we are shown his awkwardness and inexperience; she kisses him and he tries to hide his embarrassment. He waves to an imaginary person over her shoulder and falls over.

There is no fade to black before the recruiting office scene, thus implying the speed of the action. This scene is largely in long shot. After his initial rejection, we pull away from Keaton and discover the reason for it. We know why he has been rejected, but he does not. The withholding of information from characters but revealing to the audience is a key device in Hollywood narrative and most particularly in comedy (see Dale 2000: 59–91; King 2002). Johnny, however, remains the centre of the narrative and we identify with him in his attempts to make sense of his rejection. For instance, he is placed next to a very much taller man in the queue and we realise before him that he would consider this the reason for his rejection. We also admire and identify with his attempts to trick his way in (there is a slightly strange cut where he appears on opposite sides of the frame in consecutive shots taken from the same angle thus breaking the **30° rule** and thus confusing us as to where he actually is).

In the following scene there is a false **'eye-line'** match from Johnny sitting on the side of the engine to Annabelle looking from the gate (we 'know' this is false from the

30° rule
A change in camera angle at the minimum of 30° is usual for each new shot of the same scene thus ensuring the cut will edit smoothly. i.e. there will not be a jump-cut.

The **eye-line** match is another convention of Hollywood editing that encourages identification with the protagonist(s). The audience sees the action from the characters eye-line i.e. thier viewpoint.

• **Plate 2.2**
The General
(Buster Keaton,
1925)
Johnny Grey
(Keaton) and
admirers

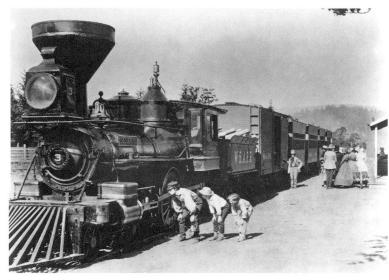

identification
The process of identification allows us to place ourselves in the position of particular characters, either throughout or at specific moments in a movie. The devices involved include subjectivity of viewpoint (we see the world through their eyes, a shared knowledge; we know what and only what they know) and a sharing in their moral world, largely through narrative construction.

economically presented
All the components are designed to help us read the narrative. An examination of the first few minutes of almost any mainstream fictional film will reveal a considerable amount of information about characters, their social situation and their motivation.

modernist device
Any device which undercuts the invisible telling of the story. A modernist device draws attention to itself and makes us aware of the construction of the narrative. It would be unclear in this instance whether the device is a consciously modernist one or a primitive one which unconsciously draws attention to itself.

journey Keaton takes to get to the house early in the film). His absence is stressed by the arrival of her father and brother who have enlisted and who are where Johnny ought to be (both physically and in the narrative).

In the final scene Annabelle accuses Johnny of not trying to enlist and therefore of being a coward. We know (because we have seen it) that this is untrue. Our identification with the unjustly treated Johnny is therefore complete. In the final shot the train accidentally takes him away, establishing that he is not in control. The dilemma is set and we know, first, that he must regain control; second, that he must prove to be a hero; and, third, that he must gain the love of Annabelle.

This sequence, although not cinematically complex, shows a strong sense of narrative and **identification**, and is **economically presented**. All elements are used to develop our knowledge of the narrative, including the use of mise-en-scène (the photographs), Keaton's body language, framing of shots and the continuity of editing. There even appears to be a **modernist device**, that of editing with a false cut. Although we cannot assume that the contemporary audience would read all that we have done into the sequence any more than would a modern audience, to make sense of the sequence does presume an understanding of film language. It is also a 'self-contained text' in that it is possible to understand the film without any previous knowledge of, for instance, the American Civil War. This is in contrast to Mèliès tableaux films such as *Ali Baba* which do not make sense without previous knowledge of the narrative.

CINEMATIC CODES

See section on editing, pp. 73–76.

With the addition of sound to film in 1927, the 'message' coming from film was relatively complete – strange experiments such as 'sensorama' or the 'smellies' notwithstanding. In normal film viewing we experience simultaneously a number of codes: visual, sound and the codes controlling the linking of one sound or image to another. The division of the components we use in reading film are relatively arbitrary, but it will help in analysis theoretically to separate them.

Mise-en-scène

This term, derived from the French, literally 'having been put into the scene', is used to describe those visual aspects that appear within a single shot. The term has been used differently by writers about film, some limiting it to those elements that are recorded by the camera – objects, movements, lighting, shadow, colour and so on – while others have included the art of recording itself, the focusing of shots and the movement of the camera. In the former sense mise-en-scène is limited to some kind of 'pro-filmic event', to those elements that are there before we start filming. In documentary films such events are perceived to have a 'real world' existence and hence appear not to be 'encoded', or at any rate only coded to the extent that the elements in the real world are. For instance, we may only expect certain categories of people with appropriate dress to be found in a hospital theatre. Not surprisingly, Early Cinema either used pre-existing events or re-staged common practices. Subsequent developments involved the use of theatrical performance, vaudeville turns, even performances of plays, albeit silent and much condensed. This history, however, reinforced a 'common-sense' notion that filming was solely the recording of reality or theatrical performance.

For further discussion of documentary film see Chapter 5.

The concept of mise-en-scène was developed by those theorists interested in issues of authorship, or the role of participants, and particularly by directors in constructing the meaning of film (see Perkins in Cameron 1972b; Maltby and Craven 1995; Gibbs 2001). During the classic period of the Hollywood studio, from 1920 to 1950, the director's control was limited to processes that were recorded during shooting. The overall narrative was clearly established, and the script would be written before the director was even engaged.

See Chapter 1 for further details on production, distribution and exhibition in the early cinema, 1900–14.

Similarly the editing of the film, and the post-dubbing of the soundtrack, were taken out of the control of the director, sometimes involving a re-cut to meet the needs of the studio or the responses of an audience at a preview. It was therefore the capacity to control what happened on the set, and the way this was recorded by the camera, which was the sign of filmic art as displayed by the director. The quality of a director's work could be read through his/her style, his/her control over the mise-en-scène.

See Chapter 4, pp. 131–151, for a detailed discussion of authorship.

We shall look now at specific elements of mise-en-scène.

Setting

In the context of studio-shooting, the predominant form of the 1920s to 1940s, all elements in front of the camera were controlled and chosen, even if sometimes the director took over an already existent set (an inheritance, perhaps, from a higher budget film). While settings are usually perceived as a signifier of authenticity, as the place where the events are happening, they are nevertheless a constructed setting for action. This becomes clear if we examine the different 'look' of the West in films such as *Shane* (George Stevens, 1953), *My Darling Clementine* (John Ford, 1946), *Johnny Guitar* (Nicholas Ray, 1954), *A Fistful of Dollars* (Sergio Leone, 1964) and *The Unforgiven* (Clint Eastwood, 1992). Although each of these five films is recognisable as 'the West', they all emphasise different kinds of settings: the wilderness, the small town and the large ranch.

Most viewers have no concept of the nature of the historic West against which the images in the films are to be judged, although films have been defined as more realistic at particular moments in time. The 'spaghetti westerns' of the 1960s, although shot in Spain, were seen as particularly authentic, settings and clothes being dirtier than the viewers were used to. The landscape and settings of a western are probably better read against the conventions of the western genre, than as a representation of the real West.

For a further discussion of genre, see Chapter 4, pp. 151–169.

Jim Kitses, in *Horizons West* (1969), describes the western in terms of the opposing focus of wilderness and civilisation, 'the contrasting images of Garden and Desert' (see also Buscombe and Pearson 1998; Saunders 2001). These oppositions permeate the themes of the western, the definition of characters and the status of particular settings and locations. The Starrett homestead in George Stevens' *Shane* is presented as an isolated place, overlooked on one side by the mountains, from where Shane comes and where he goes to, with the town, a scene of danger and evil, on the other.

• **Plate 2.3**
Shane (George Stevens, 1953)
A romantic view of the West

• **Plate 2.4**
Johnny Guitar (Nicholas Ray, 1954).
A darker view of the West.

The setting can also function to place the performers. In *The Cabinet of Doctor Caligari* (Germany, Robert Wiene, 1919) the characters are 'enclosed' in a two-dimensional set, with 'lighting' painted over the backdrop and the stage. The setting constantly suggests danger and paranoia which is revealed, at the end of the film, to be a relocation of the interior world inhabited by the 'crazy' narrator. This film was a precursor of Expressionism, a movement that can be seen in a number of influential German films from 1919 to 1931. Drawn from a contemporary movement in the visual arts, including the work of Munch and Nolde, its aim was to convey the crude force of human emotion in a total cinematic experience. It overtly rejected ideas of realism in the visual arts. While it never replaced the dominant realist aesthetic of mainstream cinema, leading protagonists of Expressionism such as Murnau and Lang moved to Hollywood in the 1920s and 1930s. The influence of Expressionism can be seen in the horror films of the early 1930s, such as James Whale's *Dracula* and *Frankenstein*, and in film noir of the 1940s. In Frank Capra's *It's a Wonderful Life* (1946), George Bailey (James Stewart), on the point of suicide, is taken by his guardian angel away from the world of middle America where he has grown up, with its model estate that he has helped to build, to a neon-lit 'modernist' rebuilt town which would have existed but for his help. Similarly, in *Blade Runner* Ridley Scott invents a futurist location that does not exist anywhere – a **dystopia** that we can recognise, possibly as much from other films (*The Fifth Element*, *The Fisher King* and *Terminator 2*) as from extensions of a contemporary inner-city location.

Locations can not only be recognised and help us to place the characters within a film, but can also through the film itself create their own space and meaning. In Douglas Sirk's *All That Heaven Allows* (1956), the principal action takes place in a family house, lived in by a family whose father has died before the film begins. While we learn little directly about this man, his presence lives on in the house, his trophies over the mantelpiece. The house with its oppressive lighting becomes almost the 'tomb' in which his

dystopia
A world of the future where everything has gone wrong.

• **Plate 2.5**
All that Heaven Allows
(Douglas Sirk, 1956)
The father still dominates the home even after his death

widow Cary (Jane Wyman) is obliged to live out the rest of her life. The main room is divided up by screens. These divide Cary from her children, and particularly the son. Throughout the film he resists any attempt to change the house from the way it was when the father lived, and most particularly resents the presence of other men in the house. However, after he decides to leave, it is the house, and the implied memory of the father, that 'gets in the way' of a new relationship with his mother.

Props

Films are also dependent on 'props' as a device for conveying meaning. In a familiar sense, props are definers of genre, such as the weapons in 'action' genres, or the arcane paraphernalia of the horror films – garlic and crosses. However, props can also become unique signifiers of meaning in a particular film. While all scenes are constructed around a number of props – to make the sequence 'look right' – our attention can be drawn to particular objects by the use of close-up and dialogue. This in itself suggests the significance of these objects – we know that such objects will be of importance in the narrative. In Hitchcock's *Strangers on a Train* (1951) a cigarette lighter changes hands from Guy, the 'innocent' tennis player with a wife he would rather be rid of, to Bruno, the plausible psychotic whom he meets on the train. The lighter is decorated with crossed tennis rackets, and the initials of Guy and his lover. The crossed rackets signify a number of 'crossings' within the movie: the 'crossed lovers', the offer of an exchange of murders by Bruno, the choices offered to Guy in the exchange, and so on. However, the lighter remains the significant 'icon' throughout the movie; it represents Bruno's threat to expose Guy if he does not keep his side of the bargain; its temporary loss delays Bruno's attempt to frame Guy; and its presence in the dying Bruno's hand at the end of the movie releases Guy from the hold that is upon him.

Props can also be used to 'anchor' characters into particular meanings (see Barthes 1977: 38–41). In the complexities of possible ways in which an individual character may

• **Plate 2.6**
Strangers on a Train
(Alfred Hitchcock, 1951)
A significant icon

be read, an object may be used to clarify meaning. While Hannibal Lecter in *The Silence of the Lambs* (Jonathan Demme, 1991) may appear increasingly civilised, even charming, in relation to his fellow inmates and warders, the danger from his mouth, whether in terms of his speech or more obviously in his capacity to bite, is exemplified by the face-guard placed over him when he is being transported. The significance of this guard is that it denies the viewer full access to him in the way that we are permitted in the earlier exchanges through the reinforced glass. In *The Godfather* the entire film is suffused with props relating to family life. At the key moment when members of the Corleone family 'go to the mattresses' to prepare for the shoot-out, the domestic world, exemplified by the cooking of a pasta sauce, is taken over by the men, exemplifying the contradiction of these family-centred and very traditional men who are prepared to murder to preserve family honour.

Costume

Costume is a variant of the prop but is, of course, tightly connected to character. Minor characters are often primarily identified on the basis of costume, which uses the codes of everyday life such as uniforms, or the cinematic codes such as the wearing of white and black to signify virtue and villainy in the early westerns. Subtle changes in the costume of a single character can be used to signify changes of status, attitude and even the passing of time. In many 1930s gangster movies such as *The Roaring Twenties* and *Scarface*, the rise of the gangster, and his increasing separation both from his roots or from 'acceptable society', are exemplified by a change into clothes that are signifiers of affluence, if not taste. In *Mildred Pierce* we see the process in reverse. Our initial viewing of Mildred Pierce is as a smart, rich and powerful woman in a fur coat. In the first flashback we are introduced to the same character wearing an apron, in a clearly suburban domestic setting. We are presented with an 'after and before', raising for us not only the dominant issue of the storyline at that moment – who killed Mildred's husband – but also the more complex issue of how this transformation has taken place.

Costume can also be used to signify mismatches. We bring to a costume a series of expectations, which are then subverted by the action. The 'false policeman' is regularly used as a plot device – either simply a robbery device, as in *The Wrong Arm of the Law*, or alternatively in films such as *The Godfather*, where police act or speak in ways that we deem to be inappropriate.

A further example of mismatch is cross-dressing, usually a male in female clothing. Normally such devices are humorous, as in *Some Like It Hot* and *Tootsie*, where our expectations of appropriate behaviour and that of the male characters in the film, given the signifying props, are a mismatch with our knowledge of the gender of the character. In *The Crying Game* our knowledge is at least problematic, and the mismatch only appears retrospectively.

See Chapter 1, Case study 3, The Crying Game, pp. 29–31.

In *Desperately Seeking Susan*, rather than using a uniform, Roberta, a suburban housewife with aspirations to a more exciting lifestyle, acquires a jacket belonging to Susan, a woman with bohemian and underworld connections. This distinctive jacket, allegedly previously worn by Jimi Hendrix, allows Roberta to be 'misread' by other characters as 'being' Susan, but equally allows the viewer to place her in her aspirational world.

Performance and movement

Probably the richest source of mise-en-scène is the performance of the actors. While there is more to consider in performance, it may help to consider the performer – whether human or animal – as an object of the camera's gaze. As with costume, there is a strong, coded element in the facial expressions and body positions held by performers. These codes, broadly referred to as 'body language', are of course part of everyday life. While there are cultural and temporal variations in body language, the body language of American film has become almost universally understood due to our

• **Plates 2.7 and 2.8** *Mildred Pierce* (Michael Curtiz, 1945). Joan Crawford translated from housewife to businesswoman

familiarity with Hollywood. Indeed one of the consequences of the spread of film has been the global penetration of particular aspects of language such as the 'thumbs up' or the 'high five' signs.

The presentation of characters by actors using body language is a key element in the creation of a 'performance'. It is perhaps significant that the much-vaunted performances of recent years – Dustin Hoffman in *Rain Man*, Tom Hanks in *Forrest Gump* – have been characterised by body styles conventionally associated with marginal figures in society. Again, body movements can be used to express both change of emotion and change of time. In *Citizen Kane*, the decline of Kane can be identified from the animated young man to the almost robotic, lumbering figure who smashes up his second wife's room when she threatens to leave him.

While early film was often dependent upon the kind of exaggerated body movements that in the theatre were recognisable from the upper gallery, the development of the close-up has meant that meaning can often be expressed by the slightest movement, whether the wringing of hands in D.W. Griffith's *Intolerance* or the maintenance of facial expressions to be observed in almost any contemporary film. In an acting master-class, Michael Caine, that most minimalist of screen actors, ably demonstrates what can be conveyed by the flickering of the eye, the raising of the eyebrows or the turning of the lip.

Finally, and briefly, the performer, and particularly the 'star', brings to the film a meaning derived merely from their presence. While some performers such as Jennifer Jason Leigh deliberately appear to present themselves differently in the films that they make, most operate with a high degree of consistency both in terms of appearance and type, a consistency which will usually be reinforced in terms of non-filmic appearances. As such, stars will bring with them a level of expectation and an implied meaning from their previous films. This becomes obvious when performers attempt to take parts that move away from type, often with disastrous effect at the box-office. It may be useful, therefore, to consider the (known) performer as part of the language of film, having a meaning that can be stretched and reused, but only to a limited extent.

'Putting into the scene'

Having assembled other components of our shots, the next procedure involves a process of recording these elements. However, such a distinction between content and form is an artificial one, in that we have already had to have recourse to concepts of close-up in order to describe individual constituents. Nevertheless, it is helpful to separate the processes, and hence those codes that characterise them from the codes of the objects themselves. While the latter are related to wider cultural artefacts and the meanings they have – like the meanings of ways of dressing – the former can be perceived either as strictly cinematic codes or as strongly related to the codes of other representational forms, such as painting, drawing and of course photography.

Lighting

Lighting of film is the first of the 'invisible' codes of cinema. While there are apparent sources of light within a shot, the lighting of a shot is off camera. Even with an outside location lighting is used to guarantee that the light level is adequate both to produce a sufficient level for recording and also to highlight particular aspects of the image. This activity is not separate from the shooting of the film, but is integral to it – hence the term 'lighting cameraman', which is applied to the principal operator within the camera crew.

Whereas Early Cinema relied on a relatively flat field of action, with the development of faster film stock it became possible, and indeed desirable, to establish a source of depth to the action. This, coupled with a small aperture lens, has enabled the camera to record over a number of fields of action. The French theorist André Bazin argued that such a form of shooting was both more 'realist' in the sense that the shots closely resemble the capacity of the eye to recognise objects across a wide depth (or at least to rapidly adjust focus to do so) and also more 'dramatic' in allowing the viewer the

For a brief discussion of Kuleshov's experiments with editing and actors in the Soviet cinema of the 1920s, see Chapter 11, pp. 394–395.

See Chapter 4, pp. 169–181 for more detailed discussion of the star.

For further discussion of Bazin and realism, see Chapter 11, p. 416.

capacity to choose, within a given shot, where to direct attention (see Bazin 1958; for a summary see Tudor 1974; see also Cardullo 1997). In practice, deep focus shots and, in particular, a number of shots in *Citizen Kane* (such as the attempted suicide of Susan Alexander, with a close-up of the sleeping draught and the distance shot of Kane breaking in through the door), allow little choice of attention. The planes of action are immediately joined as Kane rushes to the bed.

Lighting involves choices of level and direction of light. Classic Hollywood lighting involves a strong level of lighting on the main objects of a shot with fill lighting designed to eliminate shadows. The set is then backlit to enable those elements at the front of the set to be distanced from that which appears at the back, to give an illusion of depth. However, lighting is also characterised by its absence.

Light and shade can be used to direct our attention to a particular part of the frame. This is most usually done by the movement of characters through a variously lit set. A more dramatic variant can be seen in Sergio Leone's *Once Upon a Time in the West* (1968). In an early scene at the trading post a mysterious character, Harmonica (Charles Bronson), is identified as present only through his characteristic theme music. He is dramatically exposed by Cheyenne (Jason Robards) who propels an oil lamp on a horizontal wire across the room, producing a **low-key image** of Harmonica. This, the first meeting of these characters, who maintain an ambiguous relationship, is sudden, the characters revealed from out of the dark, and is followed by the flashing on and off of the light as a 'consequence' of the swinging of the oil lamp.

Sometimes, however, lighting can be used as a characteristic of the style of a whole film or over a number of scenes – rather than just as a specific light for a specific set-up. The classic realist film is usually characterised by a full lighting effect – high-key lighting – seemingly as a device to ensure that we see all the money that has been spent on constructing the effect. However, widespread use of shadows can be used to convey their own meaning. The use of reflective light scenes, and the often apparently dominant use of shadows, originated in German Expressionist cinema, but was incorporated into a Hollywood style of lighting in the 1940s and 1950s which later became known as **film noir**. This style was largely to be found in films within the detective/thriller genre, and was characterised by a world of threat and danger, but also one where characters' motivations were hidden from one another and, by implication, from the viewer. Lighting effects usually appear to be 'motivated', in that they come from sources such as table lamps that are in the shot. In an early scene of *Mildred Pierce*, the leading character Mildred 'frames' an old acquaintance Wally for a murder that she appears to have committed. The scene commences in a nightclub where the low level of lighting, together with Mildred's wide-brimmed hat, creates shots in which the face is half in shadow, with the eyes in particular in darkness. Later, returning to the beach house where the murder was committed, the interior is a kaleidoscope of lighting, coming from the low table lights and the seeming dappled effect on the ceiling which is implicitly caused by reflections from the sea. It is within this scene that Wally is apparently trapped by the shadows that cut across him at every turn. The style of film noir is one of few formal characteristics that have come to be widely recognised, and indeed it survives into contemporary films such as John Dahl's *The Last Seduction* (1994). This perhaps can be explained in part through its seeming difference from the visual effects of realist film, usually fully 'high-key' lighting, and its connection with a particular genre. The style of film noir is linked in an obvious way to themes of paranoia and alienation and other characteristics such as the *femme fatale*, a woman who is not what she immediately appears to be. In this instance the use of lighting enables the knowing viewer to be one step ahead of the protagonists within the film.

Camera and camera movement

Having created the pro-filmic event and having lit it, the next set of choices surrounds the positioning of the camera. Early Cinema was largely characterised by a steadily held

low-key image
Light from a single source producing light and shade.

film noir
A term developed by French film critics in the postwar period to describe a number of films produced in the 1940s. It has subsequently become a marketing device used to describe films with some of the lighting and narrative conventions of the period.

• **Plate 2.9** *The Last Seduction* (John Dahl, 1994). The style of film noir survives in contemporary films

camera (or at least as steady as hand-cranking permitted) and by the predominant use of the long shot incorporating all the action. Technological developments up to the Steadicam permitted greater flexibility and choice, both of movement and angle, as well as offering the option of different ratios with the variety of wide-scene formats operating since the 1950s. This 'progression' has not necessarily been continuous, particularly at the point of the introduction of sound when the cameras were initially installed within sound-proofed booths, thus restricting their movement. However, the techniques and 'language' of camera use had to be both developed by film-makers and 'learnt' by the audience.

Drawing primarily from the already existing art forms of photography and theatre, the camera was held static, with movement being derived from the actors in front of the camera. The camera was placed square onto the action, with actors moving in and out of the shot as if from the 'wings' in the theatre. The development of alternative camera positions and movements evolved in the first decade of the twentieth century. Film-makers recognised that in order to facilitate a wider degree of possible visual narrative perspectives they needed to interrogate the range of 'image' constructions available to them within the limitations afforded by the camera, and how it was used. Within the capacities of focus, the camera is able to move anywhere from the extreme close-up to the use of wide-screen shots limited to pairs of eyes, as in the final shoot-out in *Once Upon a Time in the West*, to the extreme long shot of the field hospital in *Gone with the Wind*. The close-up has a particular place in the development of film, however, permitting us to 'know intimately' the faces of leading characters, and hence by implication to read their thoughts and feelings. This operates without needing to use either the knowing subtitle of the Early Cinema, or even the voice of the narrator to take us into the character.

It is also necessary to decide on the angle of the shot (see Izod 1984; Begleiter 2001) and the relative height of the camera to the object being filmed – a low-angle shot looking up to the object or a high-angle shot looking down. Conventional accounts suggest that low-angle shots imply the power of the object – usually a human figure – and a high-angle shot its weakness. Such a rule can be seen to operate in many exchanges between characters – such as those between Kane and Susan Alexander in *Citizen Kane*, as she pieces together her jigsaw puzzle and he looks down on her. However, such rules cannot be applied to read off automatically the meaning of an individual shot. After the assault by the birds on the Brenner household in Hitchcock's *The Birds*, there is a tracking shot of the three members of the family taken from a very low angle. The suggestion is of their dominance; the birds have indeed disappeared, yet the anxious look on their faces and their isolation from one another suggest an alternative meaning. Our experience throughout the film suggests that danger comes from above – and indeed we are soon to discover that the birds have broken into the house and are waiting in an upstairs room.

While the camera is normally held level, it can also be tilted to one side. Such a shot is read as an indication of instability, either that of the characters or of the situation that the shot is recording. In an early scene in Nicholas Ray's *Rebel without a Cause* (1955) there is a series of shots on the staircase where James Dean's family is rowing. The shots are sharply tilted – an effect exaggerated by the Cinemascope screen.

While shots classically are in sharp focus, a soft focus can be used either to enhance the romantic effect of a scene or, alternatively, to expose the incapacity of a character to register the world around them.

Finally, the camera is able to move. The earliest moving shots were dependent on the movement of objects – cars or trains – so shots mimic the experience of viewing. Similarly, pans (horizontal movements) and tilts appear to reproduce eye movements and are motivated by the action that is occurring. Shots can also be developed to reproduce the movements of the characters within the set, originally using rails (hence the 'tracking shot'), or in a more liberated way using a hand-held or a Steadicam camera, walking the action. These shots give a strong sense of identity and place. For instance, in Scorsese's *GoodFellas* (1990), Henry displays his power by entering a popular restaurant through a side door and impresses both his girlfriend and us with his capacity to walk through the back passageways and the kitchen, acknowledged only by the most important figures.

While such shots are perceived as naturalistic, and replicate the natural movements of the eye, the use of the crane moves beyond this to display a degree of control by the director of the world of the film. Such shots involve positions and movements that are inaccessible to us on a day-to-day basis. Crane shots can take us from the wide panorama of a scene to focus in on the object of our attention. In Hitchcock's *Marnie* (1964) a crane shot at a party takes us from Marnie's point of view on the landing above the expansive entrance hall of her husband's mansion to a close-up of her previous employer, Strutt, who has the potential to expose her earlier misdeeds. While this shot bears no relation to any possible human movement towards Strutt, it reflects the sense of powerlessness and inevitability felt by Marnie at that moment. The crane can also be used to dramatically reveal what has previously been hidden. In *Once Upon a Time in the West* there is a connection between Harmonica and the villain Frank, although this is not known by Frank. Only at the moment of death is this link established. In a flashback, Harmonica is revealed as a boy in close-up, with the camera craning back, first to reveal his elder brother standing on his shoulders, and then literally suspended by a noose from a ruined archway in the desert, waiting for the boy to weaken and plunge the brother to his death, and finally Frank laughing. A similar effect is produced in John Carpenter's *Halloween* where, following a lengthy Steadicam shot from behind a mask where the 'camera' searches through a house and discovers and kills two lovers, the mask is removed revealing a small boy. The camera cranes back and upwards stressing both the vulnerability of the child and the judgement of the local community.

While there has been a concentration in the preceding pages on some of the more obvious effects of the camera, the predominant style of Hollywood film-making is the use of a camera which is largely invisible, a predominance of shots being within the medium distance ('le shot American'), using very slight variations from the horizontal shot and involving limited camera movement, usually motivated by the action or the interest of the characters. Yet every shot is selected from a range of possibilities, even when it continues to appear to be the 'natural', the only, one.

Editing

Having established the codes contributing to our understanding of the single shot, and hence mise-en-scène, we can now look at the combination of shots which construct a film flowing over time. While most of the characteristics of the film shot are related to codes developed in still photography, the joining of strips of film is specific to cinema, and as such has been seen as the component that is the essence of cinematic art. The Soviet film-maker Lev Kuleshov (1899–1970) engaged in a number of 'experiments' linking shots and 'proving' that with adept editing it was possible to create alternative readings of the same facial expression – or to bring together shots occurring in completely different locations. Essentially, Kuleshov attempted to prove that the meanings of shots could be changed by altering the juxtaposition of shots. This involved a close-up of an actor playing a prisoner, which was then linked to three diffent shots. The audience were said to be convinced that the actor's expression was different even though the same shot was used. However, notions of the essential nature of film are certainly unfashionable and are probably unhelpful in any attempt to read the meaning into sequences of film.

See Chapter 11, pp. 394–415, for discussion on Kuleshov and montage editing.

Historically, the first editing was between scenes, with individual extreme long shots recording a self-contained sequence at a particular time and place, followed by a cut to black. This device, drawing on the theatrical blackout, could easily be read by the early audiences, although for a contemporary audience a pre-existing knowledge of the storyline seems necessary in order to understand the narrative flow. In the first twenty years of cinema a 'vocabulary' of linking devices between scenes was established, a development largely attributed to D.W. Griffith. In particular, his method involved the distinction between 'slower' devices: the fade to and from black, and the dissolve between the image and the cut. While the fade implied a change of scene and of time, the cut was used within a scene or, in the case of cross-cut editing, signified that two events, although separated by space, were happening simultaneously (see Bordwell *et al*. 1994). This device was used particularly by Griffith to build up suspense during the rescue scene in *The Birth of a Nation*. Other devices such as the 'wipe', 'push off' and the 'turn over', while popular in the 1920s and revised as relatively simple techniques of the TV vision mixer, have largely been reduced to comic effects. The revival of linking devices by French New Wave directors such as Truffaut in *Tirez sur la pianiste* extended the use of the devices, in particular the use of the dissolve within a sequence to suggest the passing of time. The fade to black, which after time becomes almost an invisible device, was replaced by a dissolve to white, drawing attention to the uncertain status of the narrative in *Last Year in Marienbad* (Alain Resnais, 1961), and to other colours with specific emotional readings. However, the inventiveness of the New Wave directors, far from creating a universal language of the linking device, gave a number of alternative readings that had to be anchored through the mise-en-scène. The passing of time, for instance, would normally be doubly signified by use of mise-en-scène, the movement of characters, facial expressions, consumption of food and drink, or even the movement of the hands of the clock. New Wave directors felt free to ignore these conventions if the viewer was able to identify the passing of time through what was happening in the

For discussion of Birth of a Nation and the spectator and audience response, see Chapter 3, pp. 101–105.

narrative. This starts to move towards a model of 'art' or 'counter' cinema, which at one and the same time refers to classical narrative while deliberately subverting it for narrational differentiation or aesthetic effects.

While the linking devices described above have the function of signifying to the viewer the discontinuity of the action – the change of time and place – the major development in film editing has been to minimise the sense of disruption. Unlike studio TV, film is shot with considerable breaks, with changes of set, positioning and lighting. As a consequence film-makers are rarely able to record more than two to three minutes of usable stock in the course of a full working day. Those separate shots designed to be in the 'ideal' viewing place (for instance, a close-up on the speaker) have the potential to disrupt the viewers' attention. A system of conventions governing editing developed in the first two decades of cinema (although there were some changes following the introduction of sound) and these have become known as the 'rules of continuity editing'. The intention of the rules is to produce a system to tell a story in such a way as to set out the action of the narrative and its position in space and time so that it is clear to the viewer while remaining unobtrusive. In particular, the storytelling should do nothing to draw attention to itself or to the apparatus of cinema (in the physical sense of equipment), but also should be such that strategies employed appear to be 'transparent' to the viewers, in the sense that they would not be aware of their existence.

For a further discussion of how the audience watches and understands film, see Chapter 3.

These rules can be briefly summarised as follows. A scene will normally start with an 'establishing shot', a long shot which enables spectators to orient themselves to the space of the scene and to the position of the performers and objects, as well as to reorient them from the different space of the previous scene. All subsequent shots can therefore be 'read' within the space already established. Such a shot, a 'master shot', can of course be reintroduced in particular moments in the scene, whether to reestablish the space or to show any significant movements of characters. The consequence of this is the establishment of a common background space (either implicitly or explicitly) in static shots, and a clarity of direction of movement when, for instance, characters are running towards or away from one another. Important in sustaining this illusion is the principle of the 'eye-line match'. A shot of a scene looking at something off-screen is then followed by the object or person being looked at. Neither shot includes the viewer and the object together, but on the basis of the established space we presume their relationship.

The 30° rule proposes that a successive shot on the same area involves at least a 30° change of angle, or at any rate a substantial change of viewpoint. Although this involves a reorientation for the viewer, it does not involve the noticeable 'jump' of objects on the screen, which would produce a 'jump-cut'. Again, assuming the establishment of the narrative's space, the viewer is able to place the action.

Finally, the movement of actors and the reframing of the camera is so arranged and planned that the movement of the camera does not 'draw attention to itself'. This involves, for instance, the cut on action, so that the cut anticipates the movement to be made, such as a long shot of a character standing up or a cut to the person talking. The cut both takes the viewer where she/he as reader of the narrative wishes to be, and implies the control of the film-maker over the narrative. The cut appears to be 'motivated' by the need to tell the story.

This style of editing, including as it does decisions on the placement of camera and characters, is integral to the Hollywood classical narrative, a film that seemingly effaces all signs of the text's production and renders the process of that production 'invisible' by concentrating the audience upon the 'narrative' and 'sense-oriented' aspects of the cinematic experience, rather than the formal properties of cinema itself.

However, we are still made aware of these conventions when they are broken or in any way subverted. It is not unusual to commence a sequence with a close-up. In an early scene in Scorsese's *GoodFellas* we have an extreme close-up of the adolescent Henry before the reverse shot and pan reveals the gangsters across the road as the object of his gaze. Henry's voiceover stresses this boy's-eye view of the action ('They were able to stay up all night playing cards') rather than an objective narrative viewpoint. The initial close-up thus reinforces the subjective reading of the action before it is presented to us. The 180° rule noted earlier in this discussion was perhaps most obviously broken in John Ford's *Stagecoach* (1939) as the Indians attacked the coach, seemingly riding from both directions. However, the strength of the narrative line and the clear visual distinction between the Indians and the cavalry present us with no problems in identifying narrative space. In *Who's That Knocking at My Door?* (the version released in 1968, one of several cuts of the film in the period 1965–1970), the concluding dialogue between Harvey Keitel and Zina Bethune, the breaking of an 'impossible' relationship, again breaks the 180° rule as the camera plays on the invisible line. The effort is disturbing, but only reflects the concern we have about where to 'place' ourselves emotionally in the sequence. The jump-cut was used widely by the French New Wave directors, notably Jean-Luc Godard in *A bout de souffle* (1960). When used within conversations and during car journeys the device has the consequence of producing an ellipsis – the reduction of time spent on a sequence. Such a process is a necessary part of feature film narrative – films rarely operate in 'real time', equating the time of the action with what we see on the screen. However, the usual form of continuity editing hides this process by making the sequences within, say, a car journey appear continuous. It is not that Godard's use of the jump-cut makes the film's narrative incomprehensible, but rather that it draws attention to the process of selection that has taken place.

For further discussion of the French New Wave, see Chapter 12.

While continuity editing dominates classical narrative, other strategies have been used and were perhaps more formally developed in the silent era before the requirements of continuity in both sound and image restricted, at least temporarily, the expressiveness of successive images. The 'montage' sequence entailed a number of shots over a period of time to demonstrate a process of change. In *Citizen Kane*, the disintegration of Kane's first marriage is shown in a scene at breakfast, with the couple eating in silence hidden behind rival newspapers. A similar device is used in *The Godfather*, where a sequence of killings occurs in different locations, while the baptism of Michael Corleone's child is taking place. In the sequence, the soundtrack of the church service is held over the images, not only contrasting the pious words of the protagonists with their actions, but also establishing the contemporaneity of the action.

An alternative form of editing is the so-called 'non-diegetic insert' which involves a symbolic shot not involved with the time and place of the narrative to comment on or express the action in some alternative way. Eisenstein in *Strike* (1924) uses the image of a bull in a slaughterhouse to represent the killing of strikers by the mounted soldiers. The primacy of realist narrative has made this kind of device less prevalent in 'Hollywood' cinema, which tends to be less explicit in its use of overt symbols; instead, when it has cause to enhance its texts in this way, it integrates symbolic elements as motifs. Hitchcock's 'crossing' motif in *Strangers on a Train*, mentioned earlier, for example, works in this way. Such coded inserts proved useful as devices to circumscribe censorship in earlier eras. Hitchcock again used the clichéd train entering the tunnel as an expression of the consummation of Roger Thornhill's marriage at the end of *North by Northwest* (1959). In *Goodbye, Columbus* (Larry Peerce, 1969), the 'seduction' of the daughter in the attic is similarly expressed by an abrupt cut to the carving of roast meat at the family lunch.

For a further discussion of Eisenstein and Strike, *see Chapter 11 pp. 400–403.*

The cutting of film stock can also be expressive in itself. While the speed of cutting appears, particularly in dialogue sequences, to be determined by the pro-filmic event, the meaning of action sequences can be determined by editing. The length of a shot is in part determined by the amount of information within it. However, rapid or slow cutting can convey meaning in itself. Rapid cutting reflects the degree of excitement within a sequence, and cutting speeds can be accelerated to convey mood, so that the viewing of individual shots becomes almost subliminal. Perhaps most famously, the *Psycho*

• **Plate 2.10**
Psycho (Alfred
Hitchcock, 1960)
Highly fragmented
images

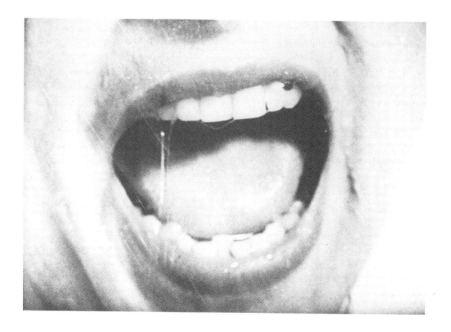

shower scene exemplifies the use of rapid and highly fragmented images to present a climactic moment. The viewer, including the original American film censor, may often claim to see things that were not actually there.

Sound

The final element in constructing the 'image' of a film is the soundtrack. Sound as an integral part of a film only developed after 1927. While films were rarely seen in silence (they were sometimes accompanied by a speaker, a piano, organ or small orchestra), the nature of the sound was rarely in the control of the originators of the film and certainly not for all showings of the film. Unlike other innovations such as colour and widescreen, sound, once introduced, became a virtually universal format in a very short period of time. Ed Buscombe (1977) argues that the speed of this innovation arose from the need for a more realistic narrative. Certainly, while Warner Brothers saw music as being the appealing part of sound, it was the talking element that attracted the first audiences. The role of the soundtrack was seen as one of reproducing the sounds that would normally be associated with the images, whether they are unenunciated words in almost any 'silent movie' or the silent but ringing alarm in Porter's *Life of an American Fireman*. In this sense sound is perceived as diegetic, arising from objects in a scene either inside the frame, or logically related outside the frame – say, for instance, the sound of knocking on a door heard within a house. 'Diegesis' refers to the specific world of the film text as we view it. Anything that occurs outside this context is 'non-diegetic'. Most obvious here is the use of a film score, where the music is not generated within a scene, for example by an orchestra playing, but nevertheless music is playing which is reinforcing the mood of the scene or even directing how the audience should respond to and understand the story events taking place.

However, it would be unwise to assume that a soundtrack can merely be read off from the visual image. Soundtracks are equally 'sound images', constructed and selected in much the same way as the visual image is created. Components on the soundtrack may be simulated at the moment of shooting, but rarely except in a documentary is the soundtrack laid down at the same time. With the development of sound mixing the quality of the track is constructed over a period of time, whether the sound is diegetic or has a music track laid over the top of it. A visual image tends to be simpli-fied, Bazin's theory of deep focus notwithstanding – the eye tends to take in different aspects of the image sequentially, whether within or between shots. The ear, by contrast, is able to absorb a number of distinct sound sources simultaneously. Early sound films tended to display a relatively unilateral soundtrack – with dialogue, sound effects and music operating successively. Sound effects, in particular, were only included because they were integral to the narrative (in much the same way as visual effects). By the 1960s, Robert Altman was developing soundtracks using the mixing devices available for music sound recording to produce dialogue where individuals interrupted or spoke over other actors (overlapping dialogue), but which also used loca-tions such as the mess-hall in *M*A*S*H**, where conversations could be picked up apparently at random. The logical extension of this were sequences in *Prêt-à-Porter* (1994), when, using multi-camera and microphones, the sound and image appear to be collected almost randomly on the set.

Sound can be used to reinforce the continuity of the action. While the image is frag-mented by the cuts from one shot to another which we 'know' can hide temporal ellipsis – a character not shown crossing a room for instance – an unbroken soundtrack signifies a continuity of time. This is perhaps best illustrated by an example that deceives the spectator. In an early scene in Scorsese's *Mean Streets* (1973), Charlie (Harvey Keitel) climbs on the stage to perform with an exotic dancer. The soundtrack, playing the Rolling Stones' 'Tell me, (you're coming back)' appears to be running contin-uously, and yet Charlie appears in consecutive shots to be on the stage and then to be in the audience viewing the dancer, thus challenging the 'reality status' of one of the shots. Our understanding of the narrative certainly suggests on subsequent viewings that the first shot is Charlie's fantasy.

Sound also has a continuity role in establishing links across scenes. Orson Welles, drawing from his radio experience, used sound to bridge between sequences. In *Citizen Kane*, Welles uses Thatcher's 'Merry Christmas' as a bridge between Kane's boyhood greeting and adulthood. Such extravagant devices do not, however, disguise transitions in the way of continuity editing but, rather, celebrate it. More commonly, soundtracks marginally precede the visual image as a preparation for what we are about to see. Sound can also access experiences not immediately evident to the viewer. In *Psycho*, Marion Crane 'remembers', while driving along, the demands of her boss to deposit the money which she has purloined. More problematically she also 'hears' the discovery of the theft of the money and the reaction of her boss and the man she has robbed. The latter sound must at the moment of hearing be a projection of the sound which she could not in reality possibly hear, as she dies before the office is opened.

Sound can also be used to direct us into the past through the use of the voiceover as in *Mildred Pierce*, where Mildred takes us back on three occasions as part of her confession in the police station. Voiceovers, while providing a seemingly useful device to accelerate storytelling, to comment on the action and to admit us into the thoughts of the protagonists in the way of a novelist, are rarely used in feature films, and even then sparingly. A flashback sequence once introduced is normally allowed to return to a conventional mode in which the visual narrative is dominant. Martin Scorsese maintains a voiceover throughout *GoodFellas*, in keeping with its presentation as a 'true life' filmic representation of the life of a sub-Mafia wise guy. Yet the voiceover narrative appears often to be contradicted by the visual narrative, at the very least suggesting Henry's explanation and indeed control of the narrative is partial. At one stage he even loses control of the voiceover, which is taken over by his wife.

A predominant form of sound, and indeed the original function of soundtracks, is the use of non-diegetic music. Primarily music is used to inform the audience of appro-priate emotional responses or, having established a response, to enhance it. The emotional pull of music and its high level of connotative meaning allow these processes to operate almost subliminally. While the impact of the *Psycho* shower scene can be attributed to the rapid cutting (see pp. 75–76), it can equally be attributed to Bernard Herrmann's 'shrieking strings', not least because they are a magnified reprise of Marion Crane's growing hysteria as she drives the car in the heavy rain. With the general denial of the use of voiceover to provide 'inner thoughts', and given the stress on the surface reality of the classic realist film, music appears to give us direct access to the emotions of the characters.

Music also plays the role of 'confirming' the emotional response of the spectator, seemingly leading us to a particular way of seeing a sequence, or at any rate editing a 'preferred reading' of the image. As such it can be seen as a way of anchoring meaning, eliminating ambiguities of response. In this sense music is often seen to be a final track. Indeed the adding of the sound to a pre-existing image and diegetic soundtrack, whether Miles Davis improvising to *Lift to the Scaffold* or a 'classical' orchestra playing a carefully choreographed score, is the more common method of construction. However, whether the final soundtrack or similar, music may be used at the editing state as a rhythmic device to inform the pace of the cutting. Sergio Leone describes the cast and crew of *Once Upon a Time in the West*, 'throughout the shooting schedules, listening to the recording [Morricone's score] acting with the music, following its rhythms and suffering its aggravating qualities, which grind the nerve' (Frayling 1998).

Sound effects are normally perceived as part of the narrative realism, authenticating the images and informing the narrative attention. At the beginning of *Mildred Pierce* we hear gunshots while viewing the exterior of the beach house, only to cut to the consequential dying body of the victim. The denial of the image of the murderer, either at the moment of shooting or the subsequent reaction shot, is a key to the remaining narrative when the murderer is revealed. Increasingly, sound effects have come to be used to evoke mood. Peripheral sound can be used to establish the wider environment. Hospital or police precinct movies will normally feature telephone rings, not as a cue to the protagonist lifting the receiver and furthering the narrative, but to create other unseen and unrecorded narratives occurring at the same time, or simply to invoke the busyness of the location. David Lynch in *Eraserhead* (1976) extends this to a non-specific industrial background sound, permeating a number of interior domestic scenes and establishing without elaborate visual images the quality of the environment. The distinction between non-diegetic music and sound effects can become blurred with the electronic production of both. At the beginning of *A Nightmare on Elm Street* (1984) we are presented with a dream sequence involving a chase among the furnaces. What sounds to be modernist, horror film mood music also includes human sighs, muffled screams and the mechanical sounds relating to the working of furnaces, all integrated into a seamless music/soundtrack, and only loosely linked to the visual images.

Music may also be used to identify character (for example, themes associated with particular performers in *Once Upon a Time in the West* and *Dr Zhivago*), locations and time. In *GoodFellas*, Scorsese uses an elaborate soundtrack with some forty-two tracks, a mixture of American commercial ballads and rock music, Italian opera and traditional songs. The music is used to contrast the Italian-American from the American-Italian and to identify age distinctions between the protagonists. It is also used to delineate the time of the action in a movie which tells a story with a twenty-five-year time span, but using only limited changes in the appearance of the characters.

NARRATIVE

Throughout our consideration of the components and coding that make up film, underlying everything has been the idea of a narrative – the idea that films have a primary function of telling a story. The images are organised and are made sense of around this function. This is particularly true of the feature film, which is developed, given a 'treatment' in terms of its plotline, and this is perceived as being what a film is 'about'. The

See Chapter 10, pp. 366–368, for a discussion of narrative in Indian cinema.

consideration of *Spider-Man*, earlier, suggested that it was a variant on 'classical narrative', and employed a three-act structure, with particular points of narrative development determined by certain inciting story events, resulting in specific crisis, climax and resolution.

It may be useful in this part of the discussion, however, to start with distinctions between parts of the narrative process that are sometimes confused. There is a distinction between the story that is represented, and the representation of that story as it is perceived by the spectator. The story, referred to by the Russian literary theorist, Shklovky, as the 'fabula', is the basic succession of events arranged in a chronological order. A film summary, appearing alongside a review in a magazine such as *Sight and Sound*, comprises the fabula. However, while this is in itself a form of narrative, it is not the narrative of the film itself. In many instances the summary as it appears bears little relationship to our experiences in trying to make sense of a film, particularly one such as *Trainspotting* (Danny Boyle, 1996), with its fractured style of storytelling. However it would be wrong to see the fabula as some kind of raw material available to the filmmaker before a film is made. As spectators, we attempt to reconstruct the fabula from the film as we view it. In some instances, for example Luis Buñuel's and Salvador Dali's *Un chien andalou* (1928), our wish to place a film into a simple cause-and-effect chain can get in the way of our understanding.

The second term that is used to describe narration is the plot, or syuzhet. The syuzhet works on the story by giving the events a logic. In particular, events are linked in a causal way, for instance by being derived from character traits and their relationship with events that have occurred. In Ang Lee's *The Ice Storm* (1997), a synopsis of the film ends with 'Ben (Kevin Kline) bursts into tears'. The syuzhet of the film has been devoted to an examination of two affluent families and their fragile personalities, confronted with a particular set of events: a wife-swapping party, teenage sexual experimentation and the death of the son in the storm. We are led to make sense of the bursting into tears from the relation of these components. Equally the syuzhet constructs the fabula in a particular temporal order and with specific spatial reference. This construction is not merely the filling-in of the details of time and space from the fabula, but establishes the relationship between the events. *The Ice Storm*, for instance, starts with its ending (the morning after the storm), and then tells us what happened up to that moment, but eschews any of the conventional signifiers of the flashback, such as the dissolve. This technique reinforces a sense of inevitability in the actions and reactions presented – we know how it is all going to end. Again, while the two families are presented as neighbours, the houses are significantly apart, separated by a woodland path, enabling actions such as adultery in the two houses to be distinctive and unknown to the other. Like the fabula, the syuzhet, is in itself media-free. However the syuzhet may in many circumstances direct the film-maker towards particular effects.

Finally we need to consider those aspects of narrative that are film-specific. These are the elements that we have already considered in this chapter: the use of editing (and in particular continuity editing), mise-en-scène in its widest sense and sound. The spectator who is both plot-literate (i.e. who understands the conventions of plotting derived from the nineteenth-century novel) and film-literate (i.e. has an understanding of the codes of cinema) will try to make sense of a narrative film. As spectators, we attempt to absorb a succession of on-screen events as a continuum, as activities occurring in particular settings, and as unified by the organisation of time and causation. In so doing we try to fit our experiences into formulae or templates that we already understand, in order to recreate for ourselves the individual fabula of the film. The closer we are able to fit the individual film into our existing templates, the easier it is for us to 'understand'.

For further discussion on film audience and spectatorship, see Chapters 3 and 7.

The cinema has often drawn its plots and, to some extent, its storytelling strategies from literature, most notably the novel. Work on film narrative has therefore often drawn from work on other media, notably literary criticism, expressing an interest in the similarities and differences in the ways stories are told in different media.

At the simplest level, narrative analysis is concerned with the extent to which those things that we see make sense. It is assumed that those elements that we see cohere in some way, that they are part of a whole. While all elements of an image will not be of equal importance, there is a supposition that if a film draws attention to something it will be of consequence in the development of the story. One of the pleasures of a film such as *The Usual Suspects* (Bryan Singer, 1995) is the attempt by the spectator to determine what are the important components or 'clues' from among the 'red herrings'. By contrast, in *North by Northwest*, Roger Thornhill lights a cigarette for Eve Kendall using a personalised matchbook bearing the initials 'ROT'. The significance of this artefact is marked by a conversation ('What does the "O" stand for?' – 'Nothing') signifying a man with nothing at the centre. Yet, at the level of the story, the matchbook re-emerges at the end when Thornhill uses the matches to alert Eve of his presence in the villain Vandamm's house. In general terms all that is of significance in the narrative has a subsequent consequence. Narrative develops on the basis of a chain of cause-and-effect. An event happens and is shown to have (likely) consequences. As experienced film-goers, we learn to expect and anticipate this chain, or at any rate to recognise the causal links when they are made. At the simplest level these links are consecutive, the effect from one cause becoming the cause of the next link, as for instance the succession of trials facing Indiana Jones in the search for the Holy Grail in *Raiders of the Lost Ark* (Steven Spielberg, 1981). However, the example from *North by Northwest* illustrates that causal links can operate over a longer period, with other plot devices intervening.

Narrative involves the viewer in making sense of what is seen, asking questions of what we see and anticipating the answers. In particular, narrative invites us to ask both what is going to happen next and when and how will it all end. Narrative operates on the tension between our anticipation of likely outcomes drawn from genre conventions and the capacity to surprise or frustrate our expectations. Some sixty minutes into *Dirty Harry* (Don Siegel, 1971) we appear to have the final link of the cause–effect chain as Inspector Callaghan arrests the serial killer Scorpio after a chase across a football field. Yet the force entailed in the arrest becomes, in turn, the cause of Scorpio's release, and the beginning of a new cause-and-effect chain leading to an apprehension from which Scorpio can never be released.

While film narrative can be viewed as a number of cause-and-effect links, it may also be perceived in terms of larger structures incorporating the entire film. Todorov sees the start of narrative as a point of stable equilibrium, where everything is satisfied, calm and normal. This stability is disrupted by some kind of force which creates a state of disequilibrium. It is only possible to recreate equilibrium through action directed against the disruption. However, the consequence of this reaction is to change the world of the narrative and/or the characters so that the final state of equilibrium is not the same as the initial state. Although this analysis is a simplified one, it is a useful starting-point in delineating the differences between individual films or genres.

The initial equilibrium state of the film is often very brief, little more than an establishing shot or, at most, an establishing sequence. Our expectation of narrative disruption, together with our capacity to 'read' the equilibrium state rapidly, has led to shorter and shorter equilibrium sequences. The beginning of *Jaws* (Spielberg, 1975) involves a brief scene of teenagers on a beach enjoying a night-time party before two of their number engage in a swim dramatically interrupted by the shark attack. Horror films, in particular, have become increasingly characterised by immediate disruption, as for instance in the dream sequence at the beginning of *A Nightmare on Elm Street*. Even when they return to a temporary equilibrium (the girl wakes up), this is an unstable state capable of easy disruption. *Vertigo* (Hitchcock, 1958) commences with a particularly disruptive act: a chase across the rooftops, culminating in Scottie's loss of nerve and consequent retirement from the police force. If there is a stable equilibrium state, it is implicit and occurs before the movie begins.

• **Plate 2.11**
Vertigo (Alfred
Hitchcock, 1958)
A disruptive act

Initial equilibrium states are also particularly unstable in melodrama. It is clear from the beginning of the flashback sequence in *Mildred Pierce*, in effect the beginning of the narrative, that this is not a harmonious family setting, despite the iconography of the mother baking cakes and wearing an apron. The nature of Mildred's relationship with Vida suggests that trouble is in store, quite apart from the somewhat incongruous image of Joan Crawford as a petit-bourgeois housewife. As a consequence the apparent cause of the disruption – Bert's decision to leave the family – is in no way an unexpected disruption to a stable state.

Equally, in the 'romance' genre the initial equilibrium is signified by an absence or a 'lack' (of a partner) by one, Richard Gere in *Pretty Woman* (Garry Marshall, 1990), or two, Billy Crystal and Meg Ryan in *When Harry Met Sally...* (Rob Reiner, 1989). The initial equilibrium is perceived as integrally unstable, to be resolved within the movie, and the 'disruption' involves the first meeting of the characters, usually disharmoniously, in which the misunderstandings of motive are the beginning of the resolution.

Disruptions similarly are variable, although they tend to be genre-specific. Action genres are often disrupted by an external threat or raid, for instance the raid of the Indians in *The Searchers* (John Ford, 1956), or the arrival of the vengeful Max Cady in *Cape Fear* (J. Lee Thompson, 1961). The leading characters may be forced to disrupt their normal lifestyle due to a chance experience – for example, Jack Lemmon and Tony Curtis try to pass as female musicians after viewing the St Valentine's Day massacre in *Some Like It Hot* (Billy Wilder, 1959). Within the genres the disruption may be equally important to the characters and their drive towards some particular goal. Travis Bickle in *Taxi Driver* (Scorsese, 1976) is not so much driven into disequilibrium by external events (his meetings with Betsy, the appearance of Iris and Sport in his cab) as by his determined drive to transform the world.

The actions to restore equilibrium, of course, become the narrative drive of the movie. Such re-equilibrating processes are resisted, whether by the protagonists or by chance events. The pleasure associated with conventional narrative is, at least in part, related to our recognition of the strategies employed to delay the pleasure. Opposition to equilibrium can be attributed to the 'villain', a function within the narrative, and the stronger the 'villain', the greater the pleasure in the triumph of the 'hero'. This will often involve a number of moments where there appears to be a temporary equilibrium – involving the seeming defeat of the hero (the 'cliff-hanger') or, more rarely, of the villain. Since the 1970s the horror film has developed the temporary equilibrium state of the defeat of the villain at the end of the movie only for him to reappear in subsequent movies (for example, the Hammer *Dracula* series, *Halloween* and *Friday the 13th*). The struggle to resolve, while usually explicit in the revenge movie, in other genres may be present and obvious to the viewer, but not to the protagonists. In romantic comedy (*Bringing Up Baby*, *What's Up Doc?*, *When Harry Met Sally…*) the resistance to an early resolution comes from the characters themselves who are unaware of the mutual attraction (of opposites) that is 'obvious' to the viewer.

The final resolution again differs between films. There is a drive towards the 'happy ending' – we assume that Hugh Grant and Andie MacDowell will end *Four Weddings and a Funeral* (Mike Newell, 1994) in domesticity rather than death. Films often end with an 'establishing' long shot which is similar to the one with which they began – even where this involves other characters with no place in the new equilibrium 'riding off into the sunset' (*Shane*, *The Searchers*). Occasionally such an ending appears ironic; the conflicts within the movie are seen as ultimately unresolvable in the way that conventional narrative demands. At the end of *All that Heaven Allows* a relationship between Rock Hudson and Jane Wyman, separated by age and class and resisted by family and community, is

• **Plate 2.12**
The Searchers (John Ford, 1956)
No place in the new equilibrium

allowed to develop, but at the cost of a fractured leg. However, the film ends with a kitsch shot of a baby deer playing in the snow, suggesting that the resolution is no more than the false harmony of a traditional Christmas card. The 'happy ending' of *Taxi Driver* similarly strains belief. The European art movie and American 'independent' cinema, while ending with a resolution, is more often associated with character development and a recognition by protagonists of the inevitability of an unsatisfactory state of affairs.

A more elaborate analysis of narrative structure has been associated with the work of Vladimir Propp (1984). Drawing on an analysis of Russian folk-tales, he concluded that regardless of individual differences in terms of plot, characters and setting, such narratives would share common structural features. There were the functions of particular characters: 'the villain', 'the donor', 'the helper', 'the princess', 'her father', 'the dispatcher', 'the hero' and 'the false hero'. There were also thirty-one narrative units descriptive of particular action, for instance: 'a member of a family leaves home', 'a prohibition or rule is imposed on the hero', 'this prohibition is broken', etc. The characters were seen as stable elements from story to story, despite individual variations of appearance or idiosyncrasies of personality. The narrative units were sufficient to describe all of the stories, although not all units appear in all of the stories, but when they do appear they are in the prescribed order. While it might appear that such narrative structures are specific to a given genre or culture, the model has proved adaptable to Hollywood movies, such as *Sunset Boulevard* (Billy Wilder, 1950), *Kiss Me Deadly* (Robert Aldrich, 1955) and *North by Northwest*. They inevitably had to be 'translated' from the original. For instance, in Peter Wollen's 1976 article on *North by Northwest*, Eve Kendall, a double agent, becomes a princess. However, the accounts do have a degree of credibility, and at the very least have the function of making the analysis of a narrative 'strange'. The very force of narrative often makes it difficult for even the trained viewer to stand back and observe what is really going on.

The Proppean analysis does, however, depend on the existence of a single narrative operating in a linear way. The examples chosen to illustrate the analysis are characterised by a strong central storyline – although one of them, *Sunset Boulevard*, does have a framing device. Even mainstream movies have tended to develop a system of subplots, often with a 'romantic' subject subservient to the action plot. While this is recognised within Propp – the resolution involves a wedding as a consequence of the success the hero has had in the action plot – the main plot and the subplot often exist in a state of tension. Police movies have increasingly stressed a tension between the demands of the job, the successful solution of a crime and the satisfaction of the hero's romantic and domestic needs. The very principle of a linear narrative is being increasingly challenged – and not merely outside the mainstream. Robert Altman's *Short Cuts* (1993) combines a number of short stories, but with many of the characters appearing in more than one story, having, in Proppean terms, alternative character functions. Quentin Tarantino's *Pulp Fiction* (1994) extends this technique, using three stories with overlapping characters, but also inserts the final resolution – Bruce Willis with girlfriend riding off on his motorbike, the final moment in the time of the narrative – around two-thirds of the way through the film. *Pulp Fiction* does not conform to mainstream narrative structure, and it is only comprehensible because we as viewers hold on to an understanding of narrative and formal conventions through our experience of the mainstream.

For further discussion of Pulp Fiction, *see Chapter 3, pp. 116–124.*

Todorov and Propp's work stresses the simplicity of film narratives which are media-specific. In particular, the classic realist text appears to narrate itself. Despite the example of *GoodFellas* (see p. 77), the film does not usually appear to have a narrator, an 'I' who tells the story. Novels can either have a 'teller', a character or observer within the text, or an author, who by implication has privileged access to some of the characters. Similarly, in much television news or documentary coverage there is either a voiceover or a presenter who operates as the authoritative voice. In the absence of a presenter, the narrative itself is seen as the embodiment of the truth of what is happening, no matter how far-fetched.

For further discussion of the challenges the French New Wave presented to conventional narrative forms, see Chapter 12.

ALTERNATIVE NARRATIVES

The concentration in this chapter has been on mainstream cinema. However, there has always been a tradition in European cinema for the production of films that challenge or at least subvert the conventions of the mainstream. Peter Wollen (1969) has distinguished a tradition of counter-cinema exemplified in the work of Jean-Luc Godard, which is contrasted with the mainstream in a succession of oppositions as follows.

See Chapter 7, pp. 247–253, for a discussion of feminism and its relation to the avant-garde and counter-cinema. For reference to experimental animation see Chapter 6, pp. 229–232.

Narrative transitivity versus narrative intransitivity

In mainstream cinema there is a flow of action with a clear developmental pattern and a cause-and-effect chain. In counter-cinema the narrative is subject to a series of breaks where the narrative's hold on the spectator is broken. This can be in the form of inserted titles, which were eliminated from mainstream cinema with the coming of sound, or the presence of scenes that break either with the narrative drive or the style of the film. In *Natural Born Killers* (Oliver Stone, 1994) we are presented with the story through a multiplicity of devices or forms: cartoon, situation comedy (including canned laughter), dance and sequences constructed in a documentary format. The culmination of this is a film in which the veracity of anything we see is challenged.

Identification versus estrangement

In mainstream cinema we are drawn into the film through the leading protagonists, sharing their experiences and learning to see the situations within the film from their point of view. In counter-cinema we are not expected to be in thrall, and indeed are distanced from the leading characters. This may be because they are presented as less than attractive as people, or because the performers are seen to step out of character, to address us directly and to reflect on the film and the characters they are playing. Karel Reisz's *The French Lieutenant's Woman* (1981) uses the device of a film within a film to allow the actors, played by Jeremy Irons and Meryl Streep, to reflect on the circumstances of their characters within the costume drama which is the main narrative.

• Plate 2.13
The French Lieutenant's Woman (Karel Reisz, 1981)
Actors playing actors: Jeremy Irons and Meryl Streep as actors discussing the plight of their characters

Transparency versus foregrounding

In mainstream cinema the film-maker hides the work of film production. In counter-cinema the film-maker may draw attention to the processes involved by, for instance, talking to the camera operator and allow the conversation to remain on the soundtrack. In Ingmar Bergman's *Persona* (1966), the film starts by showing film stock running through the projector. Bergman then cuts to the numerical countdown that appears in the leader tape on all films, but which is never shown to the audience.

Simple versus multiple diegesis

In mainstream cinema there is a single coherent storyline with a drive towards uniformity; the soundtrack is compatible with the visual images, and all disruptions, such as flashbacks or scene changes, are absorbed into a single linear narrative. In counter-cinema different narratives can not only appear within the same film, but indeed can be contradictory. In Kurosawa's *Rashomon* (1950), the same event, a rape and a killing, is told and shown from the point of view of four characters, without in the end privileging any of the four contradictory accounts over the others.

Closure versus aperture

In the mainstream, cinema narratives are designed as self-contained worlds, both understandable in themselves but also resolving all the issues raised within the film. In counter-cinema, the film will make reference to a world outside itself, for instance by referring to other films or experiences, which the spectator may or may not be able to bring to the viewing. Consequently, the experience of the individual spectator cannot be determined by the author of the film. In many of Godard's films, characters will read extracts from books without placing them for the spectator. The sense we make of these extracts, for example whether we are meant to approve of them, will depend on our cultural background and whether we can contextualise them. In this sense counter-cinema films may be more 'open' to interpretation than the mainstream text.

Finally, Wollen sees the role of mainstream films as being to produce pleasurable fictions. Hollywood films are created to be consumed and enjoyed, and the contradictions of everyday life magically resolved in the happy ending. Counter-cinema, by contrast, is designed to give an 'unpleasurable' reality, presenting a non-narrative, non-escapist world, whose contradictions have to be resolved in real life. While Wollen's presentation of oppositional tendencies was highly apposite in the 1970s when it was written and when there was a distinctive counter-cinema shown in an art-house circuit and a relatively monolithic mainstream cinema drawn from the remnants of the studio system, it is less clear whether the same distinction can be drawn today. Many of the illustrative examples above were quoted for their accessibility, and could not be regarded as a pure form of counter-cinema. One of the hit films of 1998, *Sliding Doors* (Peter Howitt), has a fractured narrative with two alternative fabula dependent on a chance event – whether the leading (female) character catches a tube train or not. The alternative narrative is foregrounded by a reverse action sequence before she is allowed to get into the second account. The film then cuts between the two narratives, sometimes privileging one rather than the other. It denies the viewer an insight into a preferred reality. Due to the fairly rapid scene changes and the absence of editing devices such as fades or cuts to black to inform us of changes in storyline, the film depends on both a familiarity with mise-en-scène, specifically different haircuts, and the constant dredging of our memory as to where we last left the other story, in order for us to make sense of what we see.

• **Plates 2.14 and 2.15** *Rashomon* (Akira Kurosawa, 1950)
Alternative realities: the same scene within *Rashomon* replayed with different accounts

☐ CASE STUDY 3: AN ALTERNATIVE TEXT – *MEMENTO* (CHRISTOPHER NOLAN, 2000)

Sliding Doors, alongside *Groundhog Day*, *Pulp Fiction*, and *The Usual Suspects*, have challenged contemporary audiences in the ways that they have used various devices in 'film form' to subvert the mainstream model of 'story-telling', and specifically, the way that classical narrative represents 'time' and 'space'. Most 'counter-cinema' or 'art-cinema', and certainly any model of 'avant-garde' cinema, has this as *its* orthodoxy, creating a more challenging exemplar of film practice. In many senses, however, where 'art-cinema', and the 'avant-garde' seek to foreground formal disruptions, the co-opting of non-mainstream strategies into popular cinema has largely been grounded in two agendas: first, to refresh 'genre' typologies and expectations; and second, to re-engage with 'subjectivity' in the construction and representation of character. There is some irony in the latter context, in the sense that in some films this represents a return to the flexibility of expression of the first-person literary tradition, and a recognition that such is the relative sophistication and cine-literacy of contemporary audiences that cinema can now accommodate models of story-telling in which non-linear, non-objective perspectives can be more readily understood. Reassurance for the modern viewer is offered in the redefinition of the expected variables in generic models. In the case of Christopher Nolan's *Memento* (2000), for example, the anticipated staple ingredients of the late millennial noir-cum-thriller are present, but subject to a 'formal' repositioning, where the 'story' is told in reverse; each scene which follows the next is actually the scene that in a linear telling of the story would have preceded the former.

Perhaps inevitably, such a strategy points to an understanding of much of contemporary cinema as a **postmodern** phenomena (see Corrigan 1991; Denzin 1995). The fragmentation of linear narrative has a tendency to signal to audiences in the contemporary era that some degree of self-reflexiveness is occurring in the narrative – this is

postmodern
A perspective on the modern world which suggests that there is no dominant social, political or artistic perspective, nor any prevailing 'narratives' (Marxism, Psychoanalysis etc.) which determine an authoritative and consensual understanding of lived experience or aesthetic culture. Rather, there are multiple readings of history and culture which question both received and perceived experience, and a recognition of increased 'reflexivity' in personal and cultural activities which rest on the pastiche, parody or ironic interpretation of past forms and experiences. The collapse of an 'orthodoxy', or the assumption of a notion of 'consensual' experience has resulted in much more 'conceptual' rather than 'craft-oriented' art forms, and a fundamental fragmentation in 'narratives' and 'structural' norms. In this model, 'style' has seemingly triumphed over 'substance'; 'High Art' is indivisible from 'Popular Culture'; and the Media are seemingly the new arbitrators of dominant, if transient, social 'narratives'.

• **Plate 2.16** *Memento* (Christopher Nolan, 2000)

normally a playful engagement with film form in which pastiche, parody, homage and self-conscious artifice are foregrounded as a model of cinematic illusionism and modern-day storytelling. Simply, if there are no more stories to tell, the *way* in which we tell the old ones might serve as innovation. It is important not to see this a mere interrogation of technique, however, and to recognise that 'film form' was and is always intrinsically related to the representation of human *perception* and *creativity*. Consequently, this inevitably leads us to address how these aspects reflect notions of 'pastness', whether this be in the representation of personal 'memory' or in the shape of film 'history' itself. These have become the preoccupations of both contemporary 'film form' and the concept of 'narrative', which are both in essence subject to constant redefinition, deconstruction and re-analysis. At one level, this has led to debates about 'the end of cinema' (see Neale and Smith 1998; Lewis 2001), which sees only the corporatised, digitalised, MTV-style, 'dumbing down' of film as an art-form, as the terminal condition of cinema; at another, it acknowledges that 'cinema' in whatever form insists on its survival and development, even if its 'canon' of classics seems ever more fixed, and film as an art form, seen to be a pre-1980 phenomenon. *Memento* in many ways speaks to many of these issues, and is worth some consideration.

Leonard Shelby (Guy Pearce) pursues his wife's killer; in the incident in which she was killed he too was attacked, and as a consequence he suffers total short-term memory loss. In effect, he can make no new memories. Shelby believes that his long-term memory is sound, but as the film proceeds, even this assumption is questionable, both in the mind of the character, and in the minds of the audience, who are given no information outside that which is given by or experienced by the main character, as he comes to know it or experience it. Our role as spectators, therefore, is a complex one. It is only possible to make sense of the scene we watch if we have stored information about, and an interpretation of, the scene before. This is usual but in this case the audience is compiling the narrative backwards.

We first see a Polaroid un-developing; witness Shelby shoot 'Teddy'; see Teddy immediately revived, and talking with Shelby in the sequence that precedes the shooting, and so on. This has the effect of making the viewer highly *empathetic* with the character because we discover things as he does, but equally, we feel *alienated* in the quest to make sense of the 'narrative' before us. Shelby uses a 'system' to remember things, composed of annotated polaroids, scrawled notes and sketches, and tattoos with key 'facts' etched on his body. Like Shelby, the audience struggles to make sense of the clues and information, especially when this is compounded by the unreliable nature of his own recollections, particularly in regard to a parallel story about 'Sammy Jankis', a man supposedly suffering the same condition. Aphorisms and 'insights' litter the script: 'Memory is treachery'; 'Facts, not memories'; 'Always get a receipt'; 'How I am supposed to heal if I can't feel time?'; 'I can't remember to forget you'; 'Don't believe his lies'; 'There are things you know for sure'; and most significantly, 'You lie to yourself to be happy'. These work as touchstones in reminding the audience of its own instability in trying to establish what is happening. There are none of the securities of classical narrative, no three-act structure, no distinct authorial voice, no easy moral or romantic centre. The audience is anchored only by some of the familiar tenets of the noir: the femme fatale, Natalie, who is revealed as an explicit manipulator; the underworld villains – Dodd and Grants, both small-time drug-dealers and misogynist hoods; and the ambiguous cop, Teddy, either a 'buddy' protecting Shelby, or like the others, exploiting his 'condition'. Most importantly, there is the alienated hero, Shelby, whose desire for revenge for his wife's death seems, at least at the outset, understandable, but as more perspectives emerge and a more relative picture is available to the viewer, it is clear that the extent of Shelby's paranoid self-delusion, revealed in the film's denouement, necessitates rethinking the whole film once more. The film works as a meditation on the ambiguities, contradictions and ambivalence of 'subjectivity', and the impossibility of an 'objective' perspective. Like Shelby, the viewer seeks evidence to validate and valorise his (cinematic) experience. This is cinema as an act of interpretation, not an act of reassurance. This is fundamentally concerned with the manipulation of 'film form' to challenge the assumptions of 'narrative', and is an extraordinary achievement.

Ironically, a film which is told 'backwards', uses black and white interludes, refuses coherence, and insists upon enigma, may point the way forward to a resurgence in cinematic styling. If there is doubt about 'cinema' and 'film culture' sustaining itself in the face of corporate determinism, mainstream mediocrity and an effects-laden, apolitical model of 'spectacle' film-making (see Davies and Wells 2002), there is always the indeterminacy of 'film form' and 'narrative' itself to be exploited and developed by the new storytellers of what might be the first stage of post-photographic cinema and the erosion of 'classical' norms.

1 Compare and contrast any film that you feel is 'mainstream' and an 'alternative' text. Why do you think these films differ? Look carefully at the ways in which the 'story' is told. How far does each text use 'classical narrative', and how far, and in what ways, does it reject it?

2 Contemporary cinema is constantly changing. Try and define what now might be meant by 'counter-cinema' or 'art cinema'. How does this differ from your understanding of 'mainstream' Hollywood cinema? How might these terms have changed in meaning – try and look at some aspects of the history of cinema to make your evaluation.

 **KEY TEXTS**

Three recommended introductory texts of increasing level of difficulty:

Turner G., *Film as Social Practice*, Routledge, London, 1988.

Andrew, D., *Concepts in Film Theory*, Oxford University Press, Oxford, 1984.

Lapsley, R. and Westlake, M., *Film Theory: An Introduction*, Manchester University Press, Manchester, 1988.

General texts

Bordwell, D., Staiger, J. and Thompson, K., *The Classical Hollywood Cinema*, Routledge and Kegan Paul, London, 1985; repr. 1994.

Ellis, J., *Visible Fictions: Cinema, Television and Video*, Routledge & Kegan Paul, London, 1982.

Lewis, J., *The End of Cinema*, Pluto Press, London, 2001.

Maltby, R. and Craven, I., *Hollywood Cinema*, Blackwell, Oxford, 1995.

Tudor, A., *Theories of Film*, Secker & Warburg for the British Film Institute, London, 1974.

FURTHER VIEWING

In a sense almost any viewing would be applicable to work on this chapter. Nevertheless, the 'non-obtrusiveness' of much mainstream cinema creates difficulties in observing the processes whereby meaning is created. This suggests that initial work on form and narrative is perhaps most productive with work characterised by 'excess'. In recent years, the impact of Tarantino, the Wachowski Brothers, Woo, Solondz, Anderson, and Korine among others has at least challenged the sustained dominance of Spielberg, Lucas, Scorsese *et al*. in Hollywood. Viewing the ways these directors challenge the orthodoxies of 'the Old Guard' is a useful tool in seeing how 'film form' and 'narrative' are changing and developing. Simply, directors of quality inevitably use 'film form' and 'narrative' in interesting and sometimes provocative ways – invest in watching as much film as possible and these differentiations will become apparent very quickly.

RESOURCE CENTRES

http: //www.filmeducation.org
http: //www.tcf.ua.edu/screensite/res/journals

Chapter 3

Spectator, audience and response

Patrick Phillips

■ Spectator, audience and response

INTRODUCTION

A central reason for studying film is to better describe and explain our response to the film experience. In a response study, we ask how and why we react as we do – both emotionally and intellectually. We may extend this to consider reasons for the uniformity or diversity of reactions among a group of people.

Film studies has distinguished between the response of social groups, collectives of people – an *audience* – and the response of the individual – a *spectator*. This chapter will consider some of the ideas that have informed thinking about the film spectator and the cinema audience and it will use these as a springboard for an introductory examination of *response*.

THE FILM SPECTATOR

Film studies has assigned great importance to spectatorship. The following are some of the working assumptions that have underpinned this work since the 1960s. Here are three, each of which can be considered open to dispute or be in need of considerable qualification:

- spectatorship is primarily concerned with the way the individual is positioned between projector and screen in a darkened space
- the audience ceases to exist for the individual spectator for the duration of the film
- although the spectator is singular, a figure alone before the screen, spectatorship studies tries to generalise about how *all* spectators behave

Let us consider each of the above.

Spectatorship is primarily concerned with the way the individual is positioned between projector and screen in a darkened space
You or I are referred to as spectators when we position ourselves in front of a screen and engage in watching a film.

It has been argued that the cinema experience is much more completely separated from the rest of our lives than the act of watching a film on a television screen. We enter a public space having paid an admission charge. We are predisposed to a certain level of investment of ourselves in the film screening – if only because we have paid for it. The fact that we have paid also indicates that we have certain expectations that will further increase our willingness to concentrate. The cinema is, in a peculiar way, both more public and more private than our own homes. As a public place it offers us the chance to enjoy a different set of comforts and facilities from those at home. While the lights are up and the advertisements or trailers are playing, we are aware of the other members of the audience. The popcorn being crunched and the drinks being slurped don't annoy us particularly. When the lights go down and the film credits appear we are suddenly alone with the images on the screen and the sounds coming from the speakers. Now the crunchers and the slurpers run the risk of seriously annoying us – we suddenly realise we have come here to lose ourselves in the images and sounds of the film.

The technology of cinema exhibition holds us much more powerfully than does television. The size (and shape) of the screen, the quality of the images, the clarity of the sound all invite much more attention – indeed they demand it. We are held in our

See Chapter 1, pp. 34–40, for further discussion of film and audience.

For an extended discussion of the differences between watching a film in a cinema and watching television, see John Ellis' *Visible Fictions* (1992).

comfortable seats; all around us is near-darkness except for exit signs. We have no control over the film. If we go to the toilet we can't put the film on 'pause'. Not only that; we can only engage in the briefest of whispers about what has happened in our absence.

It is important to consider the very significant upturn in cinema visits at a time when VCR and DVD systems and multi-channel satellite/cable TV dominate domestic enter-tainment. The cinema 'experience' is acknowledged as special and different – and is considered as worth taking seriously as a topic of study. Of course, much of the above begs the question whether we, therefore, need to develop quite different approaches to spectatorship when we watch a film on television or on a computer screen – with no projection, where the scale is so much smaller and where, most often, we cannot lose ourselves in the dark.

Certainly the similarities between watching a film in a cinema and at home on a small screen should also be considered.

The audience ceases to exist for the individual spectator for the duration of the film

Do we lose ourselves in the dark? It could be argued that the public and social nature of cinema-going works against this experience. After all, we enter the auditorium as a member of the audience, our expectations possibly enhanced by the chat around us. Many people go to the cinema with one or more other people and their physical prox-imity is something that can't easily be put out of our mind. Even if alone, we are conscious of shared reactions during a screening; sometimes this takes audible form – laughter, groans, screams – any of which can be infectious, altering the individual spec-tator's response (Hill 1997).

On a broader front we can say that we exist as audiences for a movie well away from the cinema. We are constructed as members of a 'potential' audience in at least two ways. We become exposed to the promotional and marketing hype designed to create expectations. We are also drawn into conversation about issues relating to a movie which may be circulating within our culture, resulting particularly from the profile the film enjoys in other media. In moving from 'potential' to 'actual' audience member, we have both an individual and a collective sense of what we are doing – we are self-aware. After the screening we may well engage in yet another expression of audience member-ship as we discuss our reactions in a variety of contexts – on the bus, in the pub – maybe for days afterwards.

Nevertheless, for better or for worse, theories of spectatorship have tended to isolate the self that exists more or less alone with the film for the duration of its screening. We will have more to say about this later.

Although the spectator is singular, a figure alone before the screen, spectatorship studies tries to generalise about how *all* spectators behave

Even though theories of spectatorship isolate the self, this self is an abstract concept, rather than a self with individuality and differences from other spectators. In other words, interest is not in observing and explaining the response of actual people but rather in the attempt to generalise about a 'state of being' common to all people when they position themselves before a screen and watch a film.

Generalisations about this theoretical spectator show some very interesting shifts. In the 1960s and 1970s the dominant model was of a 'passive' spectator controlled by the overwhelming mechanisms and physical presence of the film screening, so that they were made vulnerable to the assumed **ideological effects** of the film experience. The emphasis more recently has been much more on an 'active' spectator who makes meaning and 'negotiates' with the film in the act of consuming it. Either in conceiving of a 'passive' or an 'active' spectator, what we find are attempts to generalise about the complexity and significance of the film – spectator interaction.

ideological effects have political signifi-cance, manipulating the spectator into an accep-tance of specific ways of thinking about and relating to the world.

Much of the remainder of this chapter will elab-orate on these ideas of the 'active' and 'passive' spectator.

THE FILM AUDIENCE

The study of film audiences has emerged from a quite different academic base to that for spectatorship. Audiences exist in the culture, as social phenomena, and it is through media sociology and cultural studies that much of the work on audiences has developed. Here are three characteristics of film audience studies which, like those outlined above in relation to spectatorship studies, are open to question and debate:

- the audience is primarily of interest as an object of study *before* and *after* the film
- audiences are seen as constructed by mass-media institutions and exist in a dependent relationship with these institutions
- audience study, even though concerned with large collections of people, is now less likely to generalise than is spectator studies; it is concerned rather with local and specific factors that may explain audience behaviour

Let us consider each of the above.

The audience is primarily of interest as an object of study *before* and *after* the film

The audience disappears when the lights go out. Spectatorship theories, as we have already seen, kick in at this point, with the audience de-aggregated into individuals alone before the screen. This may seem odd – audiences certainly remain 'whole' at other spectator events such as music concerts and football matches. In film studies it seems that, on the one hand, the audience is the 'immanent' audience, the one forming for the event, constructed by a range of factors ranging from the influence of advertising to fan obsession. On the other, the audience is the 'virtual' audience, existing after the film, a group which remain a collective because of what they do in their wider cultural lives with the film experience they have shared. What audiences 'do' with a film is often expressed in terms of *uses and gratifications* – which is another way of talking about what needs in the audience are met by the film experience.

One concept that holds onto the audience as a collective during the film screening is that of the 'film event'. The film as an 'event' has been developed from a variety of contrasting perspectives. At one end of this spectrum we find political activist cinema, such as that of Latin America in the 1960s, where the film is something that can be stopped and argued over, where active participation in debate is the very purpose of the event. At the other end of the spectrum we have what might be called the 'carnival' film event, such as when an audience dresses up and sings along, as to *The Rocky Horror Show* or *The Sound of Music*.

The 'taming' of the audience is something discussed briefly below, pp. 100–101, in the section on Early Cinema.

The very exceptional nature of these 'events' relative to the standard movie-going experience reminds us of how oddly obedient the audience is within the standard film event. The audience remain more or less silent, more or less unmoving in the seat they have chosen or been allocated. The experience remains remarkably similar to that of going to the theatre. In light of this it is perhaps unsurprising that studies have focused on the 'before' and 'after' of this act of social conformity.

Audiences are seen as constructed by mass-media institutions and exist in a dependent relationship with these institutions

Audiences, especially fans-as-audience, can be seen to be very dependent on the media institutions that produce, promote and sell the product that they consume. Just as the spectator can be seen as engaged in a symbiotic (and dependent) relationship with the film text and cinema apparatus, so the audience may be seen as engaged in a similar kind of relationship with the cinema institution. The demands of the audience are met (sometimes? always? hardly ever?) by corporations who supply the films that occupy the multiplex screens and meet the 'home cinema' market in video and DVD formats.

One interesting debate here is the extent to which audience demand for films, particularly as expressed through fan behaviour, determines supply, that is, the actual films produced by the industry. Certainly as an industry dependent on consumer choice, it might be expected that extreme sensitivity is required in interpreting indicators of audience preference. In practice, the audience is potentially so vast and diverse in its preferences that responding to audiences often means responding to a 'core' audience – the so-called 'avids' who go to the cinema most often. Of course, the more a market strategy is designed around these 'avids' the more they will dominate the audience in a closed circle of mutual interest to the exclusion of other audiences and their film preferences (see Dale 1997).

What we find here is indeed a parallel between the way spectatorship is managed by forces outside the control of the spectator and the way audience is managed by the power-brokers of production, distribution and exhibition, operating within an international commercial market.

Audience study, even though concerned with large collections of people, is now less likely to generalise than is spectator studies; it is concerned rather with local and specific factors that may explain audience behaviour

From the earliest studies of film audiences it is clear that the routine methods of social science research could tell us a great deal. In these audience studies and in many others like them since the 1910s, what we have are deductions made from the collection of quantifiable information – information about, for example, frequency of visits to the cinema and genre preferences. (This contrasts with the inductive approach of spectatorship, which starts with a theory and then projects it onto the object of study – the person in front of the movie screen.)

The purpose of audience studies has usually been to identify – and then interpret – broad tendencies. So although information comes from actual individuals who describe their real behaviour, the interest in collecting this data has been in order to see larger patterns of behaviour. More recently, under the influence of cultural studies, there has developed an increased sensitivity to local conditions and circumstances; a move towards what are sometimes referred to as 'thicker' studies. A 'thick' approach to audience study respects the diverse backgrounds and motivations of sub-groups who constitute the larger audience.

RESPONSE STUDIES

Who is it that we should talk of as responding to a film – the spectator or the audience? Perhaps neither, so much as you or me as an individual, not quite contained within theories of the spectator or general sets of observations about the audience (both of which we will look at further in this chapter). Film studies, influenced by cultural studies, is increasingly likely to centre on local, small-scale and precise groups of people who share, perhaps, some social or political 'formation'. Their behaviour both as individuated spectators and as a collective of people forming an audience is likely to be better understood if we respect and try to understand the importance of the particular life experiences and social attitudes that they bring with them to the viewing situation.

Here is a very literal example. We could carry out a study of former members of the Women's Land Army, 'land girls', women who were sent to work on farms in Britain during the Second World War to make up for the labour shortage. These women who would now be in their eighties are invited to a screening of David Leland's *Land Girls* (UK, 1998). They form a 'community of interest', that is, a group of people who though

The goal of providing explanations for cultural forms and social practices loses its appeal in favour of an emphasis on the (preferably 'thick') interpretation of specific forms, practices and effects. It is in particulars rather than abstractions that larger generalities take on forms that have emotional impact, social effect and ideological import.

(Nichols 2000: 38)

See, for example, Altenloh's text *A Sociology of the Cinema: Audiences*, which is a 1914 study of cinemagoing in Mannheim, Germany, or that by Rev. J.J. Phelan, *Motion Pictures as a Phase of Commercialised Amusement in Toldeo, Ohio*.

• Plate 3.1
Land Girls (David Leland, 1998) What is the audience's starting point: romance, nostalgia or history? A simple film may produce wildly varied responses.

Nichols is arguing that film studies is moving away from 'master narratives', that is, theories that try to construct general overarching explanations of, for example, how people watch films and respond to them. Instead, he encourages specific and small-scale case studies, for example, of particular people in a particular place at a particular time.

One such study is by Jacqueline Bobo, who examined women watching Steven Spielberg's *The Color Purple*. Parts of this are reprinted in Turner (2001: 444–68). See Chapter 7, pp. 256–257 for further discussion of Bobo's study.

not living in physical proximity to one another are identifiable as a community because of a shared interest. In fact we would discover many individual differences, as well as collective similarities in their response. For example, they may all experience to some degree a nostalgic glow for the period of their youth and for the romance of their contribution to the war effort – even if in reality they had very varied experiences as land girls from that represented in the film. On the other hand, their sophistication as film-goers may vary enormously, with some much more able to see how the film is constructed at least as much around other films of a similar kind as it is constructed around any attempt at historical accuracy. As a result tolerance levels for what is perceived as not very 'realistic' in the film may prove very varied.

It may soon become clear that even this approach, involving an apparently homogeneous group of women watching a film that locks in to a key moment in their personal histories, is too big, too likely to produce fairly crude generalisations. We quickly become aware that the 'formation' of each person is only partly the result of their public and social selves. Each of us brings to the film event an interior self, a self of countless memories and desires, some scarcely acknowledged let alone understood. Major themes in *Land Girls*, for example, revolve around female friendship, sexuality and personal relationships. We can well imagine how, for each woman in our study, very specific memories and associations may be stimulated by these themes.

In this light we may have to consider that not only does every individual have a unique relationship with the film they are watching, but that this relationship is likely to change in subtle ways from one viewing of the film to the next. Response draws in the whole of the self, a self that includes:

- a social self who can make meaning in ways not very different from others with a similar ideological 'formation'
- a cultural self who makes particular intertextual references (to other films, other kinds of images and sounds) based on the bank of material she possesses
- a private self who carries the memories of her own experiences and who may find personal significance in a film in ways very different from others in her community of interest
- a desiring self who brings conscious and unconscious energies and intensities to the film event that have little to do with the film's 'surface' content

The land girls of history came from different class backgrounds, enjoyed different educational opportunities and would subsequently have lived very different lives from one another (indeed, this is captured in Leland's film). Each of them would watch a fiction film loosely based on their experiences of the 1940s with different needs and thus different levels of personal investment in the viewing experience.

My example is a simple one – but it raises a problem of response study that is more or less the equal and opposite one to that raised in spectator study. If spectatorship study risks losing itself in the 'master narrative' of a generalising and theoretical account of how we watch films, response study can lose itself in the very particularity of each interaction between film and spectator.

For a definition of the master narrative, see the Nichol's quote given on p. 95–96

Discuss the 'film event' with a group of friends. Consider:

1 What is said about the specific experience of watching a film in a movie auditorium...and
2 How much the experience is enhanced by the ways we engage with the film through the media, with friends etc. before and after the screening.
3 Although 'home cinema' is essentially a marketing concept, there is the possibility that the audio/visual quality of the film experience could be replicated in the home. Do you think that this will mean that the film experience – as spectator and audience – will also be replicated in the home?

Do you agree that film studies is better off avoiding large generalisations about 'spectators' or 'audiences' and is likely to produce more useful kinds of knowledge by focusing on small-scale studies of particular groups of people?

If everyone responds from within their unique 'formation', both as a social self and as an interior self, is there any point in trying to generalise about how we respond to a film?

WHAT WE CAN LEARN FROM EARLY CINEMA

We tend to take film viewing and our behaviour as consumers for granted, and so theories of spectatorship and studies in audiences can alert us to the complexities of our own response to film and the cinema experience. Very often the best way of trying to understand something we're so familiar with that we take it for granted is to take an historical perspective. Certainly one of the most fruitful ways of understanding the relationship between mainstream commercial film, spectatorship and audience construction is to study how they evolved in the period referred to as 'Early Cinema', dating from around 1895 to 1915. Here we may ask not only how spectatorship and audience developed but reflect on how they could have developed differently.

For further discussion of the development of the codes and conventions of Early Cinema, see Chapter 2, pp. 59–62.

Film historians tend to agree that by about 1917 nearly all of the fundamental features of what we now consider mainstream film 'language' were in place. Film had, in just twenty years, evolved ways of managing time and space, particularly through editing, and of managing the distance between object and audience, particularly through camera movement, which made the experience of cinema very different from that of the theatre. We must remember however that films still very clearly showed their relationship to popular forms of theatre such as melodrama and vaudeville, especially in their storylines and character-types.

For a vivid account of the evolution of film form, see Burch (1979). This work mixes short films from the period 1895–1903 with Burch's own amusing film which builds up a sequence from the static camera to the close-up and shot-reverse-shot. However, some caution is required. Burch is clearly reflecting a specific view of the development of the cinema apparatus and the spectator which is increasingly under challenge.

Narrative comprehension is a complex area of study in Early Cinema. Indeed the distinguished film historian Tom Gunning coined the term 'a cinema of attractions' to highlight the fact that this cinema was at least as much concerned with spectacle as with story-telling. In the move toward narrative clarity, a range of methods were used alongside developments in film form. For example, lecturers offered commentaries on what was screened, drawing attention to key visual details.

The evolution of film form in Early Cinema

In very early films the camera is static before action and character. This can be accounted for purely by reference to the technical limitations of the equipment. However, there is also an assumption being made about spectator viewing position – the camera 'eye' assumes the position of a member of the audience sitting in the middle of the stalls of a proscenium arch theatre. The theatre spectator cannot move closer to a key character or observe a key event in more detail. Early films seem particularly clumsy to our eyes in that they often include shots full of people and a variety of action without any guidance as to which action or indeed which character is particularly significant for the development of the plot.

Not only do early films not offer us close-ups but they don't offer any guidance as to what we should give our attention to within the mise-en-scène. Also undeveloped is any systematic organisation of point-of-view shots which just a little later became so important as a means of drawing us into the action and emotion of an event.

It is useful to list some of the ways in which the spectator began to be drawn in to a particular relationship with the screen through control exercised by camera movement, mise-en-scène and editing:

■ camera movement towards and away from an object – usually the camera fixed to a train or car – in order to give the spectator a greater sense of physical involvement

■ camera position nearer or further from an object – long, medium and close shots motivated by a concern to 'direct' the spectator's attention and increase engagement with the emotions of characters

■ mise-en-scène organised to enhance the meaning and emphasise the significance of particular actors or objects through positioning, set design and lighting

■ the frame of the mise-en-scène exploited to create interest and desire in what cannot be seen beyond the edges of the shot

■ editing used as the means by which shots can be organised and, thereby, the means by which the spectators seeing is 'managed', for example:

• **Plate 3.2**
The Great Train Robbery (Edwin S. Porter, 1903) This still illustrates the static camera of Early Silent Cinema. For a spectator accustomed to the 'standard' film language, established twelve to fourteen years after this film, Early Cinema provides major problems. For example, the static camera does not create the expected involvement or draw attention to significant objects in the frame which might help create narrative clarity.

- parallel editing so that two events can be followed simultaneously, encouraging the spectator to make and respond to assumed dramatic and thematic connections
- editing used as montage – to encourage a particular interpretation of one shot by the influence exercised on the spectator's mind by the shots either side of it
- editing used particularly to move the spectator between different points of view within the mise-en-scène.

A way of pulling much of the above together is by reference to the concept of the **look**.

The evolution of film spectatorship in Early Cinema

Early Cinema needed to find ways of controlling the look of the spectator as part of a move toward producing a more appealing and standardised 'product' for commercial exploitation. For example, it became essential to try to:

- ensure that the meanings intended by the film's makers were those taken by the members of the audience
- replicate for realism of effect the ways in which we engage in the act of looking outside the cinema
- provide greater pleasure in the act of looking

It is possible to talk about developments in the use of the camera, mise-en-scène and editing as ways of *controlling the look*.

The camera offers a particular 'eye' on the world of the film. This 'eye' may be the camera as the impersonal storytelling device or it may be the 'eye' of a character within the film as represented by the camera. These are literally 'points-of-view'. Even when the camera is not aligned with the viewing position of a particular character but is 'objectively' pointing at a mise-en-scène, the spectator look could be directed by the looks and glances exchanged by the on-screen characters in order to draw attention to a significant plot detail. Editing allows the spectator to adopt different viewing positions; to share in an exchange of looks, most commonly in a shot-reverse-shot dialogue sequence.

One spectator 'effect' of the development of film form is particularly important. It is the way in which the spectator is drawn into the world of the film, caught inside and between characters. This is achieved through editing and point-of-view and results in the *interpellation* of the spectator who is drawn inside the psychic, and physical life of the fiction. This 'effect' is at the heart of so many debates around spectatorship and manipulation in popular cinema.

Of all the ideological aspects of spectatorship, none have received as much attention as those around notions of voyeurism – the look of the peeping tom, able to see without being seen. Early Cinema very frequently represents the female, dissected by the close-up into a fetishised object of the male look. It is certainly interesting in relation to ongoing debates around the proposition that overwhelmingly in mainstream cinema the 'camera is male', that the evolution of this out of crude peepshow technology should be so evident from the beginning of popular cinema. Two of the most famous films exploring voyeurism are Hitchcock's *Rear Window* (1954) and Powell's *Peeping Tom* (1960).

Practical solutions, common sense or ideology?

It is fascinating to study these developing strategies in Early Cinema, especially as they do not appear to have been systematic. Some are used, then discarded, then used again. By trial and error, film-makers found a set of procedures that worked – aesthetically,

look
The 'look' developed as a central concept in relation to the control of the spectator. Cinematic looking has also been associated with theories of desire and pleasure, theories often founded in psychoanalysis.

This idea of the 'male look' was proposed by Laura Mulvey in 'Visual Pleasure and Narrative Cinema' (1975) and developed in 'Afterthoughts on Visual Pleasure and Narrative Cinema' (1981). *For further discussion, see Chapter 7.*

See also the reference to cognitive processing and the development of Early Cinema on p. 108.

hegemony
An important concept in this chapter. A set of ideas, attitudes or practices becomes so dominant that we forget they are rooted in choice and the exercise of power. They appear 'common sense' because they are so ingrained, any alternative seems 'odd' or potentially threatening by comparison. Hegemony is the ideological made invisible.
In relation to the development of cinema, it can be seen how Hollywood developed hegemonic status and power. The Hollywood form of genre-based narrative realist film is considered a 'common sense' use of the medium. Other forms of cinema, by comparison, are more or less 'odd'. In looking at the early history of cinema we can begin to understand how and why Hollywood assumed this position.

The interest shown in Early Cinema by avant-garde film-makers is particularly interesting. See, for example, Chapter 1 of Scott Macdonald's *Avant Garde Cinema* (1993).

emotionally, intellectually and, most of all, commercially. There are different ways to account for how mainstream commercial film form developed the way it did by 1917. It can be interpreted as entirely 'natural':

- a set of practical solutions to the problem of making the film more intelligible to an audience, motivated by commercial considerations
- a common-sense set of solutions to problems of replicating how the spectator engages with the real world through the act of looking

Alternatively, it can be interpreted as ideological:

- a reflection of the ways of seeing of Western culture and particularly of the male within Western culture
- a recognition of the medium, if only for commercial reasons, as a powerful manipulative medium, capable of controlling representation and response

In fact these two positions are not opposed: what appears 'natural' and 'common sense' is rooted in a set of **hegemonic** choices and constructions. The very naturalness of these choices simultaneously provides spectator/audience pleasure and a largely invisible and, therefore, particularly effective form of spectator/audience control.

A study of Early Cinema forces us to ask questions, the most fundamental of which is this: Could film have been different from what it is and still have attracted a mass audience? Those frustrated by the way a particular conception of cinema came to dominate (the mainstream Hollywood-type film) sometimes look to the period of Early Cinema which can be seen as a kind of Garden of Eden – a period of innocence and infinite possibility. Studies in Early Cinema often encourage us to think what other ways film form – and, therefore, spectatorship – could have developed from the way in which they did. For example, a model for a radical alternative form of cinema might be conceived as one which does not guide us every step of the way through close-up, shot-reverse-shot, and so on. In a static camera long shot, for example, we are given freedom to choose for ourselves what we wish to focus upon. In not being interpellated, we are free to engage more objectively and thoughtfully with what we see and hear. There is not the space here to explore these arguments. However, it is necessary to recognise that much of the interest in Early Cinema is motivated precisely by a desire to reflect on other kinds of spectatorship possibilities than that established by the kind of cinema which Hollywood (and not just Hollywood) had evolved into by around 1917.

The evolution of the film audience in Early Cinema

There are now several very good histories of Early Cinema. See the Key texts section at the end of this chapter for details.

In the introduction to this chapter, the inter-relationship of spectator and audience studies was pointed out. With regard to Early Cinema, just as interesting as the study of the development of film form as it relates to spectatorship is the development of film exhibition as it relates to audiences.

See Chapter 1, pp. 4–7, for more discussion of Early Cinema.

Film gradually emerged from a fairground attraction of 1895 to the nickleodeons of the early 1900s. Audiences were overwhelmingly working and lower working class. The medium of cinema had a very low cultural status. In the USA the move from nickelodeons, usually just small dark rooms with benches, to movie theatres, which accelerated in the early 1910s, was both cause and result of the move to make cinema-going more 'respectable' and controllable.

The commercial concern was to raise the social image of movies and this had to involve both making them more sophisticated products and placing them within more 'theatrical' auditoria. A key objective was, as the founder of Paramount, Adolphe

Zucker, said, 'to kill the slum tradition in the movies'. An anarchy in film response had to be contained if film-going were to be more appealing to the middle classes. This anarchy derived in part from the fact that the films were silent. This gave them a wonderful 'universality' on the one hand, but also offered them as particular to different audiences – for example, to the vast diversity of immigrant groups arriving on the East Coast of the USA. More specifically this anarchy derived from two factors. First, the lack of a controlled viewing position prior to the development of a standardised film form, as described in outline above, meant that the spectator was much freer to make meaning from the images presented on the screen. Second, the 'untrained' behaviour of the audience who used the cinema space as a noisy, interactive meeting place meant that the movie-going experience was held in very low regard by those sections of the middle classes that took it upon themselves to 'police' social behaviour. Neither the film's textual operations nor cinema's organisation of the viewing event was able to isolate and control the spectator. The peculiar nature of the film experience as both isolated (in spectatorship) and collective (in audience membership) was itself evolving – or rather, being constructed – toward greater uniformity.

The fact that film audiences were socialised into a particular cinema practice (e.g. sitting quietly) at the same time that film form had been evolved to manage the act of spectatorship (e.g. control over the look) is highly significant. The standardisation of both film form and of cinema exhibition from very early in the history of cinema has encouraged film theorists to develop ideas based on:

■ a normative spectator unified as the 'subject' addressed by the film
and
■ the viewing situation as a constant (rather than as variable according to who is the spectator, when and where they are and what they are watching)

The strengths and shortcomings of this approach to spectatorship, already high-lighted above, are further considered in the two sections that follow our first case study, which focuses on the early cinema audience and response to a particularly controversial film.

Even in the 1910s it is clear that the movie theatre was a highly political site. Audiences were presented constantly with pamphlets, petitions and projected slides – usually asking for their support against censor-ship threats. There was a strong relationship between an audience and the management, as these movie theatres were local, independent operations. 'The anti-censorship campaigns between 1912–1922 only intensified the involved, active quality of movie-going'. The idea of the 'active' audience is significant in relation to the discussion that follows later in this chapter. See also Barbas (1999: 217–229).

> **Consider the questions raised in this and the previous section.**
> **Do you think that the emergence of what we now recognise as the dominant main-stream kind of cinema, together with normative forms of exhibition and audience behaviour were**
>
> 1 the 'natural' and
> 2 the 'best solution' in developing the medium?

☐ CASE STUDY 1: THE RESPONSE TO *THE BIRTH OF A NATION* (D.W. GRIFFITH, 1915)

The purpose of this case study is to reflect on the most spectacular early experience of film – the discovery of the power of the medium to generate intense response both inside and outside the cinema auditorium. D.W. Griffith's film of 1915, *The Birth of a Nation*, is of great significance in the history of cinema. It brought together most of the developments of the previous years in film form in order to cement them in place in

Institutional Mode of Representation
The IMR is a term used by Noel Burch (1979). It attempts to capture the idea that a normative set of ideas became established around about 1915–17 as to what constitutes a mainstream feature film – and has remained the dominant conception of the feature film ever since. In fact the IMR is another example of hegemony – the establishing of an apparently 'common-sense' notion of how a film should be constructed and how it should communicate with an audience.

what we now sometimes call the **Institutional Mode of Representation (IMR)**. At the same time it offered the kind of film spectacle that accelerated the move of cinema into 'picture palaces'. The fact that the film remains one of the most racist films ever made offers a third key area of interest. In what follows the emphasis is on the evolution of audiences and the idea of the film event, and on the increasing cultural (and political) significance of cinema within a developing industrial-commercial 'public sphere'.

Griffith was a perfect figure for social reformers of early cinema to have as an ally because of his commitment to what may loosely be described as Victorian, conservative values combined with his brilliant understanding of the potential of the medium. He carried forward a complex project intended to advance cinema as an art form to be respected by the arbiters of culture and simultaneously to rein it in so that it might be experienced as a more standardised commodity. Perhaps a little harshly, Larry May describes Griffith's achievement as not one of aesthetics 'but simply size, scale, prestige'. In other words, Griffith's achievement was to synthesise developments over the previous years and turn this into a more spectacular product. The complication to this neat narrative is that the most historically significant of Griffith's films, while certainly conservative in ideology and while certainly laying down a benchmark for the standard narrative realist film form, produced a disruptive social effect on a national scale far beyond anything in the short history of cinema up until that point – or arguably since then (May 1980: chapter 4). In fact Griffith may appear as a very contradictory individual. His conservative values centred on ideas of the home, the family and on an essentially patriarchal sense of leadership by wise, enlightened men. At the same time, his defence of freedom of speech (especially in defending his own work!) seems to put him in a much more liberal camp. His eye for sensational images of sex and violence certainly seems to fly in the face of any sense of him as a Victorian prude.

The Clansman, as the film was first known after the title of Thomas Dixon's novel, started production on 4 July, 1914 and was completed at the end of October. The initial $40,000 budget was spent just on the battle scenes – the film finally cost an unbelievable $115,000 – a scale of production which tells us much about the 'invention' of cinema as fantastic spectacle. The film was previewed on 8 February, 1915 at Clunes Theatre, Los Angeles. The event was unprecedented as the entire Los Angeles Philharmonic took up their places to accompany the film. Here, Karl Brown, assistant to Griffith's great cameraman Billy Bitzer, describes in a 1976 interview the moment the film began:

…and when [the conductor] raised his baton and held it for a moment – down it came and everything blew just straight out of the can – oh it was the most tremendous gust of sound I'd ever heard.

This and the other testimony quotes in this case study come from *D.W. Griffith – the Father of Film*. This is a three-part documentary on video produced by Kevin Brownlow and David Gill in 1983.

It was renamed *The Birth of a Nation* before formerly opening on 3 March, 1915 at the Liberty Theatre, New York with usherettes dressed as southern belles. What it meant to go to the cinema was redefined by the scale of the film both as a film and as a cultural event – it changed people's idea of what cinema was, how it could be experienced, what effects, visceral, intellectual, moral it could have on a society. The film had a lot of firsts – the first to run for three hours, the first to have a musical score played by a 70-piece symphony orchestra, the first to have scheduled performances, the first to have an intermission, the first to charge $2 for reserved seats. It has also been described – flying in the face of what we might think of 'silent cinema' – as one of the noisiest films ever made. A small army of people was employed back stage in the big city screenings to produce a complete range of sound effects.

The audience was constructed by national advertising and promotional campaigns. It was the first film to use large billboards, the first to take full-page ad space in newspapers. It was the first full-length film to be screened at the White House. No one could fail to know about it as an 'event'. It made huge profits – most famously making the future founder of MGM, Louis B. Mayer, his first fortune – simply by owning the distribution rights to *The Birth of a Nation* in the New England area.

This commercial hype was, of course, compounded by the controversy the film created. Many people were outraged by the film's racism and yet caught in a double bind – as liberals many of these people were also against censorship. So *The Birth of a Nation* can also be regarded as the earliest example of a film demanding a collective response and yet dividing people as to what that response should be. Karl Brown, in his 1976 interview, recounts how when told that showing the film in Atlanta would cause race riots, Griffith replied, 'I hope to God they do'. Brown continues:

It wasn't that he was particularly anxious for a riot or people to be hurt or anything of the sort. But it's the old story that if someone gives you a tremendous pat hand, you're going to play it.

This confirms a view that Griffith was engaged in an act of provocation. Apologists for Griffith would argue that his main motive was not to promote racism but to prove and promote the idea that cinema was a new cultural form of great significance. However naive or calculating, what is clear is that Griffith was locked into a social formation in white, male, southern states culture that made it almost inevitable that the hegemonic form of representation of African-Americans – a racist representation – would manifest itself in his film.

The National Association for the Advancement of Colored People (NAACP) organised nationwide protests against the film, starting immediately after the Los Angeles preview one month before the New York premiere – even though members were in principle against censorship. There was plenty to be upset about – from the intertitle in Griffith's 'Prologue' which stated that 'The Bringing of the African to America planted the first seed of disunion' to the crudely racist representation of black men, especially in the post-Civil War second half of the film. Several screenings of the film were delayed and the Film Boards in some US cities required changes to the film in response to the protests. An Epilogue, paid for by the Hampton Institute, was made to show the positive contribution of African-Americans and this was first tagged on to the film at Boston's Tremont Cinema in 1916. A near riot broke out when a larger number of black people arrived to a screening to establish how useful the Epilogue was in correcting the damaging effects of the film – and were refused admission.

For more notes on censorship and regulation, see the end of the chapter, pp. 124–126 and also Chapter 1, pp. 40–46.

The effect of the film on black audiences, still at this time subject to segregation in cinemas, cannot be understated. Here is William Walker speaking in the early 1980s about his experience of having seen *The Birth of a Nation* in a blacks-only movie theatre in 1916:

some people were crying. You could hear people say, 'Oh, god' and some 'damn'…You had the worst feeling in the world. You just felt like you were not counted, out of existence. But I tell you, I just felt like there could have been some way so they couldn't see me so I could kill some of them. I just felt like going out to kill every white person I saw in the world.

Between 1915 and 1973, the right to screen *The Birth of a Nation* was challenged in the US courts at least 120 times. However, the very controversy surrounding the film was a key incentive for those wishing to develop the full-length motion picture as a powerful and significant form of mass entertainment. The film showed that cinema could produce 'effects' for both individual spectator and collective audience on such a scale that there was no turning back. The commercial and cultural significance of cinema was proven to a very large degree by this one film.

This brief case study (much more could be said if space were available) demonstrates that a focus on audiences and the film 'event' draws together key areas of film studies. *The Birth of a Nation* is uniquely able to force the following questions – what kind of experience does cinema offer, what kinds of social and cultural effects can a film have? What competing ideological forces are put into circulation by a film which dares to offer such amazing spectacle on the one hand and such pernicious messages and values on the other? *The Birth of a Nation* established that cinema matters. It demonstrated that some films at least enter into the public sphere, are experienced by audiences coming to the event with their different personal and community formations in ways that tell us not just about the movies but about the force-fields at work within the society.

In looking at issues of film reception, it shows us how issues of spectatorship and audience are difficult to untangle. Here is Karl Brown talking about the Ku-Klux-Klan rescue sequence with Wagner's 'Dance of the Valkyries' as accompaniment. Brown's construction by the film text as spectator is clear – but, also, by implication at least, is his predisposition to a certain response determined by his own ideological formation and his construction as a member of an enthusiastic audience, expectant of the kind of thrills provided:

It was like a call to arms – you just couldn't let go. You weren't watching people ride, you were riding with them and you weren't riding with them to rescue somebody but you were riding on a stern determination for vengeance, vengeance for the death of that little girl you'd learnt to love so much…. And the fact that the showing of 'The Clansman' started riots and put blood on the streets was proof beyond proof that this was a great picture – regardless of what critics might have to say about it. The proof was there.

The Birth of a Nation was hugely significant in the evolution of both film spectatorship and the audience experience. However, like all historical case studies it needs to be considered in its specificity – as a unique case – as well as in its function as establishing a precedent which changed people's perceptions of what a movie was and what an evening at the cinema could offer.

This case study of audience responses to *The Birth of a Nation* suggests a very active audience – and yet powerful manipulative forces at work in the act of spectatorship. These mixed messages about 'active' and 'passive' are the subjects of the next two sections.

It is interesting to identify the number of times the 'Dance of the Valkyries' has been used in dramatic film sequences. A notable one is the helicopter gunship attack of Colonel Kilgore in Coppola's *Apocalypse Now* where it is used satirically.
What are the associations of this piece of music by Richard Wagner?

• **Plate 3.3**
The Birth of a Nation
(D.W. Griffith, 1915)
A rider in Ku Klux Klan garb rides at full tilt towards the camera.
It is difficult to study Griffith's film. On the one hand it is the most important single advance in the development of narrative film and mainstream film form. On the other hand, it is obnoxiously racist and images such as this one appear to have contributed to increased recruitment to the Ku Klux Klan throughout the 1920s.

Choose another film – maybe a contemporary one – that has caused controversy. To what extent would you argue this controversy results from

1   the internal qualities of the film – its shocking effect on the spectator; or
2   the circulation of debates about the film within the culture – in the form of media coverage?
What are your views on censorship – should a film celebrating the Ku Klux Klan be banned?

THE PASSIVE SPECTATOR

The spectator of political and social science

At almost any point in film history one can find essentially negative assumptions about the behaviour of the movie-goer as spectator. Even contemporary debates about media 'effects' are based on a view that the spectator is extremely vulnerable to the manipulative qualities of the film text and the cinema experience. What is particularly interesting is the approach of critics from the political left during a period extending from the 1930s to the 1980s. One might expect support for the 'people's culture' and a positive attempt to interpret how mainstream commercial cinema was used by audiences. In practice. the approach over this fifty-year period was both critical and pessimistic.

The Frankfurt School, made up of left-wing intellectuals who escaped Nazi Germany in the 1930s, presented Hollywood-style films as a kind of twentieth century 'opium of the people', a form of mass culture which entertained and seduced people into an uncritical acceptance of the values, attitudes and fantasies presented to them.

Antonio Gramsci's reworking of traditional Marxist theory through the concept of hegemony also addressed issues of manipulation. He asked how, in a sophisticated twentieth century society, the dominant groups retain power. His work argued that it was not through physical force but through the constant reinforcement of dominant attitudes and values that ideology became re-written as 'common sense'. Popular cinema could be seen as playing a part in 'naturalising' particular ways of seeing and understanding the world – not just in particular on-screen representations but in the form of film (narrative realism) and the psychology of the communication process. Popular cinema could only reinforce in people a conventional way of making sense of their world – rather than inspiring them with new and different ways of thinking about their own lives and the lives of others.

These ideas from the social and political sciences were much elaborated in the 1970s by theorists who synthesised ideas developed respectively in linguistics, psychoanalysis and neo-Marxist thinking. This synthesis of ideas produced a model of the film spectator as seemingly controlled by overwhelming forces.

Key concepts in 'subject–apparatus' theory

The three key strands of this deterministic model of the film spectator are:

Linguistics

A theory of language derived from the work of Ferdinand de Saussure presents the individual as locked into language structures which limit our thinking to the forms – the words, the grammatical rules – already available. We cannot think outside the terms language provides us with; indeed, language does our thinking for us, *it speaks us*. We can consider popular cinema as a language which works according to its particular rules and conventions (be they on the 'macro' scale of narrative and genre or at the 'micro' scale of things, as for example the continuity edit). On this basis we can argue that both film-maker and spectator are locked into thinking structures that define and limit what

Please note that what is referred to here as 'subject–apparatus' theory may be referred to in other studies by different names – for example, 'screen theory' or simply 'high theory'.

This another variation on the idea of the establishment of an IMR (see p. 102 above)

For further discussion of psychoanalysis and feminist film theory see Chapter 7, pp. 251–255.

film is. Neither can 'speak' outside of these structures. Theoretically this means that the spectator's 'passive' role is even pronounced – not only unable to intervene in the work of the film, but unable to think outside the language-like structures it employs.

Psychoanalysis

The work of psychoanalyst Jacques Lacan encouraged a comparison to be made between the act of spectatorship and a specific period in the development of the young child. This theory argues that a child is born with a sense of incompleteness, a 'lack'. There is thus a desire from birth to fully 'be', with life spent trying to overcome or fill the lack, something that we can never accomplish. To compensate for the failure to re-establish a sense of personal completeness or unity, the child will console itself with imaginary solutions, especially idealised images of itself as 'complete'. The child's first illusion of wholeness is the mirror and the sense that 'that must be me'. More profound is the mirror provided by the mother, who 'reflects' a particular identity back onto the child. The mirror image is a kind of mirage, a narcissistic self-idealisation, a misrecognition because the imagined 'real' is always in fact unattainable. Film theory compared the act of spectatorship to this 'mirror phase' in order to explain both the pleasure and the ideo-logical effect of surrendering to the film image. The pleasure is that of experiencing, at least temporarily, 'wholeness', however imaginary. The ideological significance is that the spectator accepts images (and, by implication, the ideas they bear) which are a misrecognition, which are not truly representative of his or her identity or ideological needs. It is interesting to note the relationship between theories of language and theories of the mind. After the 'mirror stage', also referred to as the 'imaginary', Lacan talked about the child entering into language or the 'symbolic'. Because language pre-exists the child, he or she can only enter it on its terms. Or, to use the word again, the child is interpellated into language. Identity appears to be offered by the way language orders and names things. Different discourses – such as discourses of gender – seem to offer the possibility of greater self-recognition, greater wholeness. In fact these are mecha-nisms of control and containment, likely to increase misrecognition. The child must submit to the rules of language and in so doing his or her subjectivity is actually formed by language which 'speaks' the permissible roles and identities available to the child. The 'symbolic' appears to offer liberation but in fact offers constriction. Lacan further argued that everything that will not fit into the terms of language is consigned to the unconscious. These ideas (in a much more elaborated form than here!) became very influential in explaining the psychic and political effects of cinema.

On finding the 'symbolic' world of language just as incapable of answering a sense of 'lack', the child, according to Lacan, will look to some other person for an uncondi-tional love which will answer this need to achieve wholeness. A projection takes place, most obviously again onto the mother. But the mother or some other person can never provide fully what is being desired. This becomes the launch pad for a lifelong unfulfill-able search for the 'lost object', never-ending desire – something that cinema exploits.

As a footnote, it is important to recognise that there exist very different understand-ings of desire. For example, the French philosopher, Gilles Deleuze, whose work is having an increasing influence in film studies, offers a completely different model of human desire, not at all motivated by 'lack'.

Marxism

The ideological effects of cinema can be derived from both of the above. The film locks spectators into structures and plays out for them experiences that are irresistible. The language of mainstream cinema is 'invisible' in that it is the language the spectator has been born into. The endless exploitation of spectator desire becomes simultaneously a misrecognition that has both psychic and political consequences. The neo-Marxist philosopher Louis Althusser, influenced by the psychoanalytical theories of Jacques Lacan, talked about how people are locked into the controlling structures of society – interpellated into them. This is both the result of 'misrecognition' and perpetuates misrecognition in ways that prevent political change (this can be linked to Gramsci's ideas discussed above). Film Studies took this idea of interpellation to describe how the spectator is locked into place by the powerful mechanisms and effects of cinema. Arguably, interpellation – which at its most literal means the act of being called over, 'hailed' – is both one of the basic pleasures of the movie experience and one of the most obvious ways in which popular narrative realist cinema can be said to have ideological effects.

The cinema apparatus and the subject

The power of cinema as a system of communication, holding the spectator in place, was referred to as the *cinema apparatus*. The very term 'apparatus' conjures up ideas of being tied into place, controlled. The term describes the technical process and the effects produced in the act of projecting images onto large screens in darkened auditoria. We are interpellated into the space between projector (behind us) and screen (in front of us).

From the above it can be seen that it was thought appropriate to talk about the spectator as a function of the cinema apparatus, as its 'subject'. The subject is a way of talking about the hypothetical spectator. The subject within established film theory became the dummy figure who ideally demonstrated the effects of the cinema apparatus:

■ who was interpellated into the film in very specific ways
■ and who was, more or less, the passive 'subject' of overwhelming forces.

Responding to the spectator of film theory

Thus, the spectator of film theory was:

■ the 'subject' of an 'apparatus' which imposed the 'look' of the camera, a 'look' which was implicitly or explicitly ideological in its preferences,
■ within an overall physical and psychic experience, including 'interpellation' which prompted regressive behaviour
■ and thus led to 'misrecognition', suppressing critical faculties which might otherwise offer a defence against the ideological messages of the film.

Each of these three propositions can be challenged:

■ Does the spectator automatically or necessarily become the 'subject' of the cinema 'apparatus'?
    If not, then we need to find other ways to assess the psychic and ideological effects of cinema, possibly arriving at a far less dramatic, deterministic model.
■ Does the spectator really enter into a 'regressive' state through 'interpellation' – indeed, does interpellation accurately describe the process by which we enter into the cinema experience?
    If not, then we need to find different ways of talking about spectatorship, perhaps reflecting our ability to be simultaneously 'inside' and 'outside' the experience.
■ Does the spectator enter into acts of 'misrecognition' on such a scale that his or her formation as a political being, his or her gender, sexual, ethnic, cultural identity counts for nothing?
    If not, then we need to find different ways to talk about how the spectator handles the messages and representations of the film.

> **What do you think of the ideas put forward in this section? When you watch a film do you surrender to its effects or remain critically alert? Does it depend on the kind of film? Does it depend on your own state of mind at the time? Does it depend who you're with? Is it possible to surrender to the film *and* remain critically alert?**

THE ACTIVE SPECTATOR

Cognition

For discussion of a cultural studies approach to audience study, see Chapter 7, pp. 256–257.

In opposition to explanations of spectator activity deriving from what has rather loosely been described as 'subject–apparatus theory', is a much more pragmatic view of how, moment-by-moment, the brain works with the stimulus it is bombarded with by the film in order to make sense and gain emotional experience. This can be described, in broad terms, as a cognitivist approach. Rather than focusing on unconscious activity and the 'subjectification' of the spectator (as outlined in the previous section), this approach takes as its starting point the idea that response can largely be tracked and explained by reference to conscious and routine activity. The brain works to recognise, process and 'place' the stimulus in such a way that it becomes possible to 'read' the film's meaning and manage its effects. This emphasis on cognition certainly supports the idea of the 'active' spectator, even if much of the mental processing seems entirely automatic. For example, we learn to read a film in all kinds of ways – through recognition of the familiar aspects of narrative, genre conventions and the common audio-visual techniques of film's communication system (such as continuity editing and synchronised sound). We do this by bringing our knowledge and experience of previous films to bear in responding to a new film experience.

One way to explain how spectators make meaning is by reference to *schemas*, a concept used in studies of the human thinking process. When we are confronted by a new experience, we look for familiar patterns that allow us to orient ourselves and make sense of what is in front of us. In the experience of watching a film we automatically look for the schemas we have become accustomed to from our previous experience of film. As well as narrative and genre, mentioned in the previous paragraph, we may find, for example, an auteur schema or a star schema is useful in mentally processing what we are being presented with by a film.

This may suggest that competence in carrying out these cognitive procedures takes many years to learn – well, some may – such as learning to recognise an auteur structure/schema. However, the fundamental schemas relating to, for example narrative and genre, don't – and certainly learning to 'read' the basic communication system of film doesn't. One explanation for this ease with which we 'read' a film was provided as early as 1916 by a psychologist, Hugo Munsterburg (see Langdale 2002). He pointed out that what was remarkable about film was that it seemed to be organised to allow us to respond using the kinds of cognitive processes we bring to our everyday lives. Indeed, going back to the evolution of narrative film in Early Cinema, it can be argued that filmmakers were evolving by trial and error a form of cinema that made mental processing as 'natural' as possible. If cinema can be described as 'realist', then it is most profoundly realist in the way that it replicates mental rather than physical reality. Our brains effortlessly (but not passively!) function to make meaning from and manage response to the kind of stimulus the film throws at us second by second. Cognitivism could, therefore, be described as a 'realist' approach to spectatorship and response.

Cognitivist processing could be described as achieving a particular kind of hegemonic 'incorporation' – the pulling in to structures of order that which might otherwise be considered dangerous, anti-hegemonic. Cognitivism deals with processes of mental 'incorporation'. Again I quote Bill Nichols:

Analytical philosophy and cognitive psychology cling to the same assumptions of abstract rationality and democratic equality that led to a politics of consensus (based on the denial of bodily, material difference) and the repression of a politics of identity.

(Nichols 2000: 42)

However, a major criticism of cognitivist approaches is that in relating the film experience to everyday routines of mental processing, it can only emphasise the similarities rather than the differences between the film experience and other kinds of 'everyday' activity. What, for example, of the very particular ways in which films provide us with moments of intensity, mobilising our desires, triggering memory in the dark of the movie auditorium? Can it be said that cognitivist approaches actually 'domesticate' the film experience? The activity of the 'active' spectator of cognitivism involves working to make safe the film experience, repeating conventional ways of thinking and processing stimulus material – in this case stimulus produced by a film. The passive spectator of the 'subject–apparatus' theory at least has a 'target', the aspiration to think and see differently, to recognise and move beyond his or her misrecognition (see above). Indeed it could be argued that cognitivism not only 'domesticates' the film experience, it de-politicises it.

Perhaps it is a false distinction to describe cognitivism as promoting an 'active' spectator, as opposed to the subject–apparatus 'passive' spectator. The spectator of cognitivism is 'active' in a limited sense – to make familiar. The real challenge for the 'active' spectator is to be liberated by the film experience to look and think differently; to celebrate difference.

---

1 **What do you think of these arguments?**
2 **You may wish to consider whether the respect due cognitivism is its base in scientifically observable psychological processes – empirical studies, whereas the subject–apparatus theory is precisely that – just theory.**

As many 'readings' as there are readers?

A different kind of reaction to the idea of the 'passive' spectator came out of a body of ideas that derived from **post-structuralism**, and which was expressed itself from the 1980s through cultural studies. We have already gained some sense of this in the brief introductory session on reception studies.

Deriving from the work of French philosophers and cultural theorists, particularly Jacques Derrida, Roland Barthes and Michel Foucault, ideas emerged which countered, to some extent, those of Saussure, especially in claiming that there are any fixed and final meanings in language. These moved from the idea that language does our thinking for us, emphasising instead language either as a game or as a competing struggle between alternative language systems (discourses). At the very least this introduces a more active subject; one who negotiates with the given language. Meaning is much more obviously dependent on the reader/spectator.

Modifications in the adaptation of Lacan's work began to suggest that the spectator is not so much constructed and held in place by the apparatus and the film text. The structuralist description of the spectator as fixed in place by an (imaginary) unified self-image projected onto the screen was replaced. Instead the spectator was now considered capable (as in what was said about language in the previous paragraph) to 'play' or 'struggle' with different positions. He or she could occupy different and contradictory positions – male/female, hero/villain/protagonist/victim – and thus was able to exercise conflicting fantasies within the self.

More broadly, a Marxist-style ideological analysis had to adjust to incorporate the idea of a more active spectator. If the spectator was now to be seen as an active producer of meaning as much as a passive subject produced by the cinema apparatus/film text, then a simple deterministic model had to be modified. More attention would have to be given to the spectator as an individual whose response is based on a vast range of variables.

One of the most remarkable and significant swings away from the 'subject–apparatus' model of spectatorship was the 'death of the author' position that derived from the post-structuralist ideas outlined in the previous paragraphs. Rather than hold to the view that the reader/spectator is entirely at the service of the author (the text, the structures at work that the reader/spectator has no control over), the opposite was argued.

A text (a book, a film, a painting) only comes into existence in the act of 'reading' it. In this way the reader of the text is, in a way, simultaneously its creator. The actual author (writer, film-maker, painter, etc.) is 'dead'. Each of us comes to a film with our own personal 'formation' – the result of all our life experiences. These will predispose us to certain interpretations of character, certain attitudes towards moral and political issues and certain emotional responses to events. In its most dramatic form this suggests that there are in fact as many 'readings' of a film as there are spectators.

Arguably however, this idea bears as little relationship to actual experience as the opposite notion that spectators are simply steam-rollered by all-powerful mechanisms.

Post-structuralism is often closely tied to notions of postmodernism. Modernism was driven by a commitment to scientific rationalism – and hence to making sense of experience through an identification of underlying 'structures'. This has been illustrated in the outline account given of subject–apparatus theory as a way of explaining cinema, spectatorship and politics (see pp. 105–107). The 'posts' are often presented as a kind of despair at the failure of modernism.

Formation is a key idea already introduced in relation to my example of studying the response to *Land Girls* (see pp. 95–97).

Rather, what we seem to have is 'openness of meaning yet determinacy of effect' (Lapsley and Westlake 1988: 66). In other words, while there is the possibility of many different 'readers-as-authors' making meaning, reflecting their personal formations as unique individuals, in fact within a given society people share a very similarly constructed sense of social reality (in ways that take us back to the arguments of the Frankfurt School).

In addition, as we have seen in our brief consideration of cognitivism, when we watch a film we all carry out essentially the same 'work' using the same cognitive skills and strategies. We are all familiar with the structures and formulas of popular cultural forms – the plots, settings and character types of different genres (the schemas). In applying common cognitive processes, we 'handle' the experience in a fairly uniform way. We are also likely to contextualise the experience in a very similar way. As audiences we have a common 'formation' in the film's marketing and promotional 'hype'.

In brief, the 'determinacy of effect' that strangles the potential 'openness of meaning' is the result of

- shared social construction/ideological mechanisms, and
- shared cognitive processes/mental mechanisms.

These are two principal forces at work in hegemony. Hegemony embraces both film text and spectator, media producer and media consumer, ensuring a close relationship.

The idea of 'openness of meaning yet determinacy of effect' is a useful compromise for theorists who had originally proposed the highly deterministic set of theories around 'subject–apparatus' theory. It accepts that the spectator has to be reconceived as someone who brings their own identity to the film event. At the same time it rejects the romantic and, in relation to reality, simply untrue notion that 'there are as many responses as there are spectators'. This compromise produces a model of response that we may call 'limited pluralism'.

> Maybe you disagree that audiences respond in broadly the same way to a film. Is there evidence of much greater diversity of response to popular films?
>
> Doesn't the example provided earlier (see above, pp. 95–97) of land girls watching the film of the same name, suggest that there is the potential for considerable 'openness of response' – just that it isn't always articulated. Is it the case that much of the personal response to a film is too private to be spoken about and we tend to hear or have recorded those public responses that are most like everyone else's?

RESPONSE: THE NEGOTIATING SPECTATOR

What the previous two sections have outlined are quite extreme models of the cinema spectator and his/her response to the film experience. This section outlines some more pragmatic explanations for how we 'read' a film and enter into its fantasies. In each case there will be an attempt to find common ground or a middle way between the ideas outlined so far.

Working with authorial intentions

When we read an art object (book, film, painting), a practical starting point is a best guess at what the creator's intention was in producing this object. Indeed, it may be more than a 'best guess' if we take the trouble to do some research and discover the creator's own statements on what he or she was attempting to achieve. Although we could exercise complete independence and, in a post-structuralist sense, 'play' with the film, producing a very personal reading and response, we tend in practice to defer to the creator in making meaning. So although it is logically true to say that a work only comes into existence when we bring ourselves to it, the author is not dead – but 'immanent' in the encounter – and we are generally more than conscious of this. With regard to a film, we could try to develop a response to *Fight Club* (1999) without any sense of David Fincher as director – but a more normal way of managing this encounter is to think about what the author-director/screenwriter had in mind.

A '*preferred* reading' of a media text is one in which the spectator takes up the intended meaning, finding it relatively easy to align with the messages and attitudes of those who have created the text. An '*oppositional* reading' is one that rejects this intended response. Most often a 'preferred' response will be associated with pleasure, if only the pleasure of reassurance that comes from the comfortable and familiar. Most often an oppositional response will be associated with dis-, or perhaps better, un-pleasure. More crudely, there may be the temptation to associate a 'preferred' reading with the 'passive' spectator and an 'oppositional' reading with an active spectator.

If we take Spike Lee's *Do the Right Thing* (1989) or *Jungle Fever* (1990), we can identify strong differences in audience response which can be described in relation to 'preferred', 'oppositional' and 'negotiated' readings. Lee's films are also challenging in terms of analysing our alignment and allegiance with film characters (see below, pp. 112–113)

Lee's films are clear in the positions they adopt. Some films, especially those which use irony, are much more difficult to define in terms of their 'preferred' reading. Coppola's *Apocalypse Now* (1979) should be seen as an anti-war movie. Does this mean that those who enjoy its spectacular battle sequences and who consider the film to be celebrating war are giving an *aberrant* reading – one which is simply 'wrong'?

Another film that demonstrates the difficulty of describing responses in terms of 'preferred', 'oppositional', 'negotiated' or 'aberrant' is the American independent film *In the Company of Men* (Neil La Bute, 1996). The difficulty is rooted in distinguishing between the film's *intention* and its *effect*. This in turn highlights a problem with this approach in general. These descriptive terms are applied on the assumption that the film has a set of meanings separate from the spectator. An alternative view is that the film has no meaning without the spectator. His or her response cannot be measured against a 'right' or 'wrong' interpretation but only in terms of their experience of the film – the affective, physical and cognitive pleasures that are taken from the experience by a particular individual.

In fact *Fight Club* is one of several contemporary films that allow for an exploration of the issues of postmodernism, identity, consumerism and incorporation outlined on the previous page. *See also Chapter 7, pp. 273–275 for a case study of this film.*

• **Plate 3.4** *Apocalypse Now* (Francis Ford Coppola, 1979)   • **Plate 3.5** Oliver Stone's *Natural Born Killers* (1994)

Both Coppola's *Apocalypse Now* and Stone's *Natural Born Killers* (1994) are satires. However, 'preferred' readings of the two films cannot be guaranteed. For example, *Apocalypse Now*, rather than being viewed as an anti-war movie, could be seen as offering pleasure in the spectacle of war; *Natural Born Killers*, rather than being viewed as an indictment of contemporary media culture and values, could be seen as celebrating the values of the central characters. Meaning and response cannot be separated!

Maybe in practice, the most common form of response is one that involves 'negotiation'. A 'negotiated reading' is one which involves a certain give-and-take between our own views and experiences and those presented in the film text. It is a mature and complex response that is dependent on our familiarity with and experience in handling the medium, or, to put this slightly differently, it is to do with our 'competence' as spectators. We may well be aware that in a real world we would find a certain representation unacceptable, a certain moral attitude repulsive, but we can 'place' this within the context of a fictional experience. We are aware of being 'inside' and 'outside' the world of the film. In fact, one might argue that only psychotic spectators, incapable of distinguishing between fiction and reality, find it difficult to negotiate a position between themselves and the constructed fiction-as-reality with which they are presented.

Working with character

I am indebted to Murray Smith's, *Engaging Characters – Fiction, Emotion and the Cinema* (1995) for much of what is contained here about alignment and allegiance. As a counterpoint to what was argued earlier about the problems of a cognitivist approach to Film Studies (see pp. 108–109), Smith's book is an excellent example of how productive it can be.

See case study of Memento (2000), in Chapter 2, pp. 87–89.

A further illustration of the work of the 'active' spectator relates to the response to character. A character is, of course, a construct – intended by an 'author' and brought into existence through the processes of representation. As with our more general response to a film, there is the possibility for preferred, oppositional and negotiatiated responses. However, characters present us with specific challenges because our entry into and participation in the world of the film will be through these figures. In looking at our response to character, there seems possible a particular complementarity of cognitive and psychic processes.

The first thing we do with a character is enter into an act of recognition. Quite simply we must first *recognise* the character. By this I mean that we must be able to translate the fictional 'construct' – which, at one level, we know is the product of screenwriter, actor, director and others – into a credible person. This is something we do automatically most of the time, unless the film is deliberately making it difficult in order to force us to adopt a more detached position (consider the problems presented by *Fight Club* or *Memento* [Christopher Nolan, 2000]). At another level, our ability to recognise a character will depend in part on our knowledge and experience of the world. At yet another level it will depend on our knowledge and experience of the textual conventions (and mental 'schemas') at work generally in fictional film. When we are aware of the creation of a character by a well-known actor/star, there is a different kind of recognition which may have a number of consequences. Familiarity with the star persona/image may provide us with additional insights and expectations. It may lead to 'over'-recognition in that it is difficult to move beyond the star presence in order to engage with the character as a self-contained entity in the fictional world of the film.

Second, we become *aligned* with a particular character. We see and feel parts of the story through this fictional person. Classical film theory would say that this alignment is involuntary – we are placed by the complex and powerful technical and textual mechanisms described above. If we have more access to the point of view and subjectivity of a character, we may become dependent on them for our 'take' on the film as a whole and, in the process, form a particularly close bond, an 'identification' with them. However, care must be taken not to assume that in aligning or being aligned with a particular character, we identify with them – in the sense of endorsing their behaviour and attitudes. It is perfectly possible for a film to create structures of alignment which place the spectator in the point-of-view/subjective consciousness of a homicidal maniac or a robot.

Third, we show *allegiance*. In doing so we make evaluations about the 'appeal' of the character to us. This may well be a moral/ideological allegiance, but if, for example, a spectator expresses a strong allegiance with Mickey and Mallory in Stone's *Natural Born Killers*, this involves a positive evaluation of their wild anti-social, anarchic moral

• **Plate 3.6**
Brad Pitt and Edward Norton in *Fight Club* (David Fincher, 1999) It is increasingly common for the audience to be presented with highly complex ideas about identity and time. This produces real challenges in determining, for example, the reliability of the narrative information with which we are provided. This, in turn, will make for much more uncertain forms of identification, alignment and allegiance to key characters

positions. As with alignment, classical film theory would tell us that allegiance is constructed by forces outside our control, that we are manipulated into allegiance, sometimes with characters whose views are ideologically counter to our needs and circumstances in the real world. Such manipulated allegiances could be described as examples of 'misrecognition'. However, this sells short the spectator and the imaginative work they are performing. The spectator is someone who can try out different identities in aligning with different characters within a fiction film and someone who is quite capable of exercising their personal judgement when forming allegiances. Referring again to the interesting case of *Fight Club*, consider the reasons for showing allegiance to Jack (Edward Norton) or Tyler (Brad Pitt), two manifestations of the same person, as we eventually discover.

'Allegiance' does raise a particular challenge to our thinking about the 'conscious' and the 'unconscious' spectator. It could be argued that there comes a point where conscious, cognitive processes begin to be taken over in the act of 'allegiance' by unconscious forces. What kinds of appeals does a particular character have on us; what memories or fantasies are triggered? Again, the argument here is for a synthesis of different theoretical approaches to the film spectator – a cognitivist and a psychoanalytical theorist may each provide valuable insights. This becomes apparent when we consider our ways of buying into and responding to cinematic pleasure.

Take any film of your choice and consider your relationship to two contrasting characters in terms of *recognition*, *alignment* and *allegiance*.
Does your study show movement and change in your response across the length of the film? Does it show that we have a capacity to align with and even show allegiance to

1   a variety of different sorts of characters, and
2   characters whom we would not feel drawn to in our actual lives?

Pleasure

*For more on pleasure
see the discussion of
different responses to*
Pulp Fiction *below (pp.
116–124).*

Making meaning and response are not the same thing. The latter refers to a much more all-embracing sense of my interaction with the film. A useful focus for questions of response is pleasure. Lacan's psychoanalysis encouraged film theorists to see desire as central to an understanding of spectatorship. Desire is an expression of 'lack' (see above, p. 106). Our pleasure derives from the film's 'staging' of our desire, a desire for the ideal, that which will answer the lack with a sense of completeness. The emphasis is very much on staging, because, of course, a film is only a film and can never really satisfy our desire – which anyway is unfulfillable. (That's why we go back for more!) In these terms, the film experience can be seen as a pleasurable 'tease' in which we have dangled before us forms of fulfilment which we cannot actually reach out and take. This satisfying of desire operates at the level of our fantasy lives, more 'unconscious' than 'conscious'. Response to a film that may be entirely predictable, badly made and even stupid in its plot and character development, may affect us deeply.

Here we must distinguish between the 'affective' response and the 'intellectual' response – both of which may well be operative at the same time. I am watching a film that my intelligence tells me is awful – but I'm crying.

This distinction extends to our choice of film. If I choose to buy into the latest James Bond experience, it may be in the context of the hype surrounding it, the particular expectations it offers. If the information I have informs me that there is a choice between a film which is intellectually demanding, one which is politically provocative and a third which is throwaway spectacular fun, I will decide which best matches my needs at that moment. It is likely that the choices of others will reflect the same need – so again we see individual spectators united as an audience. In choosing the James Bond movie, I am not expecting to have intellectual needs met, nor am I going to take too seriously the politics of the film. In other words, I will be able to make a 'preferred/negotiated' reading – rather than an 'oppositional' one – even though I may, in a more serious frame of mind, have to acknowledge that the sexism, militarism and violence portrayed is not something I would endorse in life.

To put this differently, in responding to an impulsive need for escapist fun, it may be argued that I am freely choosing to become the spectator of 'subject–apparatus' theory. I *want* to become the 'subject' of the apparatus; I want to be interpellated into the action; I want to be aligned with the look of the camera. Rather than denying the model of spectatorship offered by 'subject–apparatus' theory, it may be that we should accept its accuracy in describing the film experience, but within the contexts of choice and pleasure.

However, this still begs a larger question. Why did I, together with my fellow spectators, make the choice that we did? Why did we choose a spectacular fun movie and why could we be so comfortable watching its formulaic representations of gender, ethnicity and so on? Or, to go back to the previous paragraph, how could we 'allow' ourselves the pleasures of the film?

*For further discussion of
institution and audience,
see Chapter 1, pp.
34–40.*

To explain this we could fall back on traditional models of media manipulation. We are persuaded by advertising and promotional hype to buy a ticket. We are then further manipulated once we 'surrender' as spectators to the medium. A more interesting explanation would be that most of us are 'subjects' of the same hegemonic values that circulate within our Western corporate capitalist culture. We are, in the abstract, capable of 'oppositional' readings but are most likely to conform to the 'common-sense' attitudes and understandings that constitute the political, social and cultural hegemony. If we look at the diagram on p. 00, we can see that we are not so much manipulated into a response as immersed in a mind-set through the wider culture in which we live and act. We find ourselves negotiating within a narrow range, rather than across the kind of broad spectrum of possible responses which a genuinely pluralist culture might be expected to encourage.

The diagram opposite attempts to draw together some of the sources of pleasure available to us as spectators and audiences when buying into the experience of a popular mainstream film.

Cinema institution
(e.g. Hollywood)

Generalises audience – through
'standardised' product (narrative
realist film form) – and appeal to
shared (hegemonic) values

Specifies audience – through
differentiated genres (and stars
and auteurs)

e.g. putting into production and distribution *Titanic* (Cameron, US, 1997)

Cinema apparatus
(the technology of the medium)

Isolates and dominates the
spectator through the physical
nature of projector, screen, etc.

Spectator interpellated as subject of
the cinema apparatus and the film
text

Film text
(e.g. *Titanic*)

'Stages' our fantasies and desires

Pleasures of looking,
hearing; projection and
identification

Pleasures of story
(including pleasurable
anxiety)

Desire for spectacle –
continuation

Desire for knowledge –
resolution/closure

Spectator pleasures

affective   sensory   cognitive
(emotions)   (sensations)   (ideas)

anticipation   shared   cultural
(pre-movie)   experience   exchange
(in-movie)   (after-movie)

Audience pleasures

**Social/cultural practice
of cinema**
(e.g. reading about *Titanic* in
the media, going to the
multiplex to see it, talking with
friends in the pub about it, etc.)

The circulation of cinema within
society in a variety of activities
and discourses

1 How might you need to reconstruct the diagram above to account for the pleasure of
watching some format of 'home cinema' through a TV screen?

2 Rather than writing a response to a film which is an interpretation of its content and
an analysis of its formal features and style, try putting together a response based
purely on desire and pleasure. This may include a critical analysis of any *un*-desire
and *un*-pleasure.

Some of the points made in this diagram incorporate ideas presented earlier, for example, the way that the cinema apparatus and the film text interpellate the spectator. For the spectator it is seductively pleasurable to surrender to this position (leaving to one side debates about how vulnerable we may be to ideological effects). The pleasures provided by the film text can be described in many different ways – one way is to talk of how the film 'stages' our desires and fantasies. In the cinema auditorium, sitting in front of the screen and its images, we are in a state that seems simultaneously to involve passive surrender and active engagement. We surrender to what we cannot control (the unfolding of the narrative, the subject positions we are given); and engage with what delights us (visual images, sound, character identification). We have a desire for the film to continue so we can continue to enjoy these pleasures. Simultaneously we have a desire for the film to end and thus 'close' the uncertainty and anxiety the narrative induces in us. We desire different kinds of knowledge (for example, relating to plot and character) and different kinds of experience (for example, relating to the stimulation offered by sight and sound).

Overall we can identify different kinds of spectator pleasure/response: emotional as in our empathy with character and situation; physical as in the stimulation our senses are provided with; cognitive as in our involvement with the complexities of plot and theme. Forms of desire may run through all of these.

While acknowledging the importance of this larger framework within which pleasure can be explored, there remains a particular attraction in focusing on desires set in motion in the act of spectatorship. We are forced to recognise the importance of unconscious as well as conscious aspects of the film experience. It is possible to talk in terms of a spectator 'actively' working to find some material in the film experience to satisfy their desire, just as much as their need for plot information? The rejection of a film because it fails to articulate with the spectator's desires is likely to lead to an 'oppositional' position every bit as strong as an oppositional response to the film's more visible, conscious material.

In practice we need to recognise that the power of the cinema apparatus and the film text lies in the way it envelops both our conscious *and* our unconscious selves. A model of spectatorship needs to account for the pleasures available to us at both levels. Maybe the fundamental reason for the fear of cinema expressed by different kinds of social and cultural analysts for almost the entire length of film's history has not been because of concern over the conscious self made passive, as described in 'subject–apparatus' theory. Maybe the real fear has been over film's capacity to make the unconscious self active! It is most interesting, for example, that censorship is never related to film passivity – it is always concerned with the potential of film to *activate* the spectator's imagination (see the brief section on censorship at the end of this chapter).

☐ CASE STUDY 2: PLEASURE AND EVALUATION – *PULP FICTION* (QUENTIN TARANTINO, 1994)

Pulp Fiction is a useful film to use in exploring spectatorship and audience. On the one hand, it is a very self-aware film which plays with some of the basic conventions of narrative realist film. On the other hand, sequence by sequence, it employs standard aspects of mainstream film form – such as those discussed below.

In this two-part case study we will consider the moment-by-moment response to a sequence from Tarantino's *Pulp Fiction*. In the first part Vincent (John Travolta) picks up Mia (Uma Thurman) on the instructions of his gangster boss, Mia's husband, and takes her out to a diner. In the second part he has to cope with her overdosing, resorting to some rather shocking emergency treatment.

In exploring the first part of the sequence, my emphasis will be on responding to character and situation. In the second part, my emphasis will be on cinematic shock. In both parts, there is the opportunity to reflect on how we make meaning and obtain pleasure from the details of a film as we engage both intellectually and affectively in the act of spectatorship. What will also become clear is that central to response are judgements that we must make constantly – judgements that express favour or disfavour, and which may be deeply rooted in our personality, in our very formation as a human being.

By thirty minutes into *Pulp Fiction* we have established that Vincent is a ruthless hitman but also a rather ordinary guy, appealing, even slightly vulnerable, in whom the audience can take an interest. (He is also John Travolta – a fact that significantly colours our sympathies.) Immediately before his arrival at Mia's house he has taken drugs. We have no significant knowledge of Mia, although our expectations based on the gangster genre (the schema we rely upon to 'navigate' through fictional films) may lead us to expect a typical 'moll' or 'femme fatale'. So, in different ways we are already working as spectators, either in placing and coming to terms with a character we have some knowledge of or in anticipating one we have yet to get to know.

It is important to acknowledge how much of our pleasure and the meanings we make derive from extra-film sources, such as our knowledge of a star.

Part One: Picking up Mia and Jack Rabbit Slim's

Vincent approaches the house of his employer Marsellus Wallace. The spectator follows him from behind, first in long and then in medium shot. As he takes a message from the door, there is a cut to close-up and we hear what we assume (from our familiarity with film conventions) is the voice of the person who has written the note, Mia. The voice invites Vincent to enter. There is a cut to the interior as Vincent feels his way gingerly – he's on unknown territory; he's high on heroin. The spectator is then presented with a shot of Mia from behind as she sits in front of four televisions relaying close-circuit surveillance pictures of Vincent. During the rest of the two-minute sequence, until Mia's fingers pick up the stylus, Dusty Springfield's version of 'Preacher Man' provides an accompaniment to what we see. There is next a big close-up of Mia's lips at a microphone. Her call 'Vincent' startles him. All his movements seem to require additional thought. The spectator processes a range of information contained in the mise-en-scène, soundtrack, dialogue and performances. The information is controlled by the film's maker. To this extent the spectator is in a dependent situation. However, it is precisely because of this limited access to information that the spectator becomes active

In terms of recognition, alignment and allegiance, the sequence is interesting. In the 22 shots before the couple leave the house, we do not see Mia's full face. The spectator's curiosity is increased, partly for this general reason, partly for the specific reason that throughout she has been in control. She is in a position of power because: (1) she is the boss's wife; (2) she controls camera and sound technology; and (3) Vincent's condition is not likely to produce assertiveness! Our alignment is increasingly with Mia, all the key point-of-view shots are hers, including ones where she prepares and then snorts cocaine. Our allegiance, however, is with Vincent. He is the object of the camera's look – which becomes the object of the female look. Our recognition is based on what we know of him from the first thirty minutes of the film. If an allegiance has formed, it is based in part on the attributes of the Vincent character as already established, in part on the attributes of the Travolta star persona. We quite literally do not recognise Mia yet (although it is almost certain we will have an image already in our minds from publicity material in circulation outside the space of the cinema auditorium) and must move towards forming an allegiance based only on her behaviour, voice (and lips).

A moral evaluation of the two characters will, for experienced film spectators, depend less on judging them against a set of moral criteria from the real world than from those that are operative within the world of Tarantino's film. The recognition given by someone with no awareness of Travolta and with little ability or willingness to engage imaginatively within the terms of the film's genre and form may well be very different. In other words, we can anticipate the spectrum of 'preferred', 'negotiated' and 'oppositional' responses. Another way of discussing this is in terms of the competence of the individual spectator. This refers to the skills possessed by the spectator, most obviously their 'cine-literateness'. One could imagine a spectator either too inexperienced in contemporary popular cinema or too unsophisticated to pick up Tarantino's tone and his attitude towards his characters.

There is a cut from the Wallace residence to a red Chevrolet. The camera pulls out and pans left to establish that Vincent and Mia have arrived in the diner car park. We see Mia's

full face for the first time. Tarantino has used 1 minute 17 seconds of screen time to establish the world of Jack Rabbit Slim's diner and get the two characters to their seats.

In looking at the sequence from Mia's 'What do you think?' to when she goes to
'powder' her nose, we are presented with a very familiar shot-reverse-shot dialogue
sequence. As is typical of such a sequence, there are a large number of edits: 75 in 5
minutes 30 seconds of screen time with an average shot length of 4.4 seconds. In such a
sequence it is appropriate to apply the concepts of interpellation and suture (see above).
The spectator is very much drawn into ('stitched' into) the space between the two characters. However, there is no obvious sense in which this involves spectator passivity. In
terms of processing the visual and verbal information with which we are provided, very
considerable 'active' processing is taking place. This is in part a consequence of the
specific nature of this shot-reverse-shot dialogue: the characters are themselves objecti-
fying the person opposite them. It is intended that the spectator becomes fascinated by
the complex forces put into play: Mia's power over Vincent; Vincent's odd mix of coolness
and vulnerability; the separate knowledge we have of the state of mind of each of them.
This becomes particularly apparent during the 'comfortable silence' when the spectator is
shifted from point-of-view shots to side-on 'observer' views of each character separately.
The sequence, and its continuation after Mia returns from the ladies, requires the spectator to be both caught up within the exchange of looks and yet remain observant,
responsive to the character information being revealed.

The spectator is very often both 'privileged' in possessing information which an on-
screen character lacks and 'restricted' in that key information is withheld. Both are ways in
which our interest is created and maintained. We may feel we have limited access to information at various points in this episode but in one important way we are in a position of
superior knowledge: we know that *both* of them are high on drugs. Relative to Vincent, the
spectator is 'privileged' on three separate occasions: before, during and after the trip to
the diner we see Mia taking cocaine. Not only does this inform our understanding of and
alignment with the Mia character, it also significantly shifts the spectator's expectations on
what dramatic results are likely to follow. Having returned from Jack Rabbit Slim's, Vincent
is observed in a bathroom of the Wallace home telling himself not to become sexually
involved with Mia but to go home. This is a darkly comic situation, intensified by the
Vincent/Travolta performance and made dramatically ironic by the knowledge given to the
spectator that Mia is in the sitting room with very different preoccupations.

• **Plate 3.7**
Uma Thurman in
medium close-up

• **Plate 3.8**
Travolta and Thurman in
two shot
The diner scene from
Pulp Fiction between Mia
(Uma Thurman) and
Vincent (John Travolta) is
made up in large part of a
classic shot-reverse-shot
rhythm which 'sutures'
(stitches) the spectator
into the space between
the characters producing
intense involvement.
Plate 3.7 is a typical
Vincent point-of-view
shot of Mia. However,
Tarantino can surprise us
as in the side-on two-
shot (Plate 3.8). Suddenly
the spectator is on the
outside in much more of
an observer role.

• **Plate 3.9**
Travolta and Thurman
re-enter apartment
Vincent returns Mia to her
home. The spectator has
been drawn into align-
ment and allegiance with
these two characters. As
a consequence of our
involvement further anticipation and tension is
created. After their very
flirtatious night out, will
Vincent risk taking things
further with the boss's
wife? Our privileged
information on Mia's
condition leads us to
consider a different
scenario. We care
because we have been
drawn into the situation
by the calculated use of
film techniques in the
previous scenes. An
unusual feature of *Pulp
Fiction* is that our caring,
our allegiance is some-
times set up only to be
wiped out by some turn
in the plotting or structure
of the film.

There is then a sudden shift in tone after Vincent's bathroom monologue

…So you're gonna go out there, drink your drink, say 'Goodnight, I've had a lovely evening,' go home and jack off. And that's all you're gonna do….

(Tarantino 1994: 69)

We do not expect a close-up of Mia's face, suddenly deathly white, sick coming from her mouth, blood from her nose.

Part two: OD'ing

After Mia has overdosed, there is a 2-minute 10-second sequence involving Vincent driving towards the house of Lance, trying all the while to communicate the desperateness of his situation on his mobile phone (while the Three Stooges play on Lance's TV). There then follows just under 2 minutes of frantic activity, much of filmed using a hand-held camera. (Tarantino's script offers the following description: '…everything in this scene is frantic, like a documentary in an emergency ward, with the big difference here being nobody knows what the fuck they're doing.') There is then a quieter but hardly calmer 1 minute 25 seconds preparing for and giving the adrenaline shot to the heart that causes Mia's instant recovery.

The entire 6 minutes 10 seconds before we see Mia, ghostly white, being driven home by Vincent is simultaneously suspenseful, shocking and comic. In the act of spectatorship there are undoubtedly some responses which are involuntary just as there are in our responses to shocks and surprises outside the cinema. In this sequence, the most obvious illustration of this involuntary response is when Vincent, after a long pause, takes aim and plunges the syringe into Mia's heart. The shock of an entire audience is audible! However, for most of an action sequence, spectator involvement is far from involuntary. We need to *care* what happens – and this is directly related to the allegiances we have formed with the two central characters, specifically here as a result of our 'participation' in the previous long sequence in the diner. In considering some of the alternative ways of responding to the 'OD'ing sequence', it is first necessary to list some of the alternative ways of responding to the episode as a whole:

A   primarily at the level of character and the emotions generated by their circumstances – a very 'affective' response.

B   primarily at the level of genre/form in which characters and situations are understood in relation to familiarity with the 'schemas' of different kinds of cinema – a 'cine-literate' if usually quite automatic response.

C   primarily at the level of the film as 'construct' in which there is a strong awareness of the film's makers – an 'intellectual' response.

These can be mapped against pleasure (1) and displeasure (2). In the abstract the alternatives look like this:

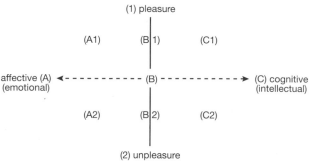

One way of interpreting these divergent responses is by reference to 'preferred', 'oppositional' and 'negotiated' readings.

In relation to the particular sequence, different responses may include the following:

A1   Intense concern for Mia (that she recovers) and for Vincent (that he does not suffer the consequences of Mia's death).
B1   Amusement at the mix of black comedy and farce.
C1   Delight in the way Tarantino mixes melodramatic intensity (1) with comedy and farce (2).

A2   Distaste for Mia and Vincent, their behaviour and the values they represent.
B2   Disorientation at the mix of black comedy and farce in a situation involving a drug overdose, and possibly outrage as a consequence.
C2   Irritation at the 'smart' way Tarantino mixes melodramatic intensity (1) with comedy and farce (2).

Of course, these can be mixed: A1 could operate alongside B2 and C2, for example. And, of course, these are not the only responses.

Try out this model on a film of your choice.

1   **What is the range of responses?**
2   **Which of these are more likely and why?**

The tone of *Pulp Fiction* needs to be carefully measured. It is most appropriately approached as a black comedy – arguably, the 'preferred' response. So, for example, Mia is hardly treated with respect or care after her overdose. She is unceremoniously dropped on the grass outside Lance's house while Vincent begs for help for his *own* survival. 'That was fucking trippy' is the summary offered by Jody, Lance's girlfriend at the end of the 'emergency', and, in relieving the tension of the situation, is meant to speak on behalf of the spectator. By contrast, one could well imagine a spectator who finds the world of the characters, the attitude towards drugs in particular, so disturbing as to 'oppose' the film. Some fairly hard 'negotiating' would be required by the spectator who is simultaneously delighted and shocked by the characters and events and the manner in which they are depicted. We could also imagine a different kind of spectator, one who is committed to crime, violence and drugs. In seeing the film as endorsing criminal lifestyles, would they be closer to a 'preferred' reading?

A complementary way of trying to explain different responses is again in relation to the concept of spectator 'competence'. In some respects 'competence' and evaluative judgement are clearly separable from one another. For example, I may be perfectly capable of appreciating artistically and cinematically what Tarantino is doing – while despising it morally and ideologically!

In other respects, however, it is more difficult to disentangle competence from evaluative judgement. For example, the inexperienced spectator may not be able to engage with fictional characters in the kind of playful, imaginative way a film such as *Pulp Fiction* clearly requires. The film invites us to take pleasure in all of A1, B1 and C1 as identified above. It is only possible to do so if the spectator is simultaneously 'inside' and 'outside' the fiction, able to empathise with character, imagine the situation and yet still recognise its fictional nature. The active spectator, like the active reader of literature, is able to use fiction to expand their experience, become capable of new insights, more mature judgements – beyond the limitations of their actual experience in the 'real' world.

Perhaps the most notorious example of the mixing of tones is in the accidental shooting of Marvin by Vincent as he sits in the back seat of a car.

In a variety of formulations this remains the key debate running through the whole of this chapter:

Is the spectator 'passive' or 'active'; 'worked upon' or 'working'? The provisional answer offered here is that the films do have 'effects' (otherwise we would not be bothered to go and see them). These effects are the product of powerful communication processes. These effects will be handled by different spectators differently – on the basis of their 'formation' and their 'competence'. Most spectators, constituted as an audience, behave in more or less the same way because, other than in personal details, their social formations and their mental formations are very similar within a given culture. This is even more so if, as is probable, the spectators making up a given audience are largely self-selecting, having made their decision to enter the cinema on the basis of information available to them about the likely nature of the film experience on offer.

Is there anything in the above summary statement that you disagree with or think should be stated somewhat differently?

Imagining

While the last paragraph attempts to summarise much of what has been said so far, one thing is missing – something that is, arguably, the central function of spectatorship: *imagining*. The 'passive' spectator is seen as one who somehow surrenders completely to the film experience in a form of imagining which can only be compared to some sort of infantile regression. The 'active' spectator is seen as one who is able, in the simple term used several times already, to be simultaneously inside and outside the world of the film. A somewhat different way of expressing this is by considering two different kinds of imagining.

In *The Thread of Life* (1999), Richard Wollheim makes a fundamental distinction, corresponding to a big divide between two modes of imagination: '*central*' imagining and '*a-central*' imagining. A rough guide to the distinction can be found in linguistic clues. While central imagining is often expressed in the form 'I imagine…', a-central imagining is expressed in the form 'I imagine that…' (M. Smith 1995: 76).

There are certain times when a spectator experiences central imagining, particularly when a film recreates a physical sensation such as falling or walking in a daze. The move toward ever more spectacular forms of visual and aural cinema – such as with the IMAX technology – we are being offered are forms of cinema providing more opportunities for central imagining: 'I imagine sitting on the rollercoaster…; I imagine the sensation of para-gliding over mountains…' What is being created is the effect recorded as early as 1896 of spectators imagining a train coming towards them in the Lumière Brothers' *Arrivée d'un train en gare à la Ciotat* and made fun of as early as 1901 in Paul's *The Countryman and the Cinematograph*.

There is a striking physical recreation of Lumière's train coming at the audience at the sensational Museo Nazionale del Cinema in Turin, Italy.

Most of the time the spectator operates in the 'I imagine that…' mode. *I imagine that it must be pretty scary to have a gangster's wife overdosing in front of you when you are responsible for her! I imagine that having to plunge a syringe into a woman's heart in order to bring her out of a coma must be, well, quite stressful and I can't imagine that I could ever do such a thing!*

By contrast, the 'subject' of classical film theory is conceived as being at one with the camera/projector and thus involved in central imagining. In practice it seems wisest to approach spectatorship as a complex mixture of central and a-central imagining.

Staying with *Pulp Fiction* a little longer, consider two further details in the 'Vincent Vega and Marcellus Wallace's Wife' episode which draw particular attention to the film as a textual construct rather than trying to disguise its construction as a film so that we may 'suspend our disbelief'.

• **Plate 3.10**
Arrivée d'un train en gare à la Ciotat (The Lumière Brothers, 1895) Movement towards the camera thrilled and terrified the first cinema audiences. There are a number of examples of the sadistic delight taken in 'running down' the audience, for example in R.W. Paul's *The Motorist* (*c.*1902), a car 'hits' the spectator head-on.

The first is a brief moment when Vincent and Mia are still in the car having just arrived outside Jack Rabbit Slim's.

Vincent: Come on, Mia, let's go get a steak.
Mia: You can get a steak here, daddy–. Don't be a…

Mia draws a square with her hands. Dotted lines appear on the screen forming a square. The lines disperse.

Vincent: After you, kitty-cat.

(Tarantino 1994: 51–2)

This is the most blatant admission to the spectator of the film as textual construct. It is a characteristic particularly common in 'postmodern' art. The spectator is invited to take pleasure in a certain complicity with the film-maker – this is a 'game' made possible because of the coming together of the 'playful' imaginations of both.

The second incident is when Mia demands that Vincent join her to dance the twist. The spectator is confronted with a fine distinction between John Travolta's role and his star identity as the dancing star of *Saturday Night Fever* (1977). The relationship between textual and extra-textual information is clearly being exploited here in order to acknowledge the star 'myth'. A model of spectatorship which presents the interaction between spectator and film text as closed off from wider contexts of audience and culture seems particularly inadequate in explaining what happens at moments such as these. Again, this can be described as a characteristic moment of postmodern cinema, this time involving a 'play' between the role of a character within the fiction and the persona-image of a star who exists outside that fiction. Tarantino mobilises a knowledge and a set of associations held by the spectator, not to enhance the fiction but to intensify a sense of the spectator and director making meaning together.

Maybe we can talk of two tendencies in contemporary cinema. One is the ever more costly attempts to produce the spectacular realist illusion, especially in action movies – moving towards the kind of IMAX experience discussed above. The other is towards an ever more 'playful' kind of cinema – such as that exemplified by *Pulp Fiction*. Maybe we need different conceptions of spectatorship for each. 'I imagine…' for the first. I imagine that…' for the second. Whichever way one looks at things, the point holds: for the majority of films it seems wisest to approach spectatorship as a complex mixture of central and a-central imagining.

MIXING APPROACHES

There has not been space in this chapter to do more than sketch a variety of approaches to the study of spectators, audiences and the responses they produce to films. The first section tried to outline some working assumptions about spectator and audience study which you may now wish to revisit and question or add to. The second section encouraged a study of Early Cinema in order to gain a better appreciation of the evolution of the spectator and audience. The remainder of the chapter has set out a 'menu' of issues and ideas that may provide you with the basis for further work in this broad area of film studies. What should be clear is that no particular theoretical or methodological approach has been particularly promoted. Rather, it is perhaps most useful to think in terms of an eclectic approach, taking whatever seems useful and productive. Here, in summary, are some of the things you should devote more time too:

- The way that the spectator is 'determined' deriving from the 'subject–apparatus' theory of 1970s film studies may be less fashionable today but it still offers valuable insights, for example in the study of unconscious processes in spectatorship.
- The way that cognitive theory allows us to talk about the 'working' spectator, constantly engaging with the audio-visual material to make meaning and respond to the stimulus offered in quite conscious ways.
- The way concepts of social formation and hegemony allow us to explain the limited range of responses usually observable in an audience made up of many different individuals.
- The ways in which contemporary cultural studies approaches encourage detailed, specific case studies which replace theoretical generalisation with 'thick' accounts of differences in responses and in the variety of uses and pleasures that motivate our film viewing.

In more general terms, there is undoubtedly the need to balance *inductive* approaches, based on theoretical work, with *deductive* approaches. The latter requires the collection of reliable empirical information – which, in keeping with too much writing on the subject, this chapter singularly lacks.

SOME NOTES ON CENSORSHIP AND REGULATION

Assumptions and biases

For further discussion about censorship in the US and the UK see Chapter 1, pp. 40–46

Debates around film regulation and censorship should be informed by *studies* of spectatorship and actual audience behaviour. Instead they are nearly always informed by *assumptions* about spectatorship and cinema audiences that are grounded in neither empirical nor theoretical studies.

In the UK there has existed for almost the entire history of cinema a paternalistic approach based on a set of assumptions about the power of the cinema 'apparatus' and the vulnerability of an audience to the manipulative potential of the film medium. The spectator has been regarded as in need of protection from the 'effects' of the cinema experience. This is particularly stridently stated during times of so-called 'moral panics'. When a different view about 'effects' has prevailed, more closely reflecting a cultural studies/response theory model of spectatorship, this has been the result of a more libertarian cultural climate in general, such as developed throughout the 1960s and 1970s.

Often the debate on film 'effects' appears characterised by no more than those in one corner of the room shouting 'Oh, yes it does…!' and those in the opposite corner shouting 'Oh, no it doesn't…!'

I wish to refer briefly now to four arguments and offer a summary overview.

Film and spectator dis-inhibition

This is a more sophisticated version of the simple stimulus–response idea that underlies much crude discussion of the spectator. Disinhibition refers to the gradual wearing down of the moral/ideological 'rules' that the spectator adheres to as a member of a particular society. So, for example, the 'effect' of a sexual crime represented on film may appear negligible but watching such events repeatedly within film fiction will, according to the argument, wear down the 'natural' inhibition the spectator has grown up with and which protects him/her from any tendency within themselves to carry out such an action.

Film and 'What If…'

By contrast, there is the view that through fiction of all kinds, including film, we 'try out' experiences, some of which are not possible, some of which are not permissible. In so doing we extend our experience – as we do when we watch television news: 'What if … such a thing happened outside my front door?' It is argued that no matter how often we watch, for example, acts of gross violence in film, we will remain just as capable of being shocked and appalled by an act of violence witnessed in reality.

Film and catharsis

An extension of the 'trying out' argument is that film is unique as an art form because of the circumstances of reception in a darkened but public place. Within this space we can 'let go' the 'darker side' of our nature in a controlled, safe and ultimately therapeutic experience. The analogy is made with Ancient Greek theatre and the notion that through the ritualistic blood-letting of theatre and religious forms, any craving to do these things in reality is safely channelled.

Liberal theories of spectatorship and 'the 10 per cent'

Even if we are relaxed about the ideas put forward in the paragraphs above, one question will not go away: What about the 10 per cent who are incapable of the imaginative processing required? (It may not be 10 per cent – this is the problem; without empirical data, numbers and percentages are thrown around quite wildly!). Some spectators may indeed be incapable of distinguishing between fiction and reality. Some spectators may seek out certain films not in order to 'safely channel' some dangerous craving but in order to stimulate it. Should all the audience be controlled by legislation in order to protect society from a relatively small minority of spectators?

At the time of writing there is some evidence that this is changing at the British Board of Film Classification (BBFC). Of course, as with similar bodies in other countries, policies on film censorship and regulation swing back and forth, reflecting much broader shifts in social attitudes.

This takes us back to a consideration of central and a-central imagining (see p. 122).

A model

In what has been written so far there is clearly a distinction to be made between forms of spectatorship behaviour which were described above as central imagining ('I imagine…') and a-central imagining ('I imagine that…'). The latter expresses the sophistication of those who 'explore' and 'channel'; the former the potential danger in the '10 per cent'.

The following attempts to superimpose political and social attitudes to censorship onto spectatorship theories. The model is crude and invites elaboration. The vertical axis represents the difference between a paternalistic government/state (such as in the UK) and a libertarian one (such as in Sweden and The Netherlands). Against each is attached a view on the spectator. The horizontal axis represents two ways in which a government/state can operate: a free market which puts as few restrictions on business as possible, promoting capitalist enterprise; the other interventionist, believing that in order to ensure values such as equal opportunity, enterprise should be controlled.

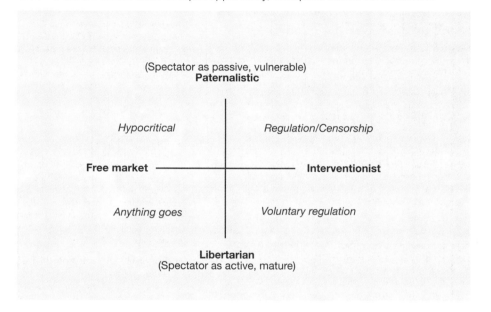

Of the four quadrants, the one which may appear to make least sense is the left upper. It may seem difficult to imagine a state system which both promotes a free market system and holds strong paternalistic tendencies – perhaps caricatured as 'You can sell anything you like at whatever price you can get to anyone prepared to buy it…but oh, how can you sell this to these people – what effects it will have on them!' Arguably this was the position of the Thatcher government in the UK in the 1980s.

As a further footnote here, it is interesting that the long-held fear of cinema 'effects' from the dominant power groups in society should be shared both by the political right and the political left for similar and different reasons. Crudely speaking, the policing function of the state has been concerned by the potential of cinema for undermining core social values. The left has feared the opposite: that cinema lulls people into a state of passivity which prevents them from challenging the system in which they live. However, both are based on the shared assumption that the apparatus and the film text are somehow irresistible and overwhelming.

The demand is repeatedly for more empirical studies of how spectators actually behave. There is the ongoing need to refine descriptions of the spectator of theory so that he or she resembles as closely as possible the spectator sitting in a seat in the darkened auditorium of the cinema.

FURTHER READING

Overview of shifts in film studies/film theory

To track the shift from 'subject–apparatus' approaches, through American pragmatism/cognitivism, to cultural studies perspectives, these three books provide a chronological map:

Lapsley, R. and Westlake, M., *Film Theory: An Introduction*, Manchester University Press, Manchester, 1988.

Bordwell, David and Carroll, Noel, *Post-Theory: Reconstructing Film Studies*, University of Wisconsin, Madison, 1996.
Gledhill, Christine and Williams, Linda (eds), *Reinventing Film Studies*, London, Arnold, 2001.

Spectatorship and film

The following are accessible, with Judith Mayne's the most useful summary of the area:

Ellis, John, *Visible Fictions: Cinema, Television and Video*, Routledge & Kegan Paul, London, 1982; repr. 1992.
Mayne, Judith, *Cinema and Spectatorship*, Routledge, London, 1993.
Phillips, Patrick, *Understanding Film Texts*, British Film Institute, London, 2000.
Stacey, Jackie, *Star Gazing: Hollywood Cinema and Female Spectatorship*, Routledge, London, 1993.
Turner Graeme, *Film as Social Practice*, Routledge, London, 1988; repr., Routledge, London, 1993.

The following list puts particular emphasis on spectatorship issues discussed from a feminist and psychoanalytical perspective. These books are more much more demanding than the first list:

Erens, Patricia (ed.), *Issues in Feminist Film Criticism*, Indiana University Press, Bloomington, 1990.
hooks, bell, 'The Oppositional Gaze: Black Female Spectators', in Manthia Diawara (ed.), *Black American Cinema: Aesthetics and Spectatorship*, Routledge/American Film Institute, London, 1993.
Kaplan, E Ann (ed.), *Psychoanalysis and Cinema*, London, American Film Institute/Routledge, London, 1990.
Mulvey, Laura, *Visual and Other Pleasures*, Macmillan, London, 1989.

Audience and response studies coming from a cultural studies perspective:

Tinkcom, Matthew and Villarejo, Amy (eds), *Keyframes: Popular Cinema and Cultural Studies*, Routledge, London, 2001.
Turner, Graeme (ed.), *The Film Cultures Reader*, Routledge, London, 2001, pp.444–68.

Cognitivist/pragmatist approaches to spectatorship and response

Particularly productive applications of this approach to film studies are:

Plantinga, Carl and Smith, Greg M. (eds), *Passionate Views: Film, Cognition and Emotion*, Baltimore, Johns Hopkins University Press, 1999.

Smith, Murray, *Engaging Characters – Fiction, Emotion and the Cinema*, Oxford University Press, Oxford, 1995.

On Early Cinema and the development of spectatorship

The first two volumes of the University of California History of the American Cinema series are particularly useful:

Bowser, Eileen, *The Transformation of Cinema 1907–1915*, University of California, Berkeley, 1994.
Musser, Charles, *The Emergence of Cinema: The American Screen to 1907*, University of California, Berkeley, 1994.

The following are also very readable:

May, Larry, *Screening Out the Past; the Birth of Mass Culture and the Motion Picture Industry*, Chicago University Press, Chicago, 1980.
Robinson, David, *From Peep Show to Palace – the Birth of American Film*, Columbia, New York, 1996.
The Silents Majority: On-line Journal of Silent Film; online at http://www.silentsmajority.com

Censorship/regulation

Five different approaches are represented here. The first two look at 'effects' and 'moral panic' debates; the third takes a cultural approach, arguing that response to violent material relates to the particular 'formation' of that society. The fourth is an interesting response study looking at audience reactions to recent violent films. The fifth considers a range of examples of censorship around the world and the various motives for this censorship:

Barker, Martin and Petley, Julian (eds), *Ill Effects – the Media Violence Debate*, Routledge, London, 1997.
Barker, Martin, Arthurs, Jane and Ramawani, Haridranath, *The Crash Controversy*, Wallflower Press, London, 2001.
Duclos, Denis, *The Werewolf Complex: America's Fascination with Violence*, Oxford University Press, New York, 1998.
Hill, Annette, *Shocking Entertainment*, John Libby, Luton, 1997.
Petrie, Ruth (ed.), *Film and Censorship – The Index Reader*, Cassell, London, 1997.

The Birth of a Nation

The script and a range of essays are contained in:

Lang, Robert (ed.), *D.W. Griffith – Birth of a Nation*, Rutgers University Press, New Brunswick, NJ, 1994.
An educational site with useful links can be found at: http://webster.edu/fatc/birth.html

Pulp Fiction

Polan, Dana, *Pulp Fiction*, British Film Institute, London, 2001.
Tarantino, Quentin, *Pulp Fiction – The Screenplay*, Faber & Faber, London, 1994.
http://www.geocities.com/Hollywood/7606/pulp.html
A site with most things a fan could wish for.

Clearly all films raise issues in relation to spectatorship and response. The following twelve films, listed chronologically, are suggested for study purposes as they raise particular questions or issues:

1915	*The Birth of a Nation* (Griffith, US)	1992	*Man Bites Dog* (Belvaux & Bonzel, Belgium)
1929	*Man with a Movie Camera* (Vertov, USSR)	1994	*Natural Born Killers* (Stone, US)
1954	*Rear Window* (Hitchcock, US)	1998	*Festen* (Vinterberg, Denmark)
1960	*Peeping Tom* (Powell, UK)	1999	*Fight Club* (Fincher, US)
1966	*Blow Up* (Antonioni, UK/Italy)	2000	*Timecode* (Figgis, US)
1972	*Klute* (Pakula, US)	2000	*Memento* (Nolan, US)

British Board of Film Classification: **http://www.bbfc.co.uk**

Chapter 4

Critical approaches to Hollywood cinema: authorship, genre and stars

Paul Watson

■ Critical approaches to Hollywood cinema: authorship, genre and stars

INTRODUCTION

The following chapter addresses three of the most influential and persistent critical approaches that have been used in film studies to explore the meanings and value of cinema, and in particular Hollywood cinema: authorship theory, genre criticism and star studies. Indeed, all three approaches have enjoyed long and interesting careers in film theory, careers which to a large extent reflect the ebb and flow between various methods of theorising film and the shifting conception of the relationship between the cinematic institution, the films it produces and the audiences who watch them. In other words, in tracing the critical heritage of authorship, genre and star studies we are necessarily also tracing the complex relationship of film theory to film culture, where 'culture' is understood as the inter-related practices of film-making, film consumption and film evaluation. As such, it is no accident that these three critical approaches have proven to be so resilient, despite numerous attempts to overwrite, debunk or simply ignore them, precisely to the extent that their respective conceptual currencies are attuned to the intangible relationship between the business of making films (the industry) and the pleasures of watching them (the audience). In short, notions of authorship, genre and stardom continue to percolate through contemporary film studies insofar as they remain central to the interests of both industry and audiences.

As such, each section addresses the historical conditions which gave rise to the critical approach under discussion as well as how its particular method seeks to expand our understanding of film. At the same time, however, these approaches are neither singular nor fixed in either their development or purview. So while on the one hand represented here is an overview of key debates and critical thinking intrinsic to each section, on the other hand there is recognition that the way films are made and exhibited has changed significantly since those approaches were first formulated. As such, the impending destabilisation of 'film' as an organising object of study brought about by digital cinema technology, as well as the dissolution of film studies as a distinct field within broader interdisciplinary configurations requires us to rethink and reframe what is *useful* about these critical approaches to studying cinema. This process involves, on the one hand, reconsideration of what is distinctive about each method, and on the other hand, consideration of the ways they now increasingly seem to overlap, and with it reconsideration of cinema's own changing role within mass-mediated, high-technology culture. For while it remains necessary to be precise about the differences between authorship, genre and star studies in terms of what each yields in the way of knowledge, it is worth stating from the outset that increasingly they share a number of important intellectual and cultural similarities:

postmodern
Used by critics in a number of different ways, it can refer to the contemporary historical moment (the period after modernity); an artistic or aesthetic style which privileges surface appearances over 'deep meaning' or 'truth' (characterised by strategies of irony, **intertextuality**, pastiche, bricolage, **eclecticism**, **recombinacy** and **self-reflexivity**); and a theoretical position which adopts a sceptical attitude towards totalising notions of truth, reality and progress.

■ All three approaches cut across the three main areas of film studies: film history, film theory and film analysis.

■ All three approaches emerge from, evolve within, and continue to be practised within both the theoretical writings of film scholars and the journalistic practices of professional film critics. Moreover, unlike psychoanalysis, semiotics or **postmodernism** for instance, all three critical approaches span the specialised vocabularies of the professional film academic and the lay vocabulary of the ordinary film spectator. Indeed, writing on authorship, genre and stardom existed long before film studies was ensconced as an academic discipline in the mid-1960s and continues to be more widely accommodated outside of the intellectually faddish sport of academic publishing.

■ By the same token, the critical currencies implied by authorship, genre and star studies as well as the acts of evaluation and classification they prompt are key to the **cultural capital** of fan communities, **cinephiles** and aficionados.

■ As such, the study of **auteurs**, genre and stars cannot proceed simply in regard to specific films, or for that matter cinema itself inasmuch as all are increasingly produced and are sustained in the **extra-textual (see p. 132)** relationships between the film text and **hypermediated culture (see p. 132)** more generally.

■ Historically all three theoretical approaches have been developed in proximity to Hollywood cinema as means of both understanding and validating popular cinema.

■ As theories of film, all three are complex and have been exposed variously as contradictory, excessively all-embracing, or too narrow. As such, and given that they have to take account of an ever-widening array of cinematic forms and practices, authorship, genre and star studies now tend to be viewed as critical attitudes, as ways of looking at film within specific practices rather than singular theories.

■ Moreover, the increasing convergence of mass entertainment forms brought about by digital media technologies has led to a significant broadening and destabilisation of the notions of authorship, genre and stardom in crucial ways that both *recast and reinvigorate* their use as tools for investigating cinema.

It is for these reasons, precisely because cinema precedes and exceeds its confinement in theory, forming part of our taken-for-granted everyday lives, that authorship, genre and star studies continue to be attractive and profitable in the rapidly changing stakes of film studies.

Authorship and Hollywood cinema

INTRODUCTION: THE THREE PARADOXES OF CINEMATIC AUTHORSHIP

This section sets itself the task of defining what is at stake when we claim that certain films are authored, that is, they are the creative expression of an individual artist, in a way more or less analogous to the way we speak of the author of a novel, a letter, a poem or a painting. In other words, we will examine the idea that a film's meanings can be attributed to a single creative source who stands behind it as its creator. But already, right here, we confront the theoretical difficulty associated with the question of cinematic authorship, where traditional and common-sense conceptions of the author fail to describe the inherent complexity of film-making, a process which director Peter Bogdanovich describes as involving '300 different opinions and 500 alternative possibilities' (2002: 9). While it is possible to make a case for a writer or painter to be the author of a work on the grounds that it might be entirely generated by a single individual, whom out of more than 350 people credited for working on *Moulin Rouge* (2001) shall we single out as its author? Because, as we will see, the question of cinematic authorship has routinely been posed as a question of directorial control over visual style and narrative themes, precisely as a question of a director's individual vision, the paradigmatic reading of *Moulin Rouge* posits Baz Luhrmann as its author just insofar as it is possible to impute to him, as its director, considerable control over textual operation and meaning. Indeed, the dominant view of cinematic authorship has been that, like novels and paintings, films have a single author usually held to be the director.

cultural capital
First originating in the work of Pierre Bourdieu to describe the unequal distribution of cultural competencies and values principally across different social classes, the term has since been appropriated more generally to refer to the specific competencies and 'knowledges' of various social groupings, as well as the 'symbolic power' attained precisely from 'affiliation' to that group.

cinephilia
The notion of cinephilia refers to an intense love of, even obsession with, cinema. It implies both a way of watching and way of speaking about film beyond the standard relationship between cinema and the spectator. Cinephiles, therefore, are people who, in Andrew Sarris' phrase, 'love cinema beyond all reason', and who engage with film in highly specific ways.

auteur
A French term that originated in the pages of the film journal *Cahiers du Cinéma* in the 1950s to refer to directors who infused their films with their distinctive personal vision through the salient manipulation of film technique. Auteurs, seen as genuine artists, were contrasted with *metteurs-en-scène* who were held to be technically competent directors who merely executed the processes of film-making without consistently stamping their 'personality' on material from one film to the next.

extra-textual (see previous page)
In a broad sense, this term designates the 'outside' of the film/text, the range of cultural texts which relate in some way to the film/text, but in a narrower sense it refers to the non-filmic inter-texts which in varying degrees relate to the film/text (such as marketing and promo-tional materials, film reviews, and so on).

hypermediated culture (see previous page)
Describes the current state of post-media-saturated culture in which forms of work, leisure and entertain-ment, as well as many of the taken-for-granted activities that structure daily life, are predicted on, and determined by, the all-pervasive pres-ence of highly integrated media forms and tech-nologies. The notion of hypermediation, there-fore, refers to the way that our experience of the world is channelled through an endless network of media texts.

The paradox of individuality in a collective practice

However, if on the one hand it is now commonplace to speak of the director as the proprietor of his or her films (the idea that a 'a Spielberg film' implies a coherence of expressive techniques and meanings in a way that, say, 'a Dreamworks picture' does not), on the other hand, it is also a given of film studies to acknowledge that the over-whelming majority of film-making, and Hollywood studio production as a whole, is a fundamentally collaborative practice, and collaborative in crucial ways that affect the textual operation and meanings of a film. As such, we might call this the first paradox of cinematic authorship: how can we attribute authorship to a single creative source in what is an essentially collaborative working and creative practice? Many critics have noted that underpinning this confusion is the question of the suitability of models of authorship developed in relation to literature and the fine arts for explaining film signifi-cation, and that while authorship may be a fuzzy concept generally, when grafted onto the study of cinema it becomes particularly slippery. For simply transposing the primary terms of traditional authorial analysis to the study of film may not only belie the intrinsic differences between the traditional arts and film, but more worryingly it may conceal more complex axes of art-making practice and expressivity that characterise cinema's mode of production. Either way, it is far from clear whether the assumed analogy between the collective and collaborative nature of most film-making and the individual novelist or painter is an appropriate one.

This already vexed issue is further complicated when we take into account the various strategies adopted by film studies to deal with the implications of the first paradox of cinematic authorship. In attempting to remedy that paradox by adding progressively finer detail to the concept of the film author, the level of complexity required to sustain the idea becomes incrementally geared up. As Berys Gaut observes:

> It has been held that the film author is the director, the screenwriter, the star or the studio; that the film author is an actual individual, or a critical construct; that there is not one film author, but several; the claim of film authorship has been held primarily as an evaluative one, or an interpretive one, or simply as the view that that there are authors of films as there are authors of literary works.
>
> (1997: 149)

It is this degree of elaboration and contradiction which leads Catherine Grant to argue that 'despite the continual attention accorded to film directors during the last four decades, film authorship has rarely been considered a wholly legitimate object of contemplation' (2000: 101).

The paradox of theory

The scepticism directed towards the idea of cinematic authorship prompts the second paradox of authorship. On the one hand, in turning away from authorship and towards such theoretical concepts as semiotics, structuralism and psychoanalysis that are abstracted from the actual practices of film-making, film theory either confined the author to the sidelines of its debates or simply ignored the question of cinematic authorship all together. On the other hand, however, and in the face of such stubborn indifference, authorship continues to survive as a going academic concern with major academic publishers commissioning series after series of books dedicated to the work of single directors to the extent that the idea of the 'director-as-author' 'remains prob-ably the most widely shared assumption in film studies today' (Bordwell and Thompson 1993: 38). So while there seems to be a tacit agreement amongst professional film scholars that the work of individual film-makers is best understood as a thread in a much more complex tapestry of technological, social, historical, institutional, cognitive and cultural practices, this stance accounts for neither the individuated creative crafts involved in film production in the first instance, nor, in the final instance, the continued fascination and identification with the figure of the cinematic author by the film industry, film critics and film audiences.

The cultural paradox

Claims that the author is somehow dead, or a theoretical irrelevancy, appear out of step not only with our intuitions, but more crucially with contemporary media culture. For instance, it is possible to argue, as does Timothy Corrigan, that far from being supplanted by the apparently more rigorous approaches of semiotics, structuralism, psychoanalysis and audience studies, the figure of the cinematic author may in fact be 'more alive now than at any other point in film history' (Corrigan, 1991: 135). With the rapid proliferation of convergent media platforms and the corresponding exponential increase in the number and variety of media texts, it seems that the visibility of the author is now more pronounced than ever. For example, in the shift from video to DVD it is now routine after watching a movie to then watch it again in order to listen to the director's commentary. Perhaps we will then watch the accompanying 'Making Of' documentary, or the director's personal video diary of the shoot, read the script and production notes on the DVD-ROM, or follow the hyperlinks to a further range of web-based material. For example, the twin-disc DVD release of *Fight Club* (David Fincher, 1999) contains in addition to the film:

For more detailed discussion of the impact of new media on film, see Chapter 1, pp. 31–33.

- four audio commentary tracks
- seventeen 'behind the scenes' vignettes with further commentary and a choice of viewing angles
- out-take footage
- a range of deleted scenes with commentary by the director discussing the reasons for not including each
- a selection of original storyboards
- a gallery of publicity material associated with the initial marketing of the film
- a gallery of the concept art behind the film's production design
- a range of further 'Hidden Features'

For a discussion on Fight Club *and audience, see Chapter 3, pp. 112–113, and in terms of masculinity and crisis, see Chapter 7, pp. 273–275.*

Film-maker Alex Cox believes that the change in the way movies are watched and comprehended brought about by the technological possibilities offered by DVD's digital mode of storing and processing information has the potential to breath new life into the debate about cinematic authorship. He argues that:

I think, in the ideal instance, DVD 'additional elements' can provide some sort of film literacy, even insight. More importantly, perhaps they represent the Return of the Director, an endangered species rarely glimpsed in recent years.... The idea that a film director is an 'author' is maintained by a tiny band of believers: the Director's Guild, people who live in Paris, and...the buyers of DVDs.

(2001: 10)

The level of film-specific information contained on DVD is, of course, in addition to the vast amount of film journalism available in both print and electronic forms, as well as the boom in televisual programming dedicated to showing films and talking about them – Film Four in the UK is an exemplary model of a channel which combines the broad-cast of films with specially commissioned documentaries and lifestyle programmes about cinema. Moreover, it is worth stressing that the new currency afforded to the cinematic author by digital media culture is neither limited to, nor entirely focused on, the director. We now have regular and easy access to a much broader range of authorial candidates: cinematographers; actors; editors; producers; stunt technicians; visual-effects supervisors; and so forth.

This is the third paradox of cinematic authorship: that at a time when film theory seems to have finally wriggled free from its fascination with the figure of the cinematic author the discourse of authorship seems once more to present itself as a vital node in understanding the relationship between the film industry, the film and its audience.

THE ALLURE OF AUTHORSHIP

In spite of its troubled theoretical career, the common-sense position – that a film bears traces of its creators – has proved remarkably durable precisely because it addresses a number of crucial questions, questions that refuse to go away, about the role of cinema as an art form, a commodity and a communicative practice: exactly how are the makers of film and the audience bound together in the activities of creation, communication and comprehension; what kind of communication is this and are there really any grounds for erecting theoretical boundaries between the practices of film-making and the experience of watching movies; and why, in the final instance, do audiences and critics continue to hanker for the cinematic author when 'the challenge to the concept of the author as source and centre of the text…has been decisive in contemporary criticism' (Caughie 1981: 1)?

As we shall see, the emergence of authorship outfitted film critics with a set of tools with which to:

mise-en-scène
Refers both to *what* is filmed (setting, props, costumes etc.) and to *how* it is filmed (cine-matographic properties of the shot such as depth of field, focus and camera movement). In an attempt to counter the imprecision of the term, this latter aspect is sometimes called *mise-en-shot*.

■ argue for the artistic and academic legitimacy of cinema by claiming that there are film artists just as there are literary or visual artists, and that the work of these artists should be afforded the same intellectual scrutiny as the traditional arts;

■ interpret films as the creative expression of those who made them by shifting the critical focus away from film narrative (what happens) towards film style (**mise-en-scène** and thematics); and

■ evaluate the relative artistic merits of both film and its makers.

It is these three principal critical procedures which continue to make the idea of author-ship not only a controversial idea, but a useful critical tool as well. There are, however, two important implications that emerge from these various dimensions of authorship. First, we cannot assume that authorship means the same thing in every context. For the question of how authorship relates to a film's meanings and enunciative techniques is not the same as how an author creates value in a film. And second, we might have to look for a more pragmatic definition of film authorship which recognises the importance of the distinct contribution of a broader range of cinematic roles to the meaning and value of films. This would involve, on the one hand, a reconsideration of the *critical function* of authorship theory (what we expect its yield to be in the way of results), and on the other, a reconsideration of *how and where we look for evidence of authorship*, and with it reconsideration of some of those elements that have, up to now, tended to be assigned to the director. Before doing so, however, it is first necessary to review some of the most salient steps in the history and development of authorship theory in order to: (1) locate the above discussion of the paradoxical nature of the authorship debate in its proper historical context; (2) identify the useful aspects arising from the various incarnations of authorship theory; and (3) to establish how it might be possible to shape those aspects into a critical method for analysing contemporary cinema that chimes with both current theoretical concerns and our intuitive attraction to the author.

THE EMERGENCE OF THE AUTEUR

Today, both film-makers and critics take for granted cinema's status as an art form. Some fifty or so years ago however, when not altogether ignored by scholars as beneath serious critical attention, cinema was often vilified along with other forms of 'mass culture' as a blemish on art, or worse, a dehumanising agent of cultural oppression. As such, the origins of cinematic authorship can be understood as a response to three simultaneous lines of argument which conspired to exile film from artistic and intellectual respectability. First, cinema's technological means of production preclude individual creativity. Second, the collaborative nature of industrial film-making and the specialised division of labour it entails forestalls self-expression. Third, the need to entertain a large audience necessitates a high degree of standardisation and conventionality which are incompatible with original artistic expression. In all of these propositions the blanket rejection of cinema as artistically illegitimate depends on the idea that art is necessarily the result of the creative activities of an individual, and can be appreciated and understood as such.

Within this context, therefore, authorship first and foremost offered a ready-made strategy for vindicating film as an aesthetic form precisely by installing in cinema the figure of the individual artist. Moreover, to a significant extent the infant discipline of film studies was underwritten by the theoretical legitimacy and disciplinary vocabulary associated with the ideas of authorship and individual artistic expression which had already been well rehearsed in literary criticism and art history. Richard Dyer neatly summarises this idea, stating that authorship:

made the case for taking film seriously by seeking to show that a film could be just as profound, beautiful and important as any other kind of art, provided, following a dominant model of value in art, it was demonstrably the work of an highly individual artist.... The power of authorship resided in its ability to mobilize a familiar argument about artistic worth and, importantly, to show that this could be used to discriminate between films. Thus, at a stroke, it was proclaimed that film could be art (with all the cultural capital this implies) and that there could be a form of criticism – indeed, study – of it.

(1998: 5)

So although film had long been discussed as art, in borrowing some of the academic legitimacy of more established disciplines by making the 'author-as-artist' a necessary and sufficient condition of the serious study of cinema, cinematic authorship entwined the notion of the value of film with the person who was deemed aesthetically responsible for it. As such, at the heart of the various complexities associated with authorship lies the idea that films are valued when they are deemed to be the work of an artist, traditionally identified as the director.

These ideas were initially cultivated in the pages of the French journal *Cahiers du Cinéma* during the 1950s, and were subsequently formulated into what was designated in the 1960s by the American critic Andrew Sarris as 'auteur theory'. While the idea that a film's director should be considered as its author certainly did not originate in the pages of *Cahiers du Cinéma*, the central role of the journal in propagating and disseminating that thesis cannot be underestimated. Likewise, despite the later critical venom directed towards Sarris' contribution, it is his work that is chiefly responsible for publicising ideas of cinematic authorship in America and shaping the idea into a critical method for analysing and evaluating the particular art of Hollywood production.

The *Cahiers* critics, as they became known – writers such as François Truffaut, André Bazin, Jean-Luc Godard, Claude Chabrol and Eric Rohmer – not only formulated the inaugural principles which Sarris later recast into auteur theory, but also implicitly and explicitly outfitted the study of cinema with an analytical method and critical vocabulary. In what is often seen as the founding document of cinematic authorship, 'A Certain Tendency of the French Cinema' (*Cahiers* no. 31, January 1954), François Truffaut chides the inclination of the dominant mode of French cinema of the 1940s and

For a further reference to the Cahiers du Cinéma *and the French New Wave, see Chapter 12, pp. 422–428.*

1950s for its bourgeois values and dependency on literary sources for its inspiration. For Truffaut this notion of 'quality cinema', motivated by traditional models of high culture and leaning on 'respectable' literature for its value, offers little in the way of art besides the technical transposition of literary scripts to the screen. Indeed, on this account the relative merits of a film are relatively unconnected with the practices of film-making, but determined rather by the putative quality of the literary pedigree of the script. In contrast, Truffaut argued for the recognition, in terms of both film-making and its critical reception, of the 'audacities' specific to the medium of film: an attention to the cinematographic properties of film style, especially the way mise-en-scène was deployed by a film-maker. This manifesto for seeing film *qua* film through an attention to the *craft* of film-making found its apotheosis in an phrase coined in the title of Bazin's 1957 article, 'On the politique des auteurs'. The cornerstone of this 'auteur policy' is the recognition of the director as a film's creative source. For the *Cahiers* critics, film ought to bear the personal stylistic signature of its director, that is, to announce what Routt (1990) has called the 'auteurprints' of its creator. Indeed, Routt goes so far as to suggest that 'On the politique des auteurs' evinces 'perhaps the most radical assertion of the shaping power of one individual in popular art'. In this way, auteurism's first provocative move was to locate the author and creative centre of a film not as its writer but as its director insofar as it is the director who orchestrates the visual aspects of cinema.

Auteurism's second, and perhaps most provocative, intervention was the championing of certain Hollywood directors as genuine, even exemplary auteurs. Indeed, to a significant extent, the idea that it is possible, even desirable to adopt a serious, critical stance towards Hollywood cinema became knotted together with the auteur approach as the *Cahiers* critics discussed the work of film-makers such as Alfred Hitchcock, Howard Hawks, Nicholas Ray, Orson Welles, John Ford and Douglas Sirk in terms previously reserved for the classical arts. For Truffaut, Bazin and others detected in the work of these Hollywood directors a style and purity of technique undiluted by the cultural dead-weight of literary heritage. It is in this sense, then, that auteurism's most profound and influential claim is not the mere attribution of individuated creative responsibility in what is a collectively produced medium, but rather the exaltation of Hollywood directors, hitherto seen as mere cogs in a vulgar commercial machine, as auteurs. Indeed, it was precisely the industrial restrictions and formal constraints that were previously evoked to define Hollywood studio productions as anonymous genre fodder that, ironically, the *Cahiers* critics valorised as the background against which the great directors' personal vision shines through: if auteurs exist in the most restrictive film-making system in the world, then they can exist anywhere.

Auteurism as method

For further discussion of auteur theory in terms of the French New Wave, see Chapter 12.

Auteurism, as it emerged from the pages of *Cahiers du Cinéma*, thus not only imbricated cinema with the traditional arts through the ascription of director-as-author, but evolved into a critical strategy for sorting the artistic wheat from the generic chaff of Hollywood cinema. The principal method by which this was achieved was the establishment of the hierarchical distinction between those directors dubbed mere 'metteurs-en-scène' and the genuine auteurs. While metteurs-en-scène were deemed technically competent directors, film-to-film their work nevertheless evinced little or no stylistic coherence or thematic consistency. By contrast, the auteur infused their work with a personal vision, leaving behind a distinctive signature across a significant number of films. Unlike the tradition of 'quality' film-making in France, for the auteur the script was merely a pretext for engaging in the proper practices of film-making – *the intentional and salient manipulation of cinematic techniques for communicative and/or expressive ends*. Privileged amongst these stylistic techniques was mise-en-scène. For it is through the specific organisation of mise-en-scène, critics argued, that a director leaves behind the footprints of his vision, individual stylistic touches that accrue to resemble the unique personality of the auteur. John Caughie argues that 'it is with the *mise-en-scene* that the *auteur* transforms the material which has been given to him; so it is in the **mise-en-scène**…that the auteur writes his individuality into the film' (1981: 12–13).

For further discussion of mise-en-scène and film form, see Chapter 2, pp. 62–70.

Of course, such a fundamentally evaluative critical method not only enabled cinema's great works and the great film artists to be ranked alongside the great works and artists from the classical arts, but presented critics with a methodology and vocabulary for studying cinema. Armed with such a method, it was possible also for the critic to contribute to the task of winkling out traces of authorship in a range of film-makers' work. Thus, the critic roves across the surfaces of a director's work explicating salient aspects of film style, in particular mise-en-scène, which can be retrospectively related back to the director-as-auteur who stands behind them as their originator. In other words, the critic's work is that of ferreting out the unique marks, flourishes and touches of a director so that they can be credited back to, or projected upon, their source: the auteur. As such, figures like Hitchcock and Welles were deemed significant in the first instance, not necessarily for advancing cinema technically, but rather for a certain aesthetic consistency and salience.

It is this evaluative method of explication that Andrew Sarris translated into North American film criticism and in so doing added a false veneer of rigour to the approach by modifying 'auteur policy' to 'auteur theory'. In a much quoted essay, 'Notes on the Auteur Theory in 1962', Sarris distilled much of the *Cahiers*' seminal polemic in arguing that 'the way a film looks and moves should have some relationship to the way a director thinks and feels' (cited in Caughie 1981: 64). Sarris proposed three criteria for establishing the auteurist credentials of a director:

- technical competency
- distinguishable personality
- the 'interior meaning' of a film arising from the tension between the director's personality and the material

On the one hand, the lineage to the *Cahiers* critics is clearly visible in this strategy inasmuch as the worth of a film remains firmly indexed to the director's ability to inscribe his/her personality across a series of films in spite of the limitations imposed on individual creativity by the industrial and commercial pressures of film-making. On the other hand, however, Sarris' legacy to the auteurist debate resides in the slippage from the *evaluative* method established in 'On the politique des auteurs' into a method explicitly based on *value judgements*. For in *The American Cinema* (1996) Sarris not only deployed the principles of auteurism to recast the history of American film as a 'pantheon' – a nine-part hierarchical system which ranked films according to his own criteria for determining value – but went further in declaring that, film for film, American cinema was superior to that of other nations.

Sarris' regressive use of auteur theory to reconstruct film history, however, represents only one snag in the frayed theoretical principles of cinematic authorship. Indeed, it is unsurprising that such an anachronistic move – the installation in the cinema of the romantic figure of the artist – would provide a broad enough and easy enough target to attract a range of far-reaching criticisms.

THE PROBLEMS OF AUTEUR THEORY

If, as Dyer suggests (1998: 5), auteurism is film studies' 'greatest hit', then it is also perhaps its most criticised and controversial idea. Indeed, as William D. Routt (1990) argues, the 'absurd pretences' on which the entire notion of cinematic authorship is historically founded 'are easy to see, and to reject, as all sober folk of good intentions have rejected and continue to reject them'. For while the desire to forge a critical method capable of bestowing intellectual and artistic credibility upon cinema, that is, a method with which to interrogate cinema's distinctive contribution to the arts, does not in itself invoke essentialist or romantic conceptions of the artist and all the elitist dead wood thus entailed, its significance nevertheless does lie in the foregrounding of a specific relationship between cinematic signification and the creative activities of individuals. And it is here that the difficulty of cinematic authorship continues to replay itself, raising uncomfortable questions about the relationship between the film text and the spectator implied by the model of communication that underpins it. For a number of crucial problems become clear once we view auteurism through the lens of subsequent developments in film theory.

First, and most obviously, auteurism was attacked for belying the collaborative conditions of cinema's mode of production. As discussed above, the analogy between writer or painter and the auteur becomes difficult to sustain when one takes into account the material contingencies and creative diversity of the film-making process in which collaboration is standard and undeniable. As a corollary to this is the idea that auteurism was insufficiently rigorous or whimsical, that at best it depended on the taste of a few specialised critics who pronounced on a film's worth by appealing to the already shop-worn principles of the traditional arts, and at worse resembled personalised and impressionistic conjecture. This prompted critics to try and correct some of these charges of imprecision by grafting auteurism onto the quasi-scientific methodology of structuralism. In an effort to counter the individualist paradigm of the Romantic artist axiomatic to its predecessor, auteur-structuralism, as it became known, was an attempt to probe beneath the surfaces of individuated agency into the 'deep' underlying socio-cultural structures which imbued a film with significance and meaning. Its apparent sophistication was in its conception of the auteur not as the figure who intentionally 'put the meaning into the film' so to speak, but as a structure identifiable in the text. As such, the concept of the auteur was, in the final instance, neither necessarily the director, nor even a person, but an indeterminate structure unearthed in the critical process of reading a film. Auteurs no longer intentionally produced films, rather films unintentionally produced auteurs.

Passing through various other theoretical modifications, this line of thinking progressively diluted auteurism's theoretical respectability to the point where Roland Barthes' 1968 article announced 'The Death of the Author' (see Barthes 1977). Underscoring Barthes' argument, as well as most of the above objections, is the suspect notion of 'ideal' comprehension, where the director's intentions coincide with the spectator's/critic's reading of a film. Often referred to as the **intentional fallacy**, the model of communication implied by the classical auteurist approach is one in which spectators are subjected to the vision of the director, a vision they reconstruct more or less faithfully in line with the map provided by the author through the film's stylistic salience. In other words, communication and signification become a closed circuit with authors jam-packing films full of meaning and spectators subsequently unpacking that meaning at its ultimate destination. This is a problematic model for a number of reasons. Not only is it at odds with cognitive models of cinematic comprehension which attribute a far more important stake to the spectator in actually creating meaning, but specifically in terms of cinematic authorship it tends to confine the significance of the auteur to the evidence of his or her activities left behind in the film text itself. To put it another way, auteurs now have an increasing cultural visibility which, in the last instance, is not tied to their role as a director. Timothy Corrigan (1991) calls this extra-textual notion of cinematic authorship 'the commerce of auteurism'. For Corrigan, auteurism has become 'a *commercial* strategy for organizing audience reception, as a critical concept bound to distribution and marketing aims' (ibid.: 103).

intentional fallacy
A phrase coined by Monroe Beardsley to describe the difference between a text's meaning(s) and what its author intended. As such, criticism dependent on, or directed towards, uncovering the intentions of the author/artist falls foul of the 'intentional fallacy' insofar as the meaning of a text is not fixed within it, but created in the historically situated act of reading.

THE COMMERCE OF AUTHORSHIP

Corrigan's intervention in the debate is to locate auteurism's critical and performative impetus not with film-making, but rather with film consumption. He argues that 'in today's commerce we want to know what our authors or auteurs look like or how they act' and that, accordingly, the concept of auteurism is now defined by institutional and commercial agencies 'almost exclusively as publicity and advertisement' (ibid.: 106). This is the idea of *auteur as star*, and like film stars auteurs peddle their celebrity currency in the promotion, marketing and publicity of the film to the extent that our primary access to the auteur is not through the film itself but through the numerous interviews, talk shows, reviews, trailers, web sites, award ceremonies and guest appearances which an auteur undertakes in selling the film to us.

The latest, and perhaps most interesting, of these strategies for exploiting the commercial potential of auteurism is the 'director's commentary' contained in the 'special features' of some DVD film releases. For not only is it in itself a means of re-promoting the film on a different platform, but it exposes an interesting slippage between textual and extra-textual models of cinematic authorship. Alex Cox describes the process of producing such commentaries:

The process of recording these [commentaries] is simple. The director sits watching a video of a film made, usually, several years previously. As the film plays, he or she is expected sagely to regale a microphone with anecdotes about the making of the film. It helps if the director has managed to snag someone as 'back-up' – the producer, the writer, an actor or the composer. Quite often, their recollections will be completely different.

(2001: 10)

Cox's anecdote prompts two observations. First, a range of possible descriptions become available of the same events and processes, and hence the possibility of *multiple or collaborative authorship*. And second, authorial agency is *deliberately foregrounded though a network of extra-textual relationships*, not only as a method of representing the artistic worth of a film and thus differentiating it within the market, but also as a way of stabilising the possible ways in which it is received. That is to say, if the conception of the auteur developed in the pages of *Cahiers du Cinéma* and circulated by Sarris depended on the discernible textual evidence of their artistic presence, auteurs are now 'placed before, after and outside a film text...in effect usurping the work of that text and its reception' (Corrigan 1991: 106). Access to a blow-by-blow account of a director's intentions, influences and ideas now permitted by developments such as DVD's multiple audio channels, that is, evidence of the relationship between individual agency and aesthetics, short-circuits the critical need to unearth those intentions since they are already provided as part of the 'package'. In this respect, developments such as the 'director's commentary' are a logical extension or complement to the model of commercial auteurism outlined by Corrigan in which a refusal of interpretation becomes tied with cinematic pleasures. He argues that many of the pleasures of contemporary cinema lie 'in being able to already know, not read, the meaning of the film in a totalising image that precedes the movie in the public images of its creator (ibid.). In this sense, the notion of authorship functions as *a precept of aesthetic expectation* insofar as the extra-textual construction of the auteur implies a particular mode of consumption and endorses a range of possible understandings *in advance* of viewing a film. The logical destination of this line of thought, therefore, is the idea that it is possible to understand and consume the work of an auteur without seeing the films. Viewed from the other end, this means that *the principle* of authorship in cinema is predicated neither on the vagaries of spectatorship, nor even on the 'fact' of the film text itself, but is rather redirected through the institutional circuits of extra-textual mediation which surround a film and which act as a pre-condition to its reception.

TOWARDS A PRAGMATIC CONCEPTION OF CINEMATIC AUTHORSHIP

While on the one hand it is undeniable that auteurs are increasingly sustained extra-textually through the journalistic practices of reviewers and critics, as well as through the institutional commodification of the director as a brand name, on the other hand *the films* of those people remain irreducible to those commercial process of mediation and branding. In other words, it is one thing to agree that auteurism is far from a unified, coherent discourse, but it is quite another to deny or unduly discard its critical useful-ness in helping us to understand cinema both as an art form and as a cultural phenomenon. The persistence of the figure of the auteur testifies to that, and although its meaning and function are historically malleable, at times ambiguous, its effective-ness has not diminished in the least. The question, then, is: what model of cinematic authorship is able to account for artistic as well as commercial concerns of film-making?

A first move would be to shake off some of the unnecessarily convoluted aspects of the critical vocabulary associated with cinematic authorship that have recently tended to sink auteur analysis even before it has begun. For what is lost at the more dizzying levels of abstraction associated with much theoretical writing on auteurism is precisely the ability to make critically interesting and useful judgements about the relative artistic and aesthetic merits of a film and its makers. As such, it is perhaps useful, instead of searching for the intangible evidence of a film's unifying figure, to think of *creativity as constitutive at every level of cinematic activity*. To put it another way, the question of cinematic authorship can usefully be posed on a range of labour, creative and commercial levels. In this respect, director Alexander Kluge's observa-tion that 'auteur cinema is not a minority phenomenon: all people relate to their experiences as authors – rather than as managers of department stores', provides a useful starting point (cited in ibid.: 118). Kluge's quip alerts us to two important ideas. First, that the people who make films understand their respective roles and practice their individual crafts in ways that can meaningfully be thought of as art-making; and second, that we need a more pragmatic, rather than romantic engagement with such questions of individual expression and aesthetic worth in order to liberate the notions of art and creative expression from under the wing of the director while simultane-ously keeping open the question of the commercial construction of certain directors as auteurs.

A first step, here, is to identify the terms on which auteurism was founded and which, despite all efforts, refuse to be exiled. These are also the terms which we cannot abandon if we wish to discuss cinema as art:

- Art
- Aesthetics
- Artist
- Craft
- Practice
- Expression
- Technique
- Creativity
- Style
- Experience

In pruning-back our vocabulary to focus on these core ideas and attending to localised descriptions of how specific artistic, creative and institutional practices relate to both a film's style and its particular comprehension, it is possible to find an exit route from the excesses of the romantic conception of auteur-as-creator as well as from the equally counter-intuitive claim that the author is nowhere to be found, or worse, dead. For these tendencies are the recto and verso of the same theoretical argument, which sees auteurism as a conceptual dead-end.

As such, a more plausible method for discussing cinematic authorship entails the tracking back and forth between the various practices of film production and the film text to see how these concepts can be deployed to help us describe and better understand those practices and their relationship to how we experience the film. Moreover, we should not expect to be able to deploy them with equal success in every case, or that the results will necessarily be comparable. For individual films may be marked by the presence, but also the absence, of a coherent authorial voice. Indeed, attention to the pragmatics of film production, to the web of crafts and industrial contingencies that interact in film-making, will determine which, if any, notions of authorship are on the critical agenda. Such a pared-down and modest theory of cinematic authorship is built from piecemeal accounts of how the images and sounds made by a film hang together in meaningful and expressive patterns, one which can be fitted into, or contrasted with, other accounts of the technological, institutional and social contingencies which intersect in any film. As Richard Shusterman argues, when conceived in this pragmatic fashion, theory is 'understood as critical, imaginative reflection on practice, emerging from practice' and also 'judged pragmatically by its fruits for that practice' (2000: 59–60).

Moreover, if we accept that there are a range of criteria available to us for deploying ideas of authorship in the effort to better understand film then auteurism is not neutralised but refurbished by the absence of singular and transcendental notions of the artist. For once we let go of such essentialist notions of art-making, a whole host of potential auteurs emerge from the theoretical sidelines: creative personnel, agencies, even corporations whose influence on the art of cinema cannot be recognised by the stifling Romanticism of previous conceptions of auteurism. In locating the study of film authorship in a *practice-based model of art* it is not only possible, but desirable, to study the work of stunt directors, production designers, visual-effects supervisors, concept illustrators, computer animators, costume designers, sound engineers, fight co-ordinators, composers, specialist post-production houses, studios as well as screenwriters, producers, editors, actors and directors in terms of film aesthetics and comprehension.

CONCLUSION

The model of auteurist analysis which emerges from this pragmatic redescription of cinematic authorship, then, recognises two necessarily simultaneous practices: (1) the particular creative, expressive, and artistic activities of the personnel who collaborate in varying degrees to make a film and whose respective individual agencies determine in complex ways film style; and (2) the socio-cultural practices of contemporary media culture which constructs the auteur as a commodity, a logo so to speak, which stands not behind the text as in Romantic notions of authorship, but rather in front of it precisely to explicate, expand and legitimise the marks of individuality, expression and style in a film.

In accepting that 'intentional fallacy' is the last word on Romantic notions of auteurism, such a pragmatic reconfiguration of cinematic authorship, attuned to the primacy and complexities of film-making *practice* as well as to the *commercial imperatives* of media culture, affords us the opportunity of capturing some of the continued allure of the auteur while locating the focus of our critical gaze back in the art of film-making. Indeed, in negotiating the moment between the textual and the extra-textual activities of the auteur, a pragmatic approach to the question of authorship confronts itself back where it began: as a tool for helping us look for the art in cinema.

□ CASE STUDY 1: DIRECTOR-AS-AUTHOR – JIM JARMUSCH

I do it my way or I don't do it. It helps me in negotiating to know that I will walk away if I don't have control…I decide how the film is cut, how long it is, what music is used, who is cast. I make films by hand.

(Jim Jarmusch 1996, cited in Levy 1999)

The dominant view of authorship interprets film as the creative expression of a single individual, usually held to be the director. And although film theory has struggled long and hard to debunk this proposition as a whimsical romantic myth, it survives as the key marker of film style, an index of the value of films and a commercial strategy for marketing cinema. Ironically, however, the grounds on which the idea of director-as-author is often attacked and the reason it lives on are both rooted in an analysis of the relationship between individual creative agency and the imperatives of a commercially driven film industry organised around the division of labour into multiple specialised roles. As such, while on the one hand the attribution of singular authorship is refuted by claiming that what is seen and heard in a film is *ipso facto* the product of the activities of more than one person, on the other hand levelling-down those diverse activities to the same creative plane, or simply ignoring them altogether, accounts neither for the creative agency of individuals nor the ways in which the specificities of their labour relates to the significant artistic features of a film. In other words, film theory has tended to turn the observation that individual creative aims are often frustrated, dissipated or simply thwarted by the commercial pressures of film-making into a theoretical principle of necessary contradiction between individual expression and collaboration.

Certainly, attributing authorship to any one individual in many mainstream films may be an empty exercise. Yet if we grant that collective production will limit individual expression in some respects then we should also grant that it can extend it in others. Which is to say, collaborative work and the particular dynamics of group work can facilitate individual creativity as well as prohibit it. Thus, it is one thing to say that a director is usually merely one figure in a highly complex productive process of film-making, but quite another to then insist that authorship can never be meaningfully attributed to the director. For even granting that, on a standard case, films have multiple authors or no discernible author at all does not foreclose the possibility that in other cases a film or groups of films might usefully be analysed in terms of the creative agency of their director.

So while on a general theoretical level there may be a number of potential authors involved in the creative process of film production – screenwriters, cinematographers, actors, editors, visual-effects supervisors and so on – sometimes a director's role within that process warrants the assertion that he or she can meaningfully be understood as the film's author. Such an assertion, however, need not imply that the director has authored each and every aspect of what we see and hear, nor that he or she is the only creative agency detectable within the film. Rather it is to assert the more modest idea that investigation of the director-as-author in certain cases can yield critical rewards in the sense of *enriching our understanding of those films and our experience of them*. In other words, the theoretical question of whether the notion of authorship in cinema is plausible *per se* is different from the piecemeal approach which asks how individual agency relates to film style. In this latter, more pared-down conception, authorship emerges not as a theoretical principle, but as a *matter of degree*, established on a case-by-case basis on the evidence of practice.

Jim Jarmusch

It is just such a piecemeal approach to film authorship which allows us to explore Jim Jarmusch as a particularly persuasive case for the director-as-author. More specifically, the stylistic and expressive significance of his films can be usefully explained through an analysis which interrogates the inter-relations between aesthetics and his individual agency. Within this context, it is possible to trace Jarmusch's authorship on three over-lapping levels: *working practice*; *thematic concerns*; and *stylistic concerns*.

Working practice

The favoured method for deciding whether or not a director is an auteur centres around an analysis of the evidence presented in the film text itself. Often referred to as a 'thematic analysis', the critic looks for a set of consistent themes that run across a series of films. However, this process tends to exclude from the analysis extra-textual and pre-textual practices which both prefigure and bear upon what is ultimately seen and heard in a film. Indeed, consideration of the context of 'working practice' is especially important given the complex economic and contractual culture of the contemporary agent-led film industry in which ideas are pitched, scripts bid for and then rewritten many times, stars signed with script approval and final cut rights written into the deal, and films are reworked in light of their test screenings. Indeed, it is precisely the elaborate commercial drama of contemporary film production that simultaneously makes the notion of director as-author unlikely in most cases, but compelling in the case of Jarmusch. For not only does Jarmusch write and direct all his feature films, work closely with his cinematographer and editor, play a central role in casting the principal characters and choose the main locations, but he takes the lead in raising the money for his projects, usually from independent and European investors. His first feature, *Permanent Vacation* (1982), cost $10,000, was shot in ten days and was financed from his scholarship fund, and while the budgets have since become progressively bigger with each of his subsequent six features they are still financed entirely independent of the major studios. In this respect, Jarmusch believes that genuine creative independence is contingent on financial independence: 'I object strongly to businessmen telling me how to make a film. The business side is there to serve the film. I don't make films so that business can exist' (cited in Arrington 1990). Moreover, Jarmusch is virtually unique amongst contemporary film-makers in that he owns the negatives to all his films.

The notions of *financial independence* and *ownership* are significant precisely insofar as they prefigure any attempt to establish the authorial credentials of a director on the evidence of his or her films. In other words, it is only possible to meaningfully demonstrate consistencies of theme or style across a range of textual instances after it has first been established that the pre-textual working practices that frame production permit the director to exercise his or her creative agency.

Analysis of working practice, however, is not merely a question of finance. It also points us towards the notion of *creative process*. Again, consideration of Jarmusch's working practice is revealing. Most films begin as a story, a set of events that will happen during the course of a film, which can be pitched to studios for development. Instead of this narrative-centred process, however, Jarmusch's creative process is char-acter-centred. He says that his films develop organically in the sense that the process 'starts from a basic perception, sometimes not even accurate, of a person, an actor, a quality of that personality, and I want to grow a character on it' (cited in Keogh 2001: 128). Given this, Jarmusch writes characters for specific performers – both professional and non-professional actors. For instance, the titular character of *Ghost Dog* (1999) as

medium of communication and understanding is often undermined as characters develop and sustain relationships on other levels, understanding each other without necessarily knowing that they do. Dispossessed of a common language, and usually a common culture as well, Jarmusch's characters communicate with, and understand, one another by recognising their points of convergence and similarity, that is, precisely by discovering their shared humanity. If this idea of non-linguistic communication is at its most comic in the exchanges between Ghost Dog and his best friend Raymond, in which they often say the same thing in different languages without being aware that they have done so, then it finds its most profound and complex articulation in the beautiful misunderstandings between Blake (who is mistaken for William Blake the poet) and Nobody (who speaks four different languages during the film) in *Dead Man* (see Plate 4.2). For although Blake at one point declares that he 'has not understood one single word' that Nobody has spoken since he's met him, the significance of their relationship resides not in their inability to communicate in language but rather in the spiritual connection forged between them. Moreover, in not providing subtitles for the dialogue delivered in the native American languages Cree, Makah and Blackfoot as well as including a running joke about tobacco that is culturally specific to those native cultures, the audience is implicated in Jarmusch's thematic exploration of the nature and limits of communication.

Recessive Jarmuschian themes

In addition to the three dominant themes outlined above, we can also identify a range of secondary, or recessive thematic consistencies in Jarmusch's films which both accompany and complement many of those principal concerns.

Poetry of the ordinary and insignificant: Jarmusch has said that he is interested in the things that are normally taken out of movies, the 'blank time' between what is normally deemed to be the significant narrative events. The way Jarmusch handles the jailbreak in *Down by Law* is exemplary of this anti-suspenseful approach to narrative. The first mention of escape comes as Bob half-whispers the idea to his cell mates at the close of one scene. The next scene begins by showing the three characters fleeing across open ground. In this way, instead of suspense, action and plotting Jarmusch's films deal in the insignificant or mundane aspects of daily life played out through an attention to the minutiae of character.

• **Plate 4.2**
Nobody (Gary Farmer) and William Blake (Johnny Depp) in *Dead Man* (Jim Jarmusch, 1995)
Despite misunderstanding each other's language, they share the same spiritual journey

Electric/PolyGram Video
Tel: 0171 580 3380

Dead Man

Nobody (GARY FARMER) and
William Blake (JOHNNY DEPP)

Chance encounters: The reduced narratives of Jarmusch's films are all driven by the coincidental or serendipitous encounter between his misfit characters (the transitory meetings of passengers and drivers in *Night on Earth*; the random encounter of inmates in *Down by Law*; the coincidental relationship between rescuer and rescued in *Dead Man* and *Ghost Dog*). Moreover, it is in these moments of coincidence/fate that what on the surface appear to be life's insignificances (a visit to an aunt; staying in the same hotel; a taxi ride; a job interview; a trip to the local shop) turn out to have life-altering consequences.

Urbanism: There is strong focus on the relationship between the physical urban environment, in particular the squalor and beauty of the American city, and identity. Indeed, we are often given a tour through the American landscape in the form of extended tracking shots precisely in order that we can register its 'personality'. As such, the notion of urbanism is squarely entwined with the more primary theme of cultural disorientation.

Stylistic concerns

There is a certain justice in appreciating Jarmusch's films as a statement of his ambition: to 'exist somewhere in between the American mainstream and the individualized European style' (cited in Cohen 1999). For while his unconventional stories of social outsiders, happenstance and cultural alienation often evoke conventional American narratives precisely as the mythical counterpoint for their own irony, the visual style and narrative form in which those stories are presented is characteristic of certain European and Japanese traditions of film-making.

Out of this general observation we can distinguish the following stylistic concerns prevalent in Jarmusch's films.

Character-driven narrative: Plot is stripped away in Jarmusch's films, with events emerging from the distinctive personality traits of the characters and the nature of their interactions. For instance, without the performances in *Night on Earth* all that remains is four uneventful taxi journeys, while in *Dead Man*, what is a principal convention of the western film – a shooting – is reduced to a mere pretext for Blake and Nobody's spiritual journey. Moreover, the idea that each character *is* the film's story chimes with Jarmusch's reduced visual style – long takes and minimal use of point-of-view shots or close-ups – in the sense that shot-duration and technique are put in the service of observing character behaviour within a specific physical environment. In these respects, then, Jarmusch's creative process of writing for specific characters becomes reflected at the level of film form.

Episodic structure: This character-centred approach to film-making also permeates the structure of Jarmusch's films. Instead of a coherent narrative strain, the films proceed thematically through either their own internal thematic logic (*Stranger than Paradise*, *Dead Man*), or by imposing an episodic structure (*Down by Law*, *Ghost Dog*), or by unifying the film's story with its structure through the theme of synchronicity (*Night on Earth*, *Mystery Train*). Either way, Jarmusch's films resist narrative linearity in favour of a segmented structure. In other words, his films tend to be organised around a series of interdependent short episodes linked thematically and/or by character. This is most obvious in the films that explore synchronicity at a formal and thematic level (*Mystery Train*, *Night on Earth*), but is characteristic of all his films. Indeed, Jarmusch often marks the transition between these segments by fading into and out of black. While this technique is particularly evident in *Stranger than Paradise* and *Down by Law*, the black spaces that punctuate scenes in *Dead Man* not only give the film its organic rhythm, but chime with Blake's own sporadic drift in and out of consciousness.

For further discussion of narrative and film structure, see Chapter 2, pp. 78–89. It would be interesting to compare this section with the reading of Spider-Man, *an example of 'blockbuster' Hollywood narrative film in Chapter 2, pp. 55–59.*

For more discussion of cinematography, see Chapter 2, pp. 70–73.

Tracking shots: In all of Jarmusch's films the screen is given over to a tour of the physical environment through which the characters pass. Indeed, the extended tracking-shot, usually through the cityscape, is, like his use of fades, one of Jarmusch's most consistent visual tics; it activates the notion of environment not merely as a backdrop to the story but rather as a 'character' in its own right, with its own distinctive personality and meanings.

The notion of the director-as-author remains, and will continue to remain a troubling paradox at the level of theory. However, it is one thing to admit that individual authorship in cinema is problematic, but quite another to then leave consideration of individual creative agency out of our analyses. Indeed, an understanding of creative agency is no less crucial to film analysis than to literary analysis. So while we may wish to dismiss the idea that Jim Jarmusch is the sole author of his films, it nevertheless remains the case that describing his films *as if he is* their author, through analysis of his working practice, thematic and stylistic concerns adds to both our understanding and pleasure of those films.

□ CASE STUDY 2: CORPORATE AUTHORSHIP – INDUSTRIAL LIGHT AND MAGIC (ILM)

The beauty of ILM is that it has done so many productions, and so many of them have been groundbreaking, that there is a technological culture there that is beyond the individuals who made those advancements.

(James Cameron, cited in *From Star Wars to Star Wars* 1999)

For further discussion of animation, digital animation and computer technology, see Chapter 6, pp. 232–235.

Andrew Darley argues that the idea of the director-as-author working within a commercially driven film industry is becoming increasingly untenable to the extent that 'quite simply it is no longer an issue' (2000: 141). Moreover, he suggests that cultural production in an age of digital visual culture becomes 'first and foremost a technical problem' in which 'technique, technicians and technology itself take command' (ibid.). Within this context, it is significant that a set of company names such as 'Industrial Light and Magic' (ILM), 'Disney' and 'PIXAR' now operate as an index of artistic style alongside or in front of individual creative agency. So while on the one hand such names do not necessarily displace the director (directors such as George Lucas, Steven Spielberg, James Cameron, Ron Howard and Robert Zemeckis all regularly collaborate with ILM while retaining a distinct creative identity, and the name of PIXAR is virtually synonymous with John Lasseter), on the other hand they now tend to 'vie with them as a way of accounting for or measuring creative worth within the popular aesthetic imagination' (ibid.: 137).

One implication of this situation is not only that authorial agency might usefully be located with creative personnel other than the director, but that it becomes possible, even desirable, to identify multiple authorial agencies within a film. Moreover, it opens up the possibility not only of collective or collaborative authorship but also that of *institutional or corporate authorship*. Indeed, if we think of recent Hollywood films such as *The Abyss* (1989), *Terminator 2* (1991), *Forrest Gump* (1995), *Titanic* (1997), *Men in Black* (1997), *Mercury Rising* (1998), *The Perfect Storm* (2000), *Artificial Intelligence: AI* (2001) and *Minority Report* (2002), as well as the entire *Star Wars* and *Jurassic Park* series, then some of their most important visual and stylistic features which would, under the classic model of auteurism, be ascribed to their respective directors can be more plausibly traced to the work of other collaborators, and in particular to Industrial Light and Magic.

Established by George Lucas to develop the visual-effects for *Star Wars* (1977), ILM has since played a pioneering role in the creation of modern special-effects techniques. And while they continue to develop and utilise the full range of those techniques, it is nevertheless in the field of digital effects that ILM now stands as emblematic of the technological thrill of the contemporary blockbuster. For not only is it now impossible to watch a mainstream film which does not employ a considerable array of *invisible* digital effects, but Hollywood's chief commodity – the blockbuster – is significantly driven by the desire to *make visible* or showcase precisely the current capabilities of visual-effects technology and techniques. It is in this respect that ILM, as perhaps the most influential visual-effects company, can be considered to be more important than any single individual in determining and advancing the visual and narrative parameters of contemporary cinema. Moreover, these insights prompt analysis of ILM as a corporate author insofar as visual effects, and in particular digital imaging techniques, are both *ubiquitous* (characteristic of Hollywood's standard production and post-production processes and thus have a significant effect on contemporary film style) and *unique* (the technological or aesthetic specificity of particular effects sequences).

Applied to *Artificial Intelligence: AI* this involves on the one hand consideration of the function of visual effects in the narrative, and on the other, attention to the creative process and individual practices implicated in creating its spectacular imagery, and with it reconsideration of a range of elements that we have, up to now, willingly attributed to the director. Thus, despite the considerable critical attention devoted to the working relationship between Steven Spielberg (the film's director) and Stanley Kubrick (who bequeathed Spielberg the project) and how this is manifested in the film's images and themes, the author of *A.I.* might credibly be considered to be ILM. For while a number of Spielbergian themes are detectable – particularly the notion of innocence played out though the 'child in peril' scenario – the film's futuristic tale is rendered possible and plausible by the specialised technical resources and creative skills represented by the corporate brand name ILM. Indeed, both the narrative and visual design of the entire second half of the film are predicated on the generation of believable synthetic characters and locations. In this way, ILM can be seen as a credible authorial voice within *A.I.* just insofar as it operates both as a pre-condition to the film's realisation in the first instance and as a corporate agency through which key enunciative and expressive techniques are executed and cohere.

These identifying characteristics of ILM's authorship can be explored in relation to the section of *A.I.* which takes place in 'Rouge City'. Taking considerable influence from Chris Baker's conceptual illustrations, the design and creation of Rouge City necessitated the collaboration of a wide range of ILM's creative and technical staff from the film's Senior Visual Effects Supervisor, Dennis Muren, to model-makers, animators, art directors and so on. Indeed, the images of Rouge City, like the aerial and underwater sequences of a half-submerged New York that follow it, are comprised from a mix of visual-effects techniques including a huge set, scale models, miniatures, blue-screen and computer-generated imagery (CGI).

In this respect, Plate 4.3 is exemplary of both *A.I.*'s hybrid imagery and ILM's central role within the film's creative processes. For although at the level of the film's narrative it is visually symbolic of Spielberg's preoccupation with 'the imperilled child', at a stylistic level it reveals ILM's fundamental role in creating the technologically dense images that frame its narrative.

The still shows a sophisticated composite image which blends live-action footage with a range of visual effects. Gigolo Joe (Jude Law) and David (Haley Joel Osment), as well as the extras heading towards the 'Tails' building, are real actors shot on a sound stage comprising the fountain behind Joe and David, the platform on which they are standing and the façades of the buildings in the background. However, the figure

• **Plate 4.3**
Gigolo Joe (Jude Law)
and David (Haley Joel
Osment) in *Artificial
Intelligence: AI* (Steven
Spielberg, 2001)
'Rouge City' is the result
of a vast range of
visual-effects tech-
niques seamlessly
blended together in a
sophisticated composite
image

dancing above the entrance to 'Tails' is entirely synthetic, generated by computer animators. Moreover, the circular high-rise building behind 'Tails' as well as the neon signs advertising various products are computer generated and were added to the scene during post-production. Likewise, while much of the complex lighting set-up for this shot was done on set, the architectural detail of Rouge City was enhanced though post-production CGI lighting techniques. As such, it is impossible not only to disentangle the thematic structure of the film from its stylistic composition, but to disentangle ILM from the technical and artistic processes which facilitated the creation of that composition.

It is in this sense, then, that 'Industrial Light and Magic' stands not merely as the name of a company which houses a set of material resources and employs certain individuals with specific technical and creative skills, but as marker of visual and stylistic imperatives in both individual films and across a series of films. As such, ILM can be seen as a corporate author precisely to the extent that its company name also acts as a sign which organises and executes highly specialised and distinctive forms of industrial aesthetic practice within cinema beyond the scope of any one of the individuals it employs.

1 **Choose a director and then:**
   a **Watch a sample of his or her films and note any consistencies of style and/or theme that occur across more than one film. Can you detect a 'personal statement' or 'worldview' in the films?**

Then:
   b **List who else involved in the production of those films has contributed to their look, feel and meaning? In what ways is it meaningful or useful to describe the director as the author of those films? Are they authored by multiple people, or do you think that it is not worthwhile pursuing the question of authorship in relation to those films?**

2 **Increasingly films are being re-released as 'Director's Cut' versions. How does the notion of the director's cut relate to the idea of film authorship in terms of both art and commerce?**

3   Explore the notion of 'corporate authorship' in relation to Disney or PIXAR. To what extent do their corporate brand names also mark out distinctive stylistic practices. Does the same apply for, say, Universal or Dreamworks?

4   When released on DVD, an increasing number of films contain a 'Director's Commentary' as part of their 'Special Features'. After initially watching the film, watch it again while listening to the Director's Commentary and explore the extent to which his or her explanation of the film's thematic and stylistic features

a   reinforces your own reading of the film

b   alters your opinion about the significance and meaning of the film.

Genre and Hollywood cinema

INTRODUCTION: WHAT IS GENRE AND WHY STUDY IT?

Common questions we ask each other before going to the cinema or renting a movie are: 'What sort of film shall we watch?'; 'What kind of film do you feel like seeing?' Alternatively, in making our selections we might say things such as: 'I don't like horror films'; 'I'm not in the mood for a weepie, lets watch a comedy'. These kinds of questions and statements identify, at least on an informal level, a film's genre, a French term imported to film theory from literary studies and meaning 'type' or 'class'. The result of such inquiries is, say, the choice of watching a thriller over a western, a comedy over a musical, a science-fiction film over a crime movie or, more generally the idea that we have particular likes or dislikes for certain types of film. Moreover, the issues that underpin such deliberations and discriminations – issues of taste, preference, identity and pleasure associated with particular kinds of film – are, of course, precisely the issues that producers of film need to take into account in the effort to make their product appealing to audiences, and, by implication, a contained economic risk. Likewise, attention to those same issues provides the film reviewer with a tactical means of evaluating a film's relative merits in terms of the way it can be said to be a classic of its genre, or, moreover, if it affords particular pleasures by extending, usurping, challenging or reworking particular generic elements. On this everyday level, genre resembles a golden thread that knits the concerns of industry together with the desires of audiences.

Seizing on this sense of continuity, much genre criticism is underpinned by the assumption that genre is a conceptual prism that allows critics to simultaneously address the activities of industry, audience and culture insofar as it functions as: (1) a financial security blanket for the industry by providing a logic or framework for organising its output so as to capitalise on previous models of success and thus minimise financial risk; (2) a set of precepts and expectations for audiences to organise their viewing; and (3) a critical framework for reviewers to arbitrate between the distinctiveness and putative success of the product and the taste of its implied audience. In this way, Peter Hutchings argues that, 'part of the appeal of studying genre is that it offers the opportunity to deal with cinema, and Hollywood cinema in particular, as both an industrial and popular medium' (1995: 61).

GENRE, HOLLYWOOD AND FILM THEORY

Partly because of its promise of theoretical ubiquity, and partly due to its apparent affinity with Hollywood cinema, genre has been a key concept in the development of film theory, and, in return, cinema has provided an important staging ground for the broader discussion of genre in relation to mass entertainment and media culture. For genre criticism is marked by the possibility it affords critics to analyse the cinema as an *industrial form of aesthetic practice*, that is, precisely as a major form of mass entertainment.

In this respect, it is important to note that genre's more extrovert and inherently inclusive critical disposition contrasts sharply with auteurism's introversion and intrinsic exclusivity. Indeed, the emergence of genre criticism in the late 1960s and early 1970s is usually understood as either a development, qualification, corrective or outright rejection of auteurism. Whereas auteurist criticism was overwhelmingly trained upon the work of relatively few directors which could be distilled from the general category of cinema by appealing to Romantic conceptions of the artist, genre, in casting its critical net wider, seemed to offer critics a far more inclusive and democratic method, one which was attuned to the industrial and commercial imperatives of Hollywood. It is in this sense that Gledhill sees genre as a 'conceptual space' in which 'issues of texts and aesthetics...intersect with those of industry and institution, history and society, culture and audiences' and describes the term as reclaiming the 'commercial products of Hollywood for serious critical appraisal' (2000: 221, 222). And Stam talks of genre as the 'crystallization of a negotiated encounter between film-maker and audience, a way of reconciling the stability of an industry with the excitement of an evolving popular art' (2000: 127). It is this holistic approach to studying cinema that seemed to early genre critics capable of extending and advancing critical interest in popular cinema in a way auteurism could not. For in trying to skim the cream from Hollywood's output, auteurism tended to either construct popular cinema as the insignificant counterpoint to genuine art, or worse, to simply ignore it altogether. In short, the logic of much auteurist writing runs that it is not the film, but in fact the *artist*, that is important, and by implication that it is a few individual geniuses that are the proper focus of film studies rather than the industrial, historical and social nexus that frames the cinematic process. Or, to put it another way, auteurism valued the exception rather than the rule inasmuch as it thrashed the artistic wheat from the generic chaff, while genre criticism, on the contrary, set itself the task of understanding precisely the 'rule'-governed practices of cinema as a mass-entertainment medium.

In trawling deeper and wider than auteurism, genre criticism can be seen as an attempt to deal with Hollywood cinema as an industrial mode of film production which is itself bound up with, not to mention limited by, a much broader economic system governed by the imperatives of commodification and commercialism. For a generic analysis of cinema offers not only the possibility of describing the systematic nature of Hollywood as an industry in which differentiation between individual films occurs only with an overarching logic of product standardisation, but also prompts consideration of different genres in terms of their collective significance or deeper meanings. In other words, exactly the same value judgement of Hollywood cinema as, first and foremost, a cinema of genres which, in the hands of auteur critics, served to marginalise the *standard* practices of Hollywood provided genre critics with a critical vocabulary appropriate to the art of those practices.

Genre theory and contemporary cinema
Ironically, such has been the success of genre criticism in describing popular cinema that Hollywood is now often equated with generic film-making. As Tom Ryall argues: 'whatever else it is, Hollywood is surely a cinema of genres, a cinema of westerns,

gangster films, musicals, melodramas and thrillers' (1998: 327). However, such an equa-tion tends to hide as much as it reveals. For such claims tend to emerge from analyses of Hollywood's classical period and cannot automatically be transposed to the contem-porary situation. Indeed, since the assimilation of Hollywood studios into larger conglomerates and the concomitant shift away from the factory-like manufacture of films towards what has been described as the 'package' model of film production, genres are no longer associated with specific studios in the way they were in the heyday of the **studio system**. In addition, cinema-going nowadays is for most people a relatively infrequent event in comparison to the time devoted to other media forms. In fact, the majority of film viewing itself now revolves around our television sets, whether that is tuning in to a movie broadcast on terrestrial networks or one of a proliferating number of dedicated satellite and cable channels; hiring a video or DVD from a local rental outlet; or watching a movie from our own personal collection. Indeed, at a time when movies resemble less the self-contained entities often implied by notions of clas-sical Hollywood, and more 'multi-purpose entertainment machines' (Schatz 1993: 9–10) that initiate 'an endless chain of other cultural products' (Wasko 1994: 4), then it is perhaps unsurprising that the film text itself is only one among many possible sites where genre condenses. Likewise, much contemporary cinema evinces a variety of technological, formal, thematic and stylistic affinities with other media forms as well as itself spawning a host of other media commodities.

Given these cultural changes, some critics have recently become less convinced of the security of genre for describing Hollywood's industrial mode of production. Steve Neale, for instance, maintains that it is not genres that are Hollywood's primary commodity but rather narratives, inasmuch as 'the system of narration adopted by mainstream cinema serves as the very currency of cinema itself' (1980: 20). On this account, genre is simply a mode, albeit it a key one, of Hollywood's narrative system. More recently, Andrew Darley has suggested that in a postmodern culture of institution-alised **intertextuality** and radical **eclecticism** brought about by new technological developments, genre, while not entirely disappearing, has 'a far more limited structural role to play', perhaps reliably referring to nothing more than 'the general level of a form itself – narrative cinema' (2000: 144). Such a move divests genre theory of precisely the critical dexterity that distinguishes it from other critical approaches to studying popular film, while some critics even suggest abandoning the term itself in favour of other terms that more plausibly describe Hollywood's commercial activities within the global medi-ascape – terms such as repetition, seriality, cycle, trend and mode.

Simply disposing of the term, however, or replacing it with other cognate terms, not only seems counter-intuitive on an everyday level but also risks unnecessarily jetti-soning some useful conceptual tools for thinking about cinema on a range of theoretical levels. For if on the one hand we do need to rethink our conceptions of film genre by looking beyond the cinema for our inspiration, to place the question of film genre squarely within the broader context of mass-mediated culture, on the other hand it is precisely this broader context of media culture that makes genre not less but more pertinent to understanding contemporary Hollywood and its more sophisticated inter-relationships with world cinema and global culture. Clearly, then, much turns on how we choose to define genre.

DEFINING GENRE(S)

At a general level work on genre seeks to understand film as a *specific form of commodity* and at a more refined level attempts to disentangle *different instances of that commodity*. In other words, genre is addressed as a system for organising produc-tion as well as groupings of individual films which have collective and singular significance. It is important to note, however, that a number of approaches have

studio system
Usually seen to have developed *c.*1920 and lasting until *c.*1950, the studio system indicates the period of Hollywood history in which the major studios controlled all aspects of the production, distribution and exhibition of their products.

For further discussion of the studio system see Chapter 1, pp. 4–15.

intertextuality
This term, strongly linked with **postmod-ernism**, designates, in its narrow sense, the ways in which a film either explicitly or implicitly refers to other films (through allusion, imitation, parody or pastiche for example), or in its broader sense, the various relationships one (film) text may have with other texts. (See also **eclecticism, palimpsest** and **recombinacy**).

eclecticism
An aesthetic style in which a new composi-tion is composed wholly or in part from elements selected from a range of previous styles, forms, texts, genres drawn from different periods and from both high and popular culture. This is one of the principal aesthetic strategies of **postmodern** art. (See also **intertextuality, palimpsest, recombi-nacy** and **self-reflexivity**.)

taxonomy
The practice of classifi-
cation. In this sense, the
practice of classifying
films into groups based
on similarities of form
and/or content.

developed that address Hollywood's generic structures, all of which are underpinned by different assumptions about the purpose of genre criticism. It is possible to trace three key lines of theoretical development here: First, the **taxonomic** view of genre, which attempts to map the boundaries between generic classes; second, the view of genre as an economic strategy for organising film production schedules; and third, the view of genre as cognition, as a contract between producers and consumers which renders films intelligible on some level.

Genre as taxonomy

Tom Ryall argues that 'if genre criticism were simply a matter of constructing taxonomies and allocating films to their places in the system, then the intellectual basis of the exercise would certainly be open to doubt' (1998: 336). While Ryall is right to caution against viewing genre criticism *merely* as a question of fitting films into their appropriate generic hole, it nevertheless remains the case that the question of genre routinely emerges as a border dispute: defining the boundaries between one genre and another. Here, defining genre involves a twofold process: describing the differences between individual genres, that is, between thrillers, westerns, musicals, horror films, gangster films, action movies and so forth; as well as mapping the common elements that members of any one genre share. Indeed, the notions of *difference* and *sameness* that taxonomies imply are, albeit in various ways, central to all generic criticism. As such, Richard Maltby argues that the genre critic seeks to 'place movies into generic categories as a way of dividing up the cinematic map of Hollywood into smaller, more manageable, and relative discrete areas' (Maltby 1995: 107). Critics have attempted to map the contours of genres in a number of ways, using a variety of methods, often producing corpuses of vastly differing size and complexity.

Theoretical taxonomy

In an attempt to unearth the essential theoretical characteristics of cinematic genres Alan Williams (1984) argues that there are only three principal film genres: narrative film, experimental or avant-garde film, and documentary. In searching for conceptual equivalence between literary and cinematic genres, he notes that, in reserving this general or theoretical level for the term genre 'then film genres will by definition have the staying power seen in literary genres' (ibid.: 122). On this account, the labels we ordinarily use to distinguish between films of various kinds – thriller, horror, comedy, romance, and so forth – actually refer to sub-genres of the narrative film.

There are, however, a number of problems with imposing theoretical generic categories onto cinema. First, and most obviously, it is counter-intuitive in the sense that genre becomes abstracted from both industrial and cultural usages of the term. Second, ascending to this level of theoretical abstraction tends to belie the inherent complexity of cinematic forms. For instance, animation doesn't fit comfortably into any of Williams' categories in the sense that animation's fundamentally graphic economy permits it to straddle Williams' categories which are clearly erected to describe the enunciation of photographic modes. One answer would be to put forward animation as a fourth principal genre, yet this simply compounds the fundamental problem of theoretical cinematic genres since the complex and highly productive relationship between animation and narrative, non-fiction and experimental film would be further obfuscated behind discrete generic walls. A similar problem arises in the distinction between narrative and documentary film in that narrative is every bit as important and complex in documentary forms as in fictional forms. Indeed, as Alan Renov notes, the distinction between fiction and documentary genres is unsustainable given that 'nonfiction contains any number of "fictive" elements' to the extent that 'it might be said that the two domains inhabit one another' (1993: 2, 3).

*For discussion of anima-
tion as a distinctive
cinematic form, see
Chapter 6.*

*For a discussion of docu-
mentary film and its
relationship to fictional
film, see Chapter 5.*

In what ways does a consideration of animation problematise the notion of film genre? Is animation a genre in itself, or is it possible to draw generic distinctions between different animated films?
Likewise, try and list some of the difficulties and problems associated with grouping all non-fiction films together under the singular generic label, 'documentary'.

Historical taxonomy

Given the problems of defining genre and drawing classificatory boundaries using a set of theoretical principles, most critical writing has adopted a more historical stance to genre in seeking to map more selective 'groupings of actual films inductively linked on the basis of common themes, styles and iconography' (Ryall 1998: 329). Instead of asking questions such as, 'What markers of cinematographic representation differentiate one genre from the next?', an historical approach to genre asks, 'What distinguishes a western from a gangster film, a thriller from a crime movie?' and so forth, and 'How does an individual western film relate to the broader category of the western?', and 'Why are certain genres popular at particular times, but not at others?' In short, unlike the essentialism implied by purely theoretical definitions of genre, this model of genre criticism attempts to cut cinema at its generic joints precisely by acknowledging the historical contingency of generic forms. A variety of tactics have been used to make the dissection, ranging from attention to a genre's relation to history; to common subject matter, themes and content; to the presence of certain shared formal elements; to their intended effect on the audience; to looser groupings around stylistic or cinematographic properties. Table 4.1 schematises some of the different ways in which genres can be seen to be held together.

If such schematisation does demonstrate *possible* criteria for differentiating genres, it also belies the inherent complexity and mutability of generic definitions. For example, as indicated in Table 4.1 film noir could quite easily sit in any one of three groupings, or all three simultaneously depending on which definitional criteria one chooses to privilege. Alternatively, we could make the case, as many critics have done, that film noir is, in fact, not a genre at all but merely a particular stylistic inflection of the crime film. Moreover, and notwithstanding a host of further possible objections one might raise, not only is it possible to relocate, say, the western and gangster film to the category demarcated by formal criteria on the basis of the presence of 'the gun fight' and 'the shoot-out' respectively, but we might also collapse all categories into the one which sees differences exclusively in terms of subject matter.

Part of the problem with this method of genre building, of course, is that genres are defined in a number of different contexts. So while some genres such as the western and the musical are established industrial categories of production readily recognised by both film-makers and audiences, others, such as the 'gross-out comedy', are constructed by critics only after the film has been released. Moreover, generic labels generated by critics are often appropriated into studio production cycles and marketing materials while the most long-standing generic categories continue to act as a key point of reference in the critical evaluation of a film.

By the same token, such highly schematised generic classifications suffer from what Stam calls the problem of extension – the implied scope of a generic category (2000: 128). For example, herding films together under the generic banner 'comedy' seems straightforward enough, but actually tells us very little about individual films beyond the intention to incite laughter. For if 'the generation of laughter' is the comedy genre's

Table 4.1

Genre	Defining criteria	Differentiating criteria
Western Gangster film Epic War film **Film noir**	**Historical subject**	American West 1920s urban America Biblical or ancient history Specific historical conflicts Postwar America
Horror Thriller Comedy	**Intended effect**	Intended to horrify Intended to thrill Generate laughter
Musical Action movie Pornography	**Formal criteria**	Presence of song and dance performances Presence of action set-pieces Presence of sex acts
Science-fiction Fantasy Disaster Crime film Melodrama Road movie **Film noir**	**Subject matter**	Futuristic technologies/future worlds Impossible worlds/fantastical characters Natural or man-made catastrophe Criminal and investigatory activities Domestic drama and heterosexual romance Journey or road-trip, usually across America Crime and institutional corruption
Blockbuster **Film noir**	**Style**	Spectacular events Chiaroscuro lighting and dark mise-en-scène

*For further discussion of
film audience see
Chapter 1, pp. 34–40.*

**Video stores routinely employ categories such as 'Family', 'Romance',
'Drama' and 'Kids' to organise their titles. Is it possible to place these categories alongside those listed in Table 4.1?
Table 4.1 doesn't list the 'Biopic'. Where would you place it? Can you fit it
into more than one category?**

self-reflexivity
Used to describe films or
texts which self-
consciously
acknowledge or reflect
upon their own status as
fictional artefacts and/or
the processes involved in
their creation. This is one
of the principal aesthetic
strategies of **post-
modern** art. (See also
eclecticism, **intertextuality**, **palimpsest**, and
recombinacy.)

definitive convention then not only does it, by definition, mark all modes of comedy –
slapstick, screwball, farce, satire, parody – but it also encompasses the comic elements
or funny moments that routinely appear in most, if not all, other genres. Indeed, the co-
presence of laughter and fear is common to the horror film, while hyphenated generic
categorisations such as romantic-comedy, sex-comedy and gross-out-comedy address
at promotional and journalistic levels precisely comedy's nomadic generic existence.

Approaching the same problem of extension from the opposite angle, if comedy
seems too broad as a class, then, 'funny films about a motley police force', or 'science-
fiction films concerning time travel' seem too narrow. Either way, the issue of extension
betrays the fundamental difficulty of demarcating generic borders in any reliable way, a
problem telescoped by the extreme eclecticism and **self-reflexivity** of much of contem-

porary Hollywood. To take just one example, *Moulin Rouge* (Baz Luhrmann, 2001) is simultaneously distinguished: historically (its depiction of *fin-de-siècle* Paris); formally (the performance of song and dance routines); stylistically (an exemplar of postmodern film-making); and in terms of its organisation of subject matter (quasi-melodramatic narrative of heterosexual romance).

Visual taxonomy

From the late 1960s onwards critics attempted to refine the ways of defining the criteria which policed generic boundaries. The notion of **iconography** seemed to offer an empirical methodology more suited to the task of classifying cinema's visual terrains. As Ed Buscombe writes: 'since we are dealing with a visual medium we ought surely to look for our defining criteria at what we actually see on the screen' (cited in Neale 1980: 12). Thus, strictly aesthetic criteria – variously referred to as 'visual conventions', 'patterns of visual imagery' and 'sign-events' – were seen as essential indicators of generic differentiation. As such, the western was distinguished by its settings, both specific and general (the West, the frontier, deserts, mountains, Monument Valley, saloons, homesteads, etc.); costume (the stetson, waistcoat, gun-belts, boots, chaps and spurs of the cowboy; the facial paint, feathered head-dress of the Indian; the tight bodiced dress and gartered stockings of the saloon whore, etc.); specificities of props (Colt 45, horses – especially pintos – bows and arrows, etc.); even individual actors (John Wayne, Gary Cooper, Clint Eastwood).

However, if an attention to iconography worked well for western and gangster films, it proved difficult to translate such a visually specific methodology to other kinds of films. For instance, it is difficult to isolate with any clarity distinct iconographic systems for crime films, thrillers, film noirs and most action films. Guns and weaponry are common in each, and unlike the western and gangster film there is not necessarily any historically specific criteria to regulate aspects of setting and costume. Moreover, consideration of comedy and animation once again tends to blunt the usefulness of iconography as a generic arbitrator. In the case of the former there is no connection between the comic elements of a film and specific iconography beyond the incidental deployment of resources (verbal, physical and material) in gag-specific scenarios, while the self-enunciating visual language of animation has an abstract or arbitrary relation to the concept of iconography insofar as the notions of setting, costume and props are always *provisional*.

More nuanced approaches to constructing generic taxonomies seek to weave iconographic elements together with stylistic, formal and thematic elements to conceive genre as 'patterns/forms/styles/structures which transcend individual films, and which supervise both their construction by the film-maker, and their reading by an audience' (Ryall, cited in ibid.: 19). On this account, each genre is a rule-governed territory, one which shares a conventionality not only of visual imagery, but more complexly of particular expectations of plot and narrative structure and how these, in turn, motivate and justify the specificities of props, costume, milieus and subject matter within and across the generic spectrum. Thus, guns are common to westerns, thrillers, gangster films, action films, film noirs, war films and science-fiction films, but their significance, function and consequences differ depending on a host of other contextualising factors established in the narrative and thematic structures of genre films.

Nevertheless, although this inclusive approach to drawing rings around generically similar films does enable discussion of a far broader array of popular genres, like all attempts to produce a taxonomy of cinematic genres it still suffers from a circular logic. Andrew Tudor explains that in order to mine, say, a western for its distinctive generic characteristics the critic must *already* know what those characteristics are in order to identify it as a western in the first place, yet such an identification ought surely to be made on the evidence of the film *after* it has been watched. Thus, the genre critic is 'caught in a circle which first requires that films are isolated, for which purposes a

iconography
A term used to describe and categorise visual motifs in films. It is usually associated with genre insofar as visual patterns of setting, dress, props and style have been used to classify and analyse films generically, but it also shares similarities with **mise-en-scène**.

criterion is necessary, but the criterion is, in turn, meant to emerge from the empirically established common characteristics of the films' (Tudor 1973: 135). The result of this logic, for Tudor at least, is that 'genre is what we collectively believe it to be' (ibid.: 139).

More recently, in an attempt to unearth the grounds for those collective beliefs, critics have turned away from the idea of genre as a textually instituted categorisation, turning instead towards extra-textual formations of genre. This return to history no longer prioritises the film itself as reliable evidence for the definition and circulation of genres, but affords primacy to institutional categories, marketing materials and journalistic practices which are seen to provide original and contemporaneous testimony to generic configurations. Indeed, in recognising the limitations of his earlier, text-centred work, Neale argues that not only do such industrial, cultural and journalistic labels constitute crucial evidence for understanding both the significance of genre to industry and audiences in the present moment, they also offer 'virtually the only available evidence for a historical study of the array of genres in circulation, or of the ways in which individual films have been generically perceived at any one point in time' (1990: 52).

Genre as economic strategy

If taxonomic approaches to genre ask questions such as 'How do we cut cinema at its generic joints?', and 'Have we drawn our lines in the correct places?', then an economic approach to genre asks 'What functions does genre perform?' Steve Neale (1980, 1990) argues that Hollywood's generic regime performs two crucial inter-related functions: to guarantee meanings and pleasures for audiences; and to offset the considerable economic risks of industrial film production by providing cognitive collateral against innovation and difference.

Generic pleasures

Genre works to stabilise or regulate particular desires, expectations and pleasures offered by the cinema. On this account, while genre is not simply an institutionalised strategy to delimit choice, if we choose to watch, say, a horror film then we expect certain pleasures in return: to encounter a monster of some description; that some characters will be killed by the monster while one, usually the lead character, will kill it; and so on. By the same token, each genre implies its own set of desires, expectations and pleasures. Indeed, Neale argues that much of the pleasure of popular cinema lies precisely in the process of 'difference *in* repetition', that is, both in the recognition of the familiar elements of a generic framework *and* in the way individual instances of that genre introduce unfamiliar elements or orchestrate familiar elements in more or less original ways. This process perhaps finds its most refined expression in films such as the *Scream* series which transposes certain familiar elements across successive sequels, most obviously the masked killer, while at the same time incorporating new material into each individual film. Yet the same pull between familiarity and difference is no less crucial to looser generic groupings. For the success of, say, any individual action film, both in terms of the profit it generates and the pleasures it affords audiences, is rooted not simply in its promise to deliver action set-pieces but, more accurately, in the expectation that *the way it delivers its action* will be, at least on some level, notably distinct from other action films.

Genre as an insurance policy

The capital-intensive nature of Hollywood film production requires a market of sufficient size in order to generate surplus to both satisfy investors and plough back into future productions. This means that, as far as possible, the economic risk associated with any individual film must be contained insofar as its potential market must be predictable. Genres, on this view, allow the film industry to offset some of its financial investments against the cognitive collateral of pre-sold generic expectations and pleasures. Neale writes that genres are crucial to industrial modes of film production inasmuch as they 'serve as basic and "convenient" units for the calculation of investment and profit, and as basic and "convenient" categories in which to organise capital assets so as to ensure that their capacity will be utilised to the maximum' (1980: 53). While this economic logic does not account for the existence of mass-produced genres *per se*, nor the emergence and popularity of any one genre at any one time, it nevertheless does, at least in part, explain why Hollywood is a cinema of genres. During the heyday of the studio system this was evidenced in the specialised production schedules of Hollywood's studios.

However, Darley argues that in an age of visual digital culture characterised by aesthetic and economic synthesis between media formats we cannot regard genre in the same way, that cultural production is now organised around principles other than generic ones. He refers to this shift as a 'poetics of repetition', a situation in which 'old categories and boundaries are breaking down, blurring in the face of self-referential impulses spawned by new technological development' (2000: 142). Darley argues that, while the modifying variable, or differential element, of the 'difference in repetition' model of commodity production 'is even more vital today, precisely because of the apparent de-differentiation that is under way', at the same time the markers of difference become 'smaller in scale and simpler in operation: a mechanism for miniscule formal or surface distinctions' (ibid.: 143). Within this intensified mode of commodity production, he claims, the idea of genre is merely nominal, and, moreover, the notion of *seriality* is 'coming to replace or subsume genre in more recent manifestations of mass visual culture' (ibid.: 126):

> Seriality is akin to genre...and yet it is subtly different from it. The serial mode appears to operate and organise – in the first instance at any rate – at a more general or inclusive level than does genre, whilst at the same time being more precise and prescriptive in terms of the processes it defines. Lacking the more open (and involved) character of genre, it appears to be tied as much to the demarcation and regulation of *forms and modes* within material production processes as to the distinguishing of types or kinds (along with their aesthetic delineation) in aesthetic ones. It seems thereby, to be more intimately bound to the standardisation involved in commodification itself.
>
> (Ibid.)

This is instructive for a number or reasons. First, the notion of seriality directs our attention towards Hollywood's predilection for sequels, prequels, series, follow-ups and franchises not in terms of their putative aesthetic paucity, but rather as the most potent distillation, besides re-releases, of the economic imperatives of genre described by Neale. Second, the notion of 'mode' is a more persuasive description of contemporary Hollywood production trends. That is, notions of the blockbuster, special-effects movie, event cinema, spectacle cinema, summer movie, even action cinema which tend to fall outside of, or between, traditional generic groupings, are more plausibly described as *modes* of film-making which, in turn, entail particular modes of viewing. Third, subsuming genre within a broader poetics of repetition which frames contemporary cultural practice permits us to see cinema as an **intermedia**, that is, as thoroughly implicated in a bi-directional system of aesthetic commodification exchange which extends far beyond its own textual and formal borders through merchandising, product tie-ins, product placements, franchise deals, branding, sequels, TV spin-offs, video games, novelisations and so on. In this sense, the notion of film genre dissolves into much more multiple and diverse commercial configurations of *themed entertainment*.

It would, however, be premature to entirely abandon the notion of genre to seriality in an economic analysis of Hollywood cinema. While the term genre struggles to cope with much of contemporary Hollywood in terms of both manufacturing principles and

For a discussion of the cinematic institution in a multimedia age see Chapter 1, pp. 31–33 and pp. 39–40.

intermedia
The relations that exist between cinema, the film industry and other media at the levels of both capitalist business practices and textual forms.

aesthetic classification, the prominence of generic motifs within marketing and promotion campaigns seems to be increasing in importance insofar as, today, 'the commercial drama surrounding a movie's promotion can say as much as the fictional drama of the film itself' (Watson 1997: 79). Indeed, the idea of film as merely a pretext or staging ground for a much more extensive commercial venture often goes hand in hand with marketing strategies which foreground generic discourses in a hypervisible display of its attractions. On this view, the modal seriality of contemporary Hollywood production and the primacy of generic imagery in promotional material are two sides of the same process – the institutionalisation of exploitation cinema: a mode of film production in which textual considerations are subordinate to the considerations of marketing and promotion (ibid.).

> **If you were to invest in a movie, which genre of film-making would you choose in order to offset the financial risk and hopefully make a profit? Who would you want to star in it? List five things that would have to occur in the movie in order for you to sign the cheque. Also, what other merchandising products or tie-ins would you sanction in order to promote your film?**

Genre as cognition

For a discussion of the relationship between the film and its spectator see Chapter 3.

Neale argues that 'genres are not simply bodies of work, however classified, labelled and designed' (1990: 46). On the contrary, he sees genre as being equally constituted by 'specific systems of expectation and hypothesis which spectators bring with them to the cinema and which interact with the films themselves during the course of the viewing process' (ibid.). The clear implication of this observation is that the question of film genre can be posed not merely along industrial and aesthetic axes of the cinematic process, but as a question of film comprehension insofar as cognitive primacy is afforded to the spectator in the act of reading a film. Another way of making this point is to say that the question of film genre is, in fact, part of a much broader question to do with cultural cognition and structures of visual communication. As such, the purpose of genre criticism can be regarded as an inquiry into how we make meaning from film.

On this cognitive view, textual conventions are important not as a means of dissecting cinema into discrete categories, but instead for the way they activate certain mental processes in what Jonathan Culler calls the 'operations of reading'. Culler argues that 'the function of genre conventions is essentially to establish a contract between writer and reader so as to make certain relevant expectations operative and thus permit both compliance and deviation from accepted modes of intelligibility' (1975: 147). As he suggests, acts of communication are rendered intelligible only within the context of a shared, conventional framework of expression. Ryall notes that for Hollywood films this communal framework is provided by the generic system, which constructs a framework for comprehension, an 'ideal world' or 'fictional reality' through which the individual film 'sustains at least some of its levels of comprehensibility and maybe its dominant level of comprehensibility' (1998: 336).

Genre, here, becomes understood not as a corpus of approximate films, but as provisional and malleable conceptual environments: a cognitive repository of images, sounds, characters, events, stories, scenarios, expectations and so on. Genre can thus be seen as part of a cognitive process which delimits the number of possible meanings of any individual film by activating certain conceptual constellations while leaving others dormant.

Such a cognitive view of film genre not only forestalls the taxonomic impulse of earlier genre criticism by reformulating genre as fundamentally an intertextual process, but is more sensitive to what Jim Collins (1995: 133) calls the '**sophisticated hyperconsciousness**' of contemporary Hollywood cinema. Collins argues that in the same way that television changed the production, circulation and consumption of popular entertainment during the 1950s and 1960s, contemporary Hollywood cinema marks a 'new form of entertainment', one which is simultaneously a response and a contribution to media saturated culture (ibid.: 156). 'Genericity' is the term he coins in order to describe the shift in production and consumption initiated 'by the ever increasing number of entertainment options and the fragmentation of what was once thought to be a mass audience into a cluster of "target audiences"' (ibid.: 128). Indeed, the eclecticism and appropriationism of popular cinema today involves levels of hybridity and intertextuality that work 'at cross-purposes with the traditional notion of genre as a stable, integrated set of narrative and stylistic conventions' (ibid.: 126). In short, many contemporary Hollywood films are composed almost entirely from generic elements hijacked from the image banks of both popular and high culture and reassembled in ways that either circumnavigate, short-circuit or contradict singular generic understanding.

For example, *Moulin Rouge*'s giddy assemblage of cinematic references, historical intertexts and cultural allusions simultaneously *defies* singular generic categorisation yet *implies* a high degree of prior orientation with precisely those generic formations in order to comprehend their disorientation and rearticulation. So while on one level the film can be described generically, and was promoted generically – as a musical which tells of the tragic love affair between a penniless writer and a starlet showgirl – this actually tells us very little either about the semiotic excess of the film or the cultural literacy it demands of its audience. Likewise, if, as many critics have hinted, *Moulin Rouge* redefines the film musical, it does so partly by wrenching itself free of musical conventions and hooking up with a range of other generic formations, most obviously the music video and MTV, but also Bollywood, television advertisements, computer animation and virtual reality. Indeed, almost every shot is an ironic collage of popular cultural images and sounds, conjuring up a highly eclectic range of intertexts from the past and the present in a sophisticated **palimpsest** image. The result is a text which is simultaneously *decorative* – demanding to be looked at – and *dense* – demanding to be read *through*.

The engorgement of the opening scene, for instance, recalls the set-piece dance extravaganzas of Busby Berkeley's Warner musicals, while Satine (Nicole Kidman) begs comparison to Lola Lola, the Cabaret artist played by Marlene Dietrich in *The Blue Angel* (1930). The sequence unfolds to a dizzyingly anachronistic soundtrack which mixes, amongst others, Nirvana, Madonna, Fat Boy Slim, Marilyn Manson, Marilyn Monroe, Elton John, David Bowie and Christina Aguilera together with vocal performances by Ewan McGregor, Nicole Kidman and Jim Broadbent in a *belle époque* milieu. The intertextual density of the sequence sacrifices notions of historical authenticity and artistic originality to an aesthetic process of uncontained **recombinacy**. Graham Fuller has traced some of the intertextual levels of pastiche, irony, quotation and allusion at work in just one image of this sequence.

[T]he film proceeds [through] innumerable quotations, which shock with risky recontextualisation of famous pop moments. This can lead to bizarre self-reflexivity…When Satine descends on a swing above the slavering punters in the Moulin Rouge, she is dressed as Marlene Dietrich in the *Blue Angel*. The song she sings (in a raspy Rosalind Russell voice) is Marilyn Monroe's 'Diamonds Are a Girls Best Friend' from *Gentlemen Prefer Blondes*. But when she segues into 'Material Girl', it's not simply Madonna who is inscribed, but Monroe again, since in her video for the song Madonna is dressed as Monroe in her pink gown from the 'Diamonds' number.

(2001: 16)

---

sophisticated hyper-consciousness
A term used by Jim Collins to describe the extreme 'knowingness' and high degree of media literacy evinced by both contemporary cinema and its audience.

For a reading of Memento (Chris Nolan, 2000) as an example of Postmodern film-making and subversive mainstream narrative, see Chapter 2, pp. 87–89.

palimpsest
Defined literally, a palimpsest is a manuscript written over a previous text that has been entirely or partly erased. In a figurative sense, however, the term is often used to describe a film or text with multiple levels of meaning created through dense layers of **intertextuality**. In this way, the term has become associated with **postmodern** aesthetics.

recombinacy
The aesthetic process of combing elements drawn from a range of genres, styles, forms and periods in a new text/film. This is one of the principal aesthetic strategies of **postmodern** art. (See also **eclecticism**, **intertextuality**, **palimpsest** and **self-reflexivity**.)

• **Plate 4.4**
Nicole Kidman as the
showgirl Satine in
Moulin Rouge (Baz
Luhrmann, 2001)
The scene proceeds
through a hypercon-
scious appropriation of a
vast range of both cine-
matic and musical texts
rendering it simultane-
ously generic and
post-generic.

Moreover, much of the film's dialogue is a montage of lines pillaged from the lyrics of popular ballads, love songs and well-known literature. 'Love is a many-splendoured thing, love lifts us up where we belong, all you need is love' Christian (Ewan McGregor) waxes lyrical to Satine. And as Fuller notes, the film's pathos is almost entirely gener-ated through the 'recasting of modern pop standards' (ibid.: 14). Thus Christian's seduction of Satine is conducted as a medley of popular love songs, while McGregor's rendition of Elton John's 'Your Song' acts as the film's emotional refrain.

As such, *Moulin Rouge*'s textual articulations are, in fact, double articulations insofar as its images and sounds relate to both the internal narrative and aesthetic 'life' of the film as well as to their external 'lives' in popular culture. In this way, then, *Moulin Rouge*, like so much of contemporary Hollywood, presents us with a generic paradox: simulta-neously being *post-generic* in the sense that the hyperconsciousness of its text spills over singular classificatory boundaries yet attaining intelligibility precisely in relation to those generic formations.

RETHINKING GENRE AS METAPHOR

It is at this point that we are able to rethink film genre not as a literal concept – as either inventories of comparable films or as an economic explanation for Hollywood's production trends – but as a *metaphorical process*. Describing film genre as a *web of metaphorical expressions* allows us to capture in our analyses some of the 'liveness', volatility and malleability of contemporary (post)generic configurations by hooking up understandings of film cognition with aesthetic and industrial aspects of the cinematic process. Another way of putting this is to say that it helps us explain *why* genre can only ever be what we collectively believe it to be. For metaphors in themselves do not tell us anything, but rather draw attention to a *relationship* between things and prompt us to start looking for ways of making meaning. Indeed, the basis of metaphor is a process of *transference*: the transference of aspects of one object to another object so that the second object has an *implied resemblance* to the first object, yet is an original expression. It is precisely the ideas of *transference* and *implied resemblance* that help us describe genre as a metaphorical process. Thus film genre becomes understood as a metaphorical redescription, reworking or redeployment of cinematic and cultural vocabularies. Individual films, likewise, become original in precisely the ways they *interfere* with those vocabularies, that is to say, in the ways they deviate from the implied intertexts which form the reservoir of cognitive resemblances that make comprehension possible. Such a metaphoric conception of film genre focuses attention on the *nature* of textual transference and the process of *interference* between intertexts, that is, on the ways in which a film deploys familiar things in unfamiliar ways.

To see the operations of genre not as a literal, circumscribed process, but as a metaphorical process is to stop asking questions such as, 'To what genre does *Moulin Rouge* belong?', and to restrict ourselves to more pragmatic questions such as, 'What other cultural objects does *Moulin Rouge* resemble?', and 'How does it cause us to compare it to other experiences?' So while on the one hand we can say that *Moulin Rouge*'s opening shot of Montmartre looks *as if* it were shot by the Lumière brothers, and that Kidman sounds *like* Madonna and Monroe, on the other hand these are not literal transferrals – it is not Lumière footage and it is Kidman's voice we hear – but metaphorical expressions that alter the meanings of those extrapolations in the specific relationship of their rearticulation. It is here that a metaphorical conception of genre chimes with cognitive approaches in the sense that the spectator has to *do* something: to explore the nature of the assemblage, transferrals and interferences in the act of comprehending the film.

Equally crucial here is the idea that metaphors are constantly being renewed, with old ones dying off and forming part of the cultural 'memory bank' which itself serves as the foil for the creation of new ones. In other words, *Moulin Rouge*'s kaleidoscope of generic metaphors are themselves unrepeatable, but will be assimilated into our shared cognitive frameworks which throws future metaphors of expression into relief. One example of this process from the film would be Madonna's 'Material Girl' video which at the time of its release itself comprised a complex set of metaphorical relations that have, over time, become a literalised part of our popular culture but are rearticulated in *Moulin Rouge* as part of a new metaphorical expression.

On this account, then, genre not only becomes a cognitive mechanism of film comprehension, but also one of the most important principles by which cinema advances, changes and develops. For metaphors stretch cultural expression by casting about for unpredictable resemblances, surprising relationships and unexpected association so that, in the process of watching a film, we have to constantly revise our hypotheses and expectations to fit the new material. And, of course, the notions of 'transference' and 'implied resemblance' are not only useful for explicating the film text, but can be mapped in relation to other industrial and commercial practices as well, from the way a producer assembles a production package; to the way a film is promoted to its audience; to the broader commercial ventures it entails. Indeed, rethinking genre as a metaphorical process allows us to situate the textual analysis of film within the context of a hypercommodity culture of symbolic exchange which sees cinema's product both being derived from and exploited across the full range of information and entertainment platforms.

☐ CASE STUDY 3: *THE MATRIX* (WACHOWSKI BROTHERS, 1999)

In looking to identify exemplars of contemporary Hollywood we could do worse than start with *The Matrix* (Larry and Andy Wachowski, 1999). For some of the most salient textual and industrial characteristics of recent modes of Hollywood film production crystallise in its technical virtuosity, stylised mise-en-scène, high-octane narrative and digital visual effects. In this case study we shall pursue two, complementary, ways in which *The Matrix* can be read as paradigmatic of generic configurations in post-Classical Hollywood: First as an example of the high-concept blockbuster; and second, as one of the most interesting instances of the fusion between Hollywood and Hong Kong film genres symptomatic of contemporary Hollywood's transcultural style.

For more information on 'the blockbuster film', see Chapter 1, pp. 26–28. Also see Chapter 2, pp. 55–59 for a case study of Spider-Man *and further discussion of cinema as spectacle.*

The blockbuster

The notion of the blockbuster enjoys widespread use by academics, journalists and audiences, not to mention within the film industry itself. Thomas Schatz argues that the rise of the blockbuster since the mid-1970s is 'the key to Hollywood's survival' and, moreover, is what post-Classical Hollywood 'is about' (1993: 8, 11). And while blockbusters constitute a relatively small percentage of Hollywood's overall output, they nevertheless account for a significant percentage of its global box-office revenues as well as for crucial profits derived from intermedia and other secondary markets. However, despite the utter dominance of the blockbuster as a cultural form – and its cognate labels, summer movie, Christmas movie, event-cinema, special-effects film – there remains little agreement amongst critics whether it constitutes a circumscribed *genre* of film, or a *mode* of post-industrial film production. Yet, on the other hand, critics who have attempted to deal with the blockbuster in formal and aesthetic terms have overwhelmingly reverted to the idea of *spectacle* as a watchword for describing its technologically dense surfaces and highly engineered effects. 'Spectacle', here, is not just descriptive of the technological sophistication of the blockbuster, or approbative of its proclivity towards spectacular visual effects, but refers to more complex transformations in film production techniques, Hollywood's role within global media markets, and to the nature of the pleasures cinema affords its audiences. Indeed, the blockbuster is commonly equated with the idea of 'high-concept' cinema.

High-concept films are market-driven, multi-functional entertainment products that are not only 'pitched' to studios and pre-sold to audiences on the basis of marketable assets – star, director, genre, special effects – but also showcase a series of further merchandising and franchise profit streams. Aesthetically speaking, many critics have noted the centrality of 'style' and 'stylisation' to the blockbuster. In other words, blockbusters tend to be structured around 'loosely linked, self-contained action sequences often built around spectacular stunts, stars and special effects' rather than the 'psychologically motivated cause–effect narrative logic' associated with classical Hollywood genres (Buckland 1998: 167). Moreover, 'deep' character psychology and complex character development are sacrificed to instrumental characterisation, that is, a device around which to organise a procession of quasi-autonomous set-piece extravaganzas. Not only is 'the story' no longer the blockbuster's principal attraction, but the idea of narrative containment of spectacle, that is, the idea that moments of visual excess or virtuosity are motivated by generic or narrative causality 'has crumbled in a manner that is quite unprecedented' (Darley 2000: 106). Indeed, one dominant characteristic of the blockbuster is its post-generic mode of address. That is to say, the blockbuster does not *merely* reconfigure plot and character in more complex hybrid generic formations – although it is still possible to discern various combinations of action-adventure, science-fiction, comedy, romance, thriller and so forth within the blockbuster – but increasingly exalts the sheer spectacle of the image itself as its key means of addressing the audience. Darley argues that reception of contemporary blockbusters, replete with impossible digital effects that are seamlessly integrated into the image, 'depends as much on a *fascinated spectator*, immersed in dazzling and "spellbinding" imagery, as on identification with character and the machinations of plot and theme' (ibid.: 107). The indistinguishable nature of digital imagery and unlimited aesthetic potential of computer animation techniques have, he claims, led to a 'new register of illusionist spectacle' in the blockbuster (ibid.: 103). This is not only a cinema of kinaesthetic thrills, vicarious physical danger and visceral sensations, but a visually sensuous and decorative cinema. As such, Darley suggests that the fascination of the blockbuster involves a curiosity with the material excess of the image, an image of such technological density that it vies with narrative for the 'perceptual attentions of the spectator' (ibid.: 114). Films such as *The Abyss* (1989), *Terminator 2: Judgement Day* (1991), *Jurassic Park* (1993), *Speed* (1994), *True Lies* (1994), *Independence Day* (1996), *Twister* (1996), *Titanic* (1997), *Volcano* (1997), *Men in Black* (1997), *The Lost World: Jurassic*

Park (1997), *Armageddon* (1998), *Deep Impact* (1998), *The Matrix* (1999), *The Mummy* (1999), *Gladiator* (2000), *Mission Impossible II* (2000), *X-men* (2000), *The Mummy Returns* (2001), *Pearl Harbour* (2001), *Lara Croft: Tomb Raider* (2001), *Artificial Intelligence: AI* (2001), *Minority Report* (2002) and *Men in Black II* (2002) can thus be understood as spectacle cinema, or event-films, as particular instances of the block-buster. The following list attempts to schematise the ways in which traditional understandings of genre are postponed, abandoned or reworked by the blockbuster, and how the blockbuster itself needs to be situated as part of a broader economic and cultural picture.

Classical Hollywood	Post-Classical Hollywood
Genre (westerns etc.)	Post-genre (blockbuster)
Narrative	Spectacle
Story / plot	Special effects / image
Structure	Surface
Psychology	Viscerality / sensation
Pleasure	Excitement
Absorption	Fascination
Text	Intertext / palimpsest
Iconography	Recombinacy
Photographic	Post-photographic / digital
Exhibition	Event / marketing
Studio / contract	Package / deal
Social	Global

The Matrix neatly fits this model of the blockbuster. It is a high-concept movie, assembled around veteran action-film producer Joel Silver and the writing and directo-rial partnership of Larry and Andy Wachowski working as a semi-independent unit yet reliant on a major studio, Warner Bros. in this case, for international distribution. Moreover, the film itself is only a stitch in a much more elaborate marketing and commodity tapestry comprising two sequels, two soundtrack CDs, video cassette, two DVD releases, not to mention a host of merchandising, tie-in and franchise deals (posters, shooting script and other print publications, sunglasses, mobile phones, comic books and so on).

Although on the one hand the film evinces a number of narrative and stylistic resem-blances to science-fiction, action-adventure, fantasy, thriller and martial arts genres, on the other hand no singular or hyphenated generic configuration adequately accounts for what Peter Hutchings (1999) calls its 'spectacularly allusive' yet 'supremely indifferent' intertextuality. Another way of putting this would be to say that it invokes a range of genres, indeed, a range of cultural forms, but is itself beyond generic classification as it is traditionally understood.

Hutchings' review is instructive in one other way. In struggling to account for why *The Matrix* appears as 'something special, something more than the usual blockbuster', he rules out its derivative plot and routine characterisation, instead hinting that its fasci-nation lies in the 'sublime beauty' of its 'completely impossible' images. Likewise, Roger Ebert (1999), film critic for the *Chicago Sun-Times*, argues that its plot is a shop-worn conceit that recycles 'the same tired ideas'. However, despite its routine narrative, he sees *The Matrix*'s 'visually dazzling' surfaces as a virtue: '[I]ts [a] great looking [film], both in its design and in the kinetic energy that powers it. It uses flawlessly integrated special effects and animation to visualise regions of cyberspace' (ibid.). As such, even though narrative is not completely annihilated in the film it is precisely its spectacular technological thrills, that is, precisely the *sensational* and *sensuous* nature of its images that fascinate in the first instance.

For instance, the film opens with Trinity (Carrie-Ann Moss) seemingly trapped in a hotel room, hemmed in by two units of cops as well as three agents of the artificial intelligence that controls the world. However, just before the handcuffs snap around her wrist, Trinity, in one assured and perfect movement, grabs the cop's arm, spins underneath it and, after breaking his nose with a deft punch, springs into the air (Plate 4.5). Using a visual-effect technique called flow-motion (developed especially for the film and dubbed 'bullet-time photography' by the Wachowski Brothers) which combines hyper-slow motion and dynamic camera movement, Trinity's body appears to hover in mid-air, defying the laws of time, space and gravity as the 'virtual' camera impossibly circles her balletic pose.

As she reaches the apex of her leap, and as the camera completes its tour of this sublime image, spatio-temporal order is re-engaged as a lightning-fast kick dispatches the cop into the opposite wall. As his partners unload their arsenal of firepower, Trinity turns, and with astonishing grace runs up and around three walls, spins off, and kills her aggressors paralysed by the brutal beauty of what they had just witnessed. Indeed, like those bewildered cops, the audience is fascinated at the sheer *excess* of this sequence: the metaphysical performance of Trinity's body, the fantastical mise-en-scène, the perceptible yet credulous impossibility of the imagery; in short, the spectacular nature of the technological and aesthetic display. Thus, along with Hutchings, we can say that, at least on the level of the text, it is the 'permission to watch' the excess of the image that defines the contemporary blockbuster, and that *The Matrix* is perhaps *not* something *more* than the usual blockbuster, but exemplary of it.

Hollywood–Hong-Kong: action–martial arts

Given that the blockbuster seems such a snug description of *The Matrix*'s aesthetic and commercial energies, why suggest another level of generic analysis? The question brings us back to the inadequacy of the term 'genre' for capturing the artistic and economic complexity of contemporary Hollywood. For it is one thing to say that 'the blockbuster' is descriptive of the dominant *mode* of Hollywood film-making, but quite another to then read individual films *merely* as blockbusters. Thomas Elsaesser makes a useful distinction between macro- and micro-level connections which frame analysis of the blockbuster. The macro-level refers to the 'relations that exist between the film industry and other forms of capitalist business practice', the web of vertical and horizontal synergies which feed into and off of cinema. The micro-level, on the other

• **Plate 4.5**
Carrie-Ann Moss as Trinity defying the laws of physics in *The Matrix* (Wachowski Brothers, 1999)
This is not only perhaps the most definitive and parodied scene of recent Hollywood cinema, but exemplary of the contemporary block-buster's blend of generic registers and spectacular imagery

hand, refers to more specific 'pleasure oriented connections' (2001: 13). As such, while at a macro-level blockbusters have a strong modal similarity insofar as their astronomical budgets demand profits be procured from the widest range of secondary markets, at the micro-level of the text itself the term blockbuster often hides as much as it reveals. In other words, an appreciation of genre as a macro-level description of Hollywood's high-concept, high-stakes mode of production should not be at the expense of the particular pleasures of the blockbuster. Nor should it mask various formal and aesthetic differences within that mode. Indeed, if we pursue genre as a micro-level question of metaphorical expressions, that is, in terms of implied resemblances and transferences crystallised in the text, then *The Matrix* offers up other readings that complement its macro-level status as a blockbuster.

If *The Matrix* is exemplary of the blockbuster as a cinematic commodity, then as a text it is simultaneously a sophisticated blend of American and Asian cultural forms. Or more precisely, reading the micro-level metaphorical connections at work in *The Matrix* reveals a congestion of transferences and resemblances from Hollywood's action-adventure, science-fiction and thriller genres as well as from the martial arts tradition of film-making popularised in Hong Kong and China. This intertextual overload works on multiple levels. Most obviously, the scene in which Morpheus (Laurence Fishburne) trains Neo (Keanu Reeves) in the art of kung fu explicitly combines a science-fiction narrative thread with the kinaesthetic performance of the martial arts film. In other words, the mise-en-scène of the Chinese kung fu school at once resembles that found in scores of martial arts films yet in this scene is appropriated for, and motivated by, a science-fiction narrative logic, and is thus reinterpreted as part of a computer simulation programme. This process of rearticulation not only disturbs generic codes *per se* by laying one cultural expression upon another so that they interpenetrate, but also wrenches the images free from their historical and traditional contexts: Chinese architecture and the cultural meanings imbibed in it are abstracted from history and relocated in an imagined future which is replayed in the present. Such *interference* between past, present and future, East and West, is also evident in the choreography and execution of the combat sequence. First, Neo and Morpheus' bout freely mixes Northern Leg and Southern Fist styles of fighting with the more preposterous and stylised tradition derived from the Peking Opera. Thus, the grounded combat combines intricate fist and arm techniques with more flashy jumping, spinning and kicking. Moreover, the kinaesthetic thrill of the aerial acrobatics is a more complex articulation which draws not only on stunt techniques developed in Peking Opera, but also on Buddhist metaphysical motifs and popular Chinese literature. However, while the superhuman powers of the Ninjas in Ang Lee's *Crouching Tiger, Hidden Dragon* (2000) are culturally specific, motivated by Chinese religious, literary and cinematic traditions, the same performance of impossible physical acts in *The Matrix* is reinterpreted and rearticulated as part of the science-fiction narrative. So while the aesthetic of airborne combat (achieved by a precise system of wires and pulleys as well as physical technique) associated with veteran martial arts action choreographer, director and stunt co-ordinator, Yuen Woo-Ping, is crucial to both films' breathtaking fight sequences, its cultural meaning and narrative significance is drastically modified by the differing generic context in which it is framed. Second, given the collocation of sci-fi and martial arts genres, what is often referred to as the pleasure of pure movement of the latter, precisely its proximity to dance, becomes, in its imbrication with the former, a pleasure of fantastical movement inasmuch as physical performance is exaggerated through special effects. Thus Neo is seen to fight at speeds faster than the human eye can register, an image made possible by digital post-production techniques. In this respect, generic boundaries and cultural traditions are supplanted by the primacy of spectacle, the important questions of narrative plausibility and historical authenticity subsumed into the all-important question of 'what looks good?' And while the martial arts film has always been concerned with preposterous acts of physical violence – and to that end has itself played fast and loose with tradition and style – and the action film trades on the exuberance of its set-pieces, then *The Matrix* can be read as a new order in trans-cultural film-making, one which recombines elements from a range of genres in a manner which postpones generic classification.

Crucially, however, these various generic echoes are not simply *mixed* together, but *remixed* into an eclectic techno-aesthetic comprised from cinema, of course, but also from video games, anime, comic books, pop videos, cyberpunk novels and postmodern philosophy, all rendered through a seamless fusion of live action and computer anima-tion. Indeed, the film lays one image upon another and runs one form into the next to the extent that they colligate to form a distinctive cinematic form which is neither generic in the classificatory sense of the term, nor entirely rid of generic traces, but which rearticulates genre through an intertextual web of metaphor. In this sense, the final showdown between Neo and Agent Smith (Hugo Weaving) in the subway (Plate. 4.6) is not merely a hybrid of cinematic genres, but more complexly a colligation of transcultural visual, formal and mythic metaphors.

The scene opens with serious of shots which mimic a classic stand-off between two gunslingers. However, we are not in a nineteenth-century frontier town of the western genre, but in a computer simulation of a present-day subway sometime in the future. A sheet of newspaper blows through the frame self-consciously recalling the tumbleweed so indelibly linked with the iconography of the western. But as guns are drawn we don't cut to a wide-angle shot showing the outlaw being killed by the hero, but instead see Neo and Smith rushing toward each other unleashing a barrage of gunfire. Simultaneously they leap into the air and continue on their collision course in flight. Grappling in mid-air, they exchange punches and bullets as the camera whisks us around this impossible display of physical grace, scarcely giving us time to catch our breath before rejoining with the dizzying hand-to-hand combat assaults.

• **Plate 4.6** Neo (Keanu Reeves) and Agent Smith (Hugo Weaving) in the final showdown of *The Matrix* (Wachowski Brothers, 1999)
The scene is a multi-layered mix of generic forms drawn from American and Asian culture

The main point, here, however, is that the sequence does not merely weave martial arts techniques into the narrative fabric of the action-adventure genre, but implies an intermedia set of generic metaphors at the level of style. For instance, the elaborate nature of the fight itself, staged in a spatially finite environment, resembles the aesthetic and formal logic of beat 'em up computer games such as *Mortal Kombat*, *Street Fighter*, *Tekken* and *Virtua Fighter*. Moreover, the hyperstylised mise-en-scène owes much to graphic traditions of comic book art, not to mention the post-apocalyptic, mutant aesthetic of much Japanese anime. Indeed, in some important respects, *The Matrix* is better understood as part of those graphic and animation traditions than simply as an extension of the action-adventure genre.

Choose a film to see at the cinema and before watching it:

1 **Describe why you chose the film that you did and consider the way your own taste in movies might relate to particular genres.**
2 **Describe what you expect to happen in the film; where you expect the action to be set; what props are likely to be present; and how you think the film will end?**
3 **Investigate how notions of genre are used in the promotion and marketing of the film. These can range from the film poster, trailers, TV spots, product tie-ins, soundtrack CDs, and so forth. How do these strategies use generic codes to pre-sell the movie to you?**

After watching the film:

4 **Explore how closely your answer to (2) relates to what actually happened in the film. To what extent does the movie's genre foreclose narrative possibilities and guarantee certain pleasures?**
5 **Make a list of all the films, TV programmes, pop videos etc. that the film prompted you to think of while watching it. Did it quote, copy, resemble or allude to any other films or texts?**
6 **Consider the range of genres present in the film and how they were manifested. How did the film 'play' with generic conventions?**

Stars and Hollywood cinema

[Gwyneth] Paltrow, in short, is not just a star. She can really act.

(Michael Billington 2002)

INTRODUCTION: THREE APPROACHES TO STARDOM

When is an actor also a star? What is the relationship between performance and stardom? What stake does the star hold in the processes of film production? Is there a difference between stardom and celebrity? And why are film stars so fascinating and alluring to us? These are some of the questions that will be addressed in this section. Yet, while these questions have always proved troubling to rigorous academic scrutiny, as we enter into cinema's third century in the all-consuming context of hypermediated culture, the answers to such questions become even more complex.

Star as commodity

Until recently there were three principal ways in which critics addressed the question of stardom. The first locates the star within the economic contexts of film production and film marketing. During the era of the studio system, in which creative and technical personnel were tied to long-term contracts, stars 'provided one of the principal means by which Hollywood offered audiences guarantees of predictability' by embodying a set of particular expectations and, by extension, particular kinds of pleasure (Maltby and Craven 1995: 92). Since the collapse of the studio system in the 1950s, stars have become arguably the key element of the 'package' around which movies are produced. Susan Hayward explains that 'producers will put up money for films that include the latest top star' and 'stars can attract financial backing for a film that otherwise might not get off the ground' (1996: 339). Moreover, even a cursory glance at the promotional material surrounding a film's launch – posters, trailers, interviews in print, on TV and online, as well as a host of further merchandising products – reveals the considerable stake stars hold in announcing its presence and generating an audience of sufficient size to recoup costs. On this account, then, the star is understood as a specific form of *industrial commodity* insofar as, like genre, stars are a 'mechanism for selling movie tickets' by guaranteeing certain pleasures and enacting a commercial strategy for marketing films (Maltby and Craven 1995: 89). However, a star's commercial capacity is inextricably bound up with their ability to 'be liked' by large amounts of people from a range of cultural and national contexts. The remaining two approaches to studying stars are sensitive to these more social and psychic aspects of stardom inasmuch as they turn away from industrial questions, focusing instead on the ways in which the figure of the film star generates specific meanings and pleasures.

Star as text

Thus, the second approach seeks to understand the star as a sign, more precisely as an *image* constructed through a network of intertextuality. This blend of semiotics, sociology and ideological criticism is the most familiar approach to questions of stardom and is associated most strongly with the seminal work of Richard Dyer (1979). Indeed, so influential is Dyer's work that the critical vocabulary it proposes for discussing stars has provided the centre of critical gravity for almost twenty five years to the extent that it is virtually impossible to discuss stardom without nodding in its direction. Central to this approach is the idea that stars are not reducible to flesh-and-blood actors but are conceived as 'complex personas made up of far more than the texts in which they appear' (Tasker 1993: 74). There are two important implications of this observation. First, while on the one hand stardom is literally *embodied* by real human beings and is, to a significant extent, therefore anchored by that person's name, physical appearance, voice quality and specific performance skills, on the other hand 'we never know them as real people, only as they are found in media texts' (Dyer 1979: 2). The second, and related, point is that stardom manifests not only in the films in which a star appears, but across all kinds of other 'official' and 'unofficial' media texts in which the star may or may not appear in person: publicity and marketing materials, newspapers, magazines, television, web sites, DVD 'special features', biographies and so forth. Indeed, within this web of intertextuality 'the star' itself becomes understood, and thus *understandable* as a specific form of text just insofar as stardom is only accessible to us through texts, and thus only *exists* as a text. The crucial point here, however, is, as Paul McDonald notes, that 'the study of stars as texts…cannot be limited to the analysis of specific films or star performances' since they are precisely 'the product of intertextuality in which the non-filmic texts of promotion, publicity and criticism interact with the film text…In other words, the star's image cannot be known outside this shifting series of texts' (1995: 83). On this account, the aim of star studies is not to peel away these layers of textuality in order to reveal the *true* self of the star, but to analyse the explicit and implicit meanings of precisely that mediated image and to read it in the context of wider ideological and social discourses.

Star as 'object of desire'

Whereas the intertextual approach focuses on the ways in which stars are realised in and through texts, the third principal approach addresses the *consumption* of stars. Indeed, if the audience remains *implicit* in the 'star as text' approach as the locus of meaning, the point where the star image is (re)constructed through the act of reading, then the politics of spectatorship and the pleasures of 'star-gazing' form the explicit foci of work which theorises the star–spectator relationship. James Donald argues that while spectatorship 'is the most hotly disputed question in the whole study of stars' there is, nevertheless, 'a good case for starting not with the return on capital invested in film production, but with the unquantifiable returns on our emotional investments in…those moments of erotic contemplation of the spectacular figure of the star' (1999: 39). On this account, the star is seen, first and foremost, as an object of desire and is studied in terms of the ways in which spectators identify with, find meaning in, and gain a certain fulfilment from, his or her image. Perhaps the most influential strain of this approach is an offshoot of feminist psychoanalytic work on gender which theorises the orchestration of visual pleasure in cinema. Classically, the female star is held to be a sexualised spectacle which disrupts narrative momentum in moments of erotic exhibitionism which exceed the bounds of the story; by contrast, the male star/hero is located as an ideal ego who controls the narrative and is thus the central mechanism for audience identification. More recently, Jackie Stacey's (1994) work has attempted to ground this attention to pleasure and spectatorship in the study of *actual audiences*, that is, historically situated movie-goers. In contrast to the general, theoretical explanation of why audiences like stars offered by psychoanalysis, Stacey develops an ethnographic approach to the star–spectator relationship which uses a combination of interviews with, and surveys of, viewers, as well as information drawn from their personal letters and diaries. From this primary data, Stacey catalogues the different ways in which female viewers respond to, identify with, and use images of stars. As such, unlike the universalising tendencies of psychoanalytic methods, Stacey is able to distinguish between various modes of identification and different types of pleasure.

For a discussion of gender, spectatorship and psychoanalysis, see Chapter 7, pp. 247–256.

For a discussion of Stacey's analysis of Desperately Seeking Susan, *see Chapter 7, p. 255.*

WHEN IS A STAR NOT A STAR?

These three approaches to stardom have held sway in film studies since the late 1970s. And as Geraghty (2000) notes, the definition of stardom that has emerged from these approaches has tended to turn on a series of dualities: between a star's performing presence and their off-screen existence, between actor and character, glamour and ordinariness, and between public and private spheres. As such, she argues that, generally speaking, 'the model for work on stars and their audiences has been that of an unstable and contradictory figure, constructed both intertextually (across different films) and extratextually (across different types of material)' (ibid.: 85). Indeed, it is precisely this putative *instability* of the film star, that is to say, the way a star might mean a number of potentially conflicting things, that has underwritten academic work on stars to the extent that, until recently, hardly anyone has noticed that such work has almost entirely been forged in the shadow cast by the star system and the stars who were deemed exemplify its operations. So although the practice of tying stars into long-term fixed contracts which ceded overall control over their public and private image to the studio was over by the 1950s, the sub-discipline of star studies remains heavily influenced by the critical vocabulary used to analyse figures such as Marilyn Monroe, James Cagney, Humphrey Bogart, Marlene Dietrich, Greta Garbo and so on. Even when critics have addressed stars from later eras, they have overwhelmingly tended to transpose the critical terminology established to describe stardom in the heyday of the studio system without necessarily worrying about its potential unsuitability for later socio-economic formations. Nor, for that matter, has there been any serious or sustained interrogation of that critical terminology and the analytical categories it proposes beyond minor tweaks or the odd extension. In short, recent work on stars has tended to proceed by simply *applying* the conceptual models established in Dyer's work to more contemporary figures of film stardom.

Stardom in the digital age

Today, however, the question of stardom is considerably more vexing than it was in the 1970s when the groundwork for star studies was being laid. In the first instance, the term 'star' itself is now culturally hierarchised alongside the celebrity, the superstar and the megastar. As such, the notion of stardom has undergone significant broadening in the sense that we now routinely speak of pop stars, rock stars, soap stars, star footballers and stars of sport generally, star DJs, star artists, star buildings, star fashion designers, star models, star politicians, even star academics. If cinema once provided 'the ultimate confirmation of stardom' (Gledhill 1991: xiii), then the growing number of Hollywood films which co-opt stars confirmed in other areas of the entertainment industries (pop princesses Jennifer Lopez, Madonna, Britney Spears, Beyoncé Knowles, Whitney Houston and Mandy Moore; WWF champion, The Rock; ex-fashion model Cameron Diaz; as well as a host of talent drawn from television, George Clooney being perhaps the most visible) certainly seems to question cinema's presumed privileged relationship to stardom.

For a discussion of the implications of digital technologies in cinema, see Chapter 6, pp. 232–235.

synthespians
A recently coined term which describes 'virtual' or non-human actors. The term relates to digitally scanned or motion-captured versions of 'real' actors, as well as entirely computer-generated characters.

In the second instance, in the information age and in the wake of transformations brought about by digital image-making technologies and computer animation, 'the definition of "film" as an object of study has not only broadened considerably but has also been destabilized as an object and form' (Sobchack 2000: 301). In this way, not only is there now a new breed of **synthespians** or computer-generated stars to contend with (in this respect figures such as Buzz Lightyear, Woody, Sully, Mike, Shrek, Donkey and Jar Jar Binks are perhaps the apotheosis of the economic logic of the star system), but increasingly the 'star' of the movie is more plausibly described as a digital entity or special effect (a twister, tsunami, volcano or storm; prehistoric dinosaurs, or mutant reptiles; a mythical, spiritual or fantastical force; or an earth-threatening or city-destroying catastrophe of either natural or alien doing). Thus, in uncoupling the filmic image and the cinematic process from photographic technology the notion of the film star is now neither necessarily a flesh-and-blood human, nor for that matter even a character in the traditional sense of the term. As such, the guest appearance at the 2002 Academy Awards of Sully and Mike from PIXAR's *Monsters Inc.* (2001) and Donkey and the titular star of Dreamworks' *Shrek* (2001) not only marked the arrival of a dedicated Oscar for the 'Best Animated Feature', but also highlights these more complex articulations of stardom in contemporary popular culture, articulations which cause us not to entirely supplant the dominant models for analysing stars, but to rethink the concepts and descriptions we use to account for these *different modes of stardom.*

Geraghty argues that while the term star should not simply be abandoned because of its non-specific, catch-all nature, we do, however, need to examine contemporary configurations of film stardom within the broader contexts of popular entertainment and media culture: 'Film stardom…has to be seen in the context of the drive in the media to create and exploit the status of being famous across the whole range of entertainment formats' (2000: 188). The notion of *being famous* is important here, since it allows us to see the notions of star, superstar, megastar, as well as celebrity and actor as points on the same fame continuum, a continuum which is itself bound up with, and fuelled by, the operations of mass-mediated culture. In other words, it permits us to speak of different modes, forms or degrees of stardom, which is to say, different articulations of 'the star' become differences of kind not circumscribed or delimited by the specificities of different media or different forms within individual mediums. In other words, contemporary configurations of film stardom must be seen as inextricably entwined with broader orchestrations of fame across and through all media platforms. It is in this sense that Geraghty attempts to rethink stardom through the categories of 'celebrity', 'professional' and 'performer' inasmuch as 'these distinctions better help us to understand what film stars have in common with and how they differ from other media public figures' (ibid.: 187).

Star-as-celebrity

Celebrity is a mode of stardom relatively unconnected to the sphere of professional work. In other words, celebrity is sustained not by someone's excellence or ability in their chosen profession, but almost entirely by notoriety and infamy. In this sense, Geraghty argues that celebrity privileges biographical information about a star to the extent that their stardom is almost entirely rooted in and 'constructed through gossip, press and television reports, magazine articles and public relations' (ibid.). As such, titbits about a film star's latest failed relationship, their love of chihuahuas or their favourite designer circulate alongside similar morsels about musicians, sportsmen and women, royals, soap stars, It-Girls, socialites, designers, TV presenters and so forth. For instance, the 8 May, 2002 edition of *Now* (Plate 4.7), a British weekly magazine explicitly devoted to celebrity reporting, leads with a feature about celebrity 'Love Splits' in which the break-ups of Tom Cruise and Penélope Cruz, and Julia Roberts and Danny Moder, struggle for prominence alongside tales of the failed romances of pop stars, soap stars, TV presenters, football coaches, footballers and celebrity wannabes.

Indeed, a cursory glance at the covers of *Hello!*, another UK photomagazine dedicated to peddling stories of celebrities' private lives, simultaneously reveals how 'knowledge of the star's "real" life is pieced together through gossip columns and

• **Plate 4.7**
The cover of *Now* (08.05.02), a British weekly photomagazine
The image indicates the ways in which film stars interact and vie with celebrities from other areas of the entertainment world

celebrity interviews' and how, when speaking of the celebrity mode of stardom, film stars 'literally interact with those from other areas' of the entertainment world (ibid.: 188). So, the cover of issue 581 of *Hello!* (October 1999) features Nicole Kidman with the Duke of York as part of a national campaign to stop child abuse; issue 620 (July 2000) features Tom Cruise, Kidman's then husband, talking about how he 'would step on landmines to protect his family'; issue 650 (February 2001) features Kidman and Cruise in one of their final public appearances together before the announcement that their marriage was over; issue 686 (October 2001) leads with 'intimate photos' of Cruise and Penélope Cruz apparently revealing 'the depth of their love' as well as a feature on Kidman talking about 'the truth' of her 'life with Tom'; the following month (issue 690, November 2001) the cover features Kidman in a passionate embrace with pop star Robbie Williams amidst a frenzy of rumours linking the two romantically; and to complete the circle, issue 711 (May 2002) leads with a feature on Penélope Cruz speaking about her relationship with Cruise and the absence of bad feeling between herself and Kidman. The main point here is the idea that attention is directed towards, and in the final instance sustained by, the drama of the star's 'private' life, not their public work as professional actors.

Generally, then, we can identify three inter-related aspects to the star-as-celebrity. First, it is the public circulation through the mass media of information about the putative 'real' private life of the star that sustains the celebrity. The same issue of *Now* which rumourmongers the end of Cruise and Cruz's relationship also contains an 'exclusive' feature on how Kidman 'turned to a tight circle of half a dozen female friends to get her through her very public divorce' (Nielsen 2002: 8). She says that 'Everyone talks about girl power these days, but without it I don't know what I'd have done these last few months...I can really share my feelings with this close group of girlfriends...I'm a woman's woman, really' (ibid.). Such 'intimate' biographical information about the star's life outside the glitz of Hollywood serves to rework Kidman's inter-filmic professional image as 'glamorous movie star' into the far more accessible picture of 'just one of the girls'.

Second, the notion of intertextuality – the construction, circulation and access of information across a whole range of media platforms – not only describes the *form* and *practice* of celebrity, but is also a primary focus of research precisely insofar as 'it is the audience's access to and celebration of intimate information from a variety of texts and sources which are important' in this mode of stardom (Geraghty 2000: 189). Thus, news of Kidman and Cruise's divorce was, to a greater or lesser extent, played out through newspapers (tabloids and broadsheets, front page and gossip columns), magazines (from celebrity publications such as *Hello!*, *OK!*, *Heat*, and *Now*, to the glossies, *Marie Claire*, *Vogue*, *Cosmopolitan*, to teen publications, film magazines and so forth), television (interviews, talk shows, news, and various lifestyle programmes), the web (fan sites, gossip sites, bulletin boards, film sites, as well as electronic forms of more traditional journalism) and photography (especially the paparazzi).

Third, and perhaps most crucially, whereas traditional models of stardom emphasise the film text as the primary site of stardom, or at least the place where the star image is completed (see Ellis 1982), the celebrity mode forestalls the primacy of the films themselves insofar as it constitutes a mode of stardom which does not necessarily involve spectatorship. In other words, it is not just that 'the star can continue to command attention as a celebrity despite failures at the box office' (Geraghty 2000: 189) but rather it is quite possible to be a fan of, to admire, or simply to 'like' Nicole Kidman *without watching the films in which she appears*. In short, it is not simply that the star image of the celebrity exceeds the film text, but instead that, potentially at least, it is dislocated from it altogether and dispersed across a range of extra-filmic texts. Indeed, the adaptability and ubiquity, as well as the proximity of 'celebrity culture' to media culture *per se* make 'celebrity' perhaps the key mode of contemporary stardom.

Star-as-professional

If star-as-celebrity is understood as part of the much broader operations of media consumption which are relatively divorced from the cinematic text, then the star-as-professional is rooted far more in the film text itself. So while on the one hand it appears increasingly the case that film stars are appreciated independently of their professional work, on the other hand 'it is quite possible to understand and enjoy the meaning of the star without the interdiscursive knowledge which the star-as-celebrity relies on' (ibid.).

Crucial to the star-as-professional mode of stardom is the degree of 'fit' between the specificities of a particular star image and the corpus of professional roles played by the actor. In other words, the star-as-professional makes sense when it *appears* that the actor's 'real' personality corresponds more or less accurately and more or less consistently with their performed personas, that is, that the actor him- or herself is *personified* in their professional roles. Maltby argues that 'classical Hollywood's star system engineered a correspondence between star and role' to the extent that 'scripts were written specifically to exhibit already established traits and mannerisms in their stars (Maltby and Craven 1995: 52). As such, 'the fact that a star's persona circulated in the media as part of the promotion of specific movies allowed for a considerable interaction between the star's performance and off-screen persona, and in many respects substituted for variation in the roles a star undertook' (ibid.). On-screen and off-screen Marilyn Monroe embodied the persona of a beautiful yet innocent sex goddess, thus dissolving her 'real' personality into her professional performances. Indeed, the idea that we can detect Monroe the star in and through her roles, that the repertoire of gestures, expressions and movements are 'the property of the star not of any individual character', is central to the economy of pleasure associated with this mode of stardom (Geraghty 2000: 191).

More recently, in light of the dissolution of the star system and the change in the distribution of films brought about in particular by the video/DVD rental market, Geraghty argues that the star-as-professional mode has become reconfigured, with the star now being associated or identified with a particular genre (ibid.: 189). In organising the vast amount of titles available to audiences in rental outlets, 'video stores tend not to use the more specific genre categorisations of westerns, gangster films and horror genres and employ vaguer descriptions…such as "action movie", "comedy" and "drama"' (ibid.). It is within these broader groupings that individual stars delineate more precise sets of expectations and pleasures. For instance, Jackie Chan, Jet Li and Steven Segal are closely linked to specific forms of martial arts/action cinema; Jim Carrey is associated with a certain form of physical comedy while one would expect different comic pleasures from a film featuring Chris Rock or Eddie Murphy; and despite the glut of male stars of the action film, figures such as Bruce Willis, Arnold Schwarzenegger, George Clooney, Tom Cruise, John Travolta, Nicolas Cage, Keanu Reeves, Harrison Ford and Jean-Claude Van Damme arguably indicate relatively precise variations of that masculine agency and thus provide a quite distinct set of expectations within the overarching category of action cinema. Indeed, Geraghty suggests that 'a stable star image' is crucial for the star-as-professional insofar as 'too much difference from established star image may lead to disappointment for the intended audience (ibid.). This perhaps accounts for why actors such as Clooney, Cruise, Willis and Cage, actors whose star image, though related to their physical appearance, is not predicated primarily on the display of muscularity or physical force, have been able to successfully work in a number of genres while similar generic transitions for Schwarzenegger, Stallone, Van Damme and, more recently, Jet Li have proved less successful. In this way, then, Geraghty suggests that stars who inhabit the star-as-professional mode 'operate for cinema and video in the same way as a character in a television series, providing the pleasures of stability and repetition and the guarantee of consistency in the apparent plethora of choice offered by the expanding media' (ibid.: 191).

If actors such as Carrey, Li and Schwarzenegger provide relatively straightforward examples of the star-as-professional inasmuch as their performances tend to be heavily contextualised within specific genres, then someone such as Michael Douglas offers a far more nuanced, yet no less compelling instance of the way the distinction between actor and character can blur. For Douglas, despite working in a number of genres and collaborating with a range of directors and screenwriters, has from the mid-1980s played roles which explicitly engage with what Carol Clover has called 'the average white male consciousness' (1993: 9) and what Jude Davies calls 'a crisis of white [American] masculinity' (1995: 215). Indeed, Nick James suggests that Douglas' character choices can be seen as 'a lightning rod for the anxieties of the US male' (2000: 34). As such, from the representation of white masculinity anxious about its putative loss of social and sexual power to women/feminism in films such as *Fatal Attraction* (1987), *War of the Roses* (1989), *Basic Instinct* (1992) and *Disclosure* (1994), to a more general anger caused by the crisis of male identity depicted in *Falling Down* (1993), to the trauma of middle-age variously represented in *The Game* (1997), *Traffic* (2000) and *The Wonder Boys* (2000), Douglas' jaw-jutting, growling male persona transcends the confines of any one film, surfacing instead across a whole career. Indeed, part of the power of *Wonder Boys* lies in the way the more furious, control-freak aspects associated with Douglas are reincarnated in 'a passive wreck of a man' (ibid.). The poignancy of the scene in which Douglas' character, Grady, a disillusioned professor and writer, sits slumped on his porch wearing a tatty woolly hat and his ex-wife's pink flannelette dressing gown watching the rain fall significantly depends precisely upon his professional star image just insofar as it can be read not only as a key moment in the film, but also as a mileage marker within an overarching star persona.

Douglas is also an example of the way a star can embody the various modes of stardom simultaneously *without* those modes necessarily overlapping to either reinforce, complicate or contradict the star image. Thus, while on the one hand Douglas is a particularly interesting example of the star-as-professional, on the other hand he has a parallel celebrity existence as the son of Kirk Douglas, the husband of Catherine Zeta-Jones, the father to two children, the owner of property and business, the topic of gossip, the feature of *Hello!* and countless other photo-spreads and so forth. However, while at times Douglas' celebrity image has informed his professional work, in general a more plausible account of his stardom within the cinema, especially latterly, is related to the consistency of his screen persona.

Star-as-performer

It would be interesting to compare the 'star-as-performer' with the discussion of the 'character', the part played and how the spectator recognised and aligned with a character. *See Chapter 3, pp. 112–113 for a discussion of this.*

In a reversal of the star-as-celebrity, Geraghty's final category shifts the emphasis away from biographical aspects of a star's private life towards notions of *performance* and deliberately focuses attention on 'the work of acting' (2000: 192). So while to some extent stars have always been understood in relation to their acting abilities and style, Geraghty suggests that the discourse of performance 'now takes on particular importance as a way for film stars to claim legitimate space in the overcrowded world of celebrity status' (ibid.). If in hypermediated culture film stars are often levelled down to celebrities and have to struggle for exposure alongside footballers, pop stars and royals then the concept of star-as-performer can be understood as perhaps the primary mechanism for reinscribing some of the cultural prestige of film stardom precisely by redirecting attention towards the film text as a privileged site of the art of acting. Indeed, such an emphasis on performance not only serves to distinguish certain film stars such as Marlon Brando, Robert De Niro, Al Pacino, Sean Penn, Johnny Depp, John Malkovich, Jodie Foster, Meryl Streep, Jeff Bridges, Philip Seymour-Hoffman, and to a lesser extent, Brad Pitt and Edward Norton from the tittle-tattle of celebrity, but also operates as a key way of 'claiming back the cinema for human stars' from special effects and a growing number of non-human or animated stars (ibid.).

We can identify two principal ways in which film stardom is legitimised through this appeal to the craft of performance and acting talent. The first concerns a particular tradition of acting associated with the Actors' Studio in New York known as the Method, an approach to acting which Maltby argues has become 'the dominant account of how actors create naturalist performances' (Maltby and Craven 1995: 258). Method acting, on the one hand, is rooted in the presence of the actor's self as the emotional and psychological basis of *all* performance. As such, in order to be able to 'get inside' the mind of a character, the Method actor must first investigate their own anxieties, repressions, motivations and drives 'as the mine from which all psychological truth must be dug' (Steve Vineberg, cited in ibid.). On the other hand, however, the authentic performance can only be fully realised and understood when the distinction between actor and character is abolished in the seamless fusion of performer and role. It is in this sense, then, that Method acting reclaims a degree of cultural prestige for the star-as-performer precisely 'by making the celebrity trappings part of the detritus which has to be discarded' if the performance is to be 'real' and thus worthwhile (Geraghty 2000: 192). Accordingly, it is not simply that actors such as Brando, De Niro and Penn often appear to work 'on the edge of disappearance into their roles', immersing themselves in the complex psyches of their characters, but that their cultural status as performers is enhanced in rejecting the 'vulgar commercialism' of Hollywood (Maltby and Craven 1995: 259). Brando is now renowned for being a semi-recluse, while James Kaplan (2001) writes that Penn 'gives interviews sparingly and reluctantly' while being a performer who 'has consistently taken roles in challenging films, as opposed to films that earn big money' and has 'effectively turned himself into an actor's actor, a remote star with a lingering air of menace and inaccessibility'.

The second way in which film stardom becomes legitimised through a collocation with performance is related to a particular actor's *selection of projects*. This works on two levels, the first reconfirming the primacy of the film text to the star-as-performer as noted by Geraghty, the second diluting such a primacy by acknowledging the rhetorical construction of the actor as serious artist precisely through an extended circuit of mediation. In the case of the former, actors such as Penn, Depp, Pitt and Foster have tended to resist roles which might compromise their pretensions towards serious acting, instead choosing parts which enable them to put on display the highly visible and recognisable mannerisms of the Method. Depp, for example, has developed a reputation for taking on challenging roles and for working with recognised auteurs. He has collaborated with Tim Burton on *Edward Scissorhands* (1990), *Ed Wood* (1994) and *Sleepy Hollow* (1999), with Lasse Hallström on *What's Eating Gilbert Grape?* (1993) and *Chocolat* (2000), and with Jim Jarmusch on *Dead Man* (1995); starred opposite Method standard-bearers Marlon Brando in *Don Juan DeMarco* (1995) and Al Pacino in *Donnie Brasco* (1997); as well as playing a number of counter-cultural historical figures such as Raoul Duke/Hunter S. Thompson in Terry Gilliam's *Fear and Loathing in Las Vegas* (1998), Jack Kerouac in *The Source* (1999) and George Jung in Ted Demme's *Blow* (2001).

In the latter case, the star-as-performer reclaims cultural value for their work through a route of extra-filmic mediation which complements and commentates on both on their performances and choice of roles. In short, often through a combination of star interviews, public pronouncements and self-authored articles, the star-as-performer sets his- or herself apart from the vacuities of celebrity and the cold commercialism of Hollywood. In a lengthy article published both in the *New York Times* and the *Guardian* which champions *The Terrorist* (Santosh Sivan, 2001), an Indian film 'costing roughly $50,000 and shot in 16 days with no lighting', John Malkovich contrasts this 'masterpiece of economy' with the publicity-fuelled process of Hollywood film-making which 'flattens everything in its path like an ancient tree falling from an immense height into a particularly soft spot of moist, dumb green grass' (Malkovich 2001: 2). Indeed, the actor waxes lyrical about the 'general tendency of the movie industry to breed the identical twins, stupidity and greed' and that pursuing interesting projects in contemporary

Hollywood is difficult 'because in the America of today, the sole arbiter of nearly every kind of art (or even entertainment) is not what it provides but only what it makes' (ibid.).

Sean Penn, while perhaps the contemporary epitome of this latter, rhetorical construction of the 'serious actor', also provides us with an example of the way in which the two aspects of the star-as-performer often inform each other. For on the one hand, after declaring that he doesn't like acting and announcing a number of pseudo-retirements, he 'came back' 'determined to attach himself only to projects of impeccable aesthetic integrity' (Pulver 2001). On this level, his performances in such films as *Carlito's Way* (1993), *Dead Man Walking*, (1995), *U-Turn* (1997), *The Thin Red Line* (1998), *Hurlyburly* (1998), *Sweet and Lowdown* (1999), and *The Weight of Water* (2000), have earned him the reputation of being 'the most powerful actor of his generation' (Ebert 1996), 'all fireworks and brooding Method' (Pulver 2001). On the other hand, however, Penn complements the status of his on-screen performances with a series of public tirades against the 'trash ethos' of Hollywood in which 'everything is about entertainment and no politics' (cited in Gibbons 2001). 'The one thing you can count on in Hollywood – across the board – is cowardice' (cited in Kaplan 2001), Penn has said, and if 'you are willing to put two ideas into a picture you are ahead of the game' (cited in Gibbons 2001). At the 2001 Edinburgh Festival, Penn made perhaps his most controversial public outburst when he accused certain big-name directors of 'raping society' and stated that they 'should be sent running home screaming with rectal cancer' because 'they don't care about the films they make, or about what is going on around them or the effect they are having on their audience…The definition of a good film now is one that makes the bank happy – not one that shines a light on people's lives' (ibid.).

As such, Penn's prestige as an actor is not only claimed through his performances in the film text, but through a more or less self-conscious rhetoric of prestige constructed extra-textually. So while 'the claim to stardom as a performer depends on the work of acting being put on display' such a display is not necessarily delimited to the films in which an actor appears but can extend, as in the case of Malkovich and Penn, to series of extra-filmic performances which serve to reinforce their putative distance from either 'stars-as-celebrities who can become famous for "being themselves" and stars-as-professionals who act as themselves' (Geraghty 2000: 193).

☐ CASE STUDY 4: JODIE FOSTER

Jodie Foster offers a particularly interesting and nuanced example of the contemporary film star. In part this is because, at some point in her career, she has embodied all three of Geraghty's categories of stardom, but it is also partly because she has been, for a number of years, one of the few female Hollywood actors who are considered able to 'carry a film' as well as being a member of that even rarer breed of female producer-directors that can wield a degree of power in Hollywood. These latter observations, as well as the simple longevity of her career, are crucial insofar as Geraghty notes that 'it is important to recognise that women stars do operate in a different context from their male counterparts' (ibid.: 196). Perhaps most interesting, however, is the way in which the various modes of stardom overlay one another in Foster's star persona and inter-penetrate to produce a relatively sophisticated image of popular feminism both on- and off-screen.

Linda Ruth Williams' (2002) discussion of Foster as Meg Altman in David Fincher's *Panic Room* (2002) draws attention to the ways in which she has, since her first screen appearance aged just three in an ad for suntan lotion, straddled the three categories of stardom identified by Geraghty. As Ruth Williams' analysis highlights, despite a 'veneer of ordinariness that encases her extraordinary success' and a private persona characterised by 'reserve rather than reclusiveness', Foster's career is not untouched by rumour and gossip about her private life that fuels the star-as-celebrity (ibid.: 12).

Indeed, her accomplished performances as a child star in such demanding roles as Audrey, the streetwise alcoholic kid in *Alice Doesn't Live Here Anymore* (1974), the 12-year-old prostitute, Iris, in *Taxi Driver* (1976), the child-broad Tallulah in *Bugsy Malone* (1976), and Rynn, the child-murderer, in *The Little Girl Who Lives Down the Lane* (1976) were thrown further into relief by publicity which sought to compare such 'fallen angel' roles with her real-life broken family. Latterly, this attention on Foster's family life has been replayed through a series of 'scandals' which have attempted to 'out' her alleged homosexuality and 'name' the father of her son.

However, while generally the category of celebrity 'works well for female stars' inasmuch as 'the common association in popular culture between women and the private sphere of personal relationships and domesticity' chimes with celebrity culture's thirst for gossip, the balance of Foster's stardom lies in her abilities as a performer and a professional (Geraghty 2000: 196). As a performer she is generally seen as 'the most respected actress of her generation' (Williams 2002: 12), 'not only a wonderful actor but an intelligent one' (Ebert 1999), someone 'whose skill and presence seem to increase with each picture' (Turan 1997). Such critical eulogies are important precisely to the extent that they focus not on the glamour and beauty of the female star, nor on the ups and downs of her private life, but rather on her intellect, craft and sheer professionalism. So it is not simply Foster's refusal of celebrity that sets her apart from the overwhelming majority of contemporary female stars, but, more complexly, that her stardom is exemplary of what Hilary Radner calls Hollywood's new women, a rare breed of female actor which defies 'the Hollywood machinery that all too often reduces femininity to her image, the flattened body that functions as a projection of masculine desire' (1998: 260). In this respect her 'Californian golden-girl looks' *are* significant precisely to the extent that they don't reduce Foster to mere 'bimbo fodder', but actually inform a reading of her as representing a 'new' feminism both on- and off-screen. As Williams charts, on-screen Foster has portrayed femininity as 'riven by dark desires rather than erotic availability', playing a number of 'feisty 'women on the edge' who 'single-handedly carry mainstream productions' (2002: 12). In such roles as rape victim Sarah Tobias in *The Accused* (1988), single-parent of child genius Dede Tate in *Little Man Tate* (1991), FBI agent Clarice Starling in *The Silence of the Lambs* (1991), radio astronomer Ellie Arroway in *Contact* (1997), and as trapped parent Meg Altman in *Panic Room* (2002), Foster has created a series of psychologically complex yet potent women who, despite their neuroses, are nevertheless 'effective agents, firmly grasping the symbolic order as they strive to wield public power' (ibid.: 14).

At the level of Foster's performance, this pull between social agency and the emotional traumas that rage just beneath the public face of her characters is registered both verbally and visually: in mesmerising 'displays of mumbled and humble inarticulacy' (ibid.: 13) to the extent that so often when she speaks 'we can almost feel each word being wrung out of her emotions' (Ebert 1988); and through her 'trademark' expression of 'strained fear' (Williams 2002: 13) that defines Foster's persuasiveness in conveying 'intelligence and single-minded passion to the point of confrontational anger' (Turan 1997) (see Plates 4.8 and 4.9).

The final jaw-clenching scenes of *The Silence of the Lambs* which pit her against serial killer Buffalo Bill evince the powerful combination of these two elements. Barely able to speak, yet sufficiently articulate to carry out her job, and with terror etched into her forehead and visible through her nervously wide stare, Clarice remains composed enough to succeed in her task of containing a version of masculinity which regards women merely as objects that can literally be tailored to male desire.

Although she is not a Method actor in the strict technical sense of the term, much of Foster's prestige as a star derives from the emotional and psychological authenticity with which characters such as Sarah Tobias, Clarice Starling and Meg Altman develop. However, Williams (2002) suggests that there is another strand of Foster's work in which the distinction between actor and role is less distinct, and that, in a manner akin to the

• **Plate 4.8**
Jodie Foster in *Panic Room* (David Fincher, 2001)
Foster's most recent performance of controlled terror as she protects her daughter from intruders

star-as-professional, it is possible to read these roles as Foster performing herself. This idea focuses on Foster's exploration of characters either side of the parent–child divide that are 'struggling to cope with the repercussions of an incomplete family' in a way that, to a greater or lesser extent, mirrors Foster's own experience as both a child and a parent (ibid.: 13). This is most obvious, perhaps, in *Little Man Tate*, Foster's directorial debut about a gifted child from a single-parent household which Foster admits has autobiographical elements in it, but it is also variously evident in *The Silence of the Lambs*, *Nell* (1994), *Contact*, *Anna and the King* (1999) and *Panic Room*.

In these ways, then, Foster inhabits all three modes of stardom described by Geraghty. And yet Foster's stardom is somehow more than the sum of these parts: more alluring, more intense and more unknowable than either category reveals. For it is the ways in which these various layers of stardom interpenetrate that not only make Foster a particularly complex version of contemporary stardom *per se*, but also position her as the embodiment of **postfeminist** womanhood, what Jacinda Read (2000) refers to as a popular, common-sense feminism. Read argues that 'film is one of the sites on, through and against which meanings of feminism are *produced*', and that to fully understand such meanings we should 'read films historically through the discourses surrounding them and explore the complex ways in which such discourses intersect and negotiate with each other' (ibid.). In this sense, it is the very complexity of Foster's stardom – not only the fact that she heads her own production company, or that she is a successful professional

postfeminism
The notion of postfeminism is a contested term used by different people, in different ways, to mean different things. It is used here to indicate a version of popularised, and to some extent individualised feminism that is different from (mainly in the sense that it comes after) the highly politicised feminism of the 1970s.

• **Plate 4.9**
Jodie Foster in *The Silence of the Lambs* (Jonathan Demme, 1991)
Foster's 'trademark expression of strained fear'

woman in a male-dominated sector, or that she is herself a single parent trying to sustain a career while raising a child, or that some aspects of her private life can be glimpsed in certain of her roles, or that a number of her performances reconcile femininity with feminist agency, nor even that she is one of the few serious female actors deemed capable of carrying mainstream productions, in fact not any single facet of her stardom – that aligns her with this less dogmatic, more pragmatic version of feminism.

In discussing Foster's eleventh-hour replacement of Nicole Kidman for the lead role in *Panic Room*, the film's director David Fincher distils the significance of Foster's stardom. He says that 'Nicole Kidman makes you make a different movie...It's about glamour and physicality'. With Foster on the other hand, 'it's about what happens in her eyes. It's more political. Jodie is someone who has spent 35 years making choices that define her as a woman and define women in film. Jodie Foster is nobody's pet, nobody's trophy wife' (cited in Brooks 2002: 16).

1 For further study, choose one male and one female contemporary film star and compare:
   a the frequency with which, and the ways in which, they are represented in celebrity magazines and the press
   b their status within the marketing of their movies
   c the ways in which knowledge of their private lives overlaps with or informs their on-screen roles.

2 To what extent do pop stars, star footballers or stars from other areas of the media fit, or resist the models of film stardom discussed in this chapter?
3 Which categories of stardom do animated stars such as Woody and Buzz Lightyear fit into, and how might we modify those categories in order to describe this phenomenon?
4 In what ways is it possible to analyse and understand a special effect such as a twister, a volcano, a tidal wave or a computer-generated dinosaur as a star?

KEY TEXTS

Authorship and Hollywood cinema

Braddock, Jeremy and Hock, Stephen, (eds) *Directed by Allen Smithee*, University of Minnesota Press, Minneapolis, 2001. An interesting and cheerfully irreverent attempt to rethink auteur theory and the idea of personal style.

Caughie, John, (ed.), *Theories of Authorship: A Reader*, Routledge and British Film Institute, London, 1988. It is symptomatic of the current disinterest in authorship theory that Caughie's anthology still remains the best conceptual book in the field despite its age.

Cotta Vaz, Mark *et al.*, *Industrial Light and Magic: Into the Digital Realm*, Virgin Books, London, 1996. This book provides a useful history of ILM as well as specific accounts of the various techniques used to produce the visual effects in a range of films.

Tasker, Yvonne (ed.), *Fifty Contemporary Film-Makers*, Routledge, London, 2002.

Allon, Yoram *et al.* (eds), *Critical Guide to North American Directors*, Wallflower Press, London, 2002.

Both of these books interpret film as the creative expression of their directors. Tasker's book contains more developed essays on the work of what it deems to be fifty of the most important contemporary directors, while the compendium compiled by Allon is a more bare-bones approach to all film-makers active in North America. Both are useful texts.

Genre and Hollywood cinema

Although it is impossible to list them here, there are a multitude of books which address individual genres from a variety of historical and theoretical standpoints. The following are some excellent introductory and more sophisticated conceptual studies of genre.

Lacey, Nick, *Narrative and Genre*, Macmillan, London, 2000. An excellent introduction to the subject.

The following two books develop more specialised and sophisticated accounts of genre but are rewarding.

Altman, Rick, *Film/Genre*, British Film Institute, London, 1999.

Neale, Stephen, *Genre and Hollywood*, Routledge, London and New York, 2000.

The following anthologies contain much of the key writing on genre.

Grant, Barry Keith (ed.), *Film Genre Reader*, University of Texas, Austin, 1986.

—— (ed.), *Film Genre Reader II*, University of Texas, Austin, 1995.

Neale, Steve, *Genre and Contemporary Hollywood*, British Film Institute, London, 2002.

Stars and Hollywood cinema

Dyer, Richard, *Stars*, British Film Institute, London, 1998 (1979). Since its first publication in 1979, Dyer's book has been the key critical work in the field of star studies to the extent that it is virtually impossible to find any work since that doesn't take *Stars* as its point of departure. The updated edition also features a useful supplementary chapter by Paul McDonald which traces more recent developments in star studies. It is also worthwhile consulting Dyer's later book, *Heavenly Bodies: Film Stars and Society*.

Geraghty, Christine, 'Re-examining Stardom: Questions of Texts, Bodies and Performance', in Christine Gledhill, and Linda Williams (eds), *Reinventing Film Studies*, Arnold, London, 2000. A short chapter in a useful general anthology which attempts to rethink stardom within the broader context of contemporary media culture.

Gledhill, Christine (ed.), *Stardom: Industry of Desire*, Routledge, London, 1991. This key anthology contains many of the most influential essays in the field of star studies.

McDonald, Paul, *The Star System: Hollywood's Production of Popular Identities*, Wallflower Press, London, 2000. A relatively short but excellent introduction to the historical emergence and development of the star system in the American film industry.

 **FURTHER VIEWING**

Authorship and Hollywood cinema

Jim Jarmusch

Stranger than Paradise (1984)
Down by Law (1986)
Mystery Train (1989)
Night on Earth (1991)
Dead Man (1995)
Ghost Dog: The Way of the Samurai (1999)
These titles are available on VHS and/or DVD.

Industrial Light and Magic

The following films contain the full range of ILM's visual-effects techniques.
Star Wars (1977)
Willow (1988)
Who Framed Roger Rabbit (1988)
The Abyss (1989)
Terminator 2 (1991)
Death Becomes Her (1992)
Jurassic Park (1993)
Forrest Gump (1995)
Titanic (1997)
Men in Black (1997)
Mercury Rising (1998)
The Perfect Storm (2000)
Artificial Intelligence: AI (2001)
Minority Report (2002)
Star Wars Episode 2 Attack of the Clones (2002)
More generally, it is worthwhile exploring the 'Special Features' on many DVDs in terms of the way they often give voice to a range of authorial candidates.

Genre and Hollywood cinema

It is useful to study the way genres change or evolve over time. As such, watch a range of films of the same genre from different periods. For example, if you were to investigate the Western genre then the following would give a good indication of both the continuities and changes that have occurred within the field.
The Great Train Robbery (Edwin S. Porter, 1903)
Stagecoach (John Ford, 1939)
My Darling Clementine (John Ford, 1946)
Shane (George Stevens, 1952)
The Searchers (John Ford, 1956)
A Fistful of Dollars (Sergio Leone, 1964)
The Wild Bunch (Sam Peckinpah, 1969)
The Outlaw Josey Wales (Clint Eastwood, 1976)
Dances with Wolves (Kevin Costner, 1990)
Back to the Future III (Robert Zemeckis, 1990)
Unforgiven (Clint Eastwood, 1992)
Dead Man (Jim Jarmusch, 1995)
The Quick and the Dead (Sam Raimi, 1995)
Last Man Standing (Walter Hill, 1996)
Shanghai Noon (Tom Dey, 2000)

Hollywood–Hong Kong

The following films are interesting examples of the fusion between action and martial arts genres. As you watch them, think about the different ways they each communicate that fusion. For instance, some employ established stars from the martial arts genre (most notably Jackie Chan and Jet Li), while in others the fusion is rendered at stylistic or aesthetic levels. Furthermore, how do the films variously weave conventions from action and martial arts genres together with conventions from other genres such as horror, science fiction, and the Western?

Lethal Weapon 4 (Richard Donner, 1998)
Rush Hour (Brett Ratner, 1998)
The Matrix (Larry and Andy Wachowski, 1999)
Romeo Must Die (Andrzej Bartkowiak, 2000)
Mission Impossible II (John Woo, 2000)
Charlie's Angels (McG, 2000)
Shanghai Noon (Tom Dey, 2000)
Crouching Tiger, Hidden Dragon (Ang Lee, 2000)
Rush Hour 2 (Brett Ratner, 2001)
Kiss of the Dragon (Chris Nahon, 2001)
The One (James Wong, 2001)
Blade II (Guillermo del Toro, 2002)

Stars and Hollywood cinema

Jodie Foster

Taxi Driver (Martin Scorsese, 1976)
The Accused (Jonathan Kaplan, 1988)
Little Man Tate (Jodie Foster, 1991)
The Silence of the Lambs (Jonathan Demme, 1991)
Nell (Michael Apted, 1994)
Contact (Robert Zemeckis, 1997)
Panic Room (David Fincher, 2002)

Michael Douglas

Falling Down (Joel Schumacher, 1993)
Disclosure (Barry Levinson, 1994)
The Game (David Fincher, 1997)
Traffic (Steven Soderbergh, 2000)
The Wonder Boys (Curtis Hanson, 2000)

Sean Penn

Dead Man Walking (Tim Robbins, 1995)
Hurlyburly (Anthony Drazan, 1998)
The Thin Red Line (Terrence Malick, 1998)
Sweet and Lowdown (Woody Allen, 1999)

Johnny Depp

Ed Wood (Tim Burton, 1994)
Dead Man (Jim Jarmusch, 1995)
Donnie Brasco (Mike Newell, 1997)
Fear and Loathing in Las Vegas (Terry Gilliam, 1998)
Sleepy Hollow (Tim Burton, 1999)
Blow (Ted Demme, 2001)

RESOURCE CENTRES

Authorship and Hollywood cinema

General

http://uk.imdb.com
The Internet Movie Database
A excellent place to begin research on authorship. Not only can you quickly compile filmographies of directors, but you can also search for the work of cinematographers, editors, visual-effects supervisors, concept artists and so on. Moreover, the site contains a vast amount of links to reviews, promotional material, stills, movie and director's 'home pages', as well as a host of other useful resources.

Jim Jarmusch

http://www.sfgoth.com/~kali/jarmusch.html
It's a Sad and Beautiful World
An excellent fan site containing a range of articles about, and interviews with, Jarmusch, as well as a series of links to material on other sites.

http://jimjarmusch.tripod.com
The Jim Jarmusch Resource Page
Another useful site established and maintained by a fan containing links to reviews of Jarmusch's movies as well as a range of other helpful information.

Visual effects

http://vfxhq.com
VFF HQ
This site provides a variety of information about visual effects as well as discussion of specific movies which employ visual-effects techniques.

Genre and Hollywood cinema

http://uk.imdb.com
The Internet Movie Database
This web site is useful for all kinds of reasons, but specifically in terms of genre it is worth exploring the way it employs the notion of genre to catalogue films (http://uk.imdb/Sections/Genres). While this is relatively straightforward process for some films and for some genres, it becomes increasingly problematic for films that are hybrids of two, three or four genres.

http://www.sensesofcinema.com
Senses of Cinema
This is an online film journal which contains a range of excellent articles and features written by some leading scholars and historians. It is particularly relevant here because it regularly contains information and articles about Hong Kong and Chinese cinema, as well as 'world cinema' generally.

http://www.brightlightsfilm.com
Bright Lights Film Journal
Another useful online journal searchable by issue or by certain genres.

It is also worthwhile investigating the ways in which genre is constructed through the journalistic practice of film reviewing. The following web sites contain the work of film critics.

http://www.suntimes.com/index/ebert.html
Roger Ebert, *Chicago Sun-Times*

http://www.calendarlive.com
Kenneth Turan, *LA Times*

http://www.guardian.co.uk/Film
Guardian newspaper

http://www.bfi.org.uk/sightandsound/reviews/index.php
British Film Institute

http://www.villagevoice.com/film/
Village Voice

http://www.salon.com/ent/index.html
Salon.com

http://popmatters.com/film/reviews/
Pop Matters

http://movie-reviews.colossus.net/
Reel Views

http://www.bbc.co.uk/films/
BBCi

http://efilmcritic.com/
e Filmcritic.com

http://filmmonthly.com/
Film Monthly

Stars and Hollywood cinema

Since the lines between stardom, celebrity and fame are becoming increasingly smudged, it is important to engage with publications such as *Hello!*, *OK!*, *Heat* and *Now*, as well as the gossip and celebrity pages in the popular press. This allows one to gauge the way in which film stardom is constructed and circulated by the media. Also useful in this respect are web sites such as *Celebrity Link* (http://www.celebrity-link.com) and *Celebrity Storm* (http://www.celebritystorm.com).

Part three

Genre forms – realism and illusion

Chapter 5

The documentary form: personal and social 'realities'

Paul Wells

■ The documentary form: personal and social 'realities'

INTRODUCTION

Recent years have seen a re-emergence of the documentary form from its cultural 'ghetto'; a shedding of its traditional connotations of 'dryness', 'fact' and 'everyday-ness', and a movement towards a proper recognition of its role as a model of cinematic and televisual practice which can entertain, provoke, persuade and affect audiences emotionally. Peter Moore, Channel 4's Senior Commissioning Editor for Documentaries, suggests 'Documentary is in a permanent state of crisis and so documentary makers, who are highly critical people, turn their critical faculties on the discipline itself. They are so inventive they keep the genre alive' (Willis 1997: 9). This has not been without some anxiety, however, as some have perceived that the integrity of the documentary form has been compromised by its evolution into 'docusoap'; the fashion in which its traditional imperatives have been borrowed by 'reality TV', and a general tendency for the documentary to be treading a fine line between entertainment and exploitation. Tracing the survival and redefinition of the genre is the subject of this chapter.

It is often the case that documentary is believed to be the recording of 'actuality' – raw footage of real events as they happen, real people as they speak, real life as it occurs, spontaneous and unmediated. While this is often the case in producing the material *for* a documentary, it rarely constitutes a documentary in itself, because such material has to be ordered, reshaped and placed in sequential form. Even in the shooting of the material, choices have to be made in regard to shot selection, point of view, lighting etc., which anticipate a certain presentation of the material in the final film. Andrew Britton extends this point by suggesting,

In the first place, truly great documentaries are analytical, in the sense that they present the corner of reality with which they deal not as a truth there to be observed, but as a social and historical reality which can only be understood in the context of the forces and actions that produced it. Secondly, they are engaged, in a sense that they lay no claim to objectivity, but actively present a case through their structure and organisation of point of view.

(Britton 1992: 29)

documentary
A non-fiction text using 'actuality' footage, which may include the live recording of events and relevant research material (i.e. interviews, statistics etc.). This kind of text is usually informed by a particular point of view, and seeks to address a particular social issue which is related to and potentially affects the audience.

It is important to stress then that, just like any 'fiction' film, the **documentary** is *constructed* and may be seen not as a recording of 'reality', but as another kind of representation of 'reality'. The documentary form is rarely innocent and is defined in a number of ways, ranging from Travelogue to Radical Essay, and these forms must be addressed in regard to their specific address and purpose.

Most people see many documentaries on television and have become very familiar with their dominant codes and conventions, so much so that they have ceased to interrogate and question these texts. Audiences regularly watch documentaries characterised by the use of voiceover, a roll-call of experts, witnesses and opinionated members of the public, an apparently 'real' set of locations, footage of live events and 'found' archive material. All of these recognisable conventions have a particular history and place in the development and expansion of the documentary as a *cinematic* form. This is an important point to stress because in many ways, the documentary form has been neglected and marginalised as a film art because it has been absorbed by the more journalistic tendencies of television. Furthermore it has essentially become cheap prime-time television, finding a large popular audience. The Discovery Channel, dedicated to broadcasting documentaries and available only through satellite and cable, for example, now broadcasts to over forty countries and has worldwide audiences of over

100 million (Willis 1997: 9). There is evidence to suggest, however, that with such a proliferation of 'news-style' documentaries there has been a movement back to a more 'cinematic' approach by individual film-makers which recall the very traditions and styles discussed here. While it is clear that there are more broadcast contexts for documentary, film-makers working in a more cinematic style still seek the widest possible distribution of their films in cinemas, colleges and universities, and film societies. Furthermore, the increasing number of festivals showing documentaries have expanded their profile, often providing the context for critical acclaim that both activates wider distribution on the major exhibition circuits and often ensures prime-time broadcast on terrestrial channels predicated on a public service ethos.

WHAT IS DOCUMENTARY?

John Grierson first coined the term documentary in a review of Robert Flaherty's film *Moana* (1925), indicating the ability of the medium to literally produce a visual 'document' of a particular event. Grierson, though fiercely committed to the educational and democratic capabilities of the documentary, clearly recognised that film itself was a relative form and, in typically combative style, suggests: 'Cinema is neither an art nor an entertainment; it is a form of publication, and may publish in a hundred different ways for a hundred different audiences' (cited in Hardy 1979: 85).

For a discussion of early feminist documentary film making, see Chapter 7, pp. 249–250.

The documentary form is one method of cinematic 'publication' which in Grierson's terms is defined by 'the creative treatment of actuality' (Greirson 1932: 8). Supporting Britton's earlier point, Grierson acknowledges that the filming of 'actuality' in itself does not constitute what might be seen as the 'truth'. He recognises that 'actuality' footage must be subjected to a creative process to *reveal* its truth. This apparent manipulation of material is both a recording of 'reality' and a statement *about* 'reality'. As screenwriter and director Bela Balazs notes: 'This presentation of reality by means of motion pictures differs essentially from all other modes of presentation in that the reality being presented is not yet completed; it is itself still in the making while the presentation is being prepared. The creative artist does not need to dip into his memory and recall what has happened – he is present at the happening itself and participates in it' (Macdonald and Cousins 1996: 31). It remains necessary, therefore, to examine the nature and extent of the intervention and manipulation of the film-maker, and the subsequent generic aspects that are being explored, and possibly redefined.

A useful starting point is Richard Barsam's list of categories which constitute and seek to define what he generically terms 'the non-fiction film' (Barsam 1992: 1). This list effectively demonstrates the different types of film which have been perceived as documentary and which clearly share some of its possible codes and conventions. The categories include

- factual film
- ethnographic film
- films of exploration
- propaganda film
- cinéma vérité
- Direct Cinema
- documentary

Barsam essentially locates the documentary itself outside the other categories because he suggests that the role of the film-maker is much more specific in determining the interpretation of the material in these types of film. In other words, he views the documentary as a medium which, despite its use of 'actuality' footage, is still what we may

reactive observation-alism
Documentary film-making in which the material recorded is filmed as spontaneously as possible subject to the immediacy of observation by the camera-operator/director.

proactive observation-alism
Documentary film-making in which specific choices are made about what material is to be recorded in relation to the previous observation of the camera-operator/director.

illustrative mode
Approach to documentary which attempts to directly illustrate what the commentary/voiceover is saying.

associative mode
Approach to documentary which attempts to use footage in a way in which it has the maximum degree of symbolic or metaphorical meaning on top of the literal information available in the image.

overheard exchange
The recording of seemingly spontaneous dialogue between two or more participants engaged in conversation/observation.

testimony
The recording of solicited observation, opinion or information by witnesses, experts and relevant participants in relation to the documentary subject; the primary purpose of the interview.

exposition
The use of voiceover or direct-to-camera address by a figure who is essentially directing the viewer in the reception of information and argument.

term an 'authored' form, and this arguably provides a useful distinction by which the other categories may be evaluated in regard to their common characteristics and divergent methods.

Barsam's categories attempt to distinguish different uses of 'actuality' footage. We may view this footage as raw footage, which although subject to processes of selection as it is photographed may be viewed as an unmediated recording of an incident, an interview, an event etc. *as it happened*. This footage then becomes subject to specific compilation and organisation which defines its context. In its turn that footage can then become

the Newsreel (record of current events), the Travelogue (description of a place, often for the purposes of promotion or advertising), the Educational or Training film (to teach an audience how to do or understand something), and the Process film (to describe how an object or procedure is constructed).

(De Nitto 1985: 325)

These films, having determined their context, that is, their purpose and perspective, are then constructed in a specific way. John Corner suggests that we may address these films and their claim to be defined as documentary by looking at three key areas which inform all non-fiction films (Corner 1986: xiii–xx). These are

1 technological factors;
2 sociological dimensions;
3 aesthetic concerns.

Clearly, technological developments have been absolutely intrinsic to the changing styles and approaches that characterise the non-fiction film. Advanced technology enables advanced technique. Light, hand-held cameras capable of recording sound and using sensitive film stocks or digital video discs, able to record footage for a considerable length of time, will obviously produce a different kind of film to that produced by a static, heavy camera unable to record sound or photograph material for more than a few minutes.

The sociological dimension of these films is important because the documentary medium is a specifically social form. In attempting to record certain aspects of 'reality' in a particular time and space, the documentary implicitly and explicitly locates itself in the historical moment and focuses on the personal and cultural codes and conventions of that time.

It is in the aesthetic concerns of documentary that there is considerable debate, because it is largely in creating an aesthetic approach that documentaries and other non-fiction films begin to challenge, distort and subvert notions of documentary 'truth' and 'authenticity'. The aesthetics of a piece ultimately determine its proper context. Useful here are Corner's four modes of visual language and three modes of verbal language in the documentary form (ibid.: 27–30). Corner suggests that **reactive observationalism** operates as the most apparently unmediated recording of actuality footage, while **proactive observationalism** includes a higher degree of choice in what is actually recorded. The **illustrative mode** looks to directly echo what is being eschewed in commentary, while the **associative mode** involves the highest degree of manipulation in the sense that the footage is used in the service of overtly symbolic and metaphoric purposes. Verbal evidence in the documentary may be in the mode of **overheard exchange** between filmed participants; **testimony**, mainly through the voices of interviewees; and finally, **exposition**, through voiceover or direct-to-camera address. These approaches in relation to visual and verbal language help to determine the kind and extent of construction and self-reflexivity in the documentary – a key tension in the evolution of the non-fiction film.

SOME DEVELOPMENTS IN NON-FICTION FILM

The history of the non-fiction film has its origins in the development of the earliest motion pictures. Following on from still photography and motion studies like those photographed by Edward Muybridge, and yet further extending a trend in the arts to record 'reality, in the most accurate way' (Barsam 1992: 13–17), 'actualities' or 'documentaries' filmed by the Lumière Brothers in 1895 constitute some of the first non-fiction films. These films included *Workers Leaving the Lumière Factory* and *Arrivée d'un train en gare à la Ciotat*, and are merely examples of everyday events recorded with a static camera. Audiences were astonished by the images because they were seeing moving pictures of 'reality' for the first time. Similar short films were recorded by Edison in America and soon the phenomenon spread worldwide with examples emerging from Spain, India and China.

Perhaps the first major examples to characterise the documentary form were the films emerging after the Russian Revolution of 1917, and particularly the work of Dziga Vertov, who edited a newsreel series called *Kino-Pravda* (literally, *Film Truth*), and developed an approach to film called 'cinema-eye', informed by twelve major theoretical points. In the space available here, I only intend to stress three of the points, but they are representative of the highly politicised and indeed highly aestheticised view Vertov had of the cinematic medium as a documentary tool:

For further discussion of Soviet montage cinema and Vertov, see Chapter 11.

The Cameraman uses many specific devices to 'attack' reality with his camera and to put facts together in a new structure; these devices help him to strive for a better world with more perceptive people.

He continues,

Knowing that 'in life nothing is accidental', the cameraman is expected to grasp the dialectical relationships between disparate events occurring in reality; his duty is to unveil the intrinsic conflict of life's antagonistic forces and lay bare the 'cause and effect' of life's phenomenon,

and concludes,

All this is necessary if kinoks [documentarists] want to show on the screen 'Life-as-it-is in its essence, including the 'life' of the film itself – the process of cinematic creation from shooting and laboratory, through editing, up to the final product i.e. the film being projected to the audience in a movie auditorium.

(Petric 1978: 41–2)

Vertov's uses of the film medium is a highly creative one, stressing simultaneously the importance of the art of film-making and the politicised 'reality' it records. It is this tension between revealing the 'form' of the recording (that is, the unusual use of the camera, complex editing etc.) and the 'content' it shows which confuses the notion of the films as documentaries, especially in regard to his later and most renowned work, *The Man with a Movie Camera* (1929). Cinéma vérité director Richard Leacock says that Vertov's newsreels were persuasive, even if they were superficial in their recording of famine or disaster, but adds,

[Vertov]…went on to film *The Man with the Movie Camera*, which was accused of being formalistic, and to me it was. It was tricks, games, and I don't see that it really has any connection with his expressed desire to show life as it is.

(Cited in Roy Levin 1971: 202)

It is Vertov's aesthetic sense which in Leacock's mind ultimately distances him from the true spirit of the documentary enterprise in showing 'reality' as it is, without the addition of foregrounded 'formalist' principles of film-making practice. A similar kind of formalism occurs in what became known as the City Symphony documentaries which include *Rien Que Les Heures* (1926), directed by Alberto Cavalcanti, and Walter Ruttman's *Berlin, Symphony of a Great City* (1927), both of which were characterised by avant-garde and surrealist techniques. The films were essentially impressions of each city, using footage of real locations to reveal the disparity between rich and poor. Despite their formalist pretensions, the films succeed in making social comment, and are influential in their achievement in using images of everyday people, objects and locations for symbolic and political effect. Arguably, Vertov, Cavalcanti and Ruttman are working primarily in an *associative* mode which would later be challenged by Leacock's preferred mode of *reactive observationalism*, which he believes is closer to authentic documentary.

FROM TRAVELOGUE TO AUTHORED DOCUMENTARY

In America, the non-fiction film had primarily been defined and sustained by the travelogue (a term coined by Burton Holmes), which was footage shot in foreign lands and shown at lectures and slide-shows to introduce audiences to different cultures and exotic locations. In 1904, at the St Louis Exposition, George C. Hale's *Tours and Scenes of the World* was particularly successful, but did not reach the mythic proportions of the footage from President Teddy Roosevelt's African safaris or Robert Scott's expedition to the South Pole. These kinds of travelogues appealed to the American public because they demonstrated the American spirit of enterprise and adventure, supporting the view that the American consciousness was informed by a pioneering spirit and an enduring sense of 'the frontier'. This outlook underpins the Romantic tradition of film-making which begins with travelogue footage of real cowboys and Indians and comes to its apotheosis in the films of Robert Flaherty. Special mention must be made though of Merian C. Cooper and Ernest B. Schoedsack who shot *Grass* (1925), a film about Iranian nomadic tribes searching for fresh pasture land, and *Chang* (1927), which followed a Thai family's experiences in the jungle, and included scenes of predatory animals attempting to abduct women and children, which had a profound influence on Cooper and Schoedsack's most famous feature film, *King Kong* (1933).

It is Robert Flaherty, though, who most embodies the development of the documentary form as an ethnographic (the scientific study of other races from a position 'within' the community) and anthropological tool.

☐ CASE STUDY 1: ROBERT FLAHERTY

His films were travelogues to places that never were.

(Barsam 1992: 53)

Flaherty's films are not just moving pictures. They are experiences, similar in a geographic sense to visiting Paris or Rome or seeing the dawn rise over the Sinai desert. Flaherty is a country, which having once seen never forgets.

(Calder-Marshall 1966: 229)

Sponsored by the fur company Revillon Freres, Robert Flaherty made *Nanook of the North* (1922), a study of the Inuit Eskimos of northern Canada, which is acknowledged as one of the most influential films within the genre. It perhaps provides us with all the clues we require to define both the documentary and its acceptable limits. As is

• **Plate 5.1**
Nanook of the North (Robert
J. Flaherty, 1922)
Filmed August 1920–August
1921 in the area around the
Hudson Strait, Canada, and
along the shore of the
Hopewell Sound, Quebec.

indicated above by Barsam and Calder-Marshall, Flaherty's films are 'authored' films with a specific intent; an intent that we might characterise as not merely to record the lives of the Eskimos, but to recall and re-stage a former, more primitive, more 'real' era of Eskimo life. This nostalgic intent only serves to mythologise Eskimo life and to some extent remove it from its 'realist' context, thus once again calling into question some of the inherent principles that we may assume are crucial in determining documentary 'truth'.

Although Flaherty was an advocate of the use of lenses that could view the subject from a long distance so as not to affect unduly the behaviour of the Eskimos, and deployed cinematography (using long uninterrupted takes) instead of complex editing, it is Flaherty's intervention in the material that is most problematic when evaluating *Nanook* as a key documentary. Flaherty was not content merely to record events; he wanted to 'dramatise' actuality by filming aspects of Eskimo culture which he knew of from his earlier travels into the Hudson Bay area between 1910 and 1916. For example,

• **Plate 5.2**
Moana (Robert
Flaherty, 1926)

he wanted to film Eskimos hunting and harpooning seals in the traditional way, instead of filming them using guns, which was their regular practice. Similarly, he rebuilt igloos to accommodate camera equipment and organised parts of the Eskimo lifestyle to suit the technical requirements of shooting footage under these conditions. In *Moana*, Flaherty staged a ritual tattooing ceremony among the Samoan Islanders, recalling a practice that had not been carried out for many years, while in *Man of Aran* (1935) shark-hunts were also staged and did not characterise the contemporary existence of the Aran Islanders.

John Grierson argues that Flaherty becomes intimate with the subject matter before he records it and thus, 'He lives with his people till the story is told "out of himself"' and this enables him to 'make the primary distinction between a method which describes only the surface value of a subject, and a method which more explosively reveals the reality of it (cited in Hardy 1979: 148). This seems to legitimise Flaherty's approach because *Nanook*, *Moana* and *Man of Aran* all succeed in revealing the practices of more 'primitive' cultures – cultures which in Flaherty's view embody a certain kind of simple and romanticised utopianism.

Clearly, then, Flaherty essentially uses 'actuality' to illustrate dominant themes and interests that he is eager to explore. In some ways Flaherty ignores the real social and political dimensions informing his subjects' lives, and indeed does not engage with the darker side of the human sensibility, preferring instead to prioritise larger, more mythic and universal topics. There is almost a nostalgic yearning in Flaherty's work to return to a simpler, more physical, pre-industrial world, where humankind could pit itself against the natural world, slowly but surely harnessing its forces to positive ends. Families and communities are seen as stoic and noble in their endeavours, surviving often against terrible odds. Flaherty obviously 'manipulates' his material and sums up one of the apparent ironies in creating documentary 'truth' by suggesting that 'Sometimes you have to lie. One often has to distort a thing to catch its true spirit' (cited in Calder-Marshall 1966: 97).

FROM SOCIAL COMMENTARY TO PROPAGANDA TO POETIC ACTUALITY

If Flaherty established a tradition of documentary which emerged out of the travelogue and aspired to celebrate humankind, then it was John Grierson in Britain who defined the documentary on more politicised terms. Grierson theorised the documentary, produced a number of films (all influenced by his political stance) and created a distribution network for them. His outlook suited a period in which the mass media (film, radio and the press) and advertising industries were having considerable impact, while the idea of mass political democracy was emerging in a way that necessitated the education of ordinary people in its principles.

Enamoured by the view that documentary could serve the processes of democracy in educating the people, Grierson pursued his aims with characteristic zeal. He was influenced by the ideas of Walter Lippmann (who believed that the complexity of modern life prohibited ordinary individuals from participating in a society to a proper extent) and the works of Sergei Eisenstein (whose film *Battleship Potemkin* [1925] Grierson admired as 'glorified newsreel' and thus organised a showing of it in England). Grierson wanted the documentary to be more sociologically aware and less formally aesthetic than the work of Vertov. Grierson's documentary film unit was initially sponsored by the Empire Marketing Board, under the leadership of Sir Stephen Tallents, who sought to reach Commonwealth nations both in a commercial and ideological sense (Tallents sought to promote Britain as much as its trade). The unit came under the auspices of the General Post Office in 1933 and finally became the Crown Film Unit in 1940, predominantly working with the Ministry of Information on wartime propaganda.

The films produced by Grierson fall into Dennis De Nitto's definition of the social commentary film, which he divides into three distinct sub-groups:

For further reference to early British cinema and the GPO film unit, see Chapter 9, pp. 331–332.

The documentary of *Social Description* has its primary purpose to present to an audience social conditions, particularly how an environment and institutions affect the lives of people. Any criticism of these conditions is oblique, implied rather than stated.

In a documentary of *Social Criticism*, the director is less objective, and his intention is to make audiences conscious that something is wrong in their society and should be remedied.

When a director is angry about a situation and wishes to induce outrage in his audience and even provoke them into action, he creates a documentary of *Social Protest*.

(De Nitto 1985: 330)

Most of Grierson's output falls into the first category, beginning with *Drifters* (1929), the only film actually directed by Grierson, and concerned with herring fisherman in the North Sea. Other significant films followed: *Granton Trawler* (1934), directed by Edgar Anstey, also about fishing; *Song of Ceylon* (1934), directed by Basil Wright, which featured the first attempt to counterpoint sound to visual images rather than use music or dialogue; *Housing Problems* (1935), co-directed by Anstey and Arthur Elton, which deployed a journalistic newsreel style in interviewing ordinary people living in slum housing conditions; *Nightmail* (1936), directed by Basil Wright and Harry Watt, which features music by Benjamin Britten and poetry by W.H. Auden in its highly lyricised view of the night-time mail train on its journey from London to Glasgow; and *North Sea* (1938), produced by Alberto Cavalcanti, and directed by Harry Watt, which tells the story of ship-to-shore radio, using dramatised reconstructions.

During the Second World War, the Ministry of Information appointed Jack Beddington as the film liaison officer to work with Grierson's newly christened 'Crown' film unit to produce works of documentary information and **propaganda**. These films addressed domestic and strategic issues and were characterised by a desire to educate the public and invoke a consensus among the people in the conduct of the war at a personal and social level. Films such as *Squadron 992* (1939), *Dover Front Line* (1940) and *Target for Tonight* (1941) established Harry Watt as one of the most important film-makers of the period, but it is the work of Humphrey Jennings which represents some of the finest and most influential aspects of British documentary film-making.

propaganda
The systematic construction of a text in which the ideological principles of a political stance are promoted, endorsed and made attractive to the viewer in order to influence the viewer's beliefs and preferences. Such a text may often include critical and exploitative ideas and imagery about oppositional stances. 'Point of view' in these texts is wholly informed by political bias and a specificity of intention to persuade the viewer of the intrinsic 'rightness' of the authorial position.

□ CASE STUDY 2: HUMPHREY JENNINGS

Having read English at Cambridge University and become interested in theatre and costume design, Humphrey Jennings immersed himself in the arts and joined the GPO film unit in 1934. He designed sets for Cavalcanti's *Pett and Pott* (1934) and directed *Post Haste and Locomotives* in his first year. By 1936, he was part of the organising committee for the International Surrealist Exhibition in London, and working on ideas concerning an 'anthropology of our own people' which would be the catalyst for the Mass Observation Movement, principally taken up and established by journalist and anthropologist Tom Harrison. Mass Observation sought to observe and record detailed aspects of human behaviour, including the 'shouts and gestures of motorists', 'Bathroom Behaviour', 'Distribution, diffusion and significance of the dirty joke' and 'Female taboos about eating' (Jennings 1982: 17). Clearly this reflects some of the aspirations of Jennings' work as a documentarist, particularly in his film following the journey of the picture postcard, *Penny Journey* (1938), and his record of working-class communities' leisure pastimes, *Spare Time* (1939).

When war broke out, Jennings made two films, *The First Days* (1939) and *Spring Offensive* (1939), but his first major achievement was in collaboration with Harry Watt. Entitled *London Can Take It*, the film dealt with how the British people survived the Blitz, demonstrating their indefatigable spirit and endurance. The film was made especially to appeal to markets in the Empire and in the USA. *Heart of Britain* (1940) followed, but it was *Words for Battle* (1941) that established Jennings as a distinctive film-maker not afraid to develop aspects of the form within which he was working. In a letter to Cicely Jennings in March 1941, he defends the technique he employed to heighten the emotional impact of Britain's purpose in fighting the war:

I have been accused of 'going religious' for putting the Hallelujah Chorus at the end of 'This is England' [Words for Battle]. This of course from Rotha and other of Grierson's little boys who are still talking as loudly as possible about 'pure documentary' and 'realism' and other such systems of self-advertisement.

(Ibid.: 27)

Jennings simultaneously demonstrates a sceptical view of documentary and signals a more poetic and emotive approach to emotional realism. *Words for Battle* is composed of seven sequences, each with a commentary by Laurence Olivier, each demonstrating a juxtaposition of images with a specific piece of poetry or public oratory – these include William Blake's 'Jerusalem', Rudyard Kipling's 'The Beginnings', Winston Churchill's speech made on the 4th June 1940 and Abraham Lincoln's Gettysburg Address. Jennings effectively poeticised 'actuality', simultaneously rehistoricising public monuments and buildings and elevating the human worth of ordinary people as they stoically endured the hardships of war. This redefined the documentary as a genre which not merely recorded events and locations but appropriated them as illustration for the poetic muse.

For further reference to British films of the 40's see Chapter 9, pp. 344–345.

Listen to Britain (1941) and *Fires Were Started* (1942) continue this approach which attempts to lyricise and celebrate ordinary working practices previously ignored until their importance was heightened and their value was acknowledged during the war. It was suggested by certain distributors and critics based at Wardour Street in London that *Fires Were Started* should be cut further. This drew a response from Jennings which is revealing about his position on documentary: 'Well, of course one expects that from spineless well known modern novelists and poets who have somehow got into the propaganda business – who have no technical knowledge and no sense of solidarity or moral courage' (ibid.: 35).

Significantly, Jennings rejects the idea that his films are propaganda, and indeed that they fit easily into any Griersonian category of documentary achievement. Moreover, he aligns himself with the power of film itself to *evoke* and *provoke* consensus through moral and emotional empathy. *A Diary for Timothy* (1946) completes Jennings' war cycle, and is perhaps his finest achievement in this mode of documentary film-making, for it anticipates the baby Timothy's growing up in postwar Britain. With a script by E.M. Forster, read by John Gielgud, the film has an elegiac and ambiguous feel because Jennings' normal emotional optimism has become emotional uncertainty. Documentary 'actuality' has been imbued with the inconsistency of 'feeling' rather than the consistency of 'fact'.

PROPAGANDA AS DOCUMENTARY MYTH

For a discussion of propaganda and Soviet cinema, see Chapter 11, pp. 392–393.

A European tradition of documentary film-making would necessitate a chapter in its own right, but figures such as Joris Ivens (Holland) and Henri Storck (Belgium) contribute a great deal to the understanding of prewar Europe in their films. Ironically, one of the greatest European documentary film-directors, Leni Riefenstahl, emerges from a more sinister context, in that she was responsible for Nazi propaganda film, and created what has become acknowledged as one of the greatest films, documentary or otherwise, of all time. In 1935, Riefenstahl made *Triumph of the Will*, a record of the 1934 Nuremberg Party rally, and with this one film initiated an enduring debate. Should such a film, which so effectively glorifies the Nazi ideal, become divorced from its propagandistic context to be celebrated as 'art' and championed as one of the finest examples of documentary? Only by addressing the approach of Leni Riefenstahl can one posit an answer.

☐ CASE STUDY 3: LENI RIEFENSTAHL

Leni Riefenstahl began her career as an actress, most commonly in Arnold Fanck's 'mountain' movies, which featured aspirant climbers scaling alpine ranges in search of spiritual truth and mythic grandeur. Riefenstahl herself directed and starred in a 'mountain' movie entitled *The Blue Light*. This served to confirm her as an emergent talent, which had already been acknowledged by Hitler himself. The themes of the 'mountain' movie – the search for purity and higher knowledge, the pursuit of personal excellence in the face of the elemental and the primitive, notions of self-discipline and spiritual purpose – chimed readily with the politicised High Romanticism of National Socialism, later distorted into the criminal agendas of Nazi policy. This inherently 'fascist' genre clearly informs Riefenstahl's later work.

Riefenstahl made *Triumph of the Will* after she completed *Victory of Faith* (1933), which celebrated Hitler's first National Socialist Party Congress, and *Day of Freedom: Our Army* (1934), a tribute to the discipline and regimented efficiency of German soldiers. *Triumph of the Will* essentially combines these two themes and develops them into the notion of documentary propaganda as myth. Seemingly fully supported by Hitler and Goebbels, and given full co-operation and funding by government agencies, Riefenstahl deployed some 120 crew members and over thirty cameras in the shooting and construction of the film. The rally itself was staged to accommodate the film and essentially operated as a highly artificial, planned piece of theatre. This directly refutes Riefenstahl's claim that *Triumph of the Will* is cinéma vérité, because as Susan Sontag indicates, 'In *Triumph of the Will*, the document (the image) is no longer simply the record of reality; "reality" has been constructed to serve the image' (cited in Nichols 1976: 34).

This construction of documentary 'myth' corresponds to the fascist aesthetics Sontag outlines in her evaluation of Riefenstahl, in which she indicates that the 'ritual' of the Nuremberg Rally is characterised by 'domination' and 'enslavement' and this is reflected symbolically in

the massing of groups of people; the turning of people into things; the multiplication of things and the grouping of people/things around an all-powerful, hypnotic leader figure or force. The fascist dramaturgy centres on the orgiastic transaction between mighty forces and their puppets. Its choreography alternates between ceaseless motion and a congealed, static, 'virile' posing. Fascist art glorifies surrender, it exalts mindlessness: it glamorises death.

(Ibid.: 40)

Sontag usefully shows how a film such as *Triumph of the Will* constructs its 'actuality' around consciously conceived choreographic principles which recognise and deliberately deploy symbolic relationships. Documentary 'actuality' acts as a set of metaphors which are informed by rich mythical and political associations. An examination of the opening sequence of the film supports this view because it begins with the emergence of a plane from parting clouds, which casts its shadow over Nuremberg as it

• **Plates 5.3, 5.4 and 5.5**
Triumph des Willens (*Triumph of the Will*, Leni Riefenstahl, 1935) Filmed 4–10 September 1934 in Nuremberg at the Nazi Party Congress. Winner of the National Film Prize of Germany, 1935, and the Venice Biennale Gold Medal, 1936.

flies over excited crowds staring up towards it in anticipation. Needless to say, this is Hitler's aircraft, which serves the symbolic function of defining Hitler's Godhead as he descends from the heavens, literally overshadowing his people as he arrives to dispense his glory and wisdom. Hitler is constantly looked up to in the film and individualised and elevated above the dehumanised masses of both people and soldiers.

In making the film in this fashion, Riefenstahl uses film form in a sophisticated way to construct power relations and define Hitler's mystical identity in the light of faceless, highly regimented groups of undifferentiated 'ordinary' people. Hitler becomes an icon which is apparently authenticated and naturalised by the 'realism' inherent in the documentary form. It is only by understanding that 'actuality' may be extensively manipulated that we can understand the relativity of documentary practice and question the whole notion of documentary 'truth'. The combination of Riefenstahl's compositional skill and the specific choreography of the proceedings succeed in making a great film 'fiction'. 'Actuality' is not actual; the filmic record of the event is highly mediated; the material is edited not to reveal the 'truth' but a set of symbolic relationships with a specific political purpose; the rally in becoming an illusion of 'reality' becomes 'documentary myth'.

FROM DOCUMENTARY BIAS TO DIRECT CINEMA AND CINÉMA VÉRITÉ

Riefenstahl's work may be understood as both highly aestheticised, and to use Corner's terms, determinedly 'associative'. Another kind of approach to political documentary informed the work of the Workers' Film and Photo League of America (1930–35). Overtly left-wing in its outlook, it championed the ordinary working people of America and sought to educate, inform and politicise blue-collar groups in securing better pay and conditions. Griersonian in spirit, the League recorded key historical moments of the Depression, which included protest marches about unemployment and pictures of families in bread-lines. The League's work was later overshadowed by the emergence of 'Nykino', who were also dedicated to socialist principles and a commitment to support union activity in working environments. Dutch documentarist Joris Ivens, while working in America, was influential upon the group's political film output, particularly in Nykino's newsreel *The World Today*, which was essentially a left-wing version of the popular mainstream newsreel *The March of Time* (satirised in Orson Welles' *Citizen Kane* [1941]) (see Barsam 1992: 163–5). Although not a left-wing sympathiser, Pare Lorentz, another key figure in American non-fiction film-making, made two important films in the style of Nykino, employing a number of the group's key personnel. These films were entitled *The Plow That Broke the Plains* (1936) and *The River* (1937), and were both sponsored by the government and attempted to sustain 'the American Dream' in spite of less than ideal social realities. In principle, Lorentz tried to create films that provided ideological justification for potentially unpopular or difficult to understand programmes of reform which necessitated a high financial commitment by the government.

The River was a thirty-minute documentary made on 16mm film, designed to be shown in farmhouses, schoolrooms and any suitable venue, in order to educate the people of the Mississippi Valley in the disastrous effects of flooding and 150 years of exploitation of the land's resources. The documentary centres on the experience of one poverty-stricken family and clearly attempts to create sympathy for the people on emotional terms, suggesting that they are 'ill-clad, ill-housed, ill-fed' and 'a share of the crop their only security'. It is suggested that the people lack 'a frontier'; they have no new continent to build, they have to be instrumental in saving their land – 'the greatest river valley in the world'. Roosevelt's 'New Deal' administration had already established the Tennessee Valley Authority and the Farm Security Administration in 1933, and successfully justified state intervention in that area. The film attempts to prove that state intervention in this instance had rehabilitated the land, so that it might gain the support of mid-western audiences in financing further state reform in the Mississippi Valley.

Significantly, the family that the film focuses on is white, when it is more likely that a black family would be working in the area, and thus be more representative. It is possible that 'the argument' of the film may have been strengthened by showing a black family, and engaging 'race' sympathy. Any film's 'argument' is targeted to specific audiences, however, and it is clear that Lorentz was using his film to engage white power élites, legislators and voters in order to secure change. In short, the film was not for black audiences, although, of course, many black families were affected by the situation. Here, it is important to note that 'actuality' is once again subjected to politicised choices and adjustments. The film attempts to relate a 'national' issue through a regional policy; thus it makes specific decisions about which audiences it can *initially* speak to, even if its intentions are ultimately more democratic and universal. Documentary film is here used as a specific tool in the process of communication between government and its people. In the American tradition of documentary, it is this very premise that over thirty years later American film-makers were to reverse. New leftist film-makers wanted to directly intervene in the process of communication between the government and its people by revealing how government created institutions which oppressed and misrepresented its people in the name of democracy.

Robert Drew headed the television production section of Time Inc. and worked with key **Direct Cinema** directors, Richard Leacock, Donn Pennebaker and Albert and David Maysles, initially within the context of ABC TV. The company were at first responsive to Drew's fresh approach to news and current affairs coverage, but scheduled the programmes unfavourably, still prioritising a more mediated style of 'talking head' analysis. Ironically, the most influential film by Drew and his associates was made before joining ABC TV. Called *Primary* (1960), it followed Hubert Humphrey and John F. Kennedy on the Democratic Party campaign trail at the Wisconsin primary election, and attempted to view the proceedings through the candidates' eyes. Using shoulder-mounted camera work, the film echoes the candidates' experience and proves very revealing in its concentration on the 'liveness' of the event. This approach greatly influenced the 'fly-on-the-wall' documentaries by many British TV documentary directors, particularly in the 'Space Between the Words' and 'Decisions' series made by Roger Graef (see Rosenthal 1980: 171–82), and in the ultimately more interventionist style of Paul Watson in *The Family* (1974). Direct Cinema seemed to record 'actuality' in a way that achieved historical authenticity and accuracy. Documentary could provide 'documents' which appeared to offer veracity, and did not apparently operate in the more self-conscious style of **cinéma vérité**.

Upon leaving Drew Associates, Pennebaker pursued his interest in the popular culture of the period, making *Don't Look Back* (1966), a film of Bob Dylan's tour of England in 1965, and *Monterey Pop*, featuring performances by The Who, Simon and Garfunkel, and Jimi Hendrix. Pennebaker, like his colleague Leacock, seemed to have an affinity with music as a barometer of popular attitudes and communal energy. He viewed his films in a less political light than his Direct Cinema colleagues, stating, 'They're not documentaries. They weren't intended to be documentaries, but they're records of some moment'. He continues,

My definition of a documentary film is a film that decides that you don't know enough about something, whatever it is, psychology or the tip of South America. Some guy goes there and says 'Holy shit, I know about this and nobody else does, so I am going to make a film about it'.

(Cited in Roy Levin 1971: 234–5)

Direct Cinema
American documentarists of the 1960s and 1970s believed that the advent of light, portable, technically sophisticated camera equipment enabled a breakthrough in the ways that documentary film-making could reveal personal and social 'truth'. The fact that the documentarist could literally film anywhere under any conditions meant that a greater intimacy could be achieved with the subject, heightening the sense that 'reality' was being directly observed, and that the viewer was party to the seemingly unmediated immediacy of the experience. Less controlled, unscripted, apparently spontaneous, the look and feel of Direct Cinema arguably demonstrated a less deliberately authored approach.

Pennebaker views documentary as the use of film for exploratory, investigative and analytical purposes. He sees his own films as films of 'record', free from these agendas. Once more, the definition of the documentary seems to be intrinsically bound up with the intention of the film-maker and the nature and emphasis of the 'intervention' in the finally produced film. Films like Pennebaker's 'records' of popular culture became the staple of non-fiction film-making and continued to test traditional views of the documentary form and make controversial statements about the era.

This is significantly illustrated by comparing Mike Wadleigh's *Woodstock* (1970) (with the sing-along 'bouncing ball' sequences directed by a young Martin Scorsese) and *Gimme Shelter* (1970), made by the Mayles brothers. If *Woodstock*, a record of the most famous rock festival of all time, was a celebration of the spiritual value of peace, love, community and the use of mind-expanding drugs, then *Gimme Shelter*, a record of the Rolling Stones' American tour, featuring a murder which takes place at the band's Altamont concert, policed by Hell's Angels, suggests the era is over.

The Maysles made many documentaries about popular cultural figures, for example, The Beatles in *What's Happening!: The Beatles in the USA* (1964), Marlon Brando in *Meet Marlon Brando* (1965), Mohammed Ali and Larry Holmes in *Mohammed and Larry* (1980) and visionary artist Christo, who wraps geographical landmarks such as islands, valleys and bridges in silk, in *Christo's Valley Curtain* (1974), *Running Fence* (1976) and *Islands* (1986). One of their most important films is *Salesman* (1969), which follows four members of the Mid-American Bible Company in their attempts to sell bibles. The Bible, of course, is more than 'a book', more than 'a commodity', so what the film ultimately becomes about is a tension between commercial and spiritual values. In order to buy or sell a bible it is necessary to address what you have 'faith' in, and Paul Brennan, 'the Badger', whom the film mainly focuses on, clearly exhibits an inner crisis in doing his job. As well as prioritising the Direct Cinema approach, the Maysles also looked for different methods of recording or deploying 'the interview', for example contextualising the footage of the murder in *Gimme Shelter* by asking Mick Jagger and Keith Richard to observe and comment upon the incident and its inclusion in the film. This raised issues about the nature of documentary, in that the film seemingly distances itself from the stabbing of a black man by a white youth and does not prioritise raw 'actuality' as enough to substantiate a viewpoint. The relativity of documentary is once again called into question – a relativity never denied by one of its greatest American exponents, Frederick Wiseman.

• **Plate 5.6**
Woodstock (Mike Wadleigh, 1970)

☐ CASE STUDY 4: FREDERICK WISEMAN

I think the objective-subjective stuff is a lot of bullshit. I don't see how a film can be anything but subjective.

(Cited in Roy Levin 1971: 321)

Ex-lawyer, Frederick Wiseman, although committed to the filming of 'actuality', recognised the role of the film-maker as intrinsic to the purpose and ultimate creation of documentary. Rather than trying to make a film with a certain ideological position, however, Wiseman wished to make socially conscious films, which essentially established his own position about the people and events he was encountering. At the same time, he attempted to work in a style that enabled his audiences to do the same. Wiseman resisted the kind of documentary approach that prioritised figures or events in popular culture. He was more concerned with a particular kind of film-making which involved the viewer in the everyday life of familiar American institutions. As Wiseman says:

What I am aiming at is a series on American institutions, using the word 'institutions' to cover a series of activities that take place in a limited geographical area with a more or less consistent group of people being involved. I want to use film technology to have a look at places like high schools, hospitals, prisons and police, which seem to be very fresh material for film.

(Cited in Rosenthal 1972: 69)

Wiseman wished to address these institutions because they operate as part of the intrinsic structure of a democratic society yet seem so integrated in that society that their activities remain unexamined and uninterrogated. By not concentrating on an individual story with an imposed 'narrative', Wiseman created a 'mosaic' of events, interactions and working processes, revealing patterns of behaviour which ultimately reflected the morality of the institution and the social values of the society that established and defined the role of that institution. In order for an audience to recognise and interpret the material it was viewing, it was important that they were not 'passive' viewers but actively engaged in perceiving the world they, like Wiseman, were encountering. Consequently, Wiseman did not use voiceover or music to guide the viewer's understanding of a film. Although Wiseman clearly wished the audience to make up its own mind, he also wanted the audience to make the imaginative leap in understanding that any institution is a model of society, and that its activities serve as symbols and metaphors for some bigger themes about power and authority.

Wiseman has made many films. Some of the most important include *Titicut Follies* (1967), *High School* (1968), *Basic Training* (1971), *Model* (1980) and *Central Park* (1989). *Titicut Follies*, Wiseman's first film, perhaps remains his most controversial, as it is about the Bridgewater State Hospital for the criminally insane in Massachusetts. Effectively banned for over twenty-five years because of continuing legal action, the film created considerable controversy in its revelation of the conditions and treatment the inmates had to endure. The film, named after the annual revue staged by the staff and patients, shows the inhumane attitudes and actions of authorities and the lack of proper care for seriously disturbed patients. It is the first example of one of Wiseman's key themes, which is the attempt by any one individual to preserve their humanity while in apparent conflict with institutional rules and regulations which have a dehumanising effect.

High School, concerning the NorthEast High School in Philadelphia, illustrates the theme in another form by showing how pupils are forced to conform unquestioningly to the rigid principles of the school. Blind obedience and a lack of personal identity are seen as practical and valuable in the school's understanding of a proper induction to the institutional frameworks operating in society as a whole. The film concludes with a

• **Plate 5.7**
High School (Frederick Wiseman, 1968)

sequence of Dr Haller, the school's principal, reading a letter from ex-student Bob Walter, who requests that his GI insurance money be given to the school if he is killed in Vietnam. In the letter, he says 'I am only a body doing a job', and this in many ways serves as Wiseman's position about the school, and indeed, the army in which the boy is to serve, a context Wiseman took up in his film, *Basic Training*. Once more illustrating the effects of the processes of dehumanisation, Wiseman shows the initiation of recruits at the Fort Knox training centre in Kentucky. Key questions are raised about the humiliation of certain soldiers (the film was later an influence on Stanley Kubrick's *Full Metal Jacket*) and the regimentation achieved through manipulative strategies which focused on the fears of individuals and the perceptions they had of their own masculinity.

Ultimately a **liberal humanist**, Wiseman raises questions about the assumptions of, and the conduct within, 'institutional' life. The irony inherent in Wiseman's approach is that it is simultaneously an intimate portrait of an institution, operating very close to its 'real' interaction, yet his style remains remote. At one and the same time Wiseman is completely *present* in making the film, but *absent* in its final completion. This achievement in itself creates documentary in a spirit which refuses to take sides, blame particular people or offer solutions to problems, but still operates with a forceful commitment. These documentaries are informed 'comments' but not overt 'opinions'.

liberal humanist
A political perspective in which the emphasis is placed upon an openness of democratic discourse and a multiplicity of perspectives which directly relate to the actual experiences of people and the fundamental principles relating to what it is to be 'human'.

FROM RADICAL DOCUMENTARY TO DOCUSOAP AND DILEMMA

The Direct Cinema school in America was significantly opposed by film-maker Emile de Antonio (see Rosenthal 1980: 205–27), who felt the ambition of such film-making – an unmediated, apparently unbiased version of 'reality' – was naive and unachievable. De Antonio imbued his films with Marxist politics and fierce intellectual criticism of American institutional hypocrisy. This meant that he was monitored by J. Edgar Hoover, the FBI and the CIA throughout his career. His films are largely compiled from found footage taken from a number of sources, particularly a lot of film taken but not used for network news coverage. He deliberately made films which created an alternative view of American culture as it had been mediated through television and government

• **Plate 5.10**
Neighbours from Hell, Carlton
International Media Limited,
courtesy British Film Institute

iconoclasts
Documentarists
committed to chal-
lenging the received
construction and mean-
ings of images, partially
through the critique of
those images, and
mainly through the
reconfiguration of
imagery in a subjective
style.

Distinctive **iconoclasts** such as Nick Broomfield, Molly Dineen, Clive Gordon, Robert Gardner and Trinh T. Minh-ha (see Renov 1993; Bruzzi 2000) are stretching the boundaries of the form, continually and sometimes controversially engaging with issues not addressed in other cinematic or journalistic contexts. This kind of specifically 'authored' work, however, while representing part of the renaissance of the form, was not its commercial lifeblood. The rise of the 'docusoap' – a hybrid of fly-on-the-wall documentary and soap opera – privileging ordinary people as 'characters' and constructing their lives as small-scale 'cliffhanging' narratives, saw a derivative of documentary enjoying prime-time, populist success. Programme-maker and television executive, John Willis, notes: 'Documentary soaps are more akin to entertainment and can be intrusive and sometimes dishonest. They're the Big Macs of documentary, bland and rather tasteless, a symbol of the terrible commodification of factual television…. And although it's easy to be dismissive, some docusoaps are revealing. Even *Neighbours from Hell* contained in its final section a more powerful portrait of brutal racial harrassment than any number of issues of *Panorama* and *Dispatches*' (cited in Bishop 2001: 24) *Driving School, Hotel* and *Airport* were exam-ples of docusoaps which configured the world as a highly *personalised* place in which the vicissitudes of individual lifestyles were offered as a currency of 'reality', free from the more pressing political and ideological concerns of the social environment in which they took place. This appealing confection of apparently 'real' people in 'dramatised' construction of their lives fell into a predictable pattern, however, in which 'victim voyeurism' became its central concern, a trend which Victoria Mapplebeck suggests draws from 'the social cari-cature of the Mad, the Bad and the Sad'. She continues: 'These victimised subjects have become nineties TV icons, a new documentary A-list: the Mad, a motley crew of stalkers, new age therapists and the man who bit his dog; the Bad, Crimewatch baddies in bala-clavas, photofits and dodgy reconstructions; and the Sad, disabled children, troubled transvestites and starving donkeys' (Mapplebeck 1997: 4–5; see also Bruzzi 2000: 75–98). This stark model of social caricaturing highlights eccentricity over economy and comedy over critique, focusing upon everyday crises rather than more substantive moments of symbolic tension in human lives. Consequently, little appears to be 'said', even while it is being observed. Mapplebeck, again, suggests, 'Documentary portraiture at its most inter-esting allows the audience their own reading. In the popular documentary we are told what to think. Viewers are "shown" that these subjects are sad but cute, hopeless but hilarious, seventies rather than nineties comedy. The docusoap leaves the social observation of *Absolutely Fabulous* seeming extremely subtle' (ibid.: 4). The kind of documentary portrai-ture that Mapplebeck alludes to, however, may be alive and well in the work of contemporary artists who are exploring the interface between the premises of programme-making in the style of 'docusoap' and the creation of conceptually driven art-forms, for example in the work of 1997 Turner Prize-winning artist, Gillian Wearing.

□ CASE STUDY 5: GILLIAN WEARING

Gillian Wearing, the Birmingham born artist, has successfully engaged in looking at the ways in which the post-craft agenda of Modern 'Brit-Art' speaks to some of the assumptions of the British documentary tradition and television's contemporary investment in 'People Programming' based on discourses of confession and exposé. Inspired to work in this area by Michael Apted's *Seven Up* (1964) and Paul Watson's fly-on-the-wall documentary series *The Family* (1974), Wearing uses photography and video to interrogate the boundaries of collusion and collaboration in the revelation of private and public identities. In this she collapses some of the assumptions about 'objectivity' in the documentary form and yet creates a model by which particular kinds of 'truth' may be revealed which merely enhance the veracity of visual 'publication'. Her work *Signs That Say What You Want Them to Say and Not Signs That Someone Else Wants You to Say* (1992–93), is simply a record of a number of people, approached in the street, who have been asked to write the first thing that comes into their head on a piece of paper and display it to camera. As Wearing notes, 'This image interrupts the logic of photo-documentary and snapshot photography by the subjects' clear collusion and engineering of their own representation'.[1] This 'act of record' becomes extraordinarily revealing, most notably, in what has become one of the iconic images of the work, a young businessman holding up a piece of paper with the words 'I'm Desperate' on it; at once an indictment of the failure of Thatcherite self-aggrandisement, and also the revelation of desperate emotion beneath formal (corporate) facades.

Wearing progresses this agenda further in *10–16* (1997) where she uses the device of adults lip-synching the confessional statements of children and vice versa. This simple device makes the viewer question the received knowledge we have about children by listening more carefully to what they say, mainly because their words are couched in an incongruous yet appropriate form as the quasi-confession of an adult. This is most acute and challenging when a child admits to the desire to kill their mother and her lesbian lover, emerging from the mouth of a naked dwarf bathing. The reverse is true as adult confessional is only enhanced in its desperation and irrationality by coming from the innocent mouths of children. Ultimately, this tests and examines the role of the spectator as much as it plays with the veracity of subjective 'histories', calling into question processes of re-enactment, reconstruction and recontextualisation – the staples of popular television 'People Programming'. *'Confess All On Video, Don't Worry You Will Be in Disguise. Intrigued?'* (1994) takes this to its

• **Plate 5.11**
Signs (Gillian Wearing, 1992/93)

logical extreme as it privileges the therapeutic discourse assumed in programmes such as *The Oprah Winfrey Show* and *Trisha!* and makes it the self-conscious agenda of an approach which seeks out the private as part of a public domain which is not contextualised as 'entertainment'. Consequently, the normally reserved protagonists who within televisual formats are encouraged to be 'sensationalist' in their self-revelation are here part-parodying that in wearing a plastic mask to disguise themselves, but ironically become more honest by virtue of its protection. Wearing plays with this in a more conventional documentary style as over a two-year gestation period she created *Drunk* (2000) in which homeless alcoholics act and talk in an unstaged way within a staged context, revealing the depth of deprivation and despair in the midst of South London. Wearing's work arguably occupies the same ground as much 'docu-soap' in potentially exploiting her subjects, rather than exploring their issues. Crucially, here, her work is vindicated by its social orientation and the recognition that only through the free expression afforded through the integrity of individual artists can the dominant and prevailing codes and conventions of representation be challenged and changed.

Arguably, these models of documentary may still be open to the contention that all late capitalist investment in the documentary form has compromised the social purpose of the form for personal or commercial gain. This may be evidenced further in a controversial film such as *Sex: The Annabel Chong Story* (1998), which treads a fine line between the titillatory illustration of the world of hardcore pornography and an implicit analysis of the complex motivations of its central protagonist, scholar and porn actress, Annabel Chong; or further, in the ways that aspects of 'documentary' have been absorbed into, or have been replaced by, 'People Programming' that runs the gamut from *The Jerry Springer Show*, to *Police Camera Action*, to *Big Brother* to *Pop Idol*. Exploiting 'ordinary people' for the sake of entertainment is not the same as creating programming which reveals human experience for the sake of democracy. The use of 'documentary' to provide cost-effective models of non-fiction spectacle and accessible narratives has further challenged the creators of authored documentary to seek to reassure broadcasters that 'serious' documentary-making can still attract substantial audiences. Hugh Thomson, winner of the Grierson Award for Best Documentary Series in 2001, for *Indian Journeys*, argues that this is about scheduling documentary correctly, and supporting it with proper promotion and publicity in the ways that other kinds of programming receive: 'Some old habits need urgently to be re-examined, particularly the idea that programmes have to come in regular weekly doses. Schedulers still treat the viewing public as if they were signing them up for an adult education class: "you will be attending at 9pm every Tuesday for the next six weeks on the subject of the Vikings"' (Thomson 2001: 18). This may be an attempt to signal the very seriousness of such programming compared to the comparative lightness of docusoap, but equally it may be a way of *contextualising* the place for the serious address of *popular* subject matter, even if it is of a solemn order. Even here, however, there is some scepticism that history is being best served. Hywel Williams argues, 'The programmes take the gravest of themes, generating an appetite for explanation, and then opt for the human interest angle' (Williams 2001: 16–17), while, at another level, the BBC scaled down its traditional documentary strands, epitomised in *Modern Times* and *Inside Story* – largely considered analyses of contemporary phenomena – in preference to news-event documentaries more tied into the immediacy of current affairs. There is still a contradiction here, however, as the human interest, testimony-led, quasi-reconstructionist documentary has still not proved as popular as documentary underpinned by authentic archive footage. *World War Two in Colour* and *Britain at War* won prime-time audiences for ITV, and Adrian Wood, archivist for the series, believes that 'Actual footage and colour film in particular enables the viewer to identify with people. I remember going through archive footage of the refugees from the fall of

Paris and the faces look so very similar to those refugees caught in Bosnia-Herzegovina at the time' (Brown 2001: 16–17). The key point here, however, is that footage still operates as a *literal* vindication of history for the popular audience, and it is this sense of *evidence* allied to human story-telling which still remains persuasive in the contemporary era, as illustrated by one of its most significant proponents, the American, Ken Burns.

□ CASE STUDY 6: KEN BURNS

Ken Burns' trilogy of documentary series – *The Civil War* (1990), *Baseball* (1994) and *Jazz* (2001) – attained the highest viewing figures for documentary ever known on American television. Composed of archive photographs and extant footage, eye-witness accounts, critical testimony and voiceover commentary drawn from pertinent letters, diaries and other relevant documents, Burns' documentaries are rooted in what he terms 'emotional archeology', in which the profoundly human stories that underpin interpretations of 'history' are evidenced through the use of the materials of record, formal and informal, personal and public, 'factual' yet open to interpretation.[2] Burns also notes: 'I see my country and its history the way someone would see a friend or a family member, that is to say in a broad, sympathetic, human way',[3] and it is clear that this strategy results in a quasi-biographic style of documentary, which although pluralistic in its sources, and the variety of individuals it talks about and speaks through, nevertheless finds focus in being located in the emblematic conscience of a key figure – Abraham Lincoln (*The Civil War*), Jackie Robinson (*Baseball*) and Louis Armstrong (*Jazz*). This relates intrinsically to Burns' perspective on America itself, which in being expressed through its most important historical event – the Civil War – and two of its indigenous creations – baseball and jazz – lends itself to the view that as a nation of immigrants, generation after generation have had to reinvent national identity and purpose. Consequently, in readily embracing the Jeffersonian dictum of 'life, love and the pursuit of happiness', individuals have constantly been engaged in a model of naive patriotism which remains celebratory of, and fiercely committed to, the 'idea' of democracy, even if social and economic reality, and government itself, cannot properly evidence it. Burns' documentaries seek to illustrate a nation constantly in transition, in pursuit of the 'idea' of democracy; a nation recording its own interrogation of the principle. *The Civil War*, Burns' seminal television history, used over 100,000 images which survived from an era in which photography was coming of age, and bore witness to the terrible self-inflicted carnage that America brought upon itself. At Shiloh, in two days, more men fell than in all previous American wars; at Cold Harbor, 7,000 men died in twenty minutes, and it is this sense of tragic and senseless 'loss' that Burns attempts to suggest as he deconstructs images, and prompts their internal drama through their juxtaposition and counterpoint with the heroic 'poetry' of the surviving written testimony of letters and diaries. Throughout everything, and in despite of the horror of personal loss, there remains a love of country which reveals the democratic spirit at the heart of the American sensibility. *Baseball* and *Jazz* evidence this further, as America comes to terms with its own racist history and properly engages with its own dilemmas and anxieties in proper recognition of what democracy means and how history must be understood if the present and future are to be properly facilitated in its spirit. Burns, in constantly 'waking the dead'[4] and insisting upon such an understanding through his work, is perhaps performing the highest function that a documentarist can.

1 How does the documentary film-maker use mise-en-scène, editing, sound, cinematography and narrative devices to create a point of view/argument? Consider *who* says *what* to *whom*, *when*, *how* and *why*, and with *what* effect.

2 The documentary film-maker in dealing with 'actuality' and real social issues may encounter certain problems in the making of a text. What might these problems be and how can the documentarist resolve them?

3 In a number of the case studies in this chapter, the political and ethical stance of the film-maker is crucial to the way we understand and perhaps support or oppose the implied or explicit argument of the documentary. When watching future documentaries consider and evaluate the behaviour, attitude or position of the film-makers. Do you believe that they are correct in the ways that they pursue 'documentary truth'?

4 For further study, consider the implications of 'hybridisation' in documentary. For example, what aspects of 'soap opera' and 'documentary' combine in a 'docu-soap' and to what effect?

NOTES

1 See Interview with Gillian Wearing, *http: //owa.chef-ingredients.com/postuk/artp/wearing.htm*
2 Cited in BBC Jazz Film Project Co, *America, America: The Films of Ken Burns*, TX: BBC 2, June 2001.

3 Ibid.
4 Ibid.

KEY TEXTS

Barsam, R., *The Non-Fiction Film*, Indiana University Press, Bloomington and Indianapolis, 1992.

Corner, J., *The Art of Record: A Critical Introduction to Documentary*, Manchester University Press, Manchester and New York, 1996.

Dovey, J., *Freakshow: First Person Media and Factual Television*, Pluto Press, London and Sterling, 2000.

Macdonald, K. and Cousins, M. (eds), *Imagining Reality: The Faber Book of Documentary*, Faber & Faber, London and Boston, 1996.

Renov, M. (ed.), *Theorising Documentary*, Routledge, London and New York, 1993.

Sobchack, V. (ed.), *The Persistence of History: Cinema, Television and the Modern Event*, Routledge, London and New York, 1996.

Winston, B., *Claiming the Real: The Documentary Film Re-Visited*, British Film Institute, London, 1996.

FURTHER VIEWING

1936	*Olympia* (Leni Riefenstahl)	1992	*The Ark* (Molly Dineen)
1937	*The Spanish Earth* (Joris Ivens)	1996	*When We Were Kings* (Leon Gast and Taylor Hackford)
1955	*Night and Fog* (Alain Resnais)	1999	*Geri* (Molly Dineen)
1970	*The Sorrow and the Pity* (Marcel Ophuls)	2000	*Exodus* (Sorious Samura)
	Woodstock (Mike Wadleigh)	2001	*Startup.com* (Chris Hegedus and Jehane Noujaim)
1985	*Naked Spaces: Living is Round* (Trinh T. Minh-ha)	2002	*Biggie and Tupac* (Nick Broomfield)
	Shoah (Claude Lanzmann)		
1990	*Paris is Burning* (Jennie Livingstone)		

RESOURCE CENTRES

The web sites cited here provide a range of both academic and information materials about the documentary genre, and engage with historical and contemporary models of documentary practice from a range of global contexts.

http: //www.city.yamagata.jp/yidff/ff/box/en
http: //www.humpc61.murdoch.edu.au/criterium/docu/links. htm
http: www2dox.dk/dox

■ Animation: forms and meanings

INTRODUCTION

Animation is one of the most prominent film-making practices of the early twenty-first century, and finally, after long years dismissed as the marginalised 'second cousin' to live-action cinema, finds critical and commercial acknowledgement as the key under-pinning language of contemporary visual cultures *per se*. From feature films to sit-coms to commercials to web sites to mobile phones, animation is omnipresent, extending its parameters, changing its definition, and still challenging other forms of visual expression, determined to constantly reinvent the world and subvert orthodox representations of 'reality'. This chapter will seek to provide an analysis of its distinctive vocabulary, aspects of its history and different models of animation which reveal its intrinsic versatility. One of the most interesting observations in the light of its current success with films such as *Chicken Run* (2000), *Shrek* (2001) and *Monsters Inc.* (2001), is that animation has been able to continually experiment aesthetically and technologically while it has increased its audience and popularity. This in itself makes it unique within entertainment forms.

WHAT IS ANIMATION?

A working definition of animation is that it is a film made frame by frame, providing an illusion of movement which has not been directly recorded in the conventional sense. Norman McLaren, one of the medium's acknowledged masters, suggests: 'Animation is not the art of drawings that move, but rather the art of movements that are drawn', noting 'what happens between each frame is more important than what happens on each frame' (Solomon 1987: 11). McLaren is suggesting that the true essence of animation is the manipulation of movements between frames. Animators of the Zagreb School in the former Yugoslavia, however, seek to enhance this definition by stressing the creative and philosophic aspects of the craft: 'To animate [is to] give life and soul to a design, not through the copying but through the transformation of reality' (cited in Holloway 1972: 9). The Zagreb School wished to emphasise that by literally 'giving life' to the inanimate was to reveal something about the figure or object in the process which could not be privileged or effectively achieved in live-action. British-based animators, John Halas and Joy Batchelor, confirm this point by suggesting that 'If it is the live-action film's job to present physical reality, animated film is concerned with metaphysical reality – not how things look but what they mean' (cited in Hoffer 1981: 3). Animation essentially offers an alternative vocabulary to the film-maker by which alternative perspectives and levels of address are possible. Julianne Burton-Carvajal goes so far as to suggest that '[T]he function and essence of cartoons is...the impression of *ir*reality, of intangible and imaginable worlds in chaotic, disruptive, subversive collision' (Smoodin 1994: 139). Walt Disney himself endorses this point when he says, '[T]he first duty of the cartoon is not to duplicate real action or things as they actually happen – but to give a caricature of life and action...to bring to life dream fantasies and imaginative fantasies that we have all thought of [based on] a foundation of fact' (cited in Barrier 1999: 142). Animation can defy the laws of gravity, contest our perceived view of space and time, and endow lifeless things with dynamic vibrant properties. In short, animation can change the world and create magical effects, but most importantly, it can interrogate previous representations of 'reality' and reinterpret how 'reality' might be understood – a point well understood by pioneer film-makers such as Georges

Méliès, and early animators, J. Stuart Blackton, Emile Cohl, Winsor McCay and Ladislaw Starawicz.

EARLY ANIMATION

The development of the animated form is specifically related to the early experiments in the creation of the moving image. As early as 70 BC there is evidence of a mechanism that projected hand-drawn moving images on to a screen, described by Lucretius in *De Rerum Natura*.

In the sixteenth century, 'Flipbooks' emerged in Europe, often containing erotic drawings which, when riffled, showed the performance of sexual acts. (So much for those 'stickman' drawings of footballers and jugglers I drew in the margins of my textbooks!)

In 1825, Peter Mark Roget developed what was later to be called the *persistence of vision* theory, determining why human beings could perceive movement. Basically, the human eye saw one image and carried with it an afterimage on to the image that followed it, thus creating an apparent continuity. This is crucial in watching moving pictures in general, of course, but of particular significance for the kind of animated cinema achieved frame by frame. With developments such as the **Phenakistoscope** in 1831; the **Kinematoscope** in 1861 and the **Praxinoscope** in 1877, there was the eventual emergence of the cinematic apparatus. Intrinsic to these diversionary 'toys' was the idea of the moving image as something magical – a colourful, playful, seemingly miraculous practice.

Also in place by the 1890s was the comic strip form of the American print media industries. This is important because the comic strip was to provide some of the initial vocabulary for the cartoon film: characters continuing from episode to episode; speech 'bubbles'; visual jokes; sequential narrative etc. By 1893, the *New York World* and *New York Journal* were using colour printing in their strips, and these may be seen as prototypes of later animated forms.

At the centre of the development of 'trick effects' in the emergent cinema was Georges Méliès. His discovery of the 'dissolve' (that is, when one image cross-fades into another) led him to pioneer a whole number of other cinematic effects that have become intrinsic to the possibilities available to animators. These included stop-motion photography, split-screen techniques, fast and slow motion and the manipulation of live action within painted backdrops and scenery. Méliès was also a 'lightning cartoonist', caricaturing contemporary personalities, speeding up their 'construction' on screen by undercranking the camera.

By 1900, J. Stuart Blackton had made *The Enchanted Drawing*. He appeared as a 'lightning cartoonist', drawing a man smoking a cigar and drinking some wine. By the use of stop-motion, one drawing at a time is revealed and the man's face is made to take on various expressions. Various similar films had preceded this including *The Vanishing Lady* (1898) and *A Visit to the Spiritualist* (1899). These films can be classified as **proto-animation** as they employ techniques which are used by later animators but are not strictly or wholly made frame by frame. Blackton achieved full animation of this sort in *Humorous Phases of Funny Faces* (1906). Although using full animation in key sequences, the film was essentially a series of tricks. Primitive notions of narrative animation followed in the early work of famous comic strip artist, Winsor McCay, who under Blackton's supervision at the Vitagraph Brooklyn Studio made an animated version of his most celebrated strip *Little Nemo in Slumberland* in 1911. Blackton clearly recognised that the animated film could be a viable aesthetic and economic vehicle outside the context of orthodox live-action cinema. His film *The Haunted Hotel* (1907) included impressive supernatural sequences, and convinced audiences and financiers alike that the animated film had an unlimited potential.

For discussions of the development of early Hollywood cinema, see Chapter 1, pp. 4–7.

Early developments in the moving image

The **Phenakistoscope** was made up of two rotating discs which appeared to make an image move. The **Kinematoscope** was more sophisticated and employed a series of sequential photographs mounted on a wheel and rotated. The **Praxinoscope**, pioneered by Emile Reynaud, was a strip of images mounted in a revolving drum and reflected in mirrors; a model later revised and renamed Theatre Optique, that may claim to be the first proper mechanism to project seemingly animated images on to a screen.

proto-animation

Early live-action cinema demonstrated certain techniques which preceded their conscious use as a method in creating animation. This is largely in regard to stop-motion, mixed media and the use of dissolves to create the illusion of metamorphosis in early 'trick' films.

incoherent cinema
Influenced by the
'Incoherents', artists
working between 1883
and 1891, a movement
principally led by Cohl,
this kind of animation
was often surreal, anar-
chistic, and playful,
relating seemingly unre-
lated forms and events
in an often irrational and
spontaneous fashion.
Lines tumble into shapes
and figures in temporary
scenarios before
evolving into other
images.

**personality/character
animation**
Many cartoons and more
sophisticated adult
animated films, for
example, Japanese
anime, are still domi-
nated by 'character' or
'personality' animation,
which prioritises exag-
gerated and sometimes
caricatured expressions
of human traits in order
to direct attention to the
detail of gesture and the
range of human emotion
and experience. This
kind of animation is
related to identifiable
aspects of the real world
and does not readily
correspond with more
abstract uses of the
animated medium.

anthropomorphism
The tendency in anima-
tion to endow creatures
with human attributes,
abilities and qualities.
This can redefine or
merely draw attention to
characteristics which are
taken for granted in live-
action representations of
human beings.

In France, caricaturist Emile Cohl's *Fantasmagorie* (1908) created animation as **inco-herent cinema**, less predicated on the comic strip, and more related to abstract art. In Russia, Ladislaw Starawicz was making extraordinary three-dimensional puppet films. *The Cameraman's Revenge* (1911) features insects in a melodramatic love-triangle and self-consciously demonstrates the power of cinema itself to show human life.

It is Winsor McCay, however, who must be properly acknowledged for his influence on Disney and American cartoonal tradition. McCay's *The Story of a Mosquito* (1912) is a mock horror story of a mosquito graphically feeding on a man until it is so bloated with blood that it explodes! Such a film anticipates his development of **personality** or **character animation** through the creation of *Gertie the Dinosaur* (1914). The playful dinosaur, Gertie, gleefully hurls a mammoth into a lake in the film and clearly displays an attitude. McCay included this film as part of his touring revue show and appeared to be talking directly to and acting upon his character. This **anthropomorphism** is key within animation in general, but most significantly in the films of Walt Disney that were to follow.

While Disney is acknowledged as the main figure in moving animation towards an industrial process, this is to neglect the work of John R. Bray who pioneered the cel animation process using translucent cels in 1913, and made a film called *The Artist's Dream*. The Bray studios then released a series of cartoons with a continuing character, Colonel Heeza Liar, and demonstrated the viability of animation as a commercial industry capable of mass production. Cartoons emerged in the marketplace in the USA at the same time that more experimental abstract animation was beginning to emerge out of European avant-garde cinema practices, particularly through film-makers such as Oskar Fischinger and Walter Ruttman. The work of individual artists like these sought to explore the aesthetic boundaries of the film-making art, while rapid advances in film-making technologies in America encouraged the emergence of a variety of organisations making films. These included the Fleischer Brothers, who made the 'Out of the Inkwell' series, and later the *Betty Boop*, *Popeye* and *Superman* cartoons. Initially working at the Bray studios, the Fleischers established an efficient streamlined anima-tion process, and were one of the first studios to experiment with sound. It is Walt

• **Plate 6.1**
Gertie the Dinosaur
(Winsor McCay, 1914)

Disney, however, who remains synonymous with animation, through his radical technical and aesthetic innovation between 1928 and 1942, perhaps the 'Golden Era' of cartoon animation.

THE LEGACY OF DISNEY

Walt Disney Productions was founded in 1923. Disney himself was a draughtsman on his first 'Laugh-O-Grams' – fairytales such as *Puss in Boots* and *Cinderella* – but soon realised that his greatest flair was as an entrepreneur and artistic director. His film *Alice in Cartoonland*, a mix of animation and live-action, was successful enough to secure distribution and finance to further develop his ideas. Fundamentally, Disney wanted to move towards the establishment of an industrial process and a studio ethos and identity which was competitive with, and comparable to, the established Hollywood studios. In 1927, Disney began working on his 'Oswald the Rabbit' series of cartoons and during this process he developed 'the pencil test', i.e. photographing a pencil-drawn sequence to check its quality of movement and authenticity before proceeding to draw it on cels, to paint it etc. In 1928, Disney premiered *Steamboat Willie*, featuring Mickey Mouse, which was the first synchronised sound cartoon. Following continuing experiments in the use of sound effects and music in differing relationships to the visual images, the cartoon began to standardise itself as a form which moved beyond the illustration of different kinds of music into one which accommodated narrative and a series of related jokes. Disney introduced Technicolor, the three-strip colour system, into his 1932 Silly Symphony, *Flowers and Trees*, which later won an Oscar.

All Disney's animators undertook programmes of training in the skills and techniques of fine art in the constant drive towards ever greater notions of **realism** in his cartoons. Even though Disney was dealing with a form that arguably was more suited to abstract, non-realist expression, he insisted on verisimilitude in his characters, contexts and narratives. He wanted animated figures to move like real figures and to be informed by plausible motivation (see Wells 2002a: 72–90). Former Disney Art Director and veteran of the 'Golden era', Zack Schwartz, suggests that even though the figures moved in an anatomically correct way, they still required an element of caricature which ironically appeared to make them 'more real' on screen, and that what Disney really wanted was a state of *conviction* in the characters that reconciled the realistic with the caricatural (see Wells 1997: 4–9). This level of 'reality' was further enhanced by the development of the multi-plane camera. Traditionally, in the two-dimensional image, the illusion of perspective had to be created by the artist. The multi-plane camera achieves the illusion of perspective in the animated film by having the relevant image painted on a series of moveable panes of glass placed directly behind each other. Elements of the image can be painted in the foreground; other elements in the mid-spaces; other elements in the receding background. In this way the camera can move *through* the elements, seemingly keeping them in perspective. This directly aped live-action shooting and was successfully demonstrated in another Oscar-winning Silly Symphony, *The Old Mill* (1937), with its most advanced aesthetic use in the first full-length, Technicolour, sound-synchronised animated cartoon feature, *Snow White and the Seven Dwarfs* (1937).

Animation had reached a position of maturity, acknowledged in this form as 'art'. *Pinocchio* (1940), *Fantasia* (1940) and *Bambi* (1941) only consolidated this prestige, moving the animated film into the contemporary era and effectively reconciling Fine Art, a sense of Classicism and a model of traditional American folk culture, ironically, drawn from many European influences (see Allan 1999). The rise of Disney and the populist utopian **ideology** which appealed to the American mass audience has resulted in the neglect of other kinds of animation, but perhaps even more significantly, the popular cartoon, as exemplified in the work of Tex Avery, Robert McKimson, Bob Clampett,

realism
Live-action cinema has inspired numerous debates about what may be recognised as 'realism'. This is really a consideration of what may be recognised as the most accurate representation of what is 'real' in recording the concrete and tangible world. Clearly, the animated form in itself most readily accommodates 'the fantastic', but Disney preferred to create a hyper-realism which located his characters in plausibly 'real' worlds which also included fantasy elements in the narrative. Crucially, Disney's version of 'realism' sought to properly reproduce perspective illusionism in the frame, and not the surreal and 'eccentric mise-en-scène' of the Fleischer Brothers' films.

ideology
Although a complex issue, ideology may be seen as the dominant set of ideas and values which inform any one society or culture, but which are imbued in its social behaviour and representative texts at a level that is not necessarily obvious or conscious. An ideological stance is normally politicised and historically determined. In the first instance, cartoons seem especially 'innocent' in this respect, but they are characterised by implicit, and sometimes explicit statements about gender, race, nationality, identity etc. which are the fabric of ideological positions, and require interrogation and inspection.

Frank Tashlin and Chuck Jones at the famous 'Termite Terrace' lot at Warner Brothers Studios (Wells 2002b). An analysis of Chuck Jones's classic cartoon, *Duck Amuck* (1953) may usefully offer, however, some points which both valorise the art of the cartoon short, offer an oppositional perspective on Disney's dominance within the field and provide a vocabulary by which 'animation' itself may be studied.

☐ CASE STUDY 1: DECONSTRUCTING THE CARTOON – *DUCK AMUCK* (CHUCK JONES, 1953)

Duck Amuck, directed by Chuck Jones, is the perfect example of a cartoon which is wholly self-conscious and reveals all the aspects of its own construction. Consequently, it is possible to recognise the cartoon as a mode of **deconstruction**. As Richard Thompson points out,

> It is at once a laff riot and an essay by demonstration on the nature and conditions of the animated film (from the inside) and the mechanics of film in general. (Even a quick checklist of film grammar is tossed in via the 'Gimme a close-up' gag.)
>
> (Cited in Peary and Peary 1980: 221)

Daffy begins the cartoon in anticipation that he is in a musketeer picture and swash-buckles with due aplomb until he realises that he is not accompanied by suitable scenery. He immediately recognises that he has been deserted by the context that both he and we as the audience are accustomed to. He drops the character he is playing and becomes Daffy, the betrayed actor who immediately addresses the camera, acknowledging both the animator and the audience. Perceiving himself as an actor he localises himself within the film-making process and signals its mechanisms, all of which are about to be revealed to us.

Trouper that he is, Daffy carries on, adapting to the new farmyard scenery with a spirited version of 'Old Macdonald had a Farm', before adjusting once again to the arctic layout that has replaced the farmyard. The cartoon constantly draws attention to the relationship between foreground and background, and principally to the relationship between the character and the motivating aspects of the environmental context. Daffy's actions are determined by the understanding of the space he inhabits. These tensions inform the basic narrative process of most cartoons: all Daffy wants is for the animator to make up his mind!

Each environment is illustrated by the visual shorthand of dominant cultural images, for example, the arctic is signified by an igloo, Hawaii by Daffy's grass skirt and banjo! The white space, however, becomes the empty context of the cartoon. Daffy is then erased by an animated pencil rubber and essentially remains only as a voice. However, as Chuck Jones has pointed out, 'what I want to say is that Daffy can live and struggle on in an empty screen, without setting and without sound, just as well as with a lot of arbitrary props. He remains Daffy Duck' (ibid.: 233). This draws attention to the prede-termined understanding of Daffy as a character, and to the notion that a whole character can be understood by any one of its parts. Cartoon vocabulary readily employs the **synecdoche**, the part that represents the whole, as a piece of narrative shorthand. Daffy can be understood through his **iconic** elements, both visually and aurally. No visual elements of Daffy need be seen for an audience to know him through his lisping voice, characterised by Mel Blanc. We need only see his manic eyes or particularly upturned beak to distinguish him from Donald Duck and other cartoon char-acters, all of whom have similar unique and distinguishing elements in their design.

Upon the point when Daffy asks 'Where am I?', even in his absence the audience know of his presence. When he is repainted by the anonymous brush as a singing cowboy we anticipate, of course, that Daffy will sing, although the genre probably

---

deconstruction
All media 'texts' are constructed. To under-stand all the components within each construction it is necessary to decon-struct the text and analyse all its elements. For example, the cartoon is made up of a number of specific aspects which define it as a unique cinematic practice, i.e. its frame-by-frame construction; its modes of representation etc.

synecdoche
The idea that a 'part' of a person, an object, a machine, etc. can be used to represent the 'whole', and work as an emotive or suggestive shorthand to the viewer, who invests the 'part' with symbolic associa-tions.

iconic
The iconic is defined by the dominant signs that signify a particular person or object – Chaplin, for example, would be defined by a bowler hat, a mous-tache, a cane and some old boots, while Hitler would be defined by a short parted hairstyle and a small 'postage stamp' moustache.

stripper (which by extension is a metaphor for arrogant, oppressive masculinity) by tearing off his G-string, exposing a small penis.

The stripper is humiliated and the women, chiefly Beryl, feel empowered by the moment. She gleefully swings the G-string around after the fashion of the stripper himself, and clearly enjoys her moment of triumph and difference. Temporarily, Beryl, in the symbolic act of challenging male dominance as it is coded through the stripper's sexual confidence and sense of superiority, undermines patriarchal norms. What Beryl achieves in the narrative, Joanna Quinn achieves in her manipulation of film form – a subversion enabled by the reclaiming of a cinematic language in the animated film, a language *not* wholly colonised by men, and often deployed by an increasing number of female animators creating a feminine aesthetic in the medium (see Pilling 1992; Wells 1998).

PERPETUAL 'MODERNITY'

Throughout its history, even in its most supposedly conservative and orthodox forms, animation has consistently sought to progress its form, resisting the notion of a dominant form created at the Disney studio. As a consequence of the strike at Disney studios in 1941, Canadian animator Stephen Busustow left the company and established United Productions of America (UPA). He, along with other talented animators, John Hubley, Pete Burness, Bob Cannon and Bill Hurtz, wanted to pursue a more individual style that the Disney 'look' could not accommodate. This led to work that was less specifically 'realist' in its approach, and in which, as Ralph Stephenson has suggested, 'the cynicism, the sophistication, the depth of adult attitudes are not ruled out' (Stephenson 1969: 48).

Ironically, this 'sophistication' was achieved through non-naturalist, fairly unsophisticated technical means. These included minimal backgrounds, 'stick' characters and non-continuous 'jerky' movements. The **squash and stretch** conception of movement in conventional cartoon characters, based on a design where the body is thought of as a set of circles, was replaced by the representation of a body as a few sharp lines. Backgrounds, which in Disney animation were positively voluptuous in their colour and detail, were defined by a surrealist minimalism, where stairs led nowhere and lights hung from non-existent ceilings. This kind of development expanded the vocabulary of the animated film and more readily defined animation's relationship to modern art, and the desired 'shock of the new' imbued in its form. More importantly, it challenged the ideological and aesthetic premises by which Disney animation came to define 'American' animation (see Wells 2002b). Crucially, the division that Disney had effected in separating the notion of 'art' from the 'artisanal' by insisting upon all of the essential 'collaborativeness' of a hierarchical production process being absorbed within the authorial 'brand' named as 'Walt Disney', was challenged by a more self-evidently and individually 'authored' model of the cartoon. UPA, although operating a studio system, nevertheless privileged the work of specific directors and artists, once more reuniting the art with the artisanal – those who produced the work were acknowledged as its intrinsic creators. In many senses, this was a more self-conscious model of what actually occurred at the Warner Brothers studio, largely because UPA were prepared to name the cartoon as 'art' and not merely comic diversion.

Most surreal, both in its aesthetic and its soundtrack, was Robert 'Bobe' Cannon's *Gerald McBoing Boing* (1951), where a little boy speaks only through incongruous sounds. More popular was the *Mr Magoo* series, featuring a short-sighted old man, voiced by Jim Bacchus and based on W.C. Fields, who had endless encounters based on mistaking the people and objects he saw for someone or something else. UPA thus established a new style based on 'new ways of seeing', evidenced in the work of the artists themselves, or in characters such as Magoo. In championing a politicised

squash and stretch
Many cartoon characters are constructed in a way that resembles a set of malleable and attached circles that may be elongated or compressed to achieve an effect of dynamic movement. When animators 'squash and 'stretch' these circles they effectively create the physical space of the character and a particular design structure within the overall pattern of the film. Interestingly, early Disney shorts had characters based on 'ropes' rather than circles and this significantly changes the look of the films.

reduced animation
Animation may be literally the movement of one line which, in operating through time and space, may take on characteristics which an audience may perceive as expressive and symbolic. This form of minimalism constitutes reduced animation, which takes as its premise 'less is more'. Literally an eye movement or the shift of a body posture becomes enough to connote a particular feeling or meaning. This enables the films to work in a mode which has an intensity of suggestion.

pixillation
The frame-by-frame recording of deliberately staged live-action movement to create the illusion of movement impossible to achieve by naturalistic means, i.e. figures spinning in mid-air or skating in mid-air. This can also be achieved by particular ways of editing material.

'auteurism' even within studio confines – in direct opposition to Disney's subjugation of individual styles to the established aesthetic – UPA also echoed a similar vision to that held at the Zagreb studios in the former Yugoslavia.

Influenced by UPA's *Gerald McBoing Boing* and *The Four Poster* (1952), designed by John and Faith Hubley, the Zagreb animation industry developed around the two key figures of Dusan Vukotic and Nikola Kostelac. Initially making advertising films, the two progressed to making cartoons deploying **reduced animation,** which is described thus by Ronald Holloway:

Some films took an unbelievable eight cels to make, without losing any of the expressive movement a large number of cels usually required. Drawings were reduced to the barest minimum, and in many cases the visual effect was stronger than with twice the number of drawings.

(Holloway 1972: 12)

Liberated from the limitations of orthodox animation, these films increased the intensity of suggestion located in the images and moved towards a more avant-garde or experimental sensibility which was able to embrace aesthetic development as a model of ideological progress and political critique. Many developmental and experimental animators saw animation itself as a vehicle by which they could challenge established forms of film-making practice, privilege their own vision and refresh any stagnation in the animated form. While Disney's work was undoubtedly a pinnacle of form, it both marginalised other 'cartoonal' forms, and their pioneer creators, and rendered more progressive work as somehow unrelated to the dominant aesthetic and cultural identity defined by the cartoon. Film-makers such as Norman McLaren, cited earlier, sought to redress this by adopting a new approach to animation almost with every film; in one, painting directly on film-stock itself; in another, making a picture evolve through the metamorphoses of pastel chalk sketching; in yet another, animating the very soundtrack on the film itself. McLaren takes this to its logical extreme in *Neighbours* (1952), where he simultaneously parodies 'live-action' film-making through his use of **pixillation**, sends up the 'violence' of the cartoon idiom and makes a political point in UPA/Zagreb style.

• **Plate 6.4**
Neighbours (Norman McLaren, 1952)

☐ CASE STUDY 3: CHALLENGING ANIMATION ORTHODOXIES – *NEIGHBOURS* (NORMAN MCLAREN, 1952)

Norman McLaren is probably the most experimental film-maker in the animated field. He has explored a number of different styles, including direct animation (drawing directly onto celluloid), paper and object animation (stop-motion frame-by-frame constructions of movement with objects and cut-outs, etc.), evolution works (the gradual evolution of a pastel or chalk drawing) and multiple printing works (where movements are recorded as they evolve through the multiple printing of each stage of the movement).

As Cecile Starr has noted: 'His films are enriched with an abundance of childish playfulness, artistic subtlety, psychological insight and human concern' (1972: 111). In *Neighbours*, these qualities are played out, revealing McLaren's insight into how the language of the cartoon could readily be applied to a form that manipulated live action, the consequence of which would be to create a commentary on the representation of violence in cartoons and the presence of violent impulses in human nature. McLaren combines 'the childish playfulness' of the cartoon with a specific contemplation of aspects of the human condition, bringing to that agenda an artistic sensibility that reworks the codes and conventions of orthodox animation.

Employing pixillation, *Neighbours* works as an affecting parable. Two neighbours, seated in deckchairs, smoking their pipes, reading newspapers with the headlines, 'War certain if no peace' and 'Peace certain if no war', become involved in a territorial dispute over the ownership of a wild flower. This dispute escalates rapidly, horrible violence takes place and the pair eventually end up killing one other. The method by which this simple yet telling narrative takes place reveals as much about orthodox strategies of animation as it does about the inevitability of human conflict and, indeed, confirms that conflict is the key underpinning theme of the orthodox animated narrative.

McLaren alludes to the two-dimensional cartoon by employing this in his scenery. He creates the illusion of two neighbouring houses in the middle of a real field by erecting two hand-painted cartoon-like housefronts. He then concentrates on establishing **symmetry** in his frame before disrupting it with the chaos, first of the ecstatic responses by the men to the fragrance of the flower, and second, of their conflict. The wild exaggeration of their movements successfully parodies the dynamics of movement in the orthodox cartoon.

symmetry
The direct balance of imagery in the composition of the frame using parallel or mirrored forms.

Similarly, the electronic soundtrack echoes the role of sound effects in such films, creating mood, accompanying actions and replacing words. The effect of using these conventions but reinventing the means to create them is to draw attention to them.

This in turn signals that to reinterpret the conventions is to reinterpret the meanings inherent within them. To create cartoon conventions *showing* violence is to ignore that the conventions are *about* violence too. It is this very point that McLaren clearly understands, taking the exaggeration of cartoon violence to its logical extreme and showing the audience primitive barbarism. Two men die, two families die, and by implication two nations die, thus illustrating the futility and tragedy of war. If the close reworking of the cartoon in another kind of animated form has not done enough to signify the presence of the artist, then the final multi-lingual sequence of titles saying 'Love thy neighbour' certainly does, in the sense that the moral and didactic purpose of the film has been revealed. Although explicit here, the ways in which animated films can simultaneously make statements and advance the self-reflexiveness and modernity of the form itself, are many and varied. Crucially, these kinds of works – as represented earlier in Joanna Quinn's film, *Girls' Night Out* – have responded to the changing creative and cultural climate in which they were made, using animation as a vehicle by which both subversive and alternative perspectives may be maintained. There is some irony here as animation still carries with it connotations of innocence and undemandingness, and this has been readily exploited by animators who know that the very 'cuteness' of their expression may be the mechanism by which they can position the viewers' expectations only to challenge them. John Kricfalusi is a case in point.

☐ CASE STUDY 4: RECALLING AND REVISING ANIMATION TRADITION – *THE REN & STIMPY SHOW*

For many years, television cartoons have only been perceived in light of their 'process-driven' presence; a form seemingly without authorship; a variety of funny narratives in which the characters seem self-determining rather than the product of known artists. This in itself is ironic given the intrinsic artifice of the form. A greater recognition of this artifice in recent times, however, has not merely recovered modes of authorship, but also a recognition that the enunciativeness in the form should operate as a signifier of the knowledge that re-promotes the importance of animation as an art form and a social signifier. John Kricfalusi's *The Ren & Stimpy Show* becomes a significant example of this process, taking on the self-conscious approach of a 'creator-driven' project, which sought to foreground the self-conscious nature of the cartoon to a known model of potential spectatorship in 'baby boomer' adults and children willing to embrace a more taboo-breaking model of expression.

In prioritising the inherent properties of the medium and speaking to a *visual* literacy in his assumed audience, Kricfalusi once more reoriented the television cartoon to reflect the contingency and aesthetics of the 'Golden era'. Kricfalusi cites Dave Fleischer's 1930s 'Talkatoons'; Grim Natwick's 'Betty Boop' designs; movement cycles in the 'Popeye' cartoons; Chuck Jones' incongruous comic juxtapositions of classical music and cartoonal slapstick; Bob Clampett's *The Great Piggy Bank Robbery* (1946) and Hanna-Barbera's 'Tom and Jerry' cartoons as the key cartoonal influences that underpin his work and provoke his dictums 'Symmetry is ungodly', 'No sharp angles, points or straight lines' and 'Need [to include] shit-eating grin', the latter a recognition of the satisfaction that the cartoon medium offers in breaking taboo areas through the artifice of the graphic medium – anything you see is not *really* happening, but demonstrates what happens if it had done.

Ren & Stimpy may be viewed as Kricfalusi's stand against what may be regarded as the least successful television cartoons. His explicit role as author, and his application of classical cartoonal aesthetics as an 'explicit' art within a popular form, marks *Ren & Stimpy* out even from successful contemporaries such as Mike Judge's *Beavis and Butthead*. Kricfalusi simultaneously wishes to recall, reappraise and revive the work of Chuck Jones, Tex Avery, Bob Clampett, and most specifically, Joe Barbera, while critiquing both the production context and history of the late television cartoon. This is achieved by using the extremes of representational possibility available within the classical animation vocabulary, particularly as it was executed within Warner Brothers and MGM cartoons of the 1940s, to portray the potential extremes of behavioural conduct and cultural mores in the late millennial period.

Furthermore, this was also known by Nickelodeon as they initially sought to exploit the retro-styling of the cartoon in the assured knowledge that the best animation had longevity – *Looney Tunes* and 'Tom and Jerry' still play after fifty years – and that the adult/child cross-over audience would engage with the known constituency of established appeal. Kricfalusi's work, however, moved beyond the 'knowing' cultural critique of *The Simpsons*, or the 'dumbed down' irony of *Beavis and Butthead*, and sought to reconfigure the design and spirit of the cartoon as a comic tension between *noir* foreboding and surreal brutalism, which criticised 'television' and the culture that produced it. Kricalfusi's use of catch-phrases from cartoons – Mr Jinx' 'I hate meeses to pieces' or Elmer Fudd's 'I'm huntin' for a wabbit' – work as aural fragments which offer a casual reminder of the way in which the cartoon restates its credentials within an updated, self-conscious form. Kricfalusi takes this considerably further however, using the cartoon to challenge views about contemporary taste and decency.

Son of Stimpy, the saga of Stimpy's search for 'Stinky', his fart-child, in its scenario alone stretches notions of credibility and acceptability. Kricfalusi opens the cartoon with Stimpy watching cartoons on the television (the audience can only assume this fact from the soundtrack, however, as no images are seen), and engaging with a ritualistic act of flatulence; in Stimpy's eyes, the protracted performance and the small 'skid-marks' left on the floor are evidence of the 'birth' of a child. From here, sustained only by the internal logic of the cartoon itself, Stimpy's 'fart-child', Stinky, is assumed to be a real, living entity. The fart's status as a gas, however, means that it apparently disappears as soon as it is born, and it is only Stimpy's faith in the existence of his 'son' that transcends Ren's scepticism about Stimpy's 'stinky fantasies', and the patronising 'just-agree-with-him, he's-mad' sensibility of the 'magic nose goblins' still living beneath a chair under which they have been wiped, and whom Stimpy consults about Stinky's possible whereabouts. Stimpy slumps into protracted depression about Stinky's absence, provoking Ren to note 'It's been three years, I'm starting to worry about you'. Ren tries to comfort Stimpy at Christmas, offering to kiss under the mistletoe, but Stimpy angrily rejects him and heads off out into the snowy night to find Stinky. Putting up 'Have you smelled me' posters of Stinky, Stimpy lives through urban oppressive-ness; false alarms – he thinks he has found Stinky at a stable selling fresh manure – and the excessive cold, ultimately returning home in an ice block. Stinky, meanwhile, is also searching, escaping two hobos who attempt to 'light' him – a reference to the schoolboy prank of attempting to ignite 'fart' gas – and living underground. Finally, however, he is reunited with Stimpy in the 'squelch' of an embrace, but almost immediately he claims his independence in order to be married to a dead cod-head. The marriage takes place and Stimpy enjoys 'a happy ending'.

Kricfalusi legitimises his narrative by bringing the melodramatic 'lost son' motif to an otherwise taboo subject: the breaking of wind, and the intimation of the emission of bodily waste. Stimpy 'values' this *reductive* act as a *productive* act. The 'fart' is now a 'figure', and with this transformation comes the address of a 'subject', rather than the abstract retention of an 'object'. The central currency of the whole cartoon is predicated on things that are impolite to talk about, but which are *actually* the object of amusement for both children and adults alike in 'real life' – farting, nose-picking, body odour etc. The 'Son of God' motif which underpins the cartoon, signalled in its title and its Christmas setting and soundtrack, allies the sacred and profane in a way that some might find provocative. Kricfalusi does not make this a coherent analogy, however, but self-evidently uses the 'openness' of the animated vocabulary for subversive purposes.

A crucial point here is that animation can work as a language of **dilution** in some circumstances and **amplification** in others. Arguably, Kricfalusi uses the animation of the children's cartoon, and the supposedly innocent environment of children's program-ming to subversive ends because the seemingly unpalatable or challenging aspects of his work are *diluted* by the assumption that this is 'merely' animation – ink and paint, and no more – and that animation does not carry with it charges of difficulty and unac-ceptability. Clearly, Kricfalusi's eventual removal by Nickelodeon from his own vehicle was testament to the view that animation can be seen as an *amplification* of challenging perspectives, equally legitimised and sustained by their artifice – a key issue in the controversies caused by Japanese anime in recent years, and summarised here in a view on the work of Mamoru Oshii.

dilution and amplification
The simultaneous capacity for animation, by virtue of its intrinsic artifice to be viewed either as a language which dilutes its outcomes and effects, rendering them 'inno-cent' and 'dismissable', or as a language which inherently amplifies its literal, aesthetic and ideological perspectives, rendering them some-times unacceptably challenging in their representational aspects.

☐ CASE STUDY 5: ADULT ANIMATION – *GHOST IN THE SHELL* (MAMORU OSHII, 1995)

In the years since the breakthrough Japanese anime *Akira* (1988) first stunned Western audiences with its bravura mix of dystopic science fiction fuelled by youth cultures, explicit violence and an apocalyptic sensibility, the form has established a wide and committed fan base. Anime has been recognised as an intrinsically adult form, and while recent years have seen more made-for-children Japanese animation in the British and American television schedules, the prevailing currency of animation from Japan is its authored preoccupations, its challenging storylines involving sex, violence and complexly entwined combinations of both, and indigenous issues which either remain misunderstood in a wider Western context, or prompt new models of audience investment in embracing different kinds of symbolism, aestheticism and social mores. Most successful in the West have been the works of Hayao Miyazaki which, ironically, are highly unrepresentative of received notions of some anime as apocalyptic, quasi-pornography, and which more closely reflect the classical tradition of Japanese live-action film-making epitomised in the work of Kurosawa, Mizoguchi and Ozu. Miyazaki's films, among them *Laputa: The Castle in the Sky* (1986), *My Neighbour Totoro* (1988), *Pocco Rosso* (1992) and *Princess Mononoke* (2000), all have a contemplative and philosophical underpinning, and a deep preoccupation with spirituality, especially when played out through the innocence and energies of young children, and most specifically, the special, sometimes magical powers of young girls. Miyazaki's attention to the design, narrative and virtuoso action sequences – particularly in relation to flight – complements the moments of epiphany and revelation in his stories, and it is in this way that he both reflects more ancient and embedded traditions in Japan, but also contemporary preoccupations and anxieties. While Miyazaki may offer hope and optimism in redemption, however, Mamoru Oshii offers a darker view, albeit one no less informed by seeking to use the animation medium distinctively.

Oshii notes

My main motivation in making movies is to create worlds which are different from our own [suggesting] the first thing I think about is the visuals, then comes the story, and finally the characters. Ages ago I had a chat with James Cameron [Director of *Terminator 2: Judgement Day*, *Aliens*

• **Plate 6.5**
Ghost in the Shell
(Mamoro Oshii, 1995)

and *Titanic*]. He told me the most important aspect of the film is the characters, then the story, and then finally, the background design. I personally think that the exact opposite is true. According to Cameron, this is necessary to succeed in Hollywood. So, I thought, oh well, my films are not made for Hollywood, so I can choose whatever I want.[1]

This is an interesting observation in the sense that Oshii privileges the visual currencies of animation, and the immediacy of the form, to suggest dramatic principles. In Oshii's films, the context is just as important a 'character' as any one of the figures, and the concepts at the heart of the films essentially form the engine for a potential narrative. Having made *Patlabor* (1990) and *Patlabor 2* (1993) – both thrillers concerned with humankind's over-reliance on technology and the terrorism which may be played out through it – Oshii brings this to its logical conclusion in *Ghost in the Shell*, which foregrounds fundamental questions about what it is to be human in an increasingly computerised cyberworld, where a computer programme gains sentience and also questions its own function in the acquisition of power, autonomy and longevity. Major Kusanagi – an 'enhanced' human – tries to come to terms both with her own identity and the omnipotence of her adversary, ultimately merging with it, a challenging concept which insists upon audiences evaluating just what 'life' may constitute in a postmodern terrain, where 'simulation' itself may be the only currency of existence. By using the very artifice and illusoriness of the animated form, the narrative considerably enhances its ambiguities and contradictions, redefining gender, reconfiguring the body, and redetermining the 'political' – ironically, all consistent aspects of animation, whether in the cartoon or a more **avant-garde** approach, since its inception. While not configured with the overt and controversial brutalities of the parallel demon worlds of the *Legend of the Overfiend* series (1987–91) or the quasi-realist paranoia of *Perfect Blue* (2000), an incisive dissection of 'celebrity', *Ghost in the Shell* endures and challenges because its lyricism – enhanced by Kenji Kawai's score – is coupled with a *noir* sensibility, and the courage to use the animation medium to ask serious questions about human value in a technologically determinist world. Oshii develops the form by refusing innocence and indifference, insisting upon the maturity of the medium. Indeed, while in an accessible, orthodox model, it only advances the case further that all animation is in some sense experimental, even within populist forms.

avant-garde
Essentially non-narrative in structure and often intellectual in content, working in opposition to mainstream cinema. Literally the 'advanced guard' of experimental film-makers who reject the dominant forms of mainstream cinema in favour of innovation and experiment in film-making, often producing non-narrative, non-illusionistic, sometimes abstract films. Avant-garde film is often self-conscious and frequently makes use of devices such as cuts to the camera crew, talking to the camera and scratching on film.

CONTINUING TO EXPERIMENT

Experimental animation, in its most readily understood form, embraces a number of styles and approaches to the animated film which inevitably cross-over into areas which we may also term avant-garde or **art films**. A great deal of animation has been constituted in new forms (computer, photocopy, sand on glass, direct on to celluloid, pinscreen etc.) and resists traditional approaches as they have been understood within the cartoonal realm. William Moritz has argued that this form of non-objective and non-linear animation is actually the purest conception of animation as its language is significantly different from its live-action counterpart and most explicitly reveals the distinctive range and extent of the animated vocabulary (see Canemaker 1988: 21–32). Fundamentally, such films exhibit the greatest degree of abstraction and are more concerned with rhythm and movement in their own right, rejecting logical and linear continuity, moving away from the depiction of conventional forms and the assumed 'objectivity' of the exterior world, enabling shapes and objects to move, and liberating the artist to concentrate on the vocabulary he/she is using *in itself* instead of giving it specific function or meaning. As Leopold Survage wrote,

art films
Art cinema is a term usually applied to films where the director has clearly exercised a high degree of control over the film-making process and thus the films can be viewed as a form of personal expression. In terms of style and content, art cinema is usually characterised by the way it differs from its commercial counterpart, Hollywood cinema.

I will animate my painting. I will give it movement. I will introduce rhythm into the concrete action of my abstract painting, born of my interior life; my instrument will be the cinematographic film, this true symbol of accumulated movement. It will execute 'the scores' of my visions, corresponding to my state of mind in its successive phases....I am creating a new visual art in time, that of coloured rhythm and of rhythmic colour.

(Cited in Russett and Starr 1976: 96)

This kind of subjective work has therefore necessitated a different response from audiences. Instead of being located in understanding narrative the audience is asked to bring its own interpretation to the work. Colour, shape and texture evoke certain moods and ideas, and give pleasure in their own right without having to be attached to a specific meaning or framework. The audience may recognise the physical nature of the paint or physical materials themselves, the associations with the colours used, the sheer spontaneity in the work, which may recall the freedoms of expression in the pre-socialised child etc. These films are largely personal, subjective, original responses, which are the work of artists seeking to use the animated form in an innovative way. Sometimes these 'visions' are impenetrable and resist easy interpretation, being merely the absolutely individual expression of the artist. This in itself, once again, draws attention to the relationship between the artist and the work, and the relationship of the audience to the artist as it is being mediated through the work. The abstract nature of the films insists upon the recognition of their individuality. Further, these films may aspire to the condition of the dream-state, or memory, or fantasy, which, of course, has its own abstract logic, but conforms to a common understanding of human experience which embraces these states of consciousness. Dreams, memories, fantasies and the interpretation of thought processes may be the vehicles for personal visions but they possess a universalised dimension. Such work often has a strong relationship to music, and, indeed, it may be suggested that if music could be visualised it would look like colours and shapes moving through time with differing rhythms, movements and speeds. Some film-makers perceive that there is a psychological and emotional relationship with sound and colour which may only be expressed through the freedoms afforded by the use of animation. Sound is important in any animated film, but has particular resonance in the experimental film as it is often resisting dialogue, the clichéd sound effects of the cartoon or the easy emotiveness of certain kinds of music. Silence, avant-garde scores, unusual sounds and redefined notions of 'language' are used to create different kinds of statement.

SOME REVEALING EXPERIMENTS...

☐ CASE STUDY 6: *A COLOUR BOX* (LEN LYE, 1935)

Len Lye's *A Colour Box* is a completely abstract film in that it is created with lines and shapes stencilled directly onto celluloid, changing colour and form throughout its five-minute duration. It has dominant lines throughout, with various circles, triangles and grids interrupting and temporarily joining the image, until it reveals its sponsors, the GPO film unit, by including various rates for the parcel post, that is, 3lbs for 6d, 6lbs for 9d etc.

The dazzling, dynamic images are set to a contemporary jazz-calypso score which has the effect of bringing further energy and spontaneity to the piece. Lye believed that this kind of work should be seen as *composing motion* as it reveals the 'body energy' which connects the music and the images (Curtis 1987: 5).

• **Plate 6.6**
A Colour Box (Len
Lye/GPO Films, 1935)

☐ CASE STUDY 7: DEADSY (DAVID ANDERSON, 1990)

David Anderson's *Deadsy* is an example of the combination of xerography and puppet animation. Xerography, in this particular instance, involves the filming of a live performance by an actor, followed by the transfer of still images of his performance onto videographic paper. These images are photocopied and enlarged, and then rendered and drawn on before being re-filmed on a rostrum. The effect is to distort and degrade the image to give a haunting and hallucinatory quality to 'the character', known as Deadsy, a symbol of apocalyptic despair aligned with shifting sexual identity.

Deadsy is located as one of the 'Deadtime Stories for Big Folk', thus signalling its relationship to the vocabulary of the dream-state and, most particularly, the nightmares experienced by adults. The film creates the dream-state of deep sleep and reveals profound anxieties about the fear of death and the instability of gender and sexuality in its central character, Deadsy, who oscillates between being represented by a skeletal model and a distorted human figure. The film continually blurs lines in regard to its representation of life and death, masculinity and femininity and the physicality of sex and violence. Particularly effective in reinforcing this uncertainty and ambiguity is the use of writer Russell Hoban's monologue for Deadsy, which echoes the corrupted nature of the images by creating a post-apocalyptic language which slurs and mixes words together: for example:

When Deadsy wuz ul he like din do nuffing big He din do nuffing only ul ooky-pooky Deadsy Byebyes like he do a cockrutch or a fly He din do nuffig big. He werkin his way up tho after wyl He kilia mowss o yes my my.

This kind of language *suggests* meaning; it does not formally fix meaning in the way that English-speaking peoples might readily understand it. It alludes to the escalation of violent behaviour in the development of humankind and the inevitability of the apocalypse. Deadsy as a character becomes aligned with the personality of a rock star motivated by inner voices and instinctive drives, and aroused by the spectacle of destruction. This sense of arousal either inspires or informs the shifting gender positions Deadsy represents. Anderson shows the phallic relationship between male genitals ('sexothingys') and missiles, illustrating the masculine imperative to violence. Deadsy has a desire to change sex, however, to justify these actions. Deadsy assumes that if he becomes feminised, that is, 'Mizz Youniverss', then 'ewabody will luv me'. These gender shifts become symptomatic of the complex relationship between sexuality and violence and the socially unacceptable thoughts and feelings each individual may experience and repress. Anderson is suggesting that this kind of complexity underpins the fundamental anxiety that humankind will inevitably destroy itself.

The film is clearly trying to break into the viewers' preconceived ideas both about animation as a form and gender, death and global politics as a set of issues. Anderson is attempting to re-engage an audience with an abstraction of visual and verbal languages which reflect an anti-rational stance. Deadsy is a notional configuration but is characterised by differing representations as a form (that is, as a photographed image and a model) and in regard to gender and expression. Dialogue is abandoned in favour of voiceover monologue, but only to privilege a corrupted language that is difficult to understand. Styles are mixed, narrative and continuity are blurred and ambiguous, sometimes resisting interpretation, and even the artist, while clearly present, is elusive too. This is an attempt to create the post-apocalypse dream-state in the only form that could properly facilitate it.

COMPUTERS AND CONVERGENCE

For further discussion of the use of computer technology in film, see Chapter 4, pp. 148–151 and 172.

Animation can create the conditions to express new visions by creating a vocabulary which is both unlimitedly expressive and always potentially progressive because it need not refer to or comply with the codes and conventions of representation and expression that have preceded it. Orthodox, developmental and experimental animation are constantly changing.[2] Computer technology, for example, is enabling a new generation of animators to work with a different tool in order to both use traditional methods and invent fresh approaches to the animated form. Science, art and the moving image are conjoining to create a new digital cinema, enabling both a redetermination of the animated film and the enhancement of special effects in mainstream movies.

From the early experimental uses of computer animation at NASA and the Massachusetts Institute of Technology, the film exercises of James Whitney senior and junior, the work of Stan Vanderbeek (*Poemfields*, 1967–69), Lillian Schwartz (*Pictures from a Gallery*, 1976) and Peter Foldes (*Hunger*, 1973), and the output at the PIXAR company, there is already a tradition of animation in computing that is continually developing a vocabulary that is extending the limits of the form. Ex-Disney animator John Lasseter created highly effective computer-animated shorts – *Luxo Jnr* (1986), *Tin Toy* (1990) and *Knick Knack* (1991) – by emulating the character animation of Disney and the gag-structures of Warner Brothers and MGM cartoons. This culminated in the first full-length fully computer-generated feature *Toy Story* (1995) and its sequel, the equally engaging *Toy Story 2* (1999), which demonstrate what computer-generated images were initially uniquely able to offer. The toys are the perfect vehicle for the three-dimensional sense of smoothness and plasticity achievable using the geometric potentialities afforded by computer programmes; furthermore, the playroom space is fully exploited for the sense of dynamic movement through three-dimensional space also afforded by the computer. Inevitably, though, and this echoes the paradigm instigated by Disney, PIXAR has continued to innovate in the area of computer-generated animation by pursuing ever greater degrees of realism (see Wells 2001a). *Monsters Inc.*

(2001), although patently a fairytale story of monsters and moral revelation, is most characterised, however, by the plausibility of its environment and the authenticity of its characters, perhaps best exemplified in a sequence when 'Sulley', the large bear-like hero of the film, crashes in the snow when sledding to a nearby town. Every hair on Sulley's body and every snowflake seems real, and the twilight reflections create an eerie effect. It must not be forgotten, however, that every aspect of this image is created by the computer, but it embraces the material world as its key referent. If *Toy Story* is PIXAR's *Snow White and the Seven Dwarfs*, then *Monsters Inc.* is PIXAR's *Bambi*, the fullest representation of 'hyper-realism' in the animated form (see Wells 2002c).

Disney's own Digital Animation Unit made *Dinosaur* (2000), which like Tim Haines' BBC Television series, *Walking with Dinosaurs* (1999), successfully combines computer-generated animation with a live-action context, once more echoing the work of the pioneers in placing animated characters in a live-action environment – the Fleischer Brothers' 'Out of the Inkwell' series of cartoons – or vice versa – Disney's *Alice* shorts.[3] The sophistication of such contemporary work makes these combinations seamless, and makes 'fantasy' – the very presence and existence of dinosaurs – absolutely plausible and 'realistic'. The animated form has a rich history of 'dinosaur' films which serve as a corroboration of the ways in which animation can facilitate and, ironically, authenticate the fantastic. From *Gertie the Dinosaur* (1914), made by Winsor McCay, to Willis O'Brien's stop-motion work in *The Lost World* (1925), to Disney's invocation of pre-history in *Fantasia* (1940), to *One Million Years BC* (1966), featuring the work of Ray Harryhausen, integrating stop-motion animation with live action, to Don Bluth's Disney-like 'emotional journey' *The Land Before Time* (1988) and Steven Spielberg's *Jurassic Park* (1993), the 'dinosaur' story has been used to test the limits of animation, the impact of new technologies and approaches, and to evidence animation's distinctive and unique properties. Arguably, now, however, the computer has already been absorbed into the production of animation in a way that may be viewed as a new 'orthodoxy', and simply operates as yet another 'tool' for the animator to express particular perspectives. The comparative 'newness' of computer-generated imagery has been quickly dissipated as its omnipresence both in film and on television has established its aesthetic as the dominant aesthetic in animation in the way that Disney determined the form in the 1930s and 1940s. Crucially, though, as more independent film-makers can afford to make and embrace the conditions by which computer-generated animation is made, this dominant aesthetic will be challenged and subverted. Already, Yoichiro Kawaguchi, in Japan, has sought to be more abstract and experimental in his computer-generated films – *Eggy* (1990), *Festival* (1991) and *Mutation* (1992) – by emulating organic forms and developing random systems which create different shapes, forms and colour combinations. British animator, William Latham, has also created software to execute designs in a similar spirit, for example, in *Biogenesis* (1993). Ruth Lingford has also successfully used computer animation to make more challenging work in the graphic starkness of *Death and the Mother* (1996) and *Pleasures of War* (1999) (see Wells 2001b: 338–9). Significantly, too, the success of Nick Park and Peter Lord's *Chicken Run* (2000) has ensured that an alternative aesthetic – model animation – has currency in the feature animation market, and that the alternative vision of British animators, so successful on the international stage in the 1980s and 1990s, continues to have prominence.

□ CASE STUDY 8: MAINSTREAMING THE MARGINAL – *SHREK* (ANDREW ADAMSON AND VICKY JENSON, 2001)

Dreamworks SKG's *Shrek* (2001) became the first winner of the newly inaugurated Academy Award for Full-length Feature Animation. In this, not merely did it defeat its main rival, Disney/PIXAR's *Monsters Inc.* (2001), but was responsible for the

Plates 6.7 and 6.8 *Shrek* (Andrew Adamson and Vicky Jenson, 2001).

mainstreaming of previous marginalised aspects of animated film. Directed by Andrew Adamson and Vicky Jenson, *Shrek*, the story of an alienated, grotesque, green ogre (voiced by Mike Myers), who with the help of his wise-cracking sidekick, Donkey (Eddie Murphy), wins the love of a fairytale princess, Fiona (Cameron Diaz), in the face of the villainy of Lord Farquaad (John Lithgow), works both as a modern fairytale and a post-modern satire of Disney's story-telling techniques and ideological stances.

On the one hand, the new Academy Award can be viewed as a long overdue acknowledgement of the distinctiveness and quality of the animated feature in relation to its live-action counterpart; on the other it may be perceived as a ghetto-isation of the form, which once more refuses its achievement in regard to other Hollywood products. *Shrek* nevertheless represents a milestone in animated features because it brings together and legitimises *both* the subversive and the sentimental, drawing from some of the excesses of 'The All Sick and Twisted Festival', pioneered by Craig Decker and Mike Gribble, and the more radical work of Kricfalusi; and the archetypal and sentimental narratives created by the Disney Studio. The more taboo aspects – from 'Cracking one off' flatulence jokes to 'Dead Broad off the Table' lack-of-respect gags to the Snow White not being 'easy' despite the fact she lives with seven men innuendo – all now familiar in the public imagination due to animated sit-coms, *The Simpsons* and *South Park* – are contained and reconciled by being played out by a green ogre. His swamp, the epitome of an organic environment and earthiness, embraces the vulgarity and carnivalesque aspects of fantasy creatures, while Lord Farquaad's castle is minimalist in decoration and pristine in construction, the embodiment of control. Indeed, Farquaad (allegedly modelled on Disney's CEO, Michael Eisner, and named with no small degree of ambiguity), presides over Duloc, a thinly veiled critique of the oppressiveness of Disney's theme parks.

This underpinning satire on Disney's representational strategies in fairytales – with hilarious gags on bluebirds, lying puppets, big-eared elephants and transforming beasts – is nevertheless reliant on Disney's tried-and-trusted model of the 'emotional journey', and the use of established archetypes. Shrek, the hero, Farquaad, the villain, Fiona, the victim, and Donkey, the investigator/partner who helps to resolve problems, all correspond to an anticipated typology in fairytale story-telling, which resolves itself in a message-laden happy ending, promoting 'self-acceptance', and cautioning about the relativity of 'beauty'. While this is augmented by the contemporary spoofing of anything from *The Matrix*, *Blind Date* (*The Dating Game* in the USA), and *Indiana Jones and the Temple of Doom*, and what may prove to be anachronous pop songs which will eventually date the film, it is clear that sentiment – our sympathy for, and empathy with, Shrek – is at the heart of the story, and tempers its more subversive elements, which actually have their source in the more adult-oriented Warner Brothers cartoons of the 1930s and 1940s (see Wells 2002c).

This is especially important because it is clear that much of the enduring success of animated film within popular culture is in the way in which 'character' transcends the film and becomes part of a social discourse. From Mickey Mouse to Woody and Buzz, this has ensured that animation has historical presence. In the case of Shrek, as it may be with Sulley and Mike from *Monsters Inc.*, this may be as much about technical innovation as it is aesthetic and marketing acumen. Five years in the making, *Shrek* has some thirty-six detailed in-film locations; uses software which enhances the persuasiveness of facial movement and gesture; enhances and advances the materiality and volume of liquid substances; and crucially, creates physical forms through a layering process in the construction of figures which echoes the skeletal/muscular/skin formation of human bodies, and essentially provokes movement from the 'inside out', thus making the anatomical processes all the more realistic. Shrek, fantasy ogre though he is, 'lives', and takes his place alongside Cruise, Crowe and Clooney as a 'film star', simultaneously mainstreaming animation's open and versatile vocabulary, story-telling engine and style.

1 **In what ways and to what advantage does animation have a greater potential for expression than live-action film-making?**
2 **In what ways does animation offer different perspectives on issues of representation, i.e. how does animation address gender, race, ethnicity, age, 'the body', etc.?**
3 **How might traditional notions of 'narrative', 'genre', 'authorship', etc. in live-action film-making be revised when defined in relation to animation?**
4 **Animation is often seen as children's entertainment or an 'innocent' medium. How might it be viewed as 'subversive' and 'challenging'?**

CONCLUSION

Even without new technological apparatus animators are finding unique ways to express their individual vision. It is the intrinsic nature of animation itself which enables this to happen and animators continually to amaze, shock and amuse with their films. There is greater recognition that animation combines all the art-forms from music to dance to painting to sculpture and that it rightfully claims to be one of the most significant, and increasingly prominent art forms of the contemporary era. More and more animation is appearing online; on college and university courses; advertisements exhibit a range of commercially funded 'experimentation'; children's programming demonstrates a huge range and variety of animation production; the animated sit-com remains a television schedule staple; the feature animation has won its own Oscar category; and the independent film continues to proliferate even in times when such work sometimes seems under threat. Animation – the art of the impossible – continues to progress, and remains *the* art-form of twenty-first century visual culture.

NOTES

1   Cited in *Out of his Shell: Mamoru Oshii*, Universal Studios, 2002, TX: July 2002, Sci-Fi Channel.
2   Obviously, in a chapter of this length, no justice can be done to the many kinds of work in the animation field, nor the gifted animators who make it. While one could mention Švankmajer, Norstein, the Quay Brothers, Pitt, de Vere, Neubauer, Driessen, Rbycynski, Plympton, Park and Dudok de Wit as important names, this already neglects many others, and it is hoped that the chapter raises a general awareness of the field in order that students will seek out new work and cultivate tastes and preferences.
3   The 'Alice in Wonderland' and 'Out of the Inkwell' series served to demonstrate the profound flexibility of the animated form set against the fixity of the real world. In a similar way, Porky Pig featured in *You Ought To Be In Pictures* (1940), playing out his role as a movie star renegotiating his contract with live-action producer, Leon Schlesinger. Years later, *Who Framed Roger Rabbit?* (Robert Zemeckis, 1988) constituted a state-of-the-art amalgam of live-action characters and contexts with seemingly three-dimensional cartoon characters out a range of studios from the Golden era – Disney, Warner Brothers, MGM and Fleischer stars mixed here for the first time. This integration further articulated the tension between the representational conventions of live-action realism and the freedoms of the cartoonal form. In 1997 *Space Jam*, featuring basketball superstar Michael Jordan and the cartoon stars from the Warner Brothers studio, Bugs Bunny, Daffy Duck and Porky Pig, continued this tradition but enhanced it still further with the use of computer-generated imagery. Cartoon characters work in a live-action space; live-action characters work in a cartoon space, and all the characters interact in a computer graphic space which is constructed as a three-dimensional virtual environment through which the figures move. Jordan's play is recorded in a green screen environment mapped with reference points that the computer can correspond to in post-production in order to map in the cartoon characters and the live-action context. The 'cybercam' creates three-dimensional images of live-action figures which may be translated into three-dimensional cartoon form and further manipulated. Cartoon characters are created in three dimensions and all is seamlessly mixed in the computer-generated environment, playing out and extending the widest dynamic of choreographed movement corresponding both to the aesthetics of physical sporting activity and the historically determined codes and conventions of animated film. Meanwhile *Osmosis Jones* (2001), made by the Farrelly Brothers, uses the juxtaposition of live action and the cartoonal to point up the extent to which animation works as model of penetration, where the internal universe of the body is revealed and re-imagined in a way that is not possible using any other form.

FURTHER READING

Barrier, M., *Hollywood Cartoons: American Animation in the Golden Age*, Oxford University Press, New York and Oxford, 1999.

Bell, E., Haas, L. and Sells, L. (eds), *From Mouse to Mermaid: The Politics of Film, Gender and Culture*, Indiana University Press, Bloomington and Indianapolis, 1995.

Crafton, D., *Before Mickey: The Animated Film 1898–1928*, University of Chicago Press, Chicago and London, 1993.

Furniss, M., *Art in Motion: Animation Aesthetics*, John Libbey, London and Montrouge, 1998.

Klein, N., *7 Minutes*, Verso, London, 1993.

Pilling, J. (ed.), *Women and Animation, A Compendium*, British Film Institute, London, 1992.

Russett, R. and Starr, C., *Experimental Animation*, Da Capo, New York, 1976.

Wasko, J., *Understanding Disney*, Polity Press, Cambridge and Malden, 2001.

Wells, P., *Understanding Animation*, Routledge, London and New York 1998.

—— *Animation: Genre and Authorship*, Wallflower Press, London, 2002a.

FURTHER VIEWING

Here are some key models of animated film which repay viewing and analysis:

1933	*Three Little Pigs* (Walt Disney)
1936	*Popeye the Sailor meets Sinbad the Sailor* (Dave Fleischer)
1943	*Bad Luck Blackie* (Tex Avery)
	Coal Black and de Sebben Dwarfs (Bob Clampett)
1946	*Springer and the S.S.* (Jiri Trnka)
1949	*Red Hot Riding Hood* (Tex Avery)
1957	*What's Opera, Doc?* (Chuck Jones)
1961	*Ersatz* (Dusan Vukotic)
1963	*The Nose* (Alexander Alexieff)
1964	*The Hat* (John and Faith Hubley)
1965	*The Hand* (Jiri Trnka)
1967	*Pas De Deux* (Norman McLaren)
1974	*Great* (Bob Godfrey)
	The Street (Caroline Leaf)
1978	*Asparagus* (Suzan Pitt)
1979	*Tale of Tales* (Yuri Norstein)
1981	*Tango* (Zbigniew Rybczynski)
1982	*Dimensions of Dialogue* (Jan Švankmajer)
1988	*Akira* (Katsuhiro Otomo)
1989	*Binky and Boo* (Derek Hayes and Phil Austen)
1990	*Body Beautiful* (Joanna Quinn)
	Fatty Issues (Candy Guard)
1991	*Knick Knack* (John Lasseter)
	The Stain (Christine Roche and Marjut Rimmenen)
1994	*Triangle* (Erica Russell)
1997	*I Married a Strange Person* (Bill Plympton)
2000	*The Boy Who Saw the Iceberg* (Paul Driessen)
	Father and Daughter (Michael Dudok de Wit)
2001	*Give Up Yer Aul Sins* (Cathal Gaffney)

RESOURCE CENTRES

The UK Directory, *Animation UK* is an invaluable resource in that it lists most animators, animation companies and facilitators, and courses running in Britain. Published annually by BECTU.

http://www.aardman.com/
Aardman Animations

http://www.annecy-animation-festival.tm.fr/
Annecy Festival

http://www.awn.com/
Animation World Network
The database section is pretty minimal, and often incorrect; the best thing is the magazine's breadth of articles, mainly written by animators, critics or festival programmers. The What's New section in AWN is convenient for updates. The Animation Village has several listings and links to animators, organisations, festivals etc. in the international animation world. Artists such as Caroline Leaf and Alison Snowden/David Fine have their own

home pages on AWN. The same has Nicole Salomon's AAA in Annecy, Folioscope, ASIFA Hollywood and ASIFA San Francisco, as well as The Society for Animation Studies, Motion Picture Screen Cartoonists Union Local 839 and The Writers Guild of America. There are also links to other similar home pages not hosted by AWN, such as ASIFA International.

http: //www.awn.com/asifa_hollywood/
ASIFA Hollywood

http: //www.awn.com/asifa-sf/
ASIFA San Francisco
ASIFA East and ASIFA San Francisco produce quite informative articles, and provide information on current (US-based) projects, both commercial and independent, as well as opinion pieces.

http: //www.awn.com/heaven_and_hell/
Animation Heaven and Hell
This site has nicely designed pages on model and stop-frame animation, including Švankmajer and George Pal.

http: //www.awn.com/safo99/
Ottawa Festival

http: //www.chapman.edu/animation/
Animation Journal

http: //www.medios.fi/animafest/
Zagreb Festival

http: //memory.loc.gov/ammem/oahtml/oahome.html
Origins of American Animation web site

http: //www.nfb.ca/E/1/1/
National Film Board of Canada
The National Film Board of Canada has a really impressive site. You can go through their whole catalogue of films with descriptions; many of the most important film-makers have their own biography; and the history of NFBC is extensively described. The main problem with the NFBC home page is that the entry page is too big, it takes minutes to download; skip it and go directly to the index.

http: //Samson.hivolda.no: 8000/asifa/
ASIFA International

http: //www.swcp.com/animate/
ASIFA Central

http: //www.yrd.com/asifa/
ASIFA East

Part four

Representation of gender and sexuality

Chapter 7

Gender and film

Jill Nelmes

In the early 1900s there was an enormous expansion of the American film industry, which was making large profits because of the vast audiences attracted to the new medium. Although the new industry was cut-throat and competitive, it was also much more receptive and open to change than the European film industry and there was significantly less discrimination against women. It has been estimated that there were at least twenty-six women directors in America before 1930, but there were probably many more who directed and acted or were screenwriters but not credited with the role.

Lois Weber was the first female American film-maker and probably the most famous, often writing, producing and starring in her films, many of which dealt with social issues such as abortion and divorce. Weber directed over seventy-five films.

By the end of the 1920s silent movies were on their way out and talkies had arrived. This, indirectly, brought about the demise of many women's careers as film-makers. Only the bigger studios could survive because of the expensive equipment needed in the change-over to sound, and it was generally the many small, independent companies (who employed the majority of women) that had to close down, and so with them went many jobs for women in the industry.

Only one woman director, Dorothy Arzner, really survived the transition to talkies. She went on to make many famous movies, for example, *Christopher Strong* (1933) with Katharine Hepburn and *Dance Girl Dance* (1940). At one time Arzner was ranked among the 'top ten' directors in Hollywood.

Ironically, the changes in America drove directors such as Elinor Glynn and Jacqueline Logan to Britain and Europe, which already had an extremely poor record of women working in film.

Britain did not give much encouragement to its indigenous women film-makers; the earliest woman known to have directed British films was Dinah Shurey, though very little is known about her other than that she made two films, *Carry On* (1927) and *Last Port* (1929).

Until the Second World War, hardly any women in Britain could be termed film-makers, but some had key roles in the film-making process: Alma Reville, married to Alfred Hitchcock, assisted him in many films such as *The 39 Steps* (1935) and *The Lady Vanishes* (1938). She also helped to write other scripts such as *Suspicion* (1941) and

• **Plate 7.1**
Christopher Strong
(Dorothy Arzner, 1933)
Dorothy Arzner was once ranked among the top ten directors in Hollywood

Shadow of a Doubt (1943). Mary Field worked in documentary from 1928 and became executive producer of children's entertainment for J. Arthur Rank from 1944 to 1950. Joy Batchelor worked mainly in animation from 1935 and co-directed the first British feature-length cartoon, *Animal Farm* (1954), continuing to make animated films until the 1970s.

In Britain and the USA more women were able to work in documentary film. The British Documentary Film Movement, of which John Grierson was the founder, had a huge influence on British film and has continued to exert its influence to the present day. Grierson's sister, Ruby, worked alongside him on a number of films and was involved in making films herself, such as *Housing Problems* (1940).

Many film-makers involved in the early documentary movement went on to make propaganda films during the war. This was one area of film where a few women could be found working as directors and assistant directors. Some women were taken on in roles usually only open to men because of the increased demand for documentary propaganda film in wartime Britain and the shortage of available manpower.

Two female British fiction feature film directors, Muriel Box and Wendy Toye, made a number of films in the 1940s and 1950s and gained an international reputation. Muriel Box made profitable mass entertainment films. Her most famous film, which she also scripted, is a melodrama, *The Seventh Veil* (1945), but she continued to make films until 1964. The lesser-known Wendy Toye made such films as *Raising a Riot* (1957) and *We Joined the Navy* (1962), with Dirk Bogarde and Kenneth More.

Very few women film-makers in Britain and the USA before 1970 could be termed commercially successful, Dorothy Arzner and Muriel Box being the outstanding exceptions. It was virtually unheard of for women to work in technical areas such as sound or camera, although women art directors and film editors were not so unusual – Ann V. Coates worked as an editor on Box's film *The Truth about Women* (1958) and David Lean's *Lawrence of Arabia* (1962). In general, however, it was rare for a woman to have a key role in film-making and, it could be argued, the rise of feminism in the 1960s was to be the great catalyst for change for women in film.

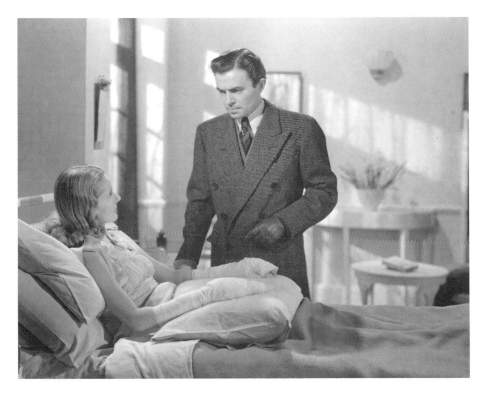

• **Plate 7.2**
The Seventh Veil (Muriel Box, 1945)
A hugely successful melodrama

By the 1990s more women were working in previously male-dominated areas such as directing, camera, sound and lighting: Diane Tammes, Sue Gibson and Belinda Parsons are all respected camerawomen; Diana Ruston and Moya Burns work in sound. Surprisingly, they have come across little sexism and feel that with more and more women coming into the industry men have no choice but to accept them. Moya Burns comments in an article entitled 'Women in Focus':

The industry has changed a lot in the last ten years, there are not so many hard-boiled areas, like big-budget features. The features that get made today are financed differently, a lot of the money seems to be coming from bodies like Channel 4. They have a different emphasis on the type of film they want to make, and this filters right down to the type of crew they want to employ.

(Burns 1992: 4)

In the field of directing many more women film-makers are now breaking into mainstream film, often from the independent sector or from the increasing number of film schools. Beeban Kidron made the highly acclaimed TV series *Oranges are Not the Only Fruit* (1990) and has regularly worked on feature films and in TV. Sally Potter moved from the avant-garde *The Gold Diggers* (1982) to *Orlando* (1993), a film based on a Virginia Woolf novel (see Case study 1, p. 258) and most recently made *The Man Who Cried* (2000), starring Johnny Depp and Cate Blanchett. Gurinder Chada's first film *Bhaji on the Beach* (1993) takes a wry and witty look at life for Asian women in Britain while *What's Cooking* (2000) is a rich and colourful film that has received international acclaim. Chada's latest film, *Bend It Like Beckham* (2002) has been a huge success in British cinemas. *Bridget Jones' Diary* (2001) was directed by Sharon Maguire and was a big hit in Britain whilst also doing very well in the USA and Europe. Internationally, more established women film-makers such as Jane Campion and Kathryn Bigelow regularly produce feature films but the spectacular box-office hits still generally come from male directors and the biggest selling films world-wide last year were in the main produced, written and directed by men.

A number of support agencies for women film-makers have been established which aim to provide the female equivalent of the 'Old Boys' Network'; 'Women in Film and TV' helps women in the mainstream sector and in the independent and workshop sector by offering seminars and screenings, while 'Networking' provides information and support for all women interested in film and video.

Whether changing attitudes towards women working in the film industry will produce more positive, realistic and varied representations of women in film is open to question. Feminism has perhaps changed the way we look at film, and there is a greater awareness

• **Plate 7.3**
Bend It Like Beckham
(Gurinder Chada, 2002)
Girls playing football is
not a traditional crowd-
puller yet this film was a
great success in the UK

of how gender is represented in the media. *Thelma and Louise* (1991) was hailed as a feminist film (directed by Ridley Scott, but scripted by a woman, Callie Khouri), although a more cynical analysis of the film reveals that the women are filmed quite conventionally, as objects of 'the look'.[1] *Charlie's Angels* (2001), whilst playing with conventions of the action genre and making the women protagonists active, uses the camera to focus on how they look and in particular the attractiveness of their bodies. *Baise-moi* (2000), a French film written and directed by Virginie Despontes and Coralie Trinh Thi, pushes the *Thelma and Louise* theme much further. The two women protagonists go on a sex and killing spree in a rape-revenge drama in which they have the power of the look. As more women writers and directors work in mainstream film, though, it does seem likely that there will be a widening out of representations of women both visually and thematically. Films such as Ang Lee's *Crouching Tiger, Hidden Dragon* (2000), has been internationally successful yet the central character is an action woman. The hugely popular *Erin Brockovich* (2000) was scripted by Susannah Grant and stars Julia Roberts in the 'rags to riches' story of a woman's struggle to sue a multinational company whilst bringing up her children as a single mother. Women's stories, told from a woman's point of view, are becoming more acceptable in mainstream cinema; hopefully this trend will continue as more women take on leading roles in the film industry and audiences continue to watch their films.

THE FEMINIST REVOLUTION

The women's movement did not suddenly arrive; since the days of the suffragettes an increasing number of women had seen the need for equality with men. A new political and social climate was evolving in the 1960s and early 1970s which questioned the established order, encouraged radical reform and produced conditions that were conducive to the rise of the feminist movement. Although this radical dissatisfaction with contemporary society began in America its message soon spread to Britain and in both countries there was a questioning of woman's role in society. Betty Friedan's book, *The Feminine Mystique*, published in 1963, touched a chord in many discontented women. The time was ripe for the spread of the feminist movement,[2] as Friedan explained:

• **Plate 7.4**
Thelma and Louise
(Ridley Scott, 1991)

stereotyping

A quick and easy way of labelling or categorising the world around us and making it understandable. Stereotypes are learned but are by no means fixed, yet are often resistant to change. They tend to restrict our understanding of the world and perpetuate beliefs that are often untrue or narrow. For instance, the concept that only thin women are attractive is a stereotype promoted by much of the media in contemporary society (though there are some exceptions, such as comediennes Dawn French and Roseanne). Stereotyping is not always negative, but tends to be very much concerned with preserving and perpetuating power relations in society. It is in the interests of those in power to continue to stereotype those with lower status in a negative light, thus preserving the status quo.

representation

The media re-presents information to its audience, who are encouraged by the mainstream media to see its output as a 'window on the world', as reflecting reality. Yet the process of representing information is highly complex and highly selective. Many feminists argue that the way notions of gender are represented by the media perpetuates and reinforces the values of patriarchal society; for instance, men tend to take on strong, active roles, while women are shown as passive and relying on their attractiveness. There are exceptions to such narrow stereotyping: the 'strong' woman shown by Ripley in the *Alien* trilogy and the two heroines in

• **Plate 7.5**
Erin Brockovich (Steven Soderburgh, 2000) More women are now working in key roles in Hollywood film production. Susannah Grant was the scriptwriter for this film

the absolute necessity for a civil rights movement for women had reached such a point of subterranean explosive urgency by 1966 that it took only a few of us to get together to ignite the spark – and it spread like a nuclear chain reaction.

(Cited in Banner 1984: 247)

Representation and stereotyping of women in the media

Feminists generally believe that the media is a contributory factor in perpetuating a narrow range of **stereotyped** images of women. How women are **represented** in the media may encourage particular expectations of women which are extremely limiting; for instance, that women are always based in the home, that they are inferior to men, that they like men who are violent, are just a few of the myths that are arguably perpetuated by the media. As Molly Haskell points out:

From a woman's point of view the ten years from, say, 1962 or 1963 to 1973 have been the most disheartening in screen history. In the roles and prominence accorded to women, the decade began unpromisingly, grew steadily worse, and at present shows no sign of improving. Directors, who in 1962 were guilty only of covert misogyny (Stanley Kubrick's *Lolita*) or kindly indifference (Sam Peckinpah's *The High Country*) became overt in 1972 with the violent abuse and brutalisation of *A Clockwork Orange* and *Straw Dogs*.

(Haskell 1973: 323)

Film, particularly in the early feminist period, was seen as one area of the media that could become a battleground for the women's movement. Film would be used as an ideological tool, which would counteract the stereotyped images of women presented by the male-dominated media and raise women's awareness of their inferior position in

patriarchal society, where women were generally relegated to a subservient role. For instance, in film, women, as the historical section indicates, have usually taken supportive roles rather than key, decision-making ones.

> Do mainstream films still represent women in a narrow range of predictable and stereotyped ways?

FEMINIST FILM THEORY AND PRACTICE

The influence of alternative, independent and avant-garde film

Alongside the expansion of feminism and the women's movement **alternative cinema** and **avant-garde** cinema was flourishing. **Independent cinema** could, at its simplest, be divided into two forms: documentary and avant-garde. British film has a strong documentary tradition, which was to some extent socialist-influenced, and feminist film initially saw documentary as a way of presenting the 'truth' about the lives of women. During the 1960s, American avant-garde film-makers produced many innovative and controversial films, some of the most well known being 'gay' and 'camp' films that challenged traditional stereotypes of gender roles such as Andy Warhol's *Lonesome Cowboys* (1968) and Kenneth Anger's *Scorpio Rising* (1965). The avant-garde developed in Europe, the French film-makers, Jean-Luc Godard and François Truffaut being its most famous exponents. Although gender roles in European films tended to be stereotypical, some feminist film-makers saw the potential of avant-garde film as a means of breaking away from the constraints of traditional cinema.

The expansion of independent film-making in Britain during the 1960s encouraged the formation of a number of workshops aiming to make film making available to all and to destroy the élitism often found in the industry. Many workshops made films that were outside the sphere of mainstream film and television, often being concerned with areas that were considered radical in politics or content. Cinema Action was one of the earliest workshops. Formed in 1968, it toured the country screening films aimed at a working-class audience. Amber Films, based in Newcastle, was founded in 1969 and The Other Cinema opened in London as a distribution agency (an essential outlet for the distribution of independent films). Perhaps the best known of the workshops is the London Film-makers Co-op, which is still in existence today.

The late 1960s and early 1970s was a period of great academic and cultural vitality. The government supported the arts and there was a commitment to film-making; in 1968 the Regional Arts Associations began funding individual films and from 1972 the Arts Council did likewise.

Thelma and Louise could be seen as positive models, although rather more cynically they could be seen merely as 'role reversal' films and so as having purely novelty value. Representations often make use of stereotypes because they are a shorthand, quick and easy way of using information. It could be argued that the media production process encourages the use of stereotypes because of the pressure of time and budget.

patriarchal society
A society in which men have the power and control. Women are generally disadvantaged and have lower status. It could be argued that we no longer live in a patriarchal society, but in a society in which men and women have equal opportunities. For instance, in the USA, Sherry Lansing is head of Paramount Pictures and in the UK a number of women now have key roles in the media, particularly at the BBC, where there are now women heads of channel programming. But many feminists would argue that we still have a long way to go in terms of politics, philosophy and economics before we live in a society in which men and women can be considered equal.

alternative cinema Provides an alternative to the codes and conventions of mainstream, narrative cinema, often both thematically and visually.

avant-garde cinema Essentially non-narrative in structure and often intellectual in content, working in opposition to mainstream cinema. Avant-garde film is often self-conscious and frequently makes use of devices such as cuts to the camera crew, talking to the camera and scratching on film.

independent cinema May be divided into two areas: first, independent mainstream cinema, such as Handmade Films, which aims to compete with the big studios, although without any large financial backing finds it difficult to survive. Palace Films was one such casualty; the success of *The Crying Game* came too late to save its demise. Second, the term is used to describe film-making outside the mainstream sector, for instance, film workshops, avant-garde film, feminist film. The boundaries between these two areas are not always clear and may overlap.

The first women's film group

The combination of the expansion of the women's movement and the rise of independent film-making brought about the conditions in which feminist film could thrive. In 1972 the first women's film group in Britain was formed. The London Women's Film Group (LWFG) aimed to spread ideas about women's liberation and enable women to learn film-making skills otherwise unavailable to them.

The LWFG, apart from making films by women, also campaigned for equal opportunities for women in the industry, and was instrumental in initiating the examination of the role of women within the industry's union, the ACCT (Association of Cinematographers, Television and Allied Technicians). Without acceptance by the union it was virtually impossible to work in the industry. In the 1970s there were no more women working in high-grade jobs in the film and television industry than there had been in the 1950s. Demystification of the learning of technical skills was considered vital, but it was also necessary to make women familiar with all the stages in the film-making process so that they had a large pool of knowledge, which they would never have been able to obtain from mainstream film. Many film groups worked co-operatively, giving all members an equal say in the production process and rejecting the strict hierarchy of roles used in mainstream film production.

The feminist film movement was intentionally political, aiming to give all women, but especially working-class women, a chance to work in film. The films were often shown to trade unions, in factories and housing estates, and it was hoped they would help to raise women's consciousness about their place in society. Many of the early feminist films fitted into the black and white documentary realist tradition, the dominant mode of alternative, political film-making in Britain. Linda Dove, of the LWFG, explained in an interview:

> We tended to reject commercial films wholesale as the ideological products of capitalist, sexist, racist society. ... Originally our aim was to change the context in which a film is seen – we wanted to break down the audience passivity by always going out with films and discussing them when they were shown.
>
> (Dove 1976: 59)

Film as a 'window on the world'

For further discussion of documentary film, see Chapter 5.

Left-wing documentary films had been seen as presenting the 'truth' and a form of reality, but the view that the visual media presented a 'window on the world' came under question in the early 1970s. The media, it was argued, are manipulated by the ruling patriarchal ideology and what is seen as natural, as clear-cut and obvious, is in fact a construct produced by society. This ambivalence about the 'meaning' of films and other media suggests its interpretation by the audience may be different to that intended by the film-maker. For instance, *Women of the Rhondda* (1972), a documentary about women who live in the South Wales Valley's, has a naturalistic style with no voiceover and the images are intended to speak for themselves. The message, though, is somewhat ambiguous for a non-feminist audience because the text has so many possible readings. This awareness resulted in a number of radical documentary film-makers becoming more didactic in their approach: for instance, *The Amazing Equal Pay Show* (LWFG, 1972) experiments with film conventions, developing links with avant-garde cinema, as does *The Night Cleaners* (Berwick Street Collective, 1972), which was concerned with better pay for office cleaners but used unconventional editing techniques.

For further discussion of Jean-Luc Goddard and the Fench New Wave, see Chapter 12.

Many feminist film-makers in the 1970s appropriated ideas from avant-garde art cinema and applied them to discuss questions that were of concern to the women's movement, such as representation. The avant-garde had always been male-dominated and narrow in its representations of women (see, for instance, Jean-Luc Godard's films such as *Breathless* [1960], *A Married Woman* [1964] and *Weekend* [1967]). But the avant-garde's political/anarchist basis gave an alternative form to the traditional use of realism in both fiction and documentary film. This influence was most profound in film-makers like Laura Mulvey and Sally Potter, whose films are discussed in more detail below.

Early feminist film theory

The ideological sense of purpose and political debate behind feminist film-making ensured the development of a film theory. Feminist film theory was, in the early period, especially concerned with representation and sexuality and its relation to the dominance of the male power structure within a patriarchal society. A number of women, often from an academic background, encouraged this development, but it was perhaps Laura Mulvey and Claire Johnston who were the progenitors of feminist film theory. Both wrote seminal articles which were to have a huge impact on the study of film and the media and which will be discussed in this chapter.

Developing a counter-cinema

Claire Johnston's 'Women's Cinema as Counter-Cinema' (1973) is one of the earliest articles on feminist film theory and practice. Johnston shows how women have been stereotyped in film since the days of the silent cinema, and argues for a cinema that challenges such narrow conventions but which will also be entertaining. In mainstream cinema woman is seen as an extension of a male vision and Johnston criticises the narrow role she is given in film: 'It is probably true to say that despite the enormous emphasis placed on woman as spectacle in the cinema, woman as woman is largely absent' (ibid.: 214).

The work of two female Hollywood directors, Dorothy Arzner and Ida Lupino, is considered by Johnston, who suggests that their films partially subvert the patriarchal viewpoint. An understanding of how these films work could be important for feminist film practice in breaking through and challenging the ruling ideology.

Johnston stresses the importance of developing a film practice that questions and challenges mainstream dominant cinema and its patriarchal basis. She terms it a counter-cinema movement which will have links with avant-garde and left-wing film.

Pleasure, looking and gender

Psychoanalytic theory, particularly the theories of Freud and Lacan, has been instrumental in the development of a feminist film theory, although **structuralist** and **Marxist theories**[3] have also been influential to a lesser extent. Laura Mulvey's article 'Visual Pleasure and Narrative Cinema' (first published in 1975) emphasises the importance of the patriarchical viewpoint in the cinema; that the pleasure gained from looking (**scopophilia** [see page 252]) is a male pleasure and 'the look' in cinema is controlled by the male and directed at the female, this is often referred to as the 'male gaze'.

Scopophilia can be directed in two areas: first, voyeurism, that is scopophilic pleasure linked to sexual attraction, and, second, scopophilic pleasure which is linked to narcissistic identification. Mulvey argues that this identification is always with the male, who is the pivot of the film, its hero, while the female is often seen as a threat. Film reflects society, argues Mulvey, and therefore society influences our understanding of film. This viewpoint is linked with psychoanalytical theory to demonstrate the influence of patriarchal society on film. Patriarchy and phallocentrism are intrinsically linked; the phallus is a symbol of power, of having (note how guns are used in film: guns = phallus = power). The woman has no phallus, she is castrated, which relates back to Freudian theory that the woman is lacking and therefore inferior because she has no phallus.

Freud's theories on scopophilia centre around voyeurism and the desire to see the erotic and the forbidden, yet this desire is male-centred. The cinema provides a perfect venue for illicit voyeuristic viewing because the audience is in a dark enclosed womblike world. Mulvey argues that the power cinema holds is so strong it can act as a temporary form of brainwashing (an argument which is still very much alive today!).

psychoanalytic theory
Based on the theories of Freud and, more recently, Lacan. Feminists argue that aspects of psychoanalysis are questionable because they are based on patriarchal assumptions that woman is inferior to man. Freud found female sexuality difficult and disturbing. Lacan argues that the mother is seen as lacking by the child because she has no phallus. Uncertainty about the role of the female in psychoanalytic theory has been picked up by a number of feminists such as Mulvey, De Lauretis and Modleski, who question the inevitability of Freud and Lacan's theories which emphasise the importance of the phallus, penis envy and patriarchal supremacy.

structuralism
A movement founded on the belief that the study of society could be scientifically based and that there are structures in society that follow certain patterns or rules. Initially, most interest was centred on the use of language; Saussure, the founder of linguistics, argued that language was essential in communicating the ideology, the beliefs, of a culture. Structuralists have applied these theories to film, which uses both visual and verbal communication, and pointed out that the text conveys an illusion of reality, so conveying the ideology of a society even more effectively.

Marxist theory
Argues that those who have the means of production have control in a capitalist society. The dominant class have control of the means of production and have an interest in perpetuating

the dominant ideology. More recently, exponents of Althusserian Marxism, particularly post-1968, have argued that mainstream narrative cinema reinforces the capitalist system and that a revolutionary cinema is needed to challenge the dominant ideology.

scopophilia
Freudian term meaning the sexual pleasure gained from looking, introduced to film analysis by Luara Mulvey, who pointed out that women are usually depicted in a passive role and are looked at, whilst men take on an active role and look.

The woman in Freudian theory represents desire, but also the fear of castration, and so there is a tension, an ambivalence towards the female form, and her 'look' can be threatening. As the male is the controller, taking the active role, the female is reduced to the icon, the erotic, but at the same time is a threat because of her difference.

Mulvey argues that woman has two roles in film: erotic object for the characters in the story and erotic object for the spectator. Recent feminist theory suggests the representation of women is far more complex, and later theory, including Mulvey's, looks at films where women do have a key role as subject rather than object. Melodrama is one such area (see Mulvey 1981).

Mulvey refers to Hitchcock because of the complicit understanding in his films that the audience gains a voyeuristic pleasure from watching a film, from looking: 'In *Vertigo* (1958) in particular, but also in *Marnie* (1964) and *Rear Window* (1954), the 'look' is central to the plot oscillating between voyeurism and fetishistic fascination' (Mulvey 1975: 813).

The denial of pleasure

Mulvey points out that devices used in the traditional Hollywood narrative film have trapped film-makers into using certain codes and conventions that place the female in a subordinate, passive position, making her role as erotic object extremely limiting. Mulvey criticises the narrowness of this role and argues that to change woman's position in film a revolutionary look at cinema needs to be taken and the denial of voyeuristic cinematic pleasure be given a priority. The exclusion of woman as object, as provider of voyeuristic pleasure will then free her from the narrow limits she has been allocated in cinema. This may seem an extreme reaction to mainstream, narrative cinema, but in the early 1970s feminists felt the only way to change female representation was to take extreme measures: a new radical cinema was needed, an alternative to the 'magic' of narrative cinema.

A new language

The importance of the creation of a female subject and the development of a new language is central to early feminist film theory, which argued that spoken, written and visual languages all placed women in a subordinate position and reflected a patriarchal ideology. A film theory and practice that had its own codes and conventions would replace the dominance of patriarchal cinema. Christine Gledhill echoes this desire in her article, 'Some Recent Developments in Feminist Criticism':

A feminist film-maker then, finds the root of patriarchy in the very tools she wishes to employ to speak about women. So what is required of her is the development of a counter-cinema that will deconstruct the language and techniques of classic cinema.

(1985: 841)

Classic narrative cinema was based on ideas that had been passed on from the literary realist tradition and many feminists felt that this realist tradition perpetuated a way of seeing, of understanding the world, that belonged to dominant patriarchal society and that feminists should break with this tradition.

Avant-garde feminist film

For further analysis of avant-garde, feminist film see Case study 1: Sally Potter, pp. 258–261.

Film-makers such as Laura Mulvey and Sally Potter were interested in a film theory and practice which worked together and would produce a new feminist language. Avant-garde film was the ideal vehicle for these ideas because it broke the normal rules and conventions of mainstream cinema. Mulvey's article 'Film, Feminism and the Avant-Garde' (1979) explores this relationship, suggesting that both forms of film can be mutually beneficial, working towards similar goals. Mulvey's films, for instance, actively avoid any sense of being constructed for the male spectator, confronting the lack of representation of women in film; they are a mixture of avant-garde, melodrama and psychoanalytic theory.

The need for an audience

Many avant-garde films were termed 'difficult' and only attracted a small audience which tended to be those familiar with 'art film'. Even though avant-garde-influenced film-makers such as Mulvey did much to aid the understanding of their films by producing hand-outs and giving lectures, some feminists felt that avant-garde film was élitist and would be of no interest to a mass audience of women. Mulvey's and Johnston's theories, they suggested, would be more useful for the development of a feminist film theory than as a guide on how to make feminist films. Kaplan (1983), for example, points out that it makes more sense to use familiar and recognisable cinematic conventions to explain that the 'realism' of mainstream cinema is a fabrication.

A period of optimism and defiance

Feminist film theory and practice in the period up to 1980 had presented a joint ideological struggle; film theory analysed the patriarchal conventions that mainstream film worked within and film practice was physically able to break these rules. But there was a very limited audience for feminist film in this period, even though there was an increasing interest in academic circles in feminist film theory. In the strongly male-dominated world of film-making, women were rarely seen as artists or film-makers, and feminist art was seen as a possible challenge to patriarchal society. As Johnston (1973) explains, the female within patriarchy is seen as the 'other' and feminist art represented a threat to these narrow conceptions of gender.

By the end of the 1970s a feminist film theory and practice had been established, giving many women a new-found confidence and a belief that society could change. In the previous decade a number of influential articles on feminist film theory and practice had been written. A body of work had been formed by feminist writers and academics, Mulvey and Johnston being the founder writers who were to influence a generation of film and media critics.

At the beginning of the 1970s the focus was on representation in film and the media, but by the end of the decade attention was being diverted to the concept of 'pleasure' and whether this should be denied in film. Some feminists expressed the concern that by denying the pleasures of mainstream cinema feminist film-makers might alienate their audience. Yet feminists generally agreed that feminist film theory and practice had an important role to play in raising consciousness as to the marginalisation of women in a patriarchal society.

A number of feminists still called for a counter-cinema and a deconstructive cinema in the early 1980s. Ann Kaplan and Annette Kuhn argued there was a need to break down the dominant forms of cinema, and the audience should become active rather than passive, gaining pleasure from learning rather than the narrative.

Both Kuhn and Kaplan and film-makers such as Sue Clayton were aware of the problems of using a cinema which rejects the mainstream, that is, which is anti-conventional and may alienate its audience. Kaplan suggested that a way forward would be to work within and manipulate the conventions of mainstream cinema.

REASSESSING FEMINIST FILM THEORY

In 1981 Mulvey published a response to her 1975 article 'Visual Pleasure and Narrative Cinema', which was so fundamental to the development of feminist film theory. Her new article was titled 'Afterthoughts on Visual Pleasure and Narrative Cinema'. In it Mulvey develops two lines of thought: first, examining whether the female spectator can gain a deep pleasure from a male-oriented text, and second, how the text and the spectator are affected by the centrality of a female character in the narrative. 'Afterthoughts' marks a shift in attitude, a move away from representation to studying the female response, to asking how women watch films and questioning the role of melodrama, which has traditionally been viewed as the woman's genre.

Feminist film theory has been especially influenced by psychoanalytic theory and particularly Freud and Lacan. Mulvey acknowledges her debt to Lacan who, she explains, has 'broadened and advanced ways of conceptualising sexual difference, emphasising the fictional, constructed nature of masculinity and femininity' (ibid.: 165).

Not all feminists supported a feminist film theory based on psychoanalytic theory. Terry Lovell, in *Pictures of Reality* (1983), criticised Lacanian theory because of its emphasis on the individual rather than the collective and argued that gaining pleasure from the text is rather more complex than a simple attribution to sexual desire.

In the latter part of the 1980s Freud's work was re-examined by many feminists because of its phallocentric basis. Tania Modleski, for instance, in her book *The Women Who Knew Too Much* (1988), argues for a less male-centred version of spectatorship and calls for the development of a feminist psychoanalytic theory which is challenging and inventive. Penley, in the introduction to *Feminism and Film Theory* (1988), states that much feminist film criticism questions the patriarchal roots of current psychoanalytic theories, especially those of Freud and Lacan.

Modleski applies her ideas to an analysis of Hitchcock's films, which have been of great interest to feminists because of his extreme use of voyeurism and the 'look'. Reassessing earlier theory, Modleski points out Mulvey's article 'Visual Pleasure and Narrative Cinema' does not allow for the complex nature of representation and raises questions about the stereotypical, passive female object and the active male. Modleski states: 'What I want to argue is neither that Hitchcock is utterly misogynistic nor that he is largely sympathetic to women and their plight in patriarchy, but that his work is characterised by a thoroughgoing ambivalence about femininity' (ibid.: 3).

Many of Hitchcock's films are seen from the point of view of a female protagonist: for instance, *Blackmail* (1929), *Rebecca* (1940), *Notorious* (1946), or when the hero or heroine is in a vulnerable or passive, female position as in *Rear Window* (1954).

Modleski re-examines aspects of Mulvey's work, especially the suggestion that the patriarchal order has banished a strong female presence. In *North by Northwest* (1959), Cary Grant's role is that of hero and sex object, the desirable male; in *Marnie* (1964), Sean Connery plays a similar role, which also serves to heighten the irony that Marnie, the heroine and his wife, is frigid. In Hitchcock's films both male and female can become objects of the 'look'.

The strong and powerful female can then exist within mainstream film, yet Hitchcock is patently not a feminist film-maker and his films express Freud's assertion that the male contempt for femininity is an expression of the repression of their bisexuality – woman is a threat who must be destroyed. As Modleski concludes: 'the male object is greatly threatened by bisexuality, though he is at the same time fascinated by it; and it is the woman who pays for this ambivalence, often with her life itself' (ibid.: 10).

Questioning psychoanalytic theory

In the 1970s and 1980s feminist film theory was dominated by a psychoanalytic approach. But the tendency to favour psychoanalytic theory has proven to be problematic when applied to feminist film theory because of its dependence on the Oedipal trajectory, in which woman is seen as not only 'lacking' but also as needing to be brought under control through the male gaze. If woman's role in film is to always be reduced to the 'other' by psychoanalytic theory, then it could be argued there is little space to open up patriarchal narratives to account for the female spectator, other than through identification with the male.

• **Plate 7.6** *North by Northwest* (Alfred Hitchcock, 1959) Cary Grant – irresistible to women

Some feminist film theorists, such as Jackie Byars, have reworked psychoanalytic theory to give it a feminist perspective. Her analysis of melodrama suggests the woman can exist as a spectator in a positive way. In *All That Heaven Allows* Byars (1995) argues that the gaze is strongly female. Jackey Stacey's analysis of *Desperately Seeking Susan* points out that the film is not about sexual difference in terms of male and female but the difference between the two women lead characters, a view which cannot be read in terms of Lacan or Freud whose theories are so phallocentric in nature (Stacey 1992). Psychoanalytic theory needs to develop a new framework which will view the woman as a positive force rather than suffering from a state of lack.

The reworking of psychoanalytic theory may provide a new model from which feminists could work. Mulvey's theories, based on Freud and Lacan, have had considerable impact in enhancing our understanding of the role of the spectator in film and how media texts place the viewer in a particular position. Application of these methods of analysis proves useful when analysing a film such as *The Piano*, which gives the female the power of the look and, to some extent, reverses conventional filming practices (see Case study 2, pp. 261–264).

A cultural studies approach

In the last decade there has been a shift away from Freudian and Lacanian theory towards a cultural studies approach to the study of film. Black feminist film theory and lesbian feminist film theory, for instance, have both suggested new ways of understanding how women from different social and ethnic groups interpret cultural messages.

The emphasis has transferred from reading media texts, a move from the study of the encoding process which asks how messages are produced, to a study of the decoding process which asks how messages are received and understood by an audience.

Cultural Studies theorists argue that **semiotic** and psychoanalytic readings of film tend to isolate the viewer from the text; cultural studies is more concerned with asking how cultural systems produce meaning and how ideology is replicated through cultural institutions, texts and practices. **Ideology** can be seen as the means by which we interpret and make sense of our lives, the viewpoint from which we see the world. Ideology, in a capitalist society, needs constant re-establishing, and this is carried out by what the critic Gramsci termed **hegemony**. This is the means by which a dominant social group maintains control of a subordinate group, a form of unconscious control, in which we take on certain beliefs, practices and attitudes as being natural or normal and carry those opinions with us, for instance, the belief that in a patriarchal society it is entirely normal for the woman to be the homemaker and to have a low-paid, menial job. Hegemony is constantly shifting; it is constantly negotiated and never fixed. From a feminist standpoint this means there is the potential for change in patriarchal society.

If cultural texts such as film are apparatus for transmitting cultural values, they are also sites for a struggle over meaning. The term given to describe the constant shifting and multiple possibilities of meaning a text may have is **polysemy**, that is, a text has no one fixed meaning. This then gives feminist film and cultural critics the opportunity to analyse audience response to texts as 'open' rather than 'closed' and the study of how gender differences work in the reception of texts becomes productive. Stuart Hall, in his early work, suggested there are three ways in which a text may be received: (1) as a *dominant reading*, as intended by its producer; (2) as a *negotiated reading*, when the text is generally accepted but is challenged in some areas; and (3) as *an oppositional reading*, when the viewer challenges the reading of the text.[4] In fact, more recent research argues for the possibility of a much more complex relationship between the reader and the text than had previously been thought.

The audience can be accredited with entering into a viewing situation with a range of skills and competences and a background of cultural knowledge. The audience is therefore more of an active than a passive receiver of the message. This understanding has implications for feminist film theory as it opens up the notion of the female as subject rather than as being permanently confined to the role of passive object. Christine Gledhill (1995) uses the term 'negotiation' of text, explaining that we negotiate with cultural texts at every level; from institutions, where feminists can apply pressure to negotiating the active meanings of texts, to the active process of reception.[5] Ethnographic research has proven to be of particular use when applied to studies of how women receive media texts. Janice Radway, in her research on romance fiction, found that the women she interviewed preferred a strong, independent heroine.[6] This contradicts previous feminist textual-based research which sees the romance novel as presenting women as passive and vulnerable. Jacqueline Bobo conducted group interviews to analyse the reception and interpretation of *The Color Purple*, the results of which she found surprising. The film contained many stereotypical images of black people and their culture and was filmed by a white, male director, Steven Spielberg, yet the black women interviewed saw the film as positive; they 'not only liked the film, but have formed a strong attachment to it. The film is significant to their lives' (Bobo 1988: 101). Bobo believes those interviewed were able to filter out negative aspects of the film and highlight areas they could relate to.

For further discussion of gender and sexuality, see Chapter 8.

semiotics
The use of semiotics in film analysis has developed out of the theories of Ferdinand de Saussure, who argued that the meanings of words are not natural but learned and socially constructed; therefore the meaning of a word, or in the case of film, an image or sound, may be complex and layered.

ideology
The dominant set of ideas and values which inform any one society or culture, but which are imbued in its social behaviour and representative texts at a level that is not necessarily obvious or conscious.

hegemony
A set of ideas, attitudes or practices which have become so dominant that we forget they are rooted in choice and the exercise of power. They appear to be 'common sense' because they are so ingrained, any alternative seems 'odd' or potentially threatening by comparison.

polysemic
A text with a multitude of possible readings.

• **Plate 7.7** *The Color Purple* (Steven Spielberg, 1985) Although directed by a white male, Steven Spielberg, many black women said they could relate to it

Black feminist theory has found it problematic to apply what could be termed white, bourgeois film theory to an ethnic group which is so noticeably under-represented in film. bell hooks explains: 'many feminist film critics continue to structure their discourse as though it speaks about "women" when in fact it only speaks about white women' (hooks 1992: 123). Because black women are largely excluded from film or given an extremely limited number of representations, a film such as *The Color Purple* is of particular significance to the many black women who read the film favourably.[7]

Lesbian and gay studies is a developing area of cultural analysis. Lesbian writers point out that a theory of lesbian desire and its relationship to media texts and representation is needed; a theory separate from previous feminist film thinking which has been concerned with the relationship of the heterosexual woman to film and places lesbian desire as other.

See Chapter 8, for a more detailed discussion of lesbian and gay studies.

The variety and wealth of theoretical approaches available to feminist film theorists in the new millennium are eclectic: psychoanalytic, social historical, semiotic-based textual analysis, postmodernist and ethnographic study are just a sample of the tools available. Some feminists have been resistant to embracing cultural studies in its totality, arguing that it has been too concerned with examining class structure. But within cultural studies there has been a shift away from solely concentrating on ideology and hegemony to studying identity and subjectivity; this can, at least in part, be attributed to the impact of feminism.

Feminist film theory needs to refer to rather than discard the range of analytical processes which have been made available and which contribute to our understanding of how women communicate, are communicated to and interpret film. The next section discusses theories of masculinity and it may be that the study of gender is as likely to reveal fresh insights into how we understand femininity as well as masculinity.

How useful a contribution has feminist film theory made to the study of film?

The following case studies apply many of the theories, concepts and approaches discussed in this section on women and film, to the following film-makers and a selection of their films.

□ CASE STUDY 1: SALLY POTTER, FILM-MAKER

Sally Potter is probably best known for three films: the film short *Thriller* (1979), the feature-length *The Gold Diggers* (1983) and the much-acclaimed *Orlando* (1993). Her recent films, *The Tango Lesson* (1997) and *The Man Who Cried* (2000), have received a rather more muted reception. Potter worked in dance and performance for many years and in the 1980s worked in television. Her work has been termed avant-garde, yet *Orlando*, although having many of the qualities of an 'art' production, has a strong narrative drive.

Potter's earlier films are feminist in tone, but in more recent years she has found the term problematic, and in an interview with Penny Florence explains, 'I can't use the word anymore because it's become debased' (Florence 1993: 279).

Whether Potter will be able to continue to make films with a strong personal vision, as Peter Greenaway and the late Derek Jarman have done, will depend very much on funding, but Potter is optimistic that there has been a change in attitude towards women film-makers, that they are now seen as just directors. *Thriller* is a feminist reading of Puccini's opera *La Bohème* (1895). Linking together feminist, Marxist and psychoanalytic theory, the film is a critique of the constraints of patriarchy, the lack of female voice and woman as object and victim. The film was funded by the British Arts Council, and although avant-garde in style was received with interest, although it was by no means a mainstream success. Ann Kaplan explains why the film aroused such interest: 'It is, first, an imaginative intervention in the dominance of a certain kind of classical narrative (the sentimental romance and the detective story) making a critique of such narratives into an alternative art form' (Kaplan 1983: 161).

The Gold Diggers (1983)

The Gold Diggers is a full-length film made with a grant from the British Film Institute (BFI). The film explores the relationship between women and power, money and patriarchy, and develops themes from *Thriller*. The film has two main characters, both women: the early nineteenth-century heroine (Julie Christie) and the modern heroine (Colette Lafone). Potter purposefully and ideologically chose an all-women crew to work on the film, including women musicians.

On its release in 1983 the film was poorly received, partly because of its complex yet plotless narrative which seemed to exemplify some of the problems of art and avant-garde cinema in the early 1980s – a lack of awareness of audience.

Potter has discussed the problems of the film, explaining the difficulties of working collaboratively with others (which was the case with *The Gold Diggers*). She has said that the film 'came out of a practice in the theatre of going with the moment, incorporating ideas, and not being completely text-bound' (Ehrenstein 1993: 3).

Imagery in the film often verges on the surreal, but the script is stilted, elliptical and difficult to follow, almost a series of vignettes. The modern heroine in the film plays the part of investigator and observer of events, an observer of patriarchy, which is seen as disempowering women. Patriarchy is threatening, bureaucratic, intimidating and ultimately ridiculous. In the scene when Colette is working at a VDU in an office with other women, the only male is the manager who imperiously surveys the scene. Colette asks him to explain what the information is on the screen, to which he patronisingly replies, 'Just do your job'.

The Gold Diggers was filmed in black and white, and is a bleak film suggesting that woman is either revered or reviled by man. *Orlando*, in contrast, is full of colour and optimism.

• **Plate 7.8** *The Gold Diggers* (Sally Potter, 1893)
A search for identity

Orlando (1993)

Potter's film is an adaptation of a Virginia Woolf novel and was made by her own company, Adventure Pictures, formed with *Orlando*'s producer Christopher Sheppard. The film budget was £2 million, making it a medium-size British film, although the quality of the production gives it a much more expensive look. In contrast to *The Gold Diggers*, in which the crew was all-female, a mixed crew worked on *Orlando*.

After the experience of *The Gold Diggers*, Potter took great care to ensure that the script was just right, doing endless rewrites until she was happy with it. The developmental process took years rather than months but ensured a clear narrative that powerfully drives the film forward.

The film is concerned with two central ideas: the concept of immortality and the fluidity of gender. Orlando travels 400 years, from the Elizabethan age (Queen Elizabeth is played by Quentin Crisp, introducing the theme of playing with gender) to the present day, changing sex in 1700. The mise-en-scène is sumptuous and exotic, richly coloured and textured, enhanced by the camera work; the scene when Orlando moves into the Victorian age, for instance, is full of movement and dynamism, the gorgeous costumes swirling forward into the future.

Aspects of feminism, gender, imperialism and politics are part of the narrative discourse – areas that are often anathema to a film's success. Yet *Orlando* has been received with much acclaim: David Ehrenstein in *Film Quarterly* compares the film to Orson Welles' *The Magnificent Ambersons*: 'Like no other film of the moment, it demonstates that art and pleasure are not mutually exclusive categories of experience' (Ehrenstein 1993: 2).

Potter is more concerned with gender than feminism, although the vulnerability of women is a key theme: when Orlando becomes female she loses her home, her financial power. She then only has her body, her femaleness to bargain with, which she refuses to share in marriage with the archduke, who sternly reminds her she has no property and will suffer the ignominy of remaining a spinster.

cate she is but also her female sexuality. The whiteness of Ada's skin is contrasted by the dark clothing she wears; her voluminous Victorian clothing is shown as impractical in the New Zealand climate, yet Ada often looks comfortable in her dress as opposed to Stewart, whose too-tight clothing makes him seem absurd and stiff (Campion purposefully made his clothes too tight to enhance this point). Baines, also a white European, has though, in contrast to Stewart, adapted to the New Zealand environment. His dress is loose and casual, reflecting a shifting of his values and an alignment with the native Maoris. The Maoris, although often seeming like comic caricatures, are shown dressed in a mix of male and female clothing, suggesting an ambivalence regarding their gender roles.

Ada's underwear becomes an object of fascination for the audience and of fetishisation for Baines. We frequently see Ada in petticoats and underwear, whilst playing with Flora but especially so in her relationship with Baines: in one scene Baines smells the top she has just taken off; in another sequence he becomes fascinated by a tiny hole in her stocking which reveals a glimpse of skin.

Campion undercuts conventional audience expectations of gender in the development of their relationship; it is Baines first removal of clothing which is so startling for both the audience and Ada, as until then it is Ada who has been placed in a vulnerable, feminine position. In this sequence there is a reversal of cinematic conventions: Ada removes the curtain (coded red for danger) which reveals Baines unclothed, but he also represents a threat; the game has moved on from being sensual to directly sexual. Ada is confronted by Baines' naked body and, as we see this sequence from her point of view, we cut to a reaction shot in which she is at first startled but does not look away. In this case the gaze, the look, is not male but female.

Much of *The Piano* is seen from Ada's point of view, emphasising our identification with her. Indeed Ada's lack of voice can be seen as a symbol of her withdrawal from patriarchal society. We hear Ada's voiceover at the beginning and end of the film, but all other communication is through the visuals and music. Although we frequently see shots of Ada's face, it is generally expressionless, almost blank, making it difficult to identify with her as one would in a conventional narrative.

The act of looking, the gaze, takes on a complex relationship between the audience, the spectator and the different characters in the film. A key sequence which exemplifies this is when the relationship between Ada and Baines changes to one of mutual attraction; firstly Flora spies on the couple and this changes her relationship with her mother, as an element of jealousy is brought in, but the scene also moves Flora to a new sphere, in which she is a voyeur made aware of her mother's sexuality. In a later scene Stewart spies on Ada and Baines making love, and stays there watching, clearly aroused by what he sees, in an instance of what is called the scopophilic drive. Yet the audience does not stay with Stewart, the film cuts to an interior medium shot and the sequence is imbued with a golden hue, sensual rather than explicit or fetishising the female body, as is so usual in patriarchal cinema. There is no sense of the couple being aware of an audience, or Ada's body being the subject of the 'male gaze'. Neither looks at the camera, yet the camera contrasts Baines' muscular, squat masculine body with Ada's tiny feminine one. The sequence concludes with a shot of Stewart surveying the couple from underneath the floorboards, when a button from Ada's dress falls through a hole onto his face. Stewart is in the position of passive voyeur, but the scene also drives home his ineffectualness, his impotence, with a deep sense of irony.

A later sequence again reverses the traditional function of the look as instrument of the male gaze; when Ada is in bed with Stewart she explores his body by touching and stroking his back down to his buttocks, strangely sensual; rather than sexual. It is unusual in film for the male body to be explored and eroticised in this way. Stewart is bathed in a warm light and has a passive position enforced upon him by Ada; when he attempts to be active Ada rejects him.

Patriarchal cinema generally fetishes sex by emphasising voyeurism and fragmenting the female body or associating it with related objects or clothing such as
underwear. Campion plays with this convention by showing Baines fetishise Ada's
clothing but extends this to include the piano; thus, although the piano functions as
Ada's voice the fetishisation takes on a surreal, almost absurd quality. In a perceptive
article on the use of clothing in *The Piano*, Stella Bruzzi points out that the film is a

> ...complex feminist displacement of the conventionalised objectification of the woman's form domi-
> nated by scopophilia and fetishism.
>
> (Bruzzi 1995: 257)

By the final stage of the film Ada's life has affected us deeply; the gradual building
up of empathy with Ada has been subtly woven into the film, so that when the final
confrontation between her and Stewart occurs we are almost as traumatised as Ada by
what happens. Stewart's retribution is terrible, acting as a symbol of phallic dismember-
ment or cliterectomy. Stewart's aim is to control Ada's sexuality and spirit. In this
sequence we continually have reaction shots of Ada and are placed to suffer with her.
She visibly shrinks before us as she falls to the ground fully punished for her transgression. Stewart has now taken on the role of evil persecutor and in the narrative of
melodrama Ada has to leave or be destroyed. The axe can be seen as a symbol of
phallic destruction associated with the Europeans: in the Bluebeard shadow play the
axe is used to kill his wives, and an acting out of the play in an earlier sequence fore-
shadows Stewart attacking Ada; Stewart is identified with the axe, seen carrying it,
chopping wood and trees which directly associate him with patriarchal and colonial
destruction.

The landscape not only acts as a metaphor for Ada's state of mind but is also used
to inform us about the people in the film and their characters. The boggy undergrowth
in which Ada finds it so difficult to move suggests her inability to escape; she is
trapped. This motif is constantly reinforced by the cinematography, where the forest is
the limit of Ada's horizons; she lives in a dense, almost knotted forest paralleling the
wild woods of folktales which are suffused with erotic symbolic significance. Stewart's
immediate world is surrounded by grey, petrified, half-dead tree trunks. He is referred to
as 'old dry balls' by the Maoris and the contrast in landscape between him and Baines
emphasises Stewart's impotence and inability to give love. Baines' hut is lush and
verdant, part of the forest, with which he is at ease.

Ada represents Western femininity in contrast with the Maori women who are
presented as coarse and loud, making lewd suggestions to Baines. Yet Ada, by her
association with Baines, is different; she is able to blend into the woods wearing
garments which seem to take on the same hues of blue and green which predominate
throughout the film. Campion uses stock stereotypes of the Maoris as noble natives,
natural and easily able to express their sexuality, thus giving a rather superficial interpretation of the race who are seen in terms of civilised versus uncivilised.

Perhaps one of the most interesting aspects of *The Piano* is the mother/daughter
relationship, a theme which is often explored through melodrama. In the film Ada and
Flora have a symbiotic relationship which is broken only by the intrusion of Stewart and
Baines. Flora is literally Ada's voice, acting as a mediator between Ada and the rest of
the world. The two are often shown in tight, claustrophobic shots and there is a sense
of almost Oedipal jealousy; for instance, Flora is in her mother's bed whenever Stewart
visits. When Flora eventually aligns with Stewart to stem Ada's affair with Baines she
precipitates his retribution on Ada; Flora chooses the path to Stewart rather than take
the piano key, inscribed with words of love from Ada, to Baines. Flora has been introduced to the dangerous forces of sexuality and the film is to some extent a rite of
passage for her. When these dark forces are unleashed Ada, in effect, uses her
daughter as a go-between and their relationship is changed.

• **Plate 7.10**
The Piano
(Jane Campion, 1993)
Mother and daughter are
isolated in an alien envi-
ronment

In the final stages of the film the piano has become a tie with the past and in a symbolic gesture, when Ada is on the boat with Baines and Flora, she insists the piano is thrown overboard. Ada is pulled in too and we think the film will end on this tragic note, but she releases herself and in voiceover tells us, 'my will has chosen life'. Yet the life she has chosen, to live with Baines in Nelson as a piano teacher, does not seem convincing or a particularly satisfactory ending, at least not for a melodramatic heroine – she is now contained by Baines.

The Piano works on a visual, poetic level which is at times dark and disturbing, yet its central discourse is an exploration of sexuality, and especially female sexuality. Patriarchal filmic conventions are reversed in portraying a heroine who often has control of the look: the woman is subject rather than object and, at times, it is the male who is the object of the female gaze. But *The Piano* is much more than a reversal of patriarchal mainstream film conventions; it is one of the few films directed by a woman to achieve critical and financial success and yet still retain its art-house character.

GENDER THEORY AND THEORIES OF MASCULINITY

Masculinity as unproblematic

Laura Mulvey's essay 'Visual Pleasure and Narrative Cinema' focused attention on cinema spectatorship in terms of binary opposites of gender: woman is defined as object of the look and man as being in control of the gaze. The importance of Mulvey's conclusions and the implications of these findings initially resulted in little further questioning of the role of the male in film because he was seen as representing patriarchy in a straightforward way. Problems with defining femininity as passive and masculinity as active had become apparent by the 1980s because seeing gender in terms of binary opposites means there is then little space left for negotiation of these boundaries.[8] Defining the masculine as the 'norm' and the female as 'other' may be valid at a particular moment in Hollywood Classical Cinema, but if gender is a social construction then constructions of gender in film are not absolute and therefore are far more complex.

Steven Neale's essay, 'Masculinity as Spectacle', published in 1983, is described by Cohan and Hark in *Screening the Male* as a 'pioneering attempt to put Mulvey's arguments in the context of those films that obviously represent a spectacular form of masculinity' (1993: 2).

Masculinity is associated with **voyeurism**, action, sadism, **fetishism** and the controlling narrative, whilst femininity is associated with passivity, exhibitionism, spectacle, masochism and narcissism. Yet these clear distinctions belie the acute anxieties and paradoxes which emerge when studying film; the binary opposites of masculinity and femininity are in fact much less opaque than may at first be apparent. The male image and the way it is represented is as complex and revealing as the female image, although it may appear 'hidden' and unrecognised, a natural part of patriarchy.

Neale's essay examines identification, looking and spectacle using Mulvey's article as a reference point. He points out that how we identify with a character in film is a complex process. We do not always clearly align ourselves with either a male or female figure depending on our gender, otherwise why would females be able to identify with Clint Eastwood in *Unforgiven* (1992) or Bruce Willis in *Die Hard* (1988).

The male hero in classical Hollywood cinema is usually recognised as powerful. He signifies omnipotence, mastering the narrative, being in control, sadistic rather than masochistic. Neale argues that the elements of violence, voyeurism and masochism in Anthony Mann's films in fact suggest a 'repressed homosexual voyeurism' (Cohan and Hark 1993: 13). The act of looking has a homoerotic quality and an anxiety which is produced as a result of the erotic possibilities that are repressed. The violence and mutilation present in these films is an expression of the anxiety that surrounds the suppression of homosexual desire that is evident in the looks between characters.

Neale's discussion of looking and spectacle further develops Mulvey's division of active male, who controls the look, and the object of the look, the passive female. Neale argues that male figures can be the subject of voyeuristic looking also. In male-centred genres such as war, action, westerns and gangster films there are binary opposites in the form of opposing forces which struggle for power and control. Mann's films use narrative outcome and spectacle to suggest male struggle, images of masculinity are fetishised and there is an emphasis on display and the spectacular.[9] Leone's westerns also work through an aggressive exchange of looks, another form of fetishisistic looking. But Neale points out that the male body is not shown purely for the purpose of erotic spectacle:

voyeurism
The sexual pleasure gained from looking at others.

fetishism
Freudian theorists argue that fetishism is linked to the castration complex and is a form of male denial of the threat and fear of castration by the female. The female is made less threatening, more reassuring, by substituting her lack of a phallus with a fetish object such as high heels, long hair or turning her into a fetish object by exaggerating or fragmenting parts of the body such as lips or breasts.

• **Plate 7.11**
Die Hard
(John McTiernan, 1988)
The 'ordinary' guy as hero

We see male bodies stylised and fragmented by close-ups, but our look is not direct, it is heavily mediated by the looks of the characters involved. And those looks are marked out not by desire but rather by fear, or hatred, or aggression.

(Ibid.: 18)

The act of aggression takes focus away from the spectacle and thus displaces the eroticism of the male body, whilst still suggesting this at a subconscious level. Some genres though, such as melodrama and the musical, do allow for the male body to be the object of the look, for instance, Rock Hudson in Sirk's melodramas and John Travolta in *Saturday Night Fever* (1977).

Neale points out the need to acknowledge and consider the eroticism and spectacle of the masculine image in terms of identification, voyeuristic looking and fetishistic representation. Mainstream cinema assumes there is a male norm, a male way of looking, while the female represents difference, that which requires investigation. But Neale argues that the male also requires investigation in the same kind of way, that masculinity is as much a mystery as femininity.

Neale's article is particularly important because he argues that the representation of the male is in no way straightforward or opaque. A number of academics researching in this area have further opened up the debate as to our understanding of masculinity and, indeed, gender in film, and this chapter will draw on some of their work in more depth. Neale's essay focuses on Freudian- and Lacanian-based psychoanalytic theory rather than cultural factors. This theoretical approach can be seen as white and phallocentric and it could also be argued, with some justification, that it is a rather limited method of study: racial and cultural differences, for instance, are ignored. There has been very little discussion of other masculinities such as the Mexican characters in Eastwood westerns or more recently the representation of Somalians in *Black Hawk Down* (2001). The focus has been on white masculinity to the exclusion of other identity-forming factors such as ethnic background, sexuality, nationality, and so on.

The construction of identity, how and why we identify with a character, is complex, a fantasy that we engage in when watching a film. Mainstream film is a site for questioning these rich and often ambiguous character identities and the study of gender in film questions what these identities are and asks how they work.

Hollywood film is much more than a straightforward, easily read transmitter of the dominant ideology. It is complex in its construction and multi-layered in meaning and, to some extent, reflects the hopes and wants and desires of the cinema-going public.

Playing with gender

It has been observed by commentators in different disciplines that the strenuousness of the masculine identities is a pointer, not to their stability, but their fragility.

(Horrocks 1995: 16)

The myth presented regarding masculinity is that it is natural, normal and universal. This myth is repeated by stories and images we see in the media and especially Hollywood film. Yet despite the certainty, the surety with which masculine identities are portrayed, closer examination reveals that masculinity is much less stable and much more easily undermined than previously thought.

See Case study 3: Fight Club, *pp. 273–275, for comparison.*

Theorists such as Barbara Creed, Yvonne Tasker and Chris Holmlund have discussed the notion of masculinity as play, as performance and masquerade. Barbara Creed suggests that the muscle-bound hero of the 1980s cinema can be understood in terms of post-modernity, of playing with the notion of manhood, and argues that the muscular hero is a 'simulcra of an exaggerated masculinity, the original lost to sight'

(1987: 65). The hero in action film is then a parody, a tongue-in-cheek play on the impossible role he has to perform. It is easy to apply this argument to Bruce Willis in the *Die Hard* films but does the same argument apply to Russell Crowe's role in *Gladiator* (2000)? Crowe's Roman general is a much more serious and weighty hero who has lost his family and is looking for revenge. He portrays a hypermasculinity but also evokes a sense of nostalgia, harking back to a time when men were strong and had a cause worth fighting for.

Whilst psychoanalysis has been used as a way of understanding the acquisition of sexual identity, postmodernism addresses the flexibility and ambiguity of popular culture. When put together, interesting ways of understanding gender emerge. Chris Holmlund combines these two approaches in 'Masculinity as Multiple Masquerade' (1993), in which she discusses the many ways that acting, playing a role on screen, is a masquerade; she argues that it is an act of gender pretence, a form of dressing up and putting on a show, and that heterosexuality is also a masquerade, a charade, in which there are often homoerotic overtones. Therefore masculinity, and thus gender, is a multiple charade of which the audience is aware yet not aware and much of the complexity of gender identity is understood by the audience at a subconscious level.

The male body

The action film, by being active, distracts from the eroticised male body on display. Dyer explains;

images of men must disavow...passivity if they are to be kept in line with the dominant ideas of masculinity-as-activity.

(Dyer 1982: 66–7)

The masculine body as spectacle and performer, having a performative function, is a key theme of Hollywood film, particularly action films of the 1980s. Yvonne Tasker's analysis of the Die Hard films suggests the particular representation of the male body in the 1980s reflects an anxiety about the roles that men and women have in their everyday lives, both at home and at work, and their concerns regarding shifts in society and gender roles. Die Hard (1988) reflects on the lack of control for the male in the workplace, where the hero finds himself in impossible situations controlled by incompetent bureaucracies:

Anxieties to do with difference and sexuality increasingly seem to be worked out over the body of the male hero.

(Tasker 1993: 236)

• **Plate 7.12**
Gladiator
(Ridley Scott, 2000)
The general seeks to avenge the murder of his wife and children

See chapter 3, pp. 116–124, for a case study of Pulp Fiction *and the audiences interaction with the film. For a discussion of the 1990's British gangster film see Chapter 9, pp. 354–356.*

that Quentin Tarantino was one of the few film-makers in that period working in the gangster genre, probably the only genre in which macho masculinity remains intact. *Pulp Fiction* (1994) has levels of irony, self-reflexivity and parody; it also contains a homophobic construction of sexuality which belies the macho strutting of the actors. Films in the latter part of the decade and the new millennium, such as *The Full Monty* (1997), *Fight Club* (1999) and *Gladiator* (2000), in their very different ways, suggest an unease with taking on a feminised role and a desire for certainty in respect of what it is to be masculine.

The feminised, enlightened new man is more fiction than reality, according to Kathleen Rowe in her 1995 article 'Melodrama and Men in Post-Classical Romantic Comedy', in which she argues that there has been an increased use of melodrama to tell the story of men's lives and male suffering. There is a darker edge to these comedies which takes away the focus from the female heroine and transfers it to the male victim, the melodramatic hero; the female becomes, if not the villain, then the lesser character.

From the late 1970s onwards romantic comedy has tapped into an unease about the notions of romance: in *Sleepless in Seattle* (1993) the lovers don't meet until the end and have no sexual contact; Woody Allen's films are often discourses about broader cultural anxieties concerning romance and masculinity. These comedies suggest an underlying fear of the impact of the changes in the status of women and their effect on men. Rowe argues they allow the male to determine the narrative outcome whilst the female is seen as lacking:

In these films it is the men who educate the women, not the reverse. Each of these heroines resists her male suitor less out of her inherent independence or recognition of his need to change than out of something wounded or underdeveloped in her – qualities which allow the hero to demonstrate his greater wisdom, charm or sensitivity.

(Kirkhan and Thumin 1995: 187)

The classical Hollywood romantic comedies undermined masculine authority whilst melodrama was seen as the women's genre, a genre which appealed to women because it related to the sufferings they endured in patriarchal culture. Suffering and loss have been more often associated with the feminine; in women melancholy is seen as disabling and negative whilst in a man, Richard Gere for instance in *Pretty Woman* (1989), or Tom Hanks in *Sleepless in Seattle* (1993), it is presented as positive, enabling the transformation of apparent loss into male power. These male transformation movies show a softer male but at the same time enhance and consolidate their hierarchical and patriarchal position by acquiring qualities traditionally regarded as feminine; in films such as *Regarding Henry* (1991), *The Fisher King* (1991), *Terminator 2* (1991), *Groundhog Day* (1993) and *Parenthood* (1989) men have emotions and are not afraid to display them but, apart from *Terminator 2*, in which Sarah Connor is sidelined in her role as mother, a role which is appropriated by Schwarzenegger, the woman's place is still in the kitchen.

Occasionally Hollywood films overturn these conventions in an interesting or challenging way; in *Jagged Edge* (1989) Jeff Bridges plays the romantic hero but is finally exposed as the killer – the romantic hero becomes the villain.

Fatherhood and the family

Many films in the 1980s and 1990s have the role of fatherhood and the family as a central discourse. The family has been central to Western society and American national identity was founded on the patriarchal family structure. The contemporary American family, however, is not stable and many families divorce or separate. Action films such as *Die Hard* and *Lethal Weapon* (1989) reflect this uncertainty. Danny

Glover's family, in *Lethal Weapon*, represents security, stability and paternal authority whilst Mel Gibson plays the outsider who is emotionally lost after his wife's death, after the woman who gave him stability has gone.

The father replacing the mother or the mother being marginalised or ignored is a theme common to a variety of films from this period. In *Terminator 2*, the Terminator becomes the minder of John Connor (the son who has lost his father) and the 'hard' man learns to be gentle and how to nurture whilst Sarah Connor is hardly involved with or even interested in motherhood. In *Three Men and a Baby* (1989) the men act as 'surrogate mothers', as well as fathers. The baby's mother is not reunited with her child until the end of the film and the audience view her as an outsider. Oliver Stone's *Wall Street* (1987) plays the 'good father' and 'the bad father' against each other, fighting to gain control of the good father's son; it is an exclusively male family scenario in which the women are either prizes or bought. More recent films such as *The Full Monty* (1997) and *Gladiator* (2000), in their very different ways explore the role of the father as patriarch and how he reacts when the family is broken up and separated from the mother or the mother and family are destroyed.

Womb envy

A number of films, from genres as diverse as comedy in *Three Men and a Baby* to horror such as *The Fly* (1986), demonstrate an unease or discomfort which at times borders on envy regarding the reproductive powers of woman. Many horror films express a fascination with building a human such as *Frankenstein* (1930) or controlling reproductive power as does the scientist in *The Fly*.

Three Men and a Baby's central theme is about man's desire to take over and control the reproductive function. The film voices male concerns about fathering, birth and female sexuality, suggesting fatherhood can be a collective male experience, rather than one man taking sole responsibility for the child. There is denial of a single responsibility for fatherhood whilst at the same time a desire to take the role of carer from the woman. A form of womb envy is apparent when one of the characters dresses as a pregnant woman.

Modleski argues that envy of woman and her procreative ability runs alongside a fear of feminisation and a wish to deny woman the role of childbearer and nurturer: 'it is possible, the film shows, for men to respond to the feminist demand for their increased participation in child rearing in such a way as to make women more marginal than ever' (2000: 525).

The protagonists in David Cronenberg's *The Fly* and *Dead Ringers* (1988) are so envious of female reproductive powers that they suffer feelings of impotence. The men

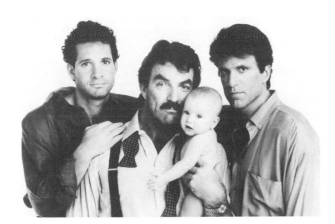

• **Plate 7.13**
Three Men and a Baby
(Leonard Nimoy, 1987)
Can men be surrogate
mothers?

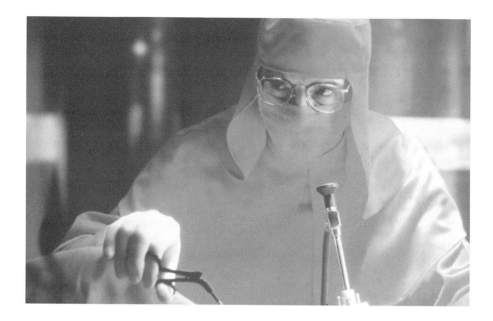

• **Plate 7.14**
Dead Ringers
(David Cronenberg,
1988)
These men want to
control the female
reproductive process

in Cronenberg's films try to control the womb or gain knowledge that gives them power over female fertility as in the twin gynaecologists in *Dead Ringers*, while in *Videodrome* (1984) the central character gains a vagina in his stomach into which a video tape is inserted.

Masculine anxiety regarding paternity and reproduction is particularly evident in the horror film: in *Alien* there is a conflict between fear and fascination with the maternal. The film contains disturbing imagery regarding birth and the female sex organs; one of the crew gives birth through his stomach, the Alien is female, she eats men, consumes them; in contrast other imagery is comforting and maternal, the sleeping places are womb-like and the crew dress in nappies.

Hurt, agony, pain – love it: the masochistic spectator

Historically the male body is viewed as the norm and the female body as a deviation, as inferior, a poor copy. Yet many monstrous figures are, on closer examination, associated with aspects of femininity: Dracula has ruby-red lips, the werewolf's lunar cycle mimics menstruation and it is reborn in the process of transformation. More recently in *The Silence of the Lambs* (1991) Buffalo Bill hopes to realise transformation by covering himself in the skin of dead women.

Barbara Creed's article 'Dark Desires' argues there are two types of horror film; the first explores man's desire for castration in order to become a woman and the second, man's desire for castration as part of a male death wish. Creed examines the rape-revenge films *I Spit on Your Grave* (1978) and *Naked Vengeance* (1984), in which the male rapist is castrated and killed by his victim. A more recent equivalent is *Species* (1997) in which the female monster kills her victim after having sex with him.

It appears that who the audience identify with in terms of gender when watching film is rather more complex than outlined by Mulvey and by Metz (1983). Carol Clover examines the nature of the male monster and the identification of the audience with the female victim and points out that the gaze of both the male and the female spectator is constructed as masochistic. In the horror film the victim is usually female and the audience mostly male. The horror film uses the female form not only for the male spectator to look at but for him to feel through and identify with, suggesting the male viewer can easily identify with a different gender. He therefore takes on the role of masochistic spectator, identifying with the fear and pain of the hero/heroine. Clover argues there has been a silence about male masochism and a silence about identification with the female, even though it is assumed that women identify with the masculine in film.

The title of this section ' Hurt, agony, pain – love it' is written on a sign at the beginning of *The Silence of the Lambs* (1991). The horror audience, whether male or female, does not have control of the look but is forced to take on a passive, classically feminine role, identifying with the pain and suffering of the protagonist, in the case of *The Silence of the Lambs*, the FBI agent Clarice Starling. Clover further argues that although the horror film is more overt in its manipulation of the audience, mainstream film makes use of similar tools to feminise the audience; we 'surrender ourselves' to a film, we expect to be manipulated, surprised and kept in suspense. Therefore the assumed dominant, sadistic role ascribed to the male viewer by Mulvey and by Metz is under question.

☐ CASE STUDY 3: *FIGHT CLUB* (DAVID FINCHER, 1999)

Fight Club is a film about masculinity in crisis. It depicts the disaffected, feminised, young white American male and his frustration with late capitalism and late twentieth-century life. The film's central discourse suggests an uncertainty about man's role in society and a lack of purpose in life; Jack, the central protagonist, expresses this as:

For a discussion of Fight Club *and audience, see Chapter 3, pp. 112–113.*

We are the middle children of history with no purpose or place

We have no great war or great depression…

We were raised by television to believe that we'd be millionaires…

But we won't…. And now we're very pissed off.

These are the 'Lost Boys', a generation of men whose fathers have left home and have given no masculine guidance to their sons; they have no clear role or function in society and their lives are without meaning.

The crisis in identity exemplified by Jack's split personality is alluded to throughout the film, although not revealed until near the end. Tyler is Jack's physically perfect alter ego and also his dark side; a role played by Brad Pitt whose muscled body is often on display. In the first half of the film Jack has an homoerotic fascination with Tyler but in the latter section the two characters, facets of his personality, battle with each other for survival and Jack's sanity. Jack represents the passive, domesticated male and Tyler the fighter who is almost Neanderthal and ultimately destructive. As Henry Giroux points out:

The central protagonists, Jack and Tyler, represent two opposing registers that link consumerism and masculinity….Jack exemplifies a form of domesticated masculinity – passive, alienated and without ambition. On the other hand Tyler exemplifies and embodies masculinity that refuses the seductions of consumerism.

(2000–2001: 33)

The emasculated male, in need of testosterone, is evident from the beginning of the film, which opens with a phallic image of Jack with a gun in his mouth. There are many references throughout the film to fear of castration and phallic inadequacy. Jack is feminised, he is obsessed with decorating his flat with IKEA furniture and has an apparently lonely, meaningless but domesticated existence. There is clearly something wrong with Jack's life; he can't sleep, and tells a doctor that he's in pain. The doctor suggests he attends classes for the terminally ill to find out what pain really is. The first class Jack goes to is for testicular cancer, where he meets Bob who has breasts because of hormone treatment. Jack consoles him that 'we're still men'. Again these references suggest fear of castration, fear of losing masculine identity and fear of losing control of the body. Tyler shows Jack a way to regain his masculinity, his place in the world. There are a number of parallels with *Falling Down*, which depicts a man's extreme reaction to losing power and control in his life.

Identity is literally torn apart in the film and this is exemplified by the fight club; fighting is not only a spectacle but a test of one's masculinity and how much pain can be taken, can be suffered. The masochistic desire for self-punishment and the belief that pain through suffering is somehow redemptive or a transformative experience is a nostalgia for the past rituals of primitive societies; there is also a nostalgia for an age when the roles of masculine and feminine are imagined as being more clearly defined. Many male secret societies and fascist groups have used pain as a test for entrance to the group. The fights between Jack and Tyler are however later shown as delusions and Jack's self-mutilation is presented as an aspect of self-hate, guilt, confusion and inner torment; we understand in retrospect that he is a deeply disturbed character.

The fight club is where men can rediscover their masculinity, can connect and overcome fear and pain. The club gives order and meaning to their lives; these men crave regulation, rules and clearly defined boundaries.

The film flirts with fascism; Jack watches with horror as the desire for a club of men and a new order is pushed to extremes. The fight club, the secret society, is transformed into an underground army which brainwashes its members who have to go through a series of masochistic initiations and tests to be considered 'man enough' to join. The paramilitary group has no real politics; Project Mayhem's aim is to destroy examples of modern art, architecture and coffee bars (the ubiquitous Starbucks?); its aim is to bring chaos and destruction. The film, through Tyler, offers a nihilist philosophy of destruction and negativity. As Tyler says:

Self-improvement is masturbation, Self-destruction is the answer.

The film links self-abuse with regaining power over the body and one's life. Jack argues in voiceover that the fight club gives him power and the people who had power over him have less and less because of his new state of mind. This is undercut however

• **Plate 7.15**
Fight Club
(David Fincher, 1999)
Fight Club suggests a
great anxiety about what
it is to be male

when he says 'by this point I could wiggle most of the teeth in my jaw', and we are made aware he is actually destroying his body. The fight club pushes self-destruction and self-loathing to its limits as the men pound each other's bodies until one gives in. As Tyler pours lye on Jack's hand he tells Jack to feel the pain and not to avoid it; this ritual becomes a repeated image later in the film, an initiation test for new members of the club, another form of self-destruction and brainwashing.

A powerful desire for male bonding is repeatedly expressed, the need to be part of a group or movement which provides a reason for their existence. There is an element of homoeroticism in the images of dirty, sweaty, bloody men which is undercut by the action and violence that is so visceral at times (see above on men and action films). The uniform of muscles becomes the uniform of a terrorist organisation, and indeed there is a fetishism of the military which is very precise in its specificity of the clothing needed to join: two pairs of black socks and so on.

Women in *Fight Club* are, on first appearance, marginalised, non-existent, apart from Marla. Yet this is contradicted by some of Jack's first words: 'all this is about Marla Singer'. Much of the film is about denying or fighting against both the female within and the female figure of Marla. *Fight Club* gives a somewhat misogynist representation of women: Marla is defined as the cause of all Jack's problems – ' She ruined everything' – and women are a threat, representing fear of castration; Tyler says to Jack 'a woman could cut off your penis and throw it out the car'. Jack is part of a generation raised by women and questions how this has affected his identity. He asks: 'I wonder if another woman is really the answer we need'. There is frequent reference to the negative effect women have on men in shaping their identities, in feminising them. Tyler tells Jack that men have lost their manhood because they have been feminised. Women are cast as binary opposites and defined in negative terms; even the woman dying at the beginning of the film is defined in terms of her sex and as being sexually unattractive. Marla's role in the film is that of an outsider and a threat to Jack's existence. She fulfils two roles, first to make Jack unhappy and second to provide sex. Yet there is a paradox here: Jack says Marla has invaded his life but this is more the unconscious denial of a want than a real desire to get rid of her. Marla is a constant, always waiting in the background, and Jack is pushed to fight against Tyler partly because of his desire to save her

On one level the film is a celebration of a hypermasculinity and violence, revelling in the visceral physicality of the fighting scenes for instance, and yet this destructive force is clearly satirised; the potential for and attraction to extreme violence by disaffected, alienated young men who have no place in society is made clear. It's rather chilling that the skyscrapers blown up at the end of the film were similar to the phallic symbols of American capitalism and wealth that were blown up on September 11, 2001 by extreme Islamic fundamentalists who were also alienated from Western society.

CONCLUSION

This chapter introduces the subject of film and gender. It is by no means a definitive study but presents a range of important viewpoints and key articles in this area of study. Mulvey's original article 'Visual Pleasure and Narrative Cinema' has inspired a whole range of theories concerning masculinity and femininity which try to unravel how meaning is produced in film. As more and more women are included in the film-making process, from writers to directors to cinematographers, it will be interesting to see if this means new theories will have to evolve to account for the new meanings and the new narratives produced.

Lesbian and gay cinema

Chris Jones

■ Lesbian and gay cinema

INTRODUCTION: REPRESENTATION

heterosexual
A word used to name
and describe a person
whose main sexual feel-
ings are for people of the
opposite sex.

gender
A name for the social
and cultural construction
of a person's sex and
sexuality. Gender, sex
and sexuality can
overlap but are by no
means an exact match. It
is this 'mismatch' which
has generated a fasci-
nating body of film
production and criticism.

sexuality
A name for the sexual
feelings and behaviour of
a person. When applied
to groups of people (e.g.
heterosexuals), ideas of
social attitude and
organisation are implied.

*For further discussion of
representation and femi-
nism, see Chapter 7, pp.
247–264.*

*For a detailed discussion
of spectatorship, see
Chapter 3.*

sex
A word used to denote
and describe a person's
physical type according
to their genital make-up.
In academic discourse,
this is primarily a scientific term.

homosexual
A word used to name
and describe a person
whose main sexual feel-
ings are for people of the
same sex. Mainly, but
not exclusively, used in
reference to males.

Representation is a social process which occurs in the interactions between a reader or viewer, and a text. It produces signs which reflect underlying sets of ideas and attitudes. In her essay, 'Visual Pleasure and Narrative Cinema' (1995), Laura Mulvey suggested ways in which a viewer of classic Hollywood films is addressed as male by being encouraged to adopt the viewpoint, the 'look' of the male protagonist. Although she later adjusted these ideas to cater for such female-oriented Hollywood genres as the melodrama, Mulvey's argument is based on the traditional psychoanalytic notion of male/female definitions and oppositions. Nowhere does she take into account the extent to which her argument is geared towards a **heterosexual** look. Nevertheless, her ideas about the positioning of the film spectator and film-maker within the **gender** system have been very influential. They have led to much constructive critical investiga-tion into how different kinds of film-makers and viewers affect meaning-making processes according to their race and **sexuality**, as well as gender. Such investigation has also started to take into account a variety of viewing formats based on video and the TV screen.

An integral part of the process of reading a film is the use of stereotyping, the depic-tion of a character according to their perceived membership of a certain social group such as Asians, mothers-in-law, businessmen, lesbians. This is a form of shorthand; a few visual or sound cues give the audience a view of a certain type of person which is widely accepted. The nature of this view is generally shaped by the dominant groups in a society.

In film, representation is organised through the signs of mise-en-scène, editing, sound and narrative patterns. Later, the chapter examines some gay and lesbian repre-sentations in a selection of films.

DEFINITIONS AND DEVELOPMENTS: HOMOSEXUAL AND GAY

Men and women who relate sexually to members of their own **sex** have always existed, but the modern term 'homosexuality' did not come into being until its inven-tion in 1869 by a Swiss doctor. It was not commonly used in the English language until the 1890s, the decade that saw the birth of cinema. The term **homosexual** was partly inherited from nineteenth-century ideas of disease. Previously, same-sex relations had been predominantly characterised by notions of sin inherited from the medieval period. These commonly held associations continued into this century as German film makers produced a number of works campaigning for more enlightened attitudes in sexual and social matters. *Different from the Others* (*Anders Als Die Andern*, 1919) was a success on first release. Even though the main character, a homosexual musician, finally poisons himself, the dour storyline is countered by sections of the film in which Dr Magnus Hirschfield puts forward an affirmative view of homosexuality. Hirschfield was a sexual researcher and social reformer whose world-renowned Institute was later destroyed by the Nazis. Within a year of its release the film was subject to censorship and now exists only in fragments, although these have since been assembled and shown. *Girls in Uniform* (*Madschen In Uniform*, Leontine Sagan, 1931) can still be seen today as a major portrayal of anti-authoritarianism, with the love of its two female protagonists for each other triumphing over the oppressive regime of their boarding school.

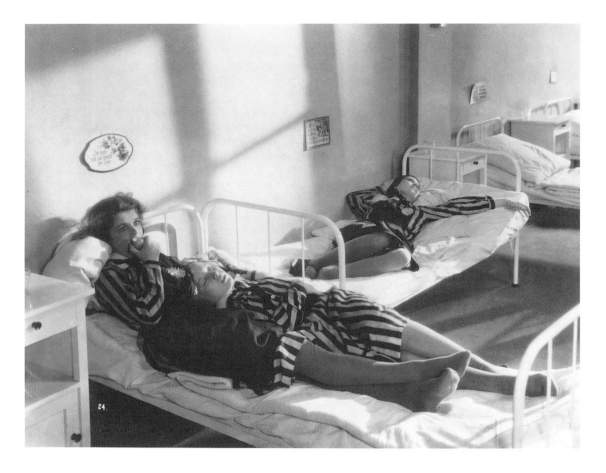

• **Plate 8.1** *Girls in Uniform* (Leontine Sagan, 1931)
Based on the play by lesbian poet Christa Winsloe, the film portrays the friendship and support given to the main character, Manuela, in her love for her teacher

During the Second World War, with its movements of population and large numbers of service men and women being thrown closely together in same-sex barracks, many people became aware of homosexuality on a personal and social level. This resulted in two parallel and contradictory developments in North America and Europe during the 1950s; increasing growth among communities of homosexuals and lesbians in big cities, and systematic attempts by those in authority to prevent such developments.

These communities began to demand and develop wider networks of meeting-places and entertainment, including film. Early examples of films made with such audiences in mind are the physique films of Dick Fontaine, who worked in San Francisco from the late 1940s. Such film activity mainly took place within the art-house world, and involved small-budget production and viewing in clubs and homes. Jean Genet's *Un Chant d'amour* (1950), with its sexually charged images of handsome male prisoners, became a cult film, as did Kenneth Anger's *Fireworks* (1947), a young man's sexual fantasy involving sailors. From the 1960s onwards the **homoerotic** films of Andy Warhol and George Kuchar began to find wider audiences. It was during this period that the word **gay** began to be used to both denote and describe a male homosexual person.

In 1969, for the first time in modern history, homosexuals in a small New York bar called the Stonewall Inn fought back against a police raid. A major riot ensued and The

homoerotic
Description of a text – prose, poem, film, painting, photograph, etc. – conveying an enjoyable sense of same-sex attraction.

gay
Description of strong, positive sexual love and attraction between members of the same sex, used by extension to describe cultural products, such as film and video, concerned with similar themes. Mainly referring to males, it can also be used for any person.

• **Plate 8.2**
Un Chant d'amour (Jean Genet, 1950)
Genet's erotic imagery has inspired many film-makers

New York Gay Liberation Front was immediately formed, soon to be followed by similar organisations across the world. Members of the new movement adopted the word 'gay' for its positive connotations of happiness, and because they wanted to use a term to describe themselves that had not been chosen by outsiders. For them, the term represented a way of demonstrating pride in their identity, the power of political organisation, and a distinct culture. The term was initially conceived as describing both men and women, but women soon began to feel marginalised within the movement, and the term **lesbian** came back in general use during the 1970s to signal the distinctness and strength of women.

It is the very different emotional connotations of these varying terms which led critic Vito Russo to say: 'There never have been lesbians or gay men in Hollywood films. Only homosexuals' (Russo 1987: 245).

AUDIENCES

Gay men, like men in general, have on average more spending power than women, despite equal opportunities legislation in many countries. With gay liberation came a greatly expanded network of related commercial goods and services; nightclubs, shops, clothing, books and magazines, the majority of which were aimed at men. The same conditions apply in the developing structures of film and cinema aimed at lesbians and gays. Men constituted the main organised audience for this type of cultural production. Even those films with non-commercial financial backing, such as the work of Derek Jarman and Isaac Julien, tended to attract funds in part because of the perceived existence of this established gay male audience.

Lesbian film and video developed in parallel with the emerging women's movement, almost always with less finance than its male equivalent, and found a base in film clubs and workshops. The American film and video artist Su Friedrich actively prefers this type of outlet as a way of reaching lesbian audiences with films such as *Damned If You Don't* (1987). As a result of this production and viewing background, and the

lesbian
A word used to name and describe a woman whose main sexual feelings are for other women. Coined as a medical term in the late nineteenth century, the word has been invested post-Stonewall with new ideas of openness and liberation. It can also be used to describe cultural products, such as film and video, dealing with lesbian themes.

See Chapter 1, pp. 34–40, and Chapter 3, for a further discussion of film audiences.

• **Plate 8.3**
Before Stonewall (Greta
Schiller and Robert
Rosenberg, 1984)
A full-length film docu-
mentary about the gay
and lesbian movement
in the US from the
1920s to the 1960s.
This film vividly evokes
lesbian and gay life in
the US before gay liber-
ation and forms part of a
growing body of work on
lesbian and gay history

modest financial levels this involves, many lesbian films of the 1970s and 1980s are less than feature-length. *Home Movie* (1972) by Jan Oxenberg is a modest but highly effective twelve-minute film, which edits home-movie footage from the director's own childhood with scenes of her adult life as a lesbian to make the viewer amusingly aware of the conventions of family life. Her *Comedy In Six Unnatural Acts* (1975, 26 minutes) presents six short, staged scenes dealing with the foibles of lesbian life, and debunking a few myths about **butch/femme** role-playing.

LESBIAN AND GAY FILM FESTIVALS

After 1945, film festivals became recognised across Europe and America as serving several useful functions. They act as a marketplace for film distributors to view and possibly buy new product and allow producers, scriptwriters and others to gather and discuss new projects. Critics attending festivals alert wider audiences to new and inter-esting work. Audiences can view and enjoy a wide range of films they would not normally see in the cinema.

Since the 1970s a worldwide circuit of Lesbian and Gay Film Festivals has grown up. San Francisco was the first to start operating, followed by London, Paris, New York, Toronto, Berlin and others. By the beginning of the twenty-first century, such festivals had begun to take place outside Europe and North America in countries such as Korea

butch
Description of behaviour patterns – such as aggression and sexual dominance – tradition-ally associated with masculinity.

femme
Description of behaviour patterns – such as gentleness, sexual passivity, concern with dress and appearance – traditionally associated with femininity.

For further discussion of film distribution and exhibition, see Chapter 1, pp. 16–22.

• **Plate 8.5** *The Boys in the Band* (William Friedkin, 1970)
This pre-liberation film contains an array of stereotypes, sometimes hilarious, often controversial

For a discussion of masculinity, See Chapter 7, pp. 264–275.

debate what exactly constitutes a 'lesbian film' or a 'gay film', gay sensibility can enrich film production and appreciation for gays and non-gays.

1 Watch a so-called 'Pepla' muscle epic of the 1950s and an action film from the 1990s starring Jean-Claude Van Damme or Dolph Lundgren. To what extent do you think these films make the male body into the focus of a homoerotic gaze?
2 Read Richard Dyer's essay on muscle epics in *The Matter of Images* (listed in the Bibliography).

CAMP AESTHETICS AND CINEMA

Dyer's ideas about searching for 'gaps and fissures' referred to above sometimes involve an attitude of conscious, ironic distancing on the part of a spectator known as

camp, traditionally associated with gay audiences. In her famous essay 'Notes on Camp', critic Susan Sontag states: 'The essence of Camp is its love of the unnatural: of artifice and exaggeration' (2001: 275). She describes camp as 'one way of seeing the world as an aesthetic phenomenon…not in terms of beauty, but in terms of degree of artifice, of stylization' (ibid.: 277).

The concept of camp is useful when considering how lesbian and gay audiences often view mainstream representations, but again the exercise of such sensibility is by no means confined to gays. The films of Ken Russell are considered to be very camp, as are many musicals, and as are muscle epics of the 1950s such as *Hercules Unchained*. In the latter, the exaggerated sexual signifiers of the hero (inflated muscles, heroic beard) and the main female figure (cleavage, diaphanous veils) come close to parodying gender stereotypes. Such exaggeration can also be seen in popular action movies, such as those starring Jean-Claude Van Damme, Dolph Lundgren, Vin Diesel and others, where camp elements intertwine with homoerotic subtext. Sontag suggested that 'Camp sensibility is disengaged, depoliticised, or at least apolitical' (ibid.). Camp continues to be a site of critical inquiry (see Farmer 2000, Chapter 3, in which he argues cogently for the political subversiveness of camp sensibility).

CRITICAL RE-READINGS

The possible meanings of a film, as with all signifying practices, reside in the interaction between the viewer and the text. Much work has been done in recent years on how sub-groups within the wider popular audience arrive at their own particular meanings when watching a mainstream film. Lesbian and gay critics have been at the forefront of such 're-readings'. The following are some examples. The books referred to can be found in the Key Reading section at the end of this chapter or in the Bibliography.

Vito Russo

Parker Tyler's book *Screening the Sexes: Homosexuality in the Movies* opened up the field of study and analysis of lesbian and gay cinema in 1972, but Russo's *The Celluloid Closet: Homosexuality in the Movies* is now regarded as a major landmark. First published in 1981 and revised in 1987, the book has continued to influence later critical work in this area.

Russo combines a historical view of lesbian and gay people's contribution to Hollywood cinema with an awareness of representation and audience. Although it deals mainly with Hollywood product, in contrast to Tyler's work, Russo's book is packed with examples and ideas that have formed the basis of further research by new generations of critics and academics. He traces the images of lesbians and gay men in Hollywood film from relatively open portrayals in the silent and early sound eras. He outlines the development of what he calls 'the sissy image' as a coded portrayal of gay men after the introduction of the Production Code and goes on to outline how 'as an outlet for unspeakable ideas, then, the sissy often became a monster or an outlaw'. One example of insights Russo has to offer is his interpretation of the monster in the horror films of gay director James Whale. He sees *Frankenstein* and *The Bride of Frankenstein* as images of unnameable experiences and feelings outside normal society. These ideas were later developed by Harry M. Benshoff (1997).

Using cogently argued examples, Russo outlines gay invisibility in the Hollywood films of the 1950s, followed by marginality and violence in the 1960s and 1970s; 'in twenty-two of twenty-eight films dealing with gay subjects from 1962 to 1978, major gay characters onscreen ended in suicide or death' (Russo 1987: 52). However, he

camp
A critical attitude which involves looking at texts less as reflections of reality than as constructed sets of words, images and sounds at a distance from reality. The attitude often involves irony or detachment when considering this distance. See 'Notes On Camp' by Susan Sontag (in Sontag 2001: 275).

makes a powerful argument about how gay men derived particular sub-cultural messages from such films as *Rebel without a cause* when empathising with the relationship between Jim (James Dean) and Plato (Sal Mineo).

The emergence of neurotic, shadowy gay characters is discussed using *The Boys in the Band* and *The Killing of Sister George* (Robert Aldrich, 1968). Russo's final argument, in the revised 1987 edition, is that worthwhile gay and lesbian cinema can only be developed and encouraged outside the traditional Hollywood power structures, and he outlines a range of examples of such positive work.

To what extent do you believe Russo's argument about Hollywood and gay film-making is still current today?

• **Plate 8.6** *Rebel Without a Cause* (Nicholas Ray, 1955)
The star images of Dean and Mineo were strong precursors of later gay images.

Richard Dyer

Richard Dyer's book, *Now You See It: Studies on Lesbian and Gay Film*, is a comprehensive academic survey of the German films outlined earlier, as well as the work of Jean Genet and Kenneth Anger. It contains a particularly useful introduction to lesbian film- and video-making of the postwar period.

Dyer is the author of many illuminating essays. His work on sexual ideology has already been mentioned, but he is perhaps best known for his work on stars. In *Heavenly Bodies: Film Stars and Society*, Dyer investigates the cultural associations between Judy Garland's star image and gay male audiences from the 1950s onwards. He shows members of this audience strongly allying themselves with Garland's much-vaunted ability to fight back against oppression and the status of outsider which her behaviour and personality often conferred on her.

His essay, 'Homosexuality in Film Noir' (Dyer 1993), coherently shows how gay characters in this classic Hollywood genre were negatively portrayed in both appearance and behaviour. He relates various homoerotic subtexts to film noir traditions and the dominant postwar view of sexual relations. This is an important genre to investigate because, as Dyer points out: 'Some of the first widely available images of homosexuality in our time were those provided by the American film noir' (ibid.: 52).

Dyer's later studies of star image include a seminal essay on Rock Hudson in relation to public perceptions of sexuality, both before and after Hudson's homosexuality became public knowledge (Kirkham and Thumin 1933). Dyer cogently argues how knowledge of Hudson's sexuality greatly enriches a viewer's appreciation of the gender-play in the 1960s sex-comedies in which he starred. He shows how such knowledge gives extra depth to Hudson's star performances in the famous sequence of 1950s melodramas directed by Douglas Sirk, such as *All That Heaven Allows* (1955).

• **Plate 8.7** *All That Heaven Allows* (Douglas Sirk, 1955)
Rock Hudson becomes a wish-fulfilment figure for both Jane Wyman and the audience

Andrea Weiss

The work of Andrea Weiss, like that of other writers on lesbian film such as Mandy Merck, B. Ruby Rich and Judith Mayne, was nurtured within the feminist movement. Weiss works primarily as a film-maker. She was chief researcher on the documentary feature *Before Stonewall* and has produced an equally well-researched book on lesbians in film, *Vampires and Violets* (1993).

In her book, Weiss clearly tackles the critical problems associated with identification and representation for lesbians. She states that:

> identification involves both conscious and unconscious processes and cannot be reduced to a psychoanalytic model that sees sexual desire only in terms of the binary opposition of heterosexual masculinity and femininity; instead it involves varying degrees of subjectivity and distance depending upon race, class and sexual differences.

(Ibid.: 40)

For further discussion of Mulvey's theories of gender and spectatorship, see Chapter 7, pp. 251–255.

Dorothy Arzner
The work of the only woman to pursue a career solely as a director in classic Hollywood is currently undergoing reassessment by critics of lesbian film. Here are some key films:
The Wild Party (1929)
Christopher Strong (1933)
The Bride Wore Red (1937)
Dance, Girl, Dance (1940).

This judgement reflects the questioning of Laura Mulvey's ideas on cinematic looking referred to earlier, a critical practice which has grown steadily since the 1980s. Weiss gives her readers a fascinating set of studies to show how lesbian audiences of classic Hollywood cinema have used their own interpretations to empower themselves, and how lesbian film-makers have been able to make their own images.

These studies range across Dorothy Arzner's *The Wild Party* (1929), star performances by Greta Garbo and Marlene Dietrich in the 1940s, lesbian vampire films and 1970s radical lesbian films by Barbara Hammer. She offers fascinating, oppositional interpretations of the way in which lesbian audiences gained positive messages from the otherwise bleak and tragic lesbian characters and relationships in *The Killing of Sister George* and *The Children's Hour* (William Wyler, 1961).

Weiss clearly outlines the ongoing critical debate about the difficulties of representing autonomous female sexuality in a system of representation which continues to focus on the male heterosexual look. A major part of this debate for lesbian film centres on the problems of producing scenes of woman-centred intimacy and lovemaking that remain satisfying for lesbian audiences while not falling into the traditional function of being a turn-on for heterosexual men.

Bearing in mind ideas of dominant heterosexual ideology, Weiss points out how Dolly, the lesbian character played by Cher in *Silkwood* (Mike Nichols, 1983), is marginalised, made to look childlike, and seen predominantly through the eyes of the heterosexual characters – what she deftly calls the 'happen to be gay' approach to the depiction of lesbians and gays in film. That is, the character is gay or lesbian but is presented within a completely heterosexual framework and outlook and is therefore found to be lacking. In a similar fusion of ideology and representation, she shows how the central lesbian relationship between Celie and Shug in Alice Walker's novel, *The Color Purple*, is downgraded and put under male control in Steven Spielberg's film version (1985).

In her section on the lesbian aspect of art film, Weiss uses some key films to show how their directors have dealt in various productive ways with the male heterosexist narrative and viewing strategies of this kind of film tradition. In this context she gives clear readings of films such as Chantal Akerman's *Je, Tu, Il, Elle* (1974) and *Joanna D'Arc of Mongolia* by Ulrike Ottinger (1988). She points out how Marlene Gorris's *A Question of Silence* (1983) sees lesbian relationships as part of a continuum of relations between women, which are privileged over those with men.

Weiss finishes her book with a look at the viewing strategies of recent film-making by and for lesbians. She has positive praise for the focus on racial and sexual diversity among women, as well as the fluid viewpoints used in Lizzie Borden's *Born in Flames* (1983). On the other hand, she analyses a well-known lesbian film of the 1980s, Sheila

● **Plate 8.8** *The Wild Party* (Dorothy Arzner, 1929)
The energetic college girls have such a fun time together that being paired off with the males at the end comes almost as an anti-climax

McLaughlin's *She Must Be Seeing Things* (1987), and sees it as being so caught up in conventional viewing strategies that it denies any positive pleasure or viewpoints for lesbian viewers. Finally, she rightly cautions against a simplistic view of lesbian film as progressing from hidden signs to liberated images, pointing out that 'the cinema has been and continues to be a contested terrain in which people and groups with often opposing interests have staked their claims' (Weiss 1993: 163).

> **In the light of Weiss's comments on viewing strategies, analyse the love-making scenes from *Desert Hearts*, *Go Fish* and any other film of your choice.**

SOME FILMS WITH GAY/LESBIAN THEMES

Stereotypes and characters

In his book, *The Matter of Images*, Richard Dyer has pointed out the dangers inherent in thinking rigidly in terms of stereotypes when dealing with representation: 'a **stereotype**

stereotype
A set of commonly expected behaviour patterns and character-istics based on role (e.g. mother) or personal features such as race, age or sexuality. In society and cultural products, the depiction of a stereotype becomes a form of communicative shorthand, and often reflects the attitudes of dominant social groups.

at the engagement party of Cay's friend Silver, Frances talks of how special the memory of Glen, her lover, is to her 'because he reached in and put a string of lights around my heart'. She tells Vivian; '…I got what I wanted. I had a love of my own'. Vivian's reply; 'You had more than most people dare hope for', sets up the main dramatic expectations of the plot as we gradually learn of Vivian's conformist marriage that she is escaping from. As she tells her lawyer; 'I want to be free of what I've been'.

Character patterns

The differences between Vivian and Cay are clearly signalled through dress and behaviour. Vivian wears a steel-grey, precisely cut 1950s skirt-suit with a matching cloche hat. Her blonde hair is up in a neat, business-like style which matches her stiff, formal movements. She is ten years older than Cay. She lectures in English Literature at Columbia University, and makes frequent references to what she calls her 'circle'. In terms of representation in American films, this brings into play a whole set of stereotypes in the contrast between the more intellectual, snobbish Easterner and the more physical Westerner. Cay shows off her long brown legs in skimpy denim shorts and cowboy boots. Her medium-length black hair flows freely. A representational tradition of associating blonde hair with aloof coolness, and dark hair with a lively, passionate nature, is being brought into play.

Cay is open and positive about her love of women. The first time Vivian visits Cay in her cottage she is disconcerted to glimpse another woman, Gwen, in Cay's bed. Vivian accepts Cay's offer of a lift into town, but is evidently awkward sitting between Gwen and Cay. Cultural differences are underlined when Cay replaces the blaring pop music on the radio with another station playing Prokofiev, whereupon Vivian recognises the music and says she likes it.

Although undeveloped in her education, Cay is open to new ideas and cultural influences, and it is for this reason that Vivian later wants to take her to New York. Cay is strong-minded, and tells Frances firmly; 'One of these days I'm gonna meet somebody that counts'. We see her resisting various social pressures to 'settle down' with Darrell, the male supervisor at the casino. She makes it clear to her friend Silver that she wants to be accepted for what she is, and Silver declares her continued friendship.

Cay tells Silver that she is very much in love with Vivian, but doesn't know whether anything will come of it. Darrell is shown protecting Cay from the unwanted advances of a client at the casino, and is polite and patient with her. His offer to 'look the other way' about Cay's affairs with women evokes her exasperation, and shows his complete misunderstanding of who Cay is.

It is Cay who makes most of the moves in bringing herself and Vivian together. At the motel, when Vivian, on the opposite side of the door, asks her to go away, Cay replies; 'I can't, honest'. Once she has let Cay into the room, Vivian turns round to find Cay naked in her bed. Cay succeeds, once again, in relaxing Vivian by making her laugh.

Vivian slowly develops a more relaxed outlook. She adopts a looser hairstyle, wears jeans and visits the casino. As she watches a rodeo, we see a close-up of her slipping her wedding ring off her finger, symbolising a new life. When she finally gets her divorce, the lawyer remarks that Vivian has found a 'pen-pal' in Reno. Her reply, 'I've found much more than that, Mr Warner', is strong and confident.

Sex and the spectator

A key scene in advancing the couple's intimacy occurs when Cay is driving Vivian home after the party, where Silver's performance of her loving country song is accompanied by shots of the two looking at each other. Cay tells Vivian that she can only find real love with a woman. When Vivian, continuing to wrap her reactions in a cloak of academic tolerance, says, 'Are you trying to shock me?', Cay replies calmly: 'No, I was only telling you the truth'. As Vivian flees to the car Cay makes her wind down the window, bends down and caresses Vivian's cheek with her lips. The romantic convention of the first kiss is made dramatic and memorable through the heavy shower that is drenching Cay and the unusual positioning of the lovers.

The love-making scene at the motel raises the vexed question of erotic voyeurism. We have a woman directing a scene of woman-to-woman love-making which generally avoids angles or shots which could echo those traditionally associated with images directed at heterosexual males. Helen Shaver as Vivian conveys pleasurable sexual awakening and a nervousness that is carried into the next scene. In a restaurant, the two declare their love for each other but Vivian is uncomfortable and her lack of 'points of reference' leads to a quarrel and reconciliation with her lover.

Given the 1950s setting, remarkably little **homophobia** is encountered by the two lovers in this film. The prejudice of Lucille, another house guest, and the incomprehension of Darrell are balanced by the tolerant support of Silver and Walter. Frances's attitudes remain ambiguous and perhaps more credible given the era in which the film is set. When they return to find Frances has kicked Vivian out of her house and booked her into a motel, this act is equally aimed at hanging on to Cay, although she says 'at least I'm normal'. The act backfires, and Cay moves out to stay with Silver. In her final conversation with Cay, Frances displays mystified antagonism: 'I just don't understand it. Women together'. Cay uses Frances's words to explain: 'She just reached in…put a string of lights around my heart' and earns a reluctant blessing and a hug, an action marred by Frances's comment that people will be talking about her.

The fragility of this lesbian relationship across the class, regional and educational differences of 1950s America is echoed by the question posed narratively at the end as the train pulls away: will it be to the next station as she claims, or will Cay stay with Vivian on that train journey to New York?

> **homophobia**
> Irrational prejudice against and hatred of a person because of her or his homosexuality.

How 'conventional' a film is *Desert Hearts* in terms of debates about essentialism and queer spectatorship?

☐ CASE STUDY 2: *LOOKING FOR LANGSTON* (ISAAC JULIEN, 1994)

Poetic meditation

Subtitled *A meditation on Langston Hughes (1902–1967) and the Harlem Renaissance*, this film is a tribute to the American poet Langston Hughes, who lived in New York and whose writings formed a key part of the flowering of black culture in that city during the 1920s, a time known as the 'Harlem Renaissance'. It is less than an hour long and was funded by Britain's Channel 4. As the word 'meditation' suggests, the work is structured in a non-narrative way around a collage of visual images and a soundtrack of poetry by Hughes, Essex Hemphill and Bruce Nugent. It is dedicated to another outstanding American writer who was also gay and black, the novelist James Baldwin.

The film opens with newsreel footage of Hughes' funeral. A female voiceover delivers an oration about the struggle of opposition, which no one undertakes easily. Later on, this idea of opposition is underlined when we see a modern article on Hughes entitled 'Black and Gay', and when we see a gang of fierce-looking skinheads attempting violence on the nightclub space occupied by the men dancing together. The skinheads are white, and when they invade the space they are seen to do so with white police officers looking on and doing nothing. The funeral footage immediately cuts to a modern re-creation, in sensuously crisp black and white, of the funeral, with large white lilies and the body laid out in its coffin. The black and white cinematography continues throughout the film as a homage and reference to famous gay images. The lilies recall the photography of Robert Mapplethorpe.

Male, black and gay

Images of the funeral recur and evoke respectful homage. They are interwoven with images of a nightclub peopled by handsome men dancing, drinking, talking and laughing together, images of enjoyment, sensuality and cultural solidarity. The men are in formal evening clothes and dancing to music which recalls the 1920s. One of the men is white and is later seen in intimate, loving surroundings with his black lover after displaying jealousy in the club. Later, the music and dancing become disco-style in a mix between 1920s and modern styles and scenes, a mix which recurs throughout the film to evoke the continuity of both black and gay culture.

The central figure in the club is a handsome man with a moustache who sees another very good-looking man. The two are attracted to each other, and the middle part of the film presents sensuous fantasy sequences of the two of them together. The man with the moustache is seen reflected in a pond in a spacious moorland setting. He comes across the other man, who is naked. His firm, well-made body is revealed to the viewer from behind, gradually, from the legs up. The poetry on the soundtrack talks of the man's 'dancer's body' and makes clear that this man is the figure of Beauty: 'Beauty's lips touched his…How much pressure does it take to awaken love?' The shots of Beauty culminate in a scene of him lying naked in bed with the other man, their bodies intertwined. This memorable image recalls a famous photograph by George Platt Lynes, once again paying homage to a major figure of gay culture.

Cultural continuity

Fantasy elements underline the sense of meditation about Hughes and the cultural tradition of which he was part. The nightclub is first seen with the men in still poses. Male angels watch over the nightclub. At one point, a beautiful young angel is seen holding a large picture of Langston Hughes, then the camera pans slowly to a large picture of James Baldwin. At another point, the camera rises from the nightclub to a scene of funeral mourning situated on the balcony above. This establishes a spatial relationship between the two main movements and moods of the film, and the words of

• **Plate 8.10**
Looking for Langston
(Isaac Julien, 1988)
The beauty of this film's images forms a vivid tribute both to Hughes as an artist and to the culture that nurtured him.

the poem on the soundtrack – 'Let my name be spoken without effect, without the ghost of shadow on it' – show that we are invited to celebrate with joy, not mourn with sadness, Hughes and the culture he represents. Nightclub images of kissing, dancing and talking are then followed by the slow pan sideways to a young man with a flower.

Archive footage underlines cultural continuity. There is footage of Hughes reading his poetry on a TV programme, literary gatherings, jazz bands in Harlem, a football team, references to poets and anthologies and to the first production of the play *Amen Corner* by James Baldwin. A sequence which evokes the milieu of Harlem in the 1920s is accompanied by a poem on the soundtrack which tells how black artists at the time were expected to produce something called 'black art', a ghetto concept which was supposed to keep such artists in their place. Black artists were not supposed to concern themselves with wider ideas such as modernism. The poem tells how black art later went out of fashion with collectors: 'History as the smiler with the knife under her cloak'.

Throughout the film, Julien juxtaposes image and sound in order to provoke thought and emotion. What both the modern and the 1920s scenes have in common is a sense of danger for gay men in public spaces, outside the safety of places such as the club, but at the same time a sense of going out into, of braving those public spaces. A young man walks into the club, and the song lyric rings out:

> You're such a beautiful black man,
> But you've been made to feel,
> That your beauty's not real.

To accompany this we see footage of a black sculptor working on a sculpture of a naked black man. The lyric, the footage of the sculptor at work, and the preceding homage to Beauty as a black man, provide a critique of sexual and aesthetic attitudes towards black men in a society dominated by ideas of beauty as white. Sound and image in collision are used to provoke questions and thoughts about how black men are sexually used by whites, black men as both objects and users of pornography, and the use of pornography for safe sex.

Strong, positive attitudes

This film takes on several controversial issues, including interracial sex and the questioning of the nature of black masculinity, and deals with them in an accomplished and stylish way. Such glamorously eroticised male images are, as Andrea Weiss points out, very different from the low-key approach taken by lesbian film-making, as in the film she and Greta Schiller made about the black lesbian jazz artist Tiny Davis, *Tiny and Ruby: Hell Drivin' Women* (1988).

The final and dominant mood of *Looking for Langston* is elegiac. A male couple is seen to leave the club and walk across Waterloo Bridge in contemporary London. While a train passes and they look at each other the voiceover poem is wistful: 'I love my friend. He went away from me. There's nothing more to say'. But life goes on, the angels overlook scenes of love and celebration, and a poem refers to Hannibal, Toussaint and other strong figures of black history. As the gang of skinheads advances down the street, the club erupts with disco music and we see the dancers enjoying themselves. The editing rhythm speeds up as it cuts between the skinheads, clubbers and police with truncheons. The expected clash is undercut when we see the police and thugs enter the club only to find it empty, followed by a shot of a laughing black angel. Is this a comment on the invisibility and/or oppression of black gay culture? Is it a demonstration of how prejudice and oppression can and will be deflected and dissipated? The final upbeat note is sounded when footage of the old TV programme is shown, with Hughes reading;

Sun's a risin'
This is gonna be my song.

---

1 Compare and contrast *Looking for Langston* with Isaac Julien's feature, *Young Soul Rebels* (1991), in terms of representations of race, sexuality and narrative structure.
2 How 'queer' is *Looking for Langston*?

☐ CASE STUDY 3: *GO FISH* (ROSE TROCHE, 1994)

Lesbian stardom

For further discussion of stardom, see Chapter 4, pp. 169–181.

Guinevere Turner, a leading actor and co-writer of this film, has become a lesbian film star. Her on-screen charisma and the intertextual effects of publicity in lesbian and gay media contain the classic ingredients for the development of the first openly lesbian film star persona. This is a trail already blazed in other media by figures such as k.d. lang (music and film) and Ellen Degeneres (television).

In the tradition of most lesbian productions, *Go Fish* is a small-budget film. The long list of helpers and contributors following the main credits attests to strong community support. Typical of such projects, many of those participating in the making of the film did several jobs; for example, V.S. Brodie is both main actor and co-producer. The film has excellent black and white cinematography by Ann T. Rossi, and an attractive, specially written score. It took two years to complete, a fact which makes the quality and consistency of Turner's performance all the more laudable.

The time was right for the success of this film. Co-producer John Pierson was aware that what he calls 'the low-budget aesthetic' was very much in vogue in 1994 and the success of *Claire of the Moon*, despite very bad reviews, had made him conscious of the vastly underserviced lesbian audience. The film was an immediate hit at the Sundance Film Festival that year, and Pierson used his considerable negotiating skills to persuade Goldwyn distributors to snap it up, the first such deal to be achieved. Nevertheless, its success with audiences, and its engaging charm, are mainly due to its lively script, direction and performances.

The script: speaking as lesbians

The screenplay of *Go Fish*, by Rose Troche and Guinevere Turner, with an introduction by Lea Delaria, is available from The Overlook Press in New York (published 1995).

Go Fish has a simple main storyline. A young lesbian student, Max (Turner), is eager to find a girlfriend. Ely (Brodie) is very reserved, nervous of commitment, and sheltering behind her fading long-distance relationship with a lover who has been living far away in Seattle for over two years. Max and Ely get together with a lot of help from their friends, which include Kia, a black college lecturer in whose apartment Max rents a room, and Evy, Kia's hispanic lover. Ely shares an apartment with Daria. These room-mates discuss the women's feelings, with each of them separately and between themselves as a group. Max is initially uninterested, but gradually changes her attitude. It emerges that Ely is very attracted to Max. Daria arranges a party in her apartment to which all the friends are invited. At the party Max and Ely get to know each other better and, soon after, arrange a big date.

This outline indicates several features that make a refreshing difference in terms of lesbian film. In contrast with the all too frequent portrayal of lesbian relationships as relatively isolated and fragile, dependent on the goodwill of a limited number of (usually straight, usually liberal) friends, Max and Ely are surrounded by a supportive lesbian culture. Daria is constantly pressing Ely to make up her mind. Kia checks through Max's college paper for her, and discusses her well-being with Evy, Daria and other friends. These women work, eat, drink, make love, have sex, play cards and care for their cats. The script is a collaboration between Guinevere Turner and director Rose Troche. During one of their get-togethers the group of friends discuss various woman-positive words for 'vagina', just one notable example of the way the dialogue crackles with lively repartee about their lived experience as lesbians.

A further example of natural-sounding dialogue occurs during the phone conversation where Max and Ely arrange their date. Gently prompted by Max, Ely admits that she considers her relationship with the woman in Seattle to be over. On hearing this admission, Max prompts Ely to ask her out on a date. They agree to meet at Max's apartment. The scene leading up to their love-making is underpinned with gentle humour. Max is late in getting ready, then tells Ely that she's having a 'fashion crisis' in deciding what to wear, and remains in her robe. The act of cutting Ely's nails, very odd for a first date as the friends later comment, brings them into close physical intimacy.

The script celebrates lesbian culture but prevents the tone of the film from becoming cosily idealistic. We see Kia fielding insults shouted in the street and hear Ely talking of being called a 'lezzie' at school. There is a scene where Evy goes home and has a major argument with her mother because her brother has informed the family that he saw her going into a local gay bar. Her mother utters a stream of homophobic insults in Spanish and English. Evy angrily declares that she is leaving home. She flees to Kia's apartment where Max comforts her in her usual clumsy way, saying, 'We can be your family'.

Direction: seeing queerly

The film has a distinct visual style based on frequent use of close-ups. The faces of Max and Ely are shot in extreme close-up, for instance, as the two of them talk on the phone, thus underlining their growing intimacy. Close-ups of hair, ear-rings, lips and

Note the visual contrast between the characters in *Go Fish* and the more overt use of make-up and high fashion in *Desert Hearts* and/or *When Night Is Falling*.

For a discussion of race and sexual role-play which parallels issues raised in *Go Fish*, see the chapter in Wilton (1995) on *She Must Be Seeing Things*.

• **Plate 8.11**
Go Fish (Rose Troche, 1994)
Guinevere Turner as Max and V.S. Brodie as Ely. A close-up shot that indicates the natural-looking, relaxed feel of this film, conveyed through close-ups.

hands make the viewer feel part of the group. This sense of intimacy through physical closeness echoes the style of other lesbian film-makers such as Sadie Benning.

There are scenes throughout the film of Kia, Evy, Daria and the latter's various girl-friends talking about their lives and discussing the progress of Max and Ely's relationship. The director presents these shots in a memorable way. We see only the women's heads in various patterns as they are lying, presumably on some kind of large bed, looking up at the ceiling, an amusing physical embodiment of them putting their heads together in order to formulate their plans.

The narrative is punctuated by shots and montage sequences which comment on the main action. Shots of a spinning top reflect the game of pairing and mating that is being played. The song on the soundtrack echoes the theme, with lyrics about love spinning round. Shots of lights being switched off and wringing hands visually embody the initial tensions of the Max–Ely relationship. A montage sequence uses shots of Max and other women looking uncomfortable in white wedding dresses while people congratulate them. Sometimes the women try to pull off the dresses. In parallel, Max's voiceover gives us her thoughts on how to live her lesbian identity, along with comment on the lures and pitfalls of conformity.

Director/scriptwriter Rose Troche uses light touches which bring the characters to life. One longer close-up of Ely's black boot being carefully laced by her, in readiness for her date with Max, embodies this character's care and nervousness. On her way home afterwards, we see Ely leaping in the air with delight and accepting a rose from a stranger. There is a comic sequence towards the end. Scenes of Ely being closely questioned by Daria about what went on during the date are cross-cut with Max giving her account to her room-mates, and these in turn are comically underpinned by contrasting scenes of the date as envisaged by Max, Ely and their friends.

New lesbian images?

For a lively visual exploration around issues of ageing, see *Nitrate Kisses* (listed in Further viewing).

The viewer is introduced to a varying array of lesbians, although there are no older women. Ages range from Kia, who is thirty, to Max, in her late teens. Kia's dress and demeanour contain overtones of the traditional butch stereotype. The fact that she is black provokes further debate about racial and sexual imaging.

The women portrayed have a refreshingly realistic, non-glamorised range of bodies and faces. Characters and attitudes also vary. Ely is firmly monogamous while Daria is happily promiscuous. Ely and Max disagree about the gay images in the film they see when they first go out together. After having sex with a male friend, Daria is waylaid by an angry group of lesbians. The ensuing discussion airs a range of views about personal freedom and sexual identity as Daria insists that she is 'a lesbian who has had sex with a man'. A queer lesbian perhaps?

Awareness of age and image is foregrounded. Max initially dismisses Ely's looks as 'seventies hippie' and with typical youthful impetuosity calls her 'ugly', to Kia's annoyance. Max learns to be less rigid in her outlook. Ely undergoes a drastic change of image, having her long hair cut into a dramatically shaved style. On her next meeting with Max, she confides her worry that the new style may be 'too butch' and the two women talk of the constraints and expectations of body image for lesbians.

The final sequence of the film, which accompanies the credits, contains an uplifting message. It shows various couples we have met during the film making love. The imagery skilfully avoids hetero-titillation and has a convincingly lesbian feel, recalling the photographic images of Della Grace. The voiceover advises viewers to keep an open mind because 'The Girl Is Out There'.

1 Compare and contrast the lesbian worlds portrayed in *Go Fish* with those in *Desert Hearts*, *When Night Is Falling* and/or *She Must Be Seeing Things*.

2 *Desert Hearts* is a romance, *Bound* is a film noir and *Better than Chocolate* is a comedy. Compare and contrast the portrayal of the lesbian lovers in each of these three films in terms of genre.

☐ CASE STUDY 4: THE HANGING GARDEN (THOM FITZGERALD, 1997)

Contrasting styles blended

A family house and garden in Nova Scotia are the setting for the action, as well as the sources of memory for the main characters. The film is predominantly naturalistic in style but, in counterpoint, we see previous incarnations of William, as a young boy and in his mid-teens, tangibly haunting William, his father and other members of the family, images which represent William's troubled childhood from which he has escaped to Toronto to build a new, confident self. There are other non-naturalistic elements. Humour is added in the critical facial expressions adopted by the ceramic figures of the Virgin Mary. Certain devices are used to indicate and comment on changes of time and scene, such as filling the screen with vivid colour or the use of time-lapse flower photography.

A montage of scenes reveals William's difficult relationship with his father during childhood. Next we cut to William, aged fifteen, carefully watering a clump of Sweet Williams, seen in point-of-view shot to underline William's fondness for the flowers, while he recites more plant names and seasons to himself. There is a major visual change in William, other than that of gaining in years; William, initially seen as a thin, wiry boy, is now very obese. The viewer is left to ponder what this may mean.

Family dramas

The remainder of the film is divided into three named sections. In the first, 'The Lady with the Locket', we see William's sister Rosemary's wedding ceremony in the garden. As we see William step out of his car, the director reveals his body and face to us only gradually to make us aware that the grown-up William is lean and handsome. Close-ups of his wary eyes as he looks round the house display his feelings about coming back home. His nervous asthma surfaces, and he reaches for his inhaler. Objects underline the change from his teenage self; the formal suit he puts on that is far too big for him, and the photo of his obese younger self reflected in grandma's display cabinet as he greets her. Most strikingly, he meets up with the teenage William in the garden as he is entering the front of the house, and eyes him uncomfortably. He picks up a sprig of Sweet William that is lying on the path.

William is the object of the gaze of Rosemary, his mother, his father and the groom, Fletcher. This play of looks establishes the reactions of the characters. Rosemary gives a contented smile, while Fletcher and his mother look surprised. His father looks disconcerted. Consequent interactions take place among Scottish jigs and fiddle music, underlining the Nova Scotian locale and William's outsider status. We learn that he left for Toronto ten years previously and has never been back since. William is introduced to a younger sibling he has never met before.

'What's his name?' asks William.

'Violet', his mother replies. William and his sister are relaxed enough with each other for William to make a joke about her husband 'coming on' to him. Later, William has to drag his drunken father to bed in a strange reversal of the earlier scene of father–son interaction. There is an intriguing point-of-view shot as William gazes at his father's naked body under the cold shower.

Throughout the film, William's look is that of the outsider looking in on the family hang-ups and dramas, while at the same time the incarnations of his younger selves are central to these dramas. William explains to his mother how he became fat 'because no-one could make me be skinny, it was the one thing you couldn't make me be', and goes on to say that because he was fat that meant 'no fights, no sport…and no girl-friends'. In the light of queer theory outlined later in this chapter, to what extent do these interactions queerify an otherwise conventional family set-up?

In reply to his mother's question about whether he has a 'friend' in Toronto, William talks of being in a happy relationship. To what extent does William become a figure of emotional normality in this film compared with those in his family milieu?

Finding yourself

It is at this point that a perennial theme of lesbian and gay films comes to the fore, that of being yourself, finding out your true nature and needs and acting on them. When William begins talking about having found himself and become happy the bitterness of his mother surfaces, the reactions of a person who feels herself a victim. As William goes upstairs, his boy-self waves to him, and is left sitting at the table with his mother. Later, halfway through clearing up the rubbish from the wedding reception, the mother flings the contents of a rubbish bag across the garden, walks away and is never seen again in the film.

A time-lapse shot of a flower opening begins the next section, 'Lad's Love'. In the first scene, William and Fletcher as teenage boys are sitting in the sun on a jetty. Fletcher takes off his T-shirt to reveal an athletic torso, and lies back. The obese young William lies back with his head near Fletcher's stomach. There is a distanced view of this scene with sunlight sparkling on the water surrounding the boys. The shot is held in a manner that traditionally connotes romance. Later, there is a long held shot as they eye each other up and slowly undress, and it is Fletcher who initiates a mutual sexual exploration, after taunting the shy, self-conscious William for not taking off his briefs.

A queer family?

With the help of his aunt, the teenage William's mother arranges for him to lose his virginity to an older local woman in need of extra money. Here, a heterosexual act imposed on a reluctant minor takes on a queerness all of its own. William's reaction next day suggests mild trauma, not least after Fletcher reveals his shallowness by refusing to meet and talk to William. In the circumstances, William's emotional need to communicate becomes the norm.

The family situation becomes steadily more fantastic and deviant. This third section of the film is entitled 'Mums', perhaps ironically. The adult William goes out, sees his young self hanging from the tree, and caresses the pale, dead face. For the first time, William directly confronts his father over the handling of grandmother. Meanwhile, father seems unconcerned about his missing wife.

• Plate 8.12
The Hanging Garden
(Thom Fitzgerald, 1997)
Erotic tension between
the teenage William and
his sister's boyfriend
Fletcher is encapsu-
lated in the scene at
the jetty.

Refer to Chapter 7, pp. 247–257. Critically assess the portrayal of William's mother in relation to feminist ideas of filmic representation.

A subsequent private conversation in the garden between William and Rosie reveals a major twist in the plot; Violet is, in fact, William's daughter, the product of his unhappy heterosexual initiation at the age of fifteen. His mother had fought for custody of her, and Rosie suggests that she wants William to take responsibility. William is initially resistant to the idea.

The adult Fletcher, alone with William, makes advances to him, starting to kiss and fondle him. This takes place on the very same jetty where they lay together as boys. In a variation of expected behaviour patterns, it is William again who shows great reluctance, not least because, as he points out, Fletcher is married to his sister.

1 How 'queer' is the portrayal of the character Fletcher in his transgression of sexual boundaries?
2 Refer to Chapter 7, pp. 264–275. Critically assess the portrayal of William's father in relation to ideas of fatherhood and masculinity in crisis.

A hanging symbol

Back in the garden, William sees his hanging former self again. This time, he is more forthright: 'I'm getting to remember why you're so fucked up', he says to the body. He takes decisive action in smashing the statue of the Virgin Mary, thereby fighting back against the belief system of his childhood, in contrast to the way his teenage self merely shrank under the gaze of the statues.

Later, Rosie drags her brother out to watch her father desperately hugging the hanging body of his obese teenage son, tears streaming down his face. She desperately makes clear to him that she has to watch this 'every fucking day'. The whole family seems haunted by this image. Even Violet expressed surprise at William not being fat when she first met him.

• **Plate 8.13**
The Hanging Garden
(Thom Fitzgerald, 1997)
The adult William has
just buried the past. This
shot indicates his devel-
oping confidence in
handling his father

Psychic resolution

William then takes his most decisive action. As Fletcher looks on, he chops violently
with a spade at the rope holding up his dysfunctional teenage self. The body drops to
the ground to William's words: 'You been hanging around here too long, buddy'. There
is a quick cut to William reclining in the garden, looking at peace with himself, contem-
plating a Sweet William flower, the other, more positive symbol in this film. This time the
wistful Gaelic voice on the soundtrack suggests a different journey into the self.

Plot resolution

Father, totally disconcerted, asks; 'Where is he?' and William replies, 'I buried him'. As
father attempts to scrape the earth away from the burial mound, William stops him,
restrains him and sits for a while with his arms around his father. 'Why did you do this? I
loved you so much' moans father. What is it exactly that William has done? Is his father
stuck in some sort of dysfunctional past, resenting the changes in his son? Father is
nowhere to be seen as William and Violet drive off. The final shot of the film takes us
through the leafiness of the beloved garden to a view of him sitting on a boulder with
William as a little boy playing around him. Is this a symbolic view of a man stuck in his
own emotional past?

1 **How does the director use the wedding as a source of personal confrontation and comedy?**
2 **Assess the significance and effectiveness of the use of flowers and the
hanging body in this film as narrative symbols.**

☐ CASE STUDY 5: *HAPPY TOGETHER* (WONG KAR WAI, 1997)

A glimpse of Chinese diversity

For another Chinese film
with a gay theme, see
The Wedding Banquet
listed in Further viewing.
In recent years, since the opening up of Chinese society, gays and lesbians in China
have become more visible, especially in traditional centres of gay life such as Shanghai.
Nevertheless, it is no surprise that a film such as *Happy Together* should have been
made in the more liberal enclave of Hong Kong, and with outside funding and locations

in Argentina. Any reference to dialogue and speech in the following analysis is based on the subtitles provided for the Artificial Eye video edition, which translate the Cantonese, Mandarin and small amount of Spanish in which the film is acted.

Ho Po-Wing is an attractive but louche good-time boy. The other half of the couple at the centre of the narrative, Lai Yiu-Fai, is a hard-working, down-to-earth man who dotes on Ho. Both parts are played by well-known Hong Kong stars. The film is initially structured around the contrasts between these two characters, and their interaction. Later a young man named Chang becomes significant in Lai's life and the narrative momentum shifts to the Lai–Chang relationship

Voiceover viewpoints

The voice of Lai on the soundtrack puts this character firmly in control of viewpoint. Lai is the one who explains to the viewer the on/off nature of his relationship with Ho, that they came on holiday to Argentina and hit the road in order to try and sort things out. Lai's voiceover explains, comments and vents emotions throughout the film.

He tells us that it was Ho's purchase of a waterfall lamp that inspired them to visit the famous landmark waterfall at Iguazu. He expresses his most intimate emotions on the soundtrack at such points when, in a later flashback showing him caring for Ho's injuries, he admits that he never told Ho that he didn't want him to recover too fast because 'these days were our happiest'. When he finally gets to see the Iguazu falls on his own, his voiceover confesses that he still feels sad, that he should be there with Ho. The visuals both complement and counteract Lai's voice. A long-shot of him as a lone figure next to the vastness of the falls makes us aware of his sense of isolation, and there is a close-up of his face splashed with tear-like water drops.

Chang enters the film about two-thirds of the way through. His viewpoint too is privileged through voiceover. His voice also comments and expresses emotions. Initially, we see his long, lean face in close-up while he is washing up in the restaurant kitchen, telling us how he loves listening to sounds. He has already noticed Lai and comments on how pleasant his voice sounds. He lets us know that he has noticed how much Lai talks on the phone and says 'he must be talking to someone he likes'.

When Chang is about to leave Buenos Aires, having saved enough money to move on, he says a fond farewell to Lai. As the two men embrace we hear Chang's voice asking himself uncertainly whether the two of them have become close. He tells us that he can hear his own heart beating, and wonders whether Lai's heart is beating too. He goes to visit the lighthouse at Ushuaia, a famous landmark. He had tried to capture Lai's voice on tape as a souvenir because he prefers sound to photos, and left Lai alone to speak into the machine, telling him to express his feelings. Lai had told him of a

• **Plate 8.14**
Happy Together (Wong Kar Wai, 1997)
Ho leans on Lai's shoulder as they go home in a taxi in a pose which connotes both tenderness and dependence.

• **Plate 8.15** *Happy Together* (Wong Kar Wai, 1997) Chang can hear his own heart beating as he gives Lai a goodbye hug. Sountrack and visuals interact intriguingly.

legend connected with the lighthouse which says that people with emotional troubles can dump them there. At the lighthouse, he plays his small, portable recorder and tells us that he is trying to help Lai, but that all he could hear on the tape was sobs. Sweeping panoramic aerial shots of Chang at the lighthouse give an airy sense of liberation and suggest that he might be successful in his chosen purpose.

1 **How effective do you consider voiceover and music to be in adding layers of meaning to this film?**
2 **Consider the waterfall and the lighthouse as symbols in this film.**

A good-time boy?

Ho is portrayed as mixed up, self-centred and immature, a character who commands little audience sympathy. He quickly decides they are to split up again and is soon parading his rich white boyfriend in front of Lai at the tango bar. Other themes in this film can be explored around relations between white and Chinese gay men. A shot of Ho lounging in his boyfriend's luxury apartment contrasts tellingly with the scenes of Lai's small, simple room and his hard work.

However, Ho does attempt to help Lai by stealing a watch, an act that misfires and results in him being beaten up and kicked out. He comes back to Lai for help. When Lai gives him a ticket and puts him on a bus he comes back again, this time with his wrists slit. During his long recovery, Lai loses his job at the bar because of an angry attack on the white boyfriend. He finds a job in the kitchen and supports Ho. Only when fully recovered through Lai's care and support does Ho run off yet again. For Lai, this is clearly the last straw. In his final scene, as we see Ho clutching a blanket and weeping copiously, there is still the question of exactly what or who he is weeping for.

A troubled man?

Lai, initially in thrall to Ho, is obviously unhappy; the film is dotted with shots showing Lai alone, looking depressed, clutching his forehead with his hand, smoking or looking wistfully from windows. In one instance, his near-naked figure is slumped against a wall in the restricted space of a harshly lit bathroom, the tiles glinting mercilessly. There is a scene where he gazes out from a boat on the river, the whole screen bathed in blue to reflect his melancholy. Other expressionist techniques are used such as the jagged blurry shot with a jolting camera as Lai runs down the street after a quarrel.

Lai is also an angry man. There are several instances of him breaking beer bottles against hard surfaces. He angrily kicks Ho out when the latter taunts him about the number of boyfriends he has had. At one point the viewer is given an outside shot of the tango bar as Lai watches the white boyfriend go in with yet another young conquest. The camera remains fixed, and all we see is Lai picking up a beer bottle, walking angrily into the bar, followed by a male scream on the soundtrack. A short while later, we learn he has lost his job for this.

As indicated earlier, Lai tries very hard to distance himself from Ho but perhaps he can't help himself when faced with Ho's child-like, dependent nature, which contrasts so strongly with his coping, caring and working which we continually view. The major instance of this inability to help himself occurs when Ho returns to his apartment with his wrists cut.

A significant shot follows immediately. After all Lai's efforts to reject Ho and put him on a bus, the camera angle reverses to reveal the love and concern on Lai's face. As Lai nurses Ho, and after he has confessed in voiceover to that time span being one of the happiest, there is surely a feeling here of unease. A relationship where one partner wants the other helpless and ill is not a healthy one and Lai seems to demonstrate this to a certain extent in his behaviour. He continues to insist on the two of them sleeping apart, one on the single bed, one on the sofa. He seems to be weaning himself off Ho.

At the same time, Lai's behaviour tends towards the obsessive and possessive, and serves to increase the viewer's sense of unease about the situation. Lai is finally strong enough to refuse to see Ho but his strong feelings for Ho continue to the end of the film. We see him gazing wistfully at the waterfall lamp just after Ho leaves and later, after Chang has left him alone with the tape recorder, we see him sobbing quietly into it as he hides his face behind it.

Finally, the script offers a possible psychological explanation for Lai's troubled nature. A phone call he attempts to make, and a long letter he writes, are accompanied in voiceover by references to seeking his father's forgiveness, not only for stealing some money from the tango bar (run by a friend of his father's) but for other unspecified things. Later, when he meets Chang's family in Taipei, he envies Chang his happy, stable home background.

Happy together?

The relationship between Ho and Lai is clearly a troubled one. Both men seem dependent on each other for reasons which do them harm. Yet there is no doubting their sexual compatibility and attraction. Their mutual attraction on this level is established in the opening scene of the film where they almost seem to eat each other up as they make passionate love in a way that is remarkably explicit but perhaps too frantic to be stable.

They come to Argentina to try and work things out, but as the film progresses, Lai seems to change. The happiest period for him may have been when he nursed Ho, but after the initial passion all we see is Ho trying to provoke, tease, caress, lick and kiss in a one-way flow of sensuality. After the break-up, we see Lai out in the gay bars and haunts of Buenos Aires, cruising.

The waterfall lamp is a powerful visual symbol of the two men's relationship. It is often foregrounded in shots of the apartment and, as indicated, used by both lovers as a focus for emotional contemplation. It ties in closely with the planned trip together to the falls, which hovers over the narrative like some kind of ideal view of how the relationship could turn out.

A sweet saviour?

After extended scenes of Ho's selfish manipulations, it is with great relief that the sweet, sensible Chang enters the narrative with the facial close-up described earlier. Chang's presence in the film puts an interesting emphasis on sound. When he and Chang are out

Further exploration of the portrayal of such troubled young men as Lai can be found in Grossman (2001). See the essay entitled 'Happy Alone? Sad Young Men in East Asian Cinema'.

drinking together as they get to know each other better, Lai finds that Chang is listening to a conversation far away at the other side of the bar. Chang explains that he had an eye problem as a child and learned to make hearing his main way of looking at the world. This is the motivation for his taping of Lai's voice, which leads to the symbolic release of Lai's woes at the lighthouse. Chang's gentle behaviour and plain style of dress combine with his dedication to listening to give him an almost mystical aura.

A similar aura of mystery remains around Chang's sexuality. He seems to be a loner, working late in the kitchen because he has nothing else to do. He tells Lai that he left home to travel in order to 'work some things out'. We see him refusing an attractive young female workmate's invitation to go to the cinema, telling Lai that he doesn't like her voice, that he prefers women whose voices are deep and low. At the same time he is eager to invite Lai out for a drink. His beating heart and tremulous musings about how much Lai likes him perhaps signal strongly that he is in love. When he returns from Buenos Aires after his trip to the lighthouse, he tries to find Lai, who has already left for home.

Although Lai doesn't get to meet Chang in Taipei, his final voiceover remark, that he will always know where to contact Chang should he want to, offers a positive ending for the audience.

> **To what extent does the appearance of Chang give the film a Hollywood-style happy ending?**

Filmic pleasures

For further discussion of mise-en-scène, see Chapter 1, pp. 62–70.

The mise-en-scène tends to reflect emotional dysfunctionality in its emphasis on harsh surfaces, empty streets and enclosed spaces. Most of the scenes of the Ho–Lai relationship are also shot in black and white. Yet there are visual and aural pleasures on offer that offset the often dismal feeling of the affair. When the two men are driving towards the waterfall, and before their car breaks down, we are treated to a panoramic, mobile aerial shot of the falls, bathed in vivid blue light and accompanied on the soundtrack by a ballad in Spanish about love and suffering, sung by a mellifluous male voice. This scene suggests a fantasy desired by both the lovers. Argentine tango music and Frank Zappa's jazz enliven the soundtrack.

There are other specific parts where the film bursts into colour photography, which is thrown into relief by the surrounding black and white: Lai's period of happiness, the scenes with Chang in the bar. The lighthouse shots accompanying Chang's 'release' of Lai's troubles are positively exhilarating. The colour and movement of Buenos Aires is a kind of backdrop for Ho and Lai, encapsulated in speeded-up shots of the downtown area with the vivid colours of traffic zooming by. The film ends on visuals of a similar urban background in Hong Kong, extended to include trains, people, high buildings and a throbbing sense of urban speed, accompanied on the soundtrack by Frank Zappa singing 'Happy Together'.

> 1 Bearing in mind ideas about queer cinema (see pp 309–314), compare the troubled relationship portrayed in this film with that in *Swoon* (see p. 309) or *The Living End*.
> 2 To what extent do Laura Mulvey's ideas about scopophilia and identification apply to *Happy Together*?

CONCLUSION: A QUEER DIVERSITY

Critic B. Ruby Rich described 1992 as 'a watershed year for independent gay and lesbian film', not only because of the number of shorts and features being made and shown, but because of the surge in critical interest which has accompanied them. During the 1990s such film and video activity came to be labelled 'Queer Cinema'. Lesbian and gay activists, critics, film-makers and audiences started to imbue the previously negative term **queer** with a range of new, exciting, positive meanings in politics, literature, art and film-making. This process of an oppressed group reclaiming and reshaping a previously negative word or idea is known as **reappropriation**; it has happened with the word 'black'. Critic Amy Taubin claimed 'American queer cinema has achieved critical mass' with the release of features such as *My Own Private Idaho* (Gus Van Sant, 1991), utilising the Hollywood star system with Keanu Reeves and River Phoenix, and Tom Kalin's *Swoon* (1992).

The key ideas behind the queer cinema movement are diversity and fluidity; a range of (homo)sexualities manifested through a variety of characters, situation, race, gender, sexual practice and film language. Film-makers are questioning the attitude, developed in the 1970s, that one must promote only positive images of lesbian and gay characters and situations. Lesbian and gay film-makers see such ideas as constraints on creativity in an era where a much wider variety of lesbian and gay images is available.

In *Swoon*, Tom Kalin examines the infamous Leopold–Loeb case of 1924, where two rich, Jewish eighteen-year-olds kidnap and murder a fourteen-year-old boy. Unlike previous film versions such as Hitchcock's *Rope* (1948), Kalin concentrates on the homosexual relationship between the two young men, and the hold which the pathological Leopold had over Loeb. In an interview, Kalin stated: 'We're in a sorry state if we can't afford to look at "unwholesome" lesbian and gay people'. Derek Jarman's *Edward II* (1991) doesn't hesitate to portray England's monarch as weak and vacillating while his male lover, Gaveston, is scheming and slimy. What Kalin's and Jarman's films do, in their very different ways, is make the audience aware of the political dimensions of homosexuality.

Happy Together (see case study 5, pp. 304–8) certainly looks in detail at gay characters that are not idealised. Ho's drawbacks and weaknesses have been commented on, and Lai's anger, violent impetuosity and attempts to smother Ho hint at inner turmoils and insecurities. In keeping with ideas of queer film-making, it is the very faults and foibles of these characters that make the film both watchable and at times challenging.

New techniques of expression

Diversity and experimentation in film language characterise those works regarded as part of the queer cinema movement. John Greyson mixes history in *Urinal* (1988) as famous figures of gay culture, including Langston Hughes and the Russian director Sergei Eisenstein, help to investigate police harassment of gays. In *Edward II*, following a style he had already used in *Caravaggio* (1986) to point to the continuing relevance of its sexual and political themes, Derek Jarman deliberately mixes and clashes the fourteenth century and the 1990s. We see Annie Lennox singing a Cole Porter song, vicars in dog-collars spitting on Gaveston after his banishment, and gay activists with placards and the **pink triangle** symbol invading the king's palace. In *Blue* (1993) Jarman's one-colour screen counterpoints the emotional range of the soundtrack's meditation on his life with, and approaching death from, HIV, and challenges received ideas about the visual portrayal of disease.

The documentary work of Stuart Marshall is challenging in subject matter and form. *Bright Eyes* (1984) presents the viewer with ever-relevant parallels between Nazi treatment of gays, Victorian medical practice and media coverage of the AIDS epidemic. Rosa Von Praunheim's *I Am My Own Woman* (1993) presents a portrait of Charlotte Von

queer
Originally a negative term for (mainly male) homosexuals, this word has been recently reappropriated by critics, artists and audiences to describe a challenging range of critical work and cultural production among lesbians, gays and transgendered people, with an emphasis on diversity of race, nationality and cultural experience.

reappropriation
The process whereby a previously oppressed group takes a negative term and turns it around to invest it with new meanings of power and liberation. Examples include 'black', 'virago' and 'queer'.

Derek Jarman
Painter, writer, activist and acclaimed British gay/queer auteur, Derek Jarman was a provocative figure and an inspiration for younger artists and film-makers. Key films are as follows:
Sebastiane (1976)
Jubilee (1978)
The Tempest (1979)
The Angelic Conversation (1985)
The Last of England (1987)

pink triangle
A symbol originally worn by homosexual prisoners in Nazi concentration camps which was later taken up by lesbian and gay people as a reminder of past oppression and an icon of liberation.

> **Critically analyse the following films by John Greyson in terms of the formal qualities that they have in common. Can these films be classified according to traditional genres?**
>
> ■ *The Making of Monsters*
> ■ *Urinal*
> ■ *Zero Patience*
> ■ *Lilies*

Mahlsdort (born Lothar Berfelde), a famous life-long transvestite who is also gay. As well as using direct interviews with him, the film dramatises scenes from his life, including his anti-Nazi work during the Second World War. At the end of many of these dramatised scenes, he himself walks onto the set and is questioned by the actors about his thoughts and motivations, a productive Brechtian-style distanciation effect and perhaps an example of queer questioning.

Film genre and film style are mixed creatively in new queer cinema. Tod Haynes' *Poison* (1991) mixes 1950s B-film sci-fi and zombie elements with a homoerotic section styled as an homage to Genet. In *Caught Looking* (1991) Constantine Giannaris takes the viewer on a journey through a spectrum of gay viewpoints with a character

• **Plate 8.16** *Edward II* (Derek Jarman, 1991)
The love between Edward (left) and Gaveston evokes mixed audience reactions.

participating in an interactive video fantasy. John Greyson's *Zero Patience* (1993) subverts the conventions of the Hollywood musical to investigate attitudes to AIDS, once again using a figure from the gay past, the Victorian explorer Richard Francis Burton, in creative and amusing ways.

Gender, race and queer cinema

Monika Treut's feature-length *Virgin Machine* (1985) accompanies its heroine on a sexual odyssey in San Francisco, but the inequality of funding for men's and women's work means that many lesbian film-makers continue to produce shorter films and videos. In *The Meeting of Two Queens* Cecilia Barriga has taken images of Garbo and Dietrich and edited them together to produce a provocatively sensual play of eye-contact and undressing between two screen goddesses. The video-work of Sadie Benning, such as the ten-minute *Jollies*, intimately explores her own body, thoughts, memories and sexuality with a bold use of camerawork intricately interacting with the soundtrack.

Critically analyse *Virgin Machine* to address the following.

1 **How is Dorothee initially portrayed?**
2 **How does she react to her explorations of the San Francisco lesbian scene?**
3 **Comment on the range of sexual situations and relationships, and their portrayal during the film.**

Pratibha Parmar is a British film-maker and critic of Asian origin who helped found the first group in Britain for black lesbians. For her, as for Isaac Julien, race is as important an issue as sexuality, and the intervention of both film-makers contributes to the new kind of diversity within queer cinema. Parmar is concerned to disrupt and change the conventional images of Asians prevalent in British society. *Khush* (1991) is a television film she made for Channel 4 about the experience of being Asian and lesbian or gay. In this piece, interviews are interwoven with images of two women in saris relaxing and dancing together, and a classic Indian musical film is provocatively re-edited so that the dancing girl's glances interplay with those of another woman.

With videos such as *Orientations* (1985), Richard Fung helps give voice to North American lesbians and gays of Chinese origin. Marlon Riggs' feature-length poetic meditation on the lives of black gay men in the USA, *Tongues Untied* (1989), is a beautifully constructed kaleidoscope of sound and image.

Queer and the mainstream – (mis)representation?

Consider varying attitudes to positive images of lesbians and gays. Should we condemn the conflation of homosexuality, violence and murder in such films as *Basic Instinct*? Or can we be confident that a wide enough variety of views of lesbian and gay life now circulates in society to balance out negative images, so that we may embrace the queer aesthetic?

Exactly how much of the queer aesthetic is being absorbed into mainstream film-making? *A Beautiful Mind* (Ron Howard, 2002), supposedly a biopic of mathematician John Nash, was called a 'lie-opic' by the *Guardian* because it excised the gay episodes from Nash's life. Hollywood is still prone to attempt a normatising process for its perceived mass audience. The publicity for *Philadelphia* (Jonathan Demme, 1993) presented the film primarily as a courtroom drama and deliberately played down its gay

• **Plate 8.17** *Khush* (Pratibha Parmar, 1991)
The title of this memorable film is the Urdu word for 'ecstatic pleasure'. In her look at some Asian lesbian and gay lives, Parmar mixes pleasurable dream sequences with interviews which recall oppression

Compare and contrast Michael Cunningham's novel, *The Hours* (Picador, 1998), with the film version (Stephen Daldry, 2003), in the light of issues around representation and mainstream expectations referred to in this section

content. In *Gods and Monsters* (Bill Condon, 1998) the theatre actor and gay activist Ian McKellen played the famous gay Hollywood director James Whale. Mark Gatiss' (1995) biography of Whale tells us that, during his last years, Whale enjoyed the company and devoted support of his young working-class lover and companion, Pierre Foegel. Yet the film version of Whale's life completely ignores this important relationship. Why did the writer/director Bill Condon make such an adjustment? Could it be that the image of a lonely old queen is more digestible for mainstream heterosexual audiences?

> Watch *Gods and Monsters* and read Chapters 10–13 of James Whale's (1995) biography by Mark Gatiss. Consider how the adjustments referred to relate to Richard Dyer's ideas about heterosexual ideology.

Queerifications

In the early twenty-first century there is no consensus in the field of lesbian/gay/queer cinema, more a developed awareness of dissolving boundaries and multiplying identities. Critics, film-makers and audiences are interested in a mapping of potentialities and possibilities. Criticism and debate is healthy, and is set to continue along with the wide, creative and growing range of this area of film- and video-making, work which will surely benefit anybody who seeks to widen and enrich their viewing experience.

What constitutes a lesbian or gay film? Do the makers of such films have to be gay or lesbian themselves? Compare the portrayal of same-sex relationships in *Desert Hearts* and *Black Widow* (Bob Rafelson, 1987). Arguably, both involve homoerotic attraction and a certain gay sensibility in the play of looks on the screen and/or between the viewer and the text. In *Black Widow* same-sex attraction and lesbian sensibility remain sub-textual. Is *Desert Hearts* therefore more 'lesbian' because of its direct portrayal of sexuality in character, situation and action? Or is *Black Widow* equally powerful in this context? What happens if we apply a similar comparison to the male-orientated films *Jeffrey* (Christopher Ashley, 1995) and *Top Gun* (Tony Scott, 1986).

Consider the concept of 'queer'. Federico Fellini and Ken Russell, both heterosexuals, made some very queer films. What does the concept tell us about the portrayal of the boundaries of gender and sexuality? In this context, consider *Priscilla, Queen of the Desert* (Kimberly Peirce, 1999) in its portrayal of a transsexual, and the treatment of transvestism in *Boys Don't Cry* (Stephen Elliott, 1994).

1   **Consider the use of homoerotic imagery in *Top Gun* in the portrayal of Tom Cruise and his companions.**
2   **Consider the varying ideas and attitudes associated with the words homosexual, gay and queer. To what extent can these terms be used to describe various kinds of film-making?**

Essentialism: to label or not to label?

For many recent critics the term 'queer' is to be preferred for its notions of opposition to mainstream representations. There are debates going on about exactly how conservative and fixed the terms 'gay' and 'lesbian' have become in both society and film. Have they become part of the mainstream against which the queer theorists strive? Such terms are seen by some as very fixed labels which form part of a rigid sexual system, in other words, as **essentialist** in nature. Those challenging this system assert that such labelling is inaccurate and misleading, in that it does not reflect either the realities of human sexuality or the fluid nature of film spectatorship. Such critics have become known as anti-essentialist.

On the other hand, defenders of gay and lesbian approaches claim that the term queer leads to an ignoring of lesbian and gay specificity; indeed, to the very kind of invisibility against which early critics such as Russo fought. A clear introduction to these debates is provided by David Alderson and Linda Anderson (2000: 2), who talk about 'queer thinking, and the anti-essentialism that underpins it'.

essentialist
A term describing the idea of a single, firmly fixed identity as regards gender, sexuality and other social elements. The opposite attitude is often described as social contructionist, implying that such identities are a product of one's society, attitudes and upbringing, and can vary or be changed.

From image-spotting to queer spectatorship: an overview

Vito Russo's book *The Celluloid Closet* proved to be very popular and influential during the 1970s for those interested in challenging dominant views of film (see pp. 287–288). The reasons for its popularity lay partly in the fact that, unlike its predecessor by Parker Tyler, *Screening the Sexes*, it concentrated almost entirely on the products of Hollywood and the question of gay invisibility, a major preoccupation of gay and lesbian campaigners at that time. Russo's critical method was to examine individual representations of gay and lesbian characters, situations and plotlines and relate them to mainstream attitudes which we would now call homophobic. His method was a form of vigilant image-spotting, politically necessary at the time but ultimately, in the words of

Ellis Hanson, concerned 'with only one gaze: the ubiquitous, prefabricated, gullible, voyeuristic gaze of homophobia'. Hanson goes on to say: 'Meanwhile, our own pleasure, that elusive gaze of delight, is left curiously undertheorised and at times inadmissible' (cited in Farmer 2000: 4).

Whatever one may think about Hanson's judgement, critics who extended Russo's work have constructively investigated gay and lesbian viewing in terms of theory. Richard Dyer and Andrea Weiss have utilised auteur theory, star study, cinema history and ideas of audience reception. They, and other critics such as Judith Mayne, Tamsin Wilton and Thomas Waugh, have contributed towards the forging of useful theories of gay, lesbian and queer viewing strategies. More recent critical work is moving towards theorising gay/lesbian/queer spectatorial pleasure. For a useful overview and development of this work, see Brett Farmer (2000).

In the introduction to his book Farmer points the way forward to the kind of theorisation that Hanson sees as vital in this area. Farmer uses key concepts of *specificity* and *performativity* (ibid.: 33–42) to ground a gay spectatorship theory that incorporates a synthesis of the social and the psychoanalytic. *Specificity* 'designates a space for the constitution of subjectivity, the arrangement of desire, and the productions of meaning in specific or particular ways', which he sees as 'a very different proposition from claiming gayness as an expressive, self-identical essence'. *Performativity* is a concept derived from cultural studies whereby social groups develop self-awareness through shared actions that develop tastes, habits and attitudes in common (ibid.: 40).

The way forward

The best way forward I can think of is to point the reader in the direction of the Further viewing section, which contains a selection of mainly feature-length narrative and documentary films. To prevent the list from becoming unwieldy, I have concentrated on presenting a cross-section of the range of viewing experiences available in terms of nationality, historical period and sexual viewpoint. Some films mentioned in the chapter have, for this reason, not been included. Foreign-language films are referred to by their recognised title in the English-speaking world.

Use the reading and viewing guides to investigate and develop the questions posed in this chapter. Watch and look into the films using the case studies as models. Above all, explore, enjoy and widen your viewing experiences.

 **KEY TEXTS**

Alderson, David and Anderson, Linda (eds), *Territories of Desire in Queer Culture*, Manchester University Press, Manchester, 2000. An excellent summary is given in the Introduction of the current debates about queer culture. It also contains a challenging essay on Jarman, and explorations of Spanish and Australian gay cinema. With an erudite historical overview, Jonathan Dollimore's concluding survey points the way to possible future developments.

Cook, Pam and Dodd, Philip (eds), *Women and Film: A Sight and Sound Reader*, British Film Institute, London, 1993. An excellent section entitled 'Queer Alternatives' contains B. Ruby Rich's seminal essay on queer cinema, Pratibha Parmar's response, and Amy Taubin's lively criticisms.

Dyer, Richard, *The Matter of Images: Essays on Representation*, Routledge, London, 1993. An ideal primer for those starting to explore sexual representation in film. Dyer illustrates the power and complexity of images across a range of films, including film noir, the seminal British film *Victim*, and the 'sad young man' tradition which fed into the star persona of James Dean and others.

Farmer, Brett, *Spectacular Passions: Cinema, Fantasy, Gay Male Spectatorships*, Duke University Press, Durham, NC, 2000. Farmer closely questions the concepts of gay and queer and proposes a theory of gay spectatorship which aptly blends psychoanalytic ideas of fantasy, identification and pleasure with social notions of performativity. He then offers fruitful textual explorations based on his theory. This is an excellent way of coming to terms with the latest debates about essentialism and gay spectatorship.

Holmlund, Chris and Fuchs, Cynthia (eds), *Between the Sheets, in the Streets: Queer, Lesbian and Gay Documentary*, University of Minnesota Press, Minneapolis, 1997. Primarily US-centred, but an extremely fruitful exploration of the nature, form and address of documentary.

Mulvey, Laura, 'Visual Pleasure and Narrative Cinema', in *The Sexual Subject: A Screen Reader in Sexualtity*, Routledge, London and New York, 1995. Suggests ways in which a viewer of classic Hollywood films is addressed as male by being encouraged to adopt the viewpoint of the male protagonist. This must be read as the seminal first step, a work that helped give voice to the study of gender and sexuality in film.

Murray, Raymond, *Images in the Dark: An Encyclopedia of Gay and Lesbian Film and Video*, TLA Publications, Philadelphia, 1996. An ideal sourcebook to make further investigations. International in its breadth, it covers mainstream and independent film and has separate sections on Queer, Lesbian, Gay Male and Transgender interest, and on Camp.

Russo, Vito *The Celluloid Closet: Homosexuality in the Movies*, Harper & Row, New York and London, 1987. The classic groundbreaking textual study of sexuality in film, concentrating mainly on Hollywood.

Weiss, Andrea, *Vampires and Violets – Lesbians in Film*, Penguin, London, 1993. Key films and the main debates about lesbian spectatorship clearly presented.

 **FURTHER VIEWING**

Aimee and Jaguar (Germany, Max Fäberböck, 1998)
A bold and sensual telling of an incredible but true story. Two women, one a Nazi super-mum and the other a Jewish resistance member, meet, fall in love and remain devoted to each other through the perils of the Nazi regime.

All Over Me (US, Alex Sichel, 1997)
A story of a group of teenage girls during the long, hot New York summers. They do the downtown music scene, dream and grapple with adult issues as the director slowly draws the viewers an intimate set of character portraits.

Another Way (Hungary, Karoly Makk, 1982)
Said to be among Eastern Europe's first films dealing with a lesbian relationship, this is an intelligent and finely observed love story set just after the Hungarian uprising of 1956.

Beautiful Thing (UK, Hettie Macdonald, 1997)
Two young men find love and comfort in each other's arms on a Bermondsey council estate and start to explore the local gay scene. Mum is eventually won over, and the young woman next door lends a hand. Liberal clichés redeemed by skilful writing and acting.

Beefcake (Canada, Thom Fitzgerald, 2000)
An entertainingly camp and affectionate look at the activities of Bob Mizer's famous 1950s physique studio, the 'Athletic Model Guild', through the eyes of a well-built country innocent learning the ways of the world in LA.

Before Night Falls (US, Julian Schnabel, 2000)
A powerful, engaging biopic of the Cuban Renaldo Arenas, whose gay sexuality, political activism and prolific writing are shown as inseparable aspects of his life. Spanish star Javier Bardem gives an excellent performance as Arenas. Also stars Johnny Depp.

Before Stonewall (US, Greta Schiller and Robert Rosenberg, 1984)
A rich documentary of ordinary lesbian and gay lives in 1940s and 1950s USA.

Bent (UK, Sean Mathias, 1997)
This film about the persecution of gays in Nazi Germany reflects the weaknesses of the stage play on which it is based. It is worth viewing, though, for its powerful performances and historically important subject matter.

Better than Chocolate (Canada, Anne Wheeler, 1998)
An entertaining lesbian romantic comedy, where Maggie meets her gorgeous dream woman just hours before her mother and brother are due to move in with her.

Blue (UK, Derek Jarman, 1993)
Jarman's most artistically audacious film. The soundtrack explores death, AIDS, Jarman's own fight against blindness and many connotations of the vivid blue that fills the screen. This is the third in Jarman's trilogy of autobiographical masterworks of social and political commentary, after *The Last of England* and *The Garden*.

Bound (US, Andy and Larry Wachowski, 1996)
A post-queer lesbian private-eye film; two consciously stereotyped babes-with-brains in steamy union. This seems set to stir up all the old debates.

The Crying Game (UK, Neil Jordan, 1992)
A political thriller which raises unsettlingly queer questions about gender and desire.

Dona Herlinda and her Son (Mexico, Jaime Hermosillo, 1985)
An entertaining comedy of sexual manners in which a perceptive mother arranges her son's love life to cater for his gay lover and her own desire for a grandchild. One of the first Latin American films to deal positively with a gay theme.

Drôle de Félix (France, Olivier Ducastel/Jacques Martineau, 2000)
After his mother's death, a young gay man goes in search of the father he has never seen, supported by his lover. A complex sense of identity and love emerges from the unaffected performances of the chaotic couple.

Forbidden Love: The Unashamed Stories of Lesbian Lives
(Canada, Aerlyn Weissman and Lynne Femie, 1992)
Wonderful to watch: a 1950s *Pulp Fiction*-style lesbian love story is interwoven with older women talking about their lives.

Gay Classics (Genet/Julien/Kwietniowski)
Three major, thought-provoking works by gay men; Genet's *Un Chant d'amour*, Julien's *Looking for Langston* and Richard Kwietniowski's stylish drama, *Flames of Passion*, a gay take on *Brief Encounter*. Available on Connoisseur Video.

Head On (Australia, Ana Kokkinos, 1998)
A powerful realisation of contemporary queer life in Australia. Centres on Ari, a young Greek-Australian battling to come to terms with his sexuality and his family. Raw and gripping. See the essay on this film in Alderson and Anderson (2000).

Je, Tu, Il, Elle (Belgium, Chantal Akerman, 1974)
This gently paced first feature by one of Europe's leading avant-garde film-makers is captivating. A young woman hitches a lift to revisit her lover. The film is sensitively imbued with a woman-centred sensuality.

Jeffrey (US, Chris Ashley, 1995)
Two beautiful New York men tread the rocky road to love in the age of AIDS, with the help of memorable supporting performances from Patrick Stewart as the arty older friend, and Sigourney Weaver as a New-Age guru.

Law of Desire (Spain, Pedro Almodovar, 1987)
A gripping gay melodrama by one of Spain's leading contemporary directors. This was the precursor of several entertaining gay films from 1990s Spain. See the essay on this film in Alderson and Anderson (2000).

The Living End (US, Gregg Araki, 1993)
A road movie featuring two comically contrasting young men, both HIV positive, who fall for each other. They undertake an anarchic and often hilarious journey, with emotional challenges, odd characters and some bad-taste jokes along the way. A landmark of the New Queer Cinema.

Macho Dancer (The Phillipines, Lino Brocka, 1988)
A young man's emotional journey through the gay underworld of Manila. A romantic and sensual film. Through his social realism and sympathy for the oppressed, the director was a leading force in the cinema of his country as well as a noted political dissident.

Madame X (Germany, Ulrike Ottinger, 1977)
An avant-garde lesbian feminist pirate adventure. Challenging viewing in its attempts to find new ways of presenting women in film, but rewarding.

Nitrate Kisses (US, Barbara Hammer, 1992)
A mixture of meditation and documentary, this richly textured film explores lesbian and gay sexuality through history, politics and poetry. Especially noteworthy for its lively portrayal of older lesbians, this is a feast for the eye and the mind.

No Skin Off My Ass (Canada, Bruce La Bruce, 1992)
New Queer Cinema with all its rough edges and unusual cinematic strategies. A punk hairdresser seduces a skinhead.

Okoge (Japan, Takehiro Nakajima, 1992)
A social comedy of love and compromise with graphic sex scenes and a background of Tokyo gay life.

Only the Brave (Australia, Ana Kokkinos, 1994)
Traces the intense and changing relationship between two daughters of Greek immigrant families in a Melbourne suburb. A grim but compelling view of their love and life.

Pandora's Box (Germany, G.W. Pabst, 1928)
A beautiful and amoral femme fatale has several male lovers, but her lesbian lover proves to be the most devoted of her followers. A classic of early German cinema, and one of the first positive and sustained portrayals of a lesbian character.

Parting Glances (US, Bill Sherwood, 1986)
A beautifully made depiction of a group of people, gay and straight, in New York City. Nick, the central character played with gently compelling humour by Steve Buscemi, has AIDS, and enjoys the love and support of his friends.

Pink Flamingoes (US, John Waters, 1972)
A cult classic which uses camp modes of expression to explore and subvert conventional sexual structures. It stars the gay idol Divine.

Salmonberries (Germany, Percy Adlon, 1991)
A close emotional involvement between an Eskimo woman, played by k.d. lang, and a teacher fleeing her past. Compulsively watchable performances and locations.

She Must Be Seeing Things (US, Sheila McLaughlin, 1987)
This film touches on many uncomfortable aspects of lesbian sex, loving and looking. It does so in a stylish and articulate way.

Skin Deep (Canada, Midi Onodera, 1997)
A male actor plays a woman passing as a man. This character, a transgender loner, becomes involved with a lesbian film-maker and her long-suffering girlfriend. Overstuffed with incident, but fascinating.

Stonewall (UK, Nigel Finch, 1996)
A passionate and funny version of the historically crucial gay riot of 1969. This film deserves particular credit for the way it puts drag queens, their music and their culture, at the centre of it all in a historically accurate way.

The Sum of Us (Australia, Kevin Dowling and Geoff Burton, 1994)
Gladiator star Russell Crowe plays a rugby-playing young gay plumber whose supportive dad comically tries to help along his love life. A slightly stagey version of a stage play, but an attractive feel-good movie.

Swoon (US, Tom Kalin, 1992)
The infamous Leopold and Loeb murder case, as seen in Hitchcock's *Rope*, revisited with a queer perspective.

Victim (UK, Basil Dearden, 1961)
A landmark early work in the portrayal of gay life and its difficulties in pre-liberation London. A detective story involving a memorable performance from Dirk Bogarde as a bravely honest gay lawyer.

Virgin Machine (Germany, Monika Treut, 1988)
A journey of lesbian self-discovery and exploration for a young German journalist in San Francisco. Wacky and provocative views of that city's lesbian scene.

The Watermelon Woman (US, Cheryl Dunye, 1997)
Cheryl, an aspiring film-maker who is making a documentary about a beautiful and elusive 1930s black film actress, is coolly seduced by the beautiful Diana. Fans of Dunye should recognise her quirky and attractive style in this feature, which seems set to widen her popularity. Stars Dunye herself and Guinevere Turner.

We Were One Man (France, Philippe Valois, 1981)
A beautifully crafted love story set in rural France during the Second World War which chronicles the affair between a wounded German pilot and a young French peasant.

The Wedding Banquet (Ang Lee, 1993)
A cross-cultural comedy full of delightful characters. A Chinese gay man living in New York with his lover puts on a show to keep visiting Mum and Dad happy.

When Night is Falling (Canada, Patricia Rozema, 1995)
A glossy and stylish lesbian romance with circus acts and a plot that closely echoes *Desert Hearts*. For a more quirky and attractively watchable film of lesbian interest see Rozema's *I've Heard the Mermaids Singing*.

Wilde (UK/US/Japan/Germany, Brian Gilbert, 1997)
At times simplistic in its account of the life and times of this great gay artist, the film offers a moving portrayal of the sexual passion that brought about Wilde's doom.

Young Soul Rebels (UK, Isaac Julien, 1991)
A gay murder is solved. In the process, two young DJs, one gay and one straight, one black and one white, find romance and promote their brand of music. A vivid evocation of the London club scene of the late 1970s, with a lively soundtrack.

 **RESOURCE CENTRES**

Video/DVD availability is very variable. All the following offer helpful, up-to-the-minute information on currently available material.
www.amazon.co.uk
www.hmv.co.uk
Search under keyword 'lesbian' and/or 'gay' for a range of books, videos and DVDs for puchase.

www.bfi.org.uk
The British Film Institute web site is especially useful for ordering their very comprehensive catalogues, of which there is one devoted to lesbian and gay material.

www.llgf.org.uk
This London Lesbian and Gay Film Festival web site gives details of their presentations at the National Film Theatre in March/April. For a few months after that, the same programme of films and videos then tours various Regional Film Theatres. All venues are indicated on the web site.

www.millivresmultimedia.com
Commercial site from the publishers of *Diva* and *Gay Times*: 'gentle romantic comedies, hard hitting coming out stories, arthouse experimental films to documentaries'. A variety of titles with helpful reviews available for sale. You can also receive their newsletter by mail.

www.planetout.com
Go to the 'PopcornQ Movies' section for helpful information and reviews of festivals and individual films. Caution: don't purchase videos or DVDs from this site unless you have a specialised player for the North American format.

www.qcinema.com
www.queerfilm.com
www.queerscreen.com
Excellent, clear, helpful databases on lesbian, gay and queer film, video, TV, actors, writers, producers. You can search for individual films and reviews, magazine articles and other material. Caution: don't purchase videos or DVDs from these sites unless you have a specialised player for the North American format.

Part five

National cinemas

■ Marking out the territory: aspects of British cinema

INTRODUCTION: DEFINING A NATIONAL CINEMA

See Chapter 11, pp. 393–394, for a discussion of how state sponsorship in Britain differed from that in Soviet Russia.

Definitions of a national cinema are determined institutionally and culturally. They vary according to country and history, and to the political status of the nation concerned. Britain, for instance, has never had a fully state-sponsored industry but the state has, on occasion, intervened through certain institutions and certain measures (such as tax breaks and levies) to support the native product. The extent to which cinema attracts national support will depend on the extent to which it is acknowledged as a significant commercial commodity and cultural force, both at home and elsewhere.

The identification of films as the product of a national cinema may depend upon the coherence of themes and imagery or the recurrence of personnel across a period of time or across a range of cultural forms. We might assume that a British film represents Britain to itself, and possibly to a foreign audience, in terms of its social and regional uniformity and diversity, its shared or diverse history, or that a British film should be the product of local funding and the combined effort of British subjects.

See Chapter 1, pp. 22–25 and 29–31, for a discussion of UK film financing and production.

However, official definitions of precisely what constitutes British cinema and British film have varied throughout the last century. The majority of films screened in Britain, for much of the twentieth century, have not been of British origin and a declining percentage of distribution and exhibition interests are British-owned. It seems useful to acknowledge that definitions of 'Britishness' have been framed differently and expediently in response to changing political, social, commercial and cultural circumstances within Britain. Equally, the commercial and cultural exchange between the domestic and imported product fluctuates over time, further questioning any fixed definition.

For present purposes, aspects of British national cinema are presented in terms of a relationship with America and Europe, a number of recurrent themes presented in British films, and the processes and products of exchange between cinema and other cultural forms.

BEGINNING AND CONTINUING

British cinema history has been privileged by the number of notable pioneers it has been able to boast, 'adventurers, crusaders and craftsmen', in the words of Rachael Low, men of 'exceptional versatility and initiative' (Low 1997: 13): Birt Acres, James Bamforth, Cecil Hepworth, G.A. Smith, James Williamson, R.W. Paul, Walter Haggar and William Friese-Greene (the last celebrated and mythologised in John Boulting's *The Magic Box*, 1951). The year 1896 is generally acknowledged as the first public cinematograph screening in Britain, with the first films being shown as items in a mixed programme in music halls and other local halls, or as an attraction at the fairground, where a number of travelling showmen might compete for attention. Recent research has expanded the quantity of material considerably (for instance, since Low wrote in the 1940s of Mitchell and Kenyon, the Lancashire firm, leaving 'little trace', more than 800 films have been discovered) and has extended our understanding of cinema's debt to pre-cinematic genres and exhibition practices. Bill Douglas' *Comrades* (1986) pays homage to the director's own enthusiasm for these precursors. Cinema is now regarded as much as a continuation of forms and procedures as a decisive innovation, and interest has shifted from 'firstings' of devices supposedly specific to film (such as cut-aways, flashbacks, close-ups, parallel action) to establishing these broader connections. Similarly, rather than dismissing early cinema and its erratic progress towards maturity as merely primitive, research in the last generation has sought to re-name and re-align it as an alternative avant-garde. The catalogue listing of distinct types of films has been absorbed in later genres, although 'fiction' and 'non-fiction' are quite difficult categories to sustain, given the staging of much material for the latter and given the preponderance of certain themes across the range: for instance, both *Rescue at a Chinese Mission* (1990) and Hepworth's 'fictional' *Rescued by Rover* (1905) culminate in chase sequences, intercutting simultaneous action in two different places. *Rescued by Rover*, the story of a baby stolen from a pram by a gypsy, finally tracked down by the family dog, was first made by Hepworth and his family in 1905, but proved so popular at home and abroad that the original negative was worn out and the film was subsequently twice re-made.

Cinema's origins as a popular and 'low-brow' form of entertainment prompted prejudice against films. With the increase of premises devoted to film screenings from 1907 onwards, concerns were levelled as much at the activities which these darkened halls were believed to encourage as at the content of the programme screened. Fleas, pickpockets and canoodling were all matters of discussion in the trade press and elsewhere. Hence, the Cinematograph Act of 1910, 'to make better provision for securing safety', endeavoured to ensure the public by regulating exhibition (Parliamentary Debates 9, 1909: 1748; 13, 1909: 379). The industry itself, keen to enhance the respectability of its product and to standardise licensing, supported interventions in favour of censorship. As ever, the physical and moral protection of children was often invoked as a primary consideration.

• **Plate 9.1** *Rescue at a Chinese Mission* (Williamson, 1900)
Reconstructed actuality.

For further discussion of film and audience, see Chapter 1, pp. 34–40.

The move to attract more middle-class viewers was accompanied by the improved decor of cinema interiors and the uniforms of the staff. A higher standard of accompaniment to the films (verbal and/or musical, either mechanical or performed live) might be expected in the new 'picture palaces'. In Britain, as elsewhere, producers looked to the older pictorial and dramatic arts for reputable material suitable for adaptation. Actors were attracted from the stage and literary adaptations (including Dickens and Shakespeare) were filmed in the studio and on location. These were programmed alongside films of topical or local interest, cartoons and science films (some of which, even in the 1900s, were coloured) in a manner somewhat akin to subsequent television scheduling: education, entertainment and information. There was some discussion in the regular and trade press and fan magazines of the discovery and promotion of British stars to rival American and European imports, but certain directors, notably Hepworth, were reluctant to 'build up' performers only to have them command inordinate fees and dominate proceedings. Films were nevertheless made as star vehicles for established comedians, such as Fred Evans in the 'Pimple' series, including the parodies of more 'respectable' productions, *Pimple's Ivanhoe* (1913) and *Pimple's Charge of the Light Brigade* (1914), and the 'Ultus' series, made as a response to the French phenomenon *Fantômas*, made a star of Aurèle Sydney (Oakley 1964: 67).

Film production in Britain, on the part of both British and foreign companies, was severely curtailed by the outbreak of war in 1914. The War Office was slow to recognise the potential of film as a means of propaganda, but some of the most famous (even notorious) footage of the front was recorded by Malins for *The Battle of the Somme* (1916) (Reeves 1986: 98 and 103). By 1918 America had consolidated its international dominance of film production and distribution.

Various attempts were made to promote the home-grown product, the less successful including the British Film Weeks campaign of 1924 and the more successful including the casting of imported talent, such as the Americans Mae Marsh (in Hithcock's 1925 *The Rat*) and Dorothy Gish (in Wilcox's 1926 *Nell Gwynne*) and the Canadian Estelle Brody in Victor Saville's *Kitty* (1929) and Maurice Elvey's *Hindle Wakes* (1927). The latter, like George Pearson's 1921–1922 *Squibs* series (starring Betty Balfour), attempted to convey colloquial spoken English in its intertitles (Lancashire and Cockney dialects respectively) and to portray regional characters and atmosphere with popular appeal. However, British high-brows, by the late 1920s, tended to disparage British films at almost any available opportunity (with the notable exception of Hitchcock's directorial debuts, *The Lodger* [1926] and *Blackmail* [1929]) and instead looked to Europe for an artistic standard and a retreat from the rampant commercial populism of America. They were especially indignant about British films which pandered to perceived and appreciable 'American' tastes, such as *Nell Gwynne*. Anthony Asquith's *Shooting Stars* (1928) portrays the operation of a British studio in the 1920s and its associated fan following, opening with an actor (Brian Aherne) playing the role of Julian, the cowboy. As ever, it was impossible to please everyone all of the time. The billing of bankable and/or respectable names, together with the imitation of well-received precedents, did not necessarily guarantee financial or critical success: Hitchcock's *Champagne* (1928), starring Betty Balfour, was roundly condemned for its ersatz interpretation of American style and subject matter.

In 1924 the total number of films 'trade shown' (films shown to exhibitors before hiring) was 56, falling to 45 in 1926 and 37 in 1927 (Dickinson and Street 1985: 5); by 1927 'something like 5% of films shown in the British Empire' were of British origin (Parliamentary Debates 203, 1927: 2047). The government was obliged to introduce legislation, originally intended as a temporary measure, to promote and protect the British industry: a 7.5% quota of British films (rising to 25% by 1935) was imposed on exhibitors. There was some discussion (as for the 1927 Act's successors) as to how 'Britishness' should be ascertained and measured, with parliament eventually deciding that 'in order to comply a film must have been made by a British subject or a British-controlled company; studio scenes must be photographed in a studio in the British Empire; the author of the scenario or of the original work must be a British subject and at least 75% salaries' would be paid to British subjects. Even in the silent period, we find an acknowledgement of film as both a culturally cohesive force and a market commodity, and the need to accommodate the different interests of producers, distributors and exhibitors (who knew that they could most easily fill their seats with imported material) in appropriate legislation. By the end of the 1940s, when the government imposed a levy on American films in favour of the British product, there were allegations from both American producers and British distributors of unfair restrictions on trade. Even in the silent period, complaints were voiced that cinema was granted protection not afforded to other industries, which were obliged to compete in an open market.

However, even in the 1927 discussion it was acknowledged that government intervention would do little to ensure quality and it was foreseen that many films would be cheaply and quickly made simply to satisfy the Act's requirements. Such 'Quota Quickies' became the object of attack of high-brow commentators, characterised by film-maker Paul Rotha's 1933 text *Celluloid: The Film Today*: 'I have excluded from this survey any mention of many directors working in British and American studios today because their films have no meaning while they themselves exhibit no understanding of, or interest in, the cinema as I accept it. They have no more pretensions to be called film directors than they have to be called plumbers or clothes-dealers' (Rotha 1933: 6). Graham Greene thought many British films of the 1930s simply 'silly'. Rotha repeats his complaint in 1949, reserving praise for the Documentary Movement of the 1930s and 1940s: 'Hopes of a significant British cinema began to fade when realism gave way to the romantic and theatrical' (Rotha 1949: 56). However, much of the British output, as in the silent period, found favour with audiences (the plumbers and clothes-dealers themselves).

For further information regarding the Documentary Movement, see Chapter 5, pp. 194–196.

Controversy and sensitivity over the issue of definition has persisted, continuing to determine which films attract subsidy and which are most leniently taxed; but when Anthony Minghella's 1996 version of *The English Patient* (ironically, taken from a novel by a Sri Lankan-born Canadian resident about a mistakenly identified Hungarian whose plane crashes in the African desert) was wreathed with Oscars, it prompted the perennial complaint that it was largely the product of American investment. Since the Second World War, many European films have drawn from cross-national sources, and from a combination of market interests. Although the response to foreign competition has differed historically with changing circumstances, the British industry has always been faced with a limited range of options: making small, such that costs can be covered and profits be made at home (such as the 'quickies' made to fulfil quota obligations, much horror and comedy production, and television spin-offs), or making large with the help of foreign investment in production and by securing foreign distribution deals favouring profits abroad.

However, undue reliance on foreign intervention has proven structural disadvantages: the withdrawal of American backing of British production at the end of the 1960s resulted in a severe downturn in available funds. Audiences, both at home and abroad, are notoriously fickle and one success does not guarantee consistent returns for a similar formula (compare the reception of writer Simon Beaufoy's *The Full Monty*, *Lucky Break* and *This Is Not a Love Song*), with production and distribution concerns often lurching from one crisis to the next (the collapse of British Lion in the 1950s, Palace Pictures [*A World Apart*, *The Crying Game*] in the 1980s and Film Four in 2002). Sometimes there has been intervention on the side of production from the industry itself, to encourage new talent (for instance, the Group Three initiative of the 1950s), sometimes from state institutions (the Arts Council and the British Film Institute's Experimental Film Fund [for Anderson's 1953 *O Dreamland*, for instance] and Production Fund [for Petit's 1979 *Radio On* and Greenaway's 1982 *The Draughtsman's Contract*]), sometimes direct intervention in terms of tax breaks for British-based companies (and whereas the erstwhile Film Fund supported projects unlikely to prove a

For further reference to
the UK Film Council, see
Chapter 1, p. 25.

commercial success, current Film Council policy, launched in 2000, favours those identified as a safe bet, arguably those least deserving of subsidy!). On the other hand, it is
sometimes claimed that distribution and exhibition merit equivalent support: for
instance, few of the National Lottery-funded productions (of which *Shooting Fish*
[Stefan Schwartz, 1997] is possibly the best-known example) of recent years have yet
achieved a widespread screening, and, in spite of the multiplexes' original declaration in
favour of 'art-house' films as a proportion of their programme, the results of the current
collaboration with the Odeon chain have yet to prove significant.

1   **What differences of interest can be identified between producers, distrib-
    utors and exhibitors, and how does government intervention address
    these?**
2   **Why does the film industry deserve preferential treatment over other
    manufactured products – or does it?**

CROSSING THE POND

'If you can't beat them, join them'

For further discussion of
film distribution and
exhibition, see Chapter 1,
pp. 16–22.

In Britain, as in other European nations, the state has intervened sporadically in an
attempt to preserve its cinema industry, culturally and commercially, from American
domination. A comparison might be made with current attempts to regulate the influx of
American-based and -produced programmes to British television. In Britain, anything
from 50–97% of films shown have been American, whereas in France (under German
occupation), Germany and Italy, for instance, there has at times of war been an
embargo or restriction on American screenings. France, which once commanded a
world lead, has often proved most vociferous in its opposition to American dominance,
notably in the 1993 discussions leading to the General Agreement on Tariffs and Trade
(Higson and Maltby 2000: 23–4). Unsustained state support of production, distribution
and exhibition in Britain has often been identified as 'too little, too late' and the loss of
personnel to Hollywood (directors, writers, actors, cinematographers, composers,
designers), especially 'key' names likely to attract investment, supposedly at the
expense of the home industry, is frequently bemoaned. There is nothing new in this, nor
is it unique to Britain, nor to the film industry, and nor is the exchange entirely one-
sided. Sometimes, those individuals who have left for America thinking that 'that's
where it's at' have become rapidly disaffected. Some British films (such as *Petulia*
[Richard Lester, 1968], *Eagle's Wing* [Anthony Harvey, 1978], *Bad Timing* [Nicholas
Roeg, 1980], *The Killing Fields* [Roland Joffo, 1984] and *Midnight Express* [Alan Parker,
1978], all involving foreign locations and American protagonists) manage to be British
without immediately appearing to be so; others are comparable to American precursors
in terms of style or content (such as musicals of the 1930s following Astaire and
Rogers; the 'B-movie' lighting of 1940s gangster films; the violence of 1970s police
films following *Dirty Harry* [Don Siegel, 1971] and the idiomatic banter of *Lock, Stock
and Two Smoking Barrels* [Guy Ritchie, 1998] following Tarantino's *Pulp Fiction* [US,
1994] and *Reservoir Dogs* [1992]). Michael Winterbottom's 1996 *Butterfly Kiss* and Mel
Smith's 2001 *High Heels and Low Life* apparently limped lamely in the wake of Ridley
Scott's *Thelma and Louise* (1991). *The Prince and the Showgirl* (Laurence Olivier, 1957)
and *Notting Hill* (Roger Michell, 1999), nominally British films, effectively cast Marilyn
Monroe and Julia Roberts, respectively, as themselves, as Hollywood stars playing
American personalities.

British talent for export

In the silent period, American companies set up British subsidiaries and American performers (such as the comedian John Bunny, the director Harold Shaw and the actor/producer Florence Turner) came to work in Britain. The music-hall talents of Stan Laurel and Charlie Chaplin were recognised by American **impresarios**, who took them to America, where they were drawn into films. In the 1920s, Clive Brook and Ronald Colman (specialists in debonair, upper-class roles, like David Niven thereafter) and the ex-boxer Victor McLaglen (known from Graham Cutts' 1924 *The Passionate Adventure* and Blackton's 1922 extravagantly coloured *The Glorious Adventure*) went to work in Hollywood (see Plate 9.2); after the encouraging reception of Alexander Korda's *The Private Life of Henry VIII* (1933), Charles Laughton and Elsa Lanchester left Britain and joined their friend, the director James Whale (the subject of Bill Conden's 1998 biopic, *Gods and Monsters*). James Mason, Merle Oberon, Olivier and Leigh and latterly Audrey Hepburn were also attached to the British 'colony', while Bristol-born Cary Grant pretty much effaced his British origins. Hitchcock was summoned by Selznick for *Rebecca* (1940); former Ealing director, Alexander MacKendrick, directed the American classic *The Sweet Smell of Success* for MGM in 1957, while Boorman (*Point Blank*, 1967), Schlesinger (*Midnight Cowboy*, 1969), Clayton (*The Great Gatsby*, 1974) and Richardson (*The Loved One*, 1965) worked in America in the 1960s and 1970s; Ridley Scott (*Blade Runner*, *Thelma and Louise*, *Gladiator*) moved stateside after *Alien* (1979) and, while Mike Figgis made *Leaving Las Vegas* (1995) and *Timecode* (2000) before returning for *Hotel* (2002), Terence Davies directed Edith Wharton's American costume drama *House of Mirth* (2000) with *The X-Files*'s Gillian Anderson .

But potential higher salaries were not in themselves sufficient to satisfy all the British émigrés. For instance, the originator of the 'It' girl, Elinor Glyn, herself an expatriate in Hollywood in the 1920s, says that fellow writer William Somerset Maugham found it difficult to adapt to the rigours of the American system and, like Aldous Huxley thereafter, resented the loss of control over his own work to the demands of the studio; David Puttnam's disappointment at Columbia, following acclaim for *The Killing Fields* (1984), is surely legendary. Looking back, Richard Burton felt similarly compromised in Hollywood, yet his enthusiasm for the film version of John Osborne's seminal *Look Back in Anger* (1959), in which he took the part of Jimmy Porter, was enough to win American backing and heralded a decade in which American institutions again decided that London was where 'it' was at. Originally staged at the Royal Court in London, the film inherits its director, Tony Richardson and Mary Ure (as Allyson, Jimmy's middle-class wife) from the original cast and the claustrophobic attic flat, complete with kitchen sink, further hemmed in by the teeming rain outside. Jimmy and the flat-mate Cliff (Gary Raymond) run a sweet stall in the market by day and Jimmy plays in a jazz club by night. Jimmy is angry because so little has changed in society ('it's pretty dreary living in the American age...unless, of course, you're American') and at his own helplessness to effect change: nevertheless, he and Cliff defend the immigrant stall-holder Kapoor against the bullying of customers and the market manager (Donald Pleasence) while Allyson bears the brunt of his frustration, leaving him and then returning after she loses their baby.

Ambivalence towards Hollywood has continued. In spite of his enormous transatlantic success (as export in *Trainspotting* [Danny Boyle, 1996] and in the *Star Wars* prequels), Ewan McGregor even now declares a professional preference, as an actor, for the smaller and more personal scale of British production, believing that this offers a better guarantee of artistic freedom. With Jude Law (*The Talented Mr Ripley*; *A.I.* [Stanley Kubrick/Steven Spielberg, 2001], Sadie Frost (*Shopping* [Paul Anderson, 1994]), Johnny Lee Miller and Sean Pertwee he set up the production company Natural Nylon (now disbanded), funding (with Film Four) *To Kill a King* (Mike Barker, 2002), starring the equally exportable Tim Roth and Rupert Everett. Tim Roth (*War Zone* [1999]) and Gary Oldman (*Nil by Mouth* [1997]), both of whom have succeeded as actors in independent and studio productions in America and Europe, have returned to Britain in order to launch themselves as directors.

impresario
Organiser of public entertainments; a manager of, especially, an operatic or concert company.

• **Plate 9.2**
Victor McLaglen in
The Glorious Adventure
(Stuart Blackton, 1922)
British beefcake for
export

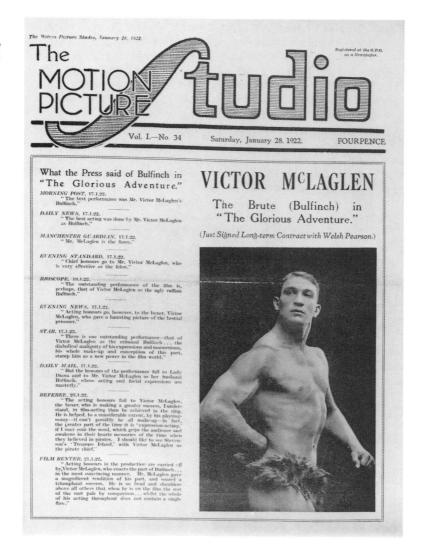

Two cultures divided by a common language

Since the advent of sound in the late 1920s, Britain might be regarded as especially vulnerable, in its susceptibility to imports and the exportability of its performers. America has continued to regard Britain as its primary export market. On the other hand, British films might be thought to be at more of an advantage than those of other European countries in seeking an American audience. However, as 'two cultures divided by a common language', the use of English has been something of a mixed blessing. In the 1930s American audiences (and, indeed, some British audiences) were resistant to the clipped accents of actors trained for the stage (Low 1985: 89); while in the 1990s, some American audiences (and some English film-goers in Britain) expressed difficulties in understanding the relatively tame Scottish English of Danny Boyle's *Trainspotting* (1996) and Ken Loach's *Sweet Sixteen* (2002). In both *Snatch* (Guy Ritchie, 2000) and *The Limey* (Steven Soderbergh, 1999), characters assert that gangland slang is impenetrable to American ears. Meanwhile, *I Know Where I'm Going* (Michael Powell, 1945) employed Gaelic to register the strangeness of the island to a newcomer and *Solomon and Gaenor* (Paul Morrison, 1999), following the example of Welsh language broadcasting, served as a salutary reminder to audiences outside Wales that English is not the only native language in Britain. *Rita, Sue and Bob, Too* (Alan Clarke, 1986), *My*

Beautiful Laundrette (Stephen Frears, 1985), *East Is East* (Damien O'Donnell, 1999), *My Son the Fanatic* (Udayan Prasad, 1997), along with *Bhaji on the Beach* (1993) and *Bend It Like Beckham* (2002) (both directed by Gurinder Chadha, who has also directed *What's Cooking* [2001]) represent British Asian communities, while *Soursweet* (Mike Newell, 1988) portrays a Hong Kong Chinese community which retains language as an element of a mixed cultural identity. American independent director John Sayles is currently at work with Robert Carlyle on *Jamie MacGillivray*, a Scottish-Canadian-US epic shot in English, French, Gaelic and Delaware Indian. Bridget Fonda (in *Scandal* [Michael Caton-Jones, 1988]), Gwyneth Paltrow (in *Sliding Doors* [Peter Howitt, 1998] and *Shakespeare in Love* [John Madden, 1998]), Renee Zellweger (in *Bridget Jones's Diary* [Sharon Maguire, 2001]) and Brad Pitt (in *Snatch* [Guy Ritchie, 2000]), American actors likely to attract an American following, were all required to learn different types of delivery of spoken English for British roles in these nominally 'British' films: Mickey in *Snatch*, notes another character, is 'not Irish not English'.

Strangers in our midst

Some Americans have chosen individually to work in Britain with British subject matter for a number of reasons. Richard Lester, for instance, came to London and was responsible for the 'fashionable' Beatles' films, *A Hard Day's Night* (1964) and *Help!* (1965), and, in 1974, the glorious multinational *The Three Musketeers*. Others, such as Joseph Losey, had less of a choice in the matter, coming to Britain to escape persecution by the House Un-American Activities in 1952. Foreigners and exiles, it has been said, often view a society more critically and sharply than those brought up in and inured to it (Palmer and Riley 1993: 2). Robert Altman's *Gosford Park* (2001), partly American financed, and featuring an American film producer conducting research for a British-style murder mystery, provides a relatively uncosy view of upstairs-downstairs life in a classic Agatha Christie setting. Its characters and cast are comparable to those of the 1974 adaptation of Christie's *Murder on the Orient*

• **Plate 9.3**
Doomed love in the Welsh-language film
Solomon and Gaenor (Paul Morrison, 1999)

Express, directed by another American, Sidney Lumet, and John Guillermin's 1978 *Death on the Nile*. Losey's *The Servant* (1963), *Accident* (1967) and *The Go-Between* (1970) are even more acerbic in their view of class deference, antagonism and retaliation. In *The Servant* (scripted by Harold Pinter), Dirk Bogarde plays Barrett, employed by Tony (James Fox) as a 'gentleman's gentleman': 'the thought of some old woman running about the place telling me what to do rather put me off', he says, at the interview which opens the film. The plot revolves around a battle of wills between Barrett and Tony's upper-class fiancée, Susan (Wendy Craig), determined to maintain control and to keep the servant in his place: 'the truth is I don't give a tinker's gob what you think', she informs him. Susan's parents, indolent and ignorant, are posed like figures in a Gainsborough portrait. But Barrett and his own fiancée/sister, Vera (Sarah Miles), find the ineffectual master easy prey and readily deceive and debauch him, while Barrett assumes the role of 'the old woman telling him what to do': 'I can't get anything done here – as soon as I get the hoover out you're up it'. Gradually their roles reverse, with Tony ingratiating himself with Barrett, acknowledging his dependence and admitting that he prefers the male company of 'two old pals' (they both had this feeling once before, in the army). Both *The Servant* and *Accident* are concerned with the manipulation of the power and glamour bestowed by aristocracy, youthful attractiveness and intellect (and even brute force). *The Remains of the Day* (James Ivory, 1993) and *Gosford Park* (Robert Altman, 2001) return, albeit more mildly, to similar class tensions in the humiliation of servants meted out by their supposed superiors: in the former, the butler (Anthony Hopkins) is asked his political opinion, when it is understood that his social role constrains him from voicing any such opinion (or, at least, not one which ventures to contradict that of his employer); in the latter, a servant/mistress (Emily Watson) of the master (Michael Gambon) is dismissed for impertinence when she dares to interrupt a conversation in which she is assumed to have no voice and no place whatsoever.

Bigger bucks, smaller pound

The transatlantic success of Richardson's early collaborations with John Osborne (*The Entertainer* and *Look Back in Anger*) and of *A Taste of Honey* invited funding from United Artists for *Tom Jones* (Tony Richardson, 1963), which, in turn, prompted the massive investment of the later 1960s: Alexander Walker suggests that at its peak this reached almost 90% (Walker 1974: ii). John Osborne's screenplay of Henry Fielding's 1749 *The History of Tom Jones* and Stanley Kubrick's adaptation of William Makepeace Thackeray's 1853 historical novel *The Memoirs of Barry Lyndon Esq., written by himself,* both assume the self-conscious conversational style of their originals in their voiceover narration and interaction with the camera (Tom hangs his tricorn hat over the camera to prevent its ogling Mrs Walters' ample bobbing bosom). Both are divided episodically, following the original chapter headings. *Tom Jones* exploits the slapstick elements of the story, to the accompaniment of a rumbustious, brassy soundtrack, and employs direct address and asides to the audience in the manner of Frankie Howerd, in addition to such explicitly cinematic devices as freeze-frame and mock iris closures on particular details. In spite of costumes and settings which clearly locate the action in the past, Tom (Albert Finney) and Barry (Ryan O'Neal) are played very much as modern adventurers, rising through the social hierarchy by dint of their wit and opportunism. Like Jimmy (Alan Bates) in *Nothing But the Best* and Joe (Laurence Harvey) in *Room at the Top* and *Life at the Top*, Barry secures wealth and position by marrying above himself. Tom, on the other hand, functions to question an accident of birth as an inalienable right to status and the hand of the girl he loves: Squire Western stalwartly opposes Tom's marriage to his daughter until he discovers him to be the only heir of Squire Allworthy, at which point he declares him to have been 'always his favourite'.

• **Plate 9.4** American backing for large-scale production: Albert Finney as an eighteenth-century adventurer in *Tom Jones* (Tony Richardson, 1963)

Consider a variety of strategies employed in the production of British films which seek to attract American investment and American audiences (for instance: personnel, subject matter, locations).

CONTINENTAL DRIFT

Visitors, exiles and émigrés

As early as 1898, a branch of the French company Gaumont was established in Britain; by 1928 Gaumont-British had become an entirely British-controlled company. Even in the 1920s there were attempts by European producers to pool resources and to employ stars deemed transnational in their appeal, as a means of countering American competition collectively. Such co-operation enabled larger-scale productions with a greater chance of securing distribution abroad. For instance, Betty Balfour, who in her *Squibs* persona was just as popular in France as in Britain, was hired by the French directors, L'Herbier and Mercanton, to play more serious dramatic roles in *Little Devil-May-Care* (1927) and *Monte Carlo* (1925). The Japanese superstar Sessue Hayakawa (whose long career extended to playing opposite Alec Guinness in David Lean's *Bridge on the River Kwai* [1957]), was hired for *The Great Prince Shan* (1924), which was produced, as were many films of the decade, in studios and on location on the Côte d'Azur. The Russian actress Olga Tschechova and the French actor Jean Bradin were hired for *Moulin Rouge* (Alfred Junge, 1928), and the Chinese-American actress Anna May Wong for *Piccadilly* (1929), produced by British International Pictures and directed by a German, E.A. Dupont.

At the end of the 1920s, where foreign actors had been cast in a British role, native English speakers might be required to provide dialogue for a sound version: such, famously, was the case with Hitchcock's *Blackmail* (1929), in which the voice of the Czech Anny Ondra was combined with that of Joan Barry. In the early 1930s, different language versions of the same subject were shot simultaneously (although language was sometimes not the only aspect in which they differed): *Atlantic* (1929), again directed by Dupont, is a notable example. Furthermore, in the 1930s, a significant

Details of the GPO Film Unit can be found in Chapter 5, pp. 195–196.

number of European directors, producers, designers and cameramen settled more permanently in Britain. The Brazilian Alberto Cavalcanti, once associated with the French avant-garde, worked in Britain with John Grierson's GPO Film Unit and with Michael Balcon at Ealing. René Clair, hired by Korda (*The Ghost Goes West*, 1936), brought a similar background to his work in Britain.

Alexander Korda, like many of his fellow Hungarians, served an apprenticeship across Europe before going to Hollywood. In 1931 he moved to Britain and his company, London Films, was responsible two years later for *The Private Life of Henry VIII* (starring Charles Laughton with Elsa Lanchester and Robert Donat). Encouraged by its success in America, Korda continued with other ambitious projects, notably *Knight Without Armour*

For further discussion of Erierson and documentary film, see Chapter 5, pp. 189, 194–195

(Jacques Feyder, 1937), starring Marlene Dietrich, and the H.G. Wells adaptations, *Things to Come* (William Cameron Menzies, 1936) and its companion piece, *The Man Who Could Work Miracles* (Lothar Mendes,1936). Wells' science-fiction fantasy envisages the collapse of civilisation into barbarism and its salvation by a phalanx of pioneers who build vast white cities, cut into the mountains, with moving walkways in place of streets. Selflessly, in spite of the dangers, these brave souls set their sights on space travel and discovery. *Things to Come* was impressively scored by Arthur Bliss and its sets for the new millennium, designed by Korda's brother Vincent, are monumental, white and spartan, with streamlined plexiglass furniture; the jersey uniforms are close-fitting and uncluttered: in terms of imagining the future, this film certainly did set a trend for the shape of things to come. Korda was also responsible for initiating the long-standing partnership of fellow Hungarian Emeric Pressburger (who moved to Britain from Berlin) with the director Michael Powell, best known for their work in the 1940s: *The Thief of Baghdad*, 1940; *The Life and Death of Colonel Blimp*, 1943, *The Red Shoes*, 1948 (*Life and Death* and *Red Shoes* with Anton Walbrook, similarly previously employed in Germany), *A Matter of Life and Death*, 1946, and *Black Narcissus*, 1946.

Other émigrés included set designers Alfred Junge (*The Man Who Knew Too Much* [Alfred Hitchcock, 1934], *The Life and Death of Colonel Blimp*, *A Canterbury Tale* [Michael Powell, 1944], *Evergreen* [Victor Saville, 1934]) and Ken Adams, whose work extends from the 'classic' Bond films of the 1960s (*Dr No* [Terence Young, 1962], *Goldfinger* [Guy Hamilton, 1964] and *From Russia, with Love* [Terence Young, 1963]) to *Chitty Chitty Bang Bang* (Ken Hughes, 1968), *Barry Lyndon* (Stanley Kubrick, 1975) and

• **Plate 9.5**
Britain's first million-dollar film
Things to Come (1936)
was produced by
Alexander Korda,
magnificently designed
by Vincent Korda and
directed by an
American, William
Cameron Menzies

• **Plate 9.6** German émigré Anton Walbrook plays the Russian ballet impresario Lermontov opposite Moira Shearer's Vicky in *The Red Shoes* (Michael Powell, 1948)

The Madness of King George (Nicholas Hytner, 1995). Producer/director Paul Czinner and his wife, Elisabeth Bergner, worked together in Britain in the 1930s before migrating to America, their British projects including *Stolen Life* (1939), in which Bergner plays both 'good' and 'bad' identical girl twins married to a British explorer (Michael Redgrave), and a glorious 1936 adaptation of Shakespeare's *As You Like It* (starring Laurence Olivier as Orlando), suggested by J.M. Barrie (who envisaged Bergner as Peter Pan).

In the 1950s, British films looking back at the war sometimes cast European actors in key roles. For instance, Anthony Asquith's *Orders to Kill* (1958) has Gerard Philippe as an American of French extraction who is sent as a spy to investigate a traitor in the Resistance; Conrad Veidt, who left Germany to escape Nazism, found himself cast frequently as an undesirable alien (*The Spy in Black* [Michael Powell, 1939], *I Was a Spy* [Victor Saville, 1933]). There were also, in the 1950s and 1960s, more lavish productions which employed multinational crews and casts and exotic locations. For instance, David Lean's 1965 version of Boris Pasternak's *Doctor Zhivago* paired Omar Sharif with Julie Christie, while *Casino Royale* (John Huston/Ken Hughes/Val Guest/Robert Parrish/Joe McGrath/Richard Talmadge, 1967) cast David Niven as James Bond with cameo appearances from Orson Welles, Woody Allen, Ursula Andress, Charles Boyer and Jean-Paul Belmondo.

Rates of exchange

In the 'Swinging Sixties' and the seventies, London attracted a number of European directors and British actors were employed in Europe. The casting of foreigners in European films frequently serves a particular dramatic purpose in addition to attracting production funding and distribution. Franco Zeffirelli made *Romeo and Juliet* (UK/Italy, 1968), Michelangelo Antonioni made *Blow-Up* (1966) and *The Passenger* (Italy/France/Spain, 1975), while Pier Paolo Pasolini shot *The Canterbury Tales* (Italy/France, 1971) in Britain with Robin Asqwith (best known for the *Confessions of…* series) and cast Terence Stamp as the enigmatic stranger in *Teorema* (Italy, 1968), shot in Italy. Ivy Close, whose career in film was launched by her success in a 1919 *Daily Mirror* beauty contest, was cast by Abel Gance for *La Roue* (France, 1920) for her 'typically English' look and style. Dirk Bogarde, formerly the hapless Sparrow of the *Doctor* series of the 1950s (for instance, *Doctor in the House* [Ralph Thomas, 1954] and *Doctor at Sea* [Ralph Thomas, 1955], with Brigitte Bardot), delivered some of his

For further discussion of Truffant and the French New Wave, see Chapter 12.

finest performances in *Death in Venice* (Luchino Visconti, Italy, 1971), *Night Porter* (Liliana Cavani, Italy, 1973) and, with John Gielgud, in *Providence* (Alain Resnais, France/Switzerland, 1977). Polanski made *Cul-de-Sac* (1966) with Jacqueline Bisset in Northumberland, *Repulsion* (1965) with Catherine Deneuve in South Kensington, and *Tess* (1979) with Nastassja Kinski in Dorset.

François Truffaut (once notorious for his deprecation of British cinema; Truffaut 1967: 100) directed an adaptation of Ray Bradbury's *Fahrenheit 451* (1966), a **dystopian** depiction of a future Britain, set in nondescript, standard suburbia, casting Julie Christie both as the wife who betrays her disaffected husband (a servant of the state – a fireman – played by Oskar Werner) and as the girl (a romantic who resists the state's suppression of books) who befriends him. Indeed, while Polanski, Antonioni and Truffaut may have been attracted to Britain by the euphoria (and, more concretely, the funds) invested in British cinema during this period, none (like Losey) provide a gratifying nor celebratory picture. *Blow-Up*, as Alexander Walker observes, serves rather as a caricature of common contemporary clichés, heightening the effect of superficiality and shift. Thomas (David Hemmings), a fashionable photographer, struts his stuff through meetings with his publisher, parties, gigs and casual attachments against a readily recognisable background peppered with guardsmen in bearskins, gays with poodles and 'happening' types in panstick make-up (Walker 1974: 320). Mere appearances cannot be trusted: Thomas is not the down and out of the film's opening; pictures, says his painter friend, are ambiguous; evidence can be assembled and constructed such that it 'tells' the story of a murder…but possibly erroneously. In recent years, Indian Bollywood films have turned to British landscapes, castles and stately homes, hitherto locations familiar in native 'heritage' film production.

The European co-funding of nominally British productions has continued and increased in both mainstream commercial and art-house cinema. Much of the support and crewing for Peter Greenaway's feature films has come from The Netherlands (*Prospero's Books* [Netherlands/France/Italy/UK/Japan, 1991], *The Cook, the Thief, His Wife and Her Lover* [France/Netherlands/UK, 1989], *The Pillow Book* [Netherlands/France/UK/Luxemburg, 1996]), while Andrew Birkin's film of Ian McEwan's 1978 novel *The Cement Garden* (UK/Germany/France, 1992) cast his niece, Charlotte Gainsbourg, as the older daughter of the family with Hanns Zischler (German) as the father, Sinead Cusack (Irish) as the mother and Jochen Horst (German) as her boyfriend. *Bend It Like Beckham* was partly funded from Germany and stages a girls' football match (lost) in Hamburg. *The Gambler* (Netherlands/Hungary, Karoly Makk, 1997), an adaptation of a novel by Fyodor Dostoyevsky starring Michael Gambon and Jodhi May, was a veritable Europudding, filmed in Prague and Sochi. For *The Barber of Siberia* (Russia/France/Italy/Czechoslovakia, 1998) (another pudding of a movie), Nikita Mikhalkov cast British actors Julia Ormond and Richard Harris.

> 1 What in the soundtrack and image track renders a film such as *Blow-Up* a typical film of the 'Swinging Sixties'?
> 2 How do tourists' impressions of cities differ from the impressions of residents?

TOWN, COUNTRY AND COAST

The outer edge and beyond

For further discussion of the importance of setting and location in film, see Chapter 2, pp. 63–66.

British cinema, as a national institution, frequently depicts Britain as a geographical entity. Elizabethan London is presented in an aerial shot at the opening of Oliviér's *Henry V* (1944) and we are shown a view of the coast with France beyond. In an admittedly small country, the distance and difference between places has been a recurrent focus of interest. Thus, for Michael Powell in 1937, the Isle of Foula is not simply a smaller island, remote from the mainland, but *The Edge of the World*. Life in the outer highlands and islands is often shown to be especially harsh and primitive, as in *The Brothers* (David Macdonald, 1947). *Another Time, Another Place* (Michael Radford, 1983) portrays the work of the farming community governed by the seasonal round of a living earned from the soil and Janie (Phyllis Logan) dreams of what it might be to escape the narrow confines of a joyless, passionless existence; *Breaking the Waves* (Lars von Trier, 1996) returns to this territory and to its severely puritan patriarchy. In *The 39 Steps* (Alfred Hitchcock, 1935) and *The Eye of the Needle* (Richard Marquand, 1981), strangers seek anonymity and safety in far-flung crofts, whereas in *The Wicker Man* (Robin Hardy, 1973) a group of islanders, under the tutelage of its laird (Christopher Lee), has set itself beyond the pale of the laws and conventions of the mainland, holding instead to pagan beliefs and rituals. The folkloric *The Secret of Roan Inish* (John Sayles, 1994) and *Venus Peter* (Ian Sellar, 1989) are both concerned with the communion of the people of the islands with the animals which share their environment. However, in *Local Hero* (Bill Forsyth, 1983), the Scottish highlands are shown to afford a welcome retreat from the stresses and strains (and absurdities) of contemporary metropolitan go-getting: here, a worldly-wise local publican-cum-banker and broker-cum-solicitor-cum-estate agent (Denis Lawson) serves as unofficial overseer of the island's transactions with the outside world, conducting trade with passing Russian trawlers without (as in *Whisky Galore!* [Alexander Mackendrick, 1948]) the bothersome interference of usual customs and excise. The islanders manage to secure the best of their traditions while resisting the threats and blandishments of modern, urbane, profit-seeking enterprises (there is a 'secret' plan to build a nuclear re-processing plant). Self-containment and safety is ensured by the patronage of a born-again Texan business tycoon (Burt Lancaster), determined to preserve the idyll as a personal haven from which to contemplate the stars. In Kirk Jones' *Waking Ned* (1998), with a soundtrack by The Waterboys and Shaun Davey, the Isle of Man substitutes for Ireland in a similar tale of canny country folk outsmarting a city boy. When Ned Devine dies in front of his television set, clutching his winning Lotto ticket, friends Jackie (Ian Bannen) and Michael (David Kelly) decide to pretend he is still alive in order to claim the £7 million jackpot and divide it equally between the fifty-two Tullymore residents. Only Lizzie, the local witch, opposes the scheme, suggesting that she could claim 10% of the total by reporting the fraud. By an act of divine intervention (or merely an accident), the returning local priest swerves into the 'phone box just as Lizzie is calling the National Lottery, sending her spinning into the sea. Maggie (Susan Lynch) confides to Jackie that dead Ned fathered her son, Maurice, but would rather marry Pig Finn (James Nesbitt), to give the boy a new father than have to tell him the truth and claim the winnings solely for Ned's only living relative.

At the other end of the country, the cliffs of Dover function as an **emblematic** edge. In *Quadrophenia* (Franc Roddam, 1979), when Jimmy (Phil Daniels) decides that there is nothing left to live for, he revs up the flashiest silver motorbike (a talisman of dashed hopes) and hurls himself into oblivion. In Kenneth Branagh's *Henry V* (1989), referring in part to its wartime precursor, Derek Jacobi strides Kate Adie-style along the ridge of the coast before the battle commences. Strangely, perhaps, for a nation so historically indebted to its mercantile and political interests overseas, the coast is relatively rarely represented by its ports. *The Long Good Friday* (John Mackenzie, 1980) shows London's docklands in decline, ripe for redevelopment. *Tiger Bay* (J. Lee Thompson, 1959) and *A Taste of Honey* (Tony Richardson, 1961) show the transience of relationships, the settlement of travellers and the mixed racial identity which may characterise such areas. *Letter to Brezhnev* (Chris Bernard, 1985), set in Liverpool, concerns a star-crossed attachment between a British girl, Elaine (Alexandra Pigg), and a Russian sailor, Peter (Peter Firth), who against the odds decide to stay together, even if this means Elaine leaving the security of her family and friends. For Elaine, looking beyond the shore is something filled with hope and optimism.

• **Plate 9.7**
Janie (Phyllis Logan)
imagines life beyond the
island in *Another Time,
Another Place* (Michael
Radford, 1983)

DIRECTOR
MICHAEL RADFORD
SCREENPLAY
MICHAEL RADFORD
PRODUCER
SIMON PERRY
EXECUTIVE PRODUCER
TIMOTHY BURRILL

PHOTOGRAPHY
ROGER DEAKINS
SOUND
DIANA RUSTON
EDITOR
TOM PRIESTLEY
ART DIRECTOR
HAYDEN PEARCE

MUSIC
JOHN MCLEOD
LEADING CAST
**PHYLLIS LOGAN,
GIOVANNI
MAURIELLO,
DENISE COFFEY,**

**TOM WATSON,
GIAN LUCA FAVILLA**
PRODUCTION COMPANY
UMBRELLA FILMS

*For further reference to
Amber Films and inde-
pendent film-making in
Britain in the 1960s and
1970s, see Chapter 7,
pp. 249–250.*

Communities, now in decline, which earn a living from boats and the sea, have featured in *Turn of the Tide* (Norman Walker, 1935), filmed in Yorkshire; Ealing's *The Maggie* (Alexander Mackendrick, 1953), filmed in Scotland; and Amber Films' *The Launch* (1974) and *Seacoal* (Murray Martin, 1985). But mostly the juncture of land and sea is depicted as a place of leisure and recreation, as a welcome and popular diversion from everyday labour. There is a social history of holidays and day-trips bound up with the seaside on film: the collective exodus of Wakes week in the North (as in *Hindle Wakes* (Arthur Crabtree, 1952); the day-long Blackpool excursion of *A Taste of Honey* and *Bhaji on the Beach*; privileged or eccentric sport, as in the London to Brighton rally in *Genevieve* (Henry Cornelius, 1953) – Rob Fleming's mum's favourite in Nick Hornby's *High Fidelity*). The day-trip offers unanticipated delights in chance encounters and encourages a sense of irresponsibility and freedom from usual constraints: pensioner mum (Edna Doré), cooped up and isolated in London in Mike Leigh's *High Hopes* (1987), says that Margate is where she would prefer to be – but Lindsay Anderson, in his short film about Margate, *O Dreamland* (1953), takes a stern view of the amusements on offer to the tripper, presenting the experience as tawdry, superficial and a sham. The sheer brazen gaudiness of the seaside recurs as a motif in *Brighton Rock* (John Boulting, 1947) (where the seaside is far from a safe haven) and in *Mona Lisa* (Neil Jordan, 1985). *The Punch and Judy Man* (Jeremy Summers, 1962), starring Tony Hancock, and *The Entertainer* (Tony Richardson, 1960), filmed at Morecombe and starring Laurence Olivier, show life from the other side of the front, both Hancock and Olivier playing performers in seaside shows struggling to compete with newer attractions (such as television) and with personalities more attractive to audiences. *Wish You Were Here* (David Leland, 1987) bears its title ironically: for Rita (Emily Lloyd), growing up in the 1950s, the seaside *is* everyday life, a seaside of polite tea-rooms and parochial constraint and hypocrisy. The promenade, under a grey sky, is deserted apart from a sad marionette figure dancing for a non-existent audience, and Rita cycling with her skirts flying in the breeze.

Although sand, sea and fun reconfigure in the British surf movie *Blue Juice* (Carl Prechezer, 1995), the depiction of the seaside as desolate, as a place in which to be alone, has continued. In *Last Orders* (Fred Schepisi, 2001) the sky is overcast and the wind fierce as Jack's ashes are scattered over the waves (Margate), and in *Some Voices*

(Simon Cellan Jones, 2000) Ray (Daniel Craig) and Laura (Kelly MacDonald) escape for a chilly weekend away from the pressure of the city. In *Last Resort* (Pawel Pawlikowski, 2000), Margate (yet again) appears as Stonehaven, as a dismal place of arrival for asylum-seekers and immigrants and as an anonymous place of retreat for Alfie (Paddy Considine) after a spell in prison. Relationships between characters are forged through a coincidence of circumstance: Alfie, manager of an amusement arcade, meets Russian Tania (Dina Korzun) and her son (Artom Strelnikov) when the attachment which has brought her to Britain falls through – but here again, the place itself seems bleak and inhospitable, at times threatening, and the relationship survives against a hostile environment.

The heart of England

The countryside, too, is often imagined as a site of retreat or forgetfulness, although it is more often glamorised than degraded. The 'heritage' films of the 1980s all too often showed an historic past in which woods and fields functioned as a passive and picturesque background to a stately home setting rather than a source of income (for example, the British locations of James Ivory's 1985 *A Room With a View* as opposed to their Tuscan counterparts). Adaptations from Thomas Hardy, adopting a key theme of the original texts, are distinguished by their concern with the land as a place of work: *Far From the Madding Crowd* (John Schlesinger, 1967); *Jude* (Michael Winterbottom, 1996); *The Woodlanders* (Phil Agland, 1997). Losey's *The Go-Between* (Joseph Losey, 1970) sets the indolence of the family at the big house, idling through the long, hot summer, against the sweated labour of Ted Burgess (Alan Bates), Lord Trymingham's tenant farmer. Again, following Hardy, Chris Menges photographs the Dorset weather in *Far from the Madding Crowd* as an essential protagonist in the narrative. In *The Land Girls* (David Leland, 1998) and in *Last Orders* (Fred Schepisi, 2002), work in the country-side is a form of escape from the normal routine and is identified with an idealised moment in characters' lives, prior to the onset of a harsher reality; in *A Month in the Country* (Pat O'Connor, 1987), rural Yorkshire provides respite from the terrors of the trenches: the country may thus become a place of personal renewal. In *Kes* (Ken Loach, 1969) and *Rita, Sue and Bob, Too* (Alan Clarke, 1987) the countryside is shown to be a place of working-class recreation; on the other hand, the group of friends at the centre of *Trainspotting* (Danny Boyle, 1996) feel entirely disconnected from the landscape when they take the train for a day-trip from Edinburgh.

For a discussion of Land Girls *and the audience response, see Chapter 3, pp. 95–97.*

The countryside is most explicitly the site of a fantastical past in the studio-staged costume melodramas of the 1940s. Elstree produced a half-timbered 'olde worlde' view of Cornish wreckers for Hitchcock's adaptation of Daphne du Maurier's *Jamaica Inn* (1939), through which Charles Laughton swaggers magnificently as the duplicitous Sir Humphrey Pangallan, intent on having his way with a feisty Irish girl, Mary Yelland (Maureen O'Hara). Gainsborough manufactured a nondescript rural ambience for *The Wicked Lady* (Leslie Arliss, 1945), with Margaret Lockwood as an aristocratic adven-turess who finds excitement in partnership with a highwayman (James Mason). Such 'bodice rippers' were enjoyed by their contemporary audiences for precisely the escape they afforded from everyday constraints (Cook 1996: 59). Mary Yelland finds the law-breaking smuggler at least as attractive as his alter-ego, the law-enforcing government agent who seeks to unmask Pengallan as ringleader of the wreckers.

Regional specificity

The representation of a specific locality (rural and urban) has been a declared objective of Amber Films, based in the north east of England, seeking to portray the concerns of a particular community, often employing the same family of semi-professional performers. In *Eden Valley* (1994), Billy (Darren Bell) receives a suspended prison sentence for stealing drugs and leaves his mother and her boyfriend in Newcastle to go live with his father (Brian Hogg) who breeds and trains horses for harness races in County Durham. At first the father is as much a stranger to the son as the environment is strange. Hoggy discovers that his field is to be sold but makes a successful bid for it by bargaining with the fixer, Danker (Mike Elliott), who in return requires Billy to throw his first race. Billy fails to comply and Danker exacts his revenge by poisoning Billy's horse. But, in the course of the film, the relationship between father and son is ultimately strengthened.

Other films have taken a specific city as location, such as Newcastle in *Stormy Monday* (Mike Figgis, 1988); Liverpool in *Gumshoe* (Stephen Frears, 1971), *Letter to Brezhnev* (Chris Bernard, 1985) and *The 51st State* (Ronny Yu, 2001); Bradford in *Billy Liar!* (John Schlesinger, 1963); Edinburgh in *Shallow Grave* and *Trainspotting* (Danny Boyle, 1994 and 1996); Glasgow in *Small Faces* (Gillies Mackinnon, 1996), *My Name is Joe* (Ken Loach, 1998, partly financed by the Glasgow Film Fund), *Sweet Sixteen* (Ken Loach, 2002) and *Ratcatcher* (Lynne Ramsay, 1999); Sheffield in *Looks and Smiles* (Ken Loach, 1981) and *The Full Monty* (Peter Cattaneo, 1997). Actor Keith Allen's brother, Kevin, returned to his roots in 1997 to direct *Twin Town* and Shane Meadows turned to Nottingham for *Twenty-Four Seven* (1997), reinforcing memories of Karel Reisz's *Saturday Night and Sunday Morning* (1960) by recording a similar tale of disaffected youth in monochrome, selecting similar territory for *A Room For Romeo Brass* (1999) and, most emphatically, *Once Upon a Time in the Midlands* (2002), financed by Film Four, the Film Council and Nottingham-based EMMI. *Butterfly Kiss* (Michael Winterbottom, 1996), financed by British Screen and The Merseyside Film Production Fund, manages never to get anywhere in particular, trailing Eunice (Amanda Plummer) and Miriam (Saskia Reeves) through a series of nondescript motorway cafes, service stations and a theme park. Others have set up an opposition between town and country, or between north and south (especially London as distinct from the provinces), or between different areas of the same city (especially the comforts and respectability of London's West End contrasted with its more dangerous and exotic foil, the East). Some films have endeavoured to show other towns to be just as swinging as London may have seemed to be in the 1960s: *Human Traffic* (Justin Kerrigan, 1998) referred to the Cardiff club scene of the 1990s, while *24 Hour Party People* (Michael Winterbottom, 2002), partly funded by Manchester-based company Granada, marked the rise and fall of the Hacienda and 'Madchester', and Factory bands Joy Division and the Happy Mondays. The image of Manchester as a happening place (and a place of migration for soft and often duplicitous southerners) has been endorsed by the small screen, in *Queer as Folk* (C4/Red, 1998), *Cold Feet* (Granada TV, 1997/98), *Bob and Rose* (BBC TV/Red, 2001) and *Cutting It* (BBC TV, 2002).

• **Plate 9.8**
Albert Finney as Nottingham's angry young man and would-be adventurer Arthur Seaton in *Saturday Night and Sunday Morning* (Karel Reisz, 1960)

Hard northerners and soft southerners

In *Life at the Top*, the sequel to *Room at the Top*, Joe Lampton (Laurence Harvey) travels to London then returns: his boss, his father-in-law Abe Brown, is the archetypical northern self-made man (from Norman McKinnell in *Hindle Wakes* to James Mason in *Georgy Girl* [Silvio Narizzano, 1966]). As the Jaguar speeds through the moorland roads, men are seen launching their trained pigeons into the skies. In Alexander Mackendrick's *The Man in the White Suit* (1951), the captain of industry is chauffered in his Rolls Royce to the company factory, past an illuminated sign which reads, simply, 'to the North'. In *Charlie Bubbles* (1967), directed by Albert Finney (whose own success as an actor in the 1960s proved for him a mixed blessing), a successful writer (whose success is due in part to the filming of his books) returns to Derbyshire to take his son to a football match. As in *Nothing But the Best* (Clive Donner, 1964), *Life at the Top* and *Get Carter* (Mike Hodges, 1971), much is made of the potential for redevelopment of old city slum areas and the willingness of local officials to secure personal profits by selling favours. Much is said about supposed London life (both admiring and distrustful) but also about Charlie's job as somehow soft and not proper work at all. He gets under the feet of his ex-wife (Billie Whitelaw), feeding the hens and the goat, busy in the kitchen (it may be rubbish but it's organic rubbish, she says), and an old friend of Charlie's dad (who played cards with him when they were sitting out the Depression together), now working as a hotel waiter, asks him: 'You just do your writing now or are you still working?'

London is often deemed especially decadent ('he can't have learned those things in Leicester', says Joe Orton's brother-in-law in Alan Bennett's biopic of Orton and his lover Kenneth Halliwell *Prick Up Your Ears* [Stephen Frears, 1987]). Often London seems to promise adventures and the potential for self-fulfilment and material gain not available in the provinces: it is its very danger that is attractive. In *Billy Liar!*, Billy (Tom Courtenay) fancies Liz (Julie Christie), whose educated and liberated attitudes appear synonymous with her having travelled not only to London but abroad, while Billy himself, in spite of his efforts, never manages to get past the railway station. In Richard Lester's *The Knack* (1965), already a pastiche of a mythologised metropolis, country mouse Nancy Jones (Rita Tushingham) arrives in London, *Honey* magazine in hand, searching for the YWCA. She encounters schoolteacher Colin (Michael Crawford in the prototype of his TV Frank Spencer role), his flat-mate Tolan (Ray Brooks) – who fashionably volunteers only the one name – and the Irish painter Tom (Donal Donnelly) – who proceeds to strip and white-wash the ground floor flat. The film provides a whistle-stop tour of visitor attractions (double-decker buses, Buckingham Palace and the Albert Hall) and of 1960s style (Mary Quant dresses, Chelsea boots, narrow slacks and cool shades). Tolan, to Nancy's alarm, taunts Colin with his expertise with women, although Tom remains unimpressed by Tolan's claim to get them in and out of his stripy black and white sheets in less than ten minutes. But *The Knack* is as much a commentary on a generation gap as it is on received notions of 'Swinging' London. Stock affirmations of shock and disgust are heard in voiceover as the foursome gallivants its way about town, proclaiming the bene-fits of national service, bemoaning the shortness of girls' skirts and so forth.

Stella Does Tricks (Coky Giedroyc, 1996) is equally a story about a young girl in the big city – a familiar theme – but here the outcome, like its 2002 variant *Nine Dead Gay Guys* (Lab Ky Mo, 2002) (two young boys arriving from Belfast), is more bleak. For Stella (like the Kings Cross girls in *Mona Lisa* [Neil Jordan, 1986]) the city is not only not paved with gold but even fails to deliver the little she asks of life. Stella (Kelly Macdonald) runs away from her abusive father (Ewan Stewart), whose own ambition has been to build a career in London, and his sister in Glasgow, only to find herself adopted by a surrogate father, Mr Peters (James Bolam), who becomes her pimp: 'you're the nice man who took me in', she says, dutifully. Stella tries to escape him by earning a living by other means – she takes a job on a flower stall – but falls in with Eddie (Hans Matheson) who steals from her in order to support his drug habit. Mr Peters is not prepared to release his hold on Stella and continues to use her for his own profit. For Stella there seems to be no escape: a

(1951) an idealist, Sidney Stratton (Alec Guinness) invents a new fibre which never needs washing and never wears out. But far from welcoming this new product, bosses and workers join forces to oppose Sidney – even Mrs Wilson, his kindly landlady, asks 'Why can't you scientists leave things alone? What about my bit of washing when there's no more washing to do?' The workers realise that they will lose their jobs with no new orders coming in; 'It'll knock the bottom out of everything' says the factory boss, Courtland, 'What about the sheep farmers, the cotton growers, the traders, the middlemen?' Ultimately, the suit disintegrates and its hapless inventor is mocked: leaving the town with suitcase in hand, silhouetted against the mill's chimneys beyond, Sidney is an isolated man.

Quintessentially English?

The films produced at Ealing under the leadership of Michael Balcon (from 1938 to 1955, when the studio was sold to the BBC) typically concern a small, contained community. *Passport to Pimlico* (Henry Cornelius, 1948) opens with the residents and shopkeepers (a fishmonger, a hardware merchant, a dressmaker, a bank manager, a policeman, a bookie) going about their everyday business in the midst of an extraordinary heatwave. Much of the film's humour is highly contemporary: 'Forget that Cripps Feeling', reads a poster, referring to the wartime minister, Sir Stafford Cripps; the 'evacuated' Burgundian children see newsreels at the cinema which intercut actual footage of mass demonstrations at Trafalgar Square, bomb sites and Churchill arriving at Downing Street with 'faked' interviews with the Burgundians, voiced-over with a stylised commentary. An unexploded bomb is set off accidentally and a document is discovered in the rubble which proves that the area still falls under the jurisdiction of Burgundia, and is outside British laws and customs. On hearing this news from the professor (Margaret Rutherford) the residents celebrate in the local pub, tearing up their ration books and identity papers. Meanwhile, the men from the ministry argue about whose responsibility the Burgundians have become – whether they are to be classified as aliens or undesirable aliens. The rest of Britain supports the bid by the 'plucky little Burgundians" for independence and their resistance to bureaucracy. Eventually, order is restored when the bank loans its treasure to Britain – and even the weather returns to normal.

For further discussion of stardom, see Chapter 4, pp. 169–181.

Although the Ealing comedies were not intended as star vehicles for individual performers, more often requiring ensemble playing from familiar key figures, Balcon nevertheless claimed that they made a star of Alec Guinness and that in America they were dubbed 'Guinness comedies' (Balcon 1969: 165–6). In *The Lavender Hill Mob* (Charles Crichton, 1951) Guinness plays Holland, a nondescript clerk, resident in a private hotel, who dreams up a plan to steal gold bullion from the Bank of England, aided and abetted by Pendlebury (Stanley Holloway), a disaffected sculptor, and Lackery Wood (Sid James), a professional crook. For a while, at least, we are happy to witness Holland outwitting the police and enjoying the fruits of his crime in the exotic climes of South America (where Audrey Hepburn makes a brief appearance as a cigarette seller). In *The Ladykillers* (Alexander Mackendrick, 1955), he assumes the role of a dark-eyed and buck-toothed maniacal 'Professor', while in *Kind Hearts and Coronets* (Robert Hamer, 1949) he plays the eight members of the d'Ascoyne family who stand in the way of the inheritance of Louis Mazzini (Dennis Price). For each he adopts a different voice and different mannerisms. The self-effacing Guinness preferred to think of himself as a character actor rather than a star, latterly becoming identified with the hapless Wormold in Greene's *Our Man in Havana* (Carol Reed, 1959) and the secret agent Smiley in BBC TV's 1970s adaptations from Le Carré, including *Tinker, Tailor, Soldier, Spy* and *The Honourable Schoolboy*. Indeed, Guinness was impatient with the disproportionate attention attracted by his appearance in the Hollywood production *Star Wars* and disliked dealing with the vast quantity of appeals and fan mail which American-style stardom engendered (Guinness 1997: 71). Guinness was not alone in his antipathy. Although, as we have seen, British films have been made as star vehicles (for Matthews, Fields, etc.) and British studios have endeavoured to create and commodify stars (such as Rank Charm School's Diana Dors), many theatrically trained British actors have been uncomfortable with the personal demands and possible professional constraints of stardom. In *The Ladykillers*, Guinness plays against the other characters and they similarly play against one another. The gang assembled by Professor Marcus and the neighbourhood in which the action takes place (like the earlier Pimlico) function as representative types: Louis (Herbert Lom) is a gangster, dressed in black with a white kipper tie and violin case; Robinson (Peter Sellers) is the Teddy boy, complete with narrow lapels and brothel creepers; while One Round (whose nickname is soon justi-fied) is the slow-witted giant who does not like the idea of little old 'Mrs Lopsided' being harmed in any way or being implicated in their caper; Mrs Wilberforce herself is archaically dressed in Edwardian style and keeps a parrot called General Gordon. She is well-known to the local constabulary (Jack Warner, of BBC TV's *Dixon of Dock Green* fame) who take a kindly interest in her welfare even while assuming that she is slightly dotty.

Decline and reconfiguration

A number of recent films have dealt more directly with the subject of traditional industry in decline, the threat which this poses to family and communal relationships, and the struggle to maintain self-respect apart from the identity and status afforded by a partic-ular job. In *High Hopes* (Mike Leigh, 1988) an old-age pensioner (Edna Doré) is increasingly isolated as a once tenanted, working-class area of London is sold-off and gentrified; when she locks herself out of her house her snooty neighbours (Lesley Manville and David Bamber) are decidedly un-neighbourly. In *The Full Monty* (1997), Gaz (Robert Carlyle), an unemployed steel worker, estranged from his wife, tries to retain his relationship with his young son, who returns his efforts by lending his post office savings when Gaz and his workmates group together to perform a striptease on stage. The community rallies around and for one night (and one night only) the men's troubles are temporarily forgotten. In *Brassed Off* (Mike Herman, 1996) the colliery band continues to compete as a gesture of solidarity against the inevitable closure of the pit (they may be down but they're not out yet); in *Billy Elliot* (Stephen Daldry, 2000) the father, Jackie (Gary Lewis), and older brother, Tony (Jamie Draven), are out on strike. Against his initial prejudices and his political principles, but determined to hang onto his pride as a father, Jackie is even prepared to return to work to earn funds for Billy's audi-tion at the Royal Ballet School in London. A raffle and a benefit is organised in the neighbourhood and Jackie pawns his dead wife's jewellery. While the Miners' Union is eventually forced to agree terms, the hopes invested in Billy are rewarded and personal ambition is fulfilled: the younger generation potentially achieves what 'might have been' (for nana in *Billy Elliot*) and what has been given up (by Jess Bhamra's father in *Bend It Like Beckham*) by going elsewhere.

For further discussion of masculinity in crisis, see Chapter 7, pp. 264–275.

A model society

Social structure is frequently mirrored within the confined environment of institutions which seek to educate or inculcate into individuals conformist behaviour. Public schools, borstals and prisons are routinely accommodated to this standard generic pattern. Lindsay Anderson's 1982 *Britannia Hospital* (the release of which coincided importunately with the outbreak of the Falklands War) takes the occasion of a royal visit to commemorate a 500th anniversary as a metaphor for the nation's ills. In *The Italian Job* (Peter Collinson, 1969) Mr Bridger (Noel Coward), the veteran con, effec-tively runs the prison and incarceration is not allowed to interfere with his continued mastery over criminal operations on the outside. With his pompous reverence for the monarchy and official protocol, Bridger gently mimics the parading of his equivalent state functionaries. Colin (Tom Courtenay), in Tony Richardson's *The Loneliness of the Long Distance Runner* (1962), Alex (Malcolm MacDowell), in Stanley Kubrick's *A Clockwork Orange* (1971), and Archer, in Alan Clarke's *Scum* (1979), refuse to comply with the system, even if this entails loss of favour and an extended term of imprisonment. Archer points out the obvious to his warder: that his keys and chain are mere tokens of authority but that he remains as ineffectually chained as the inmates; Colin, the runner, refuses to bring glory to the institution and its Governor by winning a race against a local public school, conspicuously allowing its own representative (James Fox) to pass him at the finishing line. For Colin and Archer, their only remaining pride and strength resides in not playing the game by the rules dictated by their keepers.

In Peter Brook's adaptation of William Golding's *Lord of the Flies* (1963), Lindsay Anderson's *If...* (1968), an ironic reference to Rudyard Kipling's well-known poetic homily, and Marek Kanievska's film of Julian Mitchell's stage play *Another Country* (1984), public school hierarchies, rites of passage and rituals initiate the boys into the roles they will inherit from their fathers and their fathers' fathers, assuming as adults their place in the establishment: 'Nothing's going to be so good again till I'm Ambassador in Paris', says Guy Bennett (Rupert Everett) in *Another Country*, after spending the night with his lover, James. Ultimately their loyalty is to the vested interests of their house rather than to the school as a whole, which is run by the Gods (senior prefects) and prefects rather than by the masters (whom the boys despise as mere functionaries). Tommy Judd (Colin Firth) is the obvious intellectual and political rebel, declaring himself a Bolshevik (subsequently dying in action in the Spanish Civil War), complaining that the school wastes its time playing cricket and teaching about the Tudors and Stuarts instead of economics. But Guy points out to him that, for all his talk of equality and fraternity, Tommy holds himself superior to others. Guy (based in part on the actual spy, Guy Burgess) mocks the panoply of an Officer Training Corps inspection (and the dignity of his step-father) by presenting himself improperly kitted-out, but escapes punishment by blackmail, thinking sportsmanship hypocritical. Eventually he accepts a beating after a younger boy has hung himself fearing expulsion for homosexuality (while the prefects seem to mind this less than a boy having an affair with someone from another house). As far as Guy's politics are concerned, as he tells Judd, 'What better cover for me than total indiscretion?'

Jenning's work is discussed in greater detail in Chapter 5, pp. 195–196.

The representation of a typical self-sufficient community acquires a particular potency when the nation as a whole is under attack. Just as Humphrey Jennings' poetic documentaries of the Second World War strove to depict town and country, north and south, young and old, labour and capital, officers and the ranks unified against a common threat, feature films worked to a similar purpose. Noel Coward's *In Which We Serve* (David Lean, 1942), based on the battleship commanded by Lord Mountbatten, cuts between members of the crew and the home front: unity is achieved in deference to the command of the captain (Coward). In Ealing's *Went the Day Well* (Alberto Cavalcanti, 1942), based on a story by Graham Greene, soldiers from the Gloucestershire Regiment augment the studio's cast. Biscuit-tin thatched and half-timbered cottages surround the manor house. The film is framed by a rustic directly addressing the audience as if at some future date, recalling Whitsun Weekend in 1942 when German troops planned to invade Britain. A sailor, Tom (Frank Lawton), two land girls, Peggy and Ivy (Elizabeth Allan and Thora Hird), the postmistress (Muriel George) and Mrs Fraser and the vicar's daughter, Nora, at the manor (Marie Lohr and Valerie Taylor), along with the local poacher and a rapscallion young lad, George (Harry Fowler), all show themselves alert to the signs that Major Hammond and his men are not all that they seem to be (they are in fact German soldiers). With much ingenuity, the women endeavour to pass messages to the

• **Plate 9.11**
Attempts to sustain the
camaraderie of war in
peacetime: *The League of
Gentlemen* (Basil Dearden,
1960)

outside and eventually the wounded George informs the Home Guard at a neighbouring village. Wilsford (Leslie Banks), the traitor in their midst, poignantly stands
with Hammond in front of the church memorial to the dead of the Great War,
discussing their campaign. Mrs Fraser sacrifices herself for the sake of the children.
Nora, who has previously been attracted to Wilsford, discovers him unbolting the
manor's barricaded windows and shoots him dead.

Many films of the 1950s continued to deploy similar emblematic groupings of offi-
cers and men, generally celebrating their efforts and triumphs: *The Dam Busters*
(Michael Anderson, 1955), with its monumental Eric Coates score, and *Reach for the
Sky* (Lewis Gilbert, 1956) stand as a memorial to Barnes Wallis and Douglas Bader
respectively; The *Wooden Horse* (Jack Lee, 1950) and *The Colditz Story* (Guy
Hamilton, 1954) record the escape of British officers from Nazi POW camps. Basil
Dearden's *The League of Gentlemen* (1960) has a group of disaffected men (Jack
Hawkins, Nigel Patrick, Richard Attenborough, Roger Livesey and Bryan Forbes)
reunited in peace-time, planning to sustain the bonds of male camaraderie and the
dangerous thrill of the war-game by planning a bank raid. *The Cruel Sea* (Charles
Frend, 1953; Rob Fleming's dad's favourite in Nick Hornby's *High Fidelity*) likewise
brings together in service a number of men from different areas of civilian life; a
'good' woman, who motivates survival is paired against a 'bad' woman (Morrell, the
society barrister, gives up when he recalls his wife's infidelity) and a junior officer
exhibits loyalty to his seniors and his ship at the expense of personal advancement.
But frequently the crew conclude that war is brutal, wasteful and nonsensical.
Ericson, the Captain (Jack Hawkins), sometimes proves himself fallible and regrets
decisions made in impossible circumstances: he orders a torpedo attack, thinking
that German ships are in the area and that other British ships are endangered, but
when British men in the water are killed he is accused on his own ship of murder.

1 **Compare Notting Hill as envisaged by Bryan Forbes in *The L-Shaped
   Room* (1962) with the same area of London as envisaged by Roger Michell
   in his film *Notting Hill* (1999): consider, for instance (in terms of sexuality,
   race, class and social difference), the range of characters and the setting.
   What criticisms can be levelled at either film or both?**
2 **Compare the idealism and camaraderie of *In Which We Serve* with the
   post-war readjustment of *The League of Gentlemen*. How are different
   class interests acknowledged?**

INTERMEDIAL RAIDS AND EXCHANGES

Made in Britain...for export

Rather than defining itself by the source of film financing or the origins of its film crews and casts, a national cinema may be recognised in a coherent set of attributes shared across other areas of cultural activity supported by similar social and political national institutions. Such production and reception criteria may be most readily appreciable amongst the home audience, but may also be packaged to appeal to certain foreign markets as well – for instance, the Swinging London films of the 1960s (*The Knack* [Richard Lester, 1965], *Georgy Girl* [Silvio Narizzano, 1966], *Darling* [John Schlesinger, 1965], *Blow-Up* [Michelangelo Antonioni, 1966]) and the social realism of Ken Loach and Mike Leigh (*Looks and Smiles* [1981], *Raining Stones* [1993], *My Name is Joe, Sweet Sixteen* [2002]; *Naked* [1993], *Secrets and Lies* [1996], *All or Nothing* [2002]) habitually winning praise and prizes in France for directors and actors alike (Peter Mullan in Loach's *My Name Is Joe*, David Thewlis in Leigh's *Naked* and Brenda Blethyn in Leigh's *Secrets and Lies*); heritage films of the 1980s (James Ivory's *A Room with a View, Howard's End* [1992] and *Maurice* [1987]) and the Richard Curtis series of the 1990s (*Four Weddings and a Funeral* [Mike Newall, 1994], *Notting Hill* [Roger Michell, 1999] and *Bridget Jones's Diary* [Sharon Maguire, 2001]). While the 1996 government-sponsored report, Britain™, recognised that film and other cultural products were instrumental in promoting an image of Britain abroad, concerns were expressed that Britain's image was too frequently associated with the past.

Much quality film production in Europe has taken a canon of classical and contemporary literature as its source and has frequently looked to paintings, prints, photographs and other illustrative material as some sort of guarantee of authenticity. For instance, David Lean's *Oliver Twist* (1948) and Carol Reed's *Oliver!* (1968) are both indebted to Gustave Doré's engravings of London's rookeries; *Barry Lyndon* conspicuously follows the composition and lighting of Hogarth's *The Rake's Progress* (amongst many other eighteenth-century sources); and *Mrs Brown* (John Madden, 1997) composes a shot of a solitary stag after Edwin Landseer's *Monarch of the Glen*; *Wish You Were Here* (1987) used Bert Hardy's 1950s Picture Post photographs as a source for images in the film itself and its poster campaign. Sometimes the film versions, as with the majority of 'classic' serials on television, thus stick diligently to the period of the original (*Sense and Sensibility* [Ang Lee, 1996], *Little Dorrit* [Christine Edzard, 1987]), but sometimes they may update costumes and settings in some measure to give the story particular resonance or immediacy (Derek Jarman's 1991 *Edward II*, Richard Loncraine's 1995 *Richard III*, Kenneth Branagh's Shakespeare musical *Love's Labour's Lost*, 1999, Patricia Rozema's *Mansfield Park*, 1999, Iain Softley's 1998 *The Wings of the Dove*). Such films may be supposed to attract an audience familiar with the original source but they are perennially under attack from purists for deviating from their original written text and by other critics who presume that they bolster a literary canon which may only partially represent national interests. As Andrew Higson asserted in 1993:

[the] key heritage films in the national cinema of the 1980s are fascinated by the private property, the culture and values of a particular class. By reproducing these trappings outside of a materialist historical context, they transform the heritage of the upper classes into the national heritage: private interest becomes naturalised as public interest...The national past and national identity emerge in these not only as aristocratic, but also as male-centred, while the nation itself is reduced to the soft pastoral landscape of southern England, untainted by the modernity of urbanisation or industrialisation...In each instance, the quality of the films lends the representation of the past a certain cultural validity and respectability.

(Higson in Friedman 1993: 114)

However, a large number of films have been made also from novels published closer to the time of adaptation and, indeed, from novels written with half an eye to the film rights. In addition to writing film criticism in the 1930s and producing screenplays in the 1940s for Carol Reed (*The Fallen Idol* [1948] and *The Third Man* [1949]), Graham Greene (*Our Man in Havana* [Carol Reed, 1959], *The Honorary Consul* [John MacKenzie, 1983], *The End of the Affair* [Neil Jordan, 1999]) has frequently been translated to screen; John Fowles (*The Collector* [William Wyler, 1965], *The Magus* [Guy Green, 1968], *The French Lieutenant's Woman* [Karl Reisz, 1981]); Len Deighton (*The Ipcress File* [Sidney J. Furie, 1965], *Funeral in Berlin* [Guy Hamilton, 1966]); Le Carré (*The Spy Who Came in from the Cold* [Martin Ritt, 1965], *The Looking Glass War* [Frank R. Pierson, 1969]); Beryl Bainbridge (*Sweet William* [Claude Whatham, 1979], *An Awfully Big Adventure* [Mike Newell, 1995]). The current batch of chick lit and lad lit has proved itself translatable, with Helen Fielding's Bridget Jones sequel *The Edge of Reason* forthcoming and Nick Hornby's *Fever Pitch* directed by David Evans in 1997 and *About a Boy* (2002) attracting American directors Paul and Chris Weitz, and *High Fidelity* (Stephen Frears, 2000) being transported wholesale to an American setting. Steven Soderbergh's *Traffic* (2001) was adapted from a five-part television series made for Channel 4 in Britain.

Stage to screen

In the 1920s, complaints were levelled at the British film industry for its undue reliance on adaptations and on performers (such as the matinee idol, Ivor Novello) from the West End stage. Hollywood's debt to the British stage has, of course, continued, not only with a long succession of stage-trained actors but also directors (for instance, Sam Mendes' *American Beauty* [2000] and Anthony Minghella's *The Talented Mr Ripley* [1999]). Hollywood has habitually acknowledged and exploited the commercial and artistic potential of English actors, in both British and American films, for instance casting Kate Winslett in James Cameron's blockbuster *Titanic* (US, 1996) and rewarding Judi Dench with an Academy Award for *Shakespeare in Love* and, with Jim Broadbent, for *Iris* (Richard Eyre, 2001). The favour has been returned, in recent years, with Hollywood stars Cybil Shepherd, Kevin Spacey, Gwyneth Paltrow, Nicole Kidman and even Madonna attracting punters (and, perhaps, securing West End endorsement) in London.

Adaptations of *The Vortex* (Adrian Brunel, 1928), starring Ivor Novello, and *Easy Virtue* (Alfred Hitchcock, 1927) capitalised on Noel Coward's sensational stage success; there were also silent and sound film versions of the domestic dramas of John Galsworthy, including *The Skin Game* (B.E. Doxat-Pratt, 1921, and Alfred Hitchcock, 1931, both versions starring Edmund Gwenn). There were also plays which proved themselves broadly popular on stage and screen. Maurice Elvey's 1918 and 1927 *Hindle Wakes*, drawn from Stanley Houghton's 1913 production in London and Manchester (even reproducing some of the stage performances), expanded the cast of the original and extended the action to include scenes at Blackpool's pleasure beach and the Tower Ballroom, and in a Lancashire cotton mill. The characters of *Hindle Wakes* (an independent young girl; her money-grabbing mother and a hen-pecked husband; a self-made mill-owner, whose son has a weekend escapade with the girl which the mother seeks to turn to her advantage) have proved persistently attractive, the story being remade for audiences in the 1930s (Victor Saville, 1931) and in the 1950s (Arthur Crabtree, 1952). Indeed, with the spate of 'Northern realist' dramas and novels of the 1960s, themselves readily transferred to the screen (*Saturday Night and Sunday Morning*; *The Loneliness of the Long Distance Runner*; *A Taste of Honey*; *Billy, Liar!*), Granada Television recorded a number of the Manchester plays of the earlier period, tracing a direct lineage of theme and setting. The popular legitimate stage has continued to provide material, stage and screen versions, often surviving alongside one another and serving to promote each other: for instance, the stage and screen vehicles for Novello, *I Lived with You* (Maurice Elvey, 1933), Joe Orton's *Entertaining Mr Sloane* (Douglas Hickox, 1969) and various Pinters (including *The Caretaker* [Clive Donner, 1963] and *The Birthday Party* [William Friedkin, 1968]), Willy Russell's *Shirley Valentine* (Lewis Gilbert, 1989) and *Educating Rita* (Lewis Gilbert, 1983), Richard O'Brien's *The Rocky Horror Show* (Jim Sharman, 1975), Jim Cartwright's *Little Voice* (Mike Herman, 1999), and stage and screen adaptations from Louis de Bernière's novel, *Captain Corelli's Mandolin* (John Madden, 2000) and Hanif Kureishi's *Intimacy* (Patrice Chereau, 2000). Conversely, *The Full Monty* has subsequently been produced as a Broadway musical and toured to the West End. Samuel Beckett's *Not I* (BBC TV, 1977) and *Happy Days* (BBC TV 1990), made with Billie Whitelaw, have recently been recommissioned and televised in a series of Beckett works by feature film-makers and gallery artists (*Not I* directed by Neil Jordan [with Julianne Moore]; *Endgame* directed by Conor McPherson [with Michael Gambon and David Thewlis]; *Play* directed by Anthony Minghella [with Alan Rickman, Kristin Scott Thomas and Juliet Stephenson] and *Breath* directed by Damien Hirst [with the voice of Keith Allen]).

Popular turns and celebrities

For further discussion of the performer as part of film form, see Chapter 2, pp. 67–69.

For more on the star as performer, see Chapter 4, pp. 176–178.

The silent screen attracted not only legitimate stage actors but also performers well-known for their turns in the **music hall**, pantomime and revue: the famous Drury Lane dame Dan Leno and the balladeer and comic Harry Lauder were both recorded in familiar roles. Music hall performer Arthur Lucan partnered Kitty McShane in the long-running *Mother Riley* series (1937–52).The Betty Balfour *Squibs* series was similarly based on a music hall sketch and John Baxter's 1934 *Say It With Flowers* and 1942 *Let the People Sing*, drawn from J.B. Priestley, celebrated the music hall tradition. Anna Neagle (once a Cochran revue girl) moved into film, and star vehicles were created for the popular entertainers George Formby (including *I See Ice* [Anthony Kimmins, 1938] and *Let George Do It* [Marcel Varnel, 1939]) and Gracie Fields 'before 1939 the most popular singer in Britain by far' (Frith 1988: 67) (including *Sally in Our Alley* [Maurice Elvey,1931] and *This Week of Grace* [Maurice Elvey, 1933]), and the dancers Jack Buchanan (*Goodnight, Vienna* [Herbert Wilcox, 1932], alongside Anna Neagle) and Jessie Matthews (*The Good Companions* [Victor Saville, 1933], also drawn from J.B. Priestley, *Evergreen* [Victor Saville, 1934] and *First a Girl* [Victor Saville, 1935]). The Crazy Gang (including the famous double-act of Flanagan and Allen) appeared in *O-Kay for Sound* (Marcel Varnel, 1937) and on stage in the denouement at the London Palladium of Hitchcock's 1935 *The 39 Steps*, where their appearance serves to locate and authenticate the action.

Wartime radio comics (such as Jimmy Edwards, Tony Hancock and the Goons) moved into television and (especially in the case of Peter Sellers, with a comedy role in *The Millionairess* [Anthony Asquith, 1960] and a more serious role in *Lolita* [Stanley Kubrick, 1961]) endeavoured to forge a career in film, while Spike Milligan's *Puckoon* has been posthumously adapted for the screen (Terence Ryan, 2002). Saville's *Evergreen* (from the C.B. Cochran original) featured Matthews in dual roles, as Harriet Green, an Edwardian music hall entertainer, and as her daughter. When the daughter auditions for a role in the chorus line, the theatre manager decides to put her on stage in a masquerade of her mother, as a publicity stunt to counter competition from 'the flea pit down the road'. His scheme is abetted by Harriet's former dresser and understudy (Betty Balfour). The film features many familiar songs (from 'Daddy Wouldn't Buy Me a Bow-wow' to 'Over My Shoulder'), and lavish choreography, costumes and sets in Busby Berkeley style (subsequently again imitated by Ken Russell for *The Boy Friend* [1971]).

Here, again, the career progression of singers to the screen, promoting the performer and potentially expanding the appeal of performer and film alike, has become a recurrent aspect of British national cinema, frequently in roles which called for the reproduction of established numbers or for new ones: for instance, Cliff Richard in *Summer Holiday* (Peter Yates/Herbert Ross, 1963) and *The Young Ones* (Sidney J. Furie, 1961); Sting in Chris

Petit's 1979 road movie, *Radio On* and Mike Figgis' *Stormy Monday* (1987); and David Bowie in *Absolute Beginners* (Julien Temple, 1986). The US-exiled Paul Robeson was cast in *King Solomon's Mines* (Robert Stevenson, 1937) and alongside Elizabeth Welch in *The Song of Freedom* (J. Elder Willis, 1936), the story of a black London dockhand, while Welch herself made a welcome return with the classic song 'Stormy Weather', dramatically but anachronistically employed in Jarman's *The Tempest* (1990). Jarman's Super-8 *Broken English* used Marianne Faithfull's 1979 song as its backing, track while Faithfull ('God' in the final episode of BBC television's *Absolutely Fabulous* [1996]) also appeared as an amateur dramatics society retainer in *Intimacy* and a watchful party-goer in Sam Taylor-Wood's 1999 gallery film *Third Party*. Sometimes singers are used in 'straight' roles, as with Adam Faith in *Beat Girl* (Edmond T. Greville, 1960), Keith Moon (although his Uncle Ernie is far from 'straight') in Ken Russell's *Tommy* (1975), Sting in *Brimstone and Treacle* (Richard Loncraine, 1987) and *Snatch* (Guy Ritchie, 2001), Toyah Wilcox in Derek Jarman's *Jubilee* (1987) and *The Tempest* (1979) or David Bowie in *The Man Who Fell to Earth* (Nicholas Roeg, 1976) and *Merry Christmas Mr Lawrence* (Nagisa Oshima, 1982). Sometimes films endeavour to target a particular audience by such casting (for instance, Shaznay Lewis of girl-band All Saints in *Bend It Like Beckham*). Roeg's *Performance* (1970) cast Marianne Faithfull's erstwhile lover Mick Jagger as a rock star on the wane ('I remember him when I was just a nipper', says the precocious child of the bohemian west London household), trading on his overt star celebrity as a presence without requiring him to demonstrate his vocal credentials for the part.

Sixties supermodel Veruschka appeared as herself in *Blow-Up*, and Jean Shrimpton was similarly cast by Peter Watkins for *Privilege* (1967). The aristocratic and statuesque bearing of Marisa Berenson was employed by Stanley Kubrick in *Barry Lyndon*. Meanwhile, model turned actor Twiggy, partnered dancer Christopher Gable in Ken Russell's *The Boy Friend*, and turned a face which launched the make-up and clothing company Biba to the film's advantage. Adam Cooper, dancing in Matthew Bourne's *Swan Lake* (the older Billy Elliott) has followed Christopher Gable and Robert Helpmann (*The Red Shoes* and *Chitty Chitty Bang Bang*) into film. Billy Connolly moved from television stand-up comedy to star in non-comedic roles in *Mrs Brown* (John Madden, 1997) and *Gabriel and Me* (Udayan Prasad, 2001), while personnel from BBC's *Not the Nine O'Clock News* and *Alas Smith and Jones* adapted stage and television characters or turned to large-screen direction (Rowan Atkinson in *Bean: The Ultimate Disaster Movie* [Mel Smith, 1997] and Mel Smith's *The Tall Guy* [1989] and *High Heels and Low Life* [2001]). For performers, such transitions may be regarded as career progressions, whereas for film producers, the status of celebrities and their audience-following may promise greater ticket sales for a film.

The bigger picture: competing claims

The progression from radio to television and from small screen to large screen has seemed traditionally to present a hierachical pattern for many performers, directors, producers and writers (largely, it seems, as a consequence of the remuneration and celebrity anticipated). BBC Television and Channel 4 continue to draw much of their material from radio (for instance, *Dead Ringers* [BBC TV, 2002], Chris Morris' *The Day Today* [1994] and its sequel *Brass Eye* [1997]) while vestiges of Steve Coogan's radio and television persona Alan Partridge reappear in his performances in *The Parole Officer* (John Duigan, 2001) and *24 Hour Party People*. The cast of Jimmy Croft and David Perry's long-standing television comedy series *Dad's Army* (BBC TV, 1968–1977) transferred to both radio and film (Norman Cohen, 1971). However, there is much exchange of personnel across media and the path between them is not necessarily unidirectional: Nigel Kneale's enormously successful TV series *The Quartermass Experiment* was filmed by Hammer in 1955, directed by Val Guest; the *Doctor* series of the 1950s transferred to the small screen, while adaptations from John Braine's *Room at the Top* (Jack Clayton, 1959) and *Life at the Top* (Ted Kotcheff, 1965)

For further discussion of the relationship between film, TV and other media, see Chapter 1, pp. 22–33.

spawned the teleseries *Man at the Top* (1971–73). *Lock, Stock and Two Smoking Barrels* started out as a feature film before being sold as a television series format, while *Lara Croft* was created in Britain as an interactive game character but has been exploited subsequently as a film property (*Tomb Raider* [US, Simon West, 2001]). Hugh Hudson, Alan Parker and Ridley Scott moved from advertising to feature films (and were occasionally lured back for high-profile commissions thereafter), while Guy Ritchie has lent his reputation as a film-maker to BMW for a recent campaign delivered on the internet. Artist Gillian Wearing's film *2 into 1*, purchased by the Saatchi agency, was subsequently copied for an advertising campaign managed by Saatchi (Stallabrass 1999: 2000). Derek Jarman's monologue film *Blue* (1993), the entire screen awash with ultramarine for the duration of the work, was designed by Jarman for radio and television broadcast and theatrical release in the same year.

In the 1970s it was said by many critics (not least in the industry itself, including Joseph Losey) that British cinema had become too reliant on formulaic, often studio-bound television spin-offs from such long-standing comedy series as *Till Death Us Do Part* (Norman Cohen, 1968), *Steptoe and Son* (1973) and *Up Pompeii*. In the last of these, Frankie Howerd's monologues, delivered in the role of the Roman slave, Lurcio, deployed a range of knowing glances, innuendoes and asides familiar from his own stand-up routines on television and (more generally) shared with pantomime, seaside postcards and the *Carry On* scripts of the 1960s. Hattie Jacques crossed from television (with an underweight Eric Sykes as her husband) to popular cinema (as a fearsome matron in *Carry On Nurse* [Gerald Thomas, 1959]) to art-house cinema (a plump fairy in James Broughton's *The Pleasure Garden*, 1952), and was persistently cast in roles which garnered humour from her size. The BBC TV *Monty Python* crew reappeared collectively and individually in *Monty Python and the Holy Grail* (Terry Gilliam and Terry Jones, 1974), *A Private Function* (Malcolm Mowbray, 1984), *A Fish Called Wanda* (Charles Crichton, 1988), *Clockwise* (Christopher Morahan, 1985) and in Terry Gilliam's *Brazil* (1985). Films frequently attempt to draw upon the following of television 'soaps' (or, more properly, drama series), for instance with the casting of *Brookside*'s Anna Friel in *Me without You* (Sandra Goldbacher, 2001) and *EastEnders*' Paul Nicholls in teen-pic *Goodbye Charlie Bright* (Nick Love, 2001).

Television companies were already in the 1970s funding films intended for simultaneous cinema release (for example, Peter Hall's Suffolk village saga *Akenfield*, 1974), but the launching of a fourth television channel, Channel 4, in 1982 proved to have a crucial impact on the structure, strength and style of film production for the remainder of the decade; film's aim was now to say 'something new in new ways' (Hill 1999: 53). During the 1980s the budget for 'Film on Four' (films originally intended for television transmission, subsequently for cinema release and broadcast) doubled from £6 million to £12 million with other companies, such as Granada (*The Magic Toyshop* [David Wheatley, 1986] and *My Left Foot* [Jim Sheridan, 1988]), Central (*The Hit* [Stephen Frears, 1984] and *Sid and Nancy* [Alex Cox, 1986]) and the BBC (*War Requiem* [Derek Jarman, 1988], *Mrs Brown* and *Ratcatcher*) following this example. The new channel also provided an outlet for non-commercial and experimental film (which often struggle to find distribution and venues) through *The Eleventh Hour* slot (Rees 1999: 92). Lynn Ramsey's career in features (*Ratcatcher* [2000] and *Morvern Callar* [2002]) was launched by her success with *Small Deaths* in the BBC-sponsored short film competition *The Talent*.

My Beautiful Laundrette (Stephen Frears, 1985) indicates the trend which the new channel was to follow; like the New Wave films of the early 1960s, it portrayed a younger generation at odds with the political and social ambitions of its parents, and forming new allegiances across conventional barriers of race, class and gender. Omar (Gordon Warnecke) is a young Pakistani set up in business by his uncle (Saeed Jaffrey). While Omar's father (Roshan Seth) is a socialist and former journalist who wants his son to go to college 'so that he can see clearly what is being done and to who in this country', the uncles (sometimes legally, sometimes not) fully embrace the enterprise economy promoted by Mrs Thatcher. The Olympics 'anthem for the Common People' is used somewhat ironically as the laundrette is declared open. Omar enlists the help of an old schoolfriend, Johnny (Daniel Day Lewis) who has in the past marched with the National Front and whose white friends resent his working for Omar. Tania, Omar's cousin, tells her father's mistress, Rachel (Shirley Anne Field, of *Saturday Night and Sunday Morning*), that she disapproves of women who live off men: Rachel replies that there is a difference between them of age and class but reminds Tania that she is hardly independent herself. At the end of the film, Tania leaves the family to make her own way and asks Johnny if he'd like to come with her. But Johnny is more interested in Omar and the film abounds with cheeky references to their sexual relationship (to which Omar's family seem to be oblivious, continuing to attempt to arrange a more 'suitable' marriage on his behalf).

In the 1960s, film production companies were at pains to keep films out of the reach of television transmission for as long as possible in order to extend theatrical returns; now, not only are feature films released for television transmission and video sale with increasing speed, but sales of video and DVD releases (and associated spin-offs) may provide the bulk of total profits. Certainly, for many viewers, the first experience of a feature film may well now be at home rather than in a cinema. Some 'films' may be shot on video and for theatrical release or may be distributed direct onto DVD without an intervening screening or with minimal theatrical screening (such as *Ali G indahouse* [Mark Mylod, 2002]). Many artists' films intended for gallery projection rather than cinematic release are produced or transferred to video (for instance, Gillian Wearing's video works *Trauma* [2000], in which the frame is locked-off in confessional 'Video-Box' mode or the large-scale *Drunks* [1999], and the five-screen record of the Birmingham nightclub scene *Broad Street* [2001]; Sam Taylor-Wood's *Pent-Up*, 1996 and seven-screen *Third Party*, 1999, shot on 16mm film), while Tacita Dean deliberately stages the mechanics of projection as part of the installation witnessed by the viewer (for instance, her *Delft Hydraulics* [1996] shot on 16mm, with the film looped as a Moebius strip and projected at waist height, and *Disappearance at Sea*, [1996] in which the projector is raised and encased in glass, recalling the profile of an oil rig).

Increasingly, film turns in upon itself as an object of imitation. The self-conscious stylisation of James Bond films (and the Ian Fleming originals) has often provided entertainment for commentators and material for reflection. *Modesty Blaise*, ostensibly based on a newspaper comic strip, was filmed by Joseph Losey in 1966. It gloriously spoofs the gadgetry and dandified action-heroism of Bond (by its casting of an immaculately dressed and coiffured Monica Vitti as its protagonist alongside Terence Stamp as her sex-object side-kick). Dirk Bogarde plays a fastidious evil-monger, exotically located in a Mediterranean fortress, with an equally mannered taste in parasols and cocktails (subsequently appropriated by Smirnoff ads: live goldfish swimming in improbably tall glasses). The Bond series has since resorted to self-parody (although, even in 1967 *Casino Royale* was hardly to be taken seriously): Judi Dench, as spymaster M, thinks of Bond (since 1995, Pierce Brosnan) as a bit of a dinosaur; in *The World Is Not Enough* (Michael Apted, 1999), John Cleese plays the eccentric boffin who has to render Bond's super-mobile operational. The Comic Strip films for television and theatrical release (*Five Go Mad in Dorset* [C4 TV, 1982], *The Supergrass* [C4 TV, 1985], *Strike!* [C4 TV, 1988], *Eat the Rich* [Peter Richardson, 1987]) spoof not only direct literary sources (Enid Blyton) but also Hollywood stereotyping and 'respectful' adaptations such as Gerald Landau's serial *Five on a Treasure Island* (1957).

What can be said in favour of and against the close association of British television and British cinema? Why is such an association of less significance in America?

☐ CASE STUDY 1: WEST END GIRLS – WONDERLAND (1999) AND BRIDGET JONES'S DIARY (2001)

• **Plate 9.12** Nadia (Gina McKee), Debbie (Shirley Henderson) and Molly (Molly Parker): three sisters wonder about life and love in *Wonderland* (Michael Winterbottom, 1999)

Wonderland (Michael Winterbottom, 1999) covers three days in the life of a London family: mum Eileen (Kika Markham), dad Bill (Jack Shepherd), daughters Nadia (Gina McKee), Molly (Molly Parker) and Debbie (Shirley Henderson) and their estranged brother, Darren (Enzo Cilenti). The film is very specifically located in place (bridges over the Thames, monuments, the underground, railway stations, bus routes) and time (posters at Leicester Square for *Elizabeth* [Shekhar Kapur, 1998] and at the café for the National Theatre 1998 tour of *Oh! What a Lovely War*; Tricky playing on Franklyn's radio). Nadia, like many characters in late nineties films, works in a café (here, in Soho) – compare, for instance, *Some Voices*, *Intimacy* (Patrice Chereau, 2001) and *Lawless Heart* (Tom Hunsinger/Neil Hunter, 2002) – indicating, perhaps, a shift in working-class employment to the service industries and to restaurants and bars as an artisanal form of entrepreneurial activity. The film presents itself with a sort of casualness (as if these could be any three days, denoted by intertitles, drawn at random); haphazard snatches of 'overheard' conversation, dialogue delivered with unexpurgated burps, hairdressers' clichés re a tight perm, 'dropping', information supplied which does not appear immediately functional to the narrative and so forth, busily recorded on a mixture of film stocks, sometimes with the rough patina of 'amateur' video. However, in structure the film is classically contrived in terms of the disruption and restoration of an equilibrium in each of the three sisters' different stories. It neither begins nor ends arbitrarily, privileging Nadia's story and employing (as did *Strapless* [David Hare, 1992] and *Truly, Madly, Deeply* [Anthony Minghella, 1991]) the birth of a child as an easy means of culminating and supposedly resolving plot lines.

Molly and Eddie (John Simm) are expecting their first child, and Eddie, scared and disorientated by the prospect decides to give up his job as a fitted kitchen sales assistant – seemingly his heart is no longer in it. On Southwark Bridge, he rehearses his speech to Molly but fails to deliver it and instead resigns without telling her; he then rides around London on his bike trying to sort things out in his head. Eventually he is involved in an accident and is taken to hospital. Molly does not know what to think and confides in her sisters – who rally around her. Molly goes into labour in the middle of Soho and Debbie takes her to hospital.

Before Eddie goes AWOL, Molly goes to hairdresser sister Debbie for a perm. She says that she thinks that Nadia is jealous of her, that perhaps the boyfriend, baby and kitchen thing is part of Nadia's romantic fantasy. Nadia, meanwhile, is looking for friendship, possibly romance via Lonely Hearts listings. She makes a quick getaway from the first date we see, then encounters Dublin charmer Tim (Stuart Townsend – a role reprised threefold for *About Adam* [Gerard Stembridge, 2000]). She arranges another meeting in a pub, but she (and the film's audience!) is amazed to discover that her date is Debbie's ex-husband Dan (Ian Hart). Unbeknown to her, Dan has left his young son, Jack ('he's little' is all that Debbie will admit to lover number one) at home by himself. Later, Nadia goes round to Tim's place – but finds that friendship, let alone romance, is the least of his priorities (he doesn't even share his supper with her) and she goes home alone, on the bus, in tears: mostly, it is Nadia's perspective which Michael Nyman's plaintive soundtrack underscores, a simple theme increasingly elaborated as the plot lines intersect. The next day, she telephones Tim but he's with someone else and when the doorbell rings she's disappointed to discover that it's Dan announcing Jack's disappearance. Dan and Nadia look for Jack at the fair and fireworks, to which he has been promised a trip. At first, Nadia fails to notice Franklyn's interest in her (she virtually ignores him in the café); at the end, dad (friend and neighbour of Franklyn and family) offers to introduce them … and the camera follows she and he walking off together into the grey morning light.

Debbie, separated from Dan, is out for fun (rather than romance) and has entrusted Jack to his father for a football match and a sleep-over. She's in bed with lover number two when she hears that Eddie has gone. Debbie and Molly visit Nadia at work; at the hospital, Jack telephones from a police station to say that he has been mugged at the fairground and Debbie goes to collect him, finding that Nadia and Dan have arrived already. Meanwhile, Molly's baby is delivered – she's to be called Alice (Eddie's choice, 'like in Wonderland'). Molly meets Eddie in a hospital corridor. He makes up with her and asks to hold Alice. Throughout all this, Darren has been weekending in London with his girlfriend as a birthday treat, has called Nadia and, at the station, leaves a message with dad to let him know 'he's fine'.

The extraordinary coincidences of the plot are matched by the tight editing of sound and image tracks. Fast intercutting and speeded-up pop-promo-style footage of London streets and nightscapes, panoramas and wide-shots, are interspersed with Nadia in slow motion, arms swinging, eyes down and smiling to herself amid the hustle and bustle as she daydreams about Tim. Less conspicuously contrived material includes head-shots leisurely recording the crowd at the football match, the clientele of the Irish pub where Dan meets Nadia, the weekend's casualties at the hospital and Eileen's fellow punters at the bingo-hall. Winterbottom's earlier *Butterfly Kiss* framed Miriam's 'confessional' direct address to camera (locked-off and monochrome) against flashbacks in colour while his later *24 Hour Party People* uses an even more elaborate amalgam of images, sometimes evoking club lighting, sometimes the striated, grainy and bleached picture of 1970s television as Tony Wilson (Granada TV helmsman) speaks directly to camera, sometimes hand-held mockumentary. In *Wonderland*, quick hand-held pans swipe from Debbie to Molly as she prepares for delivery, the tension heightened by the pairing of this segment with flashes of light from the crackling fireworks as Jack is mugged; Nadia's making out with Tim is cut with Bill stroking and cosying up to Eileen's back (only to be rejected) and Franklyn listening on his bed to a radio phone-in which he abruptly turns off, thereby cueing the next shot of Dan in the pub. *Wonderland* offers a distinctly less glamorised view of city life (while glorying in the city itself) than *Bridget Jones's Diary* (mum, indeed, is at her wits' end and thoroughly overwrought) but nevertheless provides an optimistic conclusion: life is something one can survive and there may even be a glimmer of hope that it could get better.

Bridget Jones's Diary, adapted from Helen Fielding's 1995–1997 newspaper column (and novel), directed by Sharon Maguire (Shazza of Fielding's original), similarly centres on the relationship of Bridget and her parents and a surrogate family of friends (Tom [James Callis], Shazza [Sally Phillips] and Jude [Shirley Henderson]), plus her would-be/won't-be relationships with Daniel Cleaver (Hugh Grant) and Mark Darcy (Colin Firth). The confidences entrusted to the diary are translated in the film to voiceover and 'hand-written' overtitles; on a good day, Bridget's tally of alcohol and tobacco consumption is displayed large scale over Piccadilly Circus. For the most part, however, the city is represented in studio reconstruction or merely as background. The soundtrack serves as commentary to

For further discussion of women film-makers, see Chapter 7, pp. 243–247.

the action: Chaka Khan's 'I'm Every Woman' as Bridget launches herself into new start mode after her showdown with Daniel; Diana Ross 'Ain't no Mountain High Enough' when she hears Darcy's account of Daniel's misbehaviour; Van Morrison singing 'I've been searching for a long time…for someone like you…but the best days are yet to come' as the film rolls from Bridget wrapped in Mark's coat into the end credits.

For reference to Working Title, the production company behind Bridget Jones's Diary, see Chapter 1, p.25

While Bridget's life appears more comfortably insulated in material terms (she inhabits the same Notting Hill as previously envisaged and produced by Richard Curtis) than that of Nadia (who works in town on weekends rather than mini-breaking in the country), both are romantic souls imagining something better for themselves than what is currently on offer. Bridget refuses Daniel's proposal on the basis that it's simply not good enough and she won't settle for less, and, in the manner of traditional romantic comedies (Cary Grant as the counterpart of Darcy) she is duly rewarded for her pains. Mark and Bridget embracing in a snowstorm echoes the thunder and lightning at the end of *Four Weddings and a Funeral*. But both *Wonderland* and *Bridget Jones* suggest that such happy endings are not to be entirely trusted: Darcy's first marriage has collapsed (one in three couples separate, he informs a gathering of 'smug marrieds') and in both films the parents' relationships are seen to require as much support and working at as those of their children.

Compare the London of *Wonderland* with that of *Bridget Jones's Diary*. Consider cinematic devices (such as overlays, camera moves, change of speed, variations in image quality) and the purposes to which they are employed. Do they provide additional information or are they intended for stylistic appeal to a particular audience?

☐ CASE STUDY 2: EAST END BOYS – THE BRITISH GANGSTER FILM POST-1990

For a case study of Tarrantino's film Pulp Fiction (1994) in relation to audience study, see Chapter 3, pp. 116–124.

A 1990s arsenal of gangster movies owed something of their style to Quentin Tarantino, but much of their content to British crime capers of the 1940s and the cult classics of the 1970s: *The Long Good Friday* (John MacKenzie,1979), *Get Carter* (Mike Hodges, 1971), *Performance* (Nicholas Roeg, 1970) and *A Clockwork Orange* (Stanley Kubrick, 1971). *Snatch* might be seen as an equivalent to Ealing's *The Ladykillers* for the New Millennium, with shooters, blades and knuckle-fights and a groovier, highly eclectic soundtrack. It hams up the black humour of Bob Hoskins in *The Long Good Friday* and *Mona Lisa* ('who'd crucify someone on Good Friday?') and the slapstick of *The Italian Job* ('you're only supposed to blow the bloody doors off', says Michael Caine, as a van goes up in smoke). 'The Self-Preservation Society' anthem from *The Italian Job* was taken up by English football supporters in Japan during the 2002 World Cup. Milk-drinking Turkish (Jason Statham), as narrator, delivers many of *Snatch*'s one-line gags and is given a film reference catch-line, constantly reminding side-kick Tommy that they must get wherever 'before ze Germans get there'.

Lock, Stock and Two Smoking Barrels and *Snatch* have a surface busyness of sound and image, employing oblique angles, freeze-frames, split screens, accelera-tion, voiceover and interjected music as commentary (for instance, 'Las Vegas' for gambling addict Frankie Four Fingers). Many of these devices are imitated small-scale by *Goodbye Charlie Bright* (Nick Love, 2001) (a sort of junior *Snatch*). While *The Krays* (Peter Medak, 1990), from which its subjects received royalties, glamorises Ronnie and Reggie by the casting of Spandau Ballet's Kemp twins (Martin Kemp later moving to BBC's *EastEnders*), and David Green cast Phil Collins as a great train robber in *Buster* (1988), in *Lock, Stock* Guy Ritchie casts Sting (formerly a 'mod' icon in *Quadrophenia* (Franc Roddam, 1979) and an angel/incubus figure in Denis Potter's television-to-film makeover *Brimstone and Treacle*) and, in *Snatch*, uses ex-footballer Vinnie Jones and DJ Goldie to lend further charisma and appeal. Both Ritchie films deploy cartoon-strip characters and buffoonery, portraying gangsters as essentially endearing geezers, loveable wayward rogues whose unseemly violence is contained within their own villainous sub-culture. There is action and reaction, bluff and counter bluff and, just occasionally, 'innocents' get caught in the crossfire (such as Mickey's mum) – which is unfortunate. Bent coppers (stock figures of 1970s film and television, resurrected in Antonia Bird's *Face* [1997]) do not merit a mention.

Gangster No. 1 (Paul McGuigan, 2000) presents a more vicious picture while still resorting to a formulaic reworking of standard motifs of mise-en-scène and plot: bespoke tailoring and Bond Street accessorising (as for Chas [James Fox] in *Performance*), a baby-faced thug (as is Pinky [Richard Attenborough] in *Brighton Rock*), the retention of authority over the manor against young pretenders, upstarts and traitors (as in *The Long Good Friday*), an appeal to vengeance (as in *Get Carter*). Malcolm McDowell plays the eponymous gangster (as in *Our Friends in the North* [BBC TV, 1997]), as if he were an older version of Alex in *A Clockwork Orange*, a misogynist who takes a perverted pleasure in 'the old ultra-violent'. The story opens with the release of Freddie Mays, the butcher of Mayfair (who killed a bent copper and got away with it – 'after that he was king'), who was sent down thirty years ago for a murder he did not commit.

Stephen Frears' *The Hit* (1984) cast Terence Stamp as Parker, a gangster who has grassed to the police and escaped to sanctuary in Spain. Philosophically, he accepts that at some point the past will catch up with him – his power resides in his ability to foresee and control the situation for himself once that time arrives. Braddick (John Hurt) and Myron, the rookie (Tim Roth), are sent out to retrieve him. Like *The Limey* (which explicitly uses footage of Stamp as a petty criminal in Ken Loach's 1967 *Poor Cow* to establish the character's 'past'), *The Hit* and *Gangster No. 1* are deliberate and reflexive in their casting. Ray Winstone, as Gary Dove, 'Gal', in *Sexy Beast* (Jonathan Glazer, 2001) could be the biker-boy from *Quadrophenia* or the borstal-boy from *Scum* (1979), now grown-up and reformed, settled to a life of domestic and conjugal bliss (the loveable rogue of *Fanny and Elvis* [Kay Mellor, 1999]) in an isolated villa on Spain's Costa del Crime. Here he stretches out poolside, watches the sun go down and takes pot shots at wild rabbits … and misses. When Don Logan (Ben Kingsley, a long way from Attenborough's 1982 *Gandhi*) is despatched to enlist him for one last job, Gal is determined to resist but his best friends Aitch and Jackie (Cavan Kendall and Julianne White) know that refusal and resignation from the fraternity is not an advisable option if he wants to save himself and his wife Deedee (Amanda Redman). Don ('a nutter' even more psyched-up and scary than gangster no. 1 and Falklands veteran Eddie in *Charlie Bright* [Phil Daniels again]) is unconcerned when the house-boy attempts to intervene. He goads Gal, taunting him with Deedee's past and Jackie's infidelity (he boasts that she has been his kinky lover): this wanton killer (who acts outside the law) nevertheless has very fixed and strict ideas of the rightness and wrongness of other people's behaviour. Far from the bonhomie of *Lock, Stock* and *Snatch*, here there is little trust and honour amongst thieves – just fear. Rather than competing with others (Freddie for gangster no. 1 is an object of lust and loathing), Gal's battle is to overcome his own demons, to bury them and start again. *Sexy Beast* is self-consciously stylish and darkly comic, but ultimately less in awe of East End lawlessness than its Ritchie precursors. It suggests, too (as does Mike Hodges' 1999 *Croupier*) that the 'respectability' of the City and the West End (through the figure of Harry [James Fox]) is itself deeply implicated: if Gal is living in luxury as a result of his illicit gains, then so are others, much nearer to home.

• **Plate 9.13**
On the Costa, Gal Dove
(Ray Winstone) enjoys
the proceeds of a life of
crime in *Sexy Beast*
(Jonathan Glazer, 2001)

> **Consider recurrent aspects of scripting, casting, costume and plot which together identify gangster films as a genre (see Chapters 4 and 7). Does the style of *Lock, Stock and Two Smoking Barrels* and *Snatch* (for instance) serve to trivialise or glamorise London's gangland? Or is it just a 'lorra fun'?**

NOTES

1 With thanks to Twentieth Century Flicks, Bristol, as ever, for putting up with all the whingeing and mingeing (only more so).

FURTHER READING

Balcon, M., *Michael Balcon Presents…A Lifetime of Films*, Hutchinson, London, 1969. Balcon's memoirs of his career in the British film industry since the silent period, including the Ealing war films and Ealing comedies; he praises the contribution of the documentary film movement and persistently asserts the need for a cinema which represents Britain to itself.

Chibnall, S. and Murphy, R., *The British Crime Film*, Routledge, London, 1999. A collection of essays, including some discussion of recent East End gangsters.

Cook, P., *Fashioning the Nation: Costume and Identity in British Cinema*, British Film Institute, London 1996. Useful to read this alongside the Ellis essay in *Dissolving Views* (Higson 1996), discussing the attraction for certain audiences of

costume film and its neglect by 'serious' critics in the 1940s and in subsequent debates.

Dickinson, M. and Street, S., *Cinema and State: The Film Industry and the Government 1927–1984*, British Film Institute, London, 1985. A survey of government intervention in British cinema and relations with the American market, from the 1927 Act onwards, amply supported by reference to primary sources, covering quota 'quickies', film production during the Second World War and the Eady system thereafter.

Friedmann, L. (ed.), *British Cinema and Thatcherism: Fires Were Started*, UCL Press, London, 1993. An anthology of essays covering aspects of British cinema in the 1980s: the discussion of films addressing the Troubles in Northern Ireland and Andrew Higson's comments on heritage cinema (subsequently revised, but typical of much contemporaneous criticism) are especially recommended.

Frith, S., *Music for Pleasure*, London, Routledge, 1988. Recommended here for the articles on Gracie Fields as singer and film star.

Geraghty, C., *British Cinema in the Fifties*, London, Routledge, 2000. An appraisal of common themes in postwar cinema and the representation of social shifts in the period.

Gledhill, C., *Reframing British Cinema*, 1918–1928, London, British Film Institute, 2003. The most comprehensive analysis to date of British cinema of the 1920s, covering many neglected directors (such as Cutts and Elvey) in addition to Hitchcock, relations of stage to screen, silent stars (such as Novello, Balfour and Brody) and recurrent themes.

Guinness, A., *My Name Escapes Me*, Penguin, Harmondsworth, 1997. 'A retiring actor's diary' (with an introduction by Le Carré), which occasionally indicates a characteristic distaste for Hollywood-style stardom.

Higson, A. (ed.), *Dissolving Views: Key Writings on British Cinema*, Cassell, London, 1996. A collection of essays. Of most interest here are Charles Barr's 'Hitchcock's British Films Revisited', Tim Bergfelder's essay on German film technicians in Britain in the 1930s, John Ellis' essay on film criticism of the 1940s, Terry Lovell's and Andrew Higson's essays on the British New Wave and Sarita Malik's 'Black British Film of the 1980s and 1990s'.

Higson, A. and Ashby, J. (eds), *British Cinema: Past and Present*, Routledge, London, 1996. A collection of essays, arranged chronologically, covering British sound cinema: see especially the discussion of radio stars in film of the 1930s and discussion of the representation of public and personal histories in film and television of the 1980s and 1990s.

Higson, A. and Maltby, R. (eds), *Film Europe Film America*, Exeter University Press, Exeter, 2000. An excellent collection of essays dealing with exchanges between Europe and America in the silent and early sound periods, making useful comparisons to current debates.

Hill, J., *British Cinema in the 1980s*, Clarendon Press, Oxford, 1999. Especially useful for its discussion of 'the state of the nation' film in the 1980s film policy and the foundation of Channel 4.

Low, R., *Film Making in 1930s Britain*, George Allen & Unwin, London, 1985.

—— *The History of the British Film*, Routledge, London, 1997. Low's exhaustive survey of British cinema, begun in the 1940s, is still invaluable.

Monk, C. and Sargeant, A. (eds), *British Historical Cinema*, Routledge, London, 2002. A collection of essays discussing history proper and the historical on film: see, especially, Claire Monk's interpretation of the heritage debate, Fidelma Farley's discussion of David Lean's *Ryan's Daughter* and Nick Cull's discussion of historical *Carry On* films.

Murphy, R. (ed.), *British Cinema of the 90s*, British Film Institute, London, 1999. Useful for coverage of the new 'gallery' films of the decade, its box-office successes (*Trainspotting*, *The Full Monty* etc.) and the revival of gangsters.

—— (ed.), *The British Cinema Book*, British Film Institute, London, 2001. A comprehensive, chronologically arranged collection: see, especially, Lawrence Napper's reappraisal of 'quota quickies' and Allen Eyle's essay on exhibition and the cinema-going experience.

Palmer, J. and Riley, M., *The Films of Joseph Losey*, Cambridge University Press, Cambridge, 1993. Useful for interview material, with Losey describing his exile and subsequent film-making in Britain.

Rotha, P., *Celluloid: The Film Today*, Longmans, Green & Co., London, 1933.

—— *The Film till Now*, Vision, London, 1949. Rotha admits his own 'high-brow' prejudices in film criticism and, with the exception of the documentary film movement, finds little to praise in British cinema of the 1930s (preferring, in general, the 'art cinema' of Europe).

Truffaut, F., *Hitchcock*, Secker & Warburg, London, 1967. A series of interviews conducted with Hitchcock by Truffaut while he was dedicated to promoting the 'politique des auteurs' (see Chapter 12), including his work in Britain, of which he is often obligingly disparaging.

Walker, A., *Hollywood, England: The British Film Industry in the Sixties*, Harrap, London, 1974. An extensive journalistic survey of American involvement in Britain and British production (including the Bond series), largely based on interviews with key personnel.

FURTHER VIEWING

Futher viewing is mentioned within the chapter.

RESOURCE CENTRES

The British Film Institute and National Film and Television Archive, and its collection of Special Materials (Stephen Street, London WC1) is not the only place at which to conduct research, but it is the main place. The British Library (Newspapers) at Colindale, London NW9 holds an excellent selection of trade and fan press (such as *The Bioscope* and *Motion Picture Studio*), some of which is also available in local public libraries (Manchester is especially good). John Rylands Library, Manchester, holds archives covering the work of Basil Dean and Robert Donat, amongst others; the Theatre Museum study room (London WC1) and the Theatre Collection, University of Bristol, hold material relating to actors and (in the latter case) runs of such journals as *Picturegoer*, while the University of East Anglia (Norwich) is currently busy indexing *Kinematograph Weekly*. The University of Exeter holds the collection of books, journals, memorabilia and much else amassed by the director Bill Douglas, while the University of Stirling holds material pertaining to the work of the director Lindsay Anderson.

Regional Film Archives (for instance, the South East Film and Video Archive in Brighton and the Welsh Film Archive in Aberystwyth) are excellent sources, as is the British Pathé collection (London NW1) for newsreel and cinemagazine material.

Indian cinema[1]

Lalitha Gopalan

■ Indian cinema

INTRODUCTION

Even the most casual tourist in India resorts to hyperbole to describe the potency of this cinema that produces a thousand films in more than twelve languages each year. For the uninitiated, most commentators will list implausible twists and turns in plots, excessive melodrama, loud song and dance sequences, and lengthy narrative as having tremendous mass appeal but little critical value. For instance, in his travelogue *Video Nights in Kathmandu*, Pico Iyer declares in a significant synecdoche that spills over its own rhetoric: 'Indian movies were India, only more so' (Iyer 1998). Other writers, such as Salman Rushdie, Alan Sealy and Farrukh Dhondy, have used various aspects of Indian film culture to spin fabulous narratives of success and failure, stardom and political life, love and villainy (Rushdie 1988; Sealy 1990; Dhondy 1990). Although the national audience has been its main address, Indian popular cinema or '**Bollywood**' has long travelled across the world – the former Soviet Union, Latin America, Africa and Southeast Asia – entertaining audiences whose personal histories bear few ties to the subcontinent.[2] Sometimes, these travel routes are visible on video copies – Arabic subtitles on Hindi films, Malay on Tamil films – telling us of a global set of viewers who watch other national cinemas besides Hollywood. More recently, *Newsweek* reported that Japan is spellbound by Tamil films, especially those starring Rajnikanth, because 'Indian films are filled with the classical entertainment movies used to offer' (*Newsweek International* 1999).[3] In Britain, Indian films are steadily enjoying a cross-over audience which includes the diaspora as well as film-curious non-Indians: Star City, located outside Birmingham, opened on 26 July 2000 and is apparently the largest multiplex in Britain, with thirty screens of which six show Bollywood movies. Over the last two years four Indian films have entered the UK top 20 on release: *Dil Se* (1998), *Kuch Kuch Hota Hai* (1998), *Biwi Number One* (1999) and *Hum Dil de Chuke Sanam* (1999). In June 2000 the Indian equivalent of the Oscar ceremony was held in the Dome in London, hosted by the Indian Miss World, Yukta Mookhey.[4] Besides the exhibition of these films characterised by a sensory excess, a range of extra-filmic events encourages us to read beyond the textual operations of individual films, cinematic aesthetics spilling into adjacent consumer economies. It is now commonplace to find the loyal Indian diaspora cultivating appreciation by sponsoring stage shows of film stars, events that read popular films as star-studded texts.

Bollywood
Bombay, the film capital of India.

It is important to note, however, that these descriptions of excess cohere most intimately to popular cinema and not the other styles that include alternative, 'parallel', middle and documentary cinemas that also inhabit the cinematic landscape in India albeit in a struggling manner. More on this later. Although it has become common to bunch together all popular Indian films under the term 'Bollywood', it is important to note that often the production of popular Tamil and Telugu films outpaces that of Hindi, each producing about 150–200 films a year, in addition to a steady crop of films from Bengal, Kerala, Maharashtra, Gujarat and Punjab that also populate the regional markets. Among the three largest producers, the Tamil industry is located in Chennai, the Telugu in Hyderabad and Chennai, and Hindi films are produced in Bombay, Hyderabad and Chennai, each marked by its own star system, director, technicians and musicians with occasional cross-over from one industry to another: Malayalam cinematographers working on Tamil and Hindi films, Bengali or Marathi directors directing Hindi films, and so on. Such a rich and varied national cinema requires a life time to understand its various contours, thus in this chapter we will limit our area of study to popular films produced in the 1980s and 1990s and to Hindi, Tamil, and diaspora productions. The task here is to understand and evaluate the form and address of popular Indian cinema so that even a rank outsider can appreciate its appeal. Such a focus reverses the standard study of national cinemas where all too often we are encouraged and even expected to understand the political, social and cultural movements of the nation and region before we can approach the films themselves. Among the many grand histories of Indian cinema, a couple of useful books spring to mind: Barnouw and Krishnaswamy's *Indian Film* (1980) offers a masterful introduction to the world of Indian cinema with its detailed history of cinema in India to the 1970s, while Yves Thoraval's *The Cinemas of India* (2000) offers an updated version of this grand sweep. Their comprehensiveness and thoroughness provide a useful reference point. but it is impossible for a novice to counter their observations without undertaking similarly extensive archival research. On the other hand, this chapter suggests that an understanding of the form of Indian cinema as a 'cinema of interruptions' allows us to understand the histories of production and reception, albeit in a less sweeping manner. Using case studies to highlight the various critical debates in the study of Indian cinema, this chapter guides the reader through different reading strategies to come to terms with the varying contextual parameters that allow one to understand this national cinematic style within the economy of global cinematic styles.

PRODUCTION AND RECEPTION CONDITIONS

However expansive the influence of cinema, Indian film-makers are acutely aware that most films fail at the box-office. Their financial anxieties have increased in recent years with the rise of adjacent entertainment industries that threaten to diminish the power of films, even if cinema as an institution is not waning in the public imagination. Trade papers from the 1980s record industry fears of the growing video industry that many worried would eventually discourage audiences from going to the cinema. Nevertheless, the arrival in India of video shops also exposed the film-going public to world cinemas, an opportunity afforded previously only by film festivals and film societies. Suddenly films from other parts of Asia, Europe and America were easily available. Film-makers were also very much part of this video-watching public, freely quoting and borrowing cinematic styles: for instance, director Ram Gopal Varma started his career as owner of a video shop. While a section of the urban rich retreated to their homes, trade papers reported an increase in film attendance in small towns and villages. Instead of assuming that one mode of watching would give way to the next evolutionary stage, we now find films coexisting alongside a robust video economy and satellite cable television. Ironically, both cable television and video shops are also responsible for renewing nostalgia for older films. Together, these different visual media have changed reception conditions by creating an audience which have developed a taste for global-style action films while simultaneously cherishing fondness for the particularities of Indian cinema.

In addition to video and satellite saturation of the visual field, American films (sometimes dubbed into Hindi) started reappearing in Indian theatres after a new agreement was signed between the Government of India and Motion Picture Producers and Distributors of America, Inc. (MPPDA) in April 1985, ending the trade embargo that began in 1971 (Pendakur 1985, 1990). Initially, Indian film-makers protested against this invasion, but slowly reconciled themselves to the foreign presence after recognising that American films did not in fact pose a threat to Indian film distribution.[5] Occasionally we find characters in Indian films taking pot-shots at American cinema: in Ram Gopal Varma's *Satya* (1998), protagonists purposely misread *Jurassic Park* (1993) as a horror film starring lizards; in Tamil films, cross-linguistic puns abound around James Cameron's *Titanic* (1997). These playful engagements with American culture confidently acknowledge that Indian cinema audiences belong to a virtual global economy where films from different production sites exist at the *same level* – a democratisation of global **cinephilia**. Perhaps I am

cinephilia
The notion of cinephilia refers to an intense love of, even obsession with, cinema. It implies both a way of watching and a way of speaking about film beyond the standard relationship between cinema and its spectator. Cinephiles are people who, in Andrew Sarris' phrase, 'love cinema beyond all reason', and who engage with film in highly specific ways.

exaggerating the dominance of Indian cinema, but the confidence of some Indian film-makers does hold out hopes for unsettling the inequalities of the global market-place where we are all too aware of American films unilaterally expanding into newer territories.

Although economic liberalisation opened Indian markets to a range of television programmes and videos, it also facilitated, however slowly, access to state-of-the-art film technology for film-makers. Within the industry there have been discernible changes in the production process. According to Manmohan Shetty, who runs a film-processing business, Adlabs, a sea change occurred in 1978 when Kodak introduced a negative film that could be processed at high ambient temperatures (105° Fahrenheit), improving colour resolution (Shetty 1994). At about the same time, professionally trained technicians in editing, cinematography and lighting began entering the commercial industry from film institutes in Pune and Chennai, vastly improving the quality of film production as well as increasing costs. Manjunath Pendakur (1985) notes that the rising costs of production since the 1980s not only includes huge salaries for film stars, but also higher wages for directors and technicians. Audiences seem attuned to these changes on screen. In Chennai, crowds get hysterical when cinematographer P.C. Sriram's name runs across the screen; directors have fan supported web sites competing with those on movie stars.

The profusion of film-making talent strengthened the Malayalam, Tamil and Telugu industries. Since 1979, film production in Tamil and Telugu has continued to keep pace with Hindi films, each producing about 140 films annually.[6] Increased production from regional industries has weakened the stronghold of Hindi films as the largest commercial industry in the nation while improvements in dubbing facilities has ensured a national audience for Tamil and Telugu films. Additionally, film-makers from the south such as S. Shankar, Sashilal Nair, Priyadarshan, Mani Ratnam and Ram Gopal Varma have been making inroads into the Hindi film industry, once a prerogative of female stars (Chopra 1997). The migration of directors also means that narratives focusing on national themes – intercommunal love stories, war and terrorism – are no longer a prerogative of Hindi cinema, but also surface in regional cinemas. Concurrently, narratives in Hindi films have receded from national-secular themes addressing an urban audience, dabbling instead with regional stories resonating with preoccupations of the Hindi belt: Rajputs, Biharis and Punjabis now crowd the Hindi film screen.

Technical and aesthetic improvements in mainstream Indian cinema remind us that commercial film-makers have benefited from narrative experiments introduced in 1970s by independent film-makers. Consciously setting themselves apart from commercial cinema, films by Adoor Gopalkrishnan, G. Aravindan, Mrinal Sen, Girish Kasarvalli, Kumar Shahini and Mani Kaul focused on social and political antagonisms to narrate their tales of disappointment with the post-colonial state, while conveying hopes for a different society.[7] Screened at film societies or special shows in large movie theatres, their films drew the urban élite to movie theatres and shaped film-viewing habits by encouraging the audience to focus more on the screen. A substantial number of commercial films made in the late 1980s borrowed from these film-making practices while continuing to improve on conventions of entertainment. Not unlike independent cinema, we now find directors gaining currency as auteurs in commercial cinema, controlling the production of their films and marking them with an unique cinematic style. In turn, the National Film Development Corporation (NFDC the state body that finances independent films) started producing films which extensively incorporated mainstream stories and stars.

Further, Indian films have, on occasion, internationalised the production process: S. Shankar's Tamil film *Kaadalan / Lover* (1994), for example, polished its special effects in a Hong Kong film studio. Critics rightly focus on the film's playful commentary on upper-caste hegemony and its attendant economies of taste, but we cannot ignore how globalisation of the production process also influences this narrative of caste contestations (Dhareshwar and Niranjana 1996). The more conventional figuration of the world in Indian popular cinema – song and dance sequences set in foreign locales – is not only spruced up to arouse the spectator's interests in tourism, but also aggressively participates in the movement of global capital. These sequences not only bring the world home, they also acknowledge a loyal audience abroad that wishes to see its own stories of migrations and displacement written into these films. A number of Hindi films – *Pardes* (1997), *Dilwale Dulhaniya Le Jayange* (1995), *Dil to Pagal Hai* (1998), *Kuch Kuch Hota Hai* (1998) – index an audience straggling between national identities, harbouring longings for an original home or possessing the capital for tourism. Considered together, these narrative and production details place the viewer of Indian films in a global cinematic economy, finally catching up with a long history of global reception.

Since independence, Indian films have travelled to the former Soviet Union, Latin America, Africa and Southeast Asia, entertaining audiences whose personal histories have few ties with the subcontinent. However, it is film-makers in the diaspora who have been openly engaging with, and in the process teaching us a lesson or two in defamiliarising Indian film conventions. In both Srinivas Krishna's Canadian production *Masala* (1992) and Gurinder Chadda's British film *Bhaji on the Beach* (1994), we find lengthy quotations from Indian cinema: protagonists express desire by resorting to song and dance sequences. Inserted in films working with small budgets and relying on art-house distribution, such sequences serve as fabulous strands expressing immigration fantasies borne out of travel and displacement. In a more abrupt manner, Rachid Bouchareb's French-Algerian film *My Family's Honor* (1997) uses Hindi film songs on the soundtrack and even splices an entire musical number from *Hum Kisise Kum Nahin / We Are Number One* (1977) into his narrative on North African immigrants living in France. Displaying no diegetic link to the narrative, the jarring disjunction of this sequence conveys the disruption brought through immigration and displacement in Bouchareb's film. Terry Zwigoff's *Ghost World* (2000), narrating traumas of the summer after high school, opens with a song and dance sequence 'Jab Jaan Pechachan / When we got to know each other' from *Gumnaam* (1965), intercutting with the main narrative. The feverish cabaret and twist number offers the bored teenager the requisite degree of exotic abandon. Baz Luhrmann confesses to not only having seen Indian popular films but being mesmerised enough to deploy several song and dance sequences in his recent film *Moulin Rouge* (2000). Benny Torathi's Israeli film *Desparado Piazza*, also called *Piazza of Dreams* (2000), splices a song sequence from *Sangam* (1964) to map a different history of migration for ethnic Jews.[8] All these films celebrate these interruptions as a way of accounting for cinephilia even when the protagonists have to adjust to arduous conditions imposed through transnational migration, ennui-ridden teenagers or a courtesan's love story. These unexpected sites of reception allow us to see, from without, how Indian films are available for a wide range of readings, including camp and cult possibilities, based on their multi-plot narratives and multiple disruptions.

For further discussion of Moulin Rouge *as an example of a film breaking genre conventions, see Chapter 4, pp. 161–163.*

Check your local papers for theatres showing Indian films in your town or city and invite a friend to go with you on an opening night. Describe in detail the entire visit including standing in the queue for a ticket, the trailers, audience reaction to stars and songs, the conversation during the interval and so on. As a comparative project, visit your local theatre for a showing of a popular British or American film.

□ CASE STUDY 1: *MONSOON WEDDING* (MIRA NAIR, 2002)

• **Plate 10.1**
Wall poster for *Monsoon Wedding* (Mira Nair, 2000).

A procession of colour, a clutch of garrulous Punjabis and a loving family crowd, Mira Nair's box-office success has emerged as the most successful Indian film to have cross-over appeal, as well as winning the Golden Lion Award at the 2001 Venice International Film Festival. Rumours have circulated that the wedding decor in the film has been imitated by non-resident Indians in the diaspora. Undoubtedly, Nair was aware of the appeal of the wedding film to audiences worldwide – *Four Weddings and a Funeral* (Mike Newell, 1994), *Hum Aap Ke Hain Koun*, *Dilwale dulhania le jayenge (DDLG)*, and so on that include the doubtful bride, a cheating groom and a chorus of relatives whose own tribulations and desires make the wedding a sideshow. This film is no different, with the wedding as the central event, but in this the bride, Aditi, and groom, Hemant, are not the main draw in the film: the bride's parents Pimmi and Lalit exhibit an 'old-shoe' affection as Nair puts in it an interview; the bride's cousin Ria who is the same age faces her demons of sexual abuse at the family gathering; the bride's trysts with her older lover; her teenage brother whose voracious appetite for cooking casts aspersions on his masculinity; and a sideshow of uncles, aunts and cousins whose own desires criss-cross with others during the days before the wedding. While the upper-class, globally conscious Punjabi family holds centre stage in the film, Nair reels into it the budding romance and eventual union of the event manager, Dube, and the maid, Alice.

In the official web site for the film, Nair acknowledges her homage to Bollywood style, particularly the songs from old films on the soundtrack, Dube's floral tribute to Alice as a nod to Raj Kapoor's *Shree 420* and the incorporation of song and dance sequences as part of the wedding festivities. It is worth noting, however, that Nair also engages with the small-film idea that has taken over film production with the advent of digital video, largely inspired by the low-budget aesthetics of the Dogma group. In fact, *Monsoon Wedding* seems to bear a structural similarity to *Festen / Celebration* (Thomas Vinterberg, 1998). In other words, the film's scale and its lack of obvious stars casts it as a small film incorporating particular elements from different world cinemas.

Having located Nair's film within the wedding genre, albeit in various global locations, it is useful to frame our reading of the film in terms of the discussion that has
developed on this genre in Hindi cinema in the mid-1990s. In a productive reading of
two such films produced in the mid 1990s – *Dilwale Dulhania le jayegne* (*DDLJ*) and
Pardes – Patricia Uberoi (1998) suggests we consider the aspirations of the Indian
middle class, both within the nation and in the diaspora, that wishes to retain a certain
configuration of Indian values while embracing the options offered by the global marketplace. Even if you haven't seen these particular films, you can imagine a series of
conflicts: tradition versus modernity; arranged versus love marriages; individual desires
versus familial obligations and so on. Uberoi suggests that these films offer the
'arranged love marriage' as the ideal, 'a style of matchmaking whereby a romantic
choice already made is endorsed, *post facto*, by parental approval and treated thereafter like an "arranged marriage"'. What Uberoi attends to in these films is the particular
problematisation of these various issues and their resolution, a framework that is
equally useful for our purposes here.

1   Describe the different signs of globalisation in *Monsoon Wedding*. How
    does the film introduce them and tackle them? Attempt to differentiate
    between elements of globalisation and modernisation in the film.
2   In a similar vein, note the different ways in which India and Indianness are
    signalled in this film. For instance, how does the film present and resolve
    Aditi's choice in the film?
3   Viewing the different intercutting sequences describe the differences
    between the two couples: Aditi and Hemant, and Dube and Alice. Why
    does the film feel the need to elaborate the romance between Dube and
    Alice? Pay close attention to Alice's identity. Where would you place
    Dube's class identity?
4   How does the film employ the song and dance sequences and to what
    end?
5   The official web site for the film points out that besides the various
    matchmaking attempts in the narrative, the film is an adoring tribute to
    Delhi. How does the film achieve this?
6   As in *Festen* (1998), here too the narration of sexual abuse of children
    breaks the familial revelry. How does the film choose to resolve the ques-
    tion of incest. In other words, describe the film's ideology in terms of
    maintaining familial relationship.

WRITING ON INDIAN CINEMA

Within India, critical writing on cinema has blossomed in the last two decades, reporting
a serious, sometimes cinephiliac, relationship to films. Published from Bangalore, *Deep
Focus* combines interviews with directors from different regions of the world, film
reviews and lengthy critical pieces. *Cinemaya*, based in Delhi, follows the festival
schedule in Asia, brings its readers news of the latest films and interviews with directors, and addresses a pan-Asian audience from Turkey to Japan. These two magazines
locate Indian cinema, both popular and alternative, and its audience, within a global
network of cinematic styles.

The short-lived *Splice*, published from Calcutta, had an exclusive focus on alternative cinematic practices and excavated the correspondences between avant-garde
practices in India and those from the former socialist republics. For a brief moment,

Splice was an integral part of a blooming film scene in Calcutta which now includes a film archive at Nandan and a brand-new film studies department at Jadavpur University. The recently launched *Journal of Moving Images* from the Department of Film Studies at Jadavpur addresses an emerging academic audience. Published by the Film and Television Institute of India (FTII) Pune, *Lensight* addresses film-makers with reports on state-of-the-art lab-processing techniques, editing equipment and cameras while also carrying lengthy interviews with film-makers on their craft. Although pitched exclusively to film-makers, *Lensight* carries a wealth of information on sociological conditions of production that are not widely available to a film critic.

Finally, publication of the *Encyclopaedia of Indian Cinema* (1994, with a revised edition in 1999) stamped the scholarly seal of approval on Indian cinema. Expansive in its scope, Ashish Rajadhyaksha and Paul Willemen's opus strings together biographies, film lists and plot summaries, providing a road map of the different features of Indian cinema, from genres to independent film movements and regional cinemas.

The emergence of a field of Indian Film Studies against this backdrop has made it possible for critics to steer away from large-scale histories of the 'national cinema' towards more intensive readings of films and cinematic institutions. Although I will focus here on these different theoretical paradigms that privilege textual analysis, it is useful to be aware of the burgeoning field of extra-cinematic studies that combine ethnographic fieldwork and archival work to look at non-filmic objects. For instance, S.V. Srinivas's careful study of fan clubs of Telugu, argues persuasively for a critical study of reception and not just close textual analysis of individual films (Srinivas 2000). Sara Dickey's ethnographic study of fan clubs in the South Indian town of Madurai and Steve Derne's study of film-going practices in the North Indian town Shimla similarly provide us with a textured analysis of extra-filmic institutions (Dickey 1993; Derne 2000). Rachel Dwyer's reading of the popular star-zine *Stardust* urges us to consider the discourse of stardom as a mode of understanding the popularity of films (Dwyer 2000).

These disparate details form the bedrock of material changes in the production and reception of Indian popular cinema. Spelling out these details undercuts a series of archaic oppositions that we find steadfastly held in the arena of film studies: between national and international cinemas overlooking alternative routes of film distribution; between Hollywood and other national cinemas casting the latter as bad copies instead of examining them as rejoinders to a hegemonic cinema; between national and regional cinemas, placing Hindi cinema at the helm of the national imaginary and ignoring a simultaneous move towards regional nationalisms; between national and global audiences by not anticipating audiences who also endow Indian popular cinema with meaning that exceeds its own intended horizon of address; between art and commercial cinema, repeating a high modernist division between high and low cultures without admitting to a more varied terrain of taste. Naming these mobile processes speaks to a post-colonial condition that according to Stuart Hall marks a 'critical interruption into that whole grand historiographical narrative which, in liberal historiography and Weberian historical sociology, as much as in the dominant traditions of Western Marxism, gave this global dimension a subordinate presence in a story which could essentially be told from within European parameters' (Hall 1996: 250).

GENRE AND FORM

For further discussion of Hollywood and genre see Chapter 4, pp. 151–169.

Some clarification of the concept of film genre is in order before I launch into particularities of Indian cinema. Identified as a narrative form developed by classical Hollywood commercial cinema, film theorists have developed a barrage of theoretical and methodological tools to understand the narrative structure, cinematic specificity and viewer's relationship to genre films. For instance, cinematic genres are differentiated by iconography: frontier landscapes in a western; city spaces in gangster films. At other times, we understand how genre verisimilitude derives from details in the mise-en-scène: monsters in horror films and horses in a western. Genre theory continues to benefit from psychoanalytical theories by allowing us to see how our viewing pleasures are dictated by a structuring of repetition and difference in films. Research on advertising and distribution practices of Hollywood films reveals that film producers were deeply invested in using genre categories to target and consolidate their audience: women's films, summer action films, etc. Instead of considering genre in either/or terms, Steve Neale (1980, 2000) suggests we see genre films as a dynamic among industry, films and viewers to better understand cinema as a modern commodity form. In a recent book on American genre films and theory, Rick Altman (1999) proposes that far from being particular, Hollywood films are constructed as multiple, overlapping genres to reach a wider audience. Discrete genres, a predilection of critics, only surface after the fact. Whatever particular features film critics or film-makers deploy to differentiate one genre from another or to see multiple genres in one film, American genre films broadly obey certain cinematic principles perfected in classical Hollywood cinema that frame the unfolding narrative: continuity editing, omniscient narration, internally coherent diegesis and character-motivated plot.

In contrast to the internally coherent narrative form generated by Hollywood genre films, genres in Indian popular cinema display a set of features that are akin to pre-classical cinema, especially several extra-diegetic sequences or sequences of attractions. Instead of concluding that these films stage the underdeveloped aspects of capitalism in the Indian economy, a different set of concerns nurtures this narrative form, including a desire to domesticate cinematic technology and develop a national cinematic style. For instance, writing on Dadasaheb Phalke's *Raja Harishchandra* (1913), Ashish Rajadhyaksha argues that the prevalence of frontal address in this film points to how narrative strategies in early cinema borrowed from painting, theatre and traditional arts to lure the viewer into this new technological apparatus (Rajadhyaksha 1993). In a similar vein, Geeta Kapur (1987) suggests through her reading of *Sant Tukaram* (Damle /Fattelal, Marathi, 1936) that frontal address in this 'saint film' was a calculated move by film-makers to draw in viewers accustomed to watching theatre, yet the sequence of miracles mandatory in a saint film highlighted cinema's ability to produce magic. Both Kapur and Rajadhyaksha alert us to how cinema in India developed in a whirl of anti-colonial struggles that included an impulse to forge an independent cultural form by both reinterpreting tradition and making technology developed in the West indigenous.

Besides the direct address, other features of Indian popular cinemas similarly undercut the hermetic universe developed in Hollywood films, by interrupting it with song and dance sequences, comedy tracks and multi-plot narratives. Spectacular, and at times excessive, the elaboration of these attractions in this cinema has invited critics to dub them '**masala movies**' – a culinary term that seeks to define a medley of narrative strands in popular cinema. Naming the films made in the 1950s and 1960s as the 'feudal family romance', Madhava Prasad (1998) argues that this super genre asserts its dominance through narrative strategies of annexations whenever new sub-genres emerge. In short, Prasad suggests that instead of discrete genres a megalomaniac genre cannibalises the formation of sub-genres. Ravi Vasudevan (1995b), on the other hand, sees popular Hindi film as a discontinuous form that includes attractions like song and dance sequences and comedic sub-plots. Instead of skipping over these moments that either break the diegetic universe or disrupt the linear trajectory of the narrative, we must simply face the fact that the most persistent narrative form found in Indian popular cinema includes several interruptions bearing a more or less systematic relationship to the narrative. In other words, we should start heeding production details that obsess over how Indian film-makers expend considerable energy experimenting with the choreography and location of these sequences and, in the process, acknowledge how

masala movie
Spicy Indian movie overloaded with emotions.

our viewing pleasure arises from these interruptions and the novel ways in which a popular film strings together these sequences.

Identifying these interruptions encourages us to start in the reverse direction, that is, by exploring how these films experiment and fortify Indian cinematic conventions, rather than mulling over how these films are derived from Hollywood genres. Moreover, attending to these interruptions throws light on how the concept of a national cinematic style emerges at the conjuncture of state interests in quality cinema, the film industry's interests in profits and global circulation of popular cinemas. To account for how these disparate interests in production and reception shape the textual make-up of popular films, I will be looking at three different kinds of interruptions that brand the narrative form of Indian cinema: song and dance sequences, the interval and censorship.

☐ CASE STUDY 2: *SHOLAY* (RAMESH SIPPY, 1975)

More than any of the above material conditions effecting the relationship between films and their viewers, Ramesh Sippy's *Sholay / Flames* (1975) was a landmark in Indian cinema, changing forever the production and reception of popular cinema. Coinciding with the state of emergency declared by Prime Minister Indira Gandhi in 1975, *Sholay* was emblematic of a slew of films feeding off what political theorists refer to as a crisis of legitimacy of the Indian state (Vanaik 1991). Film critics, media activists and film scholars agree that the unrest in civil society marked by communal riots, police brutality, violent secessionist movements and assaults against women and minorities seeped into film narratives (Das 1992). Stacked with gangsters, avenging women, brutal police and corrupt politicians, these films resolve their narratives through vigilante actions that repeatedly undercut the authority of the state (Rangoonwala 1993; Doriaswamy 1995). Activist organisations such as Delhi's Media Advocacy Group argue that representations of brutality in contemporary commercial cinema have a direct and reinforcing effect on the level of violence in civil society (The Media Advocacy Group for The National Commission for Women, n.d., 1993).[9]

However *Sholay*'s iconic status exceeds a mimetic relationship to reality, drawing in large part from its reconfiguration of the western.[10] Mixing a host of conventions from Indian popular cinema such as song and dance sequences, *Sholay* successfully

• **Plate 10.2**
Wall poster for *Sholay*
(Ramesh Sippy, 1975)

produced an Indian riposte to the classic American western. Fans of this cult film extensively quote Salim Khan and Javed Akhtar's script back to the screen; rumors abound as to the existent variations of the closing sequence; and overnight the actor Amjad Khan, who plays the villain Gabbar Singh, became one of the most popular stars in the film world. Anupama Chopra's book *Sholay: The Making of a Classic* (2000) – a requisite read for any fan – revives cinephiliac obsession with this film by journeying to its origins of production.

The film also spurred the first psychoanalytical critique of popular Indian cinema. In a much neglected essay, Madan Gopal Singh (1983) evaluates the tremendous success of this film by picking one scene as a symptom of the changing relationship between screen and spectator: the 'Mehbooba! Mehbooba!' song and dance sequence. According to Singh, in this sequence the camera gropes the dancer's body and, by extension, provides us with a point of view that was hitherto unavailable in popular Hindi cinema. Singh uses voyeurism as a conceptual tool to describe the altered relationship between screen and spectator in the film, an idea that draws extensively from certain cinematic principles found in Hollywood – omniscient narration, continuity editing, internally coherent narrative and the ideal spectator's identification with the camera – leading to the argument that the camera's groping mechanism fragments the female dancer's body and generates viewing pleasure. But he glosses over the fact that song and dance sequences explicitly distract the viewer from narrative flow and go against conventions of continuity editing. Overtly exhibitionistic, song and dance sequences break codes of realism that psychoanalytical voyeurism relies upon.[11] Nevertheless, Singh's cryptic formulation prods us to consider how even the most superficial and entertaining song and dance sequences carries an ideological charge, heightening our viewing pleasure.[12]

For further discussion of the relationship between film and the spectator, see Chapter 3.

Singh's essay also tells another story, a story of the intellectual context of his critical engagement with Hindi films. Originally published in the avant-garde *Journal of Arts and Ideas*, Singh's essay echoes the opinions of alternative film-makers such as Kumar Shahini, Mani Kaul and John Abraham all of whom were writing and making a different kind of narrative cinema. Accounting for the hegemonic potential of Hindi commercial cinema, especially its ability to throttle radical film-making, Singh bemoans the loss of freshly minted student film-makers from the Film and Television Institute of India (FTII) to the commercial industry, a move, he argues, that turns them into technicians of special effects. While *Sholay* affords Singh the occasion to critically assess the ideological manifestations of the consumerist cinema, his theoretical speculations helped shape an entire generation of film theorists working on Indian cinema.[13]

For discussion of narrative and non-narrative film, see Chapter 2, pp 78–79.

In sharp contrast to Singh's critical essay, *Sholay* is a revered master text of success for film-makers: Ram Gopal Varma confesses to knowing every shot of two of his favourite films – *Sholay* and Francis Ford Coppola's *The Godfather* (1972); more recently, Rajkumar Santoshi allegedly watched *Sholay* every morning while shooting his own *China Gate* (1999) (Naseeruddin Shah, *Filmfare*, May 1998). *Sholay* is the mythical origin spurring an entire generation of film-makers to borrow from globally circulating genres yet reincorporating conventions from Indian popular cinema with great aplomb.[14] Spawning a number of B films throughout the 1980s, the full impact of Sippy's innovative cinematic style on popular Indian cinema – accommodating Indian cinematic conventions within a Hollywood genre – was fully developed a decade later by J.P. Dutta, Mani Ratnam, Mukul Anand, Ram Gopal Varma, Rajkumar Santoshi and Shekhar Kapur.

These divergent readings of *Sholay* demonstrate a gap between critics writing on popular Indian cinema and film-makers. Simply put, critics tend to take a moralistic view of mainstream cinema, seeing very little of the 'popular', while commercial film-makers see themselves as entertainers and regard critics as élitists whose opinions rarely account for the working of the industry (Thomas 1985[15]). This stand-off between critics and commercial film-makers is as old as the practice of narrative cinema itself, and has little new to add to debates on the differences between high and low, between mass and popular cultures that as cultural critics we have learned to make and then unmake. Finally we have settled on 'popular culture' as the most viable concept that absorbs the paradoxes of our trade: we can read resistance in its form, even as we continue to be mesmerised by it (MacCabe 1986). This shifty definition seems vastly superior to the polarised definitions of cultural taste plaguing readings of Indian films. There is no doubt that we learn a great deal from vigilant readings of cinema's hegemonic influence that reveal its power to affirm ethnic stereotyping, sexism and jingoism, and caution us against being taken in by its dazzling surface. But all too often we tend to pay little attention to questions of pleasure. Inasmuch as we assume that commercial films maintain the status quo, flattening all radical possibilities in their viewers, we must also admit that film-makers are constantly invested in inviting us to return to the movies through novel cinematic conventions.

Sholay exemplified the possibility of combining ever so deftly dominant genre principles developed in Hollywood films with conventions particular to Indian cinema. Recasting the linear trajectory of genre films to include several local cinematic conventions, Indian popular films often render the former illegible to the rank outsider. What I am suggesting is that it seems presumptuous to think that when Hollywood genres are appropriated by other national cinemas, we may find straightforward application of dominant genre principles instead of reading how local contexts of production and reception intervene and prevail over genre. The end product of this encounter between global and local features can, at times, be read as a subaltern response to Hollywood, a strategy forwarded by Paul Smith in his reading of Leone's 'spaghetti westerns', or we can simply read it as a riposte that simultaneously reveals how Hollywood genres are also built around certain national cinematic styles (Smith 1993).

Describe and analyse the function of the various interruptions in *Sholay*, paying close attention to the comedy tracks and their relationship to masculine friendship.

SONG AND DANCE SEQUENCES

One of the most common and popular features of Indian films are its song and dance sequences. According to Barnouw and Krishnaswamy (1980: 69), Indian talkies always had songs: the first sound feature, Ardeshir Irani's *Alam Ara / Light of the World* (1931), had over seven songs; another early Hindi film had forty songs; not to be outdone, a Tamil film is counted as having sixty. By the 1950s 'the film song had become a key to successful film promotion' (ibid.: 157). Film-makers continue to release audio tracks before the film's release and it is now widely believed that those sales alone can recover the production costs of a movie.[16] Music directors, choreographers and singers receive awards and popular memory of these sequences often surpass the film's own story. Over the years, commercial film-makers have tried experimenting with their absence with varying commercial success: K.A. Abbas' *Munna / Lost Child* (1954), the Tamil film *Antha Nal / That Day* (1954), B.R. Chopra's *Ittefaq* (1969), P.C. Sriram's *Kurudhippunal / River of Blood* (1995), Ram Gopal Varma's *Kaun / Who?* (1998) are some examples. But, since song and dance sequences guarantee a definite income, it has been difficult to dispense with them altogether. Song and dance sequences traverse radio and television, independently of the films themselves, a phenomenon encouraging critics to rush to the conclusion that they are inserted into films only as entertaining spectacles with tangential links to the narrative.

The first sound film, *Alam Ara* (1931), included seven songs, setting the standard for popular cinema. The first decade of sound witnessed a range of experiments with sound and narrative, including introducing a number of songs into films. Musicologist Bhaskar Chankravarkar (1989) names songs of one minute and forty seconds length as 'songlets' that were rarely heard outside the cinema halls, and thus are unavailable on gramophone records of the film. Referring to films such as *Indrasabha* (1931), laden with seventy-one songs, or *Kalidas* (1931), a Tamil film with fifty songs, Ashok Ranade (1981) suggests that not all of these were strictly songs but verse-in-tune flowing between prose-based dialogue and a full-blown song, a convention that he suggests emerges from oral-based cultures. Bowing to pressures from the recording industries, songs were standardised to three to four minutes, emerging as discrete moments in films, a practice that has stayed intact for the most part. According to Theodore Baskaran (1996), dramatist P. Sambanda Mudaliyar suggested that 'ideally song sequences should take about one-fourth of the film's duration'. Besides pressures from gramophone industries that promised revenues from sales of film song records, experiments in sound recording including pre-recorded song and lip-synching by playback singers, encouraged the consolidation of film songs as distinct modules. Overseeing the composition of lyrics, managing an orchestra and choosing playback singers fortified the role of the music director.[17] Allegedly Nitin Bose's *Dhoop Chaon* (1935) was the first film systematically to use playback singing under the helm of music director R.C. Boral.[18] Film historians and musicologists suggest that the popularity and persistence of film songs points to Indian cinema's early links to conventions of nineteenth-century Parsi theatre as well as folk theatre which were similarly strung together with a number of songs. Besides these theatrical origins, Chandravarkar and Ranade point to a confluence of musical influences in the hybrid film song: Indian classical, folk, and Western tunes (Chandravarkar 1989). In recent years, in addition to star music directors, choreographers such as Prabhu Deva, Saroj Khan, Farah Khan and others have been asserting their presence by grafting together Indian dance styles with Western dance moves.

Although musicologists have written extensively on the synthetic quality of Indian film songs, on the parallel economy of star music directors and singers, there is an absence of literature on song sequences, lending support to the assumption that the sequences are extra-diegetic or, in narratological terms, achronies, outside the temporal reckoning of the narrative.[19] A flamboyant example of such an instance occurs in S. Shankar's *Indian* (1994), where the film abruptly cuts from Madras to Australia as the preferred setting for the 'Melbourne' song and dance. Declaiming such practices, Baskaran writes: 'The flow of the film would not be affected in the least if song sequences were excised, wholly or partly' (1996: 48). However, indulgent song and dance sequences remain, and a close analysis of this interruption begs us to explore how they relate to the narrative time of different kinds of films.

In addition to attending to the ways in which song and dance interrupt the narrative in various ways, the iconography of these sequences of attractions calls our attention to other interests that bolster a spectator's interests in Indian cinema. For instance, the abrupt cut to exotic locations sparks the tourist interests of the viewer and similarly the object-laden mise-en-scène endorses consumerism. Not unlike the commercial imperative towards product placement in contemporary American cinema, song and dance sequences draw in a whole host of adjacent economies such tourism and consumerism that are not so easily compartmentalised in Indian cinema. There is no doubt that the presence of several such sequences is reminiscent of a cinema of attractions found in Early Cinema where the spectacular aspects of such a scene override narrative coherence. Even in their most exhibitionistic form, when their presence rarely furthers the narrative and its 'undatedness' or achrony is most visible in their ability to circulate as self-contained segments on music television or film previews, their iconography remains available for a wide range of ideological readings.[20] But they also solicit our interests as tourists, albeit virtual tourists travelling the world within the closed confines of the movie

Although not a heterosexual love story, this first film by Forhan Akhtar focuses on the friendship between three men – Sameer, Aakash and Siddharth – assumes the form of a love story. Akhtar is no stranger to the film world, having an accomplished father, Javed Akhtar, a scriptwriter and poet who wrote the catchy songs in this film, and a mother, Honey Irani, who has moved from child star to scriptwriter. Of course, pedigree alone does not account for the success of the film which captures the lives of the three upper-class boys in the period after college graduation. The conventional battles with traditional parents or parents insisting on finding the right girl for their sons are rendered inconsequential; in fact, the parents appear to be supportive, mildly admonishing and even indulgent of their sons' development into men. Given that the narrative does not seek to displace conflicts on to the parental generation, the precipitating crisis in the film is the friendship among the three and the ways in which it is affected by their erotic development. As in most heterosexual narratives, here too women interfere and force changes in what is often perceived as a stable economy between men, a narrative conceit that has tremendous play in westerns and gangster films.[22] In a provocative reading of this film Kimberly Ringler uses Corey Creekmur's essay, 'Acting Like a Male: Masculine Performances in My Darling Clementine', which extends Sedgwick's reading of the relationship between compulsory heterosexuality and homophobia, to argue that the mise-en-scène in this film suggests, yet at the same time disavows, the possibility of an erotic union between the three men (Ringler 2002). For instance, Ringler suggests that the film employs doors to ward off intimacy between men, at the same time suggesting the possibility of a homosexual union between them. Ringler's reading encourages us to consider the mise-en-scène as a rich site to mine for erotic desire, class aspirations, national longings, etc.

For discussion of lesbian and gay cinema, see Chapter 8.

1 Describe and analyse the relationship between the song and dance sequences and the narrative in the film. Do they serve as distractions, delaying devices, or are they totally dispensable?

2 Choose at least two song and dance sequences – 'Woh ladki hai kahan?' and 'Dil Chahta Hai' for instance – to discuss the meaning of the mise-en-scène and editing. Do supplement your readings with interviews culled from the official DVD with the music directors and choreographers, as ways of understanding the discourse of production.

3 How does the film describe Siddharth's relationship with Tara? Why do you think it casts her as an alcoholic and finally kills her?

4 Re-watch the closing sequence of the film and frame your analysis in terms of Sedgwick's formulation of compulsory heterosexuality.

INTERVAL

The 'interval' is the ten-minute break in every Indian popular film taking place after eighty minutes of film screening. Lights are turned on, the projector is turned off and viewers step out of the theatre to smoke a cigarette, eat a snack or visit the bathroom. Unlike the strong imprint of song and dance sequences in the film-going experience, the location of the interval remains an elusive detail in the memory of even the most avid film-viewer. It is simply seen as a brief respite from the long screening. Trade papers, however, make passing references to which halves of the film were more, or less, interesting.

According to Theodore Baskaran, a historian of Tamil cinema, intervals have existed since the early 1930s when the feature film as a genre took root.[23] The term arises, in part, from the early years of film exhibition, when the constraints of working with a single projector would force the projectionist to stop the film more than once, in effect producing two or three intervals. Besides the whims of the projectionist, Baskaran notes that the films themselves referred overtly to this break in the narrative: in *Apoorva Sagodrigal / Strange Friends* (1949) a song and dance sequence set in a garden ends with the word 'Edivali' ('Interval' in Tamil) strung together by flowers dropping from the trees; and in *Velaikkari / Servant* (1949), Mani, one of the protagonists, conspires a plan which he gestures will take place later – after the interval. Baskaran speculates that intervals probably persisted to pace the narrative which was laden with at least a dozen songs, a feature that he thinks has retained this cinema in a primitive stage of film-making beholden to attractions.

The interval weighs in as a crucial punctuation, adjusting both opening and closing strategies of the film, in effect, producing two opening and closing sequences in every Indian film. As in the song and dance sequences, the interval is not randomly located but regulated by genre constraints and directorial style. Breaking the spell of the dark auditorium, the interval reminds us of Early Cinema's exhibition practices when a film was one of many instalments of the evening's entertainment. In its current form, the interval is a cinematic device that organises the dose of cinematic attractions manda-tory in Indian cinema as well as serving as a punctuation mark that continually directs our anticipation in surprising ways by opening and closing certain narrative strands.

Both song and dance sequences, and the interval, attune us to their structural func-tion in popular Indian films, particularly through their play on spatial and temporal disjunctions. Their articulation in specific texts highlights how films imbibe both global and local conventions: genre films adjust to song and dance sequences while the interval doubles the structuring of anticipation and pleasure found in genre films. In each case, they call attention to interruptions in the convention of the linear narrative with a single diegesis dominant in Hollywood or other commercial industries, with their attendant assumptions of realist codes.[24] The ideal spectator of film theory, cloistered from adjacent consumer economies, surfaces as a phantom figure in Indian popular cinema; the Indian spectator, in contrast, travels several circuits of pleasures generated by a multi-diegetic narrative.[25]

There is no doubt that the location of the interval is crucial to Indian film-makers as an indispensable device to organise the narrative structure. For instance, when asked 'Do you write a screenplay, like a play, in three acts?', the scriptwriter Salim Khan responds:

For comparison with Hollywood narrative structure, see Chapter 2, pp. 54–59 and 78–83.

I need a simple nice plot in which I must have a definite beginning, a middle and a crucial end. The end must be clear in my mind and then I start working on the sub-plots and the characters. I go on developing material, then I arrange it till the interval point, and then further the progress of the story.

(*Screen*, 15 July 1988)

Sagar Sarhadi, another scriptwriter, answers similarly:

No. Normally I have two. There are two dramatic movements – the interval and the end. The screen-play is written to heighten these dramatic movements.

(*Screen*, 11 July 1988)

Unlike an arbitrary break at a the halfway point, Indian films often use the intermission as a definitive break, linking it to the opening and closing segments of a film. This distinct punctuation emerges not only as a unique marker of 'Indian' cinematic style but also locates the place of innovation and authorial style. Considered in these terms, the interval stands out as an obvious strategy to pace the narrative, and instead of rational-ising it as a moment of relief from the tedium of a long film, this unique form of cinematic punctuation is the cornerstone of inventiveness in Indian cinema, a structuring device that inflects our reading of this cinema. Since it falls between two moments in a film, I suggest that we can explore the ways in which it pilfers closing strategies usually anticipated later in the film, and, at the same time, permits narrative strands to bloom in the second half. Rearranging narrative expectations instructs us to reconsider the charge of derivativeness aimed at Indian commercial cinema, a charge that overlooks the different ways in which a film accommodates Hollywood genre features within the constellation of interruptions. Alternatively, the 'interval' seems to have seeped into films produced outside India – Stanley Kubrick's *Full Metal Jacket* (1987), Quentin Tarantino's *Pulp Fiction* (1994), Wong Kar-Wai's *Chunking Express* (1994), Milcho Manchevski's *Before the Rain* (1994), Alejandro Gonzalez Inarritu's *Amores Perros / Love's a Bitch* (2001), Marzeih Meshkini's *Roozi Khe Zan Shodam / The Day I Became a Woman* (2001) and Jeremy Podeswa's *Five Senses* (2000) appear to have hijacked the interval to heighten their narratives of disjunctions and dispersal.

GANGSTER FILMS

For a discussion of the contemporary British gangster film, see Chapter 9, pp. 354–366.

Although the gangster, often cast as the villain, has long been a fixture in the urban mise-en-scène in popular films – his death reinstating a moral universe in the diegesis – his exalted status as the protagonist takes force in the mid-1970s when popular culture seemed to respond and absorb the crisis of state legitimacy set in motion by the State of Emergency of 1975. In place of the iconic masculine subject who directs the narrative from chaos to the restoration of law and order, this emerging masculine subject flaunts the conventions of law and order by railing aggressively against corrupt police and politicians through vigilante actions. Critics classify these films as the 'angry man' films that fortified Amitabh Bachchan's star status. In a compelling reading of Bachchan's films – *Zanjeer / The Chain* (Prakash Mehra,1973), *Deewar / The Wall* (Yash Chopra, 1975) and *Sholay / Flames* (Ramesh Sippy, 1975) – Madhava Prasad formulates this shift in the popular cinema narrative as the 'disggregation' of the super genre, throwing up narratives teetering between the star persona on the one hand, and the role of the subaltern hero who mobilises the populist sentiments of the masses on the other hand. Tying Bachchan's stardom to that of the star scriptwriters Salim and Javed, Prasad identifies a shift in the production conditions towards a reinstatement of the dominance of popular cinema at a time when the state was vigorously involved in the production of small-budget films. Prasad's formulation allows us to explore how Bachchan's star status initiated changes at the formal register of the film through spectacular slow-motion shots of the star, fetishisation of the masculine-star's body through extreme close-ups that willy-nilly revised the heterosexual paradigms of previous years or at least problematised the relationship between the masculine subject and social authority.

Although critics are quick to recognise Bachchan's stardom as the defining trope of the 1970s and 1980s, there is no doubt that the changing production conditions also made it possible for certain star directors such as Mukul Anand, N. Chandra, Manmohan Desai, J.P. Dutta, Rajkumar Santoshi, Ramesh Sippy, etc., to emerge as auteurs and *metteurs en scène*, wresting control from distributors who by all accounts exercised undue authority over themes and stars of individual films. Centring the male protagonist – Amitabh Bachchan in the upmarket versions; other male stars such as Firoz Khan, Mithun Chakraborty in B and C productions – these films unfold around elaborate action sequences that bear strong resemblance to Hollywood-style westerns and gangster films. As we have already seen, *Sholay* was one of the most successful ventures to combine generic themes borrowed from Hollywood with conventions developed in Indian cinema, a combination that permits us similarly to scrutinise their iconography, articulations of the city and figurations of masculinity, areas that will help us better understand the populist thrust of such films.[26]

□ CASE STUDY 5: *SATYA* (RAM GOPAL VARMA, 1998)

Ramgopal Varma's landmark gangster film is the perfect example of global and local cinematic conventions. Set against the backdrop of Bombay the film narrates the rise and fall of Bhiku Mhatre whose range of activities include bankrolling politicians, bribing the police, financing film production and prostitution, a range that makes it almost impossible for the police to arrest him. Its gritty portrayal of the Bombay underworld including the multilingual slang has made it one of India's most popular films, with gangsters offering encomiums to the actor Manoj Bajpai (Bhiku Mhatre). At the centre of the narrative is Bhiku's friendship with Satya, which, the film suggests, propels his meteoric rise in the underworld as well as his precipitous fall. The hyper-real narrative, however, does include song and dance sequences and the interval does punctuate the narrative to heighten the relationship between gangster and state.

1 Analyse how the interval punctuates the film, inflecting its formal properties as well its narrative preoccupations.
2 Ram Gopal Varma did not wish to use song and dance sequences in this film but his producer Bharat Shah insisted on their marketability. Defend the use of these attractions. What kind of a film would we have seen without these sequences?
3 After seeing films such as *Dil Par mat le yaar / Don't Take it to Heart* (Hansal Mehta, 2000) and *Vastaav* (1999), attempt to sketch out the ideological underpinnings of the urban iconography in these films.

CENSORSHIP

In addition to these two kinds of interruptions, viewers of Indian films are aware that the state monitors the relationship between cinema and society most visibly through film censorship. The most glaring manifestations of state intervention in film production is the Board of Censors certificate that precedes each film. This inaugural moment of every film publicly released in India, imported or indigenous, informs the spectator that the film has been approved by the state and carries with it traces of censored cuts. The British colonial state introduced film censorship by passing the Cinematograph Act of 1918 for at least two reasons: first, to censor film footage that might incite anti-colonial riots; second, to avoid (mis)representations of the West, particularly images of Western women. These broad concerns targeted both Indian and imported films and set a pattern for post-independence censorship practices, where the state perceives films as having a tremendous influence over its citizenry and thus directs its regulations towards the production and control of 'quality' films (see Vasudev 1978; Sarkar 1982; Razdan 1975; *The Indian Cinematograph Code* 1982). However, instead of seeing censorship as *post facto* interference from the state, I suggest that film-makers spend considerable energy in incorporating censorship regulations *during* film-making, in an attempt to pre-empt sweeping cuts that would drastically effect the flow of the narrative. Moreover, over the years, the relationship between the state and the film industry has revealed a spectrum of negotiations – from an obedient nationalism to a flagrant flouting of regulations that fuel the production of images on screen.

While the obscenity codes governing Indian cinema address a wide range of issues affecting both image and dialogue, in practice the object of greatest scrutiny is

For a discussion on Censorship in the US and the UK see Chapter 1, pp. 40–46.

the female body. I use the term *coitus interruptus* to indicate the different ways in which the film industry negotiates the code to finally produce the female body on screen. This is not a gratuitous evocation of contraception, but rather a play on the structural similarity between two mechanisms – contraceptive regulations and censorship – suggesting how the state isolates the female body as the prime site of control and regulation in the public sphere. Among the several manifestations of *coitus interruptus*, the withdrawal-of-the-camera technique is instantly recognisable in various Indian films: the camera withdraws just before a steamy love scene ensues and the film replaces it with extra-diegetic shots of waterfalls, flowers, thunder, lightning and tropical storms. The varying configurations and recurrent use of *coitus interruptus* demonstrate how the film industry, despite its laments about state control, has been preoccupied with the withdrawal-of-the-camera technique as a crucial source of surplus pleasure. With its focus on dodging censorship prescriptions as well as maintaining its interests in the female body on screen, *coitus interruptus*, as a cinematic convention, captures an intimate and tense relationship between the state and the film industry predicated on attempts, however contradictory, to align the *national* subject with the film spectator. Far from aligning perfectly with the interests of the state and the film industry, the viewer is drawn into a fetishistic scenario where s/he oscillates between a cinephiliac mourning over lost footage, on the one hand, and, on the other, acknowledges that the state employs patriarchal law to produce limits on seeing.

THE WOMAN'S FILM

For further discussion of women filmmakers, see Chapter 7, pp. 243–247.

Inasmuch as cultural critics see popular films as staging social and political anxieties, the woman's film genre – which includes women-centred narratives, female protagonists undergoing political conversion, and more or less overt gestures towards feminist politics – has drawn responses and responded to the concerns of feminists, both in India and the diaspora. As mentioned earlier, Madhava Prasad notes that a fully independent woman's film struggled to develop in the 1960s, all too often annexed to what he sees as the 'super genre', or the feudal family romance. Besides the obvious economic motives of the box-office that carries bias against women ageing on screen, we can conjecture that the inability of the woman's film to survive was the unavailability of representations of strong woman-centred narratives in the social terrain, as well as the absence of critical feminist voices evaluating popular films. In this context it is useful to browse through past issues of *Manushi* – the most important feminist magazine in India – to gauge the developing, yet shifting, feminist readings of popular cinema set in motion by a section on film reviews. Rather than dismiss popular cinema altogether and applaud the politics of 'middle', parallel or alternative cinemas, these reviews read regressive representations as well as seeing feminist possibilities in popular cinema.

For further discussion of feminism and feminist film theory, see Chapter 7, pp. 247–264.

In recent years, the burgeoning field of feminist criticism of Indian films has produced an array of reading strategies that we can bring to bear on popular films. For instance, Maithili Rao (1998) examines the avenging women films of the 1980s to reprimand popular cinema for canny representations of aggressive women that fall short of feminism. Charting a similar territory, I have argued that the avenging women genre is shaped by the ongoing tussle between the film industry's desire to mine the woman's body for a range of representations and Censor Board dictates on obscenity codes, a tussle that throws up a heady concoction between sex and violence in these narratives that are predicated on rape and revenge (Gopalan 1997a). Jyotika Virdi (1999) locates the avenging women genre within the genre of women's film of the 1970s that similarly mobilised feminist possibilities but prematurely foreclosed those very options by evoking traditional representations of the pure or good woman.

Although these readings focus on women-centred narratives in popular cinema, we can detect feminist modes of analysis in Tejawini Niranjana's (1994) reading of Mani Ratnam's *Roja*, in which she argues that the film uses the figure of the good-wife-in-distress to promote a Hindu nationalist imaginary. In addition to decoding the narrative, attending to point-of-view shots, and responding to the modes of address, critics have isolated examples of feminist offerings that are even queer at times, in popular cinema: Radha Subramanyam sights a feminist consciousness in Kalpana Lajmi's *Rudaali / The Crier* (1992) that places the gendered subaltern within an erotic economy (Subramanyam 1996).

While critics have directed their energies at popular cinema, women film-makers from middle or art cinema have long been experimenting with feminist aesthetics that include narrating the plight of Brahmin widowhood while giving them dignity (see for example Prema Karanth's *Phaniyamma*, 1983); centring on the loneliness of an Anglo-Indian teacher (see for example Aparna Sen's *36 Chowringhee Lane*, 1982); and so on. In the field of documentary film-making, Deepa Dhanaraj's careful documenting of communal riots, and policies on reproductive rights and population control has expanded the field of feminist aesthetics beyond a women-centred narrative. Similarly, the women's film collective Media Storm, based in Delhi, has employed conventional and guerrilla tactics to propose visual interventions to the ongoing debates on right-wing nationalism, state brutality and feminist subjectivity.

This rich and complicated terrain of feminist film criticism provides a productive framework to examine two controversial films, *Bandit Queen* and *Fire*.

□ **CASE STUDY 6:** *BANDIT QUEEN* **(SHEKHAR KAPUR, 1994) AND** *FIRE* **(DEEPA MEHTA, 1998)**

• **Plate 10.4**
Bandit Queen
(Shekar, Kapur, 1994)

Bandit Queen (Shekhar Kapur, 1994)

Produced in collaboration with British Channel 4 and based on Mala Sen's (1991) biography of the notorious dacoit Phoolan Devi, Shekhar Kapur's film details Phoolan's development from a child-bride to an outlaw. Its release in India was stymied by the Censor Board that recommended excising the sexually explicit scenes of sex and violence in the film. In addition, the film's claim that it was a true story provoked the late Phoolan Devi, by that time a newly elected Member of Parliament from a lower caste facing allegations from the upper caste in her constituency for a massacre in Behmai. The public debate on the film took Kapur to task for the prolonged rape scenes in the film, using the guise of feminism.[27] *Bandit Queen* was eventually released with no cuts but in several cities there were separate showings for women. Since the brouhaha surrounding its release two scholarly responses have allowed us to interrogate the film's politics: Shohini Ghosh's essay 'Deviant Pleasures and Disorderly Women' places the film within the rubric of the outlaw films in popular films, questioning the film's feminist address; while Priyamvada Gopal assesses the context of its reception and questions the ethics of representation.

1   How does the film privilege a referential reading of its narrative?
2   I have taught the film in a course of westerns because of the film's iconography and its narrative preoccupation with outlaws. Ghosh suggests that the film partakes of certain conventions from popular cinema. Attempt to describe and analyse the film's proximity and distance from popular cinema.
3   How does the film juggle inter-caste antagonisms and the rape–revenge narrative?
4   Read Mala Sen's (1991) *India's Bandit Queen: The True Story of Phoolan Devi* as a way of understanding the public response to the film. Imagine a different visual construction to the biography.

Fire (Deepa Mehta, 1998)

A Canadian-Indian co-production, Deepa Mehta's film sparked a similar debate to that on *Bandit Queen* because of its overt representations of sexual relationships between women. The right-wing Hindu party Shiv Sena called for a ban, propelling a heated debate on Hindu representations of women, lesbianism in the Hindu tradition and so on – most of this is well recorded on several web sites, including SAWNET (South Asian Women's Net). After the dust had settled there was further debate among feminists on the film's images of lesbian desire, Mehta's own distance from queer politics, the class politics in the film and the relationship between audiences in the West and in India; such positions demand we take a another look at this film.

1   Describe and analyse how the film links the friendship between Radha and Sita to Mundu's desire.
2   Using Chris Straayer's (1995) essay 'Hypothetical Lesbian Heroine in Narrative Feature Film', evaluate to what extent *Fire* is beholden to patriarchal representations of women and to what degree it recasts the debates on identity. Does the film prepare us for the closing moments of the film or does it place them outside the representational circuits we have been privy to?

These interruptions do not carry equal weight across the terrain of popular cinema. Depending on directorial style or genre pressures, each film measures these interruptions differently in such a way as to suggest a *hierarchy* of interruptions. For instance, song and dance sequences are better elaborated in a love story than in a gangster genre. In a Mani Ratnam film, irrespective of the genre, we expect an elaborate choreography of song and dance sequences flattening the temporal disjunctions of other interruptions.

☐ CASE STUDY 7: *HOUSE FULL* (PARTHIBAN, 1999)

Film-makers are constantly at work finessing the alchemy of conventions and at times generating a commentary on the sequencing of these codes. Parthiban's Tamil film *Housefull* (1999), for instance, remarks on the function of these interruptions. The plot involves a bomb threat at a movie theatre in Madurai. The police and the bomb squad try surreptitiously to control the situation by asking the projectionist to keep the audience's attention on the screen, thus preventing them from leaving the theatre. Complying with the police, the projectionist skips two crucial reels – one with song and dance sequences which he claims will bring the men out in large numbers; the other marking the interval which will open the floodgates for the entire audience. While the audience in the film is transfixed on the unfolding story of the film-within-film, our film too responds to the police dictate – although we have a clearly defined 'Intermission', the film has dispensed with song and dance sequences. At one level, Partheepan's film comments on the rash of bombings that mark Indian public life by intimidating the utopian community of film-goers – people from different communities, classes and religions – that venture to see a film at a movie house aptly called 'Bharat Theatres'. Yet, what I find compelling about the film is its ability to articulate police work as a method to discipline the narrative – bombs and attractions are managed simultaneously. *Housefull* exemplifies the conditions of contemporary film production – a film leaning towards an internally coherent narrative yet continuously commenting on its textual production, while, at the same time, maintaining the intermission as a local condition of reception. These examples reveal how we cannot simply import one theoretical paradigm over another to account for non-Hollywood narrative styles, but must work through the ways in which such styles might address a spectator who is at the cross-roads of several intersecting cinematic styles.

FOUNDATIONAL FICTIONS OF THE POST-COLONIAL NATION

Critical writings on Indian cinema frequently dwell on how Indian films are intimately linked to questions of national identity and history. Sumita Chakravarty's *National Identity in Indian Popular Cinema, 1947 – 1987* (1993) is a good example of examining the themes in Hindi popular cinema as contestations over national identity, including the shifting relationship between the gendered body and the nation-state. Theodore Baskaran's pioneering work on Tamil cinema unravels the link between Tamil cinema and nationalist politics in Tamil Nadu, a focus that forces us to acknowledge regional nationalisms and cinemas (Baskaran 1981). The recent spate of overtly nationalist films has invited the ire of critics who have taken *Roja* and *Gadar* to task for espousing and condoning Hindu nationalist politics. It is in this context that we will look at two films in order to better understand how films stage battles over national identity.

☐ CASE STUDY 8: *HEY! RAM* (KAMAL HAASAN, 1999)[28]

Kamal Haasan's *Hey! Ram* (1999) tackles a nationalist narrative of epic proportions including Partition, Gandhi's assassination and contemporary communal politics in India. Rather than working as part of the backdrop, the film intimately ties these political and social events to the fate of the male protagonist Saket Ram. The twin preoccupations of the film produces an unruly narrative that avoids resolution of the knotty issues it sets in motion yet urges us to consider the inextricable links between cinematic and national histories. Keeping pace with the narrative, the film deploys a number of formal strategies including monochromatic sequences for the contemporary scenes, digital images akin to video games, as well as a rich tapestry of quotations from world cinemas: elephants from D.W. Griffith's *Intolerance* (1916) and Pastrone's *Cabiria* (1914); dream sequences from Luis Bunuel's films; mise-en-scène from *Raiders of the Lost Ark* (Steven Spielberg, 1981), and so on. Simultaneously, it evokes these references to world cinema within a nationalist narrative and in effect revisits similar coincidences of interests in Griffith's *The Birth of a Nation* (1915), to a lesser extent in Mehboob Khan's *Mother India* (1957), and more overtly in S. Shankar's *Indian* (1996), a rich set of associations encouraging us to consider Mikhail Imapolski's (1998) suggestion that quotations in films gesture toward the past. *Hey! Ram* reconfigures the melodramatic aspects of these nationalist narratives by focusing exclusively on the male protagonist's relationship to the nation, a focus that dwells on the slow conversion of the South Indian Brahmin from a distant observer to a militant subversive by deploying digital technologies.[29]

For further reference to digital technology, see Chapter 4, pp. 148–150 and Chapter 6, pp. 232–235.

To the consternation of critics lamenting the invasion of digital technologies, there is no doubt that digital morphing as a technique vastly improves the use of dissolves and cuts to suggest corporeal transformation on screen – wolf to man, man to woman, etc. (Sobchack 2000). A similar pre-digital history obtains in Indian cinema, where cut and paste devices paper over the metamorphosis of a woman into a snake (see especially the genre of snake films including *Nagin* [1954] and *Nagina* [1986]); or the grafting of two separate frames to maintain the illusion of the multiple roles played by the same actor. In an instrumental sense, digital technologies advance the making of these illusions by rendering seamless transformations on screen, in effect suturing us into the diegesis of the story. Yet this pull into the narrative cannot completely repress the history of innovations in digital technology imbricated in military experiments that are similarly plagued with issues of time and space.[30] It is therefore not surprising that we should find the most spectacular use of digital technologies in conquest narratives such as *Independence Day* (Roland Emmerich, 1996) and *The Matrix* (Wachowski, 1999), which heighten the relationship between cinematic and military modes of representations. Although *Hey! Ram* underplays military prowess, the film's use of digital technology to simulate a different story of origins consolidates the nationalist narrative and cannot help but remind us of the militant aspects of nationalism.

Kamal Haasan's film deploys digital technology to scramble linear chronology by moving back and forth between 1999 and the period 1946–48. We see Saket Ram, a Tamil Brahmin, working as an archaeologist in Mohenjodaro in 1946; with his first wife Aparna in Calcutta during communal riots which ends in her death in 1946; a respite in Chidambaram and Madras where he marries Mythili, a little before independence in 1947; visits to Maharashtra and his joining the ranks of right-wing Hindu militants between 1947 and 1948; and finally the denouement in Delhi when he tries to assassinate Gandhi in 1948. The temporal scrambling matches the spatial journey through pre-Partition India, allowing the film to draw a continuum from communal antagonisms during Partition to contemporary tensions set in motion after Hindu militants demolished the Babri Masjid on 6 December 1992. Saket Ram's conversion proceeds from his role as a disinterested scholar to a militant Hindu nationalist after encountering gorier aspects of communal riots in Calcutta, and finally to a Gandhian pacificist, a conversion narrative that rescues the film from wholly aligning itself with Hindu nationalism. Yet it is the middle sections, the parts spelling out Ram's entry into the ranks of the Hindu right, that are replete with the film's mastery over digital technology, especially morphing, relaying its own conversion from analog to digital images.

One of the most flamboyant exhibitions of digital morphing takes places during Ram and Mythili's visit to a kingdom in Maharashtra – marking his definitive sympathies towards the right-wing Hindu party Rashtriya Sevak Sangha (RSS) – when the local king at the behest of Abhiyankar – a right-wing Hindu zealot whom Ram encounters during the riots in Calcutta – draws him into a scheme to kill Gandhi. After a fortuitous reconnection with his old friend Lalvani from Karachi, Ram and Mythili join the Ram Lila celebrations at the palace grounds where Abhiyankar offers Ram a drug-laced drink that induces Ram to conjure figures from the riot scene in Calcutta as well as heightening his sexual interest in Mythili. Seducing her away from a dance performance, he leads Mythili to their chambers. As they begin to make love, we see her morph into an enormous gun with Ram stroking its barrel. Undoubtedly this is a heavy-handed metaphoric substitution that carries a banal psychoanalytical association: the woman replaces the gun in a way that demands we understand how the libidinal drive severs itself from object identification. Clearly the excesses of the scene lead us to recognise how morphing showcases digital technology while providing only a tangential link to the narrative. Nevertheless, another reading also obtains here, one which takes us down a different road. Blinding us with technological prowess, *Hey! Ram* uses morphing to veil its relationship to censorship regulations. Instead of including a sexually explicit scene that may provoke the ire of the Board of Censors, the altered image allows us to view the scene through metaphoric substitution, a substitution that reconfigures the temporality of censorship. In its extreme form, popular films simply substitute the love-making scene with pastoral evocations, cut to a song and dance sequence to regulate the overflow of passion, or push the envelope to the limit. In all three possibilities available in the pre-digital era, we confront a linear unfolding of the narrative where a cut directs us to the next image. Morphing, on the other hand, maintains intact an old-fashioned relationship to censorship while distracting us with a showstopping spectacle that morphs objects within the frame – a spatial transformation rather than a temporal one. Cushioned in a visit that highlights Ram's political conversion, morphing in this sequence overdetermines the connectives between political and sexual desire, an overlap that the film underscores during a secret meeting in the Maharaja's chambers when from Ram's point of view we see the Maharaja's face morph into that of Aparna. In other words, morphing allows a film such as *Hey! Ram* to expand the limits of what is permissible on the Indian screen through metaphoric substitution, a substitution that inverts the relationship between space and time between frames.

The second spectacular scene of morphing occurs soon after Ram's visit to Maharashtra, detouring through scenes of riots in 1996 composed in monochromatic colours mimicking black and white documentary footage – a burst of red fire undercuts the documentary gesture swaying it towards the diegesis of the film. These excursions to the monochromatic footage focus on an ailing Ram in the care of his grandson. Escorting Ram to a hospital through streets pocked by communal riots marking the anniversary of the demolition of the Babri Masjid, his grandson is halted by the police and escorted to the safety of a bunker. From an extreme close-up shot of Ram's left pupil the film dissolves into a digitally produced target. On the soundtrack we hear the police officer's command to shoot – a sound-bridge connecting the two images. In the digitally produced scene, we see a muscular Ram at target practice; his attire clearly betrays signs of a Brahmin man including the sacred thread across his bare chest, an image that cannot completely sever its relationship to the real – Ram converts the handgun to a rifle by attaching a shoulder rest. This short scene of target practice celebrating the morphed muscular Brahmin body gives way to a simulated storm that sweeps over the entire screen. Undeterred by the ferocity of the storm he stands his ground.

For further discussion of
gender and masculinity,
see Chapter 7, pp.
264–275.

Poised to function as an explanatory segment, morphing actualises Ram's metamorphosis from a reluctant spectator into a full-fledged member of a right-wing militant Hindu political party. Clearly the digital simulation of a muscular body adds further credence to popular representations of militant masculinities that surface in Amar Chitra Katha comic books and cable television.[31]

In a compelling reading of masculinity and morphing in *Forrest Gump* (Robert Zemeckis, 1994), Joseba Gabilondo (2000) suggests that in the 1990s representations of morphing on screen ushers in a different kind of masculinity, a resolutely heterosexual masculinity, constructed after or in response to both queer and feminist politics. Rather than the hard masculinities of the 1980s, according to him we find a masculinity that is self-involved, more narcissistic and more openly engaged with queerness, without being queer.[32] Its response to feminism, however, has involved usurping reproduction, not through duplication but by inverting it – masculinity reclaims fatherhood as well as motherhood. This shift in representations, mobilised by morphing, according to Gabilondo equally effects the conventional sadomasochism underlying masculinity:

The morphed and reproductive Masculinity of the 1990s show a new arrangement of this sadomasochistic economy: masochism becomes *avowed* by traditional filmic means (narrative and camera) while sadism is *disavowed* through morphing.

(Ibid.: 197)

Although great differences separate the unwilling male protagonist who suffers in *Forrest Gump* from the very deliberate action-oriented hero in *Hey! Ram*, both films engage with narratives of placing the common man in history, both officially and on the margins. Here too we find the sections preceding the morphing segment ripe with masculine inability: Ram helplessly watches his wife Aparna getting raped; bows to family pressures by marrying again; and even bears a sentimental attachment to women, home and domesticity. The communal riots do not immediately transform him into a militant Hindu nationalist. Rather the narrative derives sufficient pleasure in his suffering, a convention familiar in several Tamil films starring Kamal Haasan: frontal shots of a body bruised by the police in *Nayakan* (1987) and *Guna* (1991); unrelenting masochistic narrative of the suffering male in *Mahanadhi* (1993) and so on. Morphing, on the other hand, provides the space to articulate a sadistic masculinity that is set into motion after Abhiyankar's death when Saket Ram is chosen to assassinate Gandhi. While we do find a fair share of masochism in the scene, morphing nevertheless constructs a hyper-real space outside the conventions of realism, allowing the passage from being subjected to a subject, from victim to agent. The narrative decisively moves towards action and resolution soon after the morphing segment: Ram leaves his wife and launches his participation in the assassination scheme. At closure, the film renders the excesses of militant masculinity as a futile excursion, choosing instead to close on a male subject whose place in history is assured after a journey through sadism.

Although *Hey! Ram* converts Kamal Haasan, the star, into a spectacular digital image that exceeds the star ideal, it is the not the first film to do so. We find a more benign version of this digital simulation in *Magalir Mattum / Ladies Only* (1994), also starring Kamal Haasan. Frustrated by sexism at work, the women office-workers conjure a computer-simulated image of an ideal man who turns out to be the star Kamal Haasan. While *Magalir Mattum* unabashedly celebrates the star's image as the ideal poster boy for women office-workers, *Hey! Ram* accentuates this available image by severing its link to an indexical referent: the digital image is a vastly improved version of the star's body. However, the muscular body in the digital space does not abdicate its commitment to other referents but seeks to find its purpose within an older regime of filmic representation that continues to battle with notions of the real. In other words, the muscular militant body in the film services the cause of the ideal male image in Hindu nationalism and not that of the simulated battle on the screen. Yet Gabilondo's proposal that 'masculinity's masochistic renunciation of reality also represents a utopian possibility for other subject positionalities' (2000: 201) provides us with a way to imagine possibilities offered by the hyper-real digital images in *Hey! Ram*.

☐ CASE STUDY 9: *LAGAAN / TAX* (ASHUTOSH GOWRIKAR, 2001)

This highly successful film about cricket and politics has been the biggest cross-over film of the Hindi film industry to date, and has shown to packed houses in Britain since summer 2001. It is currently being released in America after being nominated as one of the finalists by the Academy in the Best Foreign Film category. Set in the colonial period, the film sketches the trials and tribulations of the peasants of Champaner who are being subjected to British land tax during a long period of drought. The negotiations with the local British officers leads to an unexpected offer: if the villagers were to win a game of cricket, they would no longer have to pay taxes. Unlike the contemporary success of Indian cricket teams, the motley team put together by the protagonist Bhuvan, played by the star Aamir Khan, barely know or even understand the rudimentary rules of the game. This lacuna offers fodder for an Indo–English relationship to develop between the British captain's sister, Elizabeth, serving as the peasants' coach, a move that allows us to imagine a romantic union between Bhuvan and the white memsahib. However, Gauri from the village, who has long harboured a desire for Bhuvan, prevents this reunion, hence, a triangular erotic comedy unfolds. Besides managing these competing romantic interests, Bhuvan is focused on putting together a team that can pulverise the British, an aspect of the narrative that the film succeeds in satisfying the cricket-crazed public in India by referencing stalwarts from Indian cricketing history. Thus, although a period film, the references to corruption and match-fixing resonate with contemporary overtones. The match itself is a good hour long with chance and talent pitted against each other. In a rather canny move, the film coaches the audiences in the finer aspects of the game through the figure of Elizabeth: we learn

• **Plate 10.5**
Lagaan (Ashutosh Gowrikar, 2001)

about the game as the villagers learn to play. There is no doubt that *Lagaan* successfully fuses, at least for the Indian audiences, two obsessions: cricket and movies.

1   In his review of the film, David Chute (2002) quotes cultural critic Ashish Nandy's pithy comment that cricket is 'an Indian game that happens to have been invented by the British'. If familiar with cricket, point out the various extra-textual references to games and players in the film.

2   If read allegorically, the construction of the village team recalls the utopian visions of a secular India, a vision that seems more fragile these days with the rise of Hindu nationalism and sectarian violence. Elaborate the film's investment in a secular vision, however rife with contradictions this may be.

3   The love triangle is the other driving force in the narrative. Describe how the film uses the song and dance sequences to exacerbate the tensions of this erotic triangle and explain its desire to form an Indian couple.

4   Critics have noted that the star Aamir Khan is a crucial ingredient in the film's success. Construct an archive of fandom using internet sites, star magazines and visits to Aamir Khan fan clubs, both virtual and real, so as to plot the ways in which his star presence marks the narrative – the opening sequence would be a good place to begin – and then proceed to the song and dance sequences.

CONCLUSION

The peculiar conditions of Indian commercial film narrative are constantly shifting, undoing our assumptions of some of its constituent elements. Defying the need to make sense by importing reading strategies inspired from either classical, early or contemporary American cinema, contemporary Indian movies compel us to employ several of these theoretical positions simultaneously to read *one* film. Despite being far removed from the central engine of capitalism and its accompanying realist narrative, Indian cinema mimics, copies and rewrites these forms while simultaneously maintaining a local quotient of attractions. In a curious twist in the history of appropriation and application of film theory across national cinemas, certain ontological questions surrounding narrative cinema – questions that Eisenstein raised in his famous essay on the 'montage of attractions' – find fertile ground in contemporary Indian cinema (Eisenstein 1997). An amalgamation of the different interruptions in Indian popular cinema throws up a picture bearing an uncanny resemblance to Peter Wollen's conceptualisation of the 'multi-diegesis' in Jean Luc-Godard's *Vent D'Est / Wind from the East* (1969), a film that he claims undoes the narrative conventions of both Hollywood and Soviet films (Wollen 1982). We might be hard pressed to see any immediate link between an overtly avant-garde practice and popular Indian cinema but, not unlike Wollen, viewers of Indian films do see its digressions and interruptions as intrinsic to enjoying and understanding these films as well as comprising the location of intense ideological struggles.

For detailed discussion of Eisenstein and Soviet Montage, see Chapter 11.

For further discussion of Peter Wollen in relation to alienation narratives, see Chapter 2, pp. 84–85.

NOTES

1 This is a condensed version of the Introduction to my book *Cinema of Interruptions* (London, BFI, 2002).

2 Conversation with O.P. Dutta, April 1999. Dutta tells of the 1950s and 1960s when the Soviets purchased a number of films, but Indian film-makers never kept track of these exhibitions or purchases. On viewing Indian films in Nigeria see Brian Larkin (1997)

3 Thanks to Tejaswini Ganti for posting this article.

4 Thanks to Moira Taylor's research on the web.

5 Personal conversation with P.C. Sriram, September 1995.

6 Film production in 1979: 113 in Hindi; 139 in Tamil; and 131 in Telugu; In 1995: 157 in Hindi; 165 in Tamil; and 168 in Telugu. Figures are from Rajadhyaksha and Willemen (1999).

7 For a comprehensive evaluation of alternative film-makers, see Hood (2000).

8 I wish to thank Haim Bresheeth for this wonderful example from Israeli cinema.

9 I wish to thank Roopal Oza for alerting me to these reports.

10 Touted as a 'curry western' by film critic Ken Wlaschin, reviewing the 1976 Film Festival, Sippy's film fits quite easily into revisionist westerns such as 'spaghetti westerns'.

11 Mayne (1993) has a splendid yet sympathetic critique of the ideal spectator in psychoanalysis.

12 While Singh's formulation has critical valency, I would like to question his reading of the song: a close analysis of the scene shows the camera does not actively grope the dancer's body even if it fragments her body. Attributing movement to a phantom camera, Singh may be implicitly admitting to being taken in by the entertaining song and dance number!

13 Rashmi Doraiswamy, and Aruna Vasudev, author of the best book on Indian censorship, floated the film journal *Cinemaya* with the explicit intention of increasing interest in Asian cinema from an Asian location.

14 A survey conducted by *Filmfare* in June 1999 revealed Sholay to be the first important film in the life of several young stars.

15 Thomas outlines one of the first proposals to take the popular film industry seriously, on its 'own terms'.

16 American film producers too have started to see the commercial viability of soundtracks. Music stores now exclusively stack a separate section with movie soundtracks.

17 According to Baskaran (1996), *Ambikapathi* (1937) is the earliest Tamil film to credit a music director.

18 See the entry for R.C. Boral in Rajadhyaksha and Willemen (1999). See also Terri Skillman (1986).

19 We still lack a complete analysis of sound, technology, song writers and music directors that will help us better understand the relationship between sound and image in Indian popular cinema.

20 A good recent example is Sashilal Nair's *Kabhi na Kabhi*, where a sequence forms a separate system independent of the narrative.

21 On the travel genre in early Euro-American cinema, see Musser (1990).

22 For an elaboration of the heterosexual paradigm, see Kofosky Sedgwick (1985).

23 I am extremely grateful to Theodore Baskaran for generously sharing these filmic details with me.

24 See Mayne (1993) for a splendid exegesis on the cultural context of Hollywood production and their preferred spectator.

25 Peter Wollen uses 'multi-diegesis' to describe Jean-Luc Godard's film *Vent D'Est*. He argues that Godard is responding both to Hollywood and to Mos-film narratives characterised by a single diegesis by producing a film with multi-diegesis.

26 For a stunning reading of populism in Tamil films, see M.S.S. Pandian's (1992) foundational work on star and politician M.G. Ramachandran. A good topic of analysis would be to compare Bachchan and MGR's films as a way of coming to terms with populism. .

27 See Arundhati Roy, 'The great Indian rape trick', Sunday 26 August–3 September 1994, pp.56–84 and 'The great Indian rape trick II', Sunday 11–17 September 1994, pp.58–64; Pankaj Buttalia, 'Sanction for politics of revenge', *Times of India*, 4 September 1994.

28 My reading of Hey! Ram can be found in *Cinema of Interruptions* (2002).

29 Mantra, the digital facility at Ramoji Film City in Hyderabad, won the National Award for its special effects in *Hey! Ram*.

30 On the correlation between cinema and military technologies, see Virilio (1989).

31 See Anand Patwardhan's film *Father, Son, and Holy War* for a thorough investigation of masculinity in the Indian public sphere. See also Arvind Rajagopal (2001).

32 Gabilondo engages extensively with Susan Jeffords' argument that there is a definite shift in representations of masculinity in the Reagan era. See her *Hard Bodies* (1994).

FURTHER READING

Barnouw, Erik and Krishnaswamy, S., *Indian Film*, 2nd edn, Oxford University Press, New York, 1980.

Hood, John W., *The Essential Mystery*, Orient Longman, New Delhi, 2000.

Rajadhyaksha, Ashish and Willemen, Paul (eds), *Encyclopaedia of Indian Cinema*, 2nd edn, British Film Institute, London, 1999.

Thoraval, Yves, *The Cinemas of India*, Macmillan India, New Delhi, 2000.

The following periodicals are also useful for those interested in the field.

Cinemaya

Deep Focus

Filmfare

Lensight

Stardust

FURTHER VIEWING

The following list limits itself to the genres discussed in the chapter, but you are encouraged to use the *Encyclopedia of Indian Cinema* (Rajadhyaksha and Willemen, 1999) to direct you both to alternative cinema as well as to films from other periods.

Wedding Genres: *Hum Aapke hain koun*, *Dilwale Dulhania Le Jayenge* (1995), *Pardes* (1997).

Gangster/Crime Genres: *Parinda/Caged Bird* (1987), *Hathyar* (1987), *Deewar* (1975), *Company* (2002), *Dil Par Mat le Yaar* (2002)

Love Story: *Gadar* (2001), *1942: A Love Story* (1994)

Women's Film: *Lajja* (2001), *Mitr, My Friend* (2001), *Leela* (2002).

RESOURCE CENTRES

Most Indian popular film magazines are starzines and are highly unreliable sources for production details but they are a good place to begin research on the star system. See *Filmfare*, *Stardust*, *G*. For production details see *Screen* (published by the Express Group), *Trade Guide*, *Film Information*. *Rediff.Com* is a good online source for film reviews and interviews with film-makers and stars.

www.cscsban.org has a comprehensive listing of film reviews and other related materials that your institutions can subscribe to.

Videos from South Asia from UC Berkeley's wonderful Media Resources Center. (Via internet).

Videos/films about the South Asian diaspora, also from UC Berkeley's Media.

FilmIndia is an extensive source of Indian film information, including a directory, bibliography, newsclips, events, and links.

Hollywood Masala is a web resource for South Asian film and filmmakers.

The Internet movie database has lists of movies made in the South Asian countries. *The South Asian section of this database is fairly incomplete — you may want to contribute.*

Hindi movies and music, from the Indiaworld page, which also lists Filmfare awards and profiles of some actors. Or try this more comprehensive archive of Hindi movie songs.

Hindi and Tamil movie reviews from Indolink

Women in Cinema: a reference guide. A discussion of the role and impact of women on Western cinema. Areas of discussion include: bibliographies and guides, biographical sources, reviews and filmographies, electronic sources, and subject collections on film.

Feminist Film Reviews, mostly written by Linda Lopez McAllister. Some interesting and unusual perspectives on American and British films. Includes non-mainstream films.

RML's Movie Page, a nicely organized collection of information on directors, films, and actors. Described as 'International', meaning American and European films.

Chapter 11

The Soviet montage cinema of the 1920s

Mark Joyce

■ The Soviet montage cinema of the 1920s

INTRODUCTION: WHY STUDY THE SOVIET CINEMA?

As the lights went up at the end an emotion-charged silence reigned, broken only when Lunacharsky [the Soviet Union's Commissar for Education] jumped on his chair and began an enthusiastic speech: 'We've been witnesses at an historic cultural event. A new art has been born....'

(Cited in Barna 1973: 102)

See Chapter 2 for further discussion of film form.

Anatoli Lunacharsky's response to Sergei Eisenstein's 1925 film *Battleship Potemkin* acknowledges the importance of a new wave of film-making. The films made by the Soviet directors of the 1920s are considered by many as the most innovative and exciting to have been produced in the history of the cinema. The names of these film-makers – Eisenstein, Pudovkin, Vertov and Kuleshov among others – are far from forgotten and a number of the films and directors from this period consistently score highly in *Sight and Sound*'s critics'/directors' choice of the best ten films and directors.

Soviet cinema
This will refer to films made in the Soviet Union between October 1920 and 1991, although for the purposes of this chapter most Soviet films discussed will be confined to the 1920s.

This decade of intensive experimentation with film form produced techniques that have subsequently been widely emulated. In addition, the theoretical debates formulated by these film-makers are still relevant today. For these reasons the **Soviet cinema** of the 1920s merits detailed analysis.

ideology
There are two key definitions of this term, one provided by the nineteenth-century German philosopher, Karl Marx, the other by the twentieth-century French Marxist philosopher, Louis Althusser, drawing on Marx's original ideas. For Marx, ideology was the dominant set of beliefs and values existent within society, which sustained power relations. For Althusser, ideology consisted of the representations and images which reflect society's view of 'reality'. Ideology thus refers to 'the myths that a society lives by'.

HISTORICAL BACKGROUND

The Soviet film-makers of the 1920s reflect the **ideology** (the values and beliefs) and politics of the society in which they were produced. The early 1920s marked the end of a period of civil unrest, the causes of which lay in the great divide that separated wealthy land-owning Russians from the peasants and workers.[1] For centuries Russia had been governed by the single figure of the Tsar, who had absolute powers. The Russian serfs were not granted freedom from slavery until 1861; this liberation, however, did not mean improved conditions, as they continued to live an existence of appalling poverty. Attempts had been made prior to the revolution of October 1917 by various factions to undermine the Tsarist regime, all of which were unsuccessful. A wave of revolutionary activity in 1905 included a mutiny by Russian sailors at Odessa which formed the basis for Sergei Eisenstein's 1925 film *Battleship Potemkin*.

See Chapter 3, pp. 99–101, for discussion of ideology in relation to spectatorship.

The First World War (1914–18) eventually proved to be disastrous for Tsar Nicholas II, as it consumed vast amounts of money and resources that were sorely needed at home. It was also unpopular with the Russian people as the reasons for fighting were unclear. The peasants and the workers were the worst hit by the impact of the war, either being killed on the front or starving at home as supplies became depleted. The land-owning rich were protected by their wealth and were able to continue in their existing lifestyle.

These conditions provided the catalyst for the revolution of 25 February 1917 which resulted in the formation of a liberal provisional government led by Alexander Kerensky and later supported by Menshevik and Socialist Revolutionary factions. This caused Nicholas II to abdicate on 4 March. The provisional government decided to continue the war, and for many (especially V.I. Lenin who was in hiding in Zurich) it appeared that the new government was in effect continuing the policies of the Tsarist order.

On 25 October 1917 the Bolsheviks, taking advantage of a situation of confusion and competition between the various factions, seized power by storming the Winter Palace.[2] The new Bolshevik government agreed to Germany's demands for control of areas of land previously under Russian administration and pulled out of the war. Almost immediately, however, a fierce civil war broke out between the Bolsheviks (known as the Reds) and those still loyal to the Tsarist regime (known as the Whites).[3]

By 1920 it was clear that the Bolsheviks had seized ultimate control of the country. The new Soviet government under the leadership of V.I. Lenin was faced with the task of convincing the population of Russia of the evils of the Tsarist regime and the positive points of the new Communist one.

Selected historical dates

1905, Jan.	First revolution (abortive)
	Provides the backdrop for Eisenstein's *Battleship Potemkin*
1914, July	General strike organised by the Bolsheviks
	Outbreak of war and the crushing of the political unrest The war was a general disaster for the Russians; low morale and food shortages in the following years led to uprisings in 1917
1917, Feb.	Popular uprisings culminating in the overthrow of the Tsar, and the setting up of a provisional government
1917, Oct.	The Bolsheviks overthrow the provisional government and seize political power
1918–21	Civil war between White and Red factions, as well as fighting of hostile troops sent from abroad in an attempt to restore the power of the Tsar. The continued fighting led to the destruction of trade, agriculture, industry and film production
1922–8	NEP (New Economic Policy) adopted by Lenin. A brief return to controlled forms of capitalism to help to rebuild the shattered economy
1922–3	Soviet feature film production resumes
1924	Sergei Eisenstein's *Strike* completed
1927	The tenth anniversary of the October Revolution. A number of films are made to mark the occasion including:
	October (Eisenstein)
	The End of St Petersburg (Vsevolod Pudovkin)
	The Fall of the Romanov Dynasty (Esfir Shub)

PRE-REVOLUTIONARY RUSSIAN CINEMA

The nature of the Russian cinema

When discussing the Soviet cinema it is important to have at least an outline of the form and content of its antecedent, for although the majority of the Soviet directors had not made films prior to 1919, they would certainly have been familiar with the conventions of the pre-revolutionary cinema. Significantly, for a number of the Soviet directors, this cinema was the antithesis of their new approach to film-making. The **Russian cinema** 1907–17 was in fact markedly different from the Soviet cinema of the 1920s. The majority of the films that are available for viewing today[4] are between thirty-five and seventy minutes long and deal predominantly with the lives of the upper classes, quite frequently centring on their relationship with servants and/or the working class. Their subject matter, plot and preoccupations are often melodramatic; unfaithful husbands and wives, psychological states of mind and death predominate. The form of the films is

Russian cinema
This will refer to the body of films made in Tsarist Russia between 1907 and 1917.

The 1920s could be characterised as a period in which American and European narrative films were in effect directly subsidising the dramatic experimentation with film form undertaken by the Soviet film-makers.

Innovation and experimentation frequently arise from a lack. In the Soviet Union the lack of film stock (and even film cameras) meant that certain groups of film-makers worked on re-editing existing films (often European/American films and old Russian newsreels) to make them conform to the values of the Soviet state. Other film-makers experimented with creating films from the small amount of negative available, which often only came in short lengths. Out of this experimentation came Soviet montage cinema.

FORM: MONTAGE

The roots of Soviet montage

The innovative use of montage in film by the Soviet film-makers had its roots in art forms such as painting, literature and music from pre-revolutionary Russia. David Bordwell (1972), in 'The Idea of Montage in Soviet Art and Film', states that by 1910 a group of Russian painters had already experimented extensively with 'montage': 'the Russian futurists declared that conventional art must be destroyed and that a new art, appropriate to the machine age, must be created. Hence the futurists took their subjects from modern life and exploited a technique of shocking juxtapositions'. Poetry, in particular that of Mayakovsky,[14] was also 'shattering words and reassembling them into brutal images'.

The question needs to be asked: why didn't the Russian film-makers of the 1910s experiment with montage earlier? This lack of explicit montage experiment in the Russian cinema compared to that taking place in other art forms can perhaps be attributed to economics. The crucial difference between film and many of the other arts at the time was that the small groups of experimental artists, writers and musicians were often privately funded by rich patrons. The film industry, however, was not.[15] The revolution of October 1917 provided the right conditions for experimentation with film to take place. It is ironic that this experimentation had its roots in the élitist art forms of pre-revolutionary Russia.

The Kuleshov effect and its consequences

See Chapter 2, pp. 73, for reference to Kuleshov's experiments with editing, and pp. 73–76 for discussion of editing in mainstream narrative cinema.

The montage technique is based on the theory that when two pieces of film are placed side by side the audience immediately draws the conclusion that the two shots must be directly related in some way. In other words, the audience try to create meaning by combining the two separate images. The experimentation along these lines by Lev Kuleshov, a young Soviet film-maker, culminated in what became known as the Kuleshov effect. Vsevolod Pudovkin outlined the experiment in a lecture given at the London Film Society in February 1929:

Kuleshov and I made an interesting experiment. We took from some film or other several close-ups of the well-known Russian actor Mosjukhin. We chose close-ups which were static and which did not express any feeling at all – quiet close-ups. We joined these close-ups, which were all similar, with other bits of film in three different combinations. In the first combination the close-up of Mosjukhin was immediately followed by a shot of a plate of soup standing on a table. It was obvious and certain that Mosjukhin was looking at this soup. In the second combination the face of Mosjukhin was joined to shots showing a coffin in which lay a dead woman. In the third the close-up was followed by a shot of a little girl playing with a funny toy bear. When we showed the three combinations to an audience which had not been let into the secret the result was terrific. The public raved about the acting of the artist. They pointed out the heavy pensiveness of his mood over the forgotten soup, were touched and moved by the deep sorrow with which he looked on the dead woman, and admired the light, happy smile with which he surveyed the girl at play. But we knew that in all three cases the face was exactly the same.

(Pudovkin 1929)

Kuleshov carried out further experiments using editing in which he cut together separate shots of a walking man, a waiting woman, a gate, a staircase and a mansion.[16] When the shots were combined the audience assumed that the different elements were present at the same location. Kuleshov had discovered the cinema's ability to link entirely unrelated material into coherent sequences. He termed the technique 'creative geography'.

Kuleshov's discoveries about the nature of the cinema medium provided a number of film-makers with a new set of ideas about how film could manipulate and deceive an audience. Perhaps the most vital consequence of the Kuleshov effect, however, for later directors, was its recognition that the audience were not merely passive recipients.

Soviet montage cinema

In the 1920s a number of the film-makers carried out further experiments with editing techniques along the same lines as Kuleshov: It was discovered that when two shots were joined together meaning could be made by emphasising the difference between shots, that is, instead of trying to cover up graphic dissimilarities between shots, as with **Hollywood cinema**, the difference could be emphasised and indeed become the main way in which meaning could be created. This 'montage' cinema which demanded that audiences continually searched for the meanings created by the **juxtaposition** of two shots can thus be seen as **alternative** to the continuity editing-based Hollywood cinema. One of the Soviet film-makers who developed this idea into both a theory and a practice of film-making was Sergei Eisenstein.

Hollywood cinema In classical Hollywood cinema, the editing is designed to be 'invisible'. It is intended to allow the audience closer views and to see the point of view of different characters. The editing is used essentially to clarify what is taking place in the narrative. This type of editing had become dominant in Hollywood film-making by approximately 1920.

juxtaposition In film studies, this usually refers to two different shots that have been joined together to make a contrast.

alternative Alternative cinema is defined with reference to dominant: it is an alternative (both economically and formally) to the dominant form. In any study concerning an 'alternative' cinema, the films would not only have to be examined in their own right, but also compared to contemporary dominant Hollywood cinema. A number of questions might have to be posed when analysing these alternative films: In what ways is this group of films different to the dominant cinema of the time? What are the possible reasons for the difference: cultural? economic? social? political? Could this 'alternative' way of making films, given the right conditions, have itself turned into the dominant cinema? The Soviet cinema of the 1920s, when compared to the Hollywood cinema of the same era, certainly could be regarded as alternative. In other words, it offered a style of film-making that was radically different to the mass of films that was being produced in America.

Eisenstein believed that maximum impact could be achieved if shots in a scene were in conflict. This belief was based on the general philosophical idea that 'existence' can only continue by constant change. In other words, everything surrounding us in the world is as a result of a 'collision' of opposite elements. The existing world is itself only in a temporary state until the next collision of elements produces a completely new state. It is only through this 'collision' that change can be effected. This method of creating meaning from such collision of opposites is termed **dialectical**. When applying

dialectical
A difficult term to define, as it has many different meanings. The *Collins English Dictionary* (2nd edn, 1986), for example, defines it as a 'disputation or debate, esp. intended to resolve differences between two views rather than to establish one of them as true'. The crucial factor to grasp in the context of Eisenstein's thinking, however, is the notion of change and the creation of a new order. Eisenstein would have defined dialectic with reference to Marxist philosophy, which believed that society was contradictory and in need of change.

this idea to film, Eisenstein proposed the view that when two shots are combined a completely new meaning is formed. For example, shot A combined with shot B does not produce AB but the new meaning C. The formulation can also be presented as: thesis + anti-thesis = synthesis.

Vsevolod Pudovkin, another key Soviet film-maker, was opposed to the theoretical ideas of Eisenstein, although they both used innovative forms of montage in their films. Pudovkin, like Kuleshov, believed that shots could be likened to bricks in the sense that they could be used as building blocks to construct a scene. Pudovkin then did not see his shots as being in conflict. In Pudovkin's formulae shot A + shot B = AB rather than C. Pudovkin aimed at linkage rather than conflict in his scenes.

The montage technique was not only confined to fiction film-making. Soviet documentary film-makers such as Dziga Vertov and Esfir Shub used montage extensively in a range of films in the 1920s, including Vertov's well-known *The Man with a Movie Camera* (1929). For Vertov much of the power of cinema came from its ability to record mechanically events that took place before the camera, but he also ensured that the audience was made aware of the constructed nature of his films. His films are a whirlwind of conflicting shots which disavow conventional ideas of narrative.

The montage technique for the majority of the Soviet film-makers could also provide sequences with a sense of rhythm and momentum, which could be used to increase or decrease the speed of the action. Eisenstein, for example, frequently increases his rate of cutting prior to the climax of a scene. Violent actions could also be emphasised by using a succession of short conflicting shots from different viewpoints. Montage, the film-makers discovered, could further be used to either compress or expand time, which could heighten the effect of certain actions or events.

See Chapter 5, pp. 191–192, for further discussion of Vertov and his contribution to documentary film.

Four different types of film montage[17]

The first two categories of montage outlined below are frequently, although not exclusively, used in Soviet film; the last two categories deal with montage techniques that are often to be found in mainstream films:

- intellectual montage (also called dialectical montage or discontinuity editing)
- linkage editing (also known as constructive editing)
- Hollywood montage
- fast cutting

Intellectual montage

In this type of editing, shots are placed together to emphasise their difference. They are in 'collision' with each other. For example, in *October* a shot of a mechanical golden peacock is placed next to a shot of a man (the peacock does not form part of the world of the film, that is, it is **non-diegetic**). The audience draw the conclusion that the man is vain. In this type of editing the audience are not passive as they play an active part in producing meaning from the film.

non-diegetic
Refers to any element that remains outside the world of the film, such as voiceovers, credits and mood-setting music, that does not originate from the world of the film.

Linkage editing

Mainly used by Pudovkin, who proposed a theory of montage based on this principle. In linkage editing individual shots are used to build up scenes. The shots are not in collision with each other, but are used as fragments or parts of a whole scene. The technique can be seen in *The Mother* and *The End of St Petersburg*.

Hollywood montage

Often used to show a quick succession of events over a period of time. For example, in *Raging Bull* (1980) Martin Scorsese shows the successful career of the boxer Jack La

Motta by combining shots (mostly still photographs) taken from a number of different fights interspersed with home movie footage of La Motta's home life. The shots are clearly intended to flow into each other rather than to be in conflict. The music played on the soundtrack over the images reinforces the sense of continuity.

Fast cutting

In which editing is used primarily to build suspense or tension. For example, in the gunfight at the climax of *The Good, the Bad and the Ugly* (1966), Sergio Leone creates a dramatic effect by using a combination of music, tighter and tighter close-ups of the three characters and a shortening of shot length.

Statistical analysis of Soviet films

Soviet films, because of the use of the montage technique, contain many more shots than Hollywood films of the same period. David Bordwell (1986)[18] claims that the Soviet films of the 1920s contain on average between 600 and 2,000 shots, whereas the films made in Hollywood between 1917 and 1928 contain on average between 500 and 1,000 shots. He further suggests that Hollywood films had an average shot length of five to six seconds while for Soviet films the average shot length was two to four seconds. The comparison provides concrete evidence of the unique nature of the editing used in the Soviet films in this period.

OTHER FEATURES OF SOVIET MONTAGE CINEMA

Aside from editing, these films have other features which separate them from the **dominant** Hollywood cinema. In keeping with a Marxist analysis of society, plots frequently do not centre on the individual; for example, in Eisenstein's *Strike*, *October* and *Battleship Potemkin*, individual heroes are replaced by a mass of people. The only characters that are individuated are those that wield power or have wealth. Events in the narrative therefore are not motivated by individuals. Films such as Pudovkin's *The Mother* and *The End of St Petersburg* and Dovzhenko's *Earth* (1930) do have central characters, but it is made clear that these characters are representative of the masses. The audience is not interested in the details of the heroes, only what they represent. A number of the Soviet film-makers (including Eisenstein and Pudovkin) also used non-actors to play key parts, believing that the external appearance of the character was vital to the performance. This idea is termed 'typage'.

The montage style also means that Soviet cinema relies more heavily on the use of the close-up than Hollywood cinema. Not only are there more shots overall in a scene, but a greater proportion of them are close-ups. A number of Soviet films also rely on high levels of **symbolism** to achieve their aims. The audience must be culturally and politically aware to be able to decode the messages that are being presented. In Eisenstein's *October*, for example, great demands are made on the audience to create a 'reading' of the film which does justice to Eisenstein's political thinking. It may seem that many of the film-makers ran the risk of making films that were not understood by their audience.

Several of the montage film-makers combined the montage principle with other techniques that they believed would revitalise the cinema. Lev Kuleshov, for example, placed great emphasis on the gestures and movement of actors. FEKS (Factory of the Eccentric Actor), formed by film-makers Grigori Kozintsev and Leonid Trauberg, had similar concerns about the role of the actor, but also paid great attention to mise-en-scène.

dominant
Refers to both economic strength and also to the dominant form or convention, which at this time is realism: dominant cinema in film studies is assumed to be Hollywood.

symbolism
The means by which a film-maker can assign additional meanings to objects/characters in a film. For example, in Dovzhenko's *Earth* and Eisenstein's *Old and New*, the tractor is a symbol of progress.

THE KEY SOVIET MONTAGE FILM-MAKERS OF THE 1920s

Fiction	*Documentary*
Lev Kuleshov	Dziga Vertov
Sergei Eisenstein	Esfir Shub
Vsevolod Pudovkin	
FEKS (Kozintsev and Trauberg)	
Alexander Dovzhenko	

A film directed by Eisenstein probably provided most viewers' first experience of Soviet montage. The history of the Soviet cinema of the 1920s, however, involves more than the work of this one director. In this section, although the work of Eisenstein is discussed in detail, the vital importance of Eisenstein's contemporaries is recognised by analysing the work of such directors as Kuleshov, Pudovkin, Kozintsev and Trauberg, Dovzhenko, Vertov and Shub.

Lev Kuleshov (1899–1970)

Key films
Engineer Prite's Project (1918)
The Extraordinary Adventures of Mr West in the Land of the Bolsheviks (1924)
The Death Ray (1925)
By the Law (1926)

Shortly after the revolution, Kuleshov was recruited as a teacher by the State Film School where he set up an experimental film workshop. Kuleshov and his students carried out a number of experiments related to editing, partly inspired by a lack of raw film stock. One of these experiments included re-editing D.W. Griffith's *Intolerance* (1916), a film that had impressed Kuleshov because of its innovative use of editing. The experiments resulted in the formation of a number of principles of film-making that the group adopted. The underlying belief for Kuleshov was that 'Film-art begins from the moment when the director begins to combine and join together the various pieces of film'.[19] Kuleshov's ideas about how editing should work are similar to those of Pudovkin in that his shots, rather than being in conflict, can be seen as blocks out of which a scene can be constructed. Significantly, Kuleshov's students included Vsevolod Pudovkin and, for a brief time, Sergei Eisenstein. In Eisenstein's films and theoretical writing the influence of Kuleshov can be seen clearly.

Kuleshov's experimentation was not confined to editing, however, but also involved acting. He believed that theatre-trained actors, in particular those from the Moscow Arts Theatre[20] were not suitable for the cinema. He also rejected the idea of using non-actors or 'types' chosen for their visual suitability for a role. He set up an acting laboratory dedicated to developing a style of acting tailored specifically to the requirements of the cinema and he carefully recruited would-be film actors who were 'endowed with natural beauty, good health, and the ability to show expediency and purpose on the screen without "acting" or "recreating", unaided by makeup, wigs, and props, of course' (cited in Zorkaya 1989: 52).

For comparison and contrast see Chapter 4, pp. 169–181, for a discussion of the star in Hollywood cinema.

The techniques that Kuleshov adopted emphasised gesture and movement, the exact nature and timing of which had been practised rigorously in rehearsals. This style of acting was combined with great attention to the composition and framing of each shot to give maximum impact to the action. Kuleshov's opportunity to apply the principles that he had developed came in 1924 when he was assigned valuable imported film stock to direct the first feature film of the film school: *The Extraordinary Adventures of Mr West in the Land of the Bolsheviks*.

□ CASE STUDY 1: LEV KULESHOV, *THE EXTRAORDINARY ADVENTURES OF MR WEST IN THE LAND OF THE BOLSHEVIKS* (1924)

The film is an action-comedy which uses satire to expose the false attitudes and beliefs about the Soviet Union held by many in the West. The action centres on the fate of Mr West, an American visitor to the USSR, whose view of the Bolsheviks as savages is formed by reading the *New York Times*. Mr West falls into the hands of a group of petty criminals who frighten him into parting with his dollars by dressing up to look like the Bolsheviks that Mr West has seen in his paper. At the climax he is rescued by a 'real' Bolshevik who uncovers the deception. Mr West's stereotypical views of the Bolsheviks are dismantled and he sends a radio message to his wife telling her to hang Lenin's picture in the study.

The montage technique used in *Mr West* is largely based on a system of close-ups of the actors that emphasise facial expressions. Kuleshov frequently cuts from an action to a close-up reaction shot of a character's face. He starts the film with a separate shot of Mr West juxtaposed with another of his wife; it is only later that we see them together. Later in the film Kuleshov cuts between a shot of the 'real' Bolshevik and Mr West standing on a balcony and another shot of marching Soviet troops taken at a different place and time (the film stock is markedly different).

Kuleshov here is using his technique of creative geography to make the audience construct a location in their minds that does not actually exist. The film also fulfils Kuleshov's ideas concerning acting. The movements of the actors are stylised and precise and it is clear that attention has been paid to even the smallest action. The comical nature of the action and a plot based on individual characters meant that the film was popular with audiences.[21]

• **Plate 11.1**
The Extraordinary Adventures of Mr West in the Land of the Bolsheviks (Lev Kuleshov, 1924)
Mr West is duped by the false Bolsheviks

Sergei Eisenstein (1898–1948)[22]

Eisenstein, as his age might indicate (he was just 26 when he completed *Strike*), did not emerge from the context of the pre-revolutionary Russian cinema. Prior to his film-making career, he had experimented with a number of different art forms, including the theatre. In this experimentation, the principles of his work in film may be found. In 1923 Eisenstein produced a version of a play by Alexander Ostrovky,[23] in which he attempted to communicate the messages of the play to the audience using a series of shocks which Eisenstein termed 'attractions': 'Emotions were expressed through flamboyant physical stunts…at the finale, firecrackers exploded under spectators' seats…[he] explained that the theatre could engage its audience through a calculated assembly of "strong moments" of shock or surprise' (Bordwell 1993: 6).

Eisenstein quickly abandoned experimentation with the theatre and turned to the more popular and accessible medium of film, to which he rigorously applied his theatrical principle of 'montage of attractions'.

☐ **CASE STUDY 2: SERGEI EISENSTEIN, *STRIKE* (1924); *BATTLESHIP POTEMKIN* (1925); *OCTOBER* (1927); *OLD AND NEW* (1929)**

Strike (1924)

Strike was the first of a proposed series of eight films[24] made by the Moscow Theatre of the Proletkult, under the general subheading 'Towards the Dictatorship of the Proletariat'. *Strike* is about the repression of a group of factory workers involved in

• **Plate 11.2**
Sergei Eisenstein
(1898–1948)

an industrial dispute, which ends with the massacre of the strikers and their families by government forces. The six-part structure of *Strike* – (1) 'All Quiet at the Factory', (2) 'The Immediate Cause of Strike', (3) 'The Factory Stands Idle', (4) 'The Strike is Protracted', (5) 'Engineering a Massacre', (6) 'Slaughter' – is due in part to Eisenstein's theatrical background, but it would also have been vital for the film to be contained on single reels as many cinemas had only one projector.

The plot of *Strike*, as in Eisenstein's later films *Battleship Potemkin* (1925) and *October* (1927), is not told using individual characters as heroes. Instead, any character that is individuated is deemed to be 'bad' or corrupt. The grotesque factory-owner, for example, is shown completely isolated in a vast office. The workers themselves, however, are seen usually as a group with no one individual standing out to play the role of leader. In Part 3 these ideas are combined. The scenes depicting the four stock-holders of the factory carelessly deciding the future of the strikers are intercut with images of strikers being attacked by mounted police; the individual concern of the capitalists contrasts with the collective concern of the masses. The effect of this montage is dramatic, as parallels can immediately be drawn by the viewer between, for example, the dishonesty, greed, deviousness and wealth of the management and the poverty and honesty of the workers. The political implications of this are obvious. Eisenstein, through montage, is seeking to persuade his audience towards a certain view.

The methods applied by Eisenstein in *Strike* are derived in part from a rebellion against what Eisenstein termed the 'Bourgeois Cinema' that was still the main form of entertainment in post-revolutionary cinemas. Eisenstein explains how this cinema was rejected in favour of his own approach: 'We brought collective and mass action onto the screen...our films in this period made an abrupt deviation – insisting on an understanding of the masses as hero' (cited in Leyda 1983: 181).

In terms of the Hollywood cinema it is not difficult to imagine how the plot of *Strike* could have been adapted into a mainstream film: the story of one individual's fight against authority. The comparison may be trite, but it does emphasise the difference in approach and purpose between the two different modes of representation. Eisenstein's decision not to use individual heroes is of course deliberate; the film registers a political ideology that enshrines the notion of collective strength.

• **Plate 11.3** *Strike* (Sergei Eisenstein, 1924) Mounted police enter the factory district

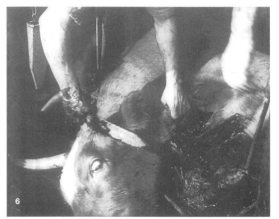

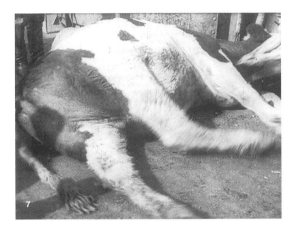

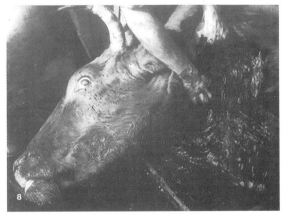

• **Plate 11.4** This sequence from *Strike* (lasting 25 seconds) illustrates Eisenstein's use of intellectual montage. An inter-title ('Rout') is inserted between shots 2 and 3

In *Strike* Eisenstein applies his principle of 'montage of attractions' to the editing. He believed that by creating visual 'jolts' between each cut, the viewer would be 'shocked' into new awarenesses. In most sequences this approach involves juxtaposing shots that are in conflict with each other in some way, either cutting between different actions taking place in a scene or emphasising the importance of certain actions or events by fragmenting them into a number of shots taken from different viewpoints. At various points in *Strike* Eisenstein juxtaposes shots which need to be interpreted by the audience. One of the best examples of this type of 'intellectual montage' is in the last part of the film ('Slaughter'), in which Eisenstein juxtaposes a non-diegetic image of a bull being slaughtered with shots of the factory workers being systematically butchered by government forces. The formula mentioned earlier can be applied: shot A (massacre of the workers) + shot B (bull being slaughtered) = NEW MEANING C (that the workers are being killed cold-bloodedly like animals in a slaughterhouse). It is the audience that is creating meaning here from the juxtaposition of the shots, thus becoming active political interpreters.

Battleship Potemkin (1925)

Eisenstein's second film, *Battleship Potemkin*, is based on the true story of a mutiny that took place on board the *Potemkin* in 1905.[25] As in *Strike*, *Battleship Potemkin* is split into a number of distinct parts: (1) 'Men and Maggots', (2) 'Drama on the Quarter Deck', (3) 'Appeal from the Dead', (4) 'The Odessa Steps', (5) 'Meeting the Squadron'.

The central scene of the film, 'The Odessa Steps', consisting of parallel lines of soldiers marching down the steps leading to the harbour systematically shooting the onlookers, provides a vivid example of the effectiveness of Eisenstein's montage technique.[26] A close examination of the sequence reveals that Eisenstein, by using montage to repeat certain key events, has expanded time.[27] The effect is to heighten the horrific nature of the slaughter as well as to hold the audience in suspense as the pram finally begins its descent. The furious and shocking climax to the scene demonstrates how Eisenstein is able to use montage to manipulate audience expectations and to shock with violent juxtapositions and graphic images.

In the last part of the film in which the sailors aboard the *Potemkin* are nervously anticipating an attack by the rest of the Russian Fleet, Eisenstein builds up tension by increasing the number of cuts in a montage finale that maintains a consistently high rate of shots per minute. The scene provides an excellent example of the way in which montage could be used to create an event that did not exist as a whole, as according to Eisenstein the shots of the 'Russian' squadron were taken from 'old newsreels of naval manoeuvres – not even of the Russian Fleet' (cited in Leyda 1983: 195).[28] It also reveals how montage can be used for rhythmic effect, as the fast cutting between the different elements gives the scene a sense of urgency which would be impossible to achieve using any other method.

The opposition of critics at the time ironically stressed the difficulties of understanding *Potemkin*'s experimental form; ironic because it was through film form that Eisenstein hoped to make his political points. It was also declared that *Potemkin* was pitched far above the intellectual level of most peasants, a damning indictment for any propaganda/revolutionary piece. However, although *Potemkin* was not successful as a piece of popular propaganda, it did, like *Strike* before it, mark a major step in the progress of revolutionary cinema. It also represented the first film that achieved recognition and acclaim for Soviet cinema. The claim that the experimental nature of *Potemkin* was not solely to blame for its unpopularity, and that it was badly let down by Sovkino's methods of distribution, is a view that should certainly be considered.

• **Plate 11.5**
Battleship Potemkin
(Sergei Eisenstein,
1925)
Drama on the quarter-
deck (the firing squad)

• **Plate 11.6**
Battleship Potemkin
(Sergei Eisenstein,
1925)
The Odessa Steps

• **Plates 11.7, 11.8 and 11.9** *Battleship Potemkin* (Sergei Eisenstein, 1925)
Immediately after the massacre on the Odessa Steps, the sailors on the battleship take their revenge by shelling the headquarters of the generals. As part of this sequence, Eisenstein juxtaposes three images of stone lions in different stages of awakening as a symbol of the awakening of the Russian people to political ideas and action.

October (1927)

October, made for the Tenth Anniversary celebrations of the Russian Revolution, depicts the build-up to the October Revolution, ending with the storming of the Winter Palace by the Bolsheviks. It is considered the most experimental of Eisenstein's films, especially in its increased use of 'intellectual montage', which demands that the audience think critically and constructively about important political issues. A demonstration of this type of montage can be found in the scene in which both Kerensky and General Kornilov are depicted as Napoleons. By intercutting between the two men and the plaster cast figures of Napoleon, Eisenstein effectively exposes both the vanity and essentially the lack of any power within the characters themselves to form a separate identity.[29] Eisenstein's 'intellectual montage' also involves **diegetic** material. For example, early in the film, shots of a soldier cowering in a trench are juxtaposed with low-angle shots of a vast cannon being unloaded elsewhere. The combination of shots initially points to the soldier being physically crushed, but then swiftly the assumption is reached that the war is oppressive, degrading and without purpose for the ordinary troops.

diegetic
The elements of a film that originate from directly within the film's narrative. For example, a popular song that is being played on the soundtrack would be diegetic if it was clear that it was coming from a source within the world of the film such as a car radio.

• **Plate 11.10**
October
(Sergei Eisenstein,
1927)
Lenin's arrival at the
Finland Railway Station

Eisenstein also combines montage techniques with visual puns and symbolism for political effect. At one point, in order to degrade the power of the church, he swiftly cuts from the image of one deity to another, starting with a magnificent statue of Christ, and ending up with a primitive wooden idol, demonstrating that all religions essentially worship crude man-made objects. Eisenstein's use of such techniques was considered by many to be obscure, inaccessible in meaning and élitist. Victor Shklovsky, writing in *Novyi Lef* in 1927, records the responses of a man connected with the cinema:

After viewing some Eisenstein sequences a man who is intelligent and conversant with cinema said to me, 'That is very good. I like that a lot but what will the masses say? What will the people we are working for say?' What can you say to that?

(Cited in Taylor and Christie 1988: 182)

Indeed, an examination of contemporary criticism of *October* reveals that far from being popular among Soviet audiences, the film was met with derision and apprehension.

Old and New (1929)

The adverse reaction to *October* prompted Eisenstein to produce *Old and New*, a film more readily understood by audiences. Despite employing a number of the techniques used in *October*, Eisenstein presents them in a simplified form. Juxtapositions, for example, are more obvious and on a less symbolic level.

• **Plate 11.11**
October
(Sergei Eisenstein, 1927)

• **Plate 11.12**
Old and New (Sergei Eisenstein, 1929)
The new tractor is eventually delivered to Martha's co-operative

The narrative of *Old and New*, concerned with the collectivisation of agriculture, unlike Eisenstein's previous films, is bound together by a central character or heroine 'Martha'. Despite its more conventional narrative form, the film contains one of Eisenstein's most effective montage sequences in which a cream separator is delivered to the collective farm. The new machine is eyed suspiciously by the peasants as milk is poured into it. In an ever-quickening flow of images, Eisenstein cuts between the glittering, spinning parts of the machine, the changing faces of the peasants and non-diegetic shots of fountains of water which symbolise the future flow of cream from the separator. The film is fascinating to study in the context of Eisenstein's earlier work and marks an attempt to address problems of understanding associated with *October*.

Key films
The Mother (1926)
The End of St Petersburg (1927)
Storm Over Asia (1928)

Vsevolod Pudovkin (1893–1953)

Editing is the language of the film director. Just as in living speech, so, one may say, in editing: there is a word – the piece of exposed film, the image; a phrase – the combination of these pieces.

(Pudovkin, cited in Perkins 1972a: 21)

Pudovkin believed that the power of cinema comes from editing. In the above quotation he claims that a 'shot' (or image) which is the equivalent of the single word in language has very limited meaning. However, when a number of words are combined together they form a 'phrase' which is dense with meaning. Pudovkin's equivalent of a 'phrase' was a number of shots edited together. He went further to support his claim by contending that:

every object-taken from a given viewpoint and shown on the screen to spectators, is a *dead object*, even though it has moved before the camera....Only if the object be placed together among a number of separate objects, only if it be presented as part of a synthesis of different separate visual images, is it endowed with filmic life.

(Ibid.: 22)

It would seem initially that Pudovkin's theoretical position regarding the effectiveness of editing was in tandem with his contemporary Eisenstein. There are, however, important differences in the specific way each director thought editing should be used.[30] Pudovkin did not agree with Eisenstein's system of montage, which created visual 'jolts' between cuts. Instead, Pudovkin believed greater impact could be made by linking shots in a constructive way. Shots were to be used as individual building blocks, made to fit together exactly. Although seemingly theoretically opposed to Eisensteinian montage, Pudovkin made extensive use of devices such as 'intellectual montage' in *The Mother* and *The End of St Petersburg*. Pudovkin's juxtapositions, however, are much less symbolic, more clearly related to the diegetic world of the film and less intent on creating conflict than those of Eisenstein. Leon Moussinac, a French historian, summed up the differences between the two directors: 'An Eisenstein film resembles a shout, a Pudovkin film evokes a song' (cited in Taylor 1979: 142).

Pudovkin, like Eisenstein, cast according to 'type' and was concerned about the problem of 'stagey acting'. He stated:

I want to work only with real material – this is my principle. I maintain that to show, alongside real water and real trees and grass, a property beard pasted on the actor's face, wrinkles traced by means of paint, or stagey acting is impossible. It is opposed to the most elementary ideas of style.[31]

Unlike Eisenstein, however, Pudovkin uses individual characters that are cast in the role of hero or heroine to carry the narrative, and although he discouraged the use of professional actors some of his lead parts were played by professional actors of the Moscow Arts Theatre.[32]

□ **CASE STUDY 3: VSEVOLOD PUDOVKIN, *THE MOTHER* (1926); *THE END OF ST PETERSBURG* (1927)**

The Mother (1926)

The scenario for Pudovkin's *The Mother* is based on the earlier play by Gorky of the same name. The plot is concerned with the political awakening of a mother after she betrays her son to the police, in the belief that he will be dealt with justly. The action is set (as in *Battleship Potemkin*) in the revolutionary context of 1905, with strikes, mass protests and a final brutal massacre of the workers.

With its focus on individuals, the film offers an interesting contrast to Eisenstein's approach to revolutionary-cinema. In *The Mother*, the role of the individual is reinstated and emphasised. The mass struggle is thus registered through the lives and fates of separate characters involved in that struggle. It is important to note that the individual characters are not highlighted in such a way that the general struggle itself becomes obscured. The audience is encouraged to make connections between individual fate and the fate of the masses. Pudovkin is thus using individual characters to make his political points, believing that the audience would be able to relate better to separate identities than to an anonymous mass.

Pudovkin's use of 'linkage' editing (shot A + shot B = AB) can be illustrated in the trial scene at the mid-point of the film. The scene is composed of a large number of shots which tend to centre on single characters or pairs of characters. The fragmentation allows Pudovkin to draw direct comparisons between, for example, the uninterested and uncaring attitude of the judges, the accused Pavel, his mother and several of the gossiping onlookers. Close shots of the soldiers guarding the courthouse are also inserted in order to demonstrate that 'justice' is being upheld by a substantial force. Pudovkin clearly reveals the judges to be vain and self-interested by highlighting their overriding concern with attire and pictures of horses, rather than the proceedings of the trial. If the same scene had been shot by Eisenstein the vanity of the judges might have been indicated in a similar way to that of Kerensky in *October* (that is, by juxtaposing him with a shot of a peacock).

The End of St Petersburg (1927)

Made to celebrate the Tenth Anniversary of the October Revolution, *The End of St Petersburg*, based on André Bely's 1916 symbolist novel *Petersburg*,[33] also uses individual characters to deal with the events preceding the revolution. One is a young peasant boy who has come to St Petersburg to seek work, as his family can no longer support him at home. Despite initial involvement with strikebreakers, the boy quickly becomes aware of the corruption and injustice of the Tsarist regime. His political awakening, however, lands him in prison and he is forced to volunteer into the Tsar's army, where he is exposed to the horrors of trench warfare.

Using montage, Pudovkin draws a contrast between the suffering of the soldiers who are fighting for the Tsar and the greed of those who are benefiting financially from the war. Horrific images of dying soldiers in mud at the front-line trenches are intercut with scenes at the St Petersburg stock market. As the fighting gets worse and worse at the front, the higher the value of the shares becomes – thereby enforcing the point that people are making money out of suffering. The old order, by supporting and being supported by the stock market, is seen to be inhumane and preoccupied with the wrong values – the acquisition of wealth at whatever cost. Pudovkin at one point intercuts

• **Plate 11.13**
The End of St Petersburg (Vsevolod Pudovkin, 1927) One of Pudovkin's central characters, a young peasant boy, is seen here demanding justice from the authorities

between the image of a soldier slashing ferociously at an opponent with his bayonet and the image of a stock market figure frenetically dealing at the stock exchange. He thus likens the barbarities of war to the barbarity inherent in the centre of the capitalist structure. Earlier Pudovkin intercut between the images of death at the front and the words 'In the name of the Tsar, the fatherland, and the capital'. This is clearly ironic as the soldiers have no idea what they are fighting for – certainly not for the Tsar.

In the final part of *The End of St Petersburg*, in the storming of the Winter Palace sequences, Pudovkin intercuts images of the advancing Bolsheviks with both fast-moving clouds and crashing waves. This emphasises the power and inevitability of the revolution – revolution is unstoppable. Earlier in a Bolshevik's speech at the Lebedev factory, images of machinery slowing down are intercut with the speaker to point to the power of his words upon the workers.

Eccentrism of the FEKS: Grigori Kozintsev and Leonid Trauberg

Key films
The Adventures of Oktyabrina (1924)
The Cloak (1926)
The New Babylon (1929)

FEKS (Factory of the Eccentric Actor), formed in December 1921 by a small group of theatre actors and directors, shared the common aim of reforming the traditional theatre and incorporating into their experimental work elements of the circus, music hall and puppet theatre. On 9 July 1922 FEKS published a manifesto which stated their aims as a group.[34] The poster shown on page 411 shows just a small sample of the material contained within the manifesto.

The extract makes it clear that FEKS valued the bold, dynamic and popular elements of circus and cinema posters. It was with these elements that they proposed to revitalise the theatre. Two of the founding members of the group, Grigori Kozintsev and Leonid Trauberg, became interested in the cinema, making a number of short experimental films between 1924 and 1927, including *The Adventures of Oktyabrina* (1924)

WE
CONSIDER ART AS A TIRELESS RAM SHATTERING THE HIGH WALLS OF HABIT AND DOGMA

———————

But we also have our own ancestors! and lots of them

———————

The brilliant creators of cinema posters, circus posters, music hall posters. Unknown designers of pulp thrillers who exalt the exploits of the King of the detectives or adventurers. In using your art, more magnificent than a clown's red nose, we spring up as if from a trampoline to perform our intripid somersault! Only the poster has escaped the pernicious scalpel of analysis and the intellect. Subject and form are indivisible, but what do they sing of?

Danger, Audacity, Violence, Pursuit, Revolution, Gold, Blood, Laxative pills, Charlie Chaplin, Catastrophes on land, sea and in the air. Fat cigars, Prima donnas of the operettas, Adventures of all sorts, Skating rinks, Tap shoes, Horses, Wrestling, Torch singers, Somersaults on bicycles and all those millions and millions of events which make splendid our Today!

THE 200 VOLUMES OF GERMAN EXPRESSIONISM DO NOT OFFER THE EXPRESSIVITY OF ONE SOLE

CIRCUS POSTER!!!

• **Plate 11.14** *The New Babylon* (Grigori Kozintsev and Leonid Trauberg, 1929)

and *The Cloak* (1926). The films primarily emphasised the artificial nature of the mise-en-scène and the stylised nature of the acting rather than the editing.

Kozintsev and Trauberg are perhaps best known for their 1929 film, *The New Babylon*, based on the events building up to the Paris Commune of 1871. As in their previous films, artificial mise-en-scène combined with stylised acting were employed, but extensive use was made also of camera movement. At one point in the film the camera moves swiftly enough to blur the image, thus conveying the sense of confusion present in the scene. The response to the film was unfavourable, as audiences failed to understand its form.

□ CASE STUDY 4: ALEXANDER DOVZHENKO, *ARSENAL* (1929); *EARTH* (1930)[35]

Inspired by the creative and political possibilities of film, Dovzhenko had approached the Odessa film studio in 1926. At this point he had little knowledge of cinema, but within a few years he had made an outstanding contribution to Soviet revolutionary cinema with such films as *Arsenal* and *Earth* which, in addition to revolutionary fervour, displayed poetic qualities and provided a demonstration of his love for the Ukraine and its people.

Arsenal surveys the devastating impact of the First World War and the political struggles between the Social Democrats and the Bolsheviks during 1917. The opening
sequences of *Arsenal* exemplify Dovzhenko's approach to film-making. There is little
camera movement or use of establishing shots and, overall, there is less concern with a
conventional rendering of space and time than with the emotional impact of the flow of
images. In these opening and further sequences Dovzhenko reveals the loss and
impoverishment of the people, as well as the unthinking callousness of the social order.

Arsenal shows that Dovzhenko is not concerned with personalised conflict between
individuals; but with the ongoing struggle between opposing social forces. This concern
is pursued further in *Earth*, which deals with class struggle in the countryside, although
like *Arsenal* it features a strong attractive male hero, Vasil. The latter is the operator of
the tractor which will allow the collective farm effectively to rid the village of the self-
seeking and more prosperous peasants, the kulaks. In the end Vasil is shot by Khoma,
the son of a kulak, although what Vasil stands for will not be defeated. Vasil's father,
hitherto hostile to the young revolutionaries of the village, commits himself to the cause
of collectivisation and rejects a religious burial in favour of the village youth singing
songs about the new life to come. The film, then, presents a strong case for the recently
instigated policy of the collectivisation of agriculture. Commentators on the film,
however, have argued that the formal and poetic qualities of the film actually undermine
the political message. Denise J. Youngblood, for example, states that:

Dovzhenko's *Earth* (1930) is a much more curious example of the collectivisation film – the politically correct story of a handsome young village Party activist murdered by an evil and dissolute
kulak opposed to collectivisation is undercut by a deeply subversive subtext related to its form. The
lyrical imagery and slow-rhythms of this film, totally unlike Eisenstein's, belie the purported theme
and in effect serve as a paean to a way of life soon to be no more.

(Youngblood 1992: 169)

• **Plate 11.15**
Earth (Alexander
Dovzhenko, 1930)

The opening sequence in which Vasil's grandfather dies would certainly seem to bear out this interpretation. He dies contented, his last act being to enjoy a pear, a product of the fruitful Ukrainian earth. Next to him a baby plays and a boy eats an apple, while the adult members of the family await the inevitable. This portrait of pastoral abundance and peacefulness with its allusions to the cycle of life and death seem to undermine the necessity for revolutionary change, but it is made clear by the old man's friend Petro that his has been a life of hard work – 'Seventy-five years behind a plough'.

Dziga Vertov (1896–1954)

Key films
Film Truth (Kino-Pravda) (1922)
Kino-Eye (1924)
A Sixth of the World (1926)
The Man With a Movie Camera (1929)
Enthusiasm (1931)

Dziga Vertov[36] (pseudonym of Denis Kaufman) was interested in the idea that the film camera had the potential to capture 'truth'; the camera could be seen simply as a mechanical device that was capable of recording the world without human intervention. Vertov led a group of film-makers called *Kinoki* ('cinema-eye') who stated in their 1923 manifesto:

I am the Cine-Eye. I am the mechanical eye.

I the machine show you the world as only I can see it.

I emancipate myself henceforth and forever from human immobility. *I am in constant motion.* I approach objects and move away from them, I creep up on them, I clamber over them, I move alongside the muzzle of a running horse, I tear into a crowd at full tilt, I flee before fleeing soldiers, I turn over on my back, I rise up with aeroplanes, I fall and rise with falling and rising bodies.

(Cited in Taylor and Christie 1988: 93)

See Chapter 5, pp. 191–192, for further discussion of Vertov's contribution to documentary film.

Vertov believed that the fiction film could not be used to reveal the 'truth' about a society. His films were based on documenting events around him; nothing should be artificially set up or staged for the camera. In 1922 Vertov had stated: 'WE declare the old films, the romantic, the theatricalised etc., to be leprous' (ibid.: 69).

Vertov's techniques were based on experimentation caused by the general scarcity of film stock and also, when available, the short lengths of the negative film. His experiments included using old newsreels as part of his films, and he found that new meanings could be created by the conflict produced by the old material and the new. Vertov soon discovered that the conflicts produced by montage were a vital element in the construction of meaning in his films.

Perhaps one of the most interesting features of Vertov's films is that great effort is taken to ensure that the audience is made aware of cameraman, editor and the whole process of producing a film. In *The Man with a Movie Camera*, for example, Vertov shows the cameraman shooting the scenes that we see before us, and later we see shots of this same film being edited. This technique of acknowledging the nature of the film-making process can be linked to documentary film-making practice in the 1970s and 1980s (in the films of Emile de Antonio and Jean-Pierre Gorin, for example) which went against the **fly-on-the-wall** practice and attempted to show the presence of the film-crew and camera and the fact that the audience are watching a manufactured film rather than 'reality'. This style of film-making which draws attention to its own process is often termed 'self-reflexive'.

fly-on-the-wall
A term associated with a style of documentary film-making which attempts to present events as though the presence of the camera and film crew had not influenced them in any way.

Esfir Shub (1894–1959)

Esfir Shub is an interesting female figure in a period of film-making dominated by men. She was initially employed by the Soviet government to re-edit foreign films to make them conform to the ideology of communism. Shub also re-edited old Tsarist newsreels to show the corrupt nature of the old order. Shub's practice of reassembling parts of existing films culminated in the adoption of the montage technique.

☐ **CASE STUDY 5: ESFIR SHUB,** *THE FALL OF THE ROMANOV DYNASTY* **(1927)**

Shub's first feature-length film, *The Fall of the Romanov Dynasty*, constructed entirely from old newsreels, was made to celebrate the Tenth Anniversary of the October Revolution, and it is claimed that 60,000 metres of film had to be examined in order to finish the project.[37] Shub provides new commentary on existing material by inserting intertitles between shots. By juxtaposing sequences of shots from different newsreels she also makes the audience draw new conclusions about the material. For example, she contrasts shots of an aristocratic gathering with shots of workers digging ditches. The intertitle reads 'by the sweat of your brow'. The intertitles and the juxtaposition of the images encourage the audience to assign an aberrant decoding to the original shots. In other words, the audience can deliberately 'misread' the images. Shub uses images which emphasise the pomp and splendour of Tsarist Russia, which in the context of the film look absurd and out of place; the audience is forced to be critical of this obvious display of wealth.

Although the film in principle uses montage in a way similar to that of Eisenstein or Pudovkin (in particular the way in which the audience are made active participants in the text), Shub does not make use of its rhythmic possibilities. The pace of the film is on the whole sedate, although it does put its political messages across in a powerful and convincing way. Recently, there has been a call by Graham Roberts for a re-evaluation of Esfir Shub; Roberts claims that Shub's contribution to the Soviet cinema has been undervalued (see Roberts 1991).

Key films
The Fall of the Romanov Dynasty (1927)
The Great Road (1927)
The Russia of Nicholas II and Lev Tolstoy (1928)

AUDIENCE RESPONSE

Viewers in the West may possibly already have an idea of the nature of the Soviet cinema after seeing extracts from films discussed previously such as Sergei Eisenstein's *Battleship Potemkin* or *October*. They may have wondered how many films such as these were made and how they were received by Soviet audiences that had only a few years previously gone through the upheaval of civil war. They may have pitied or even envied the Soviet cinema-goer – were these the only films that people could see on a Friday night? How could a largely uneducated population have coped with sophisticated material such as this?

Recent research into the Soviet cinema of the 1920s has encouraged new ideas. In the past, attention has focused on a number of key directors such as Pudovkin, Eisenstein and Vertov, whose films in the Soviet Union and later in the West were received with critical acclaim. We must, however, examine new evidence that points to the fact that Russian audiences were far more likely to be watching the Soviet 1920s equivalent of *Jurassic Park* than the likes of *Battleship Potemkin*, *Strike* and *October*.

Richard Stites, in *Russian Popular Culture: Entertainment and Society since 1900*, reveals that the majority of Soviet directors were making mainstream films that were conventional in form and content. The montage film was the exception rather than the rule:

The most popular movie genres of the revolutionary period were the same as the foreign and pre-revolutionary Russian ones: costume drama, action and adventure, literary works adapted for the screen, melodramas, and comedy. Those who patronized them were not merely the *nepmanskaya auditoriya*, that is the bourgeoisie, alleged to be addicted to lurid sex films. Working-class clubs sponsored by the Communist Party also had to show some entertainment films or risk losing their audience.

(Stites 1992: 56)

Soviet audiences also favoured foreign films which were imported in large numbers throughout the 1920s.

But why were the Soviet propaganda films relatively less successful? Why would audiences rather see foreign and conventional Soviet genre films? Were foreign films perceived as being more exciting or exotic? Denise Youngblood, in *Movies for the Masses*, cites an interview conducted in 1929 with a Soviet cinema manager that recorded audience response:

He noted that 'the public watched [Dovzhenko's *Arsenal*] with great difficulty', and that attendance dropped to 50 percent of normal when his theatre screened *New Babylon*, Kozintsev and Trauberg's famous picture about the Paris Commune. Asked about the reaction to Vertov's *The Man with the Movie Camera*, he replied sarcastically, 'One hardly need say that if *New Babylon* didn't satisfy the spectator's requirements and "lost" him, then *The Man with the Movie Camera* didn't satisfy him either'.

(cited in Youngblood 1992: 18–19)

The problem is clear. The Soviet propaganda films that were intended for the masses, from the illiterate peasant upwards, simply were not being understood by Soviet audiences, whereas the clear hero-led narrative structure of the foreign and Soviet genre films were far more straightforward and appealing. It is well documented that the American version of *Robin Hood* proved more successful in Soviet cinemas on all counts. The film-makers involved in Soviet propaganda production, although committed to the ideals of communism, were also committed to experimenting with film form. The experimentation in this case clearly did not culminate in a popular cinema that appealed to the masses.

THEORETICAL DEBATES: MONTAGE VERSUS REALISM

For further discussion of realism and Bazin, see Chapter 2, p.69.

The montage technique has been widely acknowledged as a powerful means of expression, and to many cinema theorists montage is the essence of cinema. The technique, however, does have its opponents, among them the French film critic and theorist André Bazin.[38] Bazin was concerned with the cinema's ability to record 'reality'. He saw in cinema a means of capturing a record of events before the camera with minimum mediation. Bazin regarded the montage cinema of the Soviets (among others) as essentially non-realist because scenes could be manipulated and altered in many different ways. He claimed that the audience of montage cinema was essentially passive,[39] as the director forced the audience towards certain meanings.

For further discussion of realism and documentary film, see Chapter 5.

Bazin saw montage cinema as being in direct opposition to a style of film-making associated with realism. Realism is a term often associated with the Hollywood cinema, but Bazin used it to refer to a style of film-making adopted by certain film-makers such as Jean Renoir, a French director who felt that the power of cinema came not from editing but from mise-en-scène. The realists, unlike the montage film-makers, took great pains to hide the artificial constructed nature of film. The long take, for example, was used frequently as it made editing unnecessary. The use of the long take supported the claim that what was being watched was unmediated and therefore more 'realistic'. Bazin cited further devices that could enhance the 'reality' of a scene, for example the use of deep-focus, wide-angle lenses, the long shot and a highly mobile camera, all of which meant that the film-maker could preserve real time and space in individual scenes.

POSTSCRIPT TO THE 1920s

The 1930s and after: the decline of experimentation in Soviet cinema

In the 1930s the Soviet authorities, under the guidance of Stalin, reacted to the unpopularity of many Soviet films by issuing strict guidelines on how films should be made. This set of 'rules', essentially demanding hero-led narratives and concerned with realistic subject matter, was termed 'Socialist Realism'. The head of the Soviet film industry outlined in 1933 why such a policy was necessary: 'A film and its success are directly linked to the degree of entertainment in the plot...that is why we are obliged to require our masters [the film-makers] to produce works that have strong plots and are organised around a story-line' (cited in Taylor 1986: 43).[40]

The policy of 'Socialist Realism' was combined with a complete ban on imported foreign films. By removing these positive representations of capitalism Stalin had also effectively made the Soviet film industry a monopoly; audiences could either see Soviet films or see no films at all.

The direct interest that the Soviet state took in the film industry reveals its perceived importance, but also had drastic consequences for many of the directors. It was noted by the authorities, for example, that several of these directors were not actually Communist Party members. (This might explain perhaps why they were more interested in form or technique than making positive films about communism that were easy to comprehend.) The film-makers of the 1920s discussed in this chapter were mostly not successful in the 1930s and 1940s. Eisenstein, for example, continued to make films, but the majority were either suppressed or had their funding withdrawn.

However, the decline of montage cinema could possibly be the consequence of another factor: technology. In October 1929 the first Soviet sound films were released and with this advance in cinema technology came the almost immediate downfall of film-making practices that relied on either complex camera movement or rapid editing, as sound cinema initially required non-movable cameras and fixed microphones in order to record dialogue.

The legacy of the Soviet cinema: its influence on modern cinema[41]

The impact of Soviet films of the 1920s on the analysis of film and film-making itself was immediate and continues to this day. The films, however, have not so much provided a model for successive film-makers as been an inspiration for their work. The British Documentary Movement of the 1930s, for example, was influenced by Soviet montage as well as impressed by the idea that films could be a force for education. The film-makers in this movement, however, did not conceive of films having a revolutionary role or even the role of questioning contemporary inequalities. Other film-makers have been inspired by the Soviet cinema because of its rejection of the forms and conventions of the dominant Hollywood entertainment cinema. Jean-Luc Godard, for example, demanded that audiences participate in the construction of meaning in his films and so engage directly with social and political questions. The achievements of Eisenstein continue to impress film editors as well as contemporary film directors. The editor, Ralph Rosenblum, for example, states in his discussion of *Battleship Potemkin* that '[a]lthough the movie is filled with stunning moments, the massacre on the Odessa steps outweighs them all; it remains for editors everywhere the single most intimidating piece of film ever assembled' (Rosenblum and Karen 1979).

Direct references to Eisenstein's films are numerous, ranging from Bernardo Bertolucci's subtle allusions to *Strike* in his *Tragedy of a Ridiculous Man* (1981) through Brian de Palma's opportunistic reworking of the Odessa Steps sequence in *The Untouchables* (1987)[42] to Zbigniew Rybczynski's use of the same sequence in *Steps* (1987)[43] in order to satirise cultural attitudes including the veneration of *Battleship Potemkin* as a work of art.[44] Dovzhenko's influence has not been a direct political one, but the films of Andrei Tarkovsky, a one-time pupil of Dovzhenko, and a film such as *My Childhood* (1972) by the Scottish film-maker Bill Douglas, exhibit a similar emotional intensity.

1 **Examine the relationship between Soviet cinema, theatre and the visual arts.**
2 **How successful do you think Soviet film-makers were in combining mass entertainment and revolutionary politics?**
3 **For many Soviet film-makers editing was the source of cinematic energy and impact. Did this mean that they neglected the impact of mise-en-scène and music?**
4 **Trace the influence of Soviet cinema of the 1920s on subsequent film-makers and film movements.**

NOTES

1   The term peasants is used to describe those who worked on the land in the country, and the term workers to describe those who worked within cities. This became a source of dispute in the 1920s when there was greater concern with efficiency and a more elaborate division of labour (see Thompson 1993).
2   This was a planned attack by a relatively small force, not a mass uprising as chronicled by Eisenstein in his 1927 film *October*.
3   An unusual account of this period told from the point of view of the White side can be found in Mikhail Bulgakov's 1926 novel, *The White Guard* (available in the UK as a Flamingo paperback).
4   The British Film Institute has released a number of early Russian films on video (in ten volumes).
5   See the list of selected Russian films in Further viewing.
6   The history of what happened to the migrant Russian film-makers and stars is an area worthy of study in its own right.
7   Protazanov was not in the Soviet Union for the full duration of this period; he emigrated briefly to Paris in 1920–23.
8   For more information on Protazanov, see Christie and Graffy (1993). For more information on the Russian cinema, see Leyda (1983); and Usai *et al.* (1989).
9   The first Russian studio was set up by Drankov in 1907.
10 The first half of this section is by Danny Rivers (Film Studies Lecturer, West Kent College).
11 The context of this remark can be found in Leyda (1983: 161).
12 The Museum of the Moving Image (MOMI) recreated the cinema carriage of an Agit Train complete with commentator, although the Soviet films being shown are from the period 1924–30.
13 The civil war also resulted in trade barriers being set up which prevented the importation of film stock and cinema equipment into the Soviet Union. This had a dramatic effect on the film industry as the Soviet Union initially had no means of producing its own film stock and lenses.
14 Vladimir Vladimirovich Mayakovsky (1893–1930).
15 The team effort involved in the production of a feature film would clearly cost a great deal more than an individual artist producing a painting. The Russian film industry, although economically successful, needed to produce films that would appeal to a wide audience. The desire to experi-

ment with film form, when the existing genres were popular, was therefore limited.
16 The mansion was in fact the White House.
17 Adapted from Kawin (1987: 99–101).
18 Bordwell uses a technique pioneered by Barry Salt in his article 'Statistical Style Analysis of Motion Pictures', *Film Quarterly* (Vol. 28, No. 2, Winter 1974–75).
19 Cited by Pudovkin at a lecture given at the London Film School in 1929.
20 The Moscow Arts Theatre under the direction of Konstantin Stanislavski developed a method of acting which required the actor to attempt to 'become' the character.
21 This can be inferred from the fact that Goskino made thirty-two prints of the film.
22 For fuller details and a chronology of the life of Eisenstein, see Bordwell (1993).
23 A well-known Russian playwright (1823–86).
24 The other seven films were never made.
25 Eisenstein bends historical fact in the film as the sailors on board the *Potemkin*, instead of persuading the Russian Fleet to join the struggle, were captured and the mutiny suppressed.
26 The scene has been much copied by recent film-makers: see the section on the 'Legacy of the Soviet cinema: its influence on modern cinema', on pp. 417.
27 See Bordwell (1993: 74) for an excellent analysis of the sequence.
28 Leyda also points out that the same sequence caused 'an anxious debate in the German Reichstag on the size of the Soviet Navy'.
29 Bordwell, in *The Cinema of Eisenstein* (1983: 85), claims that the peacock could be seen as a diegetic image as it forms part of the treasures contained within the Winter Palace. Yuri Tsivian, in 'Eisenstein's *October* and Russian Symbolist Culture' (see Christie and Taylor 1993), puts forward the view that 'Eisenstein was hoping to attain the effect of Kerensky entering the peacock's asshole'.
30 Pudovkin's films, like those of Eisenstein, were based on a body of theoretical writing.
31 Lecture given by Pudovkin at the London Film Society, 1929.
32 The theatre was founded in 1898 by Konstantin Stanislavski and Vladimir Nemirovich-Danchenko.

33 Published in the UK by Penguin (London, 1983).

34 The manifesto was reprinted in 1992 in a limited edition of 500 copies by Aldgate Press, London.

35 Section on Dovzhenko written by Danny Rivers (West Kent College).

36 Vertov in Russian is derived from the Russian word for 'rotation' and was thus a reflection of his approach to the arts.

37 Soviet montage cinema tended to place stress on the importance of the director (auteur) and work in post-production, rather than scriptwriting and the screen

38 Bazin was also editor of the French film journal *Cahiers du Cinema*.

39 Eisenstein rigorously opposed this view, claiming that the audience for his films played an active part in the text.

40 The head of Sovkino at this time was Boris Shumyatsky.

41 This section was written by Danny Rivers (West Kent College).

42 A statistical analysis of both scenes in terms of shot length/shot type reveals that they are also very similar in form.

43 A co-production of KTCA-TV Minneapolis and ZBIG Vision Ltd in association with Channel 4, London.

44 Woody Allen in *Love and Death* (1975), also makes reference to this sequence.

FURTHER READING

ANNOTATIONS TO FOLLOW

Aumont, J. *Montage Eisenstein*, British Film Institute, London, 1987.

Bordwell, D., *The Cinema of Eisenstein*, Harvard University Press, Cambridge, MA, 1993.

Christie, I. and Taylor, R. (eds), *Eisenstein Rediscovered*, Routledge, London, 1993.

Eisenstein, S. *Notes of a Film Director*, Dover Publications, New York, 1970.

—— *The Film Sense*, Faber & Faber, London, 1986.

—— Film scripts of *The Mother, Earth* and *Battleship Potemkin* have been published by Simon & Schuster, New York, 1973.

Kepley, V., Jr, *In the Service of the State: The Cinema of Alexander Dovzhenko*, University of Wisconsin Press, Madison, 1986.

Leyda, J. *Kino: A History of the Russian and Soviet Film*, 3rd edn, George Allen & Unwin, London, 1983.

Michelson, A. (ed.), *Kino Eye: The Writings of Dziga Vertov*, University of California Press, Berkeley, 1984.

Taylor, R., *Film Propaganda: Soviet Russia and Nazi Germany*, Croom Helm, London, 1979.

—— *The Politics of the Soviet Cinema, 1917–1929*, Cambridge University Press, Cambridge, 1979.

Taylor, R. and Christie, I. (eds), *The Film Factory: Russian and Soviet Cinema in Documents, 1896–1939*, Routledge, London, 1988.

—— (eds), *Inside the Film Factory: New Approaches to Russian and Soviet Cinema*, Routledge, London, 1991.

Youngblood, D., *Movies for the Masses: Popular Cinema and Soviet Society in the 1920s*, Cambridge University Press, Cambridge, 1992.

FURTHER VIEWING

V = available on video

16mm = available to hire on 16mm

Where neither symbol is listed, the film is not available to buy or rent

Selected Russian films of the 1910s

1908	*Sken'ka Razin*, Drankov (V)
1909	*A Sixteenth-century Russian Wedding*, Goncharov (V)
1910	*The House in Kolomna*, Petr Chardynin (V)
	The Queen of Spades, Petr Chardynin (V)
	Rusalka/The Mermaid, Goncharov (V)
1912	*The Brigand Brothers*, Goncharov (V)
	The Peasants' Lot, Vasilii Goncharov (V)
1913	*Merchant Bashkirov's Daughter*, Larin (V)
	Twilight of a Woman's Soul, Evgeny Bauer
1914	*The Child of the Big City*, Evgeny Bauer (V)
	Silent Witnesses, Evgeny Bauer (V)
1915	*After Death*, Evgeny Bauer
	Children of the Age, Evgeny Bauer
	Daydreams, Evgeny Bauer (V)
	Happiness of Eternal Night, Evgeny Bauer
1916	*The 1002nd Ruse*, Evgeny Bauer (V)
	Antosha Ruined by a Corset, Eduard Puchal'ski (V)
	A Life for a Life, Evgeny Bauer (V)
	The Queen of Spades, Yakov Protazanov (V)
1917	*For Luck*, Evgeny Bauer (V)
	Grandmother of the Revolution, B. Svetlov
	The King of Paris, Evgeny Bauer

The Revolutionary, Evgeny Bauer

Satan Triumphant, Yakov Protazanov

1918   Jenny the Maid, Yakov Protazanov

Little Ellie, Yakov Protazanov

Still, Sadness, Still, Petr Chardynin

Selected Soviet films of the 1920s–40s

1922–25   Film-Truth, Dziga Vertov (a series of newsreels)

1924   Aelita, Yakov Protazanov (16mm)

Cigarette-Girl from Mosselprom, Yuri Zhelyabuzhsky

The Extraordinary Adventures of Mr West in the Land of the Bolsheviks, Lev Kuleshov (16mm)

Kino-eye, Dziga Vertov

Strike, Sergei Eisenstein (V, 16mm)

1925   Battleship Potemkin, Sergei Eisenstein (V, 16mm)

The Death Ray, Lev Kuleshov

1926   The Mother, Vsevolod Pudovkin (V, 16mm)

A Sixth of the World, Dziga Vertov (16mm)

1927   The End of St Petersburg, Vsevolod Pudovkin (V, 16mm)

The Fall of the Romanov Dynasty, Esfir Shub (V, 16mm)

The Great Road, Esfir Shub

October, Sergei Eisenstein (V, 16mm)

1928   The Russia of Nicholas II and Lev Tolstoy, Esfir Shub

Storm Over Asia, Vsevolod Pudovkin (V, 16mm)

1929   Arsenal, Alexander Dovzhenko (V, 16mm)

The Man with a Movie Camera, Dziga Vertov (16mm)

The New Babylon, Grigori Kozintsev and Leonid Trauberg (V)

Old and New or The General Line, Sergei Eisenstein (V, 16mm)

Ranks and People, Yakov Protazanov

Turksib, Victor Turin

1930   Earth, Alexander Dovzhenko (V, 16mm)

1931   Enthusiasm, Dziga Vertov (16mm)

1934   Chapayev, Sergei and Georgy Vasiliev (V)

1935   Aerograd, Alexander Dovzhenko

The Youth of Maxim, Grigori Kozintsev, and Leonid Trauberg (16mm)

1936   Alexander Nevsky, Sergei Eisenstein (16mm)

We from Krondstadt, Yefim Dzigan (V)

1945   Ivan the Terrible: Part I, Sergei Eisenstein (V, 16mm)

1946   Ivan the Terrible: Part II, Sergei Eisenstein (V, 16mm)

Additional videos

The Secret Life of Sergei Eisenstein, British Film Institute Publishing, London, 1987

RESOURCE CENTRES

http://us.imdb.com/Sections/Countries/SovietUnion

This is the Internet Movie Data Base (US) with a listing of 2,380 Russian films including details of producers, distributors, directors, genres, casts, writers, composers of music, and other titles by which the film is known.

http://www.nd.edu/astrouni/zhiwriter/movies.htm

A Russian cinema/movies web site with films, directors, artists, critics, distributors, history, historians and Russian Cinema WWW server.

Chapter 12

The French New Wave

Chris Darke

■ The French New Wave

INTRODUCTION

The 'New Wave' (*la nouvelle vague*) refers to a group of film-makers who, between the end of the 1950s and early to mid-1960s in France, momentarily transformed French cinema and had a great impact on film-makers throughout the world. Those directors who came to prominence through the New Wave and who have remained major names in the pantheon of European 'auteur' directors include Jean-Luc Godard, François Truffaut, Eric Rohmer, Jacques Rivette, Claude Chabrol, Alain Resnais, Chris Marker and Agnès Varda.

French critic Michel Marie lists a series of key factors that dictated the aesthetics of New Wave films:

For further discussion of auteur theory, see Chapter 4, pp. 131–150.

1   the auteur-director also writes the screenplay;
2   a strictly broken-down **découpage** is not used and a significant place is left to improvisation in the conception of the sequences, the dialogue and the performances;
3   natural decor and locations are privileged over studio sets;
4   a minimal crew of a few people is used;
5   'direct sound' recorded at the moment of shooting is preferred to post-synchronisation;
6   traditional lighting set-ups, deemed to be cumbersome, are dispensed with so the director of photography tends to work with fast, ultra-sensitive film;
7   non-professional actors are used to interpret the characters;
8   if professional actors are chosen, they tend to be 'new faces' who are directed in a loose and free fashion.

découpage
A term that means the 'shot break-down' of a scene.

(Marie 1998: 63)

While it has become identified in film history with the early work of the directors named above, the term New Wave was not invented by them. It was coined by a journalist named Françoise Giroud who, in late 1957, wrote a series of articles on French youth for the weekly news magazine *L'Express*. Cinema, in the shape of this new generation of film-makers, thus became associated with a 'youth' phenomenon. The association of 'youth' with New Wave cinema was sealed by the triumph at the 1958 Cannes Film Festival of *Les Quatre cents coups* (*The 400 Blows*), the debut feature film by the 27-year-old former film critic François Truffaut. A number of successful films by other directors followed, all of which enhanced the identity of New Wave cinema as 'youthful' and 'modern'; these included *A bout de souffle* (*Breathless*, Jean-Luc Godard, 1960), *Hiroshima, mon amour* (Alain Resnais, 1959) and *Les Cousins* (Claude Chabrol, 1959).

However, these new film-makers had not emerged from out of the blue. They had all been involved in film making for the best part of the 1950s; writing film criticism, making short films and documentaries. In fact, one of the most marked characteristics of the New Wave is its association with film criticism. Many of its main directors had a long relationship with the important monthly film magazine *Les Cahiers du cinéma et de la télévision* (literally meaning 'Cinema and Television Notebooks' and referred to as *Cahiers* hereafter) which had been founded by André Bazin and Jacques Doniol-Valcroze in 1951. Truffaut, Godard, Rivette, Chabrol and Rohmer had all written for the magazine throughout the 1950s. So the New Wave was in part characterised by the unusual phenomenon of film critics becoming successful film-makers after having been influential and polemical writers. Before outlining some of the chief ideas that these film-makers advanced in their work as critics, it is worthwhile to describe the film culture that existed in France after the Second World War and on which the New Wave would have a profound impact.

• **Plate 12.1** Young French directors at the 1959 Cannes Film Festival, including François Truffaut (front row, first left), Claude Chabrol (back row, first left) and Jean-Luc Godard (back row, second right)

POSTWAR FRENCH FILM CULTURE

While France was under Nazi occupation, between 1940 and 1945, the importing of American films was banned by the collaborationist government of the Vichy regime. Shortly after the liberation of France in 1945 this backlog of American cinema started to hit the country's screens to the enthusiasm of French film-goers. This exposure to Hollywood films was a formative influence on the young critics who would become the directors of the New Wave in the late 1950s. For them, American cinema was more vital, more varied and considerably more exciting than the postwar productions of the French film industry which they derided as 'le cinéma de papa' ('Daddy's cinema'). Film culture in postwar France was bolstered by the growth in the number of magazines devoted to cinema (including *Positif*, the long standing rival of *Cahiers*, founded in 1952) and the revitalisation of a network of 'ciné-clubs', where film screenings would be accompanied by public debates and lectures by critics. Between 1948 and 1949, an important ciné-club was established, 'Objectif 49', whose organisers included Jean Cocteau, Robert Bresson, Roger Leenhardt, René Clément, Alexandre Astruc, Pierre Kast and Raymond Queneau. As Doniol-Valcroze stressed, this ciné-club would 'constitute the first link in the chain which is resulting today in what has been called the nouvelle vague, the first jolt against a cinema which has become too traditional...(and)...bought together all those – critics, film-makers and future film-makers – who dreamed of a cinéma d'auteurs' (cited in Hillier 1985: 3). One of the founders of *Cahiers*, the highly influential film critic André Bazin, was instrumental in the 'ciné-club' movement and several future members of the New Wave were already writing film criticism for publications associated with 'ciné-clubs'. In addition, the work of the curator and film archivist Henri Langlois, along with his colleague Mary Meerson, was to be of great importance to a generation of film-goers who attended screenings at the Cinémathèque Française in Paris where they could see an eclectic range of films from around the world and from different periods of cinema history. All of these components of postwar French film culture contributed to a lively **cinéphile** community of viewers. The word 'cinéphile' does not translate easily into English. It does not exactly denote a 'film buff', a 'film fan' or a 'cinema enthusiast' but someone who is intimately involved in the cultural condition of 'cinéphilia', a uniquely French approach to cinema that has traditionally argued for it as 'the seventh art'. Before they became influential critics on *Cahiers* and were internationally recognised as film directors, the chief figures in the New Wave were enthusiastic cinéphiles.

An example of the intellectual interest that was developing as regards cinema came in an essay published in 1948 by the critic, novelist and film-maker Alexandre Astruc. The essay, entitled 'The Birth of a New Avant-Garde: La caméra-stylo', argued that

> Cinema is quite simply becoming a means of expression, just as all the other arts have been before it, and in particular painting and the novel. After having been successively a fairground attraction, an amusement analogous to boulevard theatre, or a means of preserving the images of an era, it is gradually becoming a language. By a language, I mean a form in which and by which an artist can express his thoughts, however abstract they may be, or translate his obsessions exactly as he does in the contemporary essay or novel. That is why I would like to call this new age of cinema the age of '**caméra-stylo**' (camera-pen)…(by this) I mean that the cinema will gradually break free from the tyranny of what is visual, from the image for its own sake, from the immediate and concrete demands of the narrative, to become a means of writing just as flexible and subtle as written language.
>
> (Cited in Graham 1968: 17–18)

Part of the legacy of the French New Wave lies in how it can be seen to have developed – both in terms of film criticism and film-making – some of Astruc's claims for what cinema could be.

FILM CRITICISM

Cahiers du cinéma, 'la politique des auteurs' and 'mise-en-scène'.

Throughout the 1950s, the critics on *Cahiers* argued and polemicised for cinema as an art form. That is to say, they approached cinema from the point of view of the film-maker who, they argued, could be seen as the 'author' – the 'auteur' – of the work. This idea of 'authorship' was to prove highly influential in film criticism and has remained, though not without controversy, a key approach in the study of cinema. Initially, the major influence in this approach was the work of André Bazin. A humanist, left-leaning Catholic, Bazin had been deeply involved in film education and criticism after the end of the Second World War and had founded a magazine called *La Révue du cinéma* which, in 1951, was relaunched as *Les Cahiers du cinéma et de la Télévision*. It was on this magazine that the future directors of the New Wave cut their teeth as critics throughout the 1950s.

The critical agenda that was developed in the magazine throughout the 1950s claimed for certain directors the status of artist, an approach that was known as '**la politique des auteurs**' ('author politics' or 'the auteur policy'). What was unusual about

---

cinéphile
A term describing someone with a developed intellectual interest in cinema. Cinéphilia was part of the cultural climate in which the New Wave emerged.

For further discussion of counter-cinema and alternative narratives, see Chapter 2, pp. 84–89.

caméra stylo
A term coined by French writer Alexandre Astruc meaning 'camera-pen' and used to condense his argument for a 'personal' and self-expressive form of cinema.

politique des auteurs, la
Literally meaning 'auteur policy' or 'auteur politics' (although later translated by the American film critic Andrew Sarris as 'auteur theory'). It describes the position of *Cahiers du cinéma* as one that argued for the work of favoured directors as that of film artists or 'auteurs'.

such an approach was that it was developed around the work of film-makers who were working in the highly standardised and controlled industrial environment of Hollywood cinema. Those directors chiefly favoured included, among others, Alfred Hitchcock, John Ford, Howard Hawks, Fritz Lang and Otto Preminger. Hitchcock was a major reference for many of the critics who would later become film-makers. For example, François Truffaut went on to publish a famous series of interviews with Hitchcock while Claude Chabrol and Eric Rohmer co-wrote a study of his films (Truffaut 1983; Chabrol and Rohmer 1979).

The *Cahiers* critics went looking for 'art' in popular cinema. They did so because they were concentrating predominantly on the formal qualities of films to see how these might reveal a set of themes and preoccupations that could be associated with the name of the director, be it Hitchcock, Lang or Ford. The critical approach that the *Cahiers* writers used to analyse films has become known as **mise-en-scène** criticism. The term 'mise-en-scène' derives from the theatre, where it refers to the practice of stage direction in which things are 'put into the scene', or, arranged on the stage. One of the most straightforward and concise expressions of the importance of the idea of mise-en-scène to auteur criticism comes from one of the *Cahiers* critics, Fereydoun Hoveyda, who wrote in 1960:

mise-en-scène
Literally meaning 'putting in the scene' and deriving from theatre. A film's mise-en-scène is taken to describe all the elements visible in a shot – actors, objects, landscapes, etc. In terms of classic auteur criticism, a director's style can be identified only through the arrangement and orchestration of such elements, of the film's mise-en-scène in other words.

For further discussion of mise-en scène, see Chapter 2, pp. 62–70.

• **Plate 12.2** Alfred Hitchcock receiving an award from the New Wave actress Jeanne Moreau in 1969

The originality of the 'auteur' lies not in the subject matter he chooses but in the technique he employs, ie: the 'mise en scène', through which everything on the screen is expressed…the thought of a cinéaste appears through his 'mise en scène'.

(Cited in Hillier 1985: 8–9)

Hoveyda goes on to explain:

What matters in a film is the desire for order, composition, harmony, the placing of actors and objects, the movements within the frame, the capturing of a movement or a look; in short, the intellectual operation which has put an initial emotion and a general idea to work. Mise-en-scène is nothing other than the technique invented by each director to express the idea and establish the specific quality of his work.

(Ibid.)

It is useful to remember that the film criticism undertaken by writers on *Cahiers* throughout the 1950s was both highly influential and, at least initially, controversial. This controversy concerned the idea of 'art' being applied to the products of commercial American cinema. When systematically used to explore the *œuvre* (or 'body of work') of a director such as Alfred Hitchcock, John Ford or Fritz Lang, an 'auteurist' approach can discover the ways in which a director has consistently developed certain themes and how the style of that director has been developed and refined over time. However, the idea of the 'auteur' served another purpose apart from championing American cinema. It was part of a polemic against the state of French cinema which was actively developed in the pages of *Cahiers*. The most infamous expression of the journal's attitude towards postwar French cinema came in François Truffaut's article 'Une certaine tendence du cinéma français' ('A Certain Tendency of the French Cinema') which was published in *Cahiers* no. 31 in January 1954. It was in this essay (which was largely devoted to examining the role of the scriptwriter in French cinema of the 1940s and 1950s) that Truffaut made a distinction between an auteur director and what he called a 'metteur-en-scène' (or, a director deemed to lack the 'personal vision' attributed to an auteur). For Truffaut, the metteur-en-scène was a film-maker whose conception of cinema only extends as far as 'illustrating' a screenplay and being faithful to the written word: 'when they (the screenwriters) hand in their scenario, the film is done: the metteur-en-scène, in their eyes, is the gentleman who adds pictures to it' (cited in Nichols 1976: 233). It was the preponderance of films made either as literary adaptations or based on scripts by established screenwriters that Truffaut saw as evidence that French cinema was beholden primarily to literary criteria, rather than searching for specifically cinematic qualities. It is useful to remember here how critics such as Bazin and Astruc were arguing for a vision of cinema that did not wholly depend on validation by reference to the other established art forms. When Astruc wrote of the 'camera-pen' ('la caméra stylo') he was not thinking of the screenplay as a means of cinematic expression, but of film-making itself as a form of artistic creation that could be as fluent, expressive and rich as written language, rather than it merely being in the service of adapting classic literary works.

Tradition of Quality
A frequently derogatory term used by the critics on *Cahiers du cinéma* and referring to postwar, pre-New Wave French cinema characterised by its reliance on screenwriters and adaptations from literary classics.

Truffaut described the screenwriters and metteurs-en-scènes as representing French cinema's '**Tradition of Quality**': 'they force, by their ambitiousness, the admiration of the foreign press, defend the French flag twice a year at Cannes and at Venice where, since 1946, they regularly carry off medals, golden lions and *grands prix*' (ibid.: 225). In other words, the Tradition of Quality represented the mainstream of French cinema of the day – internationally recognised, nationally dominant and, for Truffaut and many of his colleagues on *Cahiers*, the enemy. In the same article Truffaut set the names of metteurs-en-scènes associated with the Tradition of Quality – for example, Yves Allegret, Claude Autant-Lara and Jean Delannoy – against the names of other French directors such as Jean Renoir, Robert Bresson, Jacques Tati and Jean Cocteau, whom he held to be 'auteurs: who often write their dialogue and some of them themselves invent the stories they direct' (ibid.: 233). Truffaut argued for an idea of the auteur within the French context that is subtly different from the idea as it was applied to Hollywood cinema. It was taken for granted that in Hollywood the director worked within a large, powerful and regimented production system and collaborated with a host of other skilled people, from actors to camera operators, screenwriters to producers, and that the opportunity to exercise artistic control and to make creative decisions was concentrated in the act of directing. The mise-en-scène of the film was where the evidence of such decisions was seen to reside. However, in the French context, Truffaut uses the term auteur for those directors whose control over their films extended to writing the dialogue and the stories, directors who were their own screenwriters; a degree of control that was impossible to conceive of in the classical Hollywood studio system. Thus Truffaut's polemic against the so-called Tradition of Quality was also a polemic against the mainstream establishment of the French film industry as well as being an assertion that it was possible to make films in another way, as is clear from his words: 'I do not believe in the peaceful coexistence of "The Tradition of Quality" and an "auteur's" cinema' (ibid.: 234). So, on one hand, the development of auteur criticism with its emphasis on mise-en-scène (finding the 'personality' of the style, one might say) was a way of arguing for the artistic worth of popular cinema. On the other hand, it was also developed as a polemical assault on what was seen as the moribund state of French cinema.

Jacques Doniol-Valcroze, who co-founded *Cahiers* with André Bazin, believed that Truffaut's article was highly significant:

A leap had been made, a trial begun with which we were all in solidarity, something bound us together. From then on, it was known that we were *for* Renoir, Rossellini, Hitchcock, Cocteau, Bresson...and against X, Y and Z. From then on there was a doctrine, the 'politique des auteurs', even if it lacked flexibility.

(Cited in Hillier 1985: 4)

• **Plate 12.3**
Roberto Rossellini, the Italian neo-realist director who greatly influenced the New Wave

Doniol-Valcroze made this statement in 1959 and the 'inflexibility' he identified in the 'politique des auteurs' had been examined by Bazin himself in an article published in *Cahiers* in April 1957 entitled 'On the politique des auteurs'. In this article Bazin examined the intellectual assumptions behind 'auteur' criticism and addressed its perceived 'inflexibility'. He also placed the idea within the editorial culture of the magazine itself:

Our readers must have noticed that this critical standpoint – whether implicit or explicit – has not been adopted with equal enthusiasm by all the regular contributors to *Cahiers*, and that there might exist serious differences in our admiration, or rather in the degree of our admiration. And yet the truth is that the most enthusiastic among us nearly always win the day. Eric Rohmer put his finger on the reason in his reply to a reader in *Cahiers* no. 64: 'When opinions differ on an important film, we generally prefer to let the person who likes it most write about it.' It follows that the strictest adherents of the 'politique des auteurs' get the best of it in the end, for, rightly or wrongly, they always see in their favourite directors the manifestation of the same specific qualities. So it is that Hitchcock, Renoir, Rossellini, Lang, Hawks or Nicholas Ray, to judge from the pages of *Cahiers*, appear as almost infallible directors who could not make a bad film.

(Cited in Graham 1968: 137–8)

□ CASE STUDY 1: *A BOUT DE SOUFFLE* (*BREATHLESS*, JEAN-LUC GODARD, 1960)

Jean-Luc Godard's debut feature was one of the films that marked the advent of the French New Wave, both in France and abroad. Its story is that of a young criminal, Michel Poiccard (Jean-Paul Belmondo), who, having casually murdered a policeman, returns to Paris to collect money he is owed and to persuade his American girlfriend, Patricia Franchini (Jean Seberg), to leave the country with him.

Patricia, who sells the *New York Herald Tribune* on the streets of Paris while attempting to establish herself as a journalist, betrays Michel to the police who shoot him dead when he tries to flee.

A bout de souffle is highly characteristic of the film-making style associated with the New Wave. The neo-documentary 'look' of the film was achieved partly through the use of a lightweight, hand-held model of film camera called the Eclair which allowed for mobility and flexibility in shooting. In addition, the film marked the first of Godard's collaboration with the cinematographer Raoul Coutard, which would continue for fifteen films between 1960 and 1968. Coutard had been a photojournalist and documentary cameraman and was accustomed to a style of shooting that was far removed from the more conventional and poised style of studio-based shooting that characterised the so-called Tradition of Quality. *A bout de souffle* was shot on black and white film stock normally used for still photography to further enhance the 'reportage' look. This 'realism' was part of the film's perceived modernity, in that it was filmed on the streets of contemporary Paris, a decision that was in part dictated by necessity – this was a low-budget film, after all, shot rapidly in only four weeks – but that emphasised the distance between the New Wave approach to film-making and that of the largely studio-bound Tradition of Quality.

A bout de souffle is heavily intertextual, a feature that would remain a constant in Godard's work. The film is scattered with allusions to painting, literature and, above all, to cinema. From the opening dedication to the small American B-movie studio Monogram Pictures, through Michel's adoration and imitation of Hollywood 'tough guy' Humphrey Bogart, Godard plays the cinéphile game of homage and quotation that would be characteristic of his own films and of the New Wave generally. Additionally, the casting of the young American actress Jean Seberg as Patricia can be read in a variety of referential ways – as an incarnation of 'America' and, more specifically, as a

• **Plate 12.4**
Jean-Paul Belmondo and Jean
Seberg in *A bout de souffle*
(*Breathless*, Jean-Luc Godard,
1960)

nod to the émigré European director Otto Preminger who, while working in Hollywood, cast Seberg in the title role of *Saint Joan* (1957). *A bout de souffle* was seen to be 'revolutionary' in the way that it directly challenged the accepted rules of cinematic language. For example, in the sequence near the opening of the film where Michel drives towards a police speed-trap, he addresses the camera – and hence, the audience – directly, breaking the 'fourth wall' that is seen to be necessary for the spectator's identification with the film's fictional world. Famously, the film's use of jerky and discontinuous editing rhythms established the 'jump cut' as a (quickly clichéd) hallmark of New Wave style. But elements such as these should be set against the film's frequent use of long-take, mobile camera shots and the lengthy mid-film sequence in which Michel and Patricia canoodle in a bedroom.

In many ways, the film can be seen as the first of Godard's (increasingly ambiguous) love-letters to Hollywood cinema. But it is a relationship marked by mutual incomprehension – as the love-affair between Michel and Patricia becomes fraught with mistrust, linguistic misunderstanding and, ultimately, betrayal. Like many of the early New Wave shorts and debut features, *A bout de souffle* was the product of a collaboration between former *Cahiers* critics: the script was based on an idea by Truffaut and Chabrol was the 'technical adviser' on the film. It was remade in America in 1983 by Jim McBride, starring Richard Gere and Valérie Kaprisky in the Belmondo and Seberg roles.

THE PRODUCTION CONTEXT OF THE NEW WAVE

One of the reasons for the worldwide influence of the French New Wave during the 1960s was its demonstration that it was possible to make exciting, dynamic and innovative films outside of an established production system. The situation that obtained within French cinema prior to the advent of the New Wave was one in which the industry was far from accessible to ambitious young film-makers. The industry was largely studio-bound and heavily regimented. The way to become a director was to serve long years of apprenticeship as an assistant director before having the possibility oneself to direct. It was this institution of production that the New Wave was seen to have changed.

cinema novo
Or, 'New Cinema'. A movement of film-makers that came to prominence in Brazil in the 1960s, the leading figure of which was Glauber Rocha. Influenced by the New Wave in France and the intellectual examples of Frantz Fanon and Che Guevara, 'cinema novo' called for film-making that emphasised 'the aesthetics of hunger' directed against a cinema of imperialism.

'movie brat' generation
A term that refers to the generation of American film-makers who, after the decline of the Hollywood studio system in the 1950s, began to make films independently and were heavily influenced by the French New Wave and European 'art cinema' of the 1960s. Such directors include Martin Scorsese and Francis Ford Coppola.

New German Cinema
A movement in German cinema in the late 1960s and 1970s that called for a personal and auteur cinema in Germany to counteract the cultural imperialism of Hollywood. Notable directors that emerged included Wim Wenders, Rainer Werner Fassbinder, Alexander Kluge and Margerethe von Trotta.

Dogme 95
The name given to a collective of Danish film-makers united around the figures of directors Lars Von Trier, Thomas Winterberg and Kristian Levering. Dogme 95 was the name of a manifesto that committed film-makers to observing a cinematic 'vow of chastity' involving an ultra-realist approach to film-making using only digital video cameras.

As films made within a certain production context, those of the New Wave can be examined from two complementary perspectives that are at the heart of any consideration of film-making: the production circumstance and the role of film-making technology.

Production circumstances

Two of the most common descriptions of New Wave films are that they were 'low-budget' productions that were made 'outside' the conventional system that obtained in France in the 1950s and 1960s. These features have held an abiding appeal for many film-makers wishing to make films of an 'independent' and 'personal' nature. One can find echoes of the New Wave's example in the Brazilian '**cinema novo**' of the 1960s, in the **'movie brat' generation** of American independent cinema of the 1960s and 1970s, in the **New German Cinema** of the late 1960s and 1970s, as well as in the **Dogme 95** movement that emerged in Denmark in the mid- to late 1990s.

In a recent study of the New Wave, the French film historian Michel Marie examined what 'low-budget' meant in terms of the production circumstances in French cinema between 1955 and 1959. Marie found that the average budget of a film in 1955 was 109 million old francs and in 1959, 149 million old francs (the conversion rate following the devaluation of the currency in 1960 saw 1 million francs being worth 10,000 francs). In 1959, of 133 films produced, 74 films cost more than 100 million old francs and 33 cost more than 200 million old francs. So, in 1959, there were 26 films made with a budget of less than 100 milllion old francs. But, as Marie stresses, the sole criteria of a 'low budget' did not qualify a film as being a New Wave production. Marie associates the relatively low budgets on which the New Wave films were made with a backlash among the *Cahiers* critics against films made on exceedingly high budgets, particularly *Notre Dame de Paris* (Jean Delannoy, 1956), a spectacular film made explicitly to compete with Hollywood films within the domestic market. Writing in *Cahiers* no. 71, April 1957, Jacques Rivette claimed that what was missing in French cinema was 'the spirit of poverty…French cinema only stands a chance now in as much as other directors will take the risk of making films for 20 or 30 million francs, or even less' (cited in Marie 1998: 51).

It was generally agreed that, while French cinema was in a state of good financial health in the mid- to late 1950s, it was deemed to be less healthy in creative terms. However, there were film-makers who had already set an example of the kind of production that would become characteristic of the New Wave. One of these was Jean-Pierre Melville who, in an interview in 1960, delivered the most concise definition of the characteristic features of New Wave films as being 'an **artisanal system of production**, shot on location, without stars, with a minimal crew and on ultra-fast stock, without necessarily having a distributor lined up, without authorisation or servitude of any kind' (ibid.: 45). Melville was the pseudonym of Jean-Pierre Grumbach, the director of such films as *Le Silence de la mer* (1947), *Bob le Flambeur* (1955) and *Le Samourai* (1967), whose influence as a predecessor of the New Wave was explicitly acknowledged by Jean-Luc Godard who cast him in a cameo role in his debut feature *A bout de souffle*.

State subsidy

Marie attributes the relative 'health' of the French film industry to a number of factors. The cinema attendance figures between 1947 and 1957 averaged out at a robust yearly figure of 390 million; the domestic market was still largely dominated by French films (it would be in the 1960s that American films began to bite into their market share) and French films were proving highly exportable, in 1956 40 per cent of receipts were generated by sales of French films abroad. However, Marie identifies another crucial aspect of the production context in the 1950s: the role of state subsidy for film-making. Drawing on a revealing interview between Bazin, Doniol-Valcroze and the director of the **CNC** (Centre Nationale de la Cinématographie), written by Jacques Flaud and published in *Cahiers* no. 71, 1957 entitled 'The Situation of French Cinema', Marie examines the importance, as well as some of the ambiguous effects, of such state aid to film-makers. Marie cites a report by Flaud that questioned the consequences of state aid on the quality of French film-making: namely, that it tended to produce films 'treating relatively easy subjects, with international stars, taken from works by well-known writers, in other words, subjects that have already been tested in other art forms, thus creating films that are adaptations or remakes' (Marie 1998: 49). The paradox that Marie identifies is that the CNC's criticisms are surprisingly close in their analysis, if not their tone, to the 'anti-Establishment' polemics of Truffaut and others on *Cahiers*:

This thesis was the institutional version of the more personal and polemical thesis put forward by François Truffaut. Jacques Flaud goes as far as to encourage producers to take risks, to try out new actors and to envisage artistic renewal…. This official programme was announced at the beginning of 1957 and one understands why the CNC would go on to do everything to support the first productions by Chabrol and Truffaut in granting their production companies the necessary dispensations, to the anger of the cinema technicians unions.

(Ibid.: 49)

What emerges from Marie's close attention both to the well-documented polemics originating in the pages of *Cahiers* as well as to the institutional discourses on the state of French cinema is an unexpected overlap between the two. According to Marie, the 1957 statement by the CNC can be seen to have played 'a decisive role in the emergence of the New Wave in the following year. This fact confirms that there was nothing "spontaneous" about the New Wave generation' (ibid.: 50).

The various types of state funding for film-makers that became effective during the 1950s support Marie's assertion. Among these was the 'prime à la qualité' ('quality subsidy') which dated from 1953 and was intended to support films whose criteria was seen to be one of 'quality', films which would 'serve the cause of French cinema or…open up new perspectives in the art of cinema' (ibid.: 48–9). Although it took until 1955 for certain films to benefit from this particular subsidy, the irony was that while the New Wave directors set themselves against what they saw as the Tradition of Quality in French cinema, they themselves would be the beneficiaries of a state subsidy promoting an idea of 'quality' in French film production.

It should be remembered that the state support of French cinema was set against the wider backdrop of policies put in place to aid French reconstruction. Principally the Blum–Byrnes agreement, signed in 1946 and amended in 1948, that, among other trade agreements, fixed a minimum quota of French films to be shown on French screens against non-French (predominantly American) films. So, state subsidy for French film-making can be seen as having been a way of preserving and encouraging domestic production in the face of international competition. In 1953, financial assistance became available for the production of short films and was instrumental in helping directors such as Chris Marker, Alain Resnais and Agnès Varda to make their first shorts. In addition, in 1959 a system of 'avances sur recettes' ('advances against earnings') was introduced, enabling producers to part-finance feature films by borrowing from a 'fonds de soutien' ('support fund') against their eventual profits. Many of the funding elements of state support remain in place to this day, although now modified by the close co-production ties established between the French film and television industries, and they account in part for the vitality of film production in France relative to other European countries which have largely capitulated to American hegemony.

artisanal system of production
A way of making films outside of an established 'industrial' means of production which emphasises a more craft-like and personal process hence allowing greater control of the film-making process.

CNC
Centre Nationale de la Cinématographie, the chief body of the French state that oversees policy affecting film-making, including the subsidies accorded to cinema.

☐ CASE STUDY 2 : *LES QUATRE CENTS COUPS* (*THE FOUR HUNDRED BLOWS*, FRANÇOIS TRUFFAUT, 1959)

Having earned himself a reputation as an 'enfant terrible' with his polemical critical writing in *Cahiers*, and having been barred from the Cannes Film Festival of 1958, in the following year, François Truffaut won Best Director at the festival for his debut feature *Les Quatre cents coups*.

The film was the first to feature the character of Antoine Doinel, played by Jean-Pierre Léaud, to whom Truffaut would return in a further five films always using the same actor. Léaud plays Doinel as Truffaut's alter-ego and *Les Quatre cents coups* was more than a little autobiographically derived. The young Antoine's unhappy home life, his troubles at school and his subsequent incarceration at a correctional centre for delinquent minors were based on Truffaut's own errant youth which saw him locked up for deserting from the army. In fact, it was the intercession of the film critic André Bazin that saved Truffaut from further punishment.

Like Godard's debut *A bout de souffle*, *Les Quatres cents coups* (the '400 blows' refers to the administering of corporal punishment) was set in the apartments and on the streets of contemporary Paris. The film's lyrical, long-take, mobile camera style owed much to the influence of the film-makers Jean Renoir, Robert Rossellini and Jean Vigo. The Italian neo-realist director Rossellini was to be an important adviser and champion of many of the young New Wave directors. Truffaut's own cinéphilia is evident throughout the film, although one might argue that it is more fully integrated into the plot and action than in Godard's debut. Whether at the level of the influence of those older directors admired by Truffaut, or simply in the scene in which Antoine steals a still from a cinema of the sultry Harriet Andersson in Ingmar Bergman's *Summer with Monika* (1952) (Bergman was an important director for both Truffaut and Godard), the cinéphilic impulse to quote from and pay homage to other films informs *Les Quatres cents coups*. Although less formally audacious than Godard's debut, *Les Quatre cents coups* ends with an arresting freeze-frame image of Antoine on a beach and at the water's edge: the sense of narrative 'closure' is uncertain and suggests an ambiguous future for the young man. It is an image that implicitly contradicts the title caption that reads 'Fin' ('End') with its suggestion that Antoine's story is 'to be continued'. As indeed it was.

• **Plate 12.5**
One of the emblematic faces of the New Wave, actor Jean-Pierre Léaud as the young Antoine Doinel in *Les Quatres cents coups* (*The 400 Blows*, François Truffaut, 1959)

• **Plate 12.6**
Actor Jean-Pierre Léaud
as Doinel years later

NEW DIRECTORS, NEW PRODUCERS

While certain young film-makers such as Agnès Varda and Claude Chabrol established their own independent production companies to assist in the making of their first feature films (in Varda's case *La Pointe Courte* [1954], in Chabrol's *Les Cousins* [1959]), there were other figures who were crucial to the production of films by New Wave directors, notably Pierre Braunberger, Anatole Dauman and Georges de Beauregard.

Pierre Braunberger began producing films in 1926 with works by Alberto Cavalcanti and Jean Renoir. The portfolio of his production company Les Films de la Pléiade was extensive, ranging from avant-garde films to commercial productions as well as works by precursors to the New Wave such as Jean-Pierre Melville (whom Braunberger supported in his adaptation of the novel *Le Silence de la mer* between 1947 and 1948) and the influential ethnographic documentarist Jean Rouch. Braunberger's involvement in producing documentaries and short fictions – both of which were genres of work important to the development of the New Wave – saw him working with figures who would become key directors in the French cinema, including Alain Resnais whose films on artists, *Van Gogh*, *Guernica* and *Gauguin*, he produced between 1947 and 1948. Other directors' short films produced by Braunberger included *O Saisons, o châteaux* (Agnès Varda, 1957), *Le Coup du berger* (Jacques Rivette, 1956) and *Tous les garçons s'appellent Patrick*, *Une histoire d'eau* and *Charlotte et son Jules* (Jean-Luc Godard, 1957, 1958 and 1959). He would continue to produce features by New Wave directors after their initial successes such as Truffaut's second film *Tirez sur le pianiste* (1960) and Godard's fourth film *Vivre sa vie* (1962).

For a more detailed discussion of La Jetée, *see Case study 3, pp. 434–435.*

Anatole Dauman founded Argos Films (with Phillipe Lifchitz) in 1951 as a company specialising in films about art and was responsible for producing important early works by two of the major 'Left Bank' New Wave film-makers Alain Resnais and Chris Marker. Dauman produced Resnais' *Nuit et brouillard* (*Night and Fog*, 1955), a seminal documentary about the memory of the mass extermination of Jews, Communists, gypsies and homosexuals in the Nazi 'death camps' of the Second World War. Dauman also produced the director's first groundbreaking feature film *Hiroshima, mon amour* (1959) and its follow-up *L'année dernière à Marienbad* (1961). As regards Marker, Argos Films produced the director's early documentary-essay films *Dimanche à Pékin* (*Sunday in Peking*, 1956) and *Lettre de Sibérie* (*Letter from Siberia*, 1958). The relationship between Argos Films and Marker also includes the production of the film-maker's singular black-and-white science-fiction short *La Jetée* (1963). Other important and influential films produced by Argos included the ethnographic cinéma-vérité exploration of Parisian life *Chronique d'un été* (1960) by Jean Rouch, as well as later works by Resnais (*Muriel, ou le temps d'un retour*, 1963), Godard (*Deux ou trois choses que je sais d'elle*, 1966, *Masculin Feminin,* 1966) and Robert Bresson (*Au Hasard, Balthazar,* 1966 and *Mouchette*, 1967).

The producer who was perhaps the principal supporter of New Wave film-makers was Georges de Beauregard. Having produced Godard's highly succesful debut *A bout de souffle*, Beauregard went on to produce six other films by the director: *Le Petit soldat* (1960), *Une Femme est une femme* (1961), *Les Carabiniers* (1963), *Le Mépris* (1963), *Made in USA* (1966) and then, years later, *Numéro Deux* (1975). Beauregard also produced films by other New Wave directors including Jacques Demy (*Lola*, 1960), Jacques Rozier (*Adieu Philippine*, 1962), Claude Chabrol (*L'Oeil du malin*, 1962), Agnès Varda (*Cléo de 5 à 7*, 1961), Jacques Rivette (*Suzanne Simonin, la Réligieuse de Diderot*, 1965) and Eric Rohmer (*La Collectioneuse*, 1966).

It is hard to conceive of New Wave cinema without the support of adventurous producers such as Dauman, Braunberger and de Beauregard who were able to support the ambitions of new film-makers on relatively low budgets, as well as to maintain the momentum of production after the first flush of New Wave successes had passed.

☐ CASE STUDY 3: *LA JETÉE* (*THE PIER*, CHRIS MARKER, 1962)

La Jetée is a 28-minute, black-and-white film made entirely from a montage of still images (with the exception of a moment when the image moves in a conventionally 'cinematic' fashion). It tells the story of a soldier who, having survived the nuclear blast of 'the third world war', finds himself the subject of time-travel experiments in post-apocalypse Paris. It was the work of the film-maker Chris Marker (real name: Christian-François Bouche-Villeneuve) who was associated with the 'Left Bank' grouping of the New Wave which was also seen to include Alain Resnais and Agnès

• **Plate 12.7**
La Jetée (*The Pier*, Chris Marker, 1962)

Varda. Having been a writer and photographer, Marker collaborated with Resnais (he co-directed *Les Statues meurent aussi* [*Statues Also Die*, 1950] and wrote the narration for Resnais' 1957 short *Le Mystère de l'atelier quinze*) and distinguished himself with a series of highly individual documentary films including *Dimanche à Pékin* (1956) and *Lettre de Sibérie* (1958). Notable for the sophistication of their editing and their allusive, poetic commentaries, Marker's documentaries are often seen as defining a genre known as 'essay films'.

La Jetée is Marker's only foray into fiction and was the basis for Terry Gilliam's big-budget Hollywood 'remake' *Twelve Monkeys* (1995). But science-fiction in *La Jetée* provides Marker with a narrative alibi – time-travel – by which to explore, with affecting poetry, the ideas of memory and history which are the key themes of all his work. Much has been written about this haunting film, acknowledged as one of the masterpieces of cinematic 'modernism'. Marker was a politically committed film-maker, closely allied to the French Left and active in the collective film-making groups that arose as a result of 'the events' of May 1968. Some of the themes that *La Jetée* touches on include the after-math of war and atomic devastation; themes that Resnais also treated in *Nuit et brouillard* (1955) and *Hiroshima, mon amour* (1959). It has also been argued that, with its protracted scenes in which the 'time-traveller' is submitted to torture, *La Jetée* uses the science-fiction narrative form as a way of commenting on the theme of political violence which was a major issue at the time. France was involved in a colonial war against Algeria, one of its former dependencies, and direct treatment of the subject could lead to censorship (as was the case with Godard's second film *Le Petit soldat* (1960, but banned until 1963)).

La Jetée alludes to a film that Marker has returned to several times in his career and which he sees as an exploration of the theme of 'impossible memory': Alfred Hitchcock's *Vertigo* (1958). When the time-traveller is sent back in time to pre-apocalypse Paris he meets a young woman and they walk together in the parks of Paris. Pausing at the stump of an ancient tree, he indicates on the rings of the tree where, in time, 'he comes from'. It is a moment that directly quotes a sequence in *Vertigo* where Madeleine (Kim Novak) shows Scottie (James Stewart) when she lived and when she died by pointing at the rings on a sequoia tree. Marker has referred to *La Jetée*, only half in jest, as a 're-make' of *Vertigo*. If there is a body of work that best exemplifies Alexandre Astruc's idea of the *caméra stylo*, it is that of Chris Marker.

☐ CASE STUDY 4: *CLÉO DE 5 À 7 (CLÉO FROM 5 TO 7,* AGNÈS VARDA, 1961)

Cléo de 5 à 7 was Agnès Varda's second feature film after her co-operatively produced and undistributed debut *La Pointe Courte* (1954) and, in characteristic New Wave style, the film is set squarely in and around contemporary Paris. In 90 minutes of film, it recounts 90 minutes in the life of Cléo Victoire (Corinne Marchand), a successful pop singer who wanders through Paris, attends a rehearsal, and meets friends and new acquaintances while she awaits the results of a medical test for cancer. The 'realism' so often associated with the New Wave's approach to film-making is here taken to a particular extreme, extended beyond a careful attention to the street-level life of Paris to a 'real-time' approach to the film's duration and the action of the plot. The running-time of the film corresponds, almost exactly, to the length and space of Cléo's journey round Paris between 17:00 and 18:30 on 21 June 1961 and uses the radio news for that day.

The film is divided into a prologue (the only sequence in colour) and thirteen sections, each with their exact time and the name of a character whose presence inflects the scene. In its attempt to develop and explore a cinematic language by which to convey a woman's subjective point of view, *Cléo de 5 à 7* relates to Varda's earlier short film *L'Opéra-Mouffe* (1958) which depicted a local Parisian neighbourhood

• **Plate 12.8**
Agnès Varda directing
actress Corinne
Marchand for *Cléo de 5
à 7* (*Cléo from 5 to 7*,
Agnès Varda, 1961)

through the mind of a pregnant woman (Varda herself) who is preoccupied by thoughts of the forthcoming birth. In its contrast between Cléo's outwardly glamorous appearance and her fear of death, *Cléo de 5 à 7* consistently probes the boundaries between the singer's appearance and her internal world which are explored through an attention to the world around her and the ways in which she sees and registers that world.

Cléo's progress through the film develops from an almost narcissistic preoccupation with her own image – the first part of the film is full of mirrors and reflections, the outside world being, for her, less of a direct experience than an 'image' – through a more direct encounter with that world and its inhabitants. In particular, there is Cléo's encounter with a gentle young man in a park who has been conscripted and is on the point of leaving to fight in Algeria. Across the film, Cléo changes from a creature whose sole function, as a beautiful woman, is to be 'looked at' to a woman who herself looks, sees and encounters the world and people around her; a transformation from being an 'object' to a 'subject'.

CHARACTERISTICS OF NEW WAVE CINEMA

Technology and aesthetics

*For further discussion of
film and technology and
its impact on
documentary film, see
Chapter 5, pp. 199–203.*

One of the most important aspects of the New Wave relates to the changes in film-making technology that occurred after the Second World War. These changes had an impact both on how films were made and how they looked. Particularly significant as regards the New Wave was the availability of relatively cheap and lightweight cameras (the Eclair, Arriflex and Cameflex being the dominant new models of lightweight cameras) and sound recording equipment (the portable Nagra tape recorder, for example). Not only did the advent of such technology allow film-makers to shoot with smaller, less cumbersome crews, it also allowed the New Wave directors to work outside the established system of French film-making. This conventional style of film-making (the so-called Tradition of Quality) privileged a studio-based method of production in which directors and cinematographers worked alongside a team of other personnel such as set designers, lighting designers and art directors. Being opposed to many of the films produced by such a system, New Wave directors were able to convert their polemical antagonism to such film-making into practice. Influenced by the examples of **cinéma vérité** documentarists such as Jean Rouch and neo-realist film-makers such as Roberto Rossellini, both of whom made films based on direct encounters with the world around them, the New Wave directors used the new cameras and sound equipment to extend this approach in the context of fiction film-making.

In his recent historical study of the New Wave, Jean Douchet (who had been a critic on *Cahiers* at the same time as Godard and Truffaut) states that '(the) hand-held camera became one of the distinctive features of the New Wave'. It is important to remember two things here. First, that television was still in the process of establishing itself as the dominant entertainment medium in France in the 1960s, so the street-level, documentary look and feel of the New Wave films would have appeared very 'new' and 'modern' at the time, coming as something of a stylistic shock in comparison to the output of much French cinema. Second, that the New Wave directors used this equipment in order to show the world of Parisian everyday life with greater 'authenticity' and 'directness' than had been hitherto possible in French cinema, but also to push at the limits of what was deemed 'acceptable' both in terms of cinematic conventions and subject matter. Douchet describes the significance of the new camera technology on the New Wave thus:

> Carried around on the operator's shoulder, it (the lightweight camera) could closely follow the actor's every movement. A new intimacy developed between the camera and its subjects. The act of filming became a close physical encounter…In terms of craft, the camera enabled film-makers to abandon the use of heavy equipment (and its operators) and provided rapidity of movement and execution (with less time required during filming). It gave them the ability to film from a variety of vehicles (the camera operator could work in anything from a car to a baby carriage) which allowed the use of camera movements that were not only unthinkable but impossible with dolly tracks. And it introduced the camera into actual spaces whose cramped quarters reinforced the impression of real life. Aesthetically, a new and unexpected style exploded across the screen and added a sense of buoyancy to otherwise serious issues.

> (Douchet 1999: 204–5)

The freewheeling style of film-making that marked the New Wave cinema was highly influential around the world. Not only would many other directors be influenced by the 'look' of the New Wave films but documentary cinema found a new lease of life with the advent of cinéma vérité and 'Direct Cinema'. And with the recent use of digital video cameras by independent film-makers it is hardly surprising that references to the stylistic example of New Wave directors such as Godard and Varda should have become commonplace (see for example Kelly 2000).

There are, of course, exceptions that prove the very 'rules' that Michel Marie outlines at the beginning of this chapter. The soundtrack for *A bout de souffle*, for example, was entirely **post-synchronised** and neither of its lead performers, Jean-Paul Belmondo and Jean Seberg, were non-professionals. Belmondo was a relatively 'new face', however and would soon become one of the leading actors associated with the New Wave generation.

Influences and precursors

In the December 1962 issue of *Cahiers*, the magazine published a 'Dictionary of 162 New Film-makers'. By this time, the New Wave was no longer deemed to be the 'phenomenon' it had been in 1958–59 but the sheer number of directors who had made one or two films in the intervening years indicated that a veritable explosion of film-making had taken place in France which, in part, contributed to this idea of the 'phenomenon' of the New Wave. Most of these films and film-makers are now forgotten

cinéma vérité
A term for one of the strands in the flourishing of new forms of documentary that took place in Europe and America from the 1950s onwards. Partly aided by lightweight camera and sound equipment, cinéma vérité saw the film-maker operating as a participant–observer relative to the reality being filmed. Another tendency in this new form of documentary was known as 'Direct Cinema'.

For further discussion of documentary cinema, cinéma vérité and direct cinema, see Chapter 5, pp. 199–203

post-synchronised
Referring to the process of adding and modifying some or all of a film's sound in a studio after the film has been shot and synchronising these sounds to the image track (also known as 'post-synching').

• **Plate 12.9**
Jean Renoir, the great
French director who was
much admired by the
New Wave, with François
Truffaut

and the New Wave is reduced to a handful of illustrious names and admittedly important, ground-breaking works. It is worth pointing out, however, a few of the figures who
influenced this phenomenon and who could be said to have been its precursors.

One can divide such figures into the following categories: 'elders', 'early contemporaries' and 'fellow travellers'. Of the elders, Jean-Pierre Melville has already been
mentioned and his importance is undeniable, both in terms of the independence with
which he produced his films but also in his abiding love of American cinema. Alexandre
Astruc should also be mentioned as an example of a critic who also became a film-
maker prior to *Cahiers* writers making the same transition, although Michel Marie argues
that Astruc's films *Les Mauvaises Rencontres* (1955) and *Une Vie* (1958) cannot be
considered as truly New Wave films because of their production circumstances and
because the latter film featured the international star Maria Schell.

Two names are worth including in the 'early contemporaries' category: Louis Malle
and Roger Vadim. Malle had been an assistant director on Robert Bresson's *Un
Condamné à mort s'est échappé* (*A Man Escaped*, 1956) and his debut feature film
Ascenseur pour l'échafaud (*Lift to the Scaffold*, 1957) had many elements that one
might identify with the New Wave – a 'film noir' atmosphere and provenance (it was
adapted from a thriller), a jazz score specially composed by the legendary musician
Miles Davis, cinematography by Henri Decaë who would go on to shoot Truffaut's *Les
Quatre cents coups,* and a lead actress in the shape of Jeanne Moreau who was to
become one of the key performers associated with the New Wave. Vadim's debut
feature *Et Dieu créa la femme* (1956) was admired by Godard and Truffaut for its
'modernity' largely because Vadim brought to the screen a new image of youthful, devil-
may-care femininity in the shape of Brigitte Bardot, who was to become the major sex
symbol of French cinema and an important signifier of many of those qualities – 'youth',
'modernity' and 'subversive' sexual freedom – that would be associated with the New
Wave as an image of modern, postwar France both at home and internationally.

As regards 'fellow travellers', this category is more fluid depending on whom one
includes. For example, Roberto Rossellini can be seen as an illustrious 'elder' relative
to the generation of the New Wave. The influence of his 'neo-realist' films on the critical ideas of André Bazin is well documented, but his significance extends beyond
this. His 1953 film *Viaggio in Italia* (*Voyage to Italy*) was a commercial and critical
failure, except with *Cahiers* critics such as Rivette, Rohmer and Godard who regarded
it as an extremely 'modern' work that 'opened a breach' in the history of cinema. It
would be through this very breach that they would propel their first films and
Rossellini was an advisor to the young directors, even co-writing the screenplay for
Godard's *Les Carabiniers* (*The Riflemen*, 1963). Jean Rouch was a documentary film-

maker who came from a background in ethnology and anthropology and his creative studies of life and rituals in 'primitive' societies as well as in European society – *Les Maîtres fous* (1955), *Moi, un noir* (1958), *La Pyramide Humaine* (1959) and *Chronique d'un été* (1960) were particularly influential works – presented the New Wave film-makers with an example of how documentary and fiction could intermingle and inform each other. The work of Agnès Varda and Alain Resnais, as part of the so-called 'Left Bank' group of film-makers who were contemporaries of the *Cahiers* critics, also demonstrated a lively interest in documentary film-making that would lead to full-length fiction films.

Actors and stars

If one of the defining features of the New Wave was its wholesale rejection of the cine-matic values of the Tradition of Quality, this is particularly marked as regards actors and actresses. The New Wave rejection of the French 'star system' can be ascribed to a number of factors: New Wave directors could not afford to employ 'stars', did not wish to be beholden to the power that a 'star' could exercise over creative decisions deemed to be in the hands of the auteur and, put plainly, 'stars' didn't correspond with the New Wave 'project' which was in search of 'youthfulness', 'modernity' and 'spontaneity'. Instead, the New Wave cast relatively unknown performers, or outright newcomers, and, in so doing, discovered a new generation of actors and, in some cases, created *bona fide* stars.

For further discussion of the star system, see Chapter 4, pp. 169–181.

• **Plate 12.10** Brigitte Bardot and Jeanne Moreau together for a press conference for the film *Viva Maria!* (Louis Malle, 1965)

One such star was Brigitte Bardot. While Bardot was by no means an archetypal New Wave actress like Anna Karina or Jeanne Moreau, she came to represent a new image of femininity that was to differentiate her and her contemporaries from the actresses who preceded them. The impact of her role in *Et Dieu créa la femme* (Vadim, 1956) was important for the New Wave for a variety of reasons. The film conformed to a certain number of the key characteristics of New Wave film-making. It was shot with a relatively small crew on location (in the then relatively 'unspoiled' fishing town of St Tropez in the South of France). While it featured a 'star' in the shape of Curt Jurgens, it was Bardot's youthful insolence and her unruffled sexual freedom that led François Truffaut to write: 'It is a film typical of our generation…despite the vast audience that *Et Dieu créa la femme* will certainly find, only young spectators will be on Vadim's side, because he shares their vision' (cited in Vincendeau 2000: 85). Bardot's association with the New Wave was actually quite limited in terms of the films she made. With the exception of *Et Dieu créa la femme*, Bardot made only two other films with directors associated with the 'young generation' of filmmakers: *Vie Privée* (*A Very Private Affair*, Louis Malle, 1961) and *Le Mépris* (*Contempt*, Godard, 1963). But there can be little doubt that her 'sex kitten' image and its connotations of a sophisticated yet earthy sexuality was important in opening up foreign markets for European art cinema abroad, particularly in the USA. As Vincendeau notes:

On the international film scene, the mid- to late 1950s saw both the break-up of the Hollywood studio system and concurrently, the rise of European art cinema: the films of Fellini, Antonioni, Resnais, Bergman, etc. As part of its drive to compete with Hollywood, European art cinema proposed a new kind of social and psychological realism which included a bid for explicit sexuality, made possible because of less stringent censorship codes. The different censorship laws and the more realistic genres of European films of the 1950s combined to produce a more 'natural' type of sexuality than Hollywood, best epitomized by Gina Lollobrigida, Sophia Loren and Silvana Mangano in Italian cinema. Women in peasant dresses, with bare feet paddling in rice fields, contrasted with the high glamour of Monroe and Lana Turner. Bardot was closer to the Italian model and *Et Dieu créa la femme* frequently features scenes of bathing, sea and beaches. European eroticism was bankable. Vadim said: 'Of course, some of (*Et Dieu créa la femme*'s) success came from its sexual frankness, and that's why so many of the first New Wave films, like Malle's *Les Amants* (1957) and Godard's *A bout de souffle* are equally casual about nudity. It's what distributors, especially American ones, were asking for.'

(Ibid.: 92–3)

For male and female performers alike, the New Wave filmmakers 'concentrated on behaviour, looks and gestures rather than psychology' (ibid.: 117). Vincendeau elaborates on these features of New Wave acting styles as follows:

Compare the ideas outlined here with the conventions of classical Hollywood cinema discussed in Chapter 2, pp. 54–83.

Its authenticity was grounded in a discourse of anti-professionalism. It was important that actors and actresses were seen not to act, especially in contrast to the Tradition of Quality cinema, which foregrounded polished performances, careful lighting and framing, experienced mastery of space, well-modulated delivery of dialogue. New Wave films foregrounded improvisation through filming on location, using available light and vernacular language. Performances matched this. Casual elocution and underplaying made performances appear 'modern' and blurred the distinction between fiction and document (reference to New Wave films as 'documentaries' on the actors are frequent). Lines are fluffed and movements are charmingly gauche.

(Ibid.)

What the New Wave auteurs required of their actors and actresses was 'male doubles or female muses' (ibid.: 115). In terms of the 'male doubles', it is particularly striking when one considers Truffaut's casting of Jean-Pierre Léaud as his alter-ego Antoine

Doinel in the suite of films beginning with *Les Quatre cent coups*. Equally, Godard's 'discovery' of the relatively unknown Jean-Paul Belmondo (who was to become one of the most popular and enduring French male leading men for several decades) often saw him playing a surrogate for the director and his cinéphilic obsessions: consider Belmondo's 'caricature' of Bogart in *A bout de souffle*, for example. But whether the actresses were *gamine* types such as Anna Karina or Chantal Goya, or sophisticated and liberated 'modern' women such as Jeanne Moreau or Emmanuelle Riva, as Ginette Vincendeau stresses: 'The close relationship between actresses and film-makers in the New Wave meant that while they played the traditional role of female object of desire, they, and not just the male alter-egos, also functioned as relayers of the film-maker's worldview' (ibid.: 116–17). Such 'close relationships' between directors and their leading actresses are often contextualised in cinéphilic terms with reference to other cinematic partnerships, such as those between Joseph von Sternberg and Marlene Dietrich or Ingmar Bergman and several of his actresses. Godard's relationship with Karina yielded seven films between 1961 and 1966, and Moreau was the partner of the directors of several of her major films in the 1960s, such as Truffaut and Malle. In fact, these 'cinéphile–svengali' partnerships could be said to be one of the characteristic features of European art cinema in the 1960s, from Federico Fellini's film's with Giullieta Masina to Michelangelo Antonioni's films with Monica Vitti.

Society and politics

The social background against which the New Wave emerged was one of postwar reconstruction and modernisation which saw France enter an economic boom period known as the 'trente glorieuses', or the 'thirty glorious years' of prosperity and techno-logical advances. Presiding over this period was the figure of Charles De Gaulle, the *résistant* war hero who, from the establishment of the Fifth Republic in 1958, was the President of France until 1969. However, during the same period, France was involved in bloody, drawn-out conflicts with countries struggling to free themselves from their former colonial masters. The involvement of the French armed forces in Indo-China saw them endure a humiliating defeat at Dien Bien Phu in May 1954, but the increasing involvement of American troops in the region set the scene for the war in Vietnam which would be one of the defining political events of the 1960s. While France negoti-ated the independence of two of its colonies, Morocco and Tunisia, the situation in France's oldest colony, Algeria, proved to be more intractable and fatally damaged the last five administrations of the French presidential structure known as the Fourth Republic. The colonial war between Algeria and France would last for eight years and claim the lives of 18,000 French soldiers and 250,000 Muslims while allowing De Gaulle to recast the presidential structure of power – the Fifth Republic – in order to resolve the crisis. Massacres and atrocities in Algeria were committed by both the Nationalist pro-independence movement, the FLN (Front de Libération Nationale), and the shadowy, colonialist 'secret army' of the French, OAS (Organisation de l'armée secrète), with the conflict spreading to the French mainland both in the shape of the attacks on civilians but also in mobilisation against the war by intellectuals, artists and those on the left-wing of the political spectrum. One such demonstration of opposition to the war in Algeria was the text supporting 'le droit à l'insoumission' (the right of soldiers to absent themselves without leave rather than serve in the war) signed by 121 prominent French intellectuals and artists including, among others, Jean-Paul Sartre, Simone de Beauvoir, Alain Resnais, Jacques Doniol-Valcroze, Pierre Kast and François Truffaut. It was immediately banned from publication and became known as the 'Manifeste des 121' ('The Manifesto of the 121'). The Evian Agreements of March 1962 finally led to full Algerian independence, despite a last ditch campaign of terror launched by the OAS.

The major political event of the 1960s in France took place in May 1968 during which widespread demonstrations and strikes took place disrupting public transport, closing banks, decimating industrial production and bringing the country to a virtual standstill. The two major forces of 'les évènements de mai' ('the events of May') were students and workers whose discontent with the French economic and social system was palliated by government action. The threat of a full-scale insurrection was thus soon snuffed out. The country's film-makers were heavily involved in the 'events' of May 1968 but the politicisation of the New Wave (often accused of having been apolitical, if not right-wing) began a little earlier. One of the main causes of such radicalisation was the perceived heavy-handedness of the state and its willingness to exercise censorship. This was an important issue during the 1960s, extending to all areas of media and culture and effecting coverage of the Algerian war just as it did the mainstream media coverage of the 'events of May'. The former writers of *Cahiers* who had avoided direct political engagement during the Algerian war came to political consciousness through a variety of confrontations with the French state in the mid- to late 1960s.

For further discussion of censorship in the US and UK, see Chapter 2, pp. 40–46, and for discussion of censorship and audience, see Chapter 3, pp. 124–126.

The censorship of film-makers' work, often resulting in the forbidding of public projection, had already alerted directors to the heavy-handedness of the state when it came to matters military – for example, Godard's *Le Petit soldat,* shot in 1960 but banned until 1963 – or clerical – Rivette's adaptation of Denis Diderot's play *La Réligieuse* was banned after protests by Catholic groups. But it was the decision of the Gaullist state in February 1968 to replace Henri Langlois as the head of the Cinémathèque Française that crystallised these misgivings and resulted in mobilisations and demonstrations that predated the events of May by several months. The concerted campaigning efforts of many film-makers protesting this decision was organised by *Cahiers* and resulted in Langlois' eventual reinstatement. Such activism generated a renewed confidence in the linking of culture and politics that would have profound repercussions throughout the milieus of film-making and criticism as well as further afield.

☐ CASE STUDY 5: JEAN-LUC GODARD

• **Plate 12.11**
Jean-Luc Godard and Anna Karina share an intimate moment

Jean-Luc Godard has endowed cinema with a vast and inexhaustibly rich body of work. Since his debut in 1990 with *A bout de souffle*, Godard has made over forty feature films, numerous short films and many hours of video, not to mention his film criticism which, throughout the 1950s, preceded and overlapped with his career as a film-maker. In fact, Godard has frequently stated that he considers his film-making as much an exercise in criticism as his writing, an assertion that allows a way into his body of work.

Godard's career is conventionally seen as dividing into three phases. First, the New Wave period that begins with *A bout de souffle* and for which his writing on *Cahiers* and his short film-making throughout the 1950s can be seen as preparation. When the New Wave period is seen to end is a matter of historical debate. Some argue that the New Wave as a 'phenomenon' was over by 1962. Others argue that it can be extended up to the political events of May 1968. With Godard's increasing politicisation around that time, the 'second phase' of his work is seen to begin when the director jettisoned his auteur celebrity status and became involved in collective, explicitly ideologically motivated film-making; this period continues until 1972. Godard's 'third phase' occurs in the early to mid-1970s when the director returned to relatively mainstream film-making with films such as *Tout va bien* (1972) and *Sauve qui peut (la vie)* (1979). One of the most important developments in this period, and which continues to the present day, has been Godard's long-standing use and exploration of video technology.

During the New Wave years (1958–1962) and in the immediate post-New Wave period (1962–68) Godard sustained a steady output of work, sometimes shooting two films simultaneously. During this period he made seventeen features and eleven shorts (including those made prior to *A bout de souffle*) and the time was marked by two consistent collaborations (excluding that with the producer Georges de Beauregard); first, with the cinematographer Raoul Coutard on fifteen features and, second, with the actress Anna Karina who was married to Godard for a period in the 1960s and with whom he made seven films and co-founded a production company, Anoushka Films.

In the films that Godard made up to 1968 a keen awareness of the history of cinema co-exists alongside a critical analysis of cinematic language and the possibilities of extending cinematic forms. As early as *A bout de souffle*, it is evident that Godard is both glorying in the generic possibilities of the Hollywood B-movie but also taking advantage of their use within a specifically French context by employing them against the backdrop of everyday Parisian life. Here, genre meets documentary. This is a crucial aspect of Godard's film-making, the desire to explore the fictional aspect of a documentary context and vice versa. He was deeply influenced in this by the work of the ethnographical documentarist Jean Rouch (Godard had studied ethnography at the Sorbonne in Paris in the late 1940s). Equally important in this regard was the example of the great Italian director Roberto Rossellini, whose 'neo-realist' films such as *Rome, Open City* (1945), *Paisan* (1946) and *Germany, Year Zero* (1947), as well as later films made with his wife Ingrid Bergman such as *Voyage to Italy* (1953), were highly influential for many New Wave film-makers in their extremely 'modern' use of documentary modes to treat fictional storylines.

Throughout the 1960s, Godard used generic forms to analyse French society, politics and consumerism. *Alphaville* (1965), for example, employs science-fiction and the spy thriller forms in a generic hybrid, as well as quoting liberally from German Expressionist cinema (the sequence printed in negative is a direct quotation from *Nosferatu, Eine Symphonie des Grauens* (F.W. Murnau, 1922), and sets these to work to produce a dystopian vision of an inhuman, technocratic society using only the existing modernist architectural forms of Paris as it was in 1965. Across a number of his films made in this period, such as *Vivre sa vie* (*My Life to Live*, 1962), *Une Femme mariée* (*A Married Woman*, 1964) and *Deux ou trois choses que je sais d'elle* (*Two or Three Things I Know about Her*, 1966), it became clear that Godard was as much a social critic with a camera as a film critic. This element of social criticism was to increase in significance in the late 1960s as Godard became more explicitly political in his analysis of consumer

● **Plate 12.12** Anna
Karina and Eddie
Constantine in *Alphaville*
(Jean-Luc Godard, 1965)

● **Plate 12.12** Anna Karina and Eddie Constantine in *Alphaville* (Jean-Luc Godard, 1965)

society (which he often likened to a form of 'prostitution' in advanced capitalist countries) and his increasing hostility towards American imperialism (this being the period of America's war in Vietnam) and what he saw as its propaganda vehicle, Hollywood cinema. By the time of *La Chinoise* (1967) and *Weekend* (1967), Godard had become fully radicalised by 'l'affaire Langlois' (see above). The political uprising of the 'events' of May 1968 – as a response to which Godard and others shut down the Cannes Film Festival in solidarity with workers' and students' protests – were to transform his career, as they would many others.

☐ CASE STUDY 6: AGNÈS VARDA

Agnès Varda's debut feature film *La Pointe Courte* (1954) was dubbed by the French film historian Georges Sadoul as 'the first film of the New Wave' and Varda has frequently been described as 'the grandmother' of the New Wave. A former art student and professional photographer, Varda made her first film with no previous experience of film-making. *La Pointe Courte* told the story of a relationship set against the location of a fishing village. It was co-operatively produced by a company that Varda established specifically in order to make the film. Ciné-Tamaris has remained Varda's production company ever since and through it she has made sixteen feature films, as well as many documentaries and shorts.

Varda is often bracketed as part of the so-called 'Left Bank' grouping of the New Wave. This term, coined by the American film critic and former director of the New York Film Festival Richard Roud, was intended to distinguish the work of Varda, Alain Resnais and Chris Marker from that of the film-makers who emerged from *Cahiers*. The 'Left Bank' film-makers were frequent collaborators with each other: Resnais was the editor of *La Pointe Courte* and Varda accompanied Marker to China to assist on the production of his 1956 documentary essay-film *Dimanche à Pekin* (*Sunday in Peking*). The 'Left Bank' film-makers were distinguished by a number of characteristics: a practical relationship with documentary film-making, their literary affinities, close contact and interest in the fine arts, and a more pronounced degree of left-leaning political commitment than the *Cahiers* directors.

For a more detailed discussion of Cléo de 5 à 7, see Case study 4, pp. 435–436.

That is not to say that these two groupings were mutually exclusive. *Cahiers* championed the work by the Left Bank group and Godard, Doniol-Valcroze and Anna Karina appear in cameo roles in a short silent film inserted into Varda's second film *Cléo de 5 à 7* (1961).

As the only woman film-maker associated with the New Wave, Varda's work is fascinating for a variety of reasons. From an early stage she practised what she called 'cinécriture' (a compound word made up of two French words, 'ciné' – cinema – and 'écriture' – writing; hence, 'cinematic-writing'). One might say that all her films are examples of Alexandre Astruc's notion of 'le caméra stylo' ('the camera-pen') in a woman's hands. Many of her films are explicitly about women's experiences and explore cinematic means of conveying female subjectivity. Varda was married for many years to another director who came to prominence during the New Wave period, Jacques Demy, who made a number of important and successful films including *Lola* (1960) and *Les Parapluies de Cherbourg* (*The Umbrellas of Cherbourg*, 1964), and who died in 1990.

The range of subjects covered by Varda's films include radical politics (*Black Panthers*, shot in the US in 1968) and the chronicle of the lives of two female friends coming to political consciousness through the 1960s and 1970s, *L'une chante l'autre pas* (*One Sings the Other Doesn't*, 1977). Many of her films are marked by her abiding interest in and love for the arts of painting, sculpture and photography. In 1985 Varda made a film about the short life and death of a young female drifter in the south of France, *Sans toit ni loi* (*Vagabond*), starring Sandrine Bonnaire, which was critically praised and reached international audiences.

More recently, Varda again claimed international attention and acclaim with her elegant and humane portrait of those living at the margins of French consumer society, *Les Glaneurs et la glaneuse* (*The Gleaners and I*, 2000), which won the European Film Academy Award for Best Documentary in 2000 as well as several prestigious American Film Critics awards. Shot on digital video, the film marked a kind of full-circle return to Varda's New Wave roots, the documentary-essay form updated with the new technology of digital video.

THE LEGACY OF THE NEW WAVE

In January 1999 *Cahiers* published a special supplement entitled 'The New Wave: a legend in question' which included seventeen articles reassessing the 'legend' of the French New Wave. The issue also featured a questionnaire in which a number of film-makers from around the world were asked to respond to a series of questions, including: 'What did the phenomenon of the New Wave represent in your life?'; 'Was its influence positive or negative?'; 'Did the New Wave help you in making films?' The directors who responded included a combination of older and contemporary French film-makers as well as illustrious international names such as Abbas Kiarostami and Martin Scorsese. It is instructive to listen to these two film-makers, each from a very different culture and industry, the one Iranian, the other American, in what they had to say about the New Wave's impact. First, Scorsese:

Whether they're aware of it or not, all the film-makers who have come since have been influenced by the New Wave...the first films of Godard, Truffaut, Chabrol, Rivette, Rohmer and others gave you the feeling that you could make a film yourself, anyhow, with anyone, no matter what the story was and that you didn't need expensive materials, famous names or powerful lights. It was enough to go out into the streets and make a film and that it would work if you had the courage of your convictions.

(*Cahiers*, January 1999: 97)

And Kiarostami:

Perhaps you won't believe me if I tell you that the movement started in French cinema by the New Wave was followed day-by-day in Iran...under the influence of New Wave film-makers my way of imagining or envisaging cinema changed. Before, I believed that cinema belonged to superstars, to studios and spectacular sets. With the New Wave, I saw myself and my neighbours in films.

(Ibid.: 96)

Before examining the considerable long-term influence of the New Wave, as attested to by Scorsese and Kiarostami, it is worthwhile considering the lifetime of the phenomenon in France. I have already explored some of the factors that encouraged the explosion of film production from 1958 onwards that became known as New Wave cinema, but it should be acknowledged how relatively short-lived this cinema was as a 'phenomenon'. That's not to say that the examples and possibilities for film-makers represented by the New Wave expired along with its sure-fire commercial prospects, but to delineate a scale of time in which this 'phenomenon' can be seen to have existed. The standard film-historical timescale in which the New Wave is seen to have been born, flourished and expired was between 1958 and 1962, between the prize-winning success of Truffaut's *Les Quatre cents coups* at Cannes in 1958 and the second films by Godard, Truffaut and Chabrol that were released between 1961 and 1962. With Godard's *Une Femme est une femme* (1961), Truffaut's *Tirez sur le pianiste* (1960) and Chabrol's *Les Godelureaux* (1960) and *L'Oeil du malin* (1962), the novelty of the New Wave was seen to have worn off, with the public staying away and the critics unenthusiastic. This strict chronology serves to delimit the New Wave as a short-term, high-profile event in French cinema that quickly fell out of favour; a caricature of these films became current as being little more than a compendium of images of 'Saint Tropez, casual relationships, whisky and ennui' (de Baecque 1991: 138). In his recent study of the period, *A Portrait of Youth* (1998), the French cultural historian Antoine de Baecque points out also that there were larger transformations underway that should be considered when examining the immediate New Wave period. The backdrop to the New Wave was 'a long-term cultural evolution', one which saw the numbers of cinema spectators gradually decline throughout the 1950s and 1960s as television became the dominant form of mass entertainment and communication. In these terms, the New Wave can be seen as the momentary phenomenon of a national cinema revitalising the domestic scene while also soliciting considerable international attention.

The New Wave certainly modified some of the conditions of film production in France. For example, the tendency to move away from studio-based production to an increased emphasis on location-based filming. It also had an effect on distribution, particularly in the importance accorded to the state-supported circuit of specialised *cinémas d'art et d'essai*, which might be seen as a precursor of the 'art cinemas' that became a feature of international film distribution from the 1960s onwards. It is in these terms that the New Wave can be seen to have had a profound and continuing influence on cinema, both in France and internationally. It can be argued that, since the New Wave period, the idea of 'auteur' cinema has become virtually institutionalised in France. During the Socialist presidency of François Mitterand in the 1980s, the Minister of Culture Jack Lang instituted a series of policies that sought to defend French film production against American domination of the domestic film scene while paying particular attention to auteur production. Many of Lang's policies remain more or less in place to this day and it has arguably been the French state's willingness to intervene, regulate and subsidise its national cinema that has contributed to it being the only European country with an active and vital national cinema.

The term 'national cinema' is increasingly questionable in a period of globalised capital and media. And it is useful to consider the extent to which the New Wave was

For further discussion of multimedia and the relationship between film and the new media, see Chapter 1, pp. 31–32.

an international phenomenon as much as it was national. Auteur film-making has been a significant part of the national industry since the 1960s and it is this form of film-making that tends to represent French cinema abroad, exporting more successfully than other, more populist, national genres such as comedies and thrillers. Thus it may be argued that the French films that successfully export abroad claim the mantle of 'art cinema' while losing some of their national specificity. Consider, for example, how the film *Amélie* (Jean-Pierre Jeunet, 2001), a huge popular success in France, was marketed as a reassuringly 'French art cinema' product in the UK.

As many critics have argued, one of the features of 'art cinema' is its simultaneously national and international character. During the 1960s, this sector of international cinema was the institutionalised space in which national cinemas competed for attention as the Hollywood studio system declined and American cinema turned to independent production. The international aspect of the New Wave legacy is complex and made up of many different strands. It should be remembered that the phenomenon of a 'new wave' of film-making was not restricted to France. In fact, 'la nouvelle vague' could be seen to have been one 'wave' (admittedly the first and perhaps most influential) following on from the international impact of Italian neo-realism, that would widen out as part of a tremendous renaissance in European national cinemas during the 1960s and 1970s and that would take in the strength of the Italian, Czech and German films of the period. The international appeal of European cinema throughout the 1960s depended on a combination of structural factors: a willingness to support domestic production, especially the work of new film-makers, and a thriving international film culture able to circulate and promote such work. It might be said that one of the major legacies of the French New Wave' was that it was responsible for circulating not just films, but critical ideas as well. This was certainly the case with *Cahiers du cinéma*, which must rank as the most influential film magazine in the history of this field. As the directors of the New Wave became international celebrities, the ideas that they had explored in their writing became international critical currency, particularly the notion of the auteur, which would become a cornerstone of early academic Film Studies. For a while in the 1960s, the magazine was published in English, a venture inaugurated by the American critic Andrew Sarris, who translated the term 'politique des auteurs' as 'auteur theory' and would go on to apply it to American film-makers in his book *The American Cinema: Directors and Directions 1929–1968* (1996). So a 'politique', as a politics and a policy, became, through mistranslation, a 'theory'.

Both as a corpus of films and as a film-making example, the New Wave has continued to influence successive generations of French film-makers. One way of considering how the memory and the myth of the New Wave still exerts a profound pull on auteur cinema – both in France and abroad – is by examining the persona of the actor Jean-Pierre Léaud. From his 1958 role as a child actor in *Les Quatre cents coups* and through his numerous reprisals of the character Antoine Doinel, Léaud has become an iconic figure in French cinema. Throughout the 1960s and 1970s he worked with a number of major auteurs, including Godard, Pier Paolo Pasolini and Bernardo Bertolucci, who cast him as a thinly disguised New Wave cinéaste in *Last Tango in Paris* (1972). It is in Bertolucci's film and in Jean Eustache's *La Maman et la putain* (*The Mother and the Whore*, 1973) that one can detect the iconic associations of Léaud's persona being modified and exploited by other directors who had been influenced by the New Wave but who were aware, sometimes uncomfortably, of coming after it. Eustache's film, a harrowing anatomisation of the emotional fall-out of the post-'68 period, put Léaud's persona as a petit-bourgeois Parisian solipsist to work in a particularly exacting fashion. Over the last decade or so, Léaud's persona – one of madcap melancholy – has featured in a number of films as a way of looking back to the past of the New Wave and considering its legacy. Having been born into a cinema of film-fixated allusions, Léaud has literally 'grown up' on screen and now finds himself frequently cast as a kind of 'quotation' of himself, as an icon in inverted commas.

Durgnat, R., *Nouvelle Vague, The First Decade*, Motion Publications, Loughton, 1963.

Graham, P. (ed.), *The New Wave: Critical Landmarks*, British Film Institute/Secker & Warburg, London, 1968. A valuable collection of texts by and about the New Wave.

Hayward, Susan, *French National Cinema*, Routledge, London, 1993. An extensive study of French cinema from the perspective of how a nation's self-image is informed by its cinematic representation.

Hayward, S. and Vincendeau, G. (eds), *French Film: Texts and Contexts*, Routledge, London, 1990. A crucial collection of essays on French cinema by major French and Anglo-Saxon critics; covers more than the New Wave period.

Hillier, J. (ed.), *Cahiers du cinéma 1: The 1950s, Neo-realism, Hollywood, The New Wave*, British Film Institute/Routledge & Kegan Paul, London, 1985. The first of four anthologies collecting translations of key *Cahiers* texts; this volume covers the New Wave period.

—— (ed.), *Cahiers du cinéma 2: 1960–1968*, British Film Institute/Routledge and Kegan Paul, London, 1986.

Marie, M., *La nouvelle vague: une école artistique*, Nathan, 1998. A highly detailed and scrupulously researched analysis of the context of the New Wave (in French).

Neale, S. 'Art Cinema as Institution', *Screen*, Vol. 22, No 1, 1981, pp. 11–41. A key essay on European art cinema as idea and institution.

Nichols, B. (ed.), *Movies and Methods*, Vol. 1, University of California Press, Berkeley, 1976.

Smith, Alison, *Agnès Varda*, Manchester University Press, Manchester, 1998. The only English language study of Varda's work; pays particular attention to Varda's interest in the 'female gaze' and fine art.

Vincendeau, G., 'France 1945–65 and Hollywood: The *Policier* as Inter-national Text', *Screen*, Vol. 33, No. 1, Spring 1992, pp. 50–63. An intertextual analysis of Godard's *Alphaville* as a film that mediates French fascination/repulsion with America and its culture.

—— *Stars and Stardom in French Cinema*, Continuum, London, 2000. A study of the major stars of French film, examining personas and acting styles; includes material on Bardot, Karina, Belmondo and Delon.

Wilson, E., *Personal Histories: French Cinema since 1950*, Duckworth, London, 1999. A contemporary, post-New Wave reading of the theme of 'first-person film-making' in French cinema. An interesting critique of auteur cinema.

FURTHER VIEWING

1957	*Les Mistons* (*The Brats*, short, F. Truffaut)
1958	*Le Beau Serge* (C. Chabrol)
1959	*Charlotte et sons Jules* (short, J.-L. Godard)
	Les Cousins (*The Cousins*, C. Chabrol)
	Le Signe du lion (E. Rohmer)
1960	*Paris nous appartient* (*Paris Belongs to Us*, J. Rivette)
	Le Petit soldat (*The Little Soldier*, J.-L. Godard)
	Tirez sur le pianiste (*Shoot the Pianist*, F. Truffaut)
1961	*Une Femme est une femme* (*A Woman is a Woman*, J.-L. Godard)
	Jules et Jim (F. Truffaut)
1962	*Vivre sa vie* (*My Life to Live*, J.-L. Godard)
1963	*Le Mépris* (*Contempt*, J.-L. Godard)
1964	*Bande à part* (*Band of Outsiders*, J.-L. Godard, 1964)

	Paris vu par... (J. Rouch, J.-L. Godard, E. Rohmer and others)
1965	*Alphaville* (J.-L. Godard)
	Pierrot le fou (*Crazy Pete*, J.-L. Godard)
1966	*Deux ou trois choses que je sais d'elle* (*Two or Three Things I Know About Her*, J.-L. Godard)
1967	*La Chinoise* (J.-L. Godard)
	Week-End (J.-L. Godard)
1968	*Ma nuit chez Maude* (*My Night at Maud's*, E. Rohmer)
1970	*Le Genou de Claire* (*Claire's Knee*, E. Rohmer)
1985	*Sans toit ni loi* (*Vagabond*, A. Varda)
1989 –	
2000	*Histoire(s) du cinéma* (J.-L. Godard)
1996	*Irma Vep* (O. Assayas)
2000	*Les Glaneurs et la glaneuse* (*The Gleaners and I*, A. Varda)
2001	*Eloge de l'amour* (*In Praise of Love*, J.-L. Godard)

RESOURCE CENTRES

British Film Institute Library, 21 Stephen Street, London W1T 1LN
Institut Français, 17 Queensbury Place, London SW7 2DT
The Institut's library and médiathèque holds a large selection of French-language books, journals and periodicals as well as videos and CDs.

Glossary

30°   A change in camera angle at the minimum of 30° is usual for each new shot at the same scene thus ensuring the cut will edit smoothly. That is, there will not be a *jump cut*.

180° rule, the   The 180° rule involves an imaginary line along the action of the scene, between actors involved in a conversation or the direction of a chase. The 'rule' dictates that this line should be clearly established and that the consecutive shots should not be taken from opposite sides of the line.

35mm film   The measurement of film in millimetres (16mm, 35mm, 70mm) describes the length of the individual film negative frames which are exposed in order to capture an image: the larger the negative, the higher the resolution of the projected image. Larger format film such as 70mm, while superior in quality, is cumbersome to use and comparatively expensive to work with. There are also fewer cinemas able to screen formats other than the now-standard 35mm print.

alternative   Alternative cinema is defined with reference to **dominant**: it is an alternative (both economically and formally) to the dominant form. In any study concerning an 'alternative' cinema, the films would not only have to be examined in their own right, but also compared to contemporary dominant **Hollywood cinema**. A number of questions might have to be posed when analysing these alternative films: In what ways is this group of films different to the dominant cinema of the time? What are the possible reasons for the difference: cultural? economic? social? political? Could this 'alternative' way of making films, given the right conditions, have itself turned into the dominant cinema? The **Soviet cinema** of the 1920s, when compared to the Hollywood cinema of the same era, certainly could be regarded as alternative. In other words, alternative cinema offered a style of film-making that was radically different to the mass of films that was being produced in America.

animation   The creation of artificial movement through a variety of techniques. Usually recorded one frame at a time, animation replicates naturalistic movement and creates the illusion of life in objects and images.

anthropomorphism   The tendency in **animation** to endow creatures with human attributes, abilities and qualities. This can redefine or merely draw attention to characteristics which are taken for granted in live-action representations of human beings.

art cinema   A term usually applied to films where the director has clearly exercised a high degree of control over the film-making process and thus the films can be viewed as a form of personal expression. This kind of film-making became common in Europe (hence the term, 'European art cinema'), especially from the 1950s onwards, due to the funding structures and nature of the European film industries, which allowed directors greater artistic freedom than was to be found within the US system. In terms of style and content, art cinema is usually characterised by the way it differs from its commercial counterpart, **Hollywood cinema**: for instance, a drifting, episodic and open-ended narrative versus the tight cause-and-effect narrative of American cinema with its characteristic closure.

art-house   A crude shorthand way of referring to films in which artistic ambition and intellectual challenge are more important than the simple motive to provide entertainment. 'Great' art-house directors such as Bergman and Godard are unquestionably considered to be **auteurs**.

artisanal mode of production   A way of making films outside of an established 'industrial' means of production by using small budgets and minimal production teams. The term emphasises a more craft-like and personal process hence allowing greater control of the film-making process.

associative mode   Approach to **documentary** which attempts to use footage in such a way as to provide the maximum degree of symbolic or metaphorical meaning on top of the literal information available in the image.

audience   Collectives of people responding to a film.

auteur   A French term that originated in the pages of the film journal *Cahiers du cinèma* in the 1950s to refer to directors who infuse their films with their distinctive personal vision through the salient manipulation of film technique. Auteurs, seen as genuine artists, were contrasted with **metteurs-en-scène** who were held to be technically competent directors who merely executed the processes of film-making without consistently stamping their 'personality' on the material from one film to the next.

auteurism   A critical approach to the study of film which identifies the director as responsible for whatever the viewer finds of thematic, stylistic or structural interest in a single film or across a body of work by one director.

avant-garde   Essentially non-narrative in structure and often intellectual in content, working in opposition to mainstream cinema. Literally the 'advanced guard' of experimental film-makers who reject the dominant forms of mainstream cinema in favour of innovation and experiment in film-making, often producing non-narrative, non-illusionistic, sometimes abstract films. Avant-garde film is often self-conscious and frequently makes use of devices such as cuts to the camera crew, talking to the camera and scratching on film.

binary analysis   An approach which derives from cultural anthropology and particularly the work of Claude Lévi-Strauss. The study of binary opposites is a useful means of identifying structures at work in, for instance, the genre of a film.

biopic   A film which dramatises the biography of a real or imaginary person. It is usually characterised by a linear narrative. Examples of musical biopics range from *The Glenn Miller Story* (Anthony Mann, 1954) to *The Doors* (Oliver Stone, 1991).

blue screen   A process that involves the subject being filmed in front of a blue screen. Optical manipulation of this footage creates imagery of the actor against a black background. Additionally, the actor's silhouette is set against a clear background. Using these two elements as **mattes** it is possible to place the action into any scene required.

Bollywood   Bombay, the film capital of India.

bricolage   The putting together of features from different genres and styles, self-consciously and usually playfully. This is one of the principal characteristics of **postmodernism**.

butch   Description of behaviour patterns – such as aggression and sexual dominance – traditionally associated with masculinity.

camp   A critical attitude which involves looking at texts less as reflections of reality and more as constructed sets of words, images and sounds at a distance from reality. The attitude often involves irony or detachment when considering this distance.

caméra stylo   A term coined by French writer Alexandre Astruc meaning 'camera-pen' and used to condense his argument for a 'personal' and self-expressive form of cinema.

carnivalesque   Term which refers to an atmosphere or attitude, found at carnivals and similar events, characterised by laughter, excess and vulgarity. Seen as a lower-class resistance to the refined tastes of the dominant (upper and middle) classes.

character/personality animation   Many cartoons and more sophisticated adult animated films, for example, Japanese anime, are still dominated by 'character' or 'personality' animation, which prioritises exaggerated and sometimes caricatured expressions of human traits in order to direct attention to the detail of gesture and the range of human emotion and experience. This kind of animation is related to identifiable aspects of the real world and does not readily correspond with more abstract uses of the animated medium.

cinema apparatus   The power of cinema as a system of communication, controlling and holding the spectator in place.

cinema novo   'New Cinema'. A movement of film-makers that came to prominence in Brazil in the 1960s, the leading figure of which was Glauber Rocha. Influenced by the New Wave in France and the intellectual examples of Frantz Fanon and Che Guevara, 'cinema novo' called for film-making that emphasised 'the aesthetics of hunger' directed against a cinema of imperialism.

cinéma vérité   A phrase often coupled with the concept of 'direct cinema'. Literally 'cinema truth', cinéma vérité emerged out of the film-making practices of Jean Rouch in France. Based on Vertov's approach, it acknowledged the impact of the film-making process upon the recording of 'actuality', and more readily recognised the subjectivity of the film-maker in securing filmic evidence of what took place. Rouch essentially suggests that the documentary form must be defined through the integrity and purpose of its author. The value and purpose of 'actuality' footage in regard to its delineation of documentary 'truth' is therefore in direct relationship to the intention of those who produce it.

cinephilia   The notion of cinephilia refers to an intense love of, even obsession with, cinema. It implies both a way of watching and a way of speaking about film beyond the standard relationship between cinema and its spectator. Cinephiles are people who, in Andrew Sarris' phrase, 'love cinema beyond all reason', and who engage with film in highly specific ways.

Classical Hollywood cinema   A particular narrative form which was exemplified by the films at the height of the studio system (1930–49). Although most Hollywood films still contain elements of classical narrative form, such as a central protagonist and a clear cause–effect relationship, film narratives, particularly since the success of movies such as *Pulp Fiction* (Tarantino, 1994), now play with plot and character with much greater flexibility.

close-up   Normally defined as a shot of the head from the neck up.

CNC   Centre Nationale de la Cinématographie, the chief body of the French state that oversees policy affecting film-making, including the subsidies accorded to cinema.

cognitivist processing   The process by which ideas that might be considered dangerous or anti-hegemonic are pulled in or incorporated into structures of order.

condensation   The compression of a set of narrative or aesthetic agendas within a minimal structural framework. Essentially, achieving the maximum amount of suggested information and implication from the minimum amount of imagery used.

consent decree   A court order made with the consent of both parties – the defendant and the plaintiff – which puts to rest the law suit brought against the former by the latter.

conventions   Conventions are established procedures within a particular form which are identifiable by both the producer and the reader. The implication of the idea of conventions is that a form does not naturally mean anything, but it is an agreement between producer and user.

cultural capital   First originating in the work of Pierre Bourdieu to describe the unequal distribution of cultural competencies and values principally across different social classes, the term has since been appropriated more generally to refer to the specific competencies and 'knowledges' of various social groupings, as well as the 'symbolic power' attained precisely from 'affiliation' to that group.

cultural studies   The cultural studies approach has gained academic respectability, partly because of the pioneering work of theorists such as Raymond Williams and Stuart Hall. Popular culture is now seen as a complex and worthy area of study, as being revealing about our society. Cultural studies has been influenced by Marxist theory, especially the theories of Antonio Gramsci, who used the term **hegemony** to describe the consensus that keeps the status quo in existence in society; capitalism keeps control by agreement of the people, yet there are still struggles for power which allow for change and adjustment in society. Cultural studies has, in more recent years, been a major influence on film studies, particularly in the study of popular film.

deconstruction   All media 'texts' are constructed. To understand all the components within each construction it is necessary to deconstruct the text and analyse all its elements. For example, the cartoon is made up of a number of specific aspects which define it as a unique cinematic practice, i.e. its frame-by-frame construction, its modes of representation and so on.

découpage   A term that means the 'shot break-down' of a scene.

developmental animation   If *Orthodox animation* emerges from Disney's 2D cel-animated tradition, developmental animation operates as the range of responses and oppositions to it. This might include the more overtly 'cartoonal' work by Warner Bros and MGM, or the range of approaches and styles from stop-motion animation, to clay animation, to cut-out animation etc., which may still possess 'mimetic' references, but are nevertheless seeking to be more non-linear and non-objective in their approaches.

dialectical   A difficult term to define, as it has many different meanings. The *Collins English Dictionary* (2nd edn, 1986), for example, defines it a 'disputation or debate, esp. intended to resolve differences between two views rather than to establish one of them as true'. The crucial factor to grasp in the context of Eisenstein's thinking, however, is the notion of change and the creation of a new order. Eisenstein would have defined dialectic with reference to **Marxist** philosophy, which believed that society was contra-dictory and in need of change.

diegetic   The elements of a film that originate from directly within the film's narrative. For example, a popular song that is being played on the soundtrack would be diegetic if it were clear that it was coming from a source within the world of the film such as a car radio. See also **non-diegetic**.

dilution and amplication   The simultaneous capacity for animation, by virtue of its intrinsic artifice, to be viewed either as a language which dilutes its outcomes and effects, rendering them 'innocent' and 'dismissable', or as a language which inherently amplifies its literal, aesthetic and ideological perspectives, rendering them sometimes unacceptably challenging in their representational aspects.

Direct Cinema   American documentarists of the 1960s and 1970s believed that the advent of light, portable, technically sophisticated camera equipment enabled a break-through in the ways that documentary film-making could reveal personal and social 'truth'. The fact that the documentarist could literally film anywhere under any condi-tions meant that a greater intimacy could be achieved with the subject, heightening the sense that 'reality' was being directly observed, and that the viewer was party to the seemingly unmediated immediacy of the experience. Less controlled, unscripted, apparently spontaneous, the look and feel of 'direct cinema' arguably demonstrated a less deliberately authored approach.

discourse systems   A discourse is a mode of speech which has evolved to express the shared human activities of a community of people. Film studies has, like other acad-emic disciplines, developed its own language – its own discourse system – to make possible the identification and 'mapping' of that area of human activity and experience with which it is concerned.

Disney dust   The term given to the glitter and sparkle that usually accompanies any form of magic or unearthly effect such as the glowing dust trail left by the flying Tinkerbell in Disney's *Peter Pan* (1953) and again in *Hook* (1991).

distribution   Division of the film industry concentrating on the marketing of film, connecting the producer with the exhibitor by leasing films from the former and renting them to the latter.

documentary   A non-fiction text using 'actuality' footage, which may include the live recording of events and relevant research material (i.e. interviews, statistics etc.). This kind of text is usually informed by a particular point of view, and seeks to address a particular social issue which is related to and potentially affects the audience.

Dogme 95   The name given to a collective of Danish film-makers united around the figures of directors Lars Von Trier, Thomas Winterberg and Kristian Levering. Dogme 95 was the name of a manifesto that committed film-makers to observing a cinematic 'vow of chastity' involving an ultra-realist approach to film-making using only digital video cameras.

dominant   Refers to both economic strength and also to the dominant form or convention: dominant cinema in film studies is assumed to be **Hollywood**.

drama-documentary   Any format which attempts to re-create historical or typical events using performers, whether actors or not.

dystopia   A world of the future where everything has gone wrong.

eclecticism   An aesthetic style in which a new composition is composed wholly or in part from elements selected from a range of previous styles, forms, texts, genres, drawn from different periods and from both high and popular culture. This is one of the prin-cipal strategies of **postmodern** art. See also **intertextuality, palimpsest, recombinacy, self-reflexivity**.

economic presentation   All the components are designed to help us read the narra-tive. An examination of the first few minutes of almost any mainstream fictional film will reveal a considerable amount of information about characters, their social situation and their motivation.

culture in which forms of work, leisure and entertainment, as well as many of the taken-for-granted activities that structure daily life, are predicted on, and determined by, the all-pervasive presence of highly integrated media forms and technologies. The notion of **hypermediation**, therefore, refers to the way that our experience of the world is channelled through an endless network of media texts.

iconic   The iconic is defined by the dominant signs that signify a particular person or object – Chaplin, for example, would be defined by a bowler hat, a moustache, a cane and some old boots; Hitler would be defined by a short, parted hairstyle and a small 'postage stamp' moustache.

iconoclasts   Film-makers and documentarists committed to challenging the received construction and meanings of images, partially through the critique of those images, and mainly through the reconfiguration of imagery in a subjective style.

iconography   The visual codes of setting, props and clothing which enable us to recognise a film as belonging to a certain genre or type. It shares similarities with **mise-en-scène**.

identification   The process of identification allows us to place ourselves in the position of particular characters, either throughout or at specific moments in a movie. The devices involved include subjectivity of viewpoint (we see the world through their eyes, a shared knowledge, we know what and only what they know), and a sharing in their moral world, largely through narrative construction.

ideological effects   Of political significance, manipulating the spectator into an acceptance of specific ways of thinking about and relating to the world.

ideological function   Ideology is the system of ideas, values and beliefs held by individuals or groups within society. Ideological function refers to the way in which ideology is disseminated through films or other cultural forms. Audiences may of course refuse to accept the dominant ideological meaning in a film.

ideology   Although a complex issue, ideology may be seen as the dominant set of ideas and values which inform any one society or culture, but which are imbued in its social behaviour and representative texts at a level that is not necessarily obvious or conscious. There are two key definitions of this term, one provided by the nineteenth-century German philosopher, Karl Marx, the other by the twentieth-century French Marxist philosopher, Louis Althusser, drawing on Marx's original ideas. For Marx, ideology was the dominant set of beliefs and values existent within society, which sustained power relations. For Althusser, ideology consisted of the representations and images which reflect society's view of 'reality'. Ideology thus refers to 'the myths that a society lives by'. An ideological stance is normally politicised and historically determined.

illustrative mode   An approach to **documentary** which attempts to illustrate directly what the commentary/voiceover is saying.

impresario   Organiser of public entertainments; a manager of, especially, an operatic or concert company.

incoherent cinema   Influenced by the 'Incoherents', artists working between 1883 and 1891, a movement principally led by Cohl. This kind of animation was often surreal, anarchistic and playful, relating seemingly unrelated forms and events in an often irrational and spontaneous fashion. Lines tumble into shapes and figures in temporary scenarios before evolving into other images.

independent   This is a highly problematic term meaning different things in different situations. In the contemporary film industry it implies a production realised outside one of the majors. It may be usefully divided into two areas. First, independent mainstream production, which aims to compete with the big studios but without any large financial backing, and thus finds it difficult to survive. Palace Films was one such casualty; the success of *The Crying Game* came too late to save its demise. Second, the term is used to describe film-making outside the mainstream sector, for instance, film work-shops, **avant-garde** film, feminist film. The boundaries between these two areas are not always clear and may overlap.

Institutional Mode of Representation/IMR   The IMR is a broad categorisation of systems of film form and narrative characterising mainstream cinema from around 1915 onwards. It was perceived as replacing the Primitive Mode of Representation (a set of conventions used in Early Cinema between 1895 and 1905) as a gradual process in the first twenty years of cinema.

intentional fallacy   A phrase coined by Monroe Beardsley to describe the difference between a text's meaning(s) and what its author intended. As such, criticism dependent on, or directed towards, uncovering the intentions of the author/artist falls foul of 'inten-tional fallacy' insofar as the meaning of a text is not fixed within it, but created in the historically situated act of reading.

intermedia   The relations that exist between cinema, the film industry and other media at the levels of both capitalist business practices and textual forms.

internet   A system of interlinking computers in a worldwide network (WWW/World Wide Web). Since the internet was privatised in April 1995 the rise in monthly traffic on the net has been such that it represents a hundredfold increase in less than three years.

interpellation   The process whereby the spectator of a film is drawn inside the psychic and physical life of the fictional world depicted by the film.

intertextuality   This term, strongly linked with **postmodernism**, designates, in its narrow sense, the ways in which a film either explicitly or implicitly refers to other films (through allusion, imitation, parody or pastiche, for example), thereby triggering ideas and associations which might enrich our response, or in its broader sense, the various relationships one (film) text may have with other texts. See also **eclecticism, intertex-tuality, palimpsest, self-reflexivity**.

jump-cut   An explicit and self-conscious editing decision to demonstrate a 'jump' in time, and to disrupt normal models of continuity editing.

juxtaposition   In film studies, this usually refers to two different shots that have been joined together to make a contrast.

Kinematoscope   Edison's first movie camera was relatively sophisticated and employed a series of sequential photographs mounted on a wheel and rotated.

lesbian   A word used to name and describe a woman whose main sexual feelings are for other women. Coined as a medical term in the late nineteenth century, the word has been invested post-Stonewall with new ideas of openness and liberation. It can also be used to describe cultural products, such as film and video, dealing with lesbian themes.

liberal humanist   A political perspective in which emphasis is placed upon an open-ness of democratic discourse and a multiplicity of perspectives which directly relate to the actual experiences of people and the fundamental principles relating to what it is to be 'human'.

'look'   Also, gaze. The 'look' and the 'gaze' developed as central concepts in relation to the control of the spectator. Cinematic looking has also been associated with theo-ries of desire and pleasure, theories often founded in psychoanalysis.

low-key image   Light from a single source producing light and shade.

magic lantern   A projection system comprising a light source and a lens, used to project an image. Usually oil-lamp fired, though many were later converted to electricity. Earliest known use was by Athanasius Kircher, recorded in a work published in 1646.

mainstream   Feature-length narrative films created for entertainment and profit. Mainstream is usually associated with **Hollywood cinema**, regardless of where the film is made.

Marxist theory   Argues that those who have the means of production have control in a capitalist society. The dominant class have control of the means of production and have an interest in perpetuating the dominant **ideology**. More recently, exponents of Althusserian Marxism, particularly post-1968, have argued that mainstream narrative cinema reinforces the capitalist system and that a revolutionary cinema is needed to challenge the dominant ideology.

masala movie   Spicy Indian movie overloaded with emotion.

match-move   Shots that have separate elements within them that need to be accurately matched, frame by frame. Usually involves live-action elements being coupled to animation or effects elements.

mattes   Opaque images that mask out certain areas of the film negative. Subsequent passes through the camera allow the initial matted-out space to be exposed with another image.

mediation   A key concept in film and media theory, it implies that there are always structures, whether human or technological, between an object and the viewer, involving inevitably a partial and selective view.

merchandising   Where manufacturers pay a film company to use a film title or image on their products.

metamorphosis   The ability for a figure, object, shape or form to relinquish its seemingly fixed properties and mutate into an alternative model. This transformation is literally enacted within the animated film, and acts as a model by which the process of change becomes part of the narrative of the film. A form starts as one thing and ends up as something different.

mise-en-scène   A theatrical term usually translated as 'staging' or *what* has been filmed (setting, props, costumes, etc.) and *how* it is filmed (cinematographic properties of the shot, such as depth of field, focus, lighting, and camera movement). Mise-en-scène is one way of producing meaning in films which can be both straightforward and extremely complex, depending upon the intentions and skill of the director. For *metteur-en-scène* see **auteur**.

modernist   A term used to describe early twentieth-century developments in art, literature, music, film and theatre which rejected **realism** as the dominant tradition in the arts. Modernist art is characterised by experiment and innovation, and modernist artists, because of their **avant-garde** practices, inevitably constitute a cultural élite.

modernist device   Any device which undercuts the invisible telling of the story. A modernist device draws attention to itself and makes us aware of the construction of the narrative. It would be unclear in this instance whether the device is a consciously modernist one or a primitive one which unconsciously draws attention to itself.

montage   From the French word meaning 'to edit', montage means the assembling of bits of footage to form a whole. In film studies it usually refers to the style of fast editing adopted by the **Soviet** film-makers of the 1920s.

'movie brat' generation   A term that refers to the generation of American film-makers who, after the decline of the Hollywood studio system in the 1950s, began to make films independently and were heavily influenced by the French New Wave and European 'art cinema' of the 1960s. Such directors include Martin Scorsese and Francis Ford Coppola.

multiple exposures   A number of exposures being made on a single frame of film. This usually entails the film being rewound in the camera for subsequent passes and further exposures. Multiple exposures are normally made with the assistance of **mattes**.

multiple run   Where a film is shown simultaneously at a number of screens.

music hall   Place for singing and dancing, variety and other entertainments.

myth   A key term within media and cultural studies, a myth is something which is not true but which is repeated so frequently that it becomes part of the 'reality' of the people who share it. In some instances it can become part of a culture's 'common sense'. Myth is a means by which the **ideology** of a culture takes form.

narrative   The idea that films have a primary function of telling a story.

national cinema   A term commonly used to describe the filmic output of a particular country and to distinguish it from **Hollywood** film-making. It has also developed as an approach within film studies to explore how films are shaped by nationally prevailing socio-political and economic conditions. This approach to the study of cinema leads to an understanding of film as expressing or articulating a sense of national identity. However, defining a national cinema and adopting this approach can be problematic. For instance, rapidly changing national geographies, the increasing trend for pan-European funding for film projects and European co-productions make it increasingly difficult to clearly delineate a single country of origin.

negotiated reading   A negotiated reading of a media text is one that involves a certain give-and-take between our own views and experiences and those presented in the film text by its creator.

noise   In the film industry, refers to any barrier to successful communication.

non-diegetic   Refers to any element that remains outside the world of the film, such as voiceovers, credits and mood-setting music, that does not originate from the world of the film.

NRA (National Recovery Administration) programme   Government programme of the 1930s designed to rescue the US economy from the Great Depression (commonly known as the 'New Deal').

obscene   A work, or part thereof, may be found 'obscene' if it has a tendency to deprave and corrupt (i.e. make morally bad) a significant proportion of those people likely to see it.

oligopoly   Where a state of limited competition exists between a small group of producers or sellers.

oppositional reading   A reading of a media text which rejects the intentions of the creator of the text. It is most often associated with dis- or unpleasure. See also **preferred reading** and **negotiated reading**.

orthodox animation   Orthodox animation emerges from Disney's cel animated tradition of work, augmented in the contemporary era by 2D and 3D computer generated applications. This kind of **animation** has a correspondence to a mimetic model of work – the use of configuration, classical narrative models, consistent aesthetic conditions etc. – and echoes live action practices, and 'real world' conventions, while embracing the more 'fantastic' possibilities of the open language of animation.

overheard exchange   The recording of seemingly spontaneous dialogue between two or more participants engaged in conversation/observation.

paid advertising   Promotion on TV, radio, billboards, printed media and the internet.

palimpsest   Defined literally, a palimpsest is a manuscript written over a previous text that has been entirely or partially erased. In a figurative sense, however, the term is often used to describe a film or text with multiple levels of meaning created through dense layers of **intertextuality**. In this way, the term has become associated with **post-modern** aesthetics.

patent pool   An association of companies, operating collectively in the marketplace by pooling the patents held by each individual company.

patriarchal society   A society in which men have power and control. Women are generally disadvantaged and have lower status. It could be argued that we no longer live in a patriarchal society, but in a society in which men and women have equal opportunities. For instance, in the US, Sherry Lansing is head of Paramount Pictures and in the UK a number of women now have key roles in the media, particularly the BBC, where there are now women heads of channel programming. But many feminists would still argue that we have a long way to go in terms of politics, philosophy and economics before we live in a society in which men and women can be considered equal.

persistence of vision   The phenomenon of persistence of vision is due to the momentary retention of an image on the eye's retina. This retention was found to be approximately one-tenth of a second by Chevalier d'Arcy in 1765 when he successfully carried out one of the first systematic scientific studies and presented his findings to the French Académie des Sciences.

Phenakistoscope   Invented by the Belgian physicist, Joseph Plateau, in 1832, this is an optical device consisting of a disk with slots cut into its edge. When rotated, images on one side can be viewed with the aid of a mirror. The resulting stroboscopic images give the illusion of movement.

pink triangle   A symbol originally worn by **homosexual** prisoners in Nazi concentration camps which was later taken up by **lesbian** and **gay** people as a reminder of past oppression and an icon of liberation.

pixillation   The frame-by-frame recording of deliberately staged live-action movement to create the illusion of movement impossible to achieve by naturalistic means, i.e. figures spinning in mid-air or skating across grass. This can also be achieved by particular ways of editing material.

play-back   Pre-recording of songs with good singers and with non-singing actors lip-synchronising on screen.

pluralistic   Multiple; refers in this instance to the fragmentation of society into different ethnic, social and cultural groups.

politique des auteurs   A term evolved from the *Cahiers du cinéma* approach to the study of French and Hollywood cinema in the 1950s, which attempted to identify directors who brought something personal to their films. It is used to describe particular bodies of film-making which are deemed to be characterised by the distinctive styles and visions of their directors. See also **auteurism**.

polysemic   Having many meanings; a polysemic text is likely to be less stable, more hotly contested by different sections of an audience.

postfeminism   The notion of postfeminism is a contested term used by different people in different ways to mean different things. It is used here to indicate a version of the popularised, and to some extent individualised, feminism that is different from (mainly in the sense that it comes after) the highly politicised feminism of the 1970s.

postmodern   A term used to describe many aspects of contemporary cultural production of the 1980s and 1990s. Among its many characteristics are an eclectic borrowing from earlier styles (see **bricolage**), an emphasis on stylish surface appearances rather than social realism or psychological depth, and a blurring of the dividing line between cultural forms, products and tastes, such as the division between 'high culture' and 'popular culture'. Postmodernism has also brought into question the 'grand narrative approach' to theory, arguing that theories such as psychoanalysis and Marxism are no longer viable because they attempt to give an all-encompassing view or understanding of society and culture. Postmodernism emphasises the fragmentation of viewpoints within our culture and the notion that there is no one philosophical truth.

post-structuralism   The critical movement away from an emphasis on the film text and the 'machinery' of cinema to an emphasis on the spectator's decoding of the text in order to create meaning. This represents a rejection of some aspects of the deterministic **Marxist**/Freudian theories at the heart of structuralism while still recognising that the spectator is himself or herself 'determined' by a range of factors (compare with **structuralism**).

post-synchronised   Referring to the process of adding and modifying some or all of a film's sound in a studio after the film has been shot and synchronising these sounds to the image track (also known as 'post-synching').

Praxinoscope   Invented by the Frenchman Emile Raynaud in 1878, this device was a more advanced and sophisticated version of the **Zoetrope**. Utilising mirrors and its own discrete light source, this was the forerunner of Raynaud's spectacular and charming, though ultimately short-lived, Theatre Optique.

preferred reading   A preferred reading of a media text is one in which the spectator takes the intended meaning, finding it relatively easy to align with the messages and attitudes of those who have created the text. See also **oppositional reading** and **negotiated reading**.

proactive observationalism   Documentary film-making in which specific choices are made about what material is to be recorded in relation to the previous observation of the camera operator/director.

production   Division of the film industry concentrating on the making of film.

propaganda   The systematic construction of a text in which the **ideological** principles of a political stance are promoted, endorsed and made attractive to the viewer in order to influence the viewer's beliefs and preferences. Such a text may often include critical and exploitative ideas and imagery about oppositional stances. 'Point of view' in these texts is wholly informed by political bias and a specificity of intention to persuade the viewer of the intrinsic 'rightness' of the authorial position.

proto-animation   Early live-action cinema demonstrated certain techniques which preceded their conscious use as a method in creating **animation**. This is largely with regard to **stop-motion**, mixed media and the use of dissolves to create the illusion of metamorphosis in early **trick films**.

psychoanalytic theory   Based on the theories of Freud and, more recently, Lacan. Feminists argue that aspects of psychoanalysis are questionable because they are based on patriarchal assumptions that woman is inferior to man. Freud found female sexuality difficult and disturbing. Lacan argues that the mother is seen as lacking by the child because she has no phallus. Uncertainty about the role of the female in psychoanalytic theory has been picked up on by a number of feminists such as Mulvey, De Lauretis and Modleski, who question the inevitability of Freud and Lacan's theories which emphasise the importance of the phallus, penis envy and patriarchal supremacy.

queer   Originally a negative term for (mainly male) **homosexuals**, this word has recently been reappropriated by critics, artists and audiences to describe a challenging range of critical work and cultural production among **lesbians** and **gays**, with an emphasis on diversity of race, nationality and cultural experience.

reactive observationalism   Documentary film-making in which the material recorded is filmed as spontaneously as possible subject to the immediacy of observation by the camera operator/director.

reading a film   Although films are viewed and heard, the concept of 'reading' a film implies an active process of making sense of what we are experiencing.

realism/reality   The concept of the 'real' is problematic in cinema, and is generally used in two different ways. First, the extent to which a film attempts to mimic reality so that a fictional film can appear indistinguishable from documentary. Second, the film can establish its own world and can, by consistently using the same conventions, establish the credibility of this world. In this later sense a science-fiction film such as *RoboCop* can be as realistic as a film set in a contemporary and recognisable world, such as *Sleepless in Seattle*.

With regard to **animation**, the animated form in itself most readily accommodates 'the fantastic', but Disney preferred to create a hyper-realism which located his characters in plausibly 'real' worlds which also included fantasy elements in the narrative.

reappropriation   The process whereby a previously oppressed group takes a negative term and turns it around to invest it with new meanings of power and liberation. Examples include 'black', 'virago' and '**queer**'.

recombinacy   The aesthetic process of combining of elements drawn from a range of genres, styles, forms and periods in a new text/film. This is one of the principal aesthetic strategies of **postmodern** art. See also **eclecticism, intertextuality, palimpsest, self-reflexivity**.

reduced animation   Animation may be literally the movement of one line which, in operating through time and space, may take on characteristics which an audience may perceive as expressive and symbolic. This form of minimalism constitutes reduced animation, which takes as its premise 'less is more'. Literally an eye movement or the shift of a body posture becomes enough to connote a particular feeling or meaning. This enables the films to work in a mode which has an intensity of suggestion.

reflexive/performative documentary   Documentary which is much more subjective and self-reflexive in its construction, foregrounding the arbitrariness and relativity of 'objectivity', '**reality**' and 'truth'.

representation   The media *re*-presents information to its audience, who are encouraged by the mainstream media to see its output as a 'window on the world', as reflecting reality. Yet the process of representing information is highly complex and highly selective. Many feminists argue that the way notions of gender are represented by the media perpetuates and reinforces the values of a **patriarchal society**; for instance, men tend to take on strong, active roles, while women are shown as passive and relying on their attractiveness. There are exceptions to such narrow stereotyping: the 'strong' woman shown by Ripley in the *Alien* series and the two heroines in *Thelma and Louise* could be seen as positive, although rather more cynically they could be seen merely as 'role reversal' films and thus as having purely novelty value. Representations often make use of **stereotypes** because they are a shorthand, quick and easy way of using information. It could be argued that the media production process encourages the use of stereotypes because of the pressure of time and budget. Many feminists point out that because so few women hold key positions in the media hierarchies, representations of women are bound to be from a male perspective.

Russian cinema   The body of films made in Tsarist Russia between 1907 and 1919.

saturation run   Where a film is shown simultaneously at an enormous number of screens (usually a minimum of 1,000 in the US/Canadian market), accompanied by heavy media promotion.

scopophilia   Freudian term meaning the 'pleasure in looking', introduced to film analysis by Laura Mulvey, who pointed out that women are usually depicted in a passive role, and are looked at whilst men take on an active role, they look.

self-reflexivity   Used to describe films or texts which self-consciously acknowledge or reflect upon their own status as fictional artefacts and/or the processes involved in their creation. This is one of the principal aesthetic strategies of **postmodern** art. See also **eclecticism, intertextuality, palimpsest, recombinacy**.

semiotics   The use of semiotics in film analysis has developed out of the theories of Ferdinand de Saussure, who argued that the meanings of words are not natural but are learned and socially constructed. Therefore, the meaning of a word, or in the case of film, an image or sound, may be complex and layered.

sex   A word used to denote and describe a person's physical type according to his or her genital make-up. In academic discourse, this is primarily a scientific term.

sexuality   A name for the sexual feelings and behaviour of a person. When applied to groups of people (e.g. **heterosexuals**), ideas of social attitude and organisation are implied.

social realism   A form of **realism** which tries to capture in a 'truthful' way the lives of industrial working-class communities. Also known as 'working-class realism' and often used in relation to the 'new wave' films of late 1950s/early 1960s British cinema.

sophisticated hyperconsciousness   A term used by Jim Collins to describe the extreme 'knowingness' and high degree of media literacy evinced by both contemporary cinema and its audience.

Soviet cinema   Films made in the Soviet Union between October 1920 and 1991.

spectator   The individual responding to a film, as distinct from the collective response of an audience. Spectator study concentrates on the consumption of films that are 'popular' and are geared towards providing typical forms of cinematic pleasure – spectacle, emotion, plot, resolution – with conventional narrative and generic forms.

squash and stretch   Many cartoon characters are constructed in a way that resembles a set of malleable and attached circles that may be elongated or compressed to achieve an effect of dynamic movement. When animators 'squash and stretch' these circles they effectively create the physical space of the character and a particular design structure within the overall pattern of the film. Interestingly, early Disney shorts had characters based on 'ropes' rather than circles and this significantly changes the look of the films.

Steadicam   A technical development from the late 1970s which permits the use of a camera held by hand which walks with the action, but with the steadiness of a camera moving on rails.

stereotyping   A quick and easy way of labelling or categorising the world around us and making it understandable. Stereotypes are learned but are by no means fixed, yet are often resistant to change. They tend to restrict our understanding of the world and perpetuate beliefs that are often untrue or narrow. For instance, the concept that only thin women are attractive is a stereotype promoted by much of the media in the late twentieth century (though there are some exceptions, for example, comediennes Dawn French and Roseanne); in other eras the opposite has been true. Stereotyping is not always negative, but tends to be very much concerned with preserving and perpetuating power relations in society. It is in the interests of those in power to continue to stereotype those with lower status in a negative light, thus preserving the status quo.

stop motion   An animation technique whereby a 3D model is filmed a single frame at a time, the model being moved by the animator between exposures.

studio system   Usually seen to have developed from about 1920 and lasting to about 1950, the studio system indicated that period of Hollywood history in which the major studios controlled all aspects of the production, distribution and exhibition of their products.

structuralism   Founded on the belief that the study of society could be scientifically based and that there are structures in society that follow certain patterns or rules. Initially, most interest was centred on the use of language; Saussure, the founder of linguistics, argued that language was essential in communicating the **ideology**, the beliefs, of a culture. Structuralists have applied these theories to film, which uses both visual and verbal communication, and pointed out that the text conveys an illusion of **reality**, so conveying the ideology of a society even more effectively.

substitution technique   An early **trick film** technique used by George Méliès. It involved one object being filmed, the camera being stopped during filming and the object being replaced by a second object before filming recommenced. This was the basis of his famous vanishing lady effect, used in many of his films.

surplus of meaning   Meaning in excess of what is required to fulfil the functional requirements of the narrative; a 'surplus' will include ambiguity, complexity rather than clarity and simplicity.

suspending disbelief   This refers to the ability a person has when engaging with a constructed object – film, play, novel – to repress his or her knowledge that the object is in fact just a 'construct', and respond to it as though it is real.

symbolism   The means by which a film-maker can assign additional meanings to objects/characters in a film. For example, in Dovzhenko's *Earth* and Eisenstein's *Old and New*, the tractor is a symbol of progress.

symmetry   Direct balance of imagery in the composition of the frame using parallel or mirrored forms.

synecdoche   The idea that a 'part' of a person, an object, a machine etc. can be used to represent the 'whole', and work as an emotive or suggestive shorthand for the viewer, who invests the 'part' with symbolic associations.

synergy strategy   Combined or related action by a group of individuals or corporations towards a common goal, the combined effect of which exceeds the sum of the individual efforts.

synthespians   A term which describes 'virtual' or non-human actors. The term relates to digitally scanned or motion-captured versions of 'real' actors, as well as entirely computer-generated characters.

taxonomy   The practice of classification. In this sense, the practice of classifying films into groups based on similarities of form and/or content.

testimony   The recording of solicited observation, opinion or information by witnesses, experts or other relevant participants in relation to the **documentary** subject; the primary purpose of the interview.

THX   A designation of sound reproduction quality in cinemas. The standards established necessitate the installation and maintenance of sound equipment to the specifications and according to the guidelines lain down by Lucasfilm Limited.

tie-ins   Mutually beneficial promotional liaisons between films and other consumer products and/or personalities.

Tradition of Quality   A frequently derogatory term used by the critics on *Cahiers du cinéma* and referring to postwar, pre-New Wave French cinema characterised by its reliance on screenwriters and adaptations from literary classics.

trick film   The generic term for the development of cinematic special effects using such techniques as **mattes, multiple exposures, proto-animation** and **substitution techniques**. Generally attributed to the pioneering French film-maker George Méliès.

trust   A group of companies operating together to control the market for a commodity. This is illegal practice in the US.

two-shot   A medium-scale shot including two characters normally taken from the waist up. A variant is the cut between the two characters assuming the same eye-level, body position and exchange.

uses and gratifications   A specific approach to the study of audiences. It considers how individuals and groups may consume a film or some other media product to satisfy their particular needs.

vertical integration   Where a company is organised so that it oversees a product from the planning/development stage, through production, through market distribution, through to the end-user – the retail consumer. In the case of the film industry, this translates to a company controlling **production, distribution** and **exhibition** of its films.

voyeurism   The sexual pleasure gained from looking at others.

wire frame   Three-dimensional shapes, with neither surface colour nor texture, illustrated through a pattern of interconnecting lines, literally a framework of 'wires' on a two-dimensional surface – the computer screen.

wire removal   The process of digitally removing any unwanted elements within a shot, such as a support for an animated object, puppet or prop. Used in the flying motorbike shot in *Terminator 2*.

Zoetrope   The forerunner of the **Praxinoscope**, this consists of a drum with vertical slots cut into the top edge. As the drum is rotated, the images on the inner surfaces, when viewed through the slots, achieve the same illusion of movement as with the **Phenakistoscope**.

zoom   A technique whereby the image appears to advance towards or recedes away from the viewer.

Bibliography

Adams, T.R., *Tom and Jerry*, Crescent Books, New York, 1991.

Adamson, J., *Tex Avery: King of Cartoons*, Da Capo, New York, 1975.

Agosterios, V., 'An Interview with Sally Potter', *Framework*, No. 14, 1979.

Alderson, David and Anderson, Linda (eds), *Territories of Desire in Queer Culture*, Manchester University Press, Manchester, 2000.

Aldgate, A. and Richards, J., *Britain Can Take It*, Basil Blackwell, London, 1986.

Allan, R., *Walt Disney and Europe*, John Libbey, London, 1999.

Allen, R. and Gomery, D., *Film History: Theory and Practice*, Newbery Award Records, New York, 1985.

Allinson, M., *A Spanish Labyrinth: The Films of Pedro Almodovar*, I.B. Taurus, London, 2001.

Allon, Yoram *et al.* (eds), *Critical Guide to North American Directors*, Wallflower Press, London, 2002.

Altenloh, Emile, *A Sociology of the Cinema: Audiences*, reprinted in *Screen*, Vol. 42, No. 3, Autumn 2001

Altman, Rick (ed.), *Genre: The Musical*, British Film Institute/Routledge & Kegan Paul, London, 1981.

—— *Film/Genre*, British Film Institute, London, 1999.

Andrew, D., *Concepts in Film Theory*, Oxford University Press, Oxford, 1984.

Angelini, S., 'The DVD Story', *Viewfinder*, No. 44, October 2001.

Armes, R., *The Ambiguous Image: Narrative Style in Modern European Cinema*, Secker & Warburg, London, 1976.

Arrington, Carl Wayne, 'Film's Avant-Guardian', *Rolling Stone*, 22 March, 1990.

Arthur, J., 'Technology and Gender', *Screen*, Vol. 30, 1989, pp. 40–59.

Aumont, J., *Montage Eisenstein*, British Film Institute, London, 1987.

Austin, B., *Immediate Seating: A Look at Movie Audiences*, Wadsworth Publishing Company, Belmont, CA, 1989.

Auty, M. and Roddick, N. (eds), *British Cinema Now*, British Film Institute, London, 1985.

Babuscio, J., *Camp and Gay Sensibility*, in Richard Dyer (ed.), *Gays and Film*, British Film Institute, London, 1977.

Bad Object Choices (ed.), *How Do I Look? Queer Film and Video*, Bay Press, Seattle, 1991.

Balazs, B. 'Filming Death', in K. Macdonald and M. Cousins (eds), *Imagining Reality: The Faber Book of Documentary*, Faber & Faber, London and Boston, 1996, pp. 29–31.

Balcon, M., *Michael Balcon presents...A Lifetime of Films*, Hutchinson, London, 1969.

Balio, T. (ed.), *The American Film Industry*, University of Wisconsin Press, Madison, 1976.

—— *Hollywood in the Age of Television*, Unwin Hyman, Boston, 1990.

Banner, L., *Women in Modern America*, Harcourt, Brace, Jovanovich, New York, 1984.

Barbas, Samantha, 'The Political Spectator: Censorship, Protest and the Moviegoing Experience, 1912–1922', *Film History*, Vol. 11, pp. 217–29.

Barker, Martin and Petley, Julian (eds), *Ill Effects – the Media Violence Debate*, Routledge, London, 1997.

Barker, Martin, Arthurs, Jane and Ramawani, Haridranath, *The Crash Controversy*, Wallflower Press, London, 2001.

Barna, Y., *Eisenstein*, Secker & Warburg, London, 1973.

Barnes, J., *The Beginnings of Cinema in England*, David & Charles, London, 1976.

Barnouw, Erik and Krishnaswamy, S., *Indian Film*, 2nd edn, Oxford University Press, New York, 1980.

Barr, C. (ed.), *All Our Yesterdays: Ninety Years of British Cinema*, British Film Institute, London, 1986.

Barrier, M., *Hollywood Cartoons: American Animation in the Golden Age*, Oxford University Press, New York and Oxford, 1999.

Barron; S. and Tuchman, M. (eds), *The Avant-Garde in Russia, 1910–1930: New Perspectives*, Los Angeles County Museum of Art, Los Angeles, 1980.

Barsam, R., *The Non-Fiction Film*, Indiana University Press, Bloomington and Indianapolis, 1992.

Barthes, Roland, *Image–Music–Text*, Fontana: London, 1977.

Baskaran, Theodore, *The Message Bearers: The Nationalist Politics and the Entertainment Media in South India, 1880–1945*, Cre-A, Madras, 1981.

—— 'Songs in Tamil Cinema', *The Eye of the Serpent*, East–West Books, Madras, 1996, pp. 38–61.

Bazin, A., *What is Cinema?*, Vol. 1, *Ontology and Language*, Editions du Cerf, Paris, 1958.

BBFC, at http://www.bbfc.co.uk.

Beck, J. and Friedwald, W., *Looney Tunes and Merrie Melodies*, Henry Holt & Co., New York, 1989.

Begleiter, M., *From Word to Image*, Michael Wiese Productions, Los Angeles, 2001.

Bell, E., Haas, L. and Sells, L. (eds), *From Mouse to Mermaid: The Politics of Film, Gender and Culture*, Indiana University Press, Bloomington and Indianapolis, 1995.

Benshoff, H., *Monsters in the Closet: Homosexuality and the Horror Film*, Manchester University Press, Manchester, 1997.

Bergan, R., *Eisenstein: A Life in Conflict*, London, Time Warner Paperbacks, 1999.

Berger, John, *Ways of Seeing*, Penguin, London, 1972.

Bergstrom, J., 'Rereading the Work of Claire Johnston', in C. Penley (ed.), *Feminism and Film Theory*, Routledge/British Film Institute, London, 1988.

Bernstein, I., *Hollywood at the Crossroads: An Economic Study of the Motion Picture Industry*, Hollywood Film Council, Los Angeles, 1957.

Berry, D., *Wales and Cinema: The First Hundred Years*, University of Wales Press, Cardiff, 1994.

Bersani, L. and Dutoit, U., *Caravaggio*, British Film Institute, London, 1999.

Betterton, R., *Looking On: Images of Femininity in the Visual Arts and the Media*, Pandora, London, 1987.

Billington, Michael, 'Proof', *Guardian*, 17/05/2002, p. 16.

Bilton, T., Bonnett, K., Jones, P., Lawsom, T., Skinner, D., Stanworth, M. and Webster, A., *Introductory Sociology*, Palgrave Macmillan, Basingstoke, 2002.

Birkos, A., *Soviet Cinema: Directors and Films*, Archon, Hamden, CT, 1976.

Bishop, L. 'Documentary Evidence', *Television*, Aug/Sept, Vol. 38, No. 7, 2001, p. 24.

Biskind, P., 'Going for Broke', *Sight and Sound*, October 1991.

Bobo, Jacquelyne, '*The Color Purple*: Black Women as Cultural Readers', in E.D. Pribram (ed.), *Female Spectator: Looking at Film and Television*, Verso, London and New York, 1988.

Bogdanovich, Peter, 'New Kid on the Block', *Guardian*, 22/02/2002.

Boral, R.C. in Ashish Rajadhyaksha and Paul Willemen (eds), *Encyclopaedia of Indian Cinema*, 2nd edn, British Film Institute, London, 1999.

Bordwell, David 'The Idea of Montage in Soviet Art and Film', *Cinema Journal*, Vol. 11, No. 2, 1972.

—— *Narration in the Fiction Film*, Routledge & Kegan Paul, London, 1986; repr. Routledge, London, 1990.

—— *The Cinema of Eisenstein*, Harvard University Press, Cambridge, MA, 1993.

Bordwell, David and Carroll, Noel, *Post-Theory: Reconstructing Film Studies*, University of Wisconsin, Madison, 1996.

Bordwell, David and Thompson, Kristin, *Film Art*, 4th edn, McGraw-Hill, London, 1993; repr. Knopf, New York, 1995.

Bordwell, D., Staiger, J. and Thompson, Kristin, *The Classical Hollywood Cinema*, Routledge and Kegan Paul, London, 1985; repr. 1994.

Bourne, S., *Brief Encounters: Lesbians and Gays in British Cinema 1930–1971*, Cassell, London, 1996.

Bowser, Eileen, *The Transformation of Cinema 1907–1915*, University of California, Berkeley, 1994.

Braddock, Jeremy and Hock, Stephen (eds.) *Directed by Allen Smithee*, University of Minnesota Press, Minneapolis, 2001.

Brion, P., *Tom and Jerry*, Crown Publishers, New York, 1990.

Britton, A., 'The Invisible Eye', *Sight and Sound*, February, 1992, p. 29.

Brooks, Xan, 'Directing Masochism', *Guardian*, G2, 24/04/2002.

Brown, M., 'The Old Ones Are the Best', *Guardian*, 26/3/2001, pp. 16–17.

Bruzzi, S., 'Tempestuous Petticoats: Costume and Desire in *The Piano*', *Screen* Vol. 36 No. 3, Autumn 1995, pp. 257–66.

—— *Undressing Cinema*, Routledge, London, 1997.

—— *New Documentary: A Critical Introduction*, Routledge, London and New York, 2000.

Brundsen, C. (ed.), *Films for Women*, British Film Institute, London, 1986.

Buckland, Warren, 'A Close Encounter with *Raiders of the Lost Ark*', in Steven Neale and Murray Smith (eds), *Contemporary Hollywood Cinema*, Routledge, London, 1998.

Bukatman, S., *Blade Runner*, British Film Institute, London, 1997.

Buncombe, A., 'Coming Soon – City Centre Cinema Boom', *Independent*, 17 September, 1998.

Burch, Noel, *Theory of Film Practice*, Secker & Warburg, London, 1973.

—— *Correction Please – or How We Got Into Movies*, Arts Council, London, 1979.

Burns, M., 'Women in Focus', *In Camera*, Spring 1992, pp. 3–5, 17–19.

Burston, P. and Richardson, C. (eds), *A Queer Romance: Gay Men, Lesbians and Popular Culture*, Routledge, London, 1995.

Burton-Carvajal, J., 'Surprise Package: Looking Southward with Disney', in E. Smoodin (ed.), *Disney Discourse*, Routledge, London and New York, 1994, pp. 131–47.

Buscombe, E., 'Sound and Colour', *Jump Cut*, No. 17, 1977.

Buscombe, E. and Pearson, R. (eds), *Back in the Saddle Again: New Essays on the Western*, British Film Institute, London, 1998.

Butler, J., *Gender Trouble: Feminism and the Subversion of Identity*, Routledge, New York and London, 1990.

—— *Bodies That Matter*, Routlege, London, 1993.

Byars, J., *All That Heaven Allows: Re-reading Gender in 1950s Melodrama*, Chapel Hill, University of North Carolina Press, 1991.

Byron, S., 'Letter to Editor', *Film Comment*, Vol. 22, No. 5, October 1986, p. 76.

Cabarga, L., *The Fleischer Story*, Da Capo, New York, 1988.

Cahiers du cinéma. Situation du cinéma français, May 1957, No.71, *Nouvelle Vague: une légende en question*, January 1999, hors séries .

Calder-Marshall, A, *The Innocent Eye: The Life of Robert J. Flaherty*, New York: Harcourt Brace Jovanovich, 1966.

Campbell, D., 'Catholics Vilify *Dogma*', *Guardian* 13 November, 1999.

Campbell, R., 'Warner Bros in the 1930s: Some Tentative Notes', *The Velvet Light Trap*, No. 1, June 1971.

Canemaker, J. (ed.), *Storytelling in Animation*, American Film Institute, Los Angeles, 1989.

Cardullo, B. (ed.), *Bazin at Work*, Routledge, London, 1997.

Caughie, John, 'Preface', in *Theories of Authorship: A Reader*, Routledge, London, 1981.

—— *Theories of Authorship: A Reader*, Routledge and British Film Institute, London, 1981.

Cerisuelo, M., *Jean-Luc Godard*, Editions des Quatre-Vents, Paris, 1989.

Chabrol, Claude and Rohmer, Eric, *Hitchcock: The First Forty-Four Films*, Frederick Ungar, New York, 1979.

Chakravarty, Sumita S., *National Identity in Indian Popular Cinema, 1947–1987*, University of Texas Press, Austin, 1993.

Champlin, C., 'What Will H. Hays Begat', *American Film*, Vol. 6, No. 1, October 1980.

Chandravarkar, Bhaskar, 'The Tradition of Music in Indian Cinema', *Cinema in India*, Vol. 1, No. 2, April 1987 to Vol. 3, No. 3, July–September 1989.

—— 'Growth of the Film Song', *Cinema in India*, Vol. 1, No. 3: 16–20.

Chapman, J., *Licensed to Thrill*, I. B. Tauris, London, 2000.

Chibnall, S. and Murphy, R., *The British Crime Film*, Routledge, London and New York, 1999.

Cholodenko, A. (ed.), *The Illusion of Life*, Power Publishers, Sydney, 1991.

Chopra, Anupama, 'Southern Invasion', *India Today*, October 13, 1997, pp. 38–40.

—— *Sholay: The Making of a Classic*, Penguin, New Delhi, 2000.

Christie, I. (ed.), *Powell Pressburger and Others*, British Film Institute, London, 1978.

—— 'From the Kingdom of Shadows', in the catalogue to *Twilight of the Tsars*, Hayward Gallery, London, 1991.

Christie, I. and Gillett, J. (eds), *Futurism/Formalism/FEKS: 'Eccentrism' and Soviet Cinema 1918–1936*, British Film Institute, Film Availability Services, London, 1978.

Christie, I. and Graffy, J. (eds), *Yakov Protazanov and the Continuity of Russian Cinema*, British Film Institute/NFT, London, 1993.

Christie, I. and Taylor, R. (eds), *Eisenstein Rediscovered*, Routledge, London, 1993.

Chute, David, Review of *Lagaan: Once Upon a Time in India*, *Film Comment*, March–April, 2002.

Clover, Carol, *Men, Women and Chainsaws: Gender in the Modern Horror Film*, British Film Institute, London, 1992.

—— 'White Noise', *Sight and Sound*, Vol. 3, No. 5 (May), 1993.

Cohan., S. and Hark, I. (eds), *Screening the Male*, Routledge, London, 1993.

Cohen, Scott, 'Strangers in Paradise', *Spin*, March 1990; online at, http://www.sfgoth.com/~kali/onsite8.html, (26/09/2001).

Collins, C., 'British Film: The Next Generation', *Guardian*, 16 November, 2001.

Collins, Jim, *Architectures of Excess: Cultural Life in the Information Age*, Routledge, London, 1995.

Collins, J., Radner, H., Preacher Collins, A. (eds), *Film Theory Goes to the Movies*, American Film Institute and Routledge, London, 1993.

Cook, P., '*The Gold Diggers*', *Framework*, Vol. 24, 1981.

—— (ed.), *The Cinema Book*, British Film Institute, London, 1985.

—— *Fashioning the Nation: Costume and Identity in British Cinema*, British Film Institute, London 1996.

—— 'No Fixed Address: The Women's Picture from *Outrage* to *Blue Steel*', in S. Neale and M. Smith (eds), *Contemporary Hollywood Cinema*, Routledge, London, 1998.

Cook, Pam and Dodd, Philip (eds), *Women and Film: A Sight and Sound Reader*, British Film Institute, London and Scarlet Press, London, 1993.

Corner, J. (ed.), *Documentary and the Mass Media*, Edward Arnold, London, 1986.

—— *The Art of Record: A Critical Introduction to Documentary*, Manchester University Press, Manchester and New York, 1996.

Corrigan, Timothy, 'The Commerce of Auteurism', in *A Cinema without Walls: Movies and Culture After Vietnam*, Routledge, London, 1991.

—— *A Cinema without Walls: Movies and Culture After Vietnam*, Routledge, London, 1991.

Cotta Vaz, Mark *et al.*, *Industrial Light and Magic: Into the Digital Realm*, Virgin Books, London, 1996.

Cox, Alex, 'Is DVD worth it?', *Guardian*, Friday Review, 23/02/2001.

Crafton, D., *Before Mickey: The Animated Film 1898–1928*, University of Chicago Press, Chicago and London, 1993.

Creed, B., 'From Here to Modernity: Feminism and Postmodernism', *Screen*, Vol. 28, No. 2, 1987, pp. 47–67.

—— 'Dark Desires: Male Masochism in the Horror Film', in S. Cohan and I. Hark (eds), *Screening the Male*, Routledge, London, 1993.

Creekmur, Corey K. and Doty, Alexander (eds), *Out in Culture: Gay, Lesbian and Queer Essays on Popular Culture*, Duke University Press, Durham, NC, 1995.

Culler, Jonathan, *Structuralist Poetics*, Routledge, London, 1975.

Curtis D., *Len Lye: Exhibition Catalogue,* Watershed, 24/10/1987–29/11/1987, Arts Council, London, 1987.

Dale, A., *Comedy is a Man In Trouble*, University of Minnesota Press, Minneapolis, 2000.

Dale, Martin, *The Movie Game: The Film Business in Britain, Europe and America*, Cassell, London, 1997.

Darke, Chris, 'Rupture, Continuity and Diversification: *Cahiers du cinéma* in the 1980s', *Screen*, Vol. 34, No .4, Winter 1993, pp. 362–80.

Darley, Andrew, *Visual Digital Culture: Surface Play and Spectacle in New Media Genres*, Routledge, London, 2002.

Das, Veena, 'Introduction', in *Mirrors of Violence: Communities and Survivors in South Asia*, Oxford University Press, New Delhi, 1992.

Davies, J., 'Gender, Ethnicity and Cultural Crisis in *Falling Down* and *Groundhog Day*', *Screen*, Vol. 36, No. 3, Autumn 1995, pp. 214–32.

Davies, J. and Smith, C.R., *Gender, Ethnicity and Sexuality in Contemporary American Film*, Edinburgh, Keele University Press, 1997.

Davies, P. and Wells, P. (eds), *American Film and Politics: Reagan to Bush Jnr*, Manchester University Press, Manchester, 2002.

de Baecque, A., *Les Cahiers du cinéma Histoire d'une revue: Tome 2 Cinéma, tours détours 1959–1981*, Editions Cahiers du cinéma, Paris, 1991.

—— *La nouvelle vague: Portrait d'une jeunesse*, Flammarion, Paris, 1998.

De Lauretis, T., 'Guerilla in the Midst – Women's Cinema in the 1980s', *Screen*, Vol. 31, No. 1, 1990.

De Nitto, D, *Film: Form and Feeling*, New York: Harper & Row, 1985.

DeAngelis, M., *Gay Fandom and Crossover Stardom: James Dean, Mel Gibson and Keanu Reeves*, Duke University Press, Durham, NC, 2001.

Denzin, N, *The Cinematic Society*, Sage, London, 1995.

Derne, Steve, *Movies, Masculinity and Modernity: An Ethnography of Men's Filmgoing in India*, Greenwood Press, Westport, CN, 2000.

Deschner, D., 'Anton Grot: Warners Art Director 1927–1948', *The Velvet Light Trap*, Vol. 15, 1975.

Dhareshwar, Vivek and Niranjana, Tejaswini '*Kaadalan* and the Politics of Resignification: Fashion, Violence and the Body', *Journal of Arts and Ideas*, Vol. 29, January 1996.

Dhondy, Farrukh, *Bombay Duck*, Cape, London, 1990.

Dickey, Sara, *Cinema and the Urban Poor in South India*, Cambridge University Press, Cambridge, 1993.

Dickinson, M. and Street, S., *Cinema and State: The Film Industry and the Government 1927–1984*, British Film Institute, London, 1985.

Dickinson, T. and de la Roche, C., *Soviet Cinema*, The Falcon Press, London, 1948.

Docherty, D., Morrison, D. and Tracey, M., *The Last Picture Show?*, British Film Institute, London, 1987.

Donald, James, 'Stars', in Pam Cook and M. Bernink (eds), *The Cinema Book*, 2nd edn, British Film Institute, London, 1999.

Donald, L. and Scanlon, S., 'Hollywood Feminism? Get Real!!', *Trouble and Strife*, Vol. 25, Winter 1992, pp. 11–16.

Donnelly, K., *Pop Music in British Cinema*, British Film Institute, London, 2001.

Doriaswamy, Rashmi, 'Hindi Commercial Cinema: Changing Narrative Strategies', in Aruna Vasudev (ed.), *Frames of Mind: Reflections on Indian Cinema*, UBS Publishers, New Delhi, 1995.

Doty, Alexander, *Making Things Perfectly Queer*, University of Minnesota Press, Minneapolis, 1993.

—— *Flaming Classics: Queering the Film Canon*, Routledge, New York and London, 2000.

Douchet, J., *French New Wave*, Distributed Art Publishers Inc./Editions Hazan/Cinémathèque Française, 1999.

Dove, L., 'Feminist and Left Independent Filmmaking in England', *Jump Cut*, Vol. 10–11, 1976.

Dovey, J., *Freakshow: First Person Media and Factual Television*, Pluto Press, London and Sterling, 2000.

Drabinsky, G., *Motion Pictures and the Arts in Canada: The Business and the Law*, Mcgraw-Hill Ryerson, Toronto, 1976.

Duclos, Denis, *The Werewolf Complex: America's Fascination with Violence*, Oxford University Press, New York, 1998.

Dudley, A., *The Major Film Theories: An Introduction*, Oxford University Press, Oxford, 1976.

Durgnat, R., *Nouvelle Vague, the First Decade*, Motion Publications, Loughton, 1963.

—— *A Mirror for England*, Faber & Faber, London, 1970.

Dwyer, Rachel, *All You Want is Money, All You Need is Love: Sexuality and Romance in Modern India*, Cassell, London, 2000.

Dyer, Richard, *Pasolini and Homosexuality*, in P. Willemen (ed.), *Pier Paolo Pasolini*, British Film Institute, London, 1977.

—— 'Resistance Through Charisma: Rita Hayworth and *Gilda*', in A.E. Kaplan (ed.), *Women in Film Noir*, British Film Institute, London, 1978.

—— *Stars*, British Film Institute, London, 1979, 1998.

—— 'Don't Look Now', *Screen*, Vol. 23, Nos. 3–4, 1982, pp. 66–7.

—— *Heavenly Bodies: Film Stars and Society*, Macmillan, Basingstoke, 1987.

—— 'Judy Garland and Gay Men', in *Heavenly Bodies: Film Stars and Society*, Macmillan, Basingstoke, 1987.

—— *Now You See It: Studies on Lesbian and Gay Film*, Routledge, London and New York, 1990.

—— *The Matter of Images: Essays on Representation*, Routledge, London, 1993.

—— *Brief Encounter*, British Film Institute, London, 1993.

—— 'Introduction to Film Studies', in John Hill and Pamela Church Gibson (eds), *The Oxford Guide to Film Studies*, Oxford University Press, Oxford, 1998.

—— *The Culture of Queers*, Routledge, New York and London, 2001.

Dyson, L., 'The Return of the Repressed? Whiteness, feminity and colonialism in *The Piano*', *Screen*, Vol. 36, No. 3, Autumn 1995, pp 269–76.

Easthope, A., *What a Man's Gotta Do, The Masculine Myth in Popular Culture*, Unwin Hyman, Winchester, 1990.

Ebert, Roger, 'Dead Man Walking', *Chicago Sun-Times*, 1/12/1996; online at http://www.suntimes.com/ebert/ebert_reviews/1996/01/1015392.html (10/05/2002).

—— 'The Accused', *Chicago Sun-Times*, 14/10/1998; online at http://www.suntimes.com/ebert/ebert_reviews/1988/10/318971.html (10/05/2002).

—— 'Anna and the King', *Chicago Sun-Times*; online at http://www.suntimes.com/ebert/ebert_reviews/1999/12/121701.html (10/05/2002).

—— 'The Matrix', *Chicago Sun-Times*, 23/04/2002; online at http://www.suntimes.com/ebert/ebert_reviews/1999/03/033101.html.

Ehrenstein, D., 'Out of the Wilderness', *Film Quarterly*, Vol. 47, No. 1, 1993, pp. 2–7.

Eisenstein, Sergei M., *Notes of a Film Director*, Dover Publications, New York, 1970.

—— *The Film Sense*, Faber & Faber, London, 1986.

—— 'The Montage of Film Attractions', in Peter Lehman (ed.), *Defining Cinema*, Rutgers University Press, New Brunswick, NJ, 1997.

Ellis, John, *Visible Fictions: Cinema, Television and Video*, Routledge & Kegan Paul, London, 1982; repr. 1992.

Elsaesser, Thomas (ed.), *Early Cinema*, British Film Institute, London, 1990.

—— 'The Blockbuster: Everything Connects, but Not Everything Goes', in Jon Lewis (ed.), *The End of Cinema as We Know It*, Pluto Press, London, 2001.

Enns, A., 'The Spectacle of Disabled Masculinity in John Woo's "Heroic Bloodshed" Films', *The Quarterly Review of Film and Video*, Vol. 17, No. 2, June 2000, pp. 137–45.

Erens, Patricia (ed.), *Issues in Feminist Film Criticism*, Indiana University Press, Bloomington, 1990.

Falcon, R., *Classified! A Teacher's Guide to Film and Video Censorship and Classification*, British Film Institute, London, 1994.

Farmer, Brett, *Spectacular Passions: Cinema, Fantasy, Gay Male Spectatorships*, Duke University Press, Durham, NC, 2000.

Farrow, B., 'Hollywood Runs Scared', *The Times*, 8 October, 1999.

Ferguson, M. and Wicke, J. (eds), *Feminism and Postmodernism*, Duke University Press, North Carolina, 1994.

Finney, A.., *The Egos Have Landed*, Mandarin, London, 1997.

Fitzgerald, T., 'Now About These Women', *Sight and Sound*, Summer 1989.

Fleming, M. and Klady, L., '"Crying" All the Way to the Bank', *Variety*, 22 March, 1993.

Florence, P., 'A Conversation with Sally Potter', *Screen*, Vol. 34, No. 3, Autumn 1993, pp. 275–84.

Forbes, J. and Kelly, M. (eds), *French Cultural Studies: An Introduction*, Oxford University Press, Oxford, 1995.

Francke, L., *Script Girls*, British Film Institute, London, 1994.

Frayling, C., *Spaghetti Westerns*, I.B. Tauris, London, 1998.

Frazer, J, *Artificially Arranged Scenes*, G. Hall, Boston, 1979.

Friedan, B., *The Feminine Mystique*, Penguin, London, 1963.

Friedmann, L. (ed.), *British Cinema and Thatcherism: Fires Were Started*, UCL Press, London, 1993.

Frith, S., *Music for Pleasure*, Routledge, London, 1988.

From Star Wars to Star Wars: The Story of Industrial Light & Magic, Film Garden/Lucas Films, 1999.

Fuller, Graham, 'Strictly Red', *Sight and Sound*, Vol. 11, No. 6, 2001.

Furniss, M., *Art in Motion: Animation Aesthetics*, John Libbey, London and Montrouge, 1998.

Fuss, D. (ed.), *Inside/Out: Lesbian Theories, Gay Theories*, Routledge, New York and London, 1991.

Gabilondo, Joseba, 'Morphing Saint Sebastian', in Vivian Sobchack (ed.), *Meta Morphing and the Culture of Quick-Change*, University of Minnesota Press, Minneapolis, 2000.

Gatiss, M., *James Whale*, Cassell, London, 1995.

Gaut, Berys, 'Film Authorship and Collaboration', in Richard Allen and Murray Smith (eds), *Film Theory and Philosophy*, Oxford University Press, Oxford, 1997.

Geraghty, Christine, *British Cinema in the Fifties*, London, Routledge, 2000.

—— 'Re-examining Stardom: Questions of Texts, Bodies and Performance', in Christine Gledhill, and Linda Williams (eds), *Reinventing Film Studies*, Arnold, London, 2000.

Gever, M., Greyson, J. and Parmar, P. (eds), *Queer Looks: Perspectives on Lesbian and Gay Video*, Between The Lines/Routledge, Toronto, 1993.

Giannetti, L., *Understanding Movies*, 6th edn, Prentice Hall, Englewood Cliffs, NJ, 1993.

Giannetti, L. and Eyman, S., *Flashback: A Brief History of Film*, 2nd edn, Prentice Hall, Englewood Cliffs, NJ, 1991.

Gibbons, Fiachra, 'Actor Lays into "Trash Ethos" of US Films', *Guardian*, 24/8/2001; online at http://film.guardian.co.uk/News_Story/Guardian/0, 4029, 541765, 00.html (10/05/2002).

Gibbs, J., *Mise-en Scène: Film Style and Interpretation*, Wallflower Press, London, 2001.

Giles, J., *The Cinema of Jean Genet: Un chant d'amour*, British Film Institute, London, 1991.

—— *The Crying Game*, British Film Institute, London, 1997.

Giroux, H., 'Brutalised Bodies and Emasculated Politics', *Third Text*, No. 53, Winter 2000/2001, pp. 31–41.

Gledhill, C., 'Some Recent Developments in Feminist Criticism', in S. Mast and M. Cohen (eds), *Film Theory and Criticism*, Oxford University Press, Oxford, 1985.

—— 'Pleasurable Negotiations', in D. Pribram (ed.), *Female Spectators: Looking at Film and Television*, Verso, London and New York, 1988.

—— 'Introduction', in *Stardom: Industry of Desire*, Routledge, London, 1991.

—— (ed.), *Stardom: Industry of Desire*, Routledge, London, 1991.

—— 'Rethinking Genre', in Christine Gledhill and Linda Williams (eds), *Reinventing Film Studies*, Arnold, London, 2000.

—— *Reframing British Cinema, 1918–1928*, London, British Film Institute, 2003.

Gledhill, Christine and Williams, Linda (eds), *Reinventing Film Studies*, London, Arnold, 2000.

Gomery, D., *The Hollywood Studio System*, Macmillan, London, 1986.

—— *Movie History: A Survey*, Wadsworth, Belmont, CA, 1991.

—— *Shared Pleasures*, British Film Institute, London, 1992.

Goodwin, J., *Eisenstein, Cinema and History*, University of Illinois Press, Urbana and Chicago, 1993.

Gopalan, Lalitha, 'Avenging Women in Indian Cinema', *Screen*, Vol. 38, No. 1, 1997a, pp. 42–59.

—— 'Coitus Interruptus and Love Story in Indian Cinema', in Vidya Dehejia (ed.), *Representing the Body: Gender Issues in Indian Art*, Kali for Women, New Delhi, 1997b, pp. 124–39.

—— *Cinema of Interruptions: Action Genres in Indian Cinema*, British Film Institute, London, 2002.

Gough-Yates, K., *Somewhere in England: British Cinema and Exile*, I. B. Tauris, London.

Graham, P. (ed.), *The New Wave: Critical Landmarks*, British Film Institute/Secker & Warburg, London, 1968.

Grant, Barry Keith (ed.), *Film Genre Reader*, University of Texas, Austin, 1986.

—— (ed.), *Film Genre Reader II*, University of Texas, Austin, 1995.

Grant, Catherine, 'www.auteur.com?', *Screen*, Vol. 41, No. 1, 2000.

Grant, J., *Masters of Animation*, Batsford, London, 2001.

Greene, G., *The Pleasure Dome*, Secker & Warburg, London, 1972.

Greer, G., *The Female Eunuch*, Flamingo, London, 1971.

Greirson, J. 'The Documentary Producer', *Cinema Quarterly*, Vol. 2, No. 1, 1932.

Grimes, C., 'Harry Potter and the Sales Team', *Financial Times*, 16 November, 2001.

Grossman, A. (ed.), *Queer Asian Cinema: Shadows in the Shade*, Harrington Park Press, New York, 2001.

Guinness, A., *My Name Escapes Me*, Penguin, Harmondsworth, 1997.

Gunning, T., 'The Cinema of Attractions: Early Film, Its Spectators and the Avant Garde', in Thomas Elsaesser (ed.), *Early Cinema: Space, Frame, Narrative*, British Film Institute, London, 1990.

Hadleigh, B., *The Lavender Screen: The Gay and Lesbian Films*, Citadel Press, New York, 1993.

Hall, Stuart, 'Encoding/decoding', in S. Hall, D. Hobson, A. Lowe and P. Willis (eds), *Culture, Media, Language*, Hutchinson, London, 1980.

—— 'When Was "Post-Colonial"? Thinking at the Limit', in Iain Chambers and Lidia Curti (eds), *The Post-Colonial Question: Common Skies, Divided Horizons*, Routledge, London, 1996.

Hamer, D. and Budge, B., *The Good, the Bad and the Gorgeous: Popular Culture's Romance with Lesbianism*, Pandora, London, 1994.

Handel, L., *Hollywood Looks at its Audience*, University of Illinois Press, Urbana, 1950.

Hanson, E., *Out Takes: Essays on Queer Theory and Film*, Duke University Press, Durham, NC, 1999.

Hardy, F. (ed.), *Grierson on Documentary*, Faber & Faber, London, 1979.

Hardy, P. (ed.), *Raoul Walsh*, Edinburgh Film Festival, 1974.

Haring, B., 'Digital Films Getting Serious', *USA Today*, 31 January, 2000.

Harper, S., *Picturing the Past: The Rise and Fall of the British Costume Film*, British Film Institute, London, 1994.

Hartsough, D., 'Soviet Film Distribution and Exhibition in Germany 1921–1933',

Harvey, S., *May '68 and Film Culture*, British Film Institute, London, 1981.

Haskell, M., *From Reverence to Rape*, New English Library, London, 1973.

Hayward, Susan, *French National Cinema*, Routledge, London, 1993.

—— *Key Concepts in Cinema Studies*, Routledge, London, 1996.

Hayward, S. and Vincendeau, G. (eds), *French Film: Texts and Contexts*, Routledge, London, 1990.

Heck-Rabi, L., *Women Filmmakers – A Critical Reception*, Scarecrow Press, London, 1984.

Henderson, B. 'Toward a Non-Bourgeois Camera Style', in B. Nichols (ed.), *Movies and Methods*, University of California Press, Berkeley, 1976.

Higson, A., *Waving the Flag: Constructing a National Cinema in Britain*, Oxford University Press, Oxford, 1985.

—— (ed.), *Dissolving Views: Key Writings on British Cinema*, Cassell, London, 1996.

—— (ed.), *Young and Innocent?*, Exeter University Press, Exeter, 2002.

Higson, A. and Ashby, J. (eds), *British Cinema: Past and Present*, Routledge, London, 1996.

Higson, A. and Maltby, R. (eds), *Film Europe Film America*, Exeter University Press, Exeter, 2000.

Hill, Annette, *Shocking Entertainment*, John Libby, Luton, 1997.

Hill, J., *Sex, Class and Realism: British Cinema 1956–1963*, British Film Institute, London, 1986.

—— *British Cinema in the 1980s*, Clarendon Press, Oxford, 1999.

Hillier, J. (ed.), *Cahiers du cinéma 1: The 1950s, Neo-realism, Hollywood, The New Wave*, British Film Institute/Routledge & Kegan Paul, London, 1985.

—— (ed.), *Cahiers du cinéma 2: 1960–1968*, British Film Institute/Routledge and Kegan Paul, London, 1986.

Historical Journal of Film, Radio and Television, Vol. 5, No. 2, 1985.

Historical Journal of Film, Radio and Television, Vol. 11, No. 2, 1991.

Hoffer, T., *Animation: A Reference Guide*, Greenwood Press, Westport, CN, 1981.

Hollis, R. and Sibley, B., *The Disney Studio Story*, Crown Publishers, New York, 1988.

Holloway, R., *Z is for Zagreb*, Tantivy Press, Cranberry NJ, 1972.

Holmes, Tim, 'Too Cool for Words', *Rolling Stone*, 6 November, 1986; online at, http://www.sfgoth.com /~kali/onsite3.html.

Holmlund, Chris, 'Impossible Bodies', in P. Kirkham and J. Thumin (eds), *You Tarzan: Masculinity, Movies and Men*, Lawrence & Wishart, London, 1993.

—— 'Masculinity as Multiple Masquerade', in S. Cohan and I. Hark, *Screening the Male*, Routledge, London, 1993.

Holmlund, Chris and Fuchs, Cynthia (eds), *Between the Sheets, in the Streets: Queer, Lesbian and Gay Documentary*, University of Minnesota Press, Minneapolis, 1997.

Hood, John W., *The Essential Mystery*, Orient Longman, New Delhi, 2000.

Hoogland, R.C., *Lesbian Configurations*, University of Columbia Press, New York, 1997.

hooks, bell, *Black Looks: Race and Representation*, Turnaround, London, 1992.

—— 'The Oppositional Gaze: Black Female Spectators', in Manthia Diawara (ed.), *Black American Cinema: Aesthetics and Spectatorship*, Routledge/American Film Institute, London, 1993.

—— *Reel to Real; Race, Class and Sex in the Movies*, Routledge, New York, 1996.

Horrocks, R., *Male Myths and Icons: Masculinity in Popular Culture*, Macmillan, London, 1995.

Hunter, J. (ed.), *Moonchild: The Films of Kenneth Anger*, Creation Books, London, 2002.

Hutchings, Peter, 'Genre Theory and Criticism', in Mark Jancovich and Joanne Hollows (eds), *Approaches to Popular Film*, Manchester University Press, Manchester, 1995.

—— 'The Matrix', *Scope*, posted, 01/11/1999; http://www.nottingham.ac.uk/film/journal/filmrev/ the_matrix.htm, (23/04/2002).

Iampolski, Mikhail, *The Memory of Tiresias: Intertextuality and Film*, trans. Harsha Ram, University of California Press, Berkeley, 1998.

The Indian Cinematograph Code, Cinematograph Laws Research Institute, Hyderabad, A.P., 1982.

Iyer, Pico, *Video Nights in Kathmandu: Reports From the Not-so-Far East*, Knopf, New York, 1988.

Izod, J., *Reading the Screen: An Introduction to Film Studies*, Longman, Harlow and York Press, Beirut, 1984.

James, Nick, 'Ballard of a Thinning Man', *Sight and Sound*, Vol. 10, No. 11 (November), 2000.

Jarman, D, *Dancing Ledge*, Quartet, London, 1984.

Jeffords, S., 'Can Masculinity Be Terminated?', in S. Cohan and I. Hark (eds), *Screening the Male*, Routledge, London, 1993.

—— *Hard Bodies: Hollywood Masculinity in the Reagan Era*, Rutgers University Press, New Brunswick, NJ, 1994.

Jennings, M.L., *Humphrey Jennings: Film-maker, Painter, Poet*, British Film Institute, London, 1982.

Johnston, C., 'Women's Cinema as Counter Cinema', *Screen Pamphlet*, No. 2, 1973.

—— 'The Subject of Feminist Film Theory/Practice', *Screen*, Vol. 21, No. 2, 1980.

Jones, C., *Chuck Amuck*, Simon & Schuster, London, 1990.

Jones, T. and Ford, R., 'Porn Laws to Tighten as Censor Defeated', *The Times*, 17 May, 2000.

Jowett, G. and Linton, J., *Movies as Mass Communication*, Sage, Newbury Park, CA, 1989.

Julien, I. and McCabe, C., *Diary of a Young Soul Rebel*, British Film Institute, London, 1991.

Kabir, S., *Lesbian Representations in Film*, Cassell, London and Washington, 1998.

Kaplan, E.A., *Women and Film: Both Sides of the Camera*, Methuen, London, 1983.

—— (ed.), *Psychoanalysis and Cinema*, American Film Institute/Routledge, London, 1990.

—— *Feminism and Film*, Oxford University Press, Oxford, 2000.

Kaplan, James, 'Give it up for Sean Penn', *Observer*, 6/05/2001; online at http://www.guardian.co.uk/ Archive/Article/0, 4273, 4181719, 00.html (10/05/2002).

Kapur, Geeta, 'Mythic Material in Indian Cinema', *Journal of Arts and Ideas*, Nos 14–15, July–December, 1987.

Kawin, B., *How Movies Work*, Collier Macmillan, London, 1987.

Kelly, Richard, *The Name of this Book is Dogme 95*, Faber & Faber, London, 2000.

Kenez, P., *The Birth of the Propaganda State: Soviet Methods of Mass Mobilization 1917–1929*, Cambridge University Press, Cambridge, 1985.

—— *Cinema and Soviet Society, 1917–1953*, Cambridge University Press, Cambridge, 1992.

Kent, N., *Naked Hollywood*, BBC Books, London, 1991.

Keogh, Peter, 'Home and Away', in Jim Hillier (ed.), *American Independent Movies*, British Film Institute, London, 2001.

Kepley, V., Jr, 'The Origins of Soviet Cinema: A Study in Industry Development', *Quarterly Review of Film Studies*, Vol. 10, No. 1, 1985.

—— *In the Service of the State: The Cinema of Alexander Dovzhenko*, University of Wisconsin Press, Madison, 1986.

Kepley, V., Jr and Kepley, B., 'Foreign Films on Soviet Screens 1922–1931', *Quarterly Review of Film Studies*, Fall 1979.

Keysaar, H., 'The Toil of Thought: On Several Non-Fiction Films by Women'. in C. Warren (ed.), *Beyond Document: Essays on Non-Fiction Film*, Wesleyan University Press, Hanover and London, 1996, pp. 101–37.

Khoklova, E, *Lev Shulov: Fifty Years in Film*, 2nd edn, Raduga Publishers, USSR, 1987.

King, G., *Film Comedy*, Wallflower Press, London, 2002.

Kirkham, P. and Thumin, J. (eds), *You Tarzan: Masculinity, Movies and Men*, Lawrence & Wishart, London, 1993.

—— *Me Jane: Masculinity, Movies and Women*, Lawrence & Wishart, London, 1995.

Kitses, J., *Horizons West*, Thames & Hudson, London, 1969.

Klein, N., *7 Minutes*, Verso, London, 1993.

Kofosky Sedgwick, Eve, *Between Men: English Literature and Male Homosocial Desire*, Columbia University Press, New York, 1985.

Koszarski, Richard, *An Evening's Entertainment*, University of California Press, Berkeley, 1994, Chapter 2.

Kuhn, A., *Women's Pictures*, British Film Institute/Routledge & Kegan Paul, London, 1982.

La Franco, R., 'E-Cinema', *Red Herring*, 13 February, 2001.

La Valley, A. and Scherr, B. (eds), *Eisenstein at 100*, NJ, Rutgers University Press, New Brunswick, 2001.

Lacey, Nick, *Narrative and Genre*, Macmillan, London, 2000.

Landau, D. (ed.), *Gladiator: The Making of the Ridley Scott Epic*, Boxtree, London, 2000.

Lang, Robert (ed.), *D.W. Griffith – Birth of a Nation*, Rutgers University. Press, New Brunswick, NJ, 1994.

Langdale, Alan (ed.), *Hugo Münsterberg on Film. The photoplay. A psychological study and Other Writings*, Routledge, London and New York, 2002.

Langdon, Matt, 'The Way of the Indie God', *If Magazine*, Vol. 13, No. 2, 2000; online at http://ifmagazine.com /common/article.asp?articleID=570.

Lant, A., *Blackout: Reinventing Women for Wartime British Cinema*, Princeton University Press, New Jersey, 1991.

Lapsley, R. and Westlake, M., *Film Theory: An Introduction*, Manchester University Press, Manchester, 1988.

Larkin, Brian, 'Indian Films and Nigerian Lovers: Media and the Creation of Parallel Modernities', *Africa,* Vol. 67m, No. 3, pp. 406–40.

Lawton, A., *The Red Screen: Politics, Society, Art in Soviet Cinema*, Routledge, London, 1992.

Leff, L. and Simmons, J., *The Dame in the Kimono*, Grove Weidenfeld, New York, 1990.

Lehman, P., 'Don't Blame this on a Girl. Female Rape revenge Films', in S. Cohan and I. Hark (eds), *Screening the Male*, Routledge, London, 1993.

—— (ed.), *Masculinity, Bodies, Movies, Culture*, American Film Institute and Routledge, New York, 2000.

Lehman, P. and Maynes, J., 'An Interview with Susan Clayton', *Wide Angle*, Vol. 6, No. 3, 1981, p. 72.

Lenin, V.I., in *Pravda*, No. 250, 7 November 1919; repr. in *Lenin: Economics and Politics in the Era of the Dictatorship of the Proletariat*, Progress Publishers, Moscow, 1978.

Levy, Emanuel, *Cinema of Outsiders: The Rise of American Independent Film*, New York University Press, New York, 1999.

Levy, Shawn, 'Postcards from Mars', in Jim Hillier (ed.), *American Independent Movies*, British Film Institute, London, 2001.

Lewis, J., *The End of Cinema*, Pluto Press, London, 2001.

Leyda, J., *Kino: A History of the Russian and Soviet Film*, 3rd edn, George Allen & Unwin, London, 1983.

Lippard, C. (ed.), *By Angels Driven: The Films of Derek Jarman*, Flick Books, Trowbridge, 1996.

Livingston, Paisley, 'Cinematic Authorship', in Richard Allen and Murray Smith (eds), *Film Theory and Philosophy*, Oxford: Oxford University Press, 1997.

Lovell, T., *Pictures of Reality: Aesthetics, Politics and Pleasure*, British Film Institute, London, 1983.

—— 'That Was the Workshop That Was', *Screen*, Vol. 31, No. 1, 1990, pp. 102–8.

Low, R., *Film Making in 1930s Britain*, George Allen & Unwin, London, 1985.

—— *The History of the British Film*, Routledge, London, 1997.

MacCabe, Colin, 'Defining Popular Culture', in Colin MacCabe (ed.), *High Theory/Low Culture: Analyzing Popular Television and Film*, St. Martin's Press, New York, 1986.

McCloud, S., *Understanding Comics*, Harper Collins, New York, 1993.

Macdonald, K. and Cousins, M. (eds), *Imagining Reality: The Faber Book of Documentary*, Faber & Faber, London and Boston, 1996.

McDonald, Paul, 'Star Studies', in Joanne Hollows and Mark Jancovich (eds), *Approaches to Popular Film*, Manchester University Press, Manchester, 1995.

—— *The Star System: Hollywood's Production of Popular Identities*, Wallflower Press, London, 2000.

Macdonald, Scott, *Avant Garde Cinema*, Cambridge University Press, Cambridge, 1993.

Malkovich, John, 'Captured by The Terrorist', *Guardian*, Friday Review, 27/04/2001.

Maltby, R. and Craven, I., *Hollywood Cinema*, Blackwell, Oxford, 1995.

Maltin, L., *Of Mice and Magic*, NAL, New York, 1987.

Mapplebeck, V., 'Voyeurs and Victim TV', *Guardian*, Media Supplement, 1/12/1997, pp. 4–5.

Marie, M., *La nouvelle vague: une école artistique*, Nathan, Paris, 1998.

Marshall, H., *Masters of the Soviet Cinema*, Routledge & Kegan Paul, London, 1983.

Mast, S. and Cohen, M. (eds), *Film Theory and Criticism*, Oxford University Press, Oxford, 1985.

May, Larry, *Screening Out the Past: The Birth of Mass Culture and the Motion Picture Industry*, Chicago University Press, Chicago, 1980.

Maynard, M., 'Current Trends in Feminist Theory', *Social Studies Review*, Vol. 2, No. 3, 1987.

Mayne, Judith, 'The Critical Audience', in *Cinema and Spectatorship*, Routledge, London and New York, 1993.

—— *Cinema and Spectatorship*, Routledge, London, 1993.

—— *Directed by Dorothy Arzner*, University of Indiana Press, Bloomington, 1994.

Media Advocacy Group for the National Commission for Women, *A Gender Perspective for the Electronic Media*, New Delhi, March 1993.

—— *People's Perception: Obscenity and Violence on the Screen*, N.D.

Mellen, J., *Big Bad Wolves: Masculinity in the American Film*, Elmtree, London, 1970.

Merck, M., '"Lianna" and the Lesbians of Art Cinema', in Charlotte Brunsdon (ed.), *Films for Women*, British Film Institute, London, 1986.

—— 'On *Desert Hearts*', in M. Gever, J. Greyson and P. Parmar (eds), *Queer Looks: Perspectives on Lesbian and Gay Video*, Between The Lines/Routledge, Toronto, 1993.

Merritt, G., *Celluloid Mavericks*, Thunder's Mouth Press, New York, 2000.

Metz, C., *Psychoanalysis and the Cinema*, Macmillan, London, 1983.

Meyer, M. (ed.), *The Politics and Poetics of Camp*, Routledge, London, 1994.

Michelson, A. (ed.), *Kino Eye: The Writings of Dziga Vertov*, University of California Press, Berkeley, 1984.

Millet, K., *Sexual Politics*, Virago, London, 1977.

Milne, T. and Narboni, J., *Godard on Godard*, Da Capo, New York, 1986.

Modleski, T., *The Women Who Knew Too Much*, Methuen, London, 1988.

—— 'Three Men and Baby M', in E.A. Kaplan (ed.), *Feminism and Film*, Oxford University Press, Oxford, 2000.

Monaco, J., *The New Wave: Truffaut, Godard, Chabrol, Rohmer, Rivette*, Oxford University Press, Oxford, 1976.

Monk, C. and Sargeant, A. (eds), *British Historical Cinema*, Routledge, London, 2002.

Movie Magazine, *The Films of Jean-Luc Godard*, Studio Vista, London, 1967.

Muir, A.R., 'The Status of Women Working in Film and Television', in L. Gammon (ed.), *The Female Gaze*, The Women's Press, London, 1988.

Mulvey, L., 'Visual Pleasure and Narrative Cinema', *Screen*, Vol. 16, No. 3, 1975.

—— *Framework*, Vol. 10, Nos 6–7, 1977, p. 7.

—— 'Film, Feminism and the Avant-Garde', 1979.

—— 'Afterthoughts on Visual Pleasure and Narrative Cinema', *Framework*, Vol. 6, Nos 15–17, 1981.

—— *Visual and Other Pleasures*, Macmillan, London, 1989.

—— 'Visual Pleasure and Narrative Cinema', in *The Sexual Subject: A Screen Reader in Sexualtity*, Routledge, London and New York, 1995.

Murphy, J., 'A Question of Silence', in C. Brundsen (ed.), *Films for Women*, British Film Institute, London, 1986.

Murphy, R., *Sixties British Cinema*, British Film Institute, London, 1992.

—— (ed.), *British Cinema of the 90s*, British Film Institute, London, 1999.

—— (ed.), *The British Cinema Book*, British Film Institute, London, 2001.

Murray, Raymond, *Images in the Dark: An Encyclopedia of Gay and Lesbian Film and Video*, TLA Publications, Philadelphia, 1996.

Musser, Charles, 'The Travel Genre in 1903–1904: Moving Towards Fictional Narrative', in Thomas Elsaesser with Adam Barker (eds), *Early Cinema: Space, Frame, Narrative*, British Film Institute, London, 1990.

—— *The Emergence of Cinema: The American Screen to 1907*, University of California, Berkeley, 1994.

Nathan, I., 'Blame-spotting', *The Times*, 11 July, 2002.

Neale, Steven, *Genre*, British Film Institute, London, 1980.

——'Art Cinema as Institution', *Screen*, Vol. 22, No 1, 1981, pp. 11–41.

—— 'Questions of Genre', *Screen*, Vol. 31, No. 1, 1990, pp. 45–67.

—— *Genre*, British Film Institute, London, 1992 (1980).

—— 'Masculinity as Spectacle', in S. Cohan and I. Hark (eds), *Screening the Male*, Routledge, London, 1993.

—— *Genre and Hollywood*, Routledge, London and New York, 2000.

—— *Genre and Contemporary Hollywood*, British Film Institute, London, 2002.

Neale, S. and Smith, M. (eds), *Contemporary Hollywod Cinema*, Routledge, London, 1998.

Newsweek International, 10 May, 1999.

Nichols, B. (ed.), *Movies and Methods*, Vol. 1, University of California Press, Los Angeles, 1976.

—— 'Performing Documentary', in *Blurred Boundaries*, Indiana University Press, Bloomington and Indianapolis, 1994, pp. 92–107.

—— 'Film Theory and the Revolt Against Master Narratives', in Christine Gledhill, and Linda Williams (eds), *Reinventing Film Studies*, Arnold, London, 2000.

Nielsen, Lars, 'Girl Power Got Me Through My Divorce', *Now*, 08/05/2002.

Niranjana, Tejaswini, 'Whose Nation? Tourists and Terrorists in *Roja*?', *Economic and Political Weekly*, Vol. 24, No. 3, 15 January, 1994.

Nussinova, T., 'The Soviet Union and the Russian Émigrés', in G. Nowell-Smith (ed.), *The Oxford History of World Cinema*, Oxford University Press, Oxford, 1996.

Oakley, C.A., *Where We Came In*, George Allen & Unwin, London, 1964.

Orr, J., *Cinema and Modernity*, Polity Press, London, 1993.

Palmer, J. and Riley, M., *The Films of Joseph Losey*, Cambridge University Press, Cambridge, 1993.

Pandian, M.S.S., *The Image Trap*, Sage, New Delhi, 1992.

Parkes, C., 'Everyone Goes to Hollywood', *Financial Times*, 13 March, 2001.

Parliamentary Debates, HMSO, London.

Paul, *The Countryman and the Cinematograph*.

Peary, D. and Peary, G. (eds), *The American Animated Cartoon*, Dutton, New York, 1980.

Pendakur, Manjunath, 'Dynamics of Cultural Policy Making: The U.S. Film Industry in India', *Journal of Communication*, Autumn 1985, pp. 52–72.

—— 'India', in John A. Lent (ed.), *The Asian Film Industry*, Texas University Press, Austin, 1990.

Penley, C. (ed.), *Feminism and Film Theory*, Routledge/British Film Institute, London, 1988.

Perkins, V., *Film as Film*, Penguin, London, 1972a.

—— 'The Cinema of Nicholas Ray', in I.F. Cameron (ed.), *Movie Reader*, November Books, London, 1972b.

Perry, G., *Forever Ealing*, Pavilion, London, 1981.

Perry, N., 'Will Sony Make it in Hollywood', *Fortune*, 9 September, 1991.

Petric, V., 'Dziga Vertov as Theorist', *Cinema Journal*, Vol. 1, Autumn 1978, pp. 41–2.

—— *Constructivism in Film: The Man with the Movie Camera – A Cinematic Analysis*, Cambridge University Press, Cambridge, 1987.

Petrie, D., *Screening Scotland*, British Film Institute, London, 2000.

Petrie, Ruth (ed.), *Film and Censorship – The Index Reader*, Cassell, London, 1997.

Phelan, Rev. J.J., *Motion Pictures as a Phase of Commercialised Amusement in Toldeo, Ohio*, reprinted in *Film History*, Vol. 13, No. 3, 2001.

Phillips, Patrick, *Understanding Film Texts*, British Film Institute, London, 2000.

Pierson, J., *Spike, Mike, Slackers and Dykes: A Guided Tour Across a Decade of Independent American Cinema*, Faber & Faber, London, 1996.

Pilcher, J., 'I'm Not a Feminist, But…', *Sociology Review*, November 1993, p. 4.

Pilling, J. (ed.), *Women and Animation, A Compendium*, British Film Institute, London, 1992.

—— (ed.), *A Reader in Animation Studies*, John Libbey, London, 1997.

Pilling, J. and O'Pray, M. (eds), *Into the Pleasure Dome: The Films of Kenneth Anger*, British Film Institute, London, 1989.

Pirie, D., *A Heritage of Horror*, Gordon Fraser, London, 1973.

Plantinga, Carl and Smith, Greg M. (eds), *Passionate Views: Film, Cognition and Emotion*, Johns Hopkins University Press, Baltimore, 1999.

Polan, Dana, *Pulp Fiction*, British Film Institute, London, 2001.

Pollock, G., *Vision and Difference*, Routledge, London, 1988.

Pollock, G. and Parker, R., *Old Mistresses*, Routledge & Kegan Paul, London, 1981.

Popple, S. and Toulmin, V., *Visual Delights*, Flicks Books, Trowbridge, 2000.

Porter, L. and Burton, A. (eds), *Pimple, Pranks and Pratfalls*, Flicks Books, Trowbridge, 2000.

—— (eds), *Crossing the Pond*, Flicks Books, Trowbridge, 2002.

Powell, D., *Films since 1939*, British Council, London, 1947.

Powell, M., *A Life in Movies*, Heinemann, London, 1986.

Prasad, M. Madhava, *Ideology of the Hindi Film: A Historical Construction*, Oxford University Press, New Delhi, 1998, pp. 138–59.

Pribram, E. (ed.), *Female Spectators: Looking at Film and Television*, Verso, London and New York, 1988.

Propp, Vladimir, *Theory and History of Folklore*, Manchester University Press, Manchester, 1984.

Pudovkin, V. *Film Technique and Film Acting*, Gollancz, London, 1929.

Pulver, Andrew, 'The Revolution Starts Here', *Guardian*, 28/08/2001; online at http://www.guardian.co.uk/Archive/Article/0, 4273, 4246163, 00.html (10/05/2002).

Radner, H., 'New Hollywood's New Women: Murder in Mind –Sarah and Margie', in S. Neale and M Smith (eds), *Contemporary Hollywood Cinema*, Routledge, London, 1998.

Radway, J., *Reading the Romance*, Verso, London, 1987.

Rajadhyaksha, Ashish, 'The Phalke Era: Conflict of Traditional Form and Modern Technology', *Journal of Arts and Ideas*, Nos 25–26, 1993.

Rajadhyaksha, Ashish and Willemen, Paul (eds), *Encyclopaedia of Indian Cinema*, British Film Institute and Oxford University Press, London, 1999.

Rajagopal, Arvind, *Politics After Television: Religious Nationalism and the Reshaping of the Indian Public*, Cambridge University Press, Cambridge, 2001.

Ranade, Ashok, 'The Extraordinary Importance of the Indian Film Song', *Cinema Vision India*, Vol. 1, No. 4, 1981, pp. 4–11.

Rangoonwala, Firoze, 'The Age of Violence', *The Illustrated Weekly of India*, 4–10 September, 1993, pp. 27–9.

Rao, Maithili, 'Victims in Vigilante Clothing', *Cinema in India*, October–December 1998, pp. 24–6.

Rawsthorn, A., 'Small Budget Movie with Big Ambitions', *Financial Times*, Weekend section, 27 January, 1996.

Razdan, C.K. (ed.), *Bare Breasts and Bare Bottoms*, Jaico, Bombay, 1975.

Read, Jacinda, 'Popular Film/Popular Feminism', *Scope*, January 2000; online at http://www.nottingham.ac.uk /film/journal/articles/popular_feminism.htm (14/02/2000).

Rees, A. L., *A History of Experimental Film and Video*, British Film Institute, London, 1999.

Reeves, N., *Official British Film Propaganda*, IWM/Croom Helm, Kent, 1986.

Reid, T. and Peek, L., 'Potter Playtime…', *The Times*, 6 November, 2001.

Reisz, K. and Millar, G., *The Technique of Film Editing*, Focal Press, London, 1953.

Renov, Alan, 'Introduction: The Truth About Non-fiction', in *Theorising Documentary*, Routledge, New York and London, 1993.

Renov, Michael (ed.), *Theorising Documentary*, Routledge, London and New York, 1993.

Richards, J., *Films and National Identity*, Manchester University Press, Manchester, 1997.

—— (ed.), *The Unknown 1930s*, I.B. Tauris, London, 1998.

Ringler, Kimberly, 'A Reading of *Dil Chahta Hai*', unpublished term paper submitted to Lalitha Gopalan for a tutorial on Indian cinema, Spring 2002.

Robbins, H.W., 'More Human Than I Alone', in S. Cohan and I. Hark (eds), *Screening the Male*, Routledge, London, 1993.

Roberts, G., 'Esfir Shub: A Suitable Case For Treatment', *Historical Journal of Film, Radio and Television*, Vol. 11, No. 2, 1991.

Robertson, J., *The British Board of Film Censors: Film Censorship in Britain, 1896–1950*, Croom Helm, Kent, 1985.

Robinson, D., *World Cinema 1895–1980*, Methuen, London, 1981.

Robinson, David, *From Peep Show to Palace – the Birth of American Film*, Columbia University Press, New York, 1996.

Roddick, N., *A New Deal in Entertainment*, British Film Institute, London, 1983.

Rosenbaum, Jonathan, *Dead Man*, British Film Institute, London, 2000.

Rosenblum, R. and Karen, R., *When the Shooting Stops…the Cutting Begins: A Film Editor's Story*, Da Capo Press, New York, 1979.

Rosenthal, A., *The New Documentary in Action*, University of California Press, Los Angeles, 1972.

—— *The Documentary Conscience*, University of California Press, Los Angeles, 1980.

Rotha, P., *Celluloid: The Film Today*, Longmans, Green & Co., London, 1933.

—— *The Film till Now*, Vision, London, 1949.

Routt, William D. (1990), 'L'Evidence', *Continuum*, Vol. 5, No. 2; online at http://wwwmcc.murdoch.edu.au/ReadingRoom/5.2/Routt.html (08/01/2002).

Rowe, K., 'Melodrama and Men in Post-Classical Romantic Comedy', in P. Kirkham and J. Thumin (eds), *You Jane: Masculinity, Movies and Women*, Lawrence & Wishart, London, 1995.

—— *The Unruly Woman*, University of Texas Press, Austin, 1995.

Roy Levin, G., *Documentary Explorations*, Doubleday, New York, 1971.

Rushdie, Salman, *The Satanic Verses*, Viking, London; New York, 1988.

Russett, R. and Starr, C., *Experimental Animation*, Da Capo, New York, 1976.

Russo, V., *The Celluloid Closet: Homosexuality in the Movies*, Harper & Row, New York and London, 1987.

Ryall, Tom, 'Genre and Hollywood', in John Hill and Pamela Church Gibson (eds), *The Oxford Guide to Film Studies*, Oxford University Press, Oxford, 1993.

Sanghera, S., 'E-movies are Ready to Roll', *Financial Times*, 7 September, 2000.

Sargeant, A., *Vsevolod Pudovkin*, I.B. Tauris, London, 2001.

Sarkar, Kobita, *You Can't Please Everyone: Film Censorship, the Inside Story*, IBH Publishing Company, Bombay, 1982.

Sarris, Andrew, *The American Cinema: Directors and Directions 1929–1968*, Da Capo, New York, 1996.

Saunders, J., *The Western Genre: From Lordsburg to Big Whiskey*, Wallflower Press, London, 2001.

Schatz, Thomas, 'The New Hollywood', in Jim Collins, Hilary Radner and Ava Preacher Collins (eds), *Film Theory Goes to the Movies*, Routledge, London, 1993.

Schnitzer, J., Schnitzer, L. and Martin, M. (eds), *Cinema in Revolution*, trans. D. Robinson, Secker & Warburg, London, 1973; repr. Da Capo Press, New York, 1987.

Screen, Vol. 12, No. 4, Winter 1971–2. A special issue centred on Soviet film of the 1920s including translations from: LEF, Novy LEF, Brik, Kuleshov, Shkiovsky, Vertov, Mayakovsky Film Scenarios.

Sealy, Allan, *Hero*, Viking India Ltd, New Delhi, 1990.

Segal, M., *Slow Motion: Changing Masculinities, Changing Men*, Virago, London, 1997.

Sen, Mala, *India's Bandit Queen: The True Story of Phoolan Devi*, Harper Collins and Pandora, London, 1991.

Sheinfeld, L., 'The Big Chill', *Film Comment*, Vol. 22, No. 3, May/June, 1986.

Shetty, Manmohan, 'Trends in Film Processing', *Lensight*, Vol. 3, No. 4, October, 1994.

Shusterman, Richard, *Pragmatist Aesthetics*, Oxford: Rowman & Littlefield, 2000.

Silents Majority, The, On-line Journal of Silent Film; online at http://www.silentsmajority.com.

Singh, Madan Gopal, 'Technique as an Ideological Weapon', in Aruna Vasudev and Phillipe Lenglet (eds), *Indian Cinema Superbazaar*, Vikas Publishing House, New Delhi, 1983.

Skillman, Terri, 'The Bombay Hindi Film Song Genre: A Historical Survey', *Yearbook for Tradition Music*, Vol. 18, 1986, pp. 133–44.

Sklar, R., 'The Making of Cultural Myths – Walt Disney', in D. Peary and G. Peary (eds), *The American Animated Cartoon*, Dutton, New York, 1980, pp. 58–65.

Slide, A., *Early Women Directors*, South Brunswick, New York, Barnes and Ysoseloff, London, 1977.

Smith, Alison, *Agnès Varda*, Manchester University Press, Manchester, 1998.

Smith, M., *Contemporary Hollywood Cinema*, Routledge, London, 1998.

Smith, Murray, *Engaging Characters – Fiction, Emotion and the Cinema*, Oxford University Press, Oxford, 1995.

Smith, Paul, *Clint Eastwood: A Cultural Production*, University of Minnesota Press, Minneapolis, 1993.

Smith, P. J., *Laws of Desire*, Clarendon Press, Oxford, 1992.

Smith, S., *Women Who Make Movies*, Hopkinson & Blake, 1975.

—— 'Byte me…'; online at www.atomfilms.com, (24 January, 2001).

Smith, Valerie, *Not Just Race, Not Just Gender*, Routledge, New York and London, 1998.

Smoodin, E. (ed.), *Disney Discourse* Routledge, London and New York, 1994.

Sobchack, Vivian (ed.), *The Persistence of History: Cinema, Television and the Modern Event*, Routledge, London and New York, 1996.

—— (ed.), *Metamorphing: Visual Transformation and the Culture of Quick-Change*, University of Minnesota Press, Minneapolis, 2000.

—— 'What is Film History?, or, the Riddle of the Sphinxes', in Christine Gledhill and Linda Williams (eds), *Reinventing Film Studies*, Arnold, London, 2000.

Solomon, C. (ed.), *The Art of the Animated Image*, American Film Institute, Los Angeles, 1987.

Sontag, S., 'Fascinating Fascism', in B. Nichols (ed.), *Movies and Methods*, University of California Press, Los Angeles, 1976, pp. 32–28.

—— 'Notes on Camp', in *Against Interpretation*, Vintage, London, 2001.

Squire, J. (ed.), *The Movie Business Book*, Columbus, London, 1986.

Srinivas, S.V., 'Devotion and Defiance in Fan Activity', in Ravi Vasudevan (ed.), *Making Meaning in Indian Cinema*, Oxford University Press, New Delhi, 2000.

Stacey, Jackie, *Desperately Seeking Difference. In the Sexual Subject: A Screen Reader in Sexuality*, London and New York, 1992.

—— *Star Gazing: Hollywood Cinema and Female Spectatorship*, Routledge, London, 1994.

Stam, Robert, *Film Theory: An Introduction*, Blackwell, Oxford, 2000.

Stan, C., *Discovering the Movies*, Van Nostrand Reinhold Co., New York, 1972.

Stephenson, R., *Animation in the Cinema*, Zwemmer Ltd, London, 1969.

Steven, P. (ed.), *Jump Cut: Hollywood, Politics and Counter Cinema*, Between The Lines, Toronto, 1985.

Stevenson, W., 'Film Jackpot Solves Nothing', *Daily Telegraph*, 15 May, 1997.

Stites, R. 'Soviet Movies for the Masses and Historians', *Historical Journal of Film, Radio and Television*, Vol. 11, No. 3, 1991.

—— *Russian Popular Culture: Entertainment and Society Since 1900*, Cambridge University Press, Cambridge, 1992.

Straayer, Chris, 'The Hypothetical Lesbian Heroine in Narrative Feature Film', in Corey K. Creekmur and Alexander Doty (eds), *Out in Culture: Gay, Lesbian and Queer Essays on Popular Culture*, Duke University Press, Durham, NC, 1995.

—— *Deviant Eyes, Deviant Bodies*, Columbia University Press, New York, 1996.

Street, S., *British National Cinema*, Routledge, London, 1997.

Street, S. and Fitzsimmons, L. (eds), *Moving Performance*, Flicks Books, Trowbridge, 2000.

Subramanyam, Radha, 'Class, Caste and Performance in "Subaltern" Feminist Film Theory and Praxis: An Analysis of, *Rudaali*'.

Sweeney, G., 'The Man in the Pink Shirt: Hugh Grant and the Dilemma of British Masculinity', *Cineaction*, No. 55, July 2001, pp. 57–67.

Tarantino, Quentin, *Pulp Fiction – The Screenplay*, Faber & Faber, London, 1994.

Tasker, Yvonne, 'Dumb Movies for Dumb People', in S. Cohan and I. Hark (eds), *Screening the Male*, Routledge, London, 1993.

—— *Spectacular Bodies: Gender, Genre and the Action Movie*, Routledge, London, 1993.

—— *Working Girls*, Routledge, London, 1998.

—— (ed.), *Fifty Contemporary Film-Makers*, Routledge, London, 2002.

Taylor, R., *Film Propaganda: Soviet Russia and Nazi Germany*, Croom Helm, London, 1979.

—— *The Politics of the Soviet Cinema, 1917–1929*, Cambridge University Press, Cambridge, 1979.

—— 'Boris Shumyatsky and the Soviet Cinema in the 1930s: Ideology as Mass Entertainment', *Historical Journal of Film, Radio and Television*, Vol. 6, No. 1, 1986.

—— (ed.), *S.M. Eisenstein: Writings 1922–1934 – Selected Works*, Vol. 1, British Film Institute, London, 1988.

—— (ed.), *Beyond the Stars: The Memoirs of Sergei Eisenstein – Selected Works*, Vol. 4, British Film Institute, London, 1995.

—— (ed.), *S.M. Eisenstein: Selected Works – Writings 1934–1947*, Vol. 3, British Film Institute, London, 1996.

—— (ed.), *The Eisenstein Reader*, British Film Institute, London, 1998.

—— *Sergei Eisenstein Biography*, Cape, 1999.

—— *October*, British Film Institute, London, 2002.

Taylor, R. and Christie, I. (eds), *The Film Factory: Russian and Soviet Cinema in Documents, 1896–1939*, Routledge, London, 1988.

—— (eds), *Inside the Film Factory: New Approaches to Russian and Soviet Cinema*, Routledge, London, 1991.

Taylor, R. and Glenny, M. (eds), *S.M. Eisenstein: Towards a Theory of-Montage – Selected Works*, Vol. 2, British Film Institute, London, 1994.

Taylor, R., Wood, N., Graffy, J. and Iordanova, D. (eds), *The British Film Institute Companion to Eastern European and Russian Cinema*, Vol. 2, British Film Institute, London, 2001.

Thomas, Rosie, 'Indian Cinema: Pleasures and Popularity', *Screen*, Vol. 26, Nos 3–4, 1985.

Thompson, K. 'Early Alternatives to the Hollywood Mode of Production', *Film History: An International Journal*, Vol. 5, No. 4, December, 1993.

Thompson, K. and Bordwell, D., *Film Art: An Introduction*, 4th edn, McGraw-Hill, New York, 1993.

—— *Film History: An Introduction*, McGraw-Hill, New York, 1994.

Thompson, R., 'Pronoun Trouble', in D. Peary and G. Peary (eds), *The American Animated Cartoon*, Dutton, New York, 1980, pp. 226–35.

Thomson, H., 'Why Did the BBC hide away my BAFTA-winning series?', *Daily Telegraph*, 22/11/2001, p. 18.

Thoraval, Yves, *The Cinemas of India*, Macmillan India, New Delhi, 2000.

Thornham, S., *Passionate Detachments*, Arnold, London, 1997.

Tincknell, E. and Chambers, D., 'Performing the Crisis, Fathering, Gender and Representation in Two 1990's Films', *Journal of Popular Film and TV*, Vol. 29. No 4, Winter 2002, pp. 146–155.

Tinkcom, Matthew and Villarejo, Amy (eds), *Keyframes: Popular Cinema and Cultural Studies*, Routledge, London, 2001.

Truffaut, François, *Hitchcock*, Secker & Warburg, London, 1967.

—— *Hitchcock/Truffaut*, Editions Ramsay, Paris, 1983.

Tsivian, Y., *Early Cinema in Russia and its Cultural Reception*, Routledge, London, 1994.

Tudor, A., *Theories of Film*, Secker & Warburg for the British Film Institute, London, 1974.

Turan, Kenneth, 'Contact', *Los Angeles Times*, 11/07/1997; online at http://www.calendarlive.com/top/1, 1419, L-LATimes-Movies-X!ArticleDetail-4490, 00.html (10/05/2002).

Turner Graeme, *Film as Social Practice*, Routledge, London, 1988; repr. London, Routledge, 1993.

—— (ed.), *The Film Cultures Reader*, Routledge, London, 2001, pp. 444–68.

Tyler, C., 'Porn Wars', *Financial Times*, 'Weekend' section, 24 October, 1998.

Tyler, P., *Screening the Sexes: Homosexuality in the Movies*, De Capo, New York, 1993.

Uberoi, Patricia, 'The Diaspora Comes Home: Disciplining Desire in DDLJ', *Contributions to Indian Sociology*, Vol. 32, No. 2, 1998.

Usai, P., Codelli, L., Montanaro, C. and Robinson, D. (eds), *Silent Witnesses: Russian Films 1908–1919*, British Film Institute, London, 1989.

Van Zoonen, L., *Feminist Media Studies*, Sage, London, 1994.

Vanaik, Achin, *The Painful Transition*, Verso, New York, 1991.

Vasudev, Aruna, *Liberty and License in Indian Cinema*, Vikas Publishing House, New Delhi, 1978.

Vasudevan, Ravi, '*Bombay* and its Public', *Journal of Arts and Ideas*, Vol. 29, January, 1996a: pp. 44–65.

—— 'Addressing the Spectator of a "Third-World" National Cinema: The Bombay Social Film of the 1940s and 1950s', *Screen*, Vol. 36, No. 4., 1995b.

Vincendeau, G., 'France 1945–65 and Hollywood: The *Policier* as Inter-national Text', *Screen*, Vol. 33, No. 1, Spring 1992, pp. 50–63.

—— *Stars and Stardom in French Cinema*, Continuum, London, 2000.

Virdi, Jyotika, 'Reverence, Rape and Then Revenge: Popular Hindi Cinema's Woman's Film', *Screen*, Vol. 40, No. 1, 1999, pp. 17–37.

Virilio, Paul, *War and Cinema: The Logistics of Perception*, Verso: London and New York, 1989.

Walker, A., *Hollywood, England: The British Film Industry in the Sixties*, Harrap, London, 1974; repr. 1986.

—— *National Heroes: British Film in the Seventies and Eighties*, Harrap, London, 1985.

—— 'The Scandal of Gambling', *Evening Standard*, 2 May, 2000.

Walters, S., *Material Girls*, University of California Press, Berkeley, 1995.

Warren, C. (ed.), *Beyond Document: Essays on Non-Fiction Film*, Wesleyan University Press, Hanover and London, 1996.

Wasko, Janet, *Hollywood in the Entertainment Age*, University of Texas Press, Austin, 1994.

—— *Understanding Disney*, Polity Press, Cambridge and Malden, 2001.

Watson, Paul, 'There's No Accounting for Taste: Exploitation Cinema and the Limits of Film Theory', in D. Cartmell *et al.* (eds), *Trash Aesthetics*, Pluto Press, London, 1997.

Waugh, T., *The Fruit Machine*, Duke University Press, Durham, NC, 2000.

Weiss, Andrea, 'A Queer Feeling When I Look at You: Hollywood Stars and Lesbian Spectatorship in the 1930s', in Christine Gledhill (ed.), *Stardom: Industry of Desire*, Routledge, London and New York, 1991.

—— *Vampires And Violets – Lesbians In Film*, Penguin, London, 1993.

Wells, P., *Art and Animation*, Academy Group/John Wiley, London, 1997.

—— (ed.), 'A Consideration of Animation and the Documentary Aesthetic', in *Art and Animation*, Academy Group/John Wiley, London, 1997, pp. 40–6.

—— *Understanding Animation*, Routledge, London and New York 1998.

—— '*Roughnecks*, Reality, Recombancy and Radical Aesthetics, *Point* 11, Spring/Summer 2001a, pp. 48–55.

—— 'Art of the Impossible', in G. Andrew (ed.), *Film: The Critic's Choice*, The Ivy Press, Lewes, 2001b, pp. 308–39.

—— *Animation: Genre and Authorship*, Wallflower Press, London, 2002a.

—— *Animation and America*, EUP/Rutgers, Edinburgh and New Jersey, 2002b.

—— 'Where the Mild Things Are', *Sight and Sound*, Vol. 12, No. 2 (NS), February 2002c, pp. 27–8.

Whatling, C., *Screen Dreams: Fantasising Lesbians in Film*, Manchester University Press, Manchester, 1997.

White, P., 'Girls Still Cry', *Screen*, Vol. 42, No. 2, 2001, pp. 217–21.

Wiegman, R., 'Feminism, "The Boyz", and Other Matters Regarding the Male', in S. Cohan and I. Hark (eds), *Screening the Male*, Routledge, London, 1993.

Willemen, Paul, 'Anthony Mann: Looking at the Male', *Framework*, Nos 15–17, 1981.

Williams Alan, 'Is a Radical Genre Criticism Possible?', *Quarterly Review of Film Studies*, Vol. 9, No. 2, 1984.

Williams, H., 'History in the Unmaking', *Guardian*, 16/4/2001, pp. 16–17.

Williams Linda Ruth, 'Mother Courage', *Sight and Sound*, Vol. 12, No. 5 (May), 2002.

Willis, J., 'What's Up, Docs?', *Guardian*, 6/10/1997, p. 9.

Willis, D.S., *High Contrast: Race and Gender in Contemporary Hollywood Film*, Duke University Press, Durham and London, 1997.

Wilson, E., *Personal Histories: French Cinema since 1950*, Duckworth, London, 1999.

Wilton, T., *Immortal Invisible: Lesbians and the Moving Image*, Routledge, London, 1995.

Winston, B., *Claiming the Real: The Documentary Film Re-Visited*, British Film Institute, London, 1996.

Wlaschin, Ken, 'Birth of the "Curry" Western: Bombay 1976', *Film and Filming*, Vol. 22, No. 7, April, 1976, pp. 20–3.

Wollen, Peter, *Signs and Meaning in the Cinema*, Secker & Warburg, London, 1969.

—— 'North by North-West: A Morphological Analysis', *Film Form*, Vol. 1, No. 2, 1976.

—— 'Godard and Counter Cinema', *Vent d'Est*', *Readings and Writings: Semiotic Counter-Strategies*, Verso, London, 1982.

Wollheim, Richard, *The Thread of Life*, Yale University Press, New Haven, CN, 1999.

Wood, R., *Hitchcock Revisited*, Faber & Faber, London, 1989.

—— 'Responsibilities of a Gay Film Critic', in Corey K. Creekmur and Alexander Doty (eds), *Out in Culture: Gay, Lesbian and Queer Essays on Popular Culture*, Duke University Press, Durham, NC, 1995.

Woolley, S., 'Last Palace Picture Show', *Guardian*, 30 October, 1992.

Youngblood, D., *Movies for the Masses: Popular Cinema and Soviet Society in the 1920s*, Cambridge University Press, Cambridge, 1992.

—— *Soviet Cinema in the Silent Era, 1918–1935*, UMI Research Press, Ann Arbor, MI, 1985.

Zorkaya, N., *The Illustrated History of Soviet Cinema*, Hippocrene Books, New York, 1989.

Index